T0188816

Communications
in Computer and Information Science 1397

More information about this series at http://www.springer.com/series/7899

Fuchun Sun · Huaping Liu ·
Bin Fang (Eds.)

Cognitive Systems and Signal Processing

5th International Conference, ICCSIP 2020
Zhuhai, China, December 25–27, 2020
Revised Selected Papers

 Springer

Editors
Fuchun Sun
Tsinghua University
Beijing, China

Huaping Liu
Tsinghua University
Beijing, China

Bin Fang
Tsinghua University
Beijing, China

ISSN 1865-0929 ISSN 1865-0937 (electronic)
Communications in Computer and Information Science
ISBN 978-981-16-2335-6 ISBN 978-981-16-2336-3 (eBook)
https://doi.org/10.1007/978-981-16-2336-3

This Springer imprint is published by the registered company Springer Nature Singapore Pte Ltd.
The registered company address is: 152 Beach Road, #21-01/04 Gateway East, Singapore 189721, Singapore

Preface

This volume contains the papers from the Fifth International Conference on Cognitive Systems and Information Processing (ICCSIP 2020), which was held in Hengqin, China, during December 25–27, 2020. ICCSIP is a prestigious biennial conference, with past events held in Beijing, China (2012, 2014, 2016, and 2018). Over the past few years, ICCSIP has matured into a well-established series of international conferences on cognitive information processing and related fields throughout the world. Similar to the previous event, ICCSIP 2020 provided an academic forum for the participants to share their new research findings and discuss emerging areas of research. It also established a stimulating environment for the participants to exchange ideas on future trends and opportunities. The theme of ICCSIP 2020 was 'Cognitive Computation for AI and Applications in Intelligent Information Processing'.

Currently, cognitive systems and information processing are applied in an increasing number of research domains such as cognitive sciences and technology, visual cognition and computation, big data and intelligent information processing, and bioinformatics and associated applications. We believe that cognitive systems and information processing will certainly exhibit greater-than-ever advances in the near future. With the aim of promoting the research and technical innovation in relevant fields domestically and internationally, the fundamental objective of ICCSIP is defined as providing the premier forum for researchers and practitioners from academia, industry, and government to share their ideas, research results, and experiences.

ICCSIP 2020 received 120 submissions, all of which were written in English. After a thorough peer review process, 59 papers were selected for presentation as full papers, resulting in an approximate acceptance rate of 49%. The accepted papers not only addressed challenging issues in various aspects of cognitive systems and information processing but also showcased contributions from related disciplines that illuminate the state of the art. In addition to the contributed papers, the ICCSIP 2020 technical program included three plenary speeches by Prof. Tianzi Jiang, Prof. Baoliang Lu, and Prof. Qinghu Meng, and three invited speeches by Prof. Yongsheng Ou, Prof. Linlin Shen, and Prof. Qing Shi. We would also like to thank the members of the Advisory Committee for their guidance, the members of the International Program Committee and additional reviewers for reviewing the papers, and the members of the Publications Committee for checking the accepted papers in a short period of time. Last but not the least, we would like to thank all the speakers, authors, and reviewers as well as the participants for their great contributions that made ICCSIP 2020 successful and all the hard work worthwhile. We also thank Springer for their trust and for publishing the proceedings of ICCSIP 2020.

March 2021

Fuchun Sun
Huaping Liu
Bin Fang

Organization

Host

Chinese Association for Artificial Intelligence

Organizers

Cognitive Systems and Information Processing Society of the Chinese Association for
  Artificial Intelligence
Zhuhai Fudan Innovation Institute

Co-organizers

Cognitive Computing and Systems Society of the Chinese Association of Automation
Zhuhai Dahengqin Development Co.
Zhuhai Dahengqin Technology Development Co.
Qinzhi Institute Co.

Conference Committee

Honorary Chairs

Bo Zhang   Tsinghua University, China
Nanning Zheng   Xi'an Jiaotong University, China

Advisory Committee Chairs

Qionghai Dai   Tsinghua University, China
Hongbin Zha   Beijing University, China
Fuji Ren   The University of Tokyo, Japan

General Chairs

Fuchun Sun   Tsinghua University, China
Jianwei Zhang   University of Hamburg, Germany
Dewen Hu   National University of Defense Technology, China

Program Committee Chairs

Zengguang Hou   Institute of Automation, Chinese Academy of Sciences,
                                        China
Xuguang Lan   Xi'an Jiaotong University, China

Organizing Committee Chairs

Huaping Liu   Tsinghua University, China
Guang-Bin Huang   Nanyang Technological University, Singapore
Hong Cheng   University of Electronic Science and Technology
                                        of China, China

Special Sessions Chair

Yixu Song   Tsinghua University, China

Publications Chair

Quanbo Ge   Tongji University, China

Publicity Chairs

Jianmin Li   Tsinghua University, China
Bin Fang   Tsinghua University, China

Finance Chair

Qianyi Sun   Tsinghua University, China

Registration Chair

Jianqin Yin   Beijjing University of Posts and Telecommunications,
                                        China

Local Arrangements Chair

Zhongyi Chu   Beihang University, China

Technical Sponsors

Intelligent Robot Society of the China Computer Federation
Tsinghua University
Science in China Press
IEEE Computational Intelligence Society

Additional Reviewers

Jibin Chen	Shenzhen University, China
Runfa Chen	Tsinghua University, China
Xiaojun Chen	Shenzhen University, China
Yang Chen	Tsinghua University, China
Ziming Chen	Tsinghua University, China
Zhongyi Chu	Beihang University, China
Xilun Ding	Beihang University, China
Mingjie Dong	Beijing University of Technology, China
Nannan Du	Beihang University, China
Bin Fang	Tsinghua University, China
Gang Guo	Tsinghua University, China
Na Guo	Tsinghua University, China
Binghui Huang	Tsinghua University, China
Haiming Huang	Shenzhen University, China
Minglie Huang	Tsinghua University, China
Wenbing Huang	Tsinghua University, China
Tianying Ji	Tsinghua University, China
Mingxuan Jing	Tsinghua University, China
Zengxin Kang	Beihang University, China
Jianfeng Li	Beijing University of Technology, China
Xiaomeng Li	Shenzhen University, China
Chunfang Liu	Beijing University of Technology, China
He Liu	Tsinghua University, China
Zhanyi Liu	Beijing Institute of Technology, China
Huaping Liu	Tsinghua University, China
Guoyi Luo	Tsinghua University, China
Yu Luo	Tsinghua University, China
Xiaojian Ma	Tsinghua University, China
Runqing Miao	Tsinghua University, China
Yue Shen	Beijing University of Posts and Telecommunications, China
Jiayan Shi	Tsinghua University, China
Shanyi Shi	Beijing Institute of Technology
Yixun Song	Tsinghua University, China
Hanbing Sun	Tsinghua University, China
Fuchun Sun	Tsinghua University, China
Chuanqi Tan	Tsinghua University, China
Tao Tao	Anhui university of Technology, China
Shuhuang Wen	Yanshan University, China
Rui Wang	Beihang University, China
Yikai Wang	Tsinghua University, China
Zongtao Wang	Yanshan University, China
Linyuan Wu	Shenzhen University, China
Shuangshuang Wu	Tsinghua University, China

Ziwei Xia	Tsinghua University, China
Binhai Xie	Beihang University, China
Chao Yang	Tsinghua University, China
Chenguang Yang	The University of Queensland
Minghao Yang	Beihang University, China
Yinfeng Yu	Tsinghua University, China
Feihu Zhang	Xidian University, China
Dan Zhao	Tsinghua University, China
Mengyi Zhao	Beihang University, China
Chenliang Zhong	Tsinghua University, China
Quan Zhou	Tsinghua University, China
Yufan Zhuo	Shenzhen University, China
Zhe Liu	Beijing University of Posts and Telecommunications, China
Yuankai Zhang	Beijing University of Posts and Telecommunications, China
Yingjian Wang	Beijing University of Posts and Telecommunications, China
Ali Shafti	Imperial College London, UK
Emmanouil Papastavridis	King's College London, UK
Chenguang Yang	University of the West of England, UK
Chengxu Zhou	University of Leeds, UK
Zhibin Li	The University of Edinburgh, UK
Arash Ajoudani	Istituto Italiano di Tecnologia, Italy
Wan-Soo Kim	Istituto Italiano di Tecnologia, Italy
Jun Morimoto	Advanced Telecommunications Research Institute International, Japan
Luka Peternel	Technische Universiteit Delft, The Netherlands
Heni Ben Amor	Arizona State University, USA
Sami Haddadin	Die Technische Universität München, Germany

Contents

Manipulation

Bioinformatics

Award

Quantized Separable Residual Network for Facial Expression Recognition on FPGA

Xinqi Fan[1], Mingjie Jiang[1(✉)], Huaizhi Zhang[2], Yang Li[3], and Hong Yan[1]

[1] Department of Electrical Engineering, City University of Hong Kong,
Hong Kong SAR, China
{xinqi.fan,minjiang5-c}@my.cityu.edu.hk
[2] College of Petrochemical and Environmental Engineering, Zhejiang Ocean
University, Zhejiang, China
[3] College of Information Science and Technology, Jinan University,
Guangdong, China

Abstract. Facial expression recognition plays an important role in human machine interaction, and thus becomes an important task in cognitive science and artificial intelligence. In vision fields, facial expression recognition aims to identify facial expressions through images or videos, but there is rare work towards real-world applications. In this work, we propose a hardware-friendly quantized separable residual network and developed a real-world facial expression recognition system on a field programming gate array. The proposed network is first trained on devices with graphical processing units, and then quantized to speed up inference. Finally, the quantized algorithm is deployed on a high-performance edge device - Ultra96-V2 field programming gate array board. The complete system involves capturing images, detecting faces, and recognizing expressions. We conduct exhaustive experiments for comparing the performance with various deep learning models and show superior results. The overall system has also demonstrated satisfactory performance on FPGA, and could be considered as an important milestone for facial expression recognition applications in the real world.

Keywords: Facial expression recognition · Separable residual network · Model quantization · FPGA

1 Introduction

Communication and information exchange between humans are important, and facial expressions are one of the most powerful sources containing human emotions [1]. In most cases, there is only a tiny difference of facial expression against different countries and races [2]. According to [3], there are six basic facial expressions, angry, disgust, fearful, happy, sad, surprised, and one extra neutral emotion. In order to facilitate the development of artificial intelligence (AI)

© Springer Nature Singapore Pte Ltd. 2021
F. Sun et al. (Eds.): ICCSIP 2020, CCIS 1397, pp. 3–14, 2021.
https://doi.org/10.1007/978-981-16-2336-3_1

and cognitive science, facial expression recognition (FER) becomes an important stage to identify human emotion for human-machine interaction (HMI) [4]. However, FER is a challenge and multi-disciplinary area including psychology, sociology, anthropology, cognitive science, and computer science [1]. The application prospects of FER in practice are broad, and there is a huge market left. For driving scenarios, FER can help to recognize human emotions to assist driving, so that it can avoid unnecessary accidents under negative emotions [5]. In terms of the polygraph, subtle expressions can be captured by FER to identify whether the subject provides correct or misleading information [1]. In addition, FER can help improve game experience through high-level information exchange [1]. In the medical industry, for some severely ill or mentally ill patients, it is possible to predict their abnormalities and take relevant preventive measures by FER systems [6].

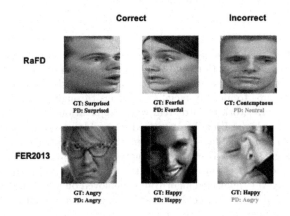

Fig. 1. Demonstration of recognition results for RaFD and FER2013 database. GT: Ground Truth; PD: Predicted Label.

There are several breakthroughs in the development of FER. Many hand-crafted features extraction methods were developed in the past several years, but most of them were replaced by convolutional neural networks (CNNs) in recent time [1]. The first successful and most famous application of CNN is LeNet-5 for recognizing digits [7]. Followed by this wonderful architecture, researchers proposed many deducted CNNs for FER, such as Incremental Boosting CNN [8], CNN with attention [9], EmotiNet [10]. Computational power becomes important at this AI era, so dedicated hardware devices such as field programmable gate array (FPGA) become popular in recent years. There are very few (i.e. 1-2) FER applications on FPGA, but the recognition models are too simple with low performance and the deployment process is too complicated [11,12]. However, most advanced algorithms for FER are too complex to fit the FPGA deployment, while existing FPGA based FER applications have a low performance with complicated deployment.

In this paper, we propose a hardware-friendly and real-world FER system on FPGA. First, we design a separable residual network (ResNet) by replacing some standard convolutional kernels in ResNet as depth-wise separable convolutional kernels to reduce the size of the model. Then, we quantize the model to speed up the inference processing by converting float to int numbers. After that, we compile the network to an executable and linkable file (ELF) for shared libraries and deployed it on FPGA. The complete system for deployment is that the system firstly captures images and sends them to the FPGA board, and then uses Viola-Jones face detector [13] to detect faces. Finally, the detected faces are fed into the quantized network to identify facial expressions, and return an expression. We demonstrate some experimental results for each database with corrected and in-corrected predictions in Fig. 1.

The rest of this paper is organized as follows. In Sect. 2, we review related works on facial expression recognition and FPGA. The proposed methodology is presented in Sect. 3. Section 4 describes datasets, experiment settings, deployment, results and analysis. Finally, Sect. 5 concludes the paper and discusses future work.

2   Related Work

2.1   Facial Expression Recognition

FER, as one of the emerging topics in computer vision and multimedia, has been through a hand-craft feature to deep learning era. Traditional machine learning methods for FER uses geometry and biomedical information to identify hand-craft features. Wang *et al.* proposed a local feature extraction method as a local binary pattern (LBP) method to automatically extract the LBP feature and then feed into a support vector machine (SVM) to perform classification [14]. Yang *et al.* perform a global feature extraction method principal component analysis (PCA) for FER [15]. In recent years, deep learning-based methods start to let people work with end-to-end feature extraction and recognition framework, which outperforms most hand-craft methods. Balahur *et al.* [10] introduced EmotiNet to recognize emotion with text built on appraisal theories but it was limited by concept nuances and complex linguistic rules. Zhang *et al.* [16] proposed a joint pose and expression of recondition architecture. Han *et al.* [17] studied sex difference of saccade patterns in FER systems. However, most research studies were only about the algorithm or software development stage, rather than deploying FER on real-world applications with both soft and hardware supports.

2.2   Field Programmable Gate Array

FPGA can provide dedicated hardware logic circuits by logic clusters or look-up tables for hardware-scale programming, so it can construct the required logic circuit and perform the logic in one clock cycle [18]. A general FPGA development process can be described as follows [18,19]. We, first, write the HLS language, then convert it into a hardware description language, then synthesize the connection of the FPGA, and then compile and run the program. There are three important points in HLS programming, namely scheduling, binding and allocation. General programming may rarely consider scheduling, but FPGA programming should consider underlying hardware clock pulses. However, most software developers can not program hardware language well, so a platform - Vitis AI from Xilinx fills this gap by providing a friendly way to convert deep learning model to hardware recognizable one through several build-in functions and simple scripts [20]. In addition, Vitis AI aims to provide a relatively easy solution to comprehensively develop softwares among heterogeneous hardwares including CPU, GPU, FPGA, etc.

3   Methodology

In this section, we describe the methodology in detail, including how and why we design the separable ResNet, model quantization for inference, and the overall system design architecture. The overall system design architecture is shown in Fig. 2, and its details are given in the following subsections.

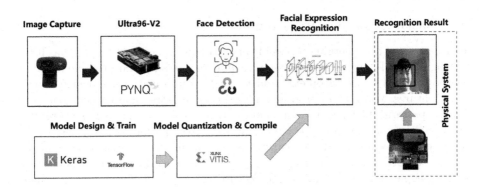

Fig. 2. Architecture of system design

3.1   Network Architecture

To balance the performance and memory cost, we propose a separable ResNet, and quantize it for inference (Fig. 3). The proposed separable ResNet is improved

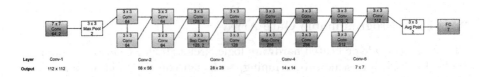

Fig. 3. Architecture of quantized separable residual network

from the original ResNet-18, which has 17 convolutional layers and 1 fully-connected layer [21]. As an important milestone in network architecture design, ResNet and Highway Network are the first network studies for allowing training with deeper architecture without degradation. The idea is to let the network learn at least original information and some other useful information by building a skip connection among several layers. For input x, the output $H(x)$ of the residual block can be shown as

$$H(x) = F(x) + x,$$

where $F(x)$ is the standard output feature map without skip connection. In particular, to balance the size and accuracy, we use 18 layers models which has a fully connected layer as the classifier in the end.

To meet the requirements of small-sized networks for FPGA deployment, we modify two middle convolutional kernels within the skip connection to depthwise separable kernels (as shown by the green and orange boxes). The philosophy is that if the separable convolution does not perform well, the skip connection should still be able to preserve enough information. Depthwise separable convolution includes depthwise convolutions for changing the size of feature maps and pointwise convolutions for changing the number of channels [22,23]. Assume the output shape is $C \times H \times W$, and there are C standard 2D convolution kernels of size $K \times K \times M$ with number of multiplication as $K \times K \times M \times C \times W \times H$, while that of depthwise separable convolution is $(K \times K \times M \times 1 + 1 \times 1 \times M \times C) \times W \times H$, which is $\frac{1}{C} + \frac{1}{K^2}$ times smaller.

The output size of our network depends on the number of classes for the output. Using maximum likelihood estimation (MLE), we derive the multi-class cross-entropy (CE) as the loss function in the proposed method for multi-class classification tasks as

$$\mathcal{L} = -\frac{1}{B} \sum_{i=1}^{B} \sum_{k=1}^{C} y_k \log(\widehat{y}_k),$$

where B is the mini-batch size; C stands for the total amount of classes; y_k and $\widehat{y}_k$ are the ground truth and the predicted score for each class k respectively. We use softmax to normalize the model's output s_k as $\widehat{y}_k = \frac{e^{s_k}}{\sum_{j=1}^{C} e^{s_j}}$.

3.2 Model Quantization

In order to make the model become more light for hardware deployment, we perform model quantization for inference. We adopt quantization with calibration approach by using a subset of data to quantize weights and calibrate activations. The quantization transforms the model from $float32$ to $int8$ data type, and converts it to a deep-learning processing unit (DPU) deployable model for FPGA implementation.

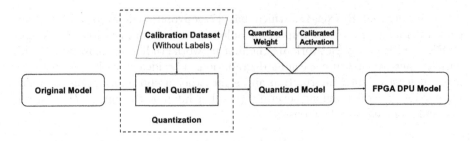

Fig. 4. Quantization process

Here we give a brief introduction of model quantization based on one popular quantization scheme [24]. The value of a fixed-point number is represented by

$$n = \sum_{i=0}^{bw-1} B_i 2^{i-f_l},$$

where $B_i \in \{0,1\}$; bw denotes the bit width; f_l is the fractional length. The quantization consists of the weight quantization phase and the data quantization phase. Weight quantization is to compute the optimal f_l which minimizes the truncation error by

$$f_l = \arg\min_{f_l} \sum |W_f - W(bw, f_l)|,$$

where W_f is a weight of float format; $W(bw, f_l)$ denotes the fixed-point format weight with the bit width bw and the fractional length f_l. In data quantization phase, it compares the output of each layer of the float model and of the fixed-point model and then finds the optimal f_l which minimizes the difference between the float model and the fixed-point model.

$$f_l = \arg\min_{f_l} \sum |x_f - x(bw, f_l)|,$$

where x_f is the output of a layer of float model; $x(bw, f_l)$ is the output of a layer of fixed-point model.

During the deployment, we perform model quantization using Vitis AI platform, the stages are listed in Fig. 4. In order to quantize the model, we need to put the original float model into model quantizer and give some calibration data without labels. After quantization, we can have an integer model with quantized weights and calibrated activation. Finally, we obtain a model with DPU support for further FPGA deployment.

3.3   System Design

We develop one of the very first real-time facial expression recognition systems on an Ultra96-V2 FPGA board, and the pipeline of which is shown in Fig. 2.

There are two main stages described in the system design, model development shown in green boxes and model deployment shown in blue boxes. The model development phase involving model design and quantization is mainly described in Sect. 3.1 and 3.2. After obtaining the quantized model, we compile the model as FPGA recognized ELF file. In terms of information flow for the system on FPGA, we firstly use a camera to capture video frames and send them to Ultra96-V2 FPGA [25] board with DPU-PYNQ environment [26]. Then, we use Viola-Jones face detector provided by OpenCV to detect face areas. After detection, only the cropped face regions are sent to quantized facial expression recognition network, and results are shown on the screen. In addition, our physical system and real-time results are also shown in the right orange box.

4   Experiment Result

4.1   Dataset and Experiment Setup

In this research, we evaluate our models on two datasets, Radboud Faces Database (RaFD) [27] and Facial Expression Recognition 2013 (FER-2013) [28]. RaFD is a dataset with 8056 images of 67 models showing 8 emotional expressions (anger, disgust, fear, happiness, sadness, surprise, contempt, and neutral). FER-2013 has 35,685 images with 7 facial expressions (happiness, neutral, sadness, anger, surprise, disgust, fear). Since RaFD does not provide the training-testing data splitting, we pick 20% images of all images as testing dataset and the rest images were used for training.

For model training, we employe data augmentation such as image horizontal flipping, image rotation and image shift. In addition, we use the stochastic gradient descent algorithm as the optimizer, and set the initial learning rate to 0.005 and momentum to 0.1. The training platform is a desktop computer equipped with NVIDIA RTX 2080Ti graphics card, running Ubuntu 16.04 system. The software environment is mainly Python 3.6.8, Tensorflow-gpu 2.0.0, Keras 2.3.1. We trained the model with 200 epochs and saved the best model.

4.2   Deployment Detail

We adopt Xilinx Ultra96-V2 FPGA board for employment. There are two main steps, environment setup and system integration. In terms of environment setup, we install PYNQ 2.5 image on the board and the related DPU drivers, including register configuration module, data controller module and convolution calculation module, for speeding up neural network operations. For system integration, we compile the quantized model to an ELF file for shared libraries, then use DPU overlay to load the model. Finally, we apply OpenCV for face detection as pre-processing, and show recognition results on the screen as post-processing.

Table 1. Comparison of Methods for Databases RaFD and FER2013

Database	Method	Accuracy
RaFD	Baseline model	85.45%
	Quantized baseline model	85.51%
	ResNet-18	95.71%
	Separable ResNet-18	93.97%
	Quantized ResNet-18	91.54%
	Quantized Separable ResNet-18	92.85%
FER-2013	Baseline model	50.57%
	Quantized baseline model	51.91%
	ResNet-18	66.26%
	Separable ResNet-18	65.90%
	Quantized ResNet-18	65.76%
	Quantized Separable ResNet-18	65.45%

4.3 Result and Analysis

We perform exhaustive experiments for both original models and quantized models on two public FER datasets, RaFD and FER2013, to demonstrate the general performance. In general, to balance the accuracy and deployment requirements, our model is still relative small, but can demonstrate sufficient performance. In addition, we deploy the quantized model on Ultra96-V2 FPGA borad as a complete real-world FER system as shown in Fig. 2. Some sample demonstrations of experimental results are shown in Fig. 1, while detailed qualitative recognition accuracy is shown in Table 1, and the confusion matrices of proposed quantized models are shown in Fig. 5. We compare experimental results on different models, including a baseline model, ResNet-18, Separable ResNet-18 and their quantized ones. The baseline model is a shallow CNN with 4 convolutional layers and 1 fully connected layer, as the similar networks are widely used in FPGA based CNN applications.

In terms of RaFD database, it can be seen that ResNet-18 and separable ResNet-18 outperform baseline model by around 9% and 6%, respectively. An interesting phenomenon found is that the accuracy of quantized models do not degrade the performance, or have similar or even higher accuracy as the original ones. There are two possible reasons which may contribute to the good performance of the quantized model: (1) The quantization with data calibration can significantly prevent the performance drop. (2) Since the data used for calibration is small, it may have the effect of regularization which can alleviate over-fitting. From the confusion matrices in Fig. 5a and 5b, we can see that our models show relatively low performance for discriminating contemptuous and neutral, but these expressions are even hard for humans to recognize. Similar results can also be found on the real-world database - FER2013 experimental results. As FER2013 is a relatively hard database with only one channel information (i.e. gray-scale image), most algorithms do not perform well on this database. As shown by the incorrect predicted samples in Fig. 1, the dataset even has face occlusion problems, which can be harmful for FER. Compared to the baseline model, ResNet-18 and separable ResNet-18 increase accuracy by more than 15%. From the confusion matrices in Fig. 5c and 5d, we found that happy, surprised and neutral are the easy expressions to recognize, while the rest ones are quite hard with around 50% accuracy only. However, this hard dataset gives researchers in this field more space to improve the performance, so that the work can be more reliable in the near future.

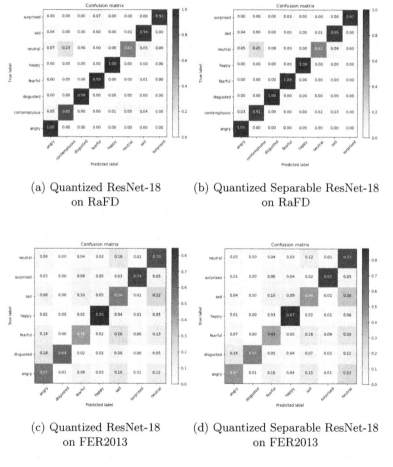

(a) Quantized ResNet-18
on RaFD

(b) Quantized Separable ResNet-18
on RaFD

(c) Quantized ResNet-18
on FER2013

(d) Quantized Separable ResNet-18
on FER2013

Fig. 5. Confusion matrix of models on RaFD and FER-2013

5   Conclusion

In this paper, we propose a hardware-friendly and read-world FER system on FPGA. First, we design a separable residual network by replacing some standard convolutional kernels in ResNet as depth-wise separable convolutional kernels to reduce the size of model. Then, we quantize the model to speed up the inference processing by converting float to int numbers. After that, we compile the network and deploy it on FPGA. The workflow of the complete system deployed on Ultra96-V2 FPGA board is that the system firstly captures images and sends them to the FPGA board, and then uses Viola-Jones face detector to detect faces. Finally, the detected faces are fed into the quantized network to identify facial expressions, and return an expression. Experimental results show the performance of quantized models do not decrease too much, so the proposed quantized ResNet-18 would be satisfactory for deployment. There are still open problems left for FER to be tackled in the future studies, including class imbalance, occlusion, illumination, domain adaptation etc.

Acknowledgement. This work is supported by the Hong Kong Innovation and Technology Commission and City University of Hong Kong (Project 7005230).

References

1. Li, S., Deng, W.: Deep facial expression recognition: a survey. IEEE Trans. Affect. Comput. (2020)
2. Gennari, R., et al.: Children's emotions and quality of products in participatory game design. Int. J. Hum. Comput. Stud. **101**, 45–61 (2017)
3. Lucey, P., Cohn, J.F., Kanade, T., Saragih, J., Ambadar, Z., Matthews, I.: The extended cohn-kanade dataset (CK+): a complete dataset for action unit and emotion-specified expression. In: IEEE Conference on Computer Vision and Pattern Recognition Workshop, pp. 94–101. IEEE (2010)
4. Filntisis, P.P., Efthymiou, N., Koutras, P., Potamianos, G., Maragos, P.: Fusing body posture with facial expressions for joint recognition of affect in child-robot interaction. IEEE Robot. Autom. Lett. **4**(4), 4011–4018 (2019)
5. Wang, Y., Ai, H., Wu, B., Huang, C.: Real time facial expression recognition with Adaboost. In: International Conference on Pattern Recognition, vol. 3, pp. 926–929. IEEE (2004)
6. He, K., Zhang, X., Ren, S., Sun, J.: Delving deep into rectifiers: surpassing human-level performance on ImageNet classification. In: IEEE International Conference on Computer Vision, pp. 1026–1034 (2015)
7. LeCun, Y., et al.: Backpropagation applied to handwritten zip code recognition. Neural Comput. **1**(4), 541–551 (1989)
8. Han, S., Meng, Z., Khan, A.S., Tong, Y.: Incremental boosting convolutional neural network for facial action unit recognition. arXiv preprint arXiv:1707.05395 (2017)
9. Fernandez, P.D.M., Pena, F.A.G., Ren, T., et al.: FERAtt: facial expression recognition with attention net. In: IEEE Conference on Computer Vision and Pattern Recognition Workshop, pp. 837–846 (2019)

10. Balahur, A., Hermida, J.M., Montoyo, A., Muñoz, R.: EmotiNet: a knowledge base for emotion detection in text built on the appraisal theories. In: Muñoz, R., Montoyo, A., Métais, E. (eds.) NLDB 2011. LNCS, vol. 6716, pp. 27–39. Springer, Heidelberg (2011). https://doi.org/10.1007/978-3-642-22327-3_4

11. Phan-Xuan, H., Le-Tien, T., Nguyen-Tan, S.: FPGA platform applied for facial expression recognition system using convolutional neural networks. Procedia Comput. Sci. **151**, 651–658 (2019)

12. Vinh, P.T., Vinh, T.Q.: Facial expression recognition system on SoC FPGA. In: International Symposium on Electrical and Electronics Engineering, pp. 1–4. IEEE (2019)

13. Viola, P., Jones, M.: Robust real-time object detection. Int. J. Comput. Vis. **4**(34–47), 4 (2001)

14. Wang, W., Chang, F., Zhao, J., Chen, Z.: Automatic facial expression recognition using local binary pattern. In: World Congress on Intelligent Control and Automation, pp. 6375–6378. IEEE (2010)

15. Yang, J., Zhang, D., Frangi, A.F., et al.: Two-dimensional PCA: a new approach to appearance-based face representation and recognition. IEEE Trans. Pattern Anal. Mach. Intell. **26**(1), 131–137 (2004)

16. Zhang, F., Zhang, T., Mao, Q., Xu, C.: Joint pose and expression modeling for facial expression recognition. In: IEEE Conference on Computer Vision and Pattern Recognition, pp. 3359–3368 (2018)

17. Han, Y., Chen, B., Zhang, X.: Sex difference of saccade patterns in emotional facial expression recognition. In: Sun, F., Liu, H., Hu, D. (eds.) ICCSIP 2016. CCIS, vol. 710, pp. 144–154. Springer, Singapore (2017). https://doi.org/10.1007/978-981-10-5230-9_16

18. Bailey, D.G.: Design for Embedded Image Processing on FPGAs. Wiley, New York (2011)

19. Kumar, A., Hansson, A., Huisken, J., et al.: An FPGA design flow for reconfigurable network-based multi-processor systems on chip. In: Design, Automation and Test in Europe Conference and Exhibition, pp. 1–6. IEEE (2007)

20. Kathail, V.: Xilinx vitis unified software platform. In: ACM/SIGDA International Symposium on Field-Programmable Gate Arrays, pp. 173–174 (2020)

21. He, K., Zhang, X., Ren, S., Sun, J.: Deep residual learning for image recognition. In: IEEE Conference on Computer Vision and Pattern Recognition, pp. 770–778 (2016)

22. Howard, A.G., Zhu, M., et al.: MobileNets: efficient convolutional neural networks for mobile vision applications. arXiv preprint arXiv:1704.04861 (2017)

23. Zhu, Y., Bai, L., Peng, W., Zhang, X., Luo, X.: Depthwise separable convolution feature learning for ihomogeneous rock image classification. In: Sun, F., Liu, H., Hu, D. (eds.) ICCSIP 2018. CCIS, vol. 1005, pp. 165–176. Springer, Singapore (2019). https://doi.org/10.1007/978-981-13-7983-3_15

24. Qiu, J., Wang, J., Yao, S., et al.: Going deeper with embedded FPGA platform for convolutional neural network. In: ACM/SIGDA International Symposium on Field-Programmable Gate Arrays, pp. 26–35 (2016)

25. Yang, Y., et al.: Synetgy: algorithm-hardware co-design for convnet accelerators on embedded FPGA. In: Proceedings of ACM/SIGDA International Symposium on Field-Programmable Gate Arrays, pp. 23–32 (2019)

26. Wu, T., Liu, W., Jin, Y.: An end-to-end solution to autonomous driving based on xilinx FPGA. In: International Conference on Field-Programmable Technology, pp. 427–430. IEEE (2019)

27. Langner, O., Dotsch, R., Bijlstra, G., Wigboldus, D.H.J., Hawk, S.T., Van Knip-penberg, A.D.: Presentation and validation of the Radboud faces database. Cogn. Emot. **24**(8), 1377–1388 (2010)
28. Goodfellow, I.J., et al.: Challenges in representation learning: a report on three machine learning contests. In: Lee, M., Hirose, A., Hou, Z.-G., Kil, R.M. (eds.) ICONIP 2013. LNCS, vol. 8228, pp. 117–124. Springer, Heidelberg (2013). https://doi.org/10.1007/978-3-642-42051-1_16

Hole-Peg Assembly Strategy Based on Deep Reinforcement Learning

Xiaodong Zhang[1(✉)] and Pengchao Ding[2]

[1] Beijing Key Laboratory of Intelligent Space Robotic Systems Technology and Application, Beijing Institute of Spacecraft System Engineering CAST, Beijing 100086, China
[2] Institute of Technology, Harbin 150001, Heilongjiang, China

Abstract. Hole-peg assembly using robot is widely used to validate the abilities of autonomous assembly task. Currently, the autonomous assembly is mainly depended on the high precision of position, force measurement and the compliant control method. The assembly process is complicated and the ability in unknown situations is relatively low. In this paper, a kind of assembly strategy based on deep reinforcement learning is proposed using the TD3 reinforcement learning algorithm based on DDPG and an adaptive annealing guide is added into the exploration process which greatly accelerates the convergence rate of deep reinforcement learning. The assembly task can be finished by the intelligent agent based on the measurement information of force-moment and the pose. In this paper, the training and verification of assembly verification is realized on the V-rep simulation platform and the UR5 manipulator.

Keywords: Deep reinforcement learning · Assembly · TD3

1 Introduction

At present, an increasing number of robots are used in a variety of assembly tasks. There are mainly two strategies for a robot to finish the assembly task, One is to preview the assembly task by teaching the robot to fulfil the task and optimize the teaching path, but it is difficult to perform the high precision assembly tasks directly; The second is to design an impedance control method for assembly strategy and make adjustments to find the best parameters, however it often can't get the good performance in unknown situations.

In this paper, deep reinforcement learning strategy is designed which can accomplish the better adaptive abilities in unknown situations. A deep reinforcement learning algorithm is adopted based on the assumption that the environmental state information of the next moment can be inferred through the current environmental state information and the actions adopted, the algorithm simulates the human learning process through designing a reward mechanism, and then finding the optimal strategy to get the reward by constant trial and error. In recent related researches, this algorithm has made some progress in intelligent grasping [1–4] and intelligent tracking of robots [5–8]. However,

© Springer Nature Singapore Pte Ltd. 2021
F. Sun et al. (Eds.): ICCSIP 2020, CCIS 1397, pp. 15–32, 2021.
https://doi.org/10.1007/978-981-16-2336-3_2

these scenes have low requirements on the motion accuracy of the robot, which cannot directly prove its applicability in the field of high-precision assembly.

Recently, many researches have been proposed on assembly [9–15]. J. Xu [10] proposed a new strategy based on traditional force control to reduce training time and used fuzzy reward mechanism to avoid the network optimization of algorithm entering local optimal, but the traditional force control actually limits the performance of the policy to some extent. Inoue. T [13] introduced a kind of LSTM neural network structure to improve the performance of network in tasks. Luo Jianlan [15] uses iLQG reinforcement learning algorithm to combine force position hybrid control and space force control, and then uses MGPS method to optimize the parameters of network, but this approach does not significantly improve the autonomous intelligence of the robot. Fan Yongxiang [9] combines the advantages of GPS and DDPG [16] to design a new framework in which the supervised learning provides guidance trajectory and the reinforcement learning carries out strategy optimization. Mel Vecerik [11] reduces the amount of work required to elaborate the reward in the reinforcement learning algorithm by adding human demonstrations. There are some problems in DDPG algorithm include the slow convergence speed and large amount of super parameter adjustment. Many scholars [9–11, 13, 14, 17] have adopted DQN algorithm, however this algorithm usually need to discretize relevant data which cannot deal with the continuity problem of large data volume.

In order to prove the feasibility of deep reinforcement learning in assembly task, this paper adopts the hole-peg assembly task, and this assembly is also the most basic assembly form of industry assembly task. At the same time, the neural network structure of TD3 algorithm [18] is improved to increase the robustness of the algorithm, a certain angle deviation is added between the axis and the hole, and the precision of the sensor in the simulation is reduced.

The rest of this article is organized as follows: The second section mainly elaborates and analyzes the tasks in detail. The third section describes the methods used in detail. The fourth section is a detailed analysis of deep reinforcement learning algorithm in V-rep training and testing process. The fifth section is the main conclusions of this paper and some prospects for the future work.

2   The Description of Problems

In the high-precision hole-peg assembly task, the corresponding assembly process is divided into the hole-searching stage and the hole-inserting stage. The assembly strategies and difficulties of these two parts are quite different, so the spatial hierarchical strategy is adopted to decompose the assembly task, the first one is the deep reinforcement learning strategy in the hole-searching stage, which is to complete the movement from any position out of the chamfering to the actual position of the hole. The second is the deep reinforcement learning strategy during inserting the hole which is to complete all the subsequent tasks. These two tasks are distinguished by determining the z position of the axis. Therefore, the researches and training in this paper are mainly carried out around these two parts. Firstly, it is the hole-searching stage. In this stage, the angle offset is so small that it is often ignored, as a result of which, the main movement dimension of the hole is three translational dimensions while the rotation action dimension is corrected by the internal position control strategy. Then it is the hole-inserting phase when the position and angle observations are so small that they usually need to be amplified. In this case, the action dimension needs not only the translational dimension but also the rotational dimension.

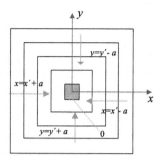

Fig. 1. The position error of the end of the shaft relative to the hole

Due to the influence of visual positioning error, the position and posture of the end of the shaft relative to the hole are measured, which is obtained by combining the forward kinematics calculation of the manipulator with the visual positioning to reduce the whole value to the origin so as to improve the ability of deep reinforcement learning to resist parameter perturbation. As shown in the Fig. 1, in the x direction, when $-a < x < a$, the value of p_x is zero; when $a < x$, the value of p_x is $x - a$; when $a > x$, the value of p_x is $x + a$. In the y direction, when $-a < y < a$, the value of p_y is zero; when $a < y$, the value of p_y is $x - a$; when $a > y$, the value of p_y is $y + a$. By this treatment, the interference error of the arm in forward operation can be reduced.

3   A Detailed Description of the Methods

In this section, two strategies of hole-searching and hole-inserting are elaborated and then the TD3 algorithm is introduced. Assume that when the current state is known, the future state is independent of the past state among the assemblies in this assembly task. So translate the solution to the assembly problem into a "Markov decision process", where the decision part is determined by the agent and the assembly process can be represented as a sequence where states and actions alternate chronologically. In this case, each action is expected to work toward the ultimate goal—maximized long-term reward, for which the value of each action contributing to the ultimate goal should be quantified. As a result, make the agent continuously interact with the environment to explore the value of each action, Q. Based on this value, an optimal strategy π is found, which determines the best action a according to the current state s to obtain the maximum reward.

$$\pi(s) = \mathrm{argmax}_a Q(s, a)$$

At the same time, in order to alleviate the sparsity problem in the exploration of reinforcement learning, the assembly process is divided into the hole-researching and hole-inserting phases, and different treatments were made for different stages.

3.1 Hole-Searching Phase

The environmental state information needed to observe is:

$$S = [p_x, p_y, p_z, \alpha, \beta, \gamma, F_x, F_y, F_z, T_x, T_y, T_z] \tag{1}$$

Where p_x, p_y, p_z are the positions relative to the hole after treatment; α, β, γ are the angles relative to the normal line of the hole after treatment; F_x, F_y, F_z, T_x, T_y are the force information detected by the six-dimensional force-moment sensor which can indirectly reflect the contact situation between the axle and hole; x, y, z are three axes in space. However, angle information is controlled by the internal strategy regulator in the hole-searching stage, for which our specific operation is to delete the three dimensions of the state information observed by the agent γ and T_z basically have no practical effect on this assembly task, so which can be deleted. Reducing dimensions can not only reduce computation and simplify neural network model, but also effectively alleviate the problem of dimension explosion. At this time the state S changes into:

$$S = [p_x, p_y, p_z, F_x, F_y, F_z] \tag{2}$$

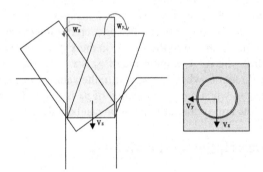

Fig. 2. The motion directions of peg

As shown in the Fig. 2, there are mainly five directions of motion in the assembly of circular hole shaft, which are v_x, v_y, v_z, w_x and w_y. The action of the agent in this stage are mainly 3-dimensional translational motions:

$$a_0 = [v_x, v_y, v_z] \tag{3}$$

Where v_x, v_y, v_z are the translational velocities respectively in the x, y and z axes, which are the three dimensions of the output of actor network. When this action is transmitted to the controller, it is denoted as:

$$a_0 = [v_x, v_y, v_z, 0, 0, 0] \tag{4}$$

The knowledge-driven action at this stage is just a simple proportional controller algorithm:

$$a_1 = [v_x, v_y, v_z, w_x, w_y, 0]$$

$$v_x = k_{x1}p_x + k_{x2}F_x$$
$$v_y = k_{y1}p_y + k_{y2}F_y$$
$$v_z = b_1$$
$$w_x = k_{x3}\alpha + k_{x4}T_x$$
$$w_y = k_{y3}\beta + k_{y4}T_y \tag{5}$$

The reinforcement learning is optimized and evaluated based on reward. At this stage, the reward designed is divided into two parts: one is the reward after successful assembly, the other is the penalty value of failure to complete the task.

The punishment at this stage is divided into two parts, force punishment and positional punishment, where the force penalty p_f is the two norm of F and the position penalty p_{pos} is the two norm of pos:

$$penalize = p_f K + p_f (1 - K) \ 0 < K < 1$$

$$p_f = f(F), F = \| F_x \ F_y \ F_z \|$$

$$p_{pos} = f(pos), pos = \| p_x \ p_y \ p_z \|$$

$$f(x) = \begin{cases} -x/xmax & xmax > x > 0 \\ -1 & x > xmax \end{cases} \tag{6}$$

Where the function $f(x)$ is a linear limiting function with respect to x and $xmax$ is the maximum value of x. By adjusting the parameter K, not only ensure that penalize is between $(0,1]$, but also adjust the proportion of each part in penalize. The reward value after successful assembly is just related to the value of the steps learned to complete the assembly action and the maximum speed of assembly is achieved by setting the reward value:

$$reward = 1 - \frac{n}{nmax} \ n \in (0, nmax] \tag{7}$$

Where n is the value of step in each episode, whose maximum value is nmax.

When the assembly of this segment is completed, the reward is the value of *reward*. In addition, the penalize is used to ensure that the value of the reward is within $(-1,1)$.

3.2 Hole-Inserting Phase

At this stage, the value of pose information is relatively small, but the deviation is large, so the state information of environment observed by agent is changed to the power information:

$$S = [p_z, F_x, F_y, F_z, T_x, T_y] \tag{8}$$

At the same time, the actions of agents are in 5 dimensions:

$$a_0 = \begin{bmatrix} v_x, v_y, v_z, w_x, w_y \end{bmatrix} \tag{9}$$

Where v_x, v_y, v_z are the translational velocities respectively in the x, y and z axes; w_x, w_y are the rotation speed along the x and y axis respectively. In this stage, the knowledge-driven action is as follows:

$$a_1 = [v_x, v_y, v_z, w_x, w_y, 0]$$
$$v_x = k_{x5}F_x$$
$$v_y = k_{y5}F_y$$
$$v_z = b_2$$
$$w_x = k_{x6}T_x$$
$$w_y = k_{y6}T_y \tag{10}$$

Then let knowledge-driven action provide supplementary guidance to agent exploration and the reward of this phase is also divided into two parts:

$$penalize = \frac{p_f + p_M}{2}K + p_h(1 - K) \quad 0 < K < 1$$

$$p_f = f(F), F = \| F_x \ F_y \ F_z \|$$

$$p_M = g(M), M = \| M_x \ M_y \ M_z \|$$

$$p_h = f_1(h), h = |p_z|$$

$$g(x) = \begin{cases} -\sqrt[3]{x/xmax} & xmax > x > 0 \\ -1 & x > xmax \end{cases}$$

$$f_1(x) = \begin{cases} -1.2x/xmax + 0.6 & xmax > x > 0 \\ -0.6 & x > xmax \end{cases}$$

$$reward = 1 - \frac{k}{kmax} \quad k \in (0, kmax] \tag{11}$$

When the assembly of the segment is completed, the reward is the value of the reward, otherwise the penalize is adopted to ensure that the value of the reward is within $(-1,1)$.

In order to get the long-term reward of every action in the current state, the reinforcement learning algorithm is designed as follows:

$$R_i = r_i + \gamma r_{i+1} + \gamma^2 r_{i+2} + \cdots + \gamma^{T-i} r_T = r_i + \gamma R_{i+1} \tag{12}$$

Where r_i is the reward value at the current moment; r_T is the reward at time T; γ is the decay rate of the effect of future reward value on current reward; R_i is the current long-term returns; R_{i+1} is the long-term return at the next moment. Calculate the value of long-term returns by iterating. However, the long-term returns bring about the rapid accumulation of fitting errors and variances when using neural network fitting. For this reason, long-term returns at the expense of longer-term returns:

$$R_i = \frac{r_i + \gamma R_{i+1}}{1 + \gamma} \tag{13}$$

Since the current size of the reward is within the range of -1 to 1, the value of the long-term reward can be effectively limited to the range of -1 to 1 by designing such a long-term reward. Compared with original formula, it can effectively reduce the influence caused by the accumulation of deviation, especially the fitting deviation for the undetected space.

In order to solve the problem that there are so many data in the continuous space of high latitude, DDPG reinforcement algorithm uses a neural network to fit the action-value function $Q(s, a)$, which means the value of taking action a under state s. In order to make the critic network fit $Q(s, a|\theta^Q)$ well, the optimized loss function of network is set to:

$$L\left(\theta^Q\right) = E_{\pi'}\left[\left(Q\left(s_i, a_i|\theta^Q\right) - y_i\right)^2\right] \tag{14}$$

$$y_i = r(s_i, a_i) + \gamma Q'\left(s_{i+1}, \mu'\left(s_{i+1}|\theta^{\mu'}\right)|\theta^{Q'}\right) \tag{15}$$

Where $r(s_i, a_i)$ is the reward of taking action a_i under states_i; $\mu'\left(s_{i+1}|\theta^{\mu'}\right)$ is the action a_{i+1} obtained by using actor neural network to fit the strategy function under the states_{i+1}; $Q'\left(s_{i+1}, a_{i+1}|\theta^{Q'}\right)$ is a neural network whose structure is identical to $Q(s, a|\theta^Q)$, which is used to calculate the value of taking action a_{i+1} in states_{i+1}; γ is the attenuation value of the influence of future value. Similar to the long-term return, get the value in the case of (s_i, a_i) throughy_i. Then by continuous training, a better actor-critic function $Q(s, a)$ can be fitted.

As mentioned above, there are four neural networks involved in the DDPG structure: the critic network, the target critic network, the actor network and the target actor network. The Actor network is the control strategy network whose main function is to calculate the corresponding actions according to the information of the sensor. The structures of the two target networks are completely similar to the corresponding network structure, but there is a certain delay for them on parameter update compared with the corresponding network. The update strategy adopted is the moving average of the corresponding network parameters:

$$\theta = \tau\theta' + 1 - \tau\theta \tag{16}$$

The main functions of the Target network are to calculate the value and to attain the action of the next moment in the time series. This dual network method can effectively alleviate the coupling problem of time. The update mode of actor network parameter θ^μ is the gradient direction of maximum value and the calculation method adopts the chain rule of gradient:

$$\nabla_{\theta^\mu} J \approx \mathbb{E}_\pi[\nabla_{\theta^\mu} Q^\mu(s_t, \mu(s_t|\theta^\mu)|\theta^\mu)$$
$$= \mathbb{E}_\pi[\nabla_{a_t^\mu} Q^\mu(s_t, a_t)\nabla_{\theta^\mu}(\mu(s_t|\theta^\mu)) \tag{17}$$

The TD3 algorithm used in this paper is improved on the basis of DDPG algorithm and the overall framework is shown in Fig. 3. There are three main improved strategies. As for the first strategy, change the critic network to a pair of independent Q-value neural

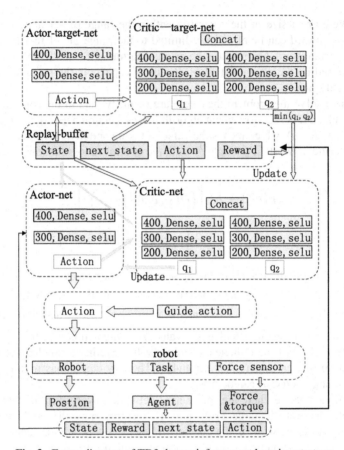

Fig. 3. Frame diagram of TD3 deep reinforcement learning strategy

networks and when optimize the network parameters, the smaller one of the two Q values is used to calculate the loss value, so as to avoid overestimation of errors:

$$y = r_i + (1 - Done) * \gamma * \min_{j=1,2} Q' \left(s_{i+1}, a_{i+1} | \theta_j^Q \right) \tag{18}$$

On the second one, the main cause of the error is the deviation of the estimation of the value function and regularization parameters are often used to eliminate deviations in machine learning. Therefore, a small area around the target action in the action space should be smoothed, which means adding some noise to the action when calculating the Q value of the target action:

$$\mu' \left(s_{i+1} | \theta^{\mu'} \right) + \epsilon$$

$$\epsilon \sim clip \left(\mathcal{N} \left(0, \tilde{\sigma} \right), -c, c \right) \tag{19}$$

About the third, delay the update of actor network, which reduce the cumulative error caused by multiple updates while reducing unnecessary repeated updates, thus solving the time coupling problems of value function and policy function.

The algorithm is divided into two threads, the first action thread is to explore the environment and storing the experience, the second learning thread is to train the network with the recovered experience. The Action thread refers to the part in bottom left of Fig. 3, Firstly, reset the assembly's initial environment including setting the initial deflection Angle within $\pm 2°$, setting the position deviation within ± 1 mm during the training jack phase and getting the feedback from the environment during the initial exploration. Secondly, select the directing actions or agent output actions with certain probability through the action selector, which is obtained through the actor network in the agent in the top of Fig. 3. Then the robot is asked to perform that action and interact with the environment to obtain new status information, which will be processed by the agent to obtain the reward value and then immediately store them in replay buffer. Finally, start a new cycle of above-mentioned state - action - state process. Replay buffer uses the FIFO method to store information and improve queue structure by taking out a block of memory in advance to explicitly store the information and the corresponding address, which speeds up the transfer of data between CPU and GPU at the expense of memory cache. At the same time, its reading method is adopted randomly to eliminate the correlation among the data and prevent overfitting.

Table 1. The learning thread of algorithm1

Algorithm 1 action thread
Initialize replay buffer: **R**
for k=1 to M **do**
Initialize the noise distribution N
S_1 = env.reset()
when the data stored in R reaches Ns
a start signal is sent to the learning thread
for t = 1 to T **do**
At a certain probability ϵ choice guiding action a_g
or $a_t = \mu(s_t|\theta^\mu) + N_t$
$s_{t+1}, reward_t, done, \_ = env.step(a_t)$
let **R** store $s_t, s_{t+1}, a_t, reward_t, done$
t = t+1
end for
k = k+1
when k is a multiple of 100
test the current actor network performance
end for
Sends a termination signal to the learning thread

The learning thread refers to the upper part of the Table 1. For updating the critic network, agent continuously replays the experience from replay buffer and obtains a smaller current Q value from the target network. After a few steps of delay, the actor network is updated by using the gradient of the critic network, and the specific content is shown in Table 2.

Table 2. The learning thread of algorithm 2

Algorithm 2 learning thread

Initialize actor network $\mu(s|\theta^\mu)$

Initialize critic network $Q(s, a|\theta_1^Q), Q(s, a|\theta_2^Q)$

Initializes the target network: $Q' \leftarrow Q, \mu' \leftarrow \mu$

Repeat

    for i=1 to I **do:**

        for t =1 to T **do:**

            randomly obtain the minibatch data (s_i, s_{i+1}, a_i, r_i) from R and the size of mini-batch is R_{batch}

$$\epsilon \sim clip(\mathcal{N}(0, \tilde{\sigma}), -c, c)$$

$$a_{i+1} = \mu'(s_{i+1}|\theta^{\mu'}) + \epsilon$$

$$y' = r_i + (1 - Done) * \gamma * \min_{j=1,2} Q'(s_{i+1}, a_{i+1}|\theta_j^Q)$$

$$y = \frac{y'}{1 + (1 - Done) * \gamma}$$

$$\theta_i \leftarrow argmin_{\theta_i} \frac{1}{N} \Sigma_i (y - Q(s, a|\theta_i^Q))^2$$

        end for

        update actor network:

$$\nabla_{\theta^\mu} J \simeq N^{-1} \sum \nabla_a Q(s, a|\theta^Q)|_{s=s_i, a=\mu(s_i)} \nabla_{\theta^\mu} \mu(s|\theta^\mu)|_{s_i}$$

        update target network:

$$\theta_i^{Q'} \leftarrow \tau\theta_i^Q + (1 - \tau)\theta_i^{Q'}$$

$$\theta^{\mu'} \leftarrow \tau\theta^\mu + (1 - \tau)\theta^{\mu'}$$

    end for

    wait **until** the star signal from the action thread is received

until receive the termination signal sent by the action thread

---

4   Simulative Training

This section mainly introduces the specific situation of our simulation training. The main robot for high precision assembly is the UR5 six-axis manipulator. The main simulation experiment platform used in the training is v-rep. The main accessory information of the computer used in the training is the GPU of NVIDIA 1660Ti with the video memory frequency of 12000 MHz and video memory of 6G and the CPU with main frequency of the 3.7 GHz AMD 2700×.

The first step is to import the axle hole assembly model and UR5 manipulator into the V-rep, as shown in Fig. 4. The diameter of the hole is 25.0 mm and the depth is 36.0 mm. The chamfering part has a maximum diameter of 40 mm and a depth of 2 mm, and the diameter of the shaft during training is 24.95 mm and its length is 10 mm.

During the training, the 2.78 version of bullet engine is adopted for the dynamic engine and select the high-precision mode. Besides, the simulation time step of the training was set to 5.0 ms and the maximum number of steps in each episode was set to 20 in the hole-seeking stage and 450 in the hole-inserting stage. The maximum Replay buffer storage is set to 1 million and the random sample size is 1024.

In order to simplify the calculation, the influence of gravity is ignored, which means setting the gravity constant G of the simulation environment to 0 and adding the gravity compensation to the dynamics control of the manipulator in the subsequent experiments. At the same time, the controller uses the internal velocity Jacobian matrix to convert the velocity of the end workspace into the velocity of each joint in the joint space in real time.

To ensure the safety of the assembly, the maximum contact force in z axis direction is set as $F_{zmax} = 50$ N. At the same time, in order to ensure that the simulation process is as close as possible to the real situation, a threshold value is set for the absolute deviation of the Angle and position of the axis in the inserting stage.

When it is greater than the threshold, namely, $abs(\theta) \leq 4°$ and $abs(\Delta p) \leq 2$ mm, the inserting process is stopped and restart a new process. At the same time, during the training process, the motion range of the axle is restricted: in the searching stage, the ranges of x and y direction are set as $(-9,9)$ mm and that of z-direction is $(27.0, 40.5)$ mm; in the inserting phase, the range of z-direction is $(0,2\ 8.5)$ mm. When the assembly process is restarted due to an uncompleted task, the reward value is set to -1.

Before formal training, in order to reduce the error accumulation caused by the large deviation and variance of the network in the initial training, the data set of initial instruction action is designed and the data set of initial reward to preliminarily train the actor network and the critic network.

To do this, according to the random generation of uniform distribution, generate a set of states within a certain range and include a state set which contains as many states as possible that may be involved in the experiment, and then obtain the action set through the directive action generator whose input is the random state set. Therefore, the elements in the two sets can be saved into state-action data sets one by one in order to train the actor network by the state-action data sets. The obtaining way of the initial reward data set is: according to the uniform distribution, in a certain range, randomly generate a data set which includes as much state action information as possible that may be involved in the experiment. At the same time, simplify the system of reward designed in the assembly process, as a result of which, the reward is fixed as 0.7 when *done*, and the reward set when restarting the assembly process is not taken into account. Then based on that, the reward data set is built and the critic network is initially trained with this data set. However, when training the critic network, set the reward decay rate to zero, which means that we only care about the immediate reward rather than the long-term return.

As for the probability ϵ, which is selected to guide action, we adopt intelligent adaptive annealing method, namely, to make the corresponding changes according the observation of the test data. Specifically, when the completion degree is greater than N for three consecutive times, the probability ϵ becomes half of the original value and N $= N + 1$. The initial value of ϵ is 0.5 and the initial value of N is 5. Specific algorithm is shown in Table 3.

Table 3. Test threat of Algorithm 3

Algorithm 3 test thread
Initialize $N_{done} = 0, R_{sum} = 0, N_{step} = 0, N = 5, N_1 = 0$
for k=1 to 10 **do**
$\quad S_1$ = env.reset()
$\quad$ **for** t = 1 to T **do**
$\quad a_t = \mu(s_t|\theta^\mu)$
$\quad s_{t+1}, reward_t, done, \_ = env.step(a_t)$
$\quad R_{sum} = R_{sum} + reward_t$
$\quad\quad$ **If** the assembly process ends, $N_{step} = N_{step} + t;$
$\quad\quad\quad$ **If** the assembly task is completed, $N_{done} = N_{done} +$
$\quad 1$
$\quad\quad$ t = t+1
$\quad$ **end for** and calculate the sum of the rewards
$\quad$ k = k+1
end for
if $N_{done} > N : N_1 = N_1 + 1$
$\quad$ **if** $N_1 > 3, \quad \epsilon = \epsilon/2, \quad N = N + 1, N_1 = 0$

4.1 Inserting Phase

In this part, a comparative experiment on the improvement of long-term returns is made. The long-term returns are changed only and the other improvements remain unchanged. The main content of the comparison includes the completion rate, the average reward value of each step and the number of steps to complete the task.

From the Fig. 4(a), the degree of completion increased steadily and finally reached 100%. From the Fig. 4(b), the average reward value of each step shows a steady increase in volatility. From the Fig. 4(c), the number of steps required to complete the task steadily decline until the training is finally stopped, and the number of steps required reduce by half compared with the early training and by three quarters compared with the pure guiding actions, resulting in two times and three times higher efficiency respectively.

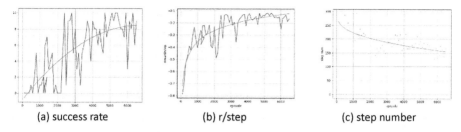

(a) success rate   (b) r/step   (c) step number

Fig. 4. Data graph after changing long-term returns

From Fig. 5, with long-term returns unchanged, the first completion case appears at the training step of 2000 and then rapidly increases to 100%, the number of steps to complete the task has reached a relatively small value since the beginning of the completion of the task and has declined in volatility. The comparison shows that the algorithm can learn the successful strategy more steadily and faster after changing the long-term return.

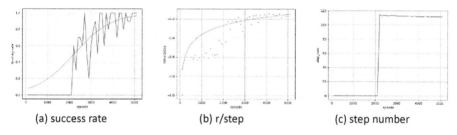

(a) success rate   (b) r/step   (c) step number

Fig. 5. Data graph without changing long-term returns

In order to verify the effect of the intelligent annealing method, a comparative experiment was made with the undirected action. The data for comparison are involved in two aspects including completion rate and average reward of each action step, as shown in Fig. 6. It can be seen from the figure that there are only a few completion cases in the 25,000 training steps while the average reward value of each action step fluctuates slowly. Compared with the previous experiments, it can be concluded that the effect of intelligent annealing method is very significant.

Then, in order to verify the effect of network pre-training, experiments without pre-training and the data are simulated and the cooperation are completed about the rate and the average reward of each action step as shown in Fig. 7. It can be seen from the figure that there are no case of completion in the training steps within 16,000, while the reward values of each action step slowly increase with some fluctuates. Compared with the previous experiments, it can be concluded that network pre-training has a very significant effect.

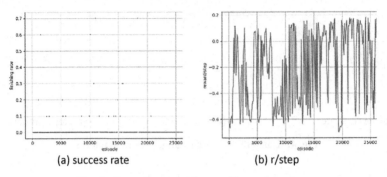

Fig. 6. Data changes without guidance to explore

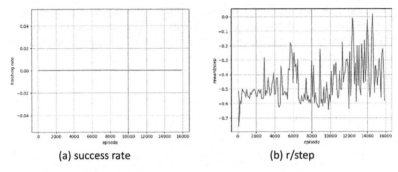

Fig. 7. Data changes without network pretraining

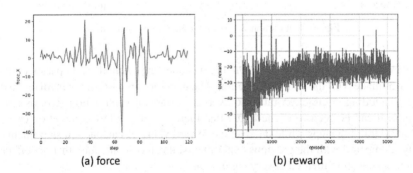

Fig. 8. Some other related data graphs

From the data information corresponding to each moment in assembly activities, as shown in Fig. 8(a), it can be found that the contact force is maintained in a relatively small range to ensure the rapid completion of the task. In Fig. 8(b), it shows that the change of total reward value in the training process whose reward value declines first and then rises rapidly in the volatility.

4.2 Performance of Anti-Jamming

This part mainly studies the anti-interference ability of strategies derived from reinforcement learning. This paper mainly studies the change of the measured contact force after adding the interference signal to the control signal or the acquired sensor signal. The interference signals tested are common Gaussian interference signals and mean interference signals. In the absence of interference signal, the change of contact force in x, y and Z direction is shown in Fig. 9.

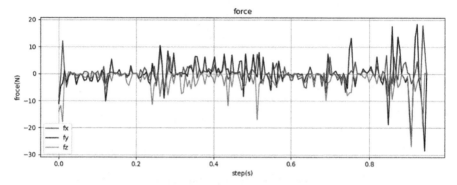

Fig. 9. The contact forces in the x,y, and Z directions

When interference signal is added to the control signal, the change of contact force in the direction of X, Y and Z is shown in Fig. 10. By comparing the Fig. 9 and Fig. 10(a), it is clear that the amplitude of contact force variation under Gaussian noise increases to a certain extent globally but the maximum amplitude does not change significantly, which means the contact force is still within the acceptable range although the fluctuation increases, so it proves that the strategies has the capability to resists Gaussian interference signal which is added to controller. By comparing Fig. 9 and Fig. 10(b–d), it can be concluded that the strategies has the capability to resists the Gaussian or mean interference signal which are added to controller or force sensor.

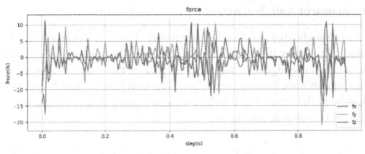

(a) Add Gaussian noise to the control signal

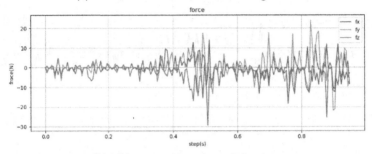

(b) Add mean noise to control signal

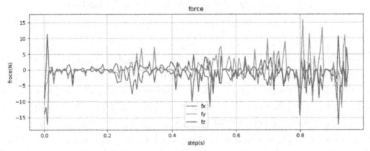

(c) Add Gaussian noise to the force sensor

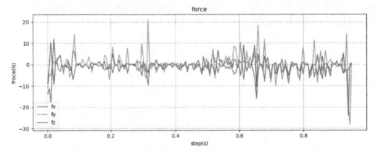

(d) Add a constant value bias to the force sensor

Fig. 10. The change of contact force

5   Conclusions

This paper presents an assembly method based on TD3 deep reinforcement learning algorithm, and designs an adaptive annealing guide method in the exploration process, which greatly accelerates the convergence rate of deep reinforcement learning. In addition, this paper improves the form of traditional reward function to reduce the possibility of divergence of the deep reinforcement learning algorithm, and the effect of the improved algorithm in accelerating convergence is proved by several comparison experiments. Finally, the interference signals is added to prove that the network trained by deep reinforcement learning algorithm and validate the abilities of anti-interference signals in the simulation.

A future direction is to introduce LSTM networks to the deep reinforcement learning to perceive time-ordered data for further improving the control effect which is similar to the performance of differential and integral terms in traditional control theory. The other direction is to study the generalization ability of reinforcement learning for multiple assemblies with different assembly shapes or more complex assembly process.

References

1. Quillen, D., Jang, E., Nachum, O., et al.: Deep reinforcement learning for vision-based robotic grasping: a simulated comparative evaluation of off-policy methods (2018). arXiv Robot
2. Zeng, A., Song, S., Welker, S., et al.: Learning synergies between pushing and grasping with self-supervised deep reinforcement learning. Intell. Robots Syst. 4238–4245 (2018)
3. Gu, S., Holly, E., Lillicrap, T., et al.: Deep reinforcement learning for robotic manipulation with asynchronous off-policy updates. In: International Conference on Robotics and Automation, pp. 3389–3396 (2017)
4. De Andres, M.O., Ardakani, M.M., Robertsson, A., et al.: Reinforcement learning for 4-finger-gripper manipulation. In: International Conference on Robotics and Automation, pp. 1–6 (2018)
5. Yang, P., Huang, J.: TrackDQN: visual tracking via deep reinforcement learning. In: 2019 IEEE 1st International Conference on Civil Aviation Safety and Information Technology (ICCASIT). IEEE (2019)
6. Kenzo, LT., Francisco, L., Javier, R.D.S.: Visual navigation for biped humanoid robots using deep reinforcement learning. IEEE Robot. Autom. Lett. **3**, 1–1 (2018)
7. Yang, Y., Bevan, M.A., Li, B.: Efficient navigation of colloidal robots in an unknown environment via deep reinforcement learning. Adv. Intell. Syst. (2019)
8. Zeng, J., Ju, R., Qin, L., et al.: Navigation in unknown dynamic environments based on deep reinforcement learning. Sensors **19**(18), 3837 (2019)
9. Fan, Y., Luo, J., Tomizuka, M., et al.: A learning framework for high precision industrial assembly. In: International Conference on Robotics and Automation, pp. 811–817 (2019)
10. Xu, J., Hou, Z., Wang, W., et al.: Feedback deep deterministic policy gradient with fuzzy reward for robotic multiple peg-in-hole assembly tasks. IEEE Trans. Ind. Informat. **15**(3), 1658–1667 (2019)
11. Roveda, L., Pallucca, G., Pedrocchi, N., et al.: Iterative learning procedure with reinforcement for high-accuracy force tracking in robotized tasks. IEEE Trans Ind. Informat. **14**(4), 1753–1763 (2018)
12. Chang, W., Andini, D.P., Pham, V., et al.: An implementation of reinforcement learning in assembly path planning based on 3D point clouds. In: International Automatic Control Conference (2018)

13. Inoue, T., De Magistris, G., Munawar, A. et al.: Deep reinforcement learning for high precision assembly tasks. In: Intelligent Robots and Systems, pp. 819–825 (2017)
14. Vecerik, M., Hester, T., Scholz, J., et al.: leveraging demonstrations for deep reinforcement learning on robotics problems with sparse rewards (2017). arXiv: Artificial Intelligence
15. Luo, J., Solowjow, E., Wen, C., et al.: Reinforcement learning on variable impedance controller for high-precision robotic assembly. In: International Conference on Robotics and Automation, pp. 3080–3087 (2019)
16. Lillicrap, T., Hunt, J.J., Pritzel, A., et al.: Continuous control with deep reinforcement learning (2015). arXiv Learning
17. Mnih, V., Kavukcuoglu, K., Silver, D., et al.: Playing Atari with deep reinforcement learning (2013). arXiv Learning
18. Fujimoto, S., Van Hoof, H., Meger, D. et al.: Addressing function approximation error in actor-critic methods (2018) . arXiv: Artificial Intelligence

EEG-Based Emotion Recognition Using Convolutional Neural Network with Functional Connections

Hongbo Wang[1], Ke Liu[1(✉)] (iD), Feifei Qi[2(✉)], Xin Deng[1], and Peiyang Li[3]

[1] Chongqing Key Laboratory of Computational Intelligence, Chongqing University of Posts and Telecommunications, Chongqing 400065, China
liuke@cqupt.edu.cn
[2] School of Internet Finance and Information Engineering, Guangdong University of Finance, Guangzhou 510521, China
20-081@gduf.edu.cn
[3] School of Bioinformatics, Chongqing University of Posts and Telecommunications, Chongqing 400065, China

Abstract. Emotion recognition plays a vital role in Brain-Computer Interaction. To extract and employ the inherent information implied by functional connections among EEG electrodes, we propose a multichannel EEG emotion recognition method using convolutional neural network (CNN) with functional connectivity as input. Specifically, the phase synchronization indices are employed to compute the EEG functional connectivity matrices. Then a CNN is proposed to effectively extract the classification information of these functional connections. The experimental results based on the DEAP and SEED datasets validate the superior performance of the proposed method, compared with the input of raw EEG data. The code of the proposed model is available at https://github.com/deep-bci/ERBCPSI.

Keywords: Electroencephalography (EEG) · Emotion recognition · Phase synchronization indices (PSI) · Convolutional neural network

1 Introduction

Brain-computer interfaces (BCIs) establish direct communication and control channels between the brain and computers or other electronic devices [1], which has been widely used for medical care, education, entertainment, marketing and

This work was supported in part by the National Natural Science Foundation of China under Grants 61703065, 61906048 and 61901077. Chongqing Research Program of Application Foundation and Advanced Technology under Grant cstc2018jcyjAX0151, the Science and Technology Research Program of Chongqing Municipal Education Commission under Grant KJQN201800612.

F. Sun et al. (Eds.): ICCSIP 2020, CCIS 1397, pp. 33–40, 2021.
https://doi.org/10.1007/978-981-16-2336-3_3

monitoring [3]. Emotions play an important role for decision-making, communication, attention and learning mechanisms. Intelligent BCI requires systems that are adaptive, able to detect user emotions and respond accordingly.

Compared with other neurophysiological signals, such as electrocardiogram (ECG) and electromyography (EMG), electroencephalogram (EEG) can provide reliable features for emotional states recognition as it's more sensitive and real-time to fluctuations in emotional states. However, accurately recognizing emotions from the non-stationary and low signal-noise-ratio (SNR) EEG signals is a long-standing challenging problem.

Many emotion recognition studies have been proposed based on EEG signals. Among them, the study in [9] constructed emotion-related brain networks using phase locking value and adopted a multiple feature fusion approach to combine the compensative activation and connection information for emotion recognition. Xu et al. [12] employed the model stacking method to ensemble three models including GBDT, RF and SVM in the experiment, and the mean accuracy of their framework achieved about 81.30%.

Due to the severe non-stationary and noise in EEG signals, extracting effective features manually from the raw EEG is not a trival task. Owing to the powerful ability for feature representation, deep neural networks (DNNs) have been widely used in BCI and emotion recognition. For example, Schirrmeister et al. [10] proposed Deep ConvNet and Shallow ConvNet to extract features from raw EEG signals. The study in [7] proposed EEGNet, a compact convolutional network to extract the hidden temporal and spatial patterns from the raw EEG data. Recently, Ding et al. [4] derived TSception for emotion classification, which uses temporal and spatial convolutional layers to learn spatiotemporal representations, achieving superior performance than EEGNet and LSTM.

These DNNs mainly focused on extracting feature representation from the raw EEG signals. However, the cognitive tasks are mainly the results of the interactions among various cortical areas. Hence, the functional connections among the EEG electrodes may contain abundant information for the classification of different cognitive tasks [2]. Indeed, the study in [8] has validated the effectiveness of brain connectivity for emotion recognition. To further exploit the information of EEG functional connections, in this work, we proposed a convolutional neural network (CNN) to extract the features within the functional connections computed by phase synchronization indices (PSI) among EEG electrodes. The numerical results using DEAP and SEED datasets also validate the superior and robust performance of the proposed method.

The rest of the paper is organized as follows. In Sect. 2, we introduce the datasets used in the experiment. Section 3 presents the details of the proposed method. In Sect. 4, we present the numerical experimental results, followed by a brief conclusion in Sect. 5.

2   The Dataset

This study was carried on two public datasets, i.e., DEAP [6] and SEED [13]. The DEAP dataset composed of 32 subjects, and its emotion stimulus was a selection of 40 one-min long music video to ensure a single desired target emotion could be evoked. When subjects were watching these materials, their physiological signals were recorded. The resulting dataset includes 32 channels of EEG signals and 8 channels of peripheral physiological signals. Each subject underwent 40 emotion-eliciting tests and each corresponding to an emotion triggered by a music video. After each trial, the participants were asked to score their emotion reflection on a scale of 1–9 in five levels of arousal, valence, liking and dominance. The rating value from small to large indicated that each index was from negative to positive, from weak to strong, respectively. In this work, the pre-processed EEG signals of DEAP dataset were employed for emotion recognition, which had been downsampled 128 Hz, band-pass filtered to 4–45 Hz. We extracted the last 60 s stimulus-related signals and removed the first 3 s stimulus-independent signals for each trial.

For SEED dataset, there are 15 subjects (7 males and 8 females). The emotion stimuli materials were 15 Chinese movie clips. The emotion labels were divided into positive, neutral, and negative according to the valence axis, with five clips in each category, and each clip duration was about 4 min. The EEG data of SEED was first downsampled 200 Hz and band-pass filtered to 0–75 Hz.

For the numerical experiments, the EEG data were filtered into five sub-bands (δ: 1–4 Hz; θ: 4–8 Hz; α: 8–13 Hz; β: 13–30 Hz; γ: 30–50 Hz) respectively. To obtain sufficienSincet training data, each trial of DEAP data was divided into a 5-s segment with a 2.5-s overlap window, obtaining 23 segments for each trial. Since the lengths of each trial are inconsistent in SEED, the first two minutes of each trial were used for the experiment to ensure data balance. Each trial of SEED data is divided into a 5-s segment with no overlap, obtaining 24 segments for each trial.

3   Method

3.1   Functional Connection Computation

The cognitive process involves not only the activities of local brain regions, but also the information propagation and interactions among different functional areas [11]. Hence, the functional connections imply important and useful information for the analysis of cognition process, such as emotion recognition. To construct the functional network, we employ the Phase Synchronization Index (PSI), which is reported to be more robust than correlation [8]. The PSI is computed based on the instantaneous phases $\phi_m(t)$ and $\phi_n(t)$ of the signals, which is derived from Hilbert transform.

Given a continuous signal $x(t)$, its Hilbert transform $\widetilde{x}(t)$ is defined as

$$\widetilde{x}(t) = \frac{1}{+u} \int_{-\infty}^{+\infty} \frac{x(t')}{t-t'} dt' = x(t) \frac{1}{\pi t'} \tag{1}$$

Then we obtain the analytical signal of $x(t)$ as

$$Z_x(t) = x(t) + i\widetilde{x}(t) = A_x(t) \exp^{i\phi_x(t)} \tag{2}$$

Similarly, for signal $y(t)$, we obtain the instantaneous phases $\phi_x(t)$ and $\phi_y(t)$. Assuming that the phase lock ratio of x and y is n/m (where n and m are integers, usually n = m = 1), the phase difference between the two analytical signals is

$$\phi_{xy}(t) \equiv n\phi_x(t) - m\phi_y(t) \tag{3}$$

Finally, the PSI value γ is obtained as

$$\gamma \equiv \left| \left\langle \exp^{i\phi_{xy}(t)} \right\rangle_t \right| = \sqrt{\langle \cos \phi_{xy}(t) \rangle_t^2 + \langle \sin \phi_{xy}(t) \rangle_t^2} \tag{4}$$

where $\langle \rangle_t$ denotes the average over time. The value of γ is in the range of [0, 1]. When $\gamma = 0$, there is no phase synchronization between the two signals; when $\gamma = 1$, there is a stable phase difference between the two signals, i.e., the physiological performance is phase synchronization.

3.2   The Proposed Convolutional Neural Network

To extract the classification information implied by the functional connections among EEG electrodes, we employ the functional connectivity matrix obtained in Sect. 3.1 as the input of our proposed CNN model. The architecture of the proposed model is shown in Fig. 1. Similar as EEGNet [7], the proposed CNN starts with a depthwise convolution, connected to the functional connectivity matrices of each sub-band individually, to learn frequency-specific spatial filters. Then a separable convolution is used, to learn spatial summary of each feature map individually and mix them together. We apply batch normalization along the feature map dimension before applying the ELU activation function. To solve the problem of over-fitting, we use the Dropout technique (dropout probability is 0.5) and early-stopping techniques. To optimize the network parameters, we adopt the Adam [5] method to iteratively update the network parameters until the desired criterion is achieved. Cross-entropy cost is used as the cost function.

To validate the effectiveness of the functional connections, we compared the performance of the proposed model with EEGNet [7], which shares the same depthwise convolution and separable convolution layer, but uses the raw EEG data as the input. Additionally, the performance of the proposed model was also compared with three widely used CNN in the field of EEG analysis, i.e., Deep ConvNet [10], Shallow ConvNet [10] and Tsception [4].

In this work, all the models were applied for the subject-dependent analysis. For DEAP, we adopted the five-fold cross-validation strategy to evaluate the performance of each model. Specifically, for each subject, we divide the 40 trials into five sections. For each cross-validation, the segments of one section are treated as the test data, while 80% of the other four sections as training data, and 20% as validation data. For SEED, the leave-one-session-out cross-validation was employed. In each cross-validation, we used one session as test data, and the other two sessions as training data and validation data, with the same allocation strategy as DEAP. Notably, due to high correlation of adjacent segments, to avoid the problem of "data leakage", we employed the trial-wise randomization

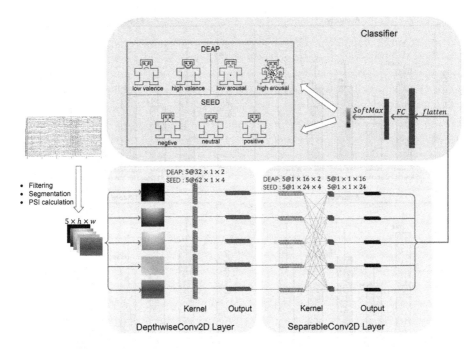

Fig. 1. The architecture of the proposed model. The h, w and kernel size of convolution layer int the model are determined by the number of channels in the dataset.

for cross-validation. Specifically, all segments belonging to one trial is allocated either as the training set, or test set or validation set. The classification accuracy and F1-score were employed as the performance metrics.

4 Experimental Results

Figure 2 and 3 depict the averaged performance metrics across subjects for DEAP and SEED datasets, respectively. Compared with EEGNet, the proposed model achieves larger accuracy ($p < 0.05$, Wilcoxon rank sum test) and F1-score ($p < 0.05$, Wilcoxon rank sum test), indicating the superior performance of the proposed CNN model and the effectiveness of the functional connections. Among all the five CNN models, the proposed model always provides the largest classification accuracy and F1-score.

To characterize the features learned by our proposed model, we visualize the kernel weights of the DepthwiseConv2D Layer, which can be treated as spatial filters learned by the proposed model. Figure 4 depicts one example of DEAP dataset. As shown in Fig. 4, the two spatial filters depict different characteristics and behave differently in each frequency band. In Gamma band, the spatial filters have greater weights around the occipital and parietal lobes. The lateral temporal

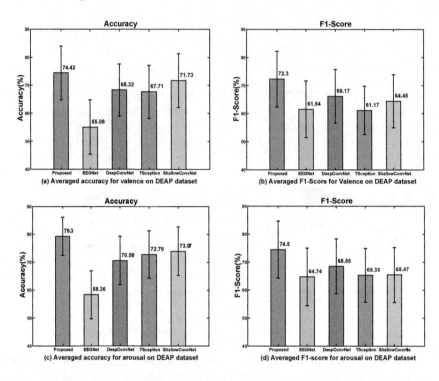

Fig. 2. Mean accuracy and F1-score across subjects for the valence and arousal of DEAP dataset. The results are shown as mean±std.

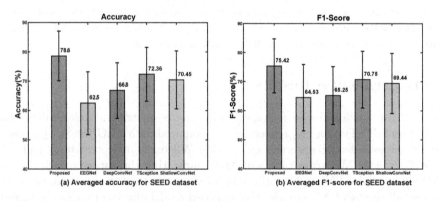

Fig. 3. Mean accuracy and F1-score across subjects for SEED dataset. The results are shown as mean±std.

areas activate more in the Beta and Gamma bands, which are in line with the previous study [14]. The delta, theta and alpha bands are almost weighted around the prefrontal site.

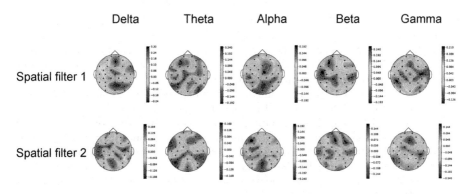

Fig. 4. Visualization of the features for each sub-band derived from the spatial filter for subject 1 of DEAP dataset.

5   Conclusion

In summary, we proposed a CNN model to extract the information implied by EEG functional connections for emotion recognition. According to our numerical results on DEAP and SEED datasets, the proposed model can effectively learn the frequency and spatial information to recognize different emotions from EEG. The interactions of different brain regions, which is represented by the EEG functional connections, can also be used as effective features for emotion classification. Since the current work mainly aims to validate the effectiveness of functional connections, we did not employ other features. However, the current work can easily be extended by fusing the functional connections with other features, such as differential entropy (DE) and power spectral density (PSD), to further improve the performance of the proposed model. Additionally, we will also apply the proposed method for cross-subject emotion recognition.

References

1. Abiri, R., Borhani, S., Sellers, E.W., Jiang, Y., Zhao, X.: A comprehensive review of EEG-based brain-computer interface paradigms. J. Neural Eng. **16**(1), 011001 (2019)
2. de Abril, I.M., Yoshimoto, J., Doya, K.: Connectivity inference from neural recording data: challenges, mathematical bases and research directions. Neural Networks **102**, 120–137 (2018)
3. Chaudhary, P., Agrawal, R.: Brain computer interface: a new pathway to human brain. In: Mallick, P.K., Pattnaik, P.K., Panda, A.R., Balas, V.E. (eds.) Cognitive Computing in Human Cognition. LAIS, vol. 17, pp. 99–125. Springer, Cham (2020). https://doi.org/10.1007/978-3-030-48118-6_10
4. Ding, Y., et al.: Tsception: a deep learning framework for emotion detection using EEG. arXiv preprint arXiv:2004.02965 (2020)
5. Kingma, D.P., Ba, J.: Adam: A method for stochastic optimization. arXiV:abs/1412.6980 (2014)

6. Koelstra, S., et al.: Deap: a database for emotion analysis; using physiological signals. IEEE Trans. Affect. Comput. **3**(1), 18–31 (2011)
7. Lawhern, V.J., Solon, A.J., Waytowich, N.R., Gordon, S.M., Hung, C.P., Lance, B.J.: EEGNet: a compact convolutional neural network for EEG-based brain-computer interfaces. J. Neural Eng. **15**(5), 056013 (2018)
8. Lee, Y.Y., Hsieh, S.: Classifying different emotional states by means of EEG-based functional connectivity patterns. PloS one **9**(4), e95415 (2014)
9. Li, P., et al.: EEG based emotion recognition by combining functional connectivity network and local activations. IEEE Trans. Biomed. Eng. **66**(10), 2869–2881 (2019)
10. Schirrmeister, R.T., et al.: Deep learning with convolutional neural networks for EEG decoding and visualization. Hum. Brain Mapp. **38**(11), 5391–5420 (2017)
11. Wang, Y., Chiew, V.: On the cognitive process of human problem solving. Cogn. Syst. Res. **11**(1), 81–92 (2010)
12. Xu, T., Yin, R., Shu, L., Xu, X.: Emotion recognition using frontal EEG in VR affective scenes. In: 2019 IEEE MTT-S International Microwave Biomedical Conference (IMBioC), vol. 1, pp. 1–4. IEEE (2019)
13. Zheng, W.L., Lu, B.L.: Investigating critical frequency bands and channels for EEG-based emotion recognition with deep neural networks. IEEE Trans. Auton. Mental Dev. **7**(3), 162–175 (2015)
14. Zheng, W.L., Zhu, J.Y., Lu, B.L.: Identifying stable patterns over time for emotion recognition from EEG. IEEE Trans. Affect. Comput. **10**, 417 (2017)

Fast Barcode Detection Method Based on ThinYOLOv4

Liwei Zhang, Yuzhao Sui, Fuwei Zhu, Mingzhu Zhu, Bingwei He, and Zhen Deng[✉]

School of Mechanical Engineering and Automation, Fuzhou University, Fuzhou 350116, China
{lw.zhang,zdeng}@fzu.edu.cn

Abstract. Barcode detection is a key step before decoding so that achieving a fast and accurate detection algorithm is of significant importance. In the present study, we propose to guide the pruning of channels and shortcut layers in YOLOv4 through sparse training to obtain the compressed model ThinYOLOv4 for barcode detection. Then a binary classification network is established to remove the prediction boxes that do not contain a barcode, thereby obtaining a fast and accurate barcode detection model. In order to evaluate the performance of the proposed method, a barcode dataset consisting of 16,545 images is provided. This dataset contains common types of barcodes in the market and covers different practical scenarios. Furthermore, interference factors such as blur, low-contrast are considered in the dataset purposefully. Obtained results show that the proposed method achieves a recall rate of 93.8% on the provided dataset, Meanwhile, parameters of YOLOv4 are reduced from 63,943,071 to 400,649, and the model size is reduced from 250,037 KB to 1,587 KB, while the corresponding detection speed is increased to 260% of YOLOv4. When the experiment is performed on the 1050Ti GPU, a detection speed of 23.308 ms/image is achieved.

Keywords: Barcode detection · Deep learning · YOLOv4 · Model compression · Dual network

1 Introduction

As a simple, fast, accurate, reliable, and economic data acquisition method, barcode has been widely utilized in diverse applications. Barcode detection is a specific application in the field of object detection. During the decoding process, only the area with a barcode contains useful information. However, such an area may have a low share (even less than one percent) of a captured image. Therefore, finding the barcode position quickly can effectively reduce the computational amount of the subsequent decoding unit.

The majority of existing barcode detection methods are based on the traditional methods, such as morphological processing [15], Hough transform [23]. Most of them are only suitable for certain specific scenarios. In order to resolve

© Springer Nature Singapore Pte Ltd. 2021
F. Sun et al. (Eds.): ICCSIP 2020, CCIS 1397, pp. 41–55, 2021.
https://doi.org/10.1007/978-981-16-2336-3_4

this shortcoming, inspired by the application of the deep learning in other object detection fields such as face detection [9] and license plate detection [27], we propose a method based on YOLOv4 [3], which is applied to barcode detection.

Methods based on deep learning mainly rely on complex neural networks so that they require high-performance equipment support. However, there are limitations to have sufficient performance support in real scenarios such as portable mobile devices. Therefore, it is of great significance to compress the model size as much as possible so that the model can operate properly on low-performance devices.

The main contributions of the present study can be summarized as followed:

1. We have established a complete, diverse, and well-labeled barcode dataset with a total of 16545 images.
2. We propose to guide the pruning of channels and layers in YOLOv4 through sparse training to obtain the compressed model ThinYOLOv4 for barcode detection.
3. We propose to use a binary classification network to classify ThinYOLOv4's prediction boxes, and eliminate the prediction boxes without barcodes, thereby improving the precision of ThinYOLOv4. Finally, a model with good speed and precision was obtained.

Contents of this paper are organized as the following: A comprehensive literature review is performed in Sect. 2 and then details of the proposed algorithm are discussed in Sect. 3. Then, obtained results are presented in Sect. 4. Finally, conclusions and main achievements are presented in Sect. 5.

2   Related Works

2.1   Traditional Methods

Many investigations have been conducted so far using traditional methods for detecting the barcode. Gallo [8] proposed an approach for barcode decoding that bypasses the binarization and has reasonable performance for UPC-A codes. However, the barcode orientation should be initially estimated with an error less than 45°. Tekin [24] used the direction histogram to locate the barcode position and calculated the gradient direction of the whole image. He showed that the shape characteristics of the one-dimensional barcode cause a certain significant direction in the statistics. But it is not true when identifying high-density barcodes. Since the barcode area is small, it can hardly affect the global statistics. Yun [29] proposed to use the orientation histogram of the image to remove the background regions and small clutter, and then analyzes a local entropy-based orientation for the segmentation of a large region that is highly likely to be barcodes, and finally judge whether the selected candidate region is a barcode. Moreover, Creusot [7] proposed a method based on the Parallel Segment Detection (PSD) technology for the visually impaired group. It should be indicated that all of the foregoing methods have been proposed for detecting one-dimensional barcodes.

Szentandrsi [23] proposed a matrix code recognition algorithm based on the Hough transform, which can quickly process high-resolution images above the megapixel level. Furthermore, Katona proposed a morphological operation method based on the bottom-hat filtering. However, studies showed that this method is sensitive to noise. Bodnar [4–6] proposed a series of barcode detection methods. He first proposed a detection method using the texture analysis [5], but he found that this method is sensitive to noise and blur. Then he improved the scanning line analysis and replaced it with a circle [4]. Finally, he proposed a method based on the distance transformation [6]. Based on the matrix structure proposed by Ando [1], Soros [22] found rectangles in the image and determined the barcode type according to the proportion of edges to corners in the rectangle set. Investigations demonstrate that although this method is effective, it is not fast enough. Wang [26] used the Local Binary Pattern (LBP) feature for the image feature extraction and the support vector machine classification to localize the barcode. Then he obtained the angle invariance through the Hough transform. Puri [18] used the Scharr gradient calculation, image blurring, kernel application, and erosion expansion to build an Android application for detecting the barcode.

2.2 Deep Learning Methods

In the past few years, the deep learning technology has achieved remarkable results in diverse fields. However, it has very few applications in the field of barcode inspection. Hansen [11] proposed a method based on the YOLO:9000 [20] detection algorithm. However, he only tested the proposed method on public datasets. It should be indicated that the background of these datasets is not complicated. Yang [28] used convolutional neural networks to recognize one-dimensional barcodes in clothing images.

Although complex deep learning models certainly have better performance, the corresponding high storage space and computing resources are enormous challenges for their real-life applications. In order to resolve this shortcoming, MobileNet [13] and ShuffleNet [30] use group convolution and depthwise separable convolution structure respectively; Furthermore, the Neural Architecture Search(NAS) [2,16,19], which can automatically seek a high-performance neural network; Han [10] used improved quantization techniques to achieve a compression rate of $35X$ to $49X$ on AlexNet and VGGNet, respectively; Liu [17] proposed a method based on model pruning to eliminate redundant parameters in the network, and we adopted this method.

3 Fast Barcode Detection Based on ThinYOLOv4

We adopted a deep learning method, using YOLOv4 as the basic network. Then use the pruning method to compress YOLOv4. Since the precision of the model after pruning will decrease, we use a binary classification network with fewer parameters than the YOLOv4 to break this state. By binary classification of the prediction boxes of the YOLOv4, the prediction boxes without barcode is eliminated, thereby improving the precision of model. Figure 1 illustrates the framework of the proposed approach.

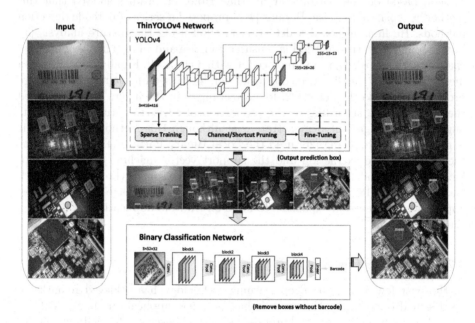

Fig. 1. Overview of the barcode detection framework

3.1 Basic Model

In practical industrial scenarios, when the detecting algorithm meets certain detection accuracy requirements, it cannot be applied without a fast enough speed. The YOLO series of algorithms can be applied to carry out a good trade-off between the detection speed and the precision. Accordingly, YOLOv4 is applied in the present study as the basic model. On the premise of ensuring the speed advantage, the YOLOv4 algorithm improves the prediction accuracy and strengthens the recognition ability of small objects. It is worth noting that YOLOv4 has the following improvements:

1. The mosaic data enhancement method is used to splice each batch of pictures in a random scaling, random cropping, and random arrangement. It greatly enriches the detection dataset. More specifically, the random scaling adds many small targets to the base dataset. In this way, the network robustness remarkably increases.
2. Learning from the CSPNet [25] and improving the backbone network Darknet53 based on the YOLOv3 [21] algorithm, a backbone structure with 72 layers is obtained, which contains 5 CSP modules. Moreover, the Mish activation function (see Eq. (1)) is adopted in the backbone structure.

3. The SPP module with the maximum pooling index of $k = \{1*1, 5*5, 9*9, 13*13\}$ is used in the YOLOv3 algorithm. Then different scale feature maps are used for the concatenation operation. This process effectively increases the reception range of backbone features.

4. Applying the CIoU loss [31] to estimate the bounding box regression loss through Eqs. (2), (3) and (4). In this regard, three important geometric factors of the prediction box regression function, including overlap area, center point distance and aspect ratio, are considered. Then the prediction box regression is improved from speed and accuracy points of view.

$$Mish = x * tanh(ln(1 + e^x)) \tag{1}$$

$$v = \frac{4}{\pi^2}(arctan\frac{w^{g^t}}{h^{g^t}} - arctan\frac{w}{h})^2 \tag{2}$$

$$\alpha = \frac{v}{(1 - IoU) + v} \tag{3}$$

$$L_{CIoU} = 1 - IoU + \frac{\rho^2(b, b^{g^t})}{c^2} + \alpha v \tag{4}$$

In order to classify the prediction boxes, DenseNet [14] is applied in this study, which is consistent with ResNet's [12] idea. By establishing the skip connection between the front and the back layers, DenseNet helps the backpropagation of the gradient during the training process. On the other hand, DenseNet uses a more aggressive dense connection mechanism for connecting all layers to each other. Under this circumstance, each layer accepts all previous layers as its additional input so that feature reuse can be achieved, fewer parameters are used and the efficiency improves. In the implementation process, inputs with the dimension of 32 * 32 and four DenseBlock structures are utilized. Finally, the output with two values is obtained, which represents the scores with and without barcodes, respectively. Meanwhile, the prediction boxes with high scores without barcodes are excluded.

3.2 Sparsity Training

We carry out pruning work at the channel and layer level. Before pruning, it is necessary to evaluate the importance of channels or layers to determine which channels and layers should be removed. For the YOLOv4, there is a BN layer behind each convolutional layer to accelerate the convergence and improve the generalization. The BN layer applies a small batch of static correction to normalize the convolution features. This can be mathematically expressed as Eq. (5).

$$y = \frac{\gamma}{\sqrt{Var\,[x] + \varepsilon}} \cdot x + \left(\beta - \frac{\lambda E\,[x]}{\sqrt{Var\,[x] + \varepsilon}}\right) \tag{5}$$

Where $E[x]$ and $Var[x]$ denote the expectation and variance of a small batch of input features, respectively. Moreover, γ and β are trainable scaling factor and offset, respectively. Since each scaling factor corresponds to a specific convolution channel, the scaling factor γ is used as an indicator to evaluate the importance of channels and layers. Sparse training is performed by applying L1 regularization to the γ value, pushing the γ value close to 0. The loss function of the sparsity training can be expressed as Eq. (6).

$$L = l_{coord} + l_{classes} + l_{confidence} + \theta \sum_{\gamma \in \Gamma} s(\gamma) \tag{6}$$

Where l_{coord}, $l_{confidence}$ and $l_{classes}$ are the coordinate loss, confidence loss and class loss of the target frame, respectively. Moreover, $\sum_{\gamma \in \Gamma} s(\gamma) = \sum_{\gamma \in \Gamma} |\gamma|$ represents the L_1 regularization, and θ is the penalty factor for balancing newly added loss terms.

3.3   Pruning

Since each scale factor corresponds to a single channel, it can be used to trim the channel and remove its incoming and outgoing connections and corresponding weights. After performing the sparse training, a part of the scale factor γ in the BN layer approaches to zero, which means that this part of the channel has little impact on the result so that it can be removed.

Then a threshold is set for the sparsely trained network parameters, which represents the amount of pruning parameters. Therefore, the degree of pruning can be flexibly controlled to iterate a model with less precision loss and larger compression amplitude.

After pruning the channel, the shortcut layer are pruned as well, sorting the γ value of the previous convolution channel of each shortcut layer to determine its importance. Also a threshold is set to adjust the number of shortcut deletions, and finally get a compression model ThinYOLOv4. It should be indicated that only the shortcut layer in the backbone is considered in the present study.

3.4   Fine-Tuning

After pruning the network model, the performance of the model temporarily decreases, so fine-tuning should be conducted to restore its performance. When the model is pruned, the obtained new model should be trained again on the dataset using the normal training hyper-parameters to restore its temporarily reduced performance due to the network structure mutation.

3.5   Binary Classification Network

In the present study, DenseNet is utilized to implement the classification task of prediction boxes. Considering significant differences between 1D and 2D barcodes, the corresponding features are more distinctive. Therefore, recognition errors between 1D and 2D barcodes are almost rare. In most cases, some backgrounds are recognized as barcodes, so the classification network only needs to

determine whether the prediction boxes is a background or a barcode. It classifies the prediction boxes into two types, including with and without barcodes.
Then the prediction boxes that do not contain barcodes are removed. In this
way, the detection precision of the overall model is improved.

4   Experiments

Experiments are conducted on GTX 1080Ti GPU. However, the detection speed
experiment was carried out on GTX 1050Ti GPU to evaluate the model performance on low-computing power devices.

4.1   Datasets

In this paper, a dataset is established. This dataset covers the mainstream barcodes in the market. Such as 39 codes, DM codes, QR codes, etc. Considering
different scenarios, Such as circuit board, logistics, etc. Some examples are shown
in Fig. 2. Then from the perspective of influencing factors of detection, each scene
is subdivided into the following subsets: normal, highly bright, high density, low
contrast, etc. In addition, during the data collection process, consciously collect
single object and multi-object images.

Fig. 2. Samples of each scene: (a) metal plate scene; (b) plastic plate, circuit board
scene; (c) logistics, express delivery scene; (d) paper code scene

In total, 16,545 images are collected. Among all collected images, 11,914,
2,978 and 1,653 images are dedicated to training, verification, and testing, respectively. Most images have a resolution of 1×10^6 pixels. Table 1 presents the characteristics of the dataset, while the structure of the dataset is shown in Fig. 3.

Table 1. Barcode detection dataset

Barcode category	train	val	test	trainval
Code-39	441	110	61	551
Code-93	363	91	50	454
GS1-128	390	98	54	488
EAN-13	363	91	50	454
UPC-E	342	85	47	427
Code-2of5 interleaved	414	103	57	517
Unclassified 1D barcode	755	189	105	944
Data matrix	6172	1543	857	7715
QR code	1662	415	231	2077
Aztec	276	69	38	345
PDF417	350	88	49	438
Han Xin	386	96	54	482
Total images	11914	2978	1653	14892

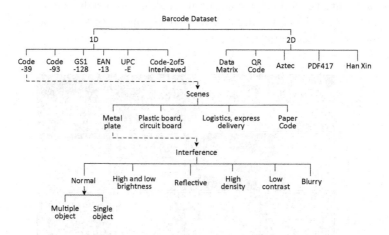

Fig. 3. Structure composition of the dataset

4.2 Normal Training

In this section, a cluster analysis is performed on the dataset as shown in the Fig. 4. A set of anchor values suitable for the dataset is obtained as the following: $(21, 28)$, $(30, 40)$, $(39, 52)$, $(53, 67)$, $(68, 92)$, $(129, 68)$, $(94, 120)$, $(123, 171)$ and $(250, 119)$.

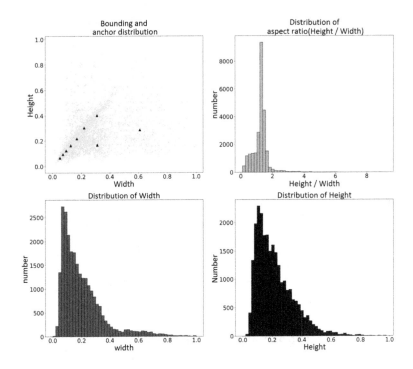

Fig. 4. Cluster of the dataset

In this section, normal training is started directly from zero on the barcode detection dataset without using the pre-training model. The number of each mini-batch is set to 8 and 270 training iterations are performed. Then the size of the input image is set to 416 × 416. Meanwhile, the momentum, decay factor and the initial learning rate are set to 0.949, 0.0005 and 0.002324, respectively. Finally, the learning rate is adjusted in the middle and final training. Variations of the loss value during the training process are monitored to determine whether the network has converged or not.

Figure 5 shows the training process. It is observed that after 270 iterations of training, the loss value tends to be stable and no longer decreases. It is concluded that the network converges and the normal training is completed at this time.

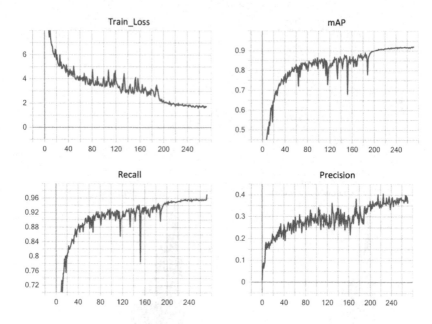

Fig. 5. Normal training process curve

4.3 Sparse Training

In this section, a sparse training is performed on the network YOLOv4, sparse rate is set to 0.001, load the weights obtained in normal training. Figure 6 shows the variation of γ value in the normal and sparse training processes. It is observed that when 90 iterations are performed in the sparse training, most of the γ values in the BN layer approach to zero. It is worth noting that since many channels with unimportant evaluation results have been obtained, it is possible to carry out subsequent pruning operations.

Fig. 6. Variations of γ during the normal and sparse trainings

4.4 Pruning and Fine-Tuning

Figure 6 shows that the sparsely trained model produces many scaling factors close to zero. Then the pruning threshold is set to prune the sparsely trained model. In the present study, different pruning rates, including 75%, 85% and 95% are considered for pruning experiments. After pruning each channel and fine-tuning the recovery performance, obtained performances from different pruning rates are compared to find the most appropriate pruning rate.

Table 2. Model performance at different channel pruning rates

Rate (%)	Model size	Parameter	mAP (%)	P (%)	R (%)	Speed (ms)
0	250,037 KB	63,943,071	92.3	65.4	95.1	55.029
75	23,708 KB	6,044,104	88.8	58.7	93.7	23.074
85	8,855 KB	2,250,428	87.4	57.0	93.5	19.561
95	1,625 KB	409,793	88.4	56.0	93.7	18.396

Table 2 shows the result of fine-tuning after pruning with different pruning rates, illustrating that when the pruning rate is 95%, the maximum speed increase is obtained without losing too much recall rate.

For the channel pruning rate of 95%, the pruning of the shortcut layer is performed, and the different pruning numbers are respectively set to: 8, 10, 12, 14, 16, 18, 20 and a comparative experiment is carried out. It should be indicated that YOLOv4 has 23 shortcut layers. Table 3 shows the experimental results of fine-tuning after pruning with different number of shortcut layer pruning.

Table 3. Model performance under different shortcut pruning numbers

Number	Model size	Parameter	mAP (%)	P (%)	R (%)	Speed (ms)
8	1,618 KB	408,109	88.8	56.1	94.3	15.972
10	1,611 KB	406,421	87.9	57.0	93.0	15.755
12	1,604 KB	404,733	87.8	56.8	93.8	14.927
14	1,597 KB	403,045	88.3	57.6	93.7	14.745
16	1,591 KB	401,625	88.5	58.9	93.7	14.693
18	1,588 KB	400,869	89.3	58.5	94.3	14.557
20	1,587 KB	400,649	88.3	58.7	93.8	14.363

4.5 Binary Classification Network

In this section, we classify the prediction boxes and eliminate the erroneous prediction boxes to improve the precision of the model. Based on the previous experiment, it is found that when the number of the shortcut pruning has a different value, the precision and recall change are small. Accordingly, channel pruning rate and layer pruning amount are set to 95% and 20, respectively. The obtained model is called ThinYOLOv4. Then the ThinYOLOv4 is applied to detect the training set and the test set to obtain a new prediction boxes dataset. Figure 7 indicates that this dataset is divided into two types: Barcode and None.

Fig. 7. Some examples of classification datasets for different prediction boxes

In the dataset of prediction boxes, the training set has a total of 35,707 images, including 25,231 Barcode images (9,629 1D and 15,602 2D) and 10,476 None images. The test set has a total of 3,983 images, including 2,792 Barcode images (1,062 1D and 1,730 2D) and 1,191 None images.

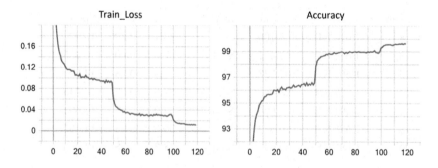

Fig. 8. Training loss and accuracy during classification network training

Based on this dataset, a network is built for the binary classification training and then it is trained to distinguish the presence or absence of barcodes in the prediction boxes. Figure 8 shows the changes in the loss value and classification accuracy during the training process. It indicates that a total of 120 epochs are trained in the experiment. It is observed that the classification accuracy on the test set reaches 96.6% and the detection speed reaches 8.945 ms/image, while the model size is only 597 KB, which definitely meets designing requirements. In the combination of the classification network with ThinYOLOv4, ThinYOLOv4 is responsible for generating prediction boxes, while the classification network is responsible for excluding the non-barcode boxes and outputting the detection result.

4.6   Experimental Results

The final dual network model is tested on the test dataset to obtain the final experimental results. Table 4 presents results in this regard. It is observed that

Table 4. The results of the final improved model

Model	Model size	Parameter	mAP (%)	P (%)	R (%)	Speed (ms)
YOLOv4	250,037 KB	63,943,071	92.3	65.4	95.1	55.029
Ours	2,184 KB	540,613	90.6	73.2	93.8	23.308

the proposed method achieves a very high size compression ratio, removes a lot of redundant parameters, and improves the detection speed to 260% of the YOLOv4 model, at the cost of only a little loss of the recall rate. More specifically, when the experiment is carried out on the NVIDIA GEFORCE GTX 1050Ti GPU graphics card, a detection speed of 23.308 ms/image is achieved. It should be indicated that the same process takes 14.363 ms for ThinYOLOv4 and 8.945 ms for the binary classification network. Moreover, the classification network improves the accuracy of the ThinYOLOv4 model to 73.2%, reaching 111.9% of the YOLOv4 model.

5   Conclusion

The present study aims to resolve the barcode detection problem for datasets with different shortcomings, including images with blur, reflection and high-density problems. These are common problems in conventional barcode detection systems in the market. To this end, an algorithm is proposed based on YOLOv4 that uses sparse training for YOLOv4, pruning it at the channel level and the layer level. Obtained results show that the proposed compression model, called ThinYOLOv4, significantly improves the processing speed. Then a classification network is utilized to classify the prediction boxes of ThinYOLOv4 and remove the redundant prediction boxes with no barcode, thereby improving the detection accuracy. In order to evaluate the performance of the proposed method, a barcode dataset with a total amount of 16,545 datasets is provided, which covers all types of conventional barcodes on the market and sets common inter-ference factors to enrich the dataset. The experimental results show that when our method is applied, the processing speed and detection precision increase by 260% and 116%, respectively, compared to that of YOLOv4.

Acknowledgements. This work is supported by the National Natural Science Foun-dation of China (Project No.: 61673115). This work is also partly funded by the Ger-man Science Foundation (DFG) and National Science Foundation of China (NSFC) in project Cross Modal Learning under contract Sonderforschungsbereich Transregio 169.

References

1. Ando, S.: Image field categorization and edge/corner detection from gradient covariance. IEEE Trans. Pattern Anal. Mach. Intell. **22**(2), 179–190 (2000)
2. Baker, B., Gupta, O., Naik, N., Raskar, R.: Designing neural network architectures using reinforcement learning. arXiv preprint arXiv:1611.02167 (2016)
3. Bochkovskiy, A., Wang, C.Y., Liao, H.Y.M.: YOLOv4: optimal speed and accuracy of object detection. arXiv preprint arXiv:2004.10934 (2020)
4. Bodnár, P., Nyúl, L.G.: A novel method for barcode localization in image domain. In: Kamel, M., Campilho, A. (eds.) ICIAR 2013. LNCS, vol. 7950, pp. 189–196. Springer, Heidelberg (2013). https://doi.org/10.1007/978-3-642-39094-4_22
5. Bodnár, P., Nyúl, L.G.: Barcode detection with morphological operations and clus-tering (2012)
6. Bodnár, P., Nyúl, L.G.: Barcode detection with uniform partitioning and distance transformation (2013)
7. Creusot, C., Munawar, A.: Low-computation egocentric barcode detector for the blind. In: 2016 IEEE International Conference on Image Processing (ICIP), pp. 2856–2860. IEEE (2016)
8. Gallo, O., Manduchi, R.: Reading 1D barcodes with mobile phones using deformable templates. IEEE Trans. Pattern Anal. Mach. Intell. **33**(9), 1834–1843 (2010)
9. Guo, G., Zhang, N.: A survey on deep learning based face recognition. Comput. Vis. Image Underst. **189**, 102805 (2019)
10. Han, S., Mao, H., Dally, W.J.: Deep compression: compressing deep neural net-works with pruning, trained quantization and Huffman coding. arXiv preprint arXiv:1510.00149 (2015)
11. Hansen, D.K., Nasrollahi, K., Rasmussen, C.B., Moeslund, T.B.: Real-time barcode detection and classification using deep learning. In: IJCCI, vol. 1, pp. 321–327 (2017)
12. He, K., Zhang, X., Ren, S., Sun, J.: Deep residual learning for image recognition. In: Proceedings of the IEEE Conference on Computer Vision and Pattern Recognition, pp. 770–778 (2016)
13. Howard, A.G., et al.: MobileNets: efficient convolutional neural networks for mobile vision applications. arXiv preprint arXiv:1704.04861 (2017)
14. Huang, G., Liu, Z., Van Der Maaten, L., Weinberger, K.Q.: Densely connected convolutional networks. In: Proceedings of the IEEE Conference on Computer Vision and Pattern Recognition, pp. 4700–4708 (2017)
15. Katona, M., Nyúl, L.G.: A novel method for accurate and efficient barcode detec-tion with morphological operations. In: 2012 Eighth International Conference on Signal Image Technology and Internet Based Systems, pp. 307–314. IEEE (2012)

16. Liu, H., Simonyan, K., Yang, Y.: DARTS: differentiable architecture search. arXiv preprint arXiv:1806.09055 (2018)
17. Liu, Z., Li, J., Shen, Z., Huang, G., Yan, S., Zhang, C.: Learning efficient convolutional networks through network slimming. In: Proceedings of the IEEE International Conference on Computer Vision, pp. 2736–2744 (2017)
18. Puri, R., Jain, V.: Barcode detection using OpenCV-python. Science **4**(1), 97–99 (2019)
19. Real, E., et al.: Large-scale evolution of image classifiers. arXiv preprint arXiv:1703.01041 (2017)
20. Redmon, J., Farhadi, A.: YOLO9000: better, faster, stronger. In: Proceedings of the IEEE Conference on Computer Vision and Pattern Recognition, pp. 7263–7271 (2017)
21. Redmon, J., Farhadi, A.: YOLOv3: an incremental improvement. arXiv preprint arXiv:1804.02767 (2018)
22. Sörös, G.: GPU-accelerated joint 1D and 2D barcode localization on smartphones. In: 2014 IEEE International Conference on Acoustics, Speech and Signal Processing (ICASSP), pp. 5095–5099. IEEE (2014)
23. Szentandrási, I., Herout, A., Dubská, M.: Fast detection and recognition of QR codes in high-resolution images. In: Proceedings of the 28th Spring Conference on Computer Graphics, pp. 129–136 (2012)
24. Tekin, E., Coughlan, J.: BLaDE: barcode localization and decoding engine. Technical report 2012-RERC. 01 (2012)
25. Wang, C.Y., Liao, H.Y.M., Wu, Y.H., Chen, P.Y., Hsieh, J.W., Yeh, I.H.: CSPNet: a new backbone that can enhance learning capability of CNN. In: Proceedings of the IEEE/CVF Conference on Computer Vision and Pattern Recognition Workshops, pp. 390–391 (2020)
26. Wang, Z., Chen, A., Li, J., Yao, Y., Luo, Z.: 1D barcode region detection based on the Hough transform and support vector machine. In: Tian, Q., Sebe, N., Qi, G.-J., Huet, B., Hong, R., Liu, X. (eds.) MMM 2016. LNCS, vol. 9517, pp. 79–90. Springer, Cham (2016). https://doi.org/10.1007/978-3-319-27674-8_8
27. Wu, P., Lin, Y.: Research on license plate detection algorithm based on SSD. In: Proceedings of the 2nd International Conference on Advances in Image Processing, pp. 19–23 (2018)
28. Yang, Q., Golwala, G., Sundaram, S., Lee, P., Allebach, J.: Barcode detection and decoding in on-line fashion images. Electron. Imaging **2019**(8), 413-1–413-7 (2019)
29. Yun, I., Kim, J.: Vision-based 1D barcode localization method for scale and rotation invariant. In: TENCON 2017–2017 IEEE Region 10 Conference, pp. 2204–2208. IEEE (2017)
30. Zhang, X., Zhou, X., Lin, M., Sun, J.: ShuffleNet: an extremely efficient convolutional neural network for mobile devices. In: Proceedings of the IEEE Conference on Computer Vision and Pattern Recognition, pp. 6848–6856 (2018)
31. Zheng, Z., Wang, P., Liu, W., Li, J., Ye, R., Ren, D.: Distance-IoU loss: faster and better learning for bounding box regression. In: AAAI, pp. 12993–13000 (2020)

The Realtime Indoor Localization Unmanned Aerial Vehicle

Yimin Zhou[1(✉)], Zhixiong Yu[2], and Zhuang Ma[1,2]

[1] Shenzhen Institutes of Advanced Technology, Chinese Academy of Sciences,
Shenzhen, China
{ym.zhou,zhuang.ma}@siat.ac.cn
[2] The University of Chinese Academy of Sciences, Beijing, China
zx.yu@siat.ac.cn

Abstract. Localization is an important issue for UAV (Unmanned Aerial Vehicle) applications. This paper proposes a localization algorithm based on the combination of direct method and feature-based method. The visual odometer uses the photometric error to directly match and track the camera's pose to improve the real-time performance. Then the ORB (Oriented FAST and Rotated Brief) features are extended from key frames, and local and global optimization can be achieved through key frames to improve map consistency by Bundle Adjustment. A depth filter is also introduced to optimize the map points by accumulating depth information of multiple frames. Then the localization accuracy can be improved by building a more accurate map. The proposed algorithm can achieve faster pose estimation and higher real-time performance while ensuring localization accuracy in indoor environments.

Keywords: Visual simultaneous localization and mapping · Depth filter · Indoor localization · UAV

1 Introduction

With the rapid technology development of unmanned aerial vehicles (UAVs), UAVs have been widely used in various fields such as public safety, weather monitoring, terrain survey, emergency rescue [1,2]. Localization is an important issue for UAV applications. In outdoor environments, the positioning technology represented by GPS is already quite mature. However, in indoor environments, GPS usually fails to provide location information, while visual SLAM (Simultaneous Localization and Mapping) technology is widely used in indoor localization with its high accuracy and cost-effective advantages [3,4]. Indoor localization technology based on UAVs is of great significance in the academic and technical fields.

Motion and observation are two important components in visual SLAM. Motion describes the estimation of the camera pose, while observation describes the position estimation of the map points. The movement of the camera can be

© Springer Nature Singapore Pte Ltd. 2021
F. Sun et al. (Eds.): ICCSIP 2020, CCIS 1397, pp. 56–70, 2021.
https://doi.org/10.1007/978-981-16-2336-3_5

determined by the visual odometer, and the position of the spatial point can be measured by the movement [5]. Visual odometry can be used to estimate the motion between adjacent frames, usually with two patterns: feature-based method and direct method [6].

In the feature-based method, feature points are used to match between adjacent frames [8,9], and to construct a minimum reprojection error to estimate the camera pose. The most representative one is the ORB-SLAM [10,11], with a three-thread structure, using ORB (Oriented FAST and Rotated Brief) [7] feature points to match among frames. The front-end visual odometry is used to estimate frame poses by extracting and matching ORB feature points, while the back-end is used to optimize the poses and map points through BA (Bundle Adjustment) [12]. Since the descriptor is calculated in the process of feature extraction, the system can detect loop by the bag-of-words model to avoid the cumulative errors, and it can relocate after tracking loss. However, in the environment with less texture, ORB-SLAM will fail to track due to insufficient feature points. On this basis, PLSLAM (Points and Lines SLAM) [13] is proposed to add line features so as to improve the tracking performance in the less texture environment. However, as these feature-based methods require feature point extraction and descriptor calculation for each frame, it is quite time-consuming.

Different from feature-based method, the direct method can directly estimate the motion of the camera through the pixel brightness between frames. Since it does not extract feature points, the connection among frames can be established through the assumption of luminosity invariance with faster speed, such as LSD-SLAM (Large Scale Direct monocular SLAM) [14]. The LSD-SLAM can calculate the gray level of pixels to make full use of the information in the image, so it has better tracking performance in the less texture environment. However, LSD-SLAM is too sensitive to the camera parameters and illumination varieties, easily resulting in tracking lost during fast movement. Meanwhile, Jakob Engel proposed the sparse direct method system DSO (Direct Sparse Odometry) [15]. Since the camera exposure is calibrated and the luminosity parameter is added during optimization, it can have higher performance in the varied light environment. However, these direct methods usually cannot achieve global optimization. With an inevitable accumulative error, the overall accuracy is unsatisfied.

Aiming at the problems of direct methods and feature-based methods, some researchers try to combine the advantages of both methods, such as SVO (Semi-direct Visual Odometry) [16]. For the front-end tracking part, SVO can optimize the pose by minimizing the photometric error which is similar to the direct method. SVO can also extract feature points in the key frames. Since the descriptor is not calculated, SVO can have an extremely fast running speed. However, SVO requires to assume that all points are on the same plane at the initialization stage, so it will fail to track during head-up. Besides, SVO does not have a loop detection part, so it is unable to optimize the map globally. SVO2.0 enhanced the performance of tracking edges and corners [17], and IMU (Inertial Measurement Unit) is added for pre-integration so as to improve the overall processing speed and robustness. Other researches [18–20] fuse IMU integration into visual information to improve the accuracy of SLAM, however, it would increase the complexity of the algorithm and the calibration of vision and IMU. Besides, neural networks can be applied for feature extraction [21,22], loop detection [23], map segmentation [24,25] and semantic detection [26–29] to improve the robustness of visual SLAM, however, neural networks usually require GPU (Graphics Processing Unit) to accelerate the calculation, so it is difficult to be implemented on the UAV in real-time.

In this paper, only stereo vision is used to construct with the combination of the direct method and the feature-based method to track camera poses so as to improve the localization speed. The proposed algorithm is improved based on ORB-SLAM2 where one of the defects of the ORB-SLAM2 is that the feature points should be extracted and the descriptor should be calculated in each frame during visual odometry with more time consumption. Hence, the feature points are matched directly via the proposed method so as to improve the real-time performance. Furthermore, the depth of the map points are estimated by only triangulating with two frames which will bring depth error in the map points by causal wrong measurements. Therefore, the depth filter is introduced to optimize the spatial position of the feature points through multi-frame information so that the accuracy of positioning is improved with a more accurate map.

The remainder of the paper is organized as follows. Section 2 describes the proposed method with the framework with the direct feature points match and depth filter introduction. The experiments and result analysis are provided in Sect. 3. Conclusion is given in Sect. 4.

2   Method of Indoor Localization

The proposed method is based on ORB-SLAM2, as shown in Fig. 1, which is composed of four threads, including tracking thread, feature extraction & depth filter thread, local mapping thread and loop closing thread. The local mapping thread and loop closing thread are the same as in ORB-SLAM2. The first algorithm proposed in this paper is the visual odometer based on direct method which is contained in the tracking thread. The proposed second algorithm is the space point depth estimation based on the stereo depth filter which is contained in the feature extraction and depth filter thread. The tracking thread is based on the direct method, while the feature-based method and direct method are combined by extracting ORB feature in the key frames during the thread of feature extraction and depth filter. The pose of the key frames and the map points are optimized through local mapping thread and loop closing thread by feature matching in the key frames. The main functions of each thread are explained as follows.

Tracking Threads
The initial pose and the depth of the initial map points are calculated after the initialization of the system by receiving the stereo images. Then the preliminary pose of the current frame is estimated by minimizing the luminosity error of the image patches between adjacent frames. The positions of the pixel in the

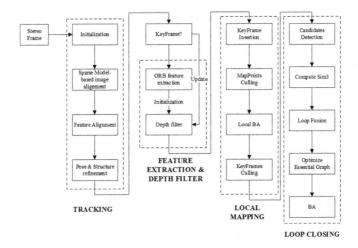

Fig. 1. The proposed localization algorithm framework

current frame which aligns to reference frames are estimated by constructing the minimum luminosity error with the preliminary pose. Then the poses and the corresponding map point positions of the current frame and the key frames nearby are optimized by constructing the minimum reprojection error. Then the current frame can be concluded whether it is a keyframe.

Feature Extraction and Depth Filter Thread
If the current frame is a keyframe, our method will extract the ORB feature and calculate the descriptor. The depths of the feature points are calculated by stereo triangulation, then sent to the depth filter to initialize the depth of seed points. If the current frame is not a keyframe, the depth will be calculated by polar searching and sent to the depth filter to update the depth of seed points until the depth converges.

Local Mapping Thread
In this thread, the converged depth points are fused with the existing map points, and the new space points are inserted into the map. The pose and spatial point coordinates of the keyframes are optimized by constructing a minimum reprojection error function with BA. Finally, the thread filters out the redundant keyframes and send the rest to the loop closing thread.

Loop Closing Thread
The main function of the loop closing thread is closed-loop detection and closed-loop correction. The new keyframe is compared with other keyframes by the bag-of-words description. If the similarity exceeds a dynamic threshold, it means that a loop is closed. The current frame and the repeated map points of the closed-loop keyframe will be merged by the closed-loop fusion and graph optimization, then the pose of the new keyframe and the loop-back keyframes will be adjusted. The thread will optimize the pose of all keyframes by BA globally.

2.1   Visual Odometer Based on Direct Method

In this paper, the optical center of the left lens of the stereo camera is considered as the origin of the camera coordinate. The specific steps of the algorithm are as follows.

Step 1. Pose Estimation with Direct Method
The preliminary pose and map points are calculated after initialization of the system by using the homography matrix and the essential matrix. As it is shown in Fig. 2, the image intensity is denoted as I_k at the current time k^{th} moment, while I_{k-1} is denoted as the image intensity at the previous $(k-1)^{th}$ moment, and the pose from the $(k-1)^{th}$ moment to the kth moment is denoted as $T_{k,k-1}$. The projection process from three-dimensional space to the image space is denoted with Ω, and the process of back projection is denoted as Ω^{-1}.

The initial pose of the current frame is usually considered as the same as the pose of the previous frame or identity matrix pose, so we assume $T_{k,k-1}$ is known. The position and depth of the feature points in the $(k-1)^{th}$ frame have also been calculated from the previous multiple frames. The position of the feature point p_i and the depth d_i in the $(k-1)^{th}$ frame are known, and this feature point can be projected to the three-dimensional space at point P_i, which can be transformed to $P_{i,k}$ in the coordinate of frame k through $T_{k,k-1}$, and then projected to the image space at p'_i.

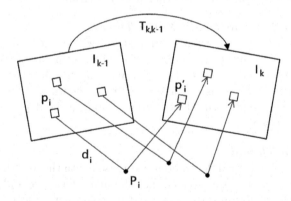

Fig. 2. The pose estimation with direct method

Since the interval between two frames is quite short, we assume that the brightness value of the same point of the image in the space at two moments is basically unchanged [6]. A function can be constructed with the image patch near the feature points of the previous frame and the reprojected point of the current frame, written as,

$$\delta I\left(T_{k,k-1}, p_i\right) = I_k\left(\pi \cdot \left(T_{k,k-1} \cdot \pi^{-1}\left(p_i, d_i\right)\right)\right) - I_{k-1}\left(p_i\right) \qquad (1)$$

where $\delta I\,(T_{k,k-1}, p_i)$ is the variation of the intensity at p_i during the movement of $T_{k,k-1}$. By minimizing the photometric error, the maximum likelihood estimation can be constructed to optimize the pose $T_{k,k-1}$:

$$T_{k,k-1} = \arg\min_{T_{k,k-1}} \frac{1}{2} \sum_{i \in R} \|\delta I\,(T_{k,k-1}, p_i)\|^2 \qquad (2)$$

where R is the image point space that the depth d_i is known at the $k - 1^{th}$ moment while the point is visible in the current frame after back-projection. Equation (2) can be solved by G-N (Gauss-Newton) or L-M (Levenberg-Marquadt) methods [30], and the estimation of $T_{k,k-1}$ can be updated after each iteration.

Step 2. Feature Points Alignment
The pose estimation between the two frames is initially obtained through the previous step, then the coordinate of the feature points reprojected from the previous frame will be biased to the real coordinate of the current frame due to noise. So the coordinate of feature pixels can be optimized through the established map points.

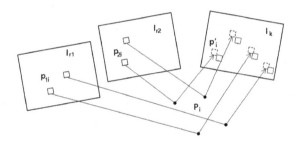

Fig. 3. Feature alignment between the keyframe and the current frame

As the map points are saved in the previously established keyframes, there will be keyframes I_{r1}, I_{r2} that share the same view of the map point P_i with the current frame I_k, as shown in Fig. 3. The current preliminary frame pose $T_{k,k-1}$ is estimated from the previous step, and we reproject the points in the keyframes that are in common view with the current frame to the current frame. Then a residual function can be constructed to optimize the feature coordinates in the current frame by minimizing the luminosity error based on the assumption of luminosity invariance:

$$p'_i = \arg\min_{p'_i} \frac{1}{2} \|I_k\,(p'_i) - A_i \cdot I_r\,(p_i)\|^2 \qquad (3)$$

As the keyframe may be far away from the current frame, it is necessary to process the feature patch in the keyframe by rotating and stretching the affine transformation A_i. The optimized estimation coordinates of the feature points in the current frame can be obtained at the coordinate p_i'.

Step 3. Pose Optimization

A more accurate match between the features of the two frames can be obtained through the previous steps, and the poses of the camera $T_{w,k}$ and the map points P_i can be optimized by constructing a reprojection model, as shown in Fig. 4. The reprojection function is,

$$\|\delta p_i\| = \|p_i - \pi \cdot (T_{k,w} P_i)\| \tag{4}$$

and the maximum likelihood function is,

$$T_{k,w} = \arg \min_{T_{k,w}} \frac{1}{2} \sum_i \|p_i - \pi \cdot (T_{k,w} P_i)\|^2 \tag{5}$$

It can be solved by the least square method [30].

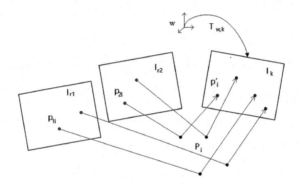

Fig. 4. The pose optimization of the established frames

2.2   Space Point Depth Estimation

Since the camera pose is calculated by observing spatial map points, building a more accurate and reliable map is the premise to improve the accuracy of positioning. The map points are usually obtained by matching the features and calculating by triangulation with only two frames. However, the depth calculated by triangulation is highly affected by the parallax of the two frames. Moreover, the non-key frames are not used to optimize the depth of the map points, resulting in a waste of information. Therefore, a depth filter is introduced to use multi-frame information to accumulate and optimize the map point depth. Considering that the convergence speed of the depth filter is affected by the initial values, this paper uses a calibrated stereo camera to obtain the initial value of the seed point depth, and optimize the depth by updating the depth filter.

(1) Triangulation ranging

The ideal stereo camera model is that the imaging surfaces of the left and right are coplanar, the optical axes are parallel, the focal lengths are same, and the pole is at infinity, as shown in Fig. 5. However, the camera cannot be achieved in practice, so it is necessary to rectify the stereo camera before it can be used for depth measurement [31].

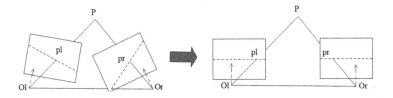

Fig. 5. Rectification of the stereo camera

After stereo calibration, the optical axes are parallel, and the ordinates of the images *pl* and *pr* of the same spatial point *P* on the left and right cameras are the same. The geometric relationship is depicted in Fig. 6.

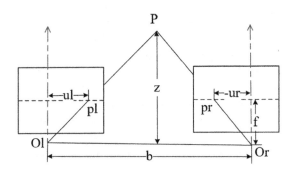

Fig. 6. Triangulation measurement with stereo camera

In Fig. 6, b is the baseline length of the stereo camera, f is the focal length of the camera. According to the principle of similar triangles, it has,

$$\frac{z - f}{z} = \frac{b - ul + ur}{b}, \quad d = ul - ur \tag{6}$$

where d is the parallax and the depth z can be calculated with Eq. (7).

As it is shown in the depth calculation Eq. (6), the accuracy of the parallax d has a greater impact on the depth calculation of the map points. Since the depth estimation of map points can be regarded as a state estimation problem, a depth filter is introduced to optimize the depth of map points with multiple observations in multiple frames.

The depth distribution is usually considered as the normal distribution [32,33]. For the spatial point P, the depth d_p follows the normal distribution $N(\mu, \sigma^2)$. The new depth d_k can be calculated by the new observation of the kth frame, and they are also followed by the normal distribution $N(\mu_o, \sigma_o^2)$. The new observation data can be fused with the existing data, and they still follow normal distribution $N(\mu_f, \sigma_f^2)$, where

$$\mu_f = \frac{\sigma_O^2 \mu + \sigma^2 \mu_o}{\sigma^2 + \sigma_o^2} \tag{7}$$

$$\sigma_f^2 = \frac{\sigma_o^2 \sigma^2}{\sigma^2 + \sigma_o^2} \tag{8}$$

When σ_f is less than the threshold, the depth is considered to be converged. In the depth estimation, the uncertainty of the depth σ_o also requires to be estimated. For a point P in the space, it can project on the two frames, p_1 and p_2. The optical centers of the two frames are O_1 and O_2, as demonstrated in Fig. 7.

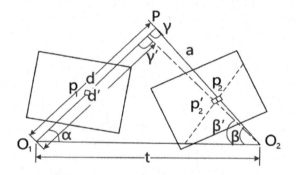

Fig. 7. Uncertainty of depth estimation

Considering the error is one pixel [25], according to the geometric relationship, it has,

$$\|d'\| = \|t\| \frac{\sin \beta'}{\sin \gamma'} \tag{9}$$

where β is the angler between $O_2 P$ and $O_1 O_2$, γ is the angler between $O_1 P$ and $O_1 O_2$, d is the distance from P to O_1, and d' is the distance changed by the error match of one pixel.

Since the inverse depth obeys normal distribution, the variance σ_o is,

$$\sigma_o = \left\| \frac{1}{d} \right\| - \left\| \frac{1}{d'} \right\| \tag{10}$$

For each seed point, when the pose of a new frame is calculated, the depth and depth uncertainty can be merged into the depth filter to obtain a smaller uncertainty until the uncertainty is less than the threshold, then the depth is considered to be converged.

(2) Depth estimation
As shown in Fig. 8, there is a point P in the space, where the left frame is the keyframe KF, the baseline of the stereo camera is b, and the distance between the non-keyframe and the left camera of the stereo is t.

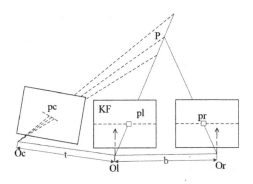

Fig. 8. Depth estimation of seed point

For the keyframes, ORB features are be extracted in the left and the right frames, and the depth can be calculated directly through feature matching, then the depth filter is initialized. For the non-key frames, they are matched with the keyframes by searching through epipolar lines, and the depth filter can be updated. If the depth converges, a map point is generated.

3   Experiments and Analysis

The EuRoC [34] dataset contains indoors sequences from UAV with stereo camera. The stereo camera uses a global shutter and the resolution of each camera is 752 × 480, the frame rate is 20fps, and the real trajectory collected by the Leica MS50 laser tracking scanner are provided for comparison. Sequence MH01, MH02, MH03, V201 are used to evaluate the processing time and pose accuracy of the proposed method. The information of the sequence is show in Table 1.

The proposed method and ORB-SLAM2 are used to run these four dataset, and the trajectory and processing time are saved for evaluation. Table 2 shows the processing environment of the experiments.

Table 1. Dataset sequence information

Sequence	Scenario	Number of frames
MH01	Large industrial environment	3682
MH02	Large industrial environment	3040
MH03	Large industrial environment	2700
V201	Room	2280

Table 2. Experiment environments

Item	Parameter
Processor	Intel i7-8750
Memory	16 GB
Operating System	Ubuntu 16.04
Language	C++

3.1 Processing Time Evaluation

We compare the time from processing each frame of image to obtain the pose by the proposed algorithm and ORB-SLAM2. Figure 9 shows the distribution for processing time spent in pose estimation of each frame. The abscissa represents frame number, and the ordinate represents time in seconds of processing each frame. Table 3 shows the average processing time of the proposed method and ORB-SLAM2.

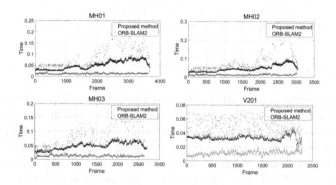

Fig. 9. Image processing time distribution per frame

The red points in Fig. 9 represent the processing time of ORB-SLAM2 and the blue points represent the processed time of the proposed method. It can be seen that the processing time of the proposed method is significantly faster than that of the ORB-SLAM2, mainly because the method feature points are directly matched with the photometric error during tracking.

Table 3. Processing time per frame

	Proposed method	ORB-SLAM2
MH01	0.0128	0.0539
MH02	0.0129	0.0502
MH03	0.0127	0.0511
V201	0.0111	0.0357

3.2 Pose Accuracy Evaluation

Since the actual value of 3D map points are difficult to obtain, the error of the camera motion track is usually used to evaluate the effect of visual odometry or visual SLAM algorithm.

Figure 10 shows the deviation of the proposed algorithm and ORB-SLAM2 from the real trajectory on the four data sets. The blue trajectory represents the trajectory of the algorithm proposed, the green trajectory represents the trajectory of ORB-SLAM2, and the dashed line represents the real trajectory.

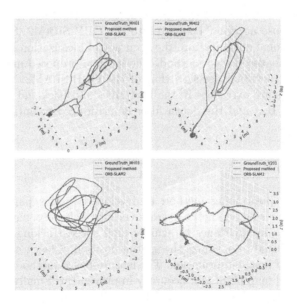

Fig. 10. Keyframe trajectory comparison on EuRoc datasets

Table 4 lists the pose accuracy of the proposed method and ORB-SLAM2, ATE (Absolute Trajectory Error) and RMSE (Root Mean Square Error) is used to evaluate among the estimated poses and the real poses,

$$RMSE = \sqrt{\frac{1}{n}\sum_i^n \left(\hat{X}_i - X_i\right)^2} \tag{11}$$

where $\hat{X}_i$ is the estimated poses and X_i is the real poses. "Max" and "Mean" represent the maximum difference and the average difference between the estimated pose and real pose.

Table 4. Keyframe trajectory accuracy comparison

	The proposed method			ORB-SLAM2		
	Max	Mean	RMSE	Max	Mean	RMSE
MH01	0.0902	0.0274	0.0347	0.0810	0.0307	0.0363
MH02	0.0900	0.0276	0.0331	0.1012	0.0312	0.0375
MH03	0.1112	0.0338	0.0378	0.1071	0.0391	0.0421
V201	0.1182	0.0588	0.0613	0.0964	0.0392	0.0458

It can be seen from Table 4 that the proposed method has roughly the same performance of pose accuracy compared to the ORB-SLAM2. Since the direct method has no global optimization, the accuracy of localization is usually worse than that of the feature-based method. The method proposed in this paper can achieve the same accuracy level as that of the ORB-SLAM2, mainly because the feature points are extracted in the keyframes and back-end optimization is constructed with BA, and the depth filter is introduced to optimize the depth of map points.

4   Conclusion

An indoor rapid positioning method is developed in this paper. The direct method is used in visual odometry to track the camera's pose, and ORB features are only extracted in keyframes to achieve high speed tracking. The depth filter is then introduced to optimize the spatial position of feature points through multiple frames of image information. The feature-based method is used to optimize the pose and map points for accuracy improvement. Finally, the speed and accuracy of the algorithm are evaluated through the dataset of EuRoc MAV. The experiments demonstrate that the proposed method has a faster processing time but also the satisfied accuracy level as ORB-SLAM2.

Acknowledgement. This work was supported under the National Key Research and Development Program of China (2018YFB1305505), National Natural Science Foundation of China (NSFC) (61973296) and Shenzhen Basic Research Program Ref. JCYJ20170818153635759, Science and Technology Planning Project of Guangdong Province Ref. 2017B010117009.

References

1. GNSS I, MIT.: Draper Research Team Equips UAV with Vision for GNSS-Denied Navigation. Inside GNSS (2017). https://insidegnss.com/mit-draper-research-team-equips-uav-with-vision-for-gnss-denied-navigation

2. Kong, L., Gong, P., Wang, L.: A review of the development status of micro-UAV. In: Proceedings of the 2019 World Transport Congress (ii). China Association for Science and Technology, Ministry of Transport, PRC, Chinese Academy of Engineering: China Highway Society, pp. 435–444 (2019). (in Chinese)

3. Li, Y., Mu, R., Shan, Y.: A brief analysis of the development status of unmanned systems vision SLAM technology. Control Decis. 1–10 (2020). (in Chinese). https://doi.org/10.13195/j.kzyjc.2019.1149

4. Lu, X.: Application research of wireless Positioning Technology on indoor Mobile platform. Ph.D. thesis. University of Science and Technology of China, Hefei (2020)

5. Schonberger, J.L., Frahm, J.-M.: Structure-from-motion revisited. In: Proceedings of the IEEE Conference on Computer Vision and Pattern Recognition, pp. 4104–4113 (2016)

6. Nistér, D., Naroditsky, O., Bergen, J.: Visual odometry. In: IEEE Computer Society Conference on Computer Vision and Pattern Recognition, vol. 1 (2004)

7. Rublee, E., Rabaud, V., Konolige, K., et al.: ORB: an efficient alternative to sift or Surf. In: IEEE International Conference on Computer Vision, pp. 2564–2571 (2011)

8. Lowe, D.G.: Distinctive image features from scale-invariant keypoints. Int. J. Comput. Vision 60(2), 91–110 (2004)

9. Bay, H., Tuytelaars, T., Van Gool, L.: SURF: speeded up robust features. In: Leonardis, A., Bischof, H., Pinz, A. (eds.) ECCV 2006. LNCS, vol. 3951, pp. 404–417. Springer, Heidelberg (2006). https://doi.org/10.1007/11744023_32

10. Mur-Artal, R., Montiel, J.M., Tardos, J.D.: ORB-SLAM: a versatile and accurate monocular SLAM system. IEEE Trans. Rob. 31(5), 1147–1163 (2015)

11. Mur-Artal, R., Tardos, J.D.: ORB-SLAM2: an open-source SLAM system for monocular, stereo, and RGB-D cameras. IEEE Trans. Rob. 33, 1255–1262 (2017)

12. Triggs, B., McLauchlan, P.F., Hartley, R.I., Fitzgibbon, A.W.: Bundle adjustment — a modern synthesis. In: Triggs, B., Zisserman, A., Szeliski, R. (eds.) IWVA 1999. LNCS, vol. 1883, pp. 298–372. Springer, Heidelberg (2000). https://doi.org/10.1007/3-540-44480-7_21

13. Pumarola, A., Vakhitov, A., Agudo, A., et al.: PL-SLAM: real-time monocular visual SLAM with points and lines. In: IEEE International Conference on Robotics and Automation, pp. 4503–4508 (2017)

14. Engel, J., Schöps, T., Cremers, D.: LSD-SLAM: large-scale direct monocular SLAM. In: Fleet, D., Pajdla, T., Schiele, B., Tuytelaars, T. (eds.) ECCV 2014. LNCS, vol. 8690, pp. 834–849. Springer, Cham (2014). https://doi.org/10.1007/978-3-319-10605-2_54

15. Wang, R., Schworer, M., Cremers, D.: Stereo DSO: large-scale direct sparse visual odometry with stereo cameras. In: IEEE International Conference on Computer Vision. IEEE Computer Society, pp. 3923–3931 (2017)

16. Forster, C., Pizzoli, M., Scaramuzza, D.: SVO: fast semi-direct monocular visual odometry. In: IEEE International Conference on Robotics and Automation, pp. 15–22 (2014)

17. Forster, C., Zhang, Z., Gassner, M., et al.: SVO: semidirect visual odometry for monocular and multicamera systems. IEEE Trans. Rob. 33(2), 249–265 (2016)

18. Spaenlehauer, A., Frémont, V., Şekercioğlu, Y.A., et al.: A loosely-coupled app-roach for metric scale estimation in monocular vision-inertial systems. In: IEEE International Conference on Multisensor Fusion and Integration for Intelligent Systems, pp. 137–143 (2017)

19. Leutenegger, S., Lynen, S., Bosse, M., et al.: Keyframe-based visual-inertial odom-etry using nonlinear optimization. Int. J. Robot. Res. **34**(3), 314–334 (2015)

20. Qin, T., Shen, S.: Robust initialization of monocular visual-inertial estimation on aerial robots. In: IEEE International Conference on Intelligent Robots and Systems, pp. 4225–4232 (2017)

21. Wang, S., Clark, R., Wen, H., et al.: DeepVO: towards end-to-end visual odom-etry with deep recurrent convolutional neural networks. In: IEEE International Conference on Robotics and Automation (2017)

22. DeTone, D., Malisiewicz, T., Rabinovich, A.: Toward geometric deep SLAM. ArXiv abs/1707.07410 (2017)

23. Lianos, K.N., Schonberger, J.L., Pollefeys, M., et al.: VSO: visual semantic odome-try. In: Proceedings of the European Conference on Computer Vision, pp. 234–250 (2018)

24. Cui, L., Ma, C.: SDF-SLAM: semantic depth filter SLAM for dynamic environ-ments. IEEE Access **8**, 95301–95311 (2020)

25. Vincent, J., Labbé, M., Lauzon, J.S., et al.: Dynamic object tracking and masking for visual SLAM. ArXiv abs/2008.00072 (2020)

26. Zhang, L., Wei, L., Shen, P., et al.: Semantic SLAM based on object detection and improved Octomap. IEEE Access **6**, 75545–75559 (2018)

27. Kang, X., Yuan, S.: Robust data association for object-level semantic SLAM. ArXiv abs/1909.13493 (2019)

28. Bavle, H., De La Puente, P., How, J.P., et al.: VPS-SLAM: visual planar semantic SLAM for aerial robotic systems. IEEE Access **8**, 60704–60718 (2020)

29. Nicholson, L., Milford, M., Sünderhauf, N.: Dual quadrics from object detections as landmarks in object-oriented SLAM. IEEE Robot. Autom. Lett. **4**(1), 1–8 (2019)

30. Nocedal, J., Wright, S.: Numerical Optimization. Springer, New York (2006). https://doi.org/10.1007/978-0-387-40065-5

31. Kaehler, A., Bradski, G.: Learning Opencv3. Tsinghua University Press, Beijing (2018)

32. Civerra, J., Davison, A.J., Montiel, J.M.M.: Inverse depth parametrization for monocular SLAM. IEEE Trans. Rob. **24**(5), 932–945 (2008)

33. Vogiatzis, G., Hernández, C.: Video-based. Real-time multi-view stereo. Image Vis. Comput. **29**(7), 434–441 (2011)

34. ASL Datasets-The EuRoC MAV Dataset [EB/OL]. Projects.asl.ethz.ch. https://projects.asl.ethz.ch/datasets/

Algorithm

Algorithm

L1-Norm and Trace Lasso Based Locality Correlation Projection

Sen Yuan[✉], Si Chen, Feng Zhang, and Wentao Huang

Information Science Academy of China Electronics Technology Group Corporation,
Beijing 100086, China

Abstract. L1-norm based dimensionality reduction methods are the most effective techniques in computer vision and pattern recognition. However, they emphasize the robustness to outliers too much and overlook the correlation information among data so that they usually encounter the instability problem. To overcome this problem, in this paper, we propose a method called L1-norm and trace Lasso based locality correlation projection (L1/TL-LRP), in which the robustness, sparsity, and correlation are jointly considered. Specifically, by introducing the trace Lasso regularization, L1/TL-LRP is adaptive to the correlation structure that benefits from both L2-norm and L1-norm. Besides, an effective procedure based on Alternating Direction Method of Multipliers is proposed for solving L1/TL-LRP. Finally, we conduct extensive experiments on several databases for data classification. The inspiring experimental results demonstrate the effectiveness of the proposed method.

Keywords: Dimensionality reduction · L1-norm · L2-norm · Trace Lasso · Outliers

1 Introduction

Dimensionality reduction technique is of great importance in the area of computer vision and bioinformatics [1–3]. It aims to represent the original data in a lower dimensional space, and more importantly, to reveal the intrinsic structure of data. Over the past few decades, many useful techniques for dimensionality reduction have been developed. Principal components analysis (PCA) [4], linear discriminant analysis (LDA) [5] locality preserving projection (LPP) [6], and neighborhood preserving embedding (NPE) [7] are the most famous techniques due to their well-documented merits in various applications.

To discover the most important manifold for pattern discrimination tasks, complete global-local LDA (CGLDA) [8] was proposed and it incorporated three kinds of local information into LDA. As an unsupervised method, unsupervised discriminant projection (UDP) [9] introduces the concept of non-locality and can learn the low-dimensional representation of data by maximizing the ratio of nonlocal scatter to local scatter. In [10], the authors incorporate the advantage of both the local geometry and global Euclidean information of data and propose elastic preserving projections (EPP). Recently, a robust version of EPP named exponential EPP (EEPP) was proposed in [11].

© Springer Nature Singapore Pte Ltd. 2021
F. Sun et al. (Eds.): ICCSIP 2020, CCIS 1397, pp. 73–84, 2021.
https://doi.org/10.1007/978-981-16-2336-3_6

It must be point out that most of the aforementioned algorithms are based on L2-norm. Since the square operation amplifies the effect of outliers, the L2-norm based methods are prone to influence by outliers. It is commonly known that the L1-norm is more robust to the outliers than the L2-norm [12]. So L1-norm based methods have been developed for dimensionality reduction. Kwak [13] proposed PCA-L1 by applying the L1-norm to measure the variance of projected data in feature space. Further, Nie et al. [14] developed a non-greedy strategy to solve PCA-L1, which can find the principal maximum L1-norm projection component of data. To use L1-norm as a constraint instead of the L2-norm for discriminant learning, LDA based on L1-norm (LDA-L1) was proposed in [15]. Motivated by previous works, more L1-norm based methods have emerged, such as LPP-L1 [16], DLPP-L1 [17], PCA-L1S [18], etc.

The L1-norm regularization can work optimally on high-dimensional low-correlation data [19, 20], but this does not always hold in practical application since the presence of correlations among data is inevitable. In this situation, the L1-norm based methods will suffer from the instability problem [20].

In this paper, we propose a new framework called L1-norm and trace Lasso based locality correlation projection (L1/TL-LRP), in which the robustness, sparsity, and correlation are jointly considered. Particularly, to improve the robustness to outliers, L1/TL-LRP adopts L1-norm to characterize the geometric structure. In addition, to overcome the instability problem, L1/TL-LRP introduces the trace Lasso [19–21], which can balance the L1-norm and L2-norm, to form a correlation adapter that considers both correlation and sparsity. An iterative method based on Alternating Direction Method of Multipliers is also presented for solving L1/TL-LRP. Experimental results on several databases demonstrate the effectiveness of the proposed method. Last but importantly, the idea behind L1/TL-LRP is quite general and can be potentially extended to other dimensionality reduction techniques.

The reminder of this paper is organized as follows. Section 2 reviews the related work. In Sect. 3, we propose the L1/TR-LEP method and present the specific alternating direction method of multipliers based iteration algorithm. The experimental results are reported in Sect. 4. Finally, Sect. 5 concludes the paper.

2   Related work

2.1   LPP

LPP is a famous dimensionality reduction technique with locality preserving property. Given a data set $X = [x_1, x_2, \ldots, x_N] \in \mathbb{R}^{D \times N}$, LPP aims to find a transformation matrix W of size $D \times d$ by minimizing the following objective function:

$$\arg \min_{ij} \sum \left\| w^T x_i - w^T x_j \right\|_2^2 S_{ij} \tag{1}$$

where $\|\cdot\|_2$ is the L2-norm, and S_{ij} is the element of similarity matrix $S \in \mathbb{R}^{N \times N}$, which is usually defined as:

$$
S_{ij} = \begin{cases} \exp(-\|x_i - x_j\|_2^2/2t^2) & \text{if} x_j \in O_K(x_i) \\ 0 & \text{otherwise} \end{cases} \tag{2}
$$

where $O_K(x_i)$ denotes the set of K nearest neighbors of x_i and t is a kernel parameter.

Seen from Eq. (1), the objective function incurs a heavy penalty if two neighbor points are mapped far apart. Thus, minimizing (1) is an attempt to preserve locality, i.e., if x_i and x_j are close, their corresponding projections are close as well. To avoid trivial solutions, a constraint $w^T XDX^T w = 1$ is added to Eq. (1). Finally, the optimization problem can be reduced to a generalized eigenvalue decomposition problem:

$$
XLX^T w = \lambda XDX^T w \tag{3}
$$

where $L = D - S$ is the Laplacian matrix, D is a diagonal matrix and its entries $D_{ii} = \sum_j S_{ij}$. Generally, d generalized eigenvectors $w_1, w_2, ..., w_d$ associated with the first d smallest eigenvalues compose the column vectors of transformation matrix W. But in many cases, XDX^T is always singular since the dimensionality of image is larger than the number of samples. One popular method of overcoming it is to use PCA as a pre-processing step.

2.2 LPP-L1

To improve the robustness of LPP against outliers, LPP-L1 is achieved by replacing the L2-norm with L1-norm. The original cost function of LPP-L1 can be represented as:

$$
\arg\min \sum_{ij} \left\| w^T x_i - w^T x_j \right\|_1 S_{ij} \tag{4}
$$

$$
s.t. \ w^T XDX^T w = 1
$$

where $\| \bullet \|_1$ is the L1-norm. However, it is difficult to solve Eq. (4) directly. To make the optimization tractable, Eq. (4) is converted to a general maximization problem:

$$
\arg\max \sum_{ij} \left\| w^T x_i - w^T x_j \right\|_1 d_{ij} \tag{5}
$$

$$
s.t. \ w^T w = 1.
$$

where $d_{ij} = 1 - S_{ij}$. Inspired by PCA-L1, an iteration procedure can be adopted to solve the optimization problem in (5), which has been justified to converge to a global maximum. The objective function (5) is an alternative one to objective function (4). Moreover, from the above description, LPP-L1 does not need to deal with eigenvalue computation so that it can overcome singular value problem completely.

3 L1-Norm and Trace Lasso Based Locality Correlation Projection (L1/TL-LRP)

3.1 Problem Formulation

In this subsection, we will introduce the proposed L1-norm and trace Lasso based locality correlation projection (L1/TL-LRP) in detail.

The criterion in Eq. (1) can be represented as:

$$
\begin{aligned}
\frac{1}{2} \min \sum_{ij} \left\| w^T x_i - w^T x_j \right\|_2^2 S_{ij} \\
= \frac{1}{2} \min \sum_{ij} (w^T x_i - w^T x_j)\left(w^T x_i - w^T x_j\right)^T S_{ij} \\
= \min w^T X L X^T w
\end{aligned}
\tag{6}
$$

where $L = D - S, D \in \mathbb{R}^{N \times N}$ is a diagonal matrix and its entries $D_{ii} = \sum_j S_{ij}$, S is the similarity matrix which measures the relationship of neighboring points.

Let the eigenvalue decompositions of L be

$$
L = \begin{bmatrix} U_L, & \tilde{U}_L \end{bmatrix} \begin{bmatrix} D_L & 0 \\ 0 & 0 \end{bmatrix} \begin{bmatrix} U_L^T \\ \tilde{U}_L^T \end{bmatrix}
\tag{7}
$$

where $\begin{bmatrix} U_L, \tilde{U}_L \end{bmatrix}$ is a orthogonal matrix, $D_L \in \mathbb{R}^{H \times H}$ is a diagonal matrix, and $H = \text{rank}(L)$. Then, Eq. (6) can be rewritten as

$$
\min w^T X L X^T w = \min w^T X U_L D_L U_L^T X^T w = \min \left\| w^T X U_L D_L^{\frac{1}{2}} \right\|_2^2
\tag{8}
$$

As L2-norm metric is more sensitive to outliers and noises than L1-norm, we adopt L1-norm to design the objective function of our proposed method. In addition, to overcome the instability problem encountered by L1-norm regularization, we also introduce trace Lasso to regularize the projection vector w. Finally, the objective function of proposed L1/TL-LRP can be defined as:

$$
\arg \min_w = \left\| w^T X U_L D_L^{\frac{1}{2}} \right\|_1 + \gamma \left\| X^T Diag(w) \right\|_*
\tag{9}
$$

where $\|\cdot\|_*$ is the trace-norm of a matrix, i.e., the sum of its singular values, $Diag(\cdot)$ denotes the conversion of a vector to a diagonal matrix, and $\gamma > 0$ is a balance parameter. The second term in Eq. (9) is called trace Lasso [19]. It can be found that trace Lasso involves the data matrix X, which makes it adaptive to the correlation of data. If the data are uncorrelated, i.e., $XX^T = I$, we have

$$
\left\| X^T Diag(w) \right\|_* = tr\left[Diag(w) X X^T Diag(w) \right]^{\frac{1}{2}} = \|w\|_1
\tag{10}
$$

In that case, the trace Lasso is equal to L1-norm. In the case that the data are highly correlated (the data points are all the same, i.e., $X = 1x$, and $XX^T = 11^T$), the trace Lasso is essentially equal to the L2-norm:

$$X^T Diag(w)_* = x^T w_* = x_2 w_2 = w_2 \tag{11}$$

For other cases, trace Lasso interpolates between L1-norm and L2-norm [19]:

$$w_1 \leq X^T Diag(w)_* \leq w_2 \tag{12}$$

The above discussion indicates that the trace Lasso can balance the L1-norm and L2-norm with adaptive consideration of data structure.

3.2 Optimization of L1/TL-LRP

Let $F = XU_L D_L^{\frac{1}{2}}$, we can reformulate Eq. (9) as

$$\underset{w}{\arg\min} \|P\|_1 + \gamma \|Q\|_* \tag{13}$$

$$s.t.\ P = w^T F, Q = X^T Diag(w)$$

To solve the optimization problem (13), the alternating direction method of multipliers (ADMM) [22] can be used. The augmented Lagrangian function of (13) is

$$L(P, w, Q) = P_1 + \gamma Q_* + \mathrm{tr}\left[Y_1^T\left(P - w^T F\right)\right] + \mathrm{tr}\left[Y_2^T\left(Q - X^T Diag(w)\right)\right]$$
$$+ \frac{\mu}{2}\left(P - w^T F_2^2 + Q - X^T Diag(w)_2^2\right) \tag{14}$$

where Y_1 and Y_2 are Lagrange multipliers, and $\mu > 0$ is a penalty parameter.

The above problem (14) is unconstrained and it can be minimized one by one with respect to variables P, Q, w by fixing the other variables, respectively, and then updating the Lagrange multipliers Y_1 and Y_2. Now we provide details of the solution of Eq. (14) below.

Step 1. Updating Q by fixing P and w. Then, Eq. (14) is equivalent to solve the following optimization problem:

$$Q^* = \underset{Q}{\arg\min}\ \gamma Q_* + \mathrm{tr}\left(Y_2^T Q\right) + \frac{\mu}{2}Q - X^T Diag(w)_2^2$$
$$= \underset{Q}{\arg\min}\ \frac{\gamma}{\mu}Q_* + \frac{1}{2}Q - \left(X^T Diag(w) - \frac{1}{\mu}Y_2\right)_2^2 \tag{15}$$

The problem (15) can be solved by the well-known singular value thresholding (SVT) operator [23]. The optimal Q^* can be updated by:

$$Q^* \leftarrow \mathrm{SVT}_{\frac{\gamma}{\mu}}\left(X^T Diag(w) - \frac{1}{\mu}Y_2\right) \tag{16}$$

where $SVT_{\frac{\gamma}{\mu}}(M) = U\mathrm{Diag}((\sigma - \frac{\gamma}{\mu})_+)V^T$, the singular value decomposition of matrix M is given by $U\mathrm{Diag}((\sigma_i)_{1 \le i \le r})V^T$, and $(\sigma - \frac{\gamma}{\mu})_+ = \max(\sigma - \frac{\gamma}{\mu}, 0)$.

Step 2. Updating P by fixing Q and w. Then we have

$$
\begin{aligned}
P^* &= \underset{P}{\mathrm{argmin}} \|P\|_1 + tr\left(Y_1^T P\right) + \frac{\mu}{2}\|P - w^T F\|_2^2 \\
&= \underset{P}{\mathrm{argmin}} \frac{1}{\mu}\|P\|_1 + \frac{1}{2}\left\|P - \left(w^T F - \frac{1}{\mu}Y_1\right)\right\|_2^2
\end{aligned}
\tag{17}
$$

The solution to the optimization problem (17) can be obtained by a shrinkage operator [24] directly. For the shrinkage purposes, we define the soft thresholding operator as:

$$
Z_\theta[x] = \mathrm{sign}(x) \cdot \max(|x| - \theta, 0)
\tag{18}
$$

So, there exists the following closed-form solution of (17):

$$
P^* = Z_{\frac{1}{\mu}}\left[w^T F - \frac{1}{\mu}Y_1\right]
\tag{19}
$$

Step 3. Updating w by fixing Q and P. Then Eq. (14) is equivalent to solve the following optimization problem:

$$
\begin{aligned}
w^* &= \arg\min_w -tr\left[Y_1^T w^T F\right] - tr\left[Y_2^T X^T Diag(w)\right] \\
&\quad + \frac{\mu}{2}\left(P - w^T F_2^2 + Q - X^T Diag(w)_2^2\right) \\
&= \arg\min_P -tr\left[Y_1^T w^T F\right] - tr\left[Y_2^T X^T Diag(w)\right] \\
&\quad + \frac{\mu}{2}\left(w^T FF^T w - 2PF^T w + tr\left(Diag(w)XX^T Diag(w)\right) - 2tr\left(Q^T X^T Diag(w)\right)\right) \\
&= \arg\min_P \frac{\mu}{2}w^T\left(FF^T + Diag\left(\Theta\left(XX^T\right)\right)\right)w \\
&\quad - \left(w^T FY_1^T + \mu PF^T w + \mu\Theta\left(Q^T X^T\right)^T w + \Theta\left(Y_2^T X^T\right)^T w\right)
\end{aligned}
\tag{20}
$$

where $tr(\cdot)$ represents the trace operator, and $\Theta(\cdot)$ denotes the diagonal of a matrix. Equation (20) is a smooth convex programming problem. By differentiating the objective function with respect to w and set it zero, the optimal w^* can be updated by

$$
w^* = \left(\mu FF^T + \mu Diag\left(\Theta\left(XX^T\right)\right)\right)^{-1}\left[FY_1^T + \mu PF^T + \mu\Theta\left(Q^T X^T\right)^T + \Theta\left(Y_2^T X^T\right)^T\right]
\tag{21}
$$

Step 4. Updating Y_1, Y_2 and μ.

$$
Y_1 = Y_1 + \mu(P - wF)
$$

$$
Y_2 = Y_2 + \mu\left(Q - X^T Diag(w)\right)
$$

$$\mu = \min(\rho\mu, \mu_{\max}) \tag{22}$$

where $\rho > 1$ is a constant.

The detailed algorithm steps of the iterative method based on ADMM are presented in Algorithm 1.

Algorithm 1: L1/TL-LRP

Input: Training samples $X = [x_1, x_2, ..., x_N] \in \mathbb{R}^{D \times N}$ and the learning rate parameter γ.

Initialize: $P = 0, Q = 0, Y_1 = 0, Y_2 = 0, \mu = 10^{-6}, \rho = 1.1, \epsilon = 10^{-7}, \mu_{max} = 10^6$

while not converge **do**

1. Update Q by (16):
2. Update P by (19);
3. Update w by (21);
4. Update Lagrange multipliers and μ by (22);
5. Check the convergence conditions:
$$\|P - w^T F\|_\infty \le \epsilon, \|Q - X^T Diag(w)\|_\infty \le \epsilon$$
6. **End while.**

Output: Optimal projection vector w.

3.3 Extension to Multiple Projection Vectors

In the above section, we have presented the process of L1/TL-LRP that extracts only one optimal projection vector (i.e., one feature), which may be not enough for representing the distinct data in low-dimension space. Based on the following process, we can easily extend it to extract multiple projection vectors. Suppose that the first l projection vectors $W_l = [w_1, \ldots, w_l]$ have been obtained by the iteration algorithm, then we can update the samples to compute the $(l + 1)$-th projection vector w_{l+1}:

$$x_i^{(l+1)} = \left(I_D - W_l W_l^T\right) x_i \tag{23}$$

After all samples $x_i^{l+1} (i = 1, 2, ..., N)$ are updated, we use them to form a new data matrix X and compute F by $F = X U_L D_L^{\frac{1}{2}}$. Then, Algorithm 1 can be used to compute the projection vector w_{l+1}. Given the newly obtained w_{l+1}, the projection matrix W_{l+1} is formed by padding W_{l+1} as $W_{l+1} = [W_l, w_{l+1}]$.

4 Experiments

In this section, we conduct a set of experiments on public available image databases (COIL-20, AR, and YFW) to show the effectiveness of the proposed L1/TL-LRP. Seven closely related methods: t-SNE [25], EPP-L2 [10], LPP-L2 [6], LPP-L1 [16], LDA-L2, LDA-L1, and DLPP-L1 are included for comparison. t-SNE is a nonlinear dimensionality reduction technique which converts similarities between data points to joint probabilities and tries to minimize the Kullback-Leibler divergence between the joint probabilities of the low- dimensional embedding and the high-dimensional data. For LPP-L2, LPP-L1, EPP-L2, DLPP-L1, and L1/TL-LRP, the K-nearest neighborhood parameter K is set to l-1, where l denotes the number of training samples per class. The value of α in EPP-L2 was fixed as 0.5 in all experiments. The recognition accuracy of different methods is evaluated based on the nearest neighbor classifier for its simplicity.

4.1 Experiments on COIL-20 Database

The COIL-20 database consists of 1440 images from 20 objects. For each object, 72 images were captured with a black background from varying angles at pose intervals of five degree. All the images were converted into a gray-level image of 32×32 pixels for computational efficiency in the experiments.

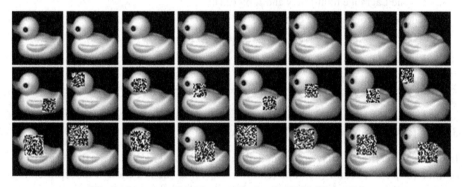

Fig. 1. Images with/without occlusion in COIL-20 database.

In the experiments, we randomly selected 10 images of each object for training and the remaining for testing. During the experiment, 50 percent of the training samples are randomly selected to be contaminated by rectangle noise. Some sample images of one object are shown in Fig. 1. We design two groups of experiments. The first group is called "Outlier 1", where the size of rectangle noise added to image is 8×8. The second group is called "Outlier 2", where the size of rectangle noise added to image is 12×12. Table 1 lists the recognition rate and the corresponding standard deviation of each method on this database. Figure 2 shows the recognition rate curve versus the variation of dimensions. From the results, we see that the curves of all the methods are smooth. The recognition rates of L2-norm based methods decrease more remarkably than L1-norm based methods with more and more occlusion in images, which well indicates the robustness of L1-norm. Although DLPP-L1 introduces the label information of data, it performs worse than LPP-L1 when dimension varies from 1 to 40. It is also noted that L1/TL-LRP outperforms the others under different dimension.

Table 1. The recognition rates and the standard deviation on COIL-20 database.

	LPP-L1	LPP-L2	LDA-L1	LDA-L2	DLPP-L1	EPP-L2	t-SNE	L1/TL-LRP
1	90.17 ± 2.35	78.20 ± 2.41	93.08 ± 2.15	83.77 ± 3.44	81.18 ± 2.84	80.55 ± 3.39	91.52 ± 1.13	**97.30 ± 2.27**
2	87.37 ± 1.81	66.57 ± 2.72	86.90 ± 1.23	74.28 ± 2.98	72.75 ± 3.20	71.40 ± 3.80	88.13 ± 1.76	**95.62 ± 1.91**

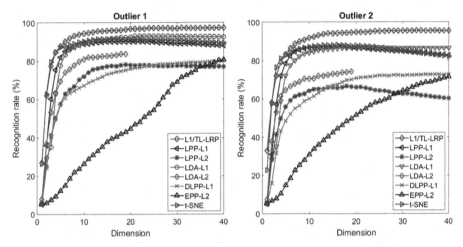

Fig. 2. Recognition rate vs. dimension of reduced space on COIL-20 database.

4.2 Experiments on AR Database

To evaluate the performance of different algorithms on real occlusions of face image, we conduct experiments on the AR database which contains over 4000 color face images of 126 people (56 women and 70 men). The images of most people were taken in two sessions (separated by two weeks). For each session, there are 3 images obscured by sunglasses, 3 images obscured by scarves, and 7 clean images with expressions and illuminations variations. The images with sun glasses and scarf are viewed as outliers. In our experiments, we utilize the subset of AR database consisting of 50 women and 50 men. For the sake of efficient computation, each image is resized to 32×32 pixels. Figure 3 shows some image examples in the AR database.

Fig. 3. Sample images in the AR database.

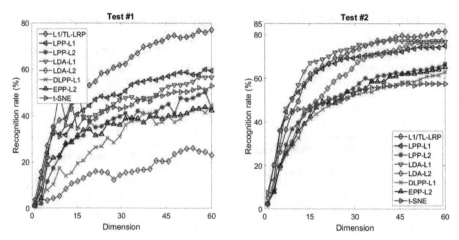

Fig. 4. Recognition accuracy versus feature dimension on AR database for (left) Test #1 and (right) Test #2.

Based on the experimental subset, we design two tests called Test #1 and Test #2. In Test #1, the 7 clean images are selected for training and 3 images with sun glasses for testing. In Test #2, to consider the case where images are both occluded by sunglasses and scarf, we select the 13 images in first session per person for training and the 13 images in second session for testing. Figure 4 shows the recognition accuracy versus feature dimension variation on AR database. From Fig. 4, one can see that, L1-norm based algorithms perform better than the corresponding L2-norm based algorithms. Specifically, in Test #1, the best results of LPP-L1 and LDA-L1 are 60.33% and 57.67%, while LPP-L2 and LDA-L2 just arrive at 50.33% and 36.67%, respectively. In Test #2, the best results of LPP-L1 and LDA-L1 are 75.00% and 77.50%, while LPP-L2 and LDA-L2 just arrive at 67.12% and 77.18%, respectively. DLPP-L1 is inferior to LDA-L1, LPP-L1, and L1/TL-LRP. Moreover, the proposed L1/TL-LRP is significantly better than all the other methods, when the reduced dimensionality varies from 40 to 60.

4.3 Experiments on LFW Database

The LFW database aims at studying the problem of the unconstrained face recognition. It contains more than 13,000 images from 5749 people. All the images were collected from web with great variations in age, pose, lighting and expression. To concentrate on the recognition task, we firs extract the face area of each image, and then resize it to 30 × 30 pixels. Figure 5 shows some sample images and the extracted face area from LFW database. Since the image number of each subject is different, 50% of the images of each people were used for training and the rest for testing. Table 2 gives the best recognition accuracy of different methods. As shown in Table 2, the proposed algorithm consistently outperforms over the other methods.

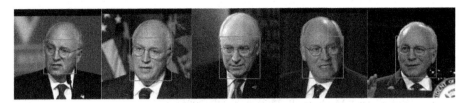

Fig. 5. Sample images in the FERET database.

Table 2. Optimal recognition rates of different methods on LFW database

Methods	LPP-L1	LPP-L2	LDA-L1	LDA-L2	DLPP-L1	EPP-L2	t-SNE	L1/TL-LRP
Accuracy	67.17	57.75	72.00	67.92	75.92	71.67	72.50	**77.28**

4.4 Discussion

From the above experiments, we have several interesting observations as follows:

(1) In most cases, L1-norm based methods obtain higher recognition rate than L2-norm based methods. This is because L1-norm criterion is more robust to outliers than L2-norm.

(2) According the curves, it can be seen that the proposed L1/TL-LRP provide good performance even with small feature dimensions. This means that L1/TL-LRP is superior to the other methods even in the low-dimensional projection space.

(3) L1/TL-LRP gets the best classification results in our experiments. The reason is that L1/TL-LRP uses L1-norm to regularize the geometric structure and simultaneously adopts trace Lasso to form a correlation adapter that considers both correlation and sparsity.

5   Conclusions

In this paper, we proposed a novel dimensionality reduction method, called L1/TL-LRP, to learn the discriminative features of data. Benefiting from L1-norm and trace Lasso, L1/TL-LRP not only has well robustness to outliers, but also considers the correlation and sparsity in data. In addition, we present a feasible solution for solving L1/TL-LRP. The experimental results manifest that L1/TL-LRP performs better than other related methods.

References

1. Paul, A., Chaki, N.: Dimensionality reduction of hyperspectral images using pooling. Pattern Recogn. Image Anal. **29**(1), 72–78 (2019). https://doi.org/10.1134/S1054661819010085
2. De Bodt, C., Mulders, D., Verleysen, M., et al.: Nonlinear dimensionality reduction with missing data using parametric multiple imputations. IEEE Trans. Neural Netw. Learn. Syst. **30**(4), 1166–1179 (2019)

3. Yuan, S., Mao, X., Chen, L.: Multilinear spatial discriminant analysis for dimensionality reduction. Image Process. IEEE Trans. **26**(6), 2669–2681 (2017)
4. Turk, M., Pentland, A.: Eigenfaces for recognition. J. Cogn. Neurosci. **3**(1), 71–86 (1991)
5. Belhumeur, P.N., Hespanha, J.P., Kriegman, D.J.: Eigenfaces vs. fisherfaces: recognition using class specific linear projection. IEEE Trans. Pattern Anal. Mach. Intell. **19**(7), 711–720 (1997)
6. He, X., Yan, S., Hu, Y., Niyogi, P., Zhang, H.-J.: Face recognition using Laplacianfaces. IEEE Trans. Pattern Anal. Mach. Intell. **27**(3), 328–340 (2005)
7. He, X.F., Cai, D., Yan, S., Zhang, H.J.: Neighborhood preserving embedding. In: The 10th IEEE International Conference on Computer Vision (ICCV), vol. 2, pp. 1208–1213 (2005)
8. Zhang, D., He, J., Zhao, Y., Luo, Z., Du, M.: Global plus local: a complete framework for feature extraction and recognition. Pattern Recogn. **47**(3), 1433–1442 (2014)
9. Yang, J., Zhang, D., Yang, J., Niu, B.: Globally maximizing, locally minimizing: unsupervised discriminant projection with applications to face and palm biometrics. IEEE Trans. Pattern Anal. Mach. Intell. **29**(4), 650–664 (2007)
10. Zang, F., Zhang, J., Pan, J.: Face recognition using elasticfaces. Pattern Recogn. **45**(11), 3866–3876 (2012)
11. Yuan, S., Mao, X.: Exponential elastic preserving projections for facial expression recognition. Neurocomputing **275**, 711–724 (2018)
12. Wang, H., Lu, X., Hu, Z., Zheng, W.: Fisher discriminant analysis with L1-norm. IEEE Trans. Cyber. **44**(6), 828–842 (2014)
13. Kwak, N.: Principal component analysis based on L1-norm maximization. IEEE Trans. Pattern Anal. Mach. Intell. **30**(9), 1672–1680 (2008)
14. Nie, F., Huang, H., Ding, C., Luo, D., Wang, H.: Robust principal component analysis with non-greedy L1-norm maximization. In: Proceedings of the 22nd International Joint Conference on Artificial Intelligence (IJCAI), pp. 1433–1438. Barcelona (2011)
15. Zhong, F., Zhang, J.: Linear discriminant analysis based on L1-norm maximization. IEEE Trans. Image Process. **22**(8), 3018–3027 (2013)
16. Pang, Y., Yuan, Y.: Outlier-resisting graph embedding. Neurocomputing **73**(4), 968–974 (2010)
17. Zhong, F., Zhang, J., Li, D.: Discriminant locality preserving projections based on L1-norm maximization. IEEE Trans. Neural Netw. Learn. Syst. **25**(11), 2065–2074 (2014)
18. Meng, D., Zhao, Q., Xu, Z.: Improve robustness of sparse PCA by L1-norm maximization. Pattern Recogn. **45**(1), 487–497 (2012)
19. Grave, E., Obozinski, G., Bach, F.: Trace Lasso: a trace norm regularization for correlated designs. Adv. Neural Inf. Process. Syst. 2187–2195 (2011)
20. Lu, G.F., Zou, J., Wang, Y., Wang, Z.: L1-norm-based principal component analysis with adaptive regularization. Pattern Recogn. **60**(C), 901–907 (2016)
21. Wang, J., Lu, C., Wang, M., Li, P., Yan, S., Hu, X.: Robust face recognition via adaptive sparse representation. IEEE Trans. Cybern. **44**(12), 2368–2378 (2014)
22. Lin, Z., Chen, M., Ma, Y.: The Augmented Lagrange Multiplier Method for Exact Recovery of Corrupted Low-Rank Matrices. UIUC Technical Report, UILU-ENG-09-2215 (2009)
23. Cai, J.-F., Candès, E.J., Shen, Z.: A singular value thresholding algorithm for matrix completion. SIAM J. Optim. **20**(4), 1956–1982 (2010)
24. Donoho, D.L.: For most large underdetermined systems of linear equations the minimal L1-norm solution is also the sparsest solution. Commun. Appl. Math. **59**(6), 797–829 (2006)
25. Hinton, G.E.: Visualizing high-dimensional data using t-SNE. J. Mach. Learn. Res. **9**(2), 2579–2605 (2008)

Episodic Training for Domain Generalization Using Latent Domains

Bincheng Huang[1,2(✉)], Si Chen[1,2], Fan Zhou[3], Cheng Zhang[4], and Feng Zhang[1,2]

[1] Key Laboratory of Cognition and Intelligence Technology, China Electronics Technology Group Corporation, Beijing 100086, China
[2] Information Science Academy, China Electronics Technology Group Corporation, Beijing 100086, China
[3] Faculty of Science and Engineering, University of Laval, Quebec G1V 06, Canada
[4] State Key Laboratory of Fluid Power and Mechatronic Systems, Zhejiang University, Hangzhou 310027, China

Abstract. Domain generalization (DG) is to learn knowledge from multiple training domain, and build a domain-agnostic model that could be used to an unseen domain. In this paper, take advantage of aggregating data method from all source and latent domains as a novel, we propose episodic training for domain generalization, aim to improve the performance during the trained model used for prediction in the unseen domain. To address this goal, we first designed an episodic training procedure that train a domain-generalized model without using domain labels. Firstly, we divide samples into latent domains via clustering, and design an episodic training procedure. Then, trains the model via adversarial learning in a way that exposes it into domain shift which decompose the model into feature extractor and classifier components, and train each component on the episodic domain. We utilize domain-invariant feature for clustering. Experiments show that our proposed method not only successfully achieves un-labeled domain generalization but also the training procedure improve the performance compared conventional DG methods.

1 Introduction

Machine learning have achieved great success, under the assumption that the training and test data are come from the same distribution. However, in the real-world, this assumption may be impossible to achieve during the domain shift, for example, the model trained by the data from sunny day, the accurate predictions may be drop obviously in the rainy day. To address this limitation, domain adaptation (DA) methods is proposed to learn the domain-invariant discriminative feature to improve the generalization ability of prediction model.

DA aims to address in the case where there is few labelled or un-labelled data from the target domain. However, in many situations, may not have enough data of the target domain in training, but intense demand is still required to build a precise model for the "unseen" target domain. This is a common case in many machine learning tasks. For example, medical diagnosis may need abundant data to train an accurate model though

© Springer Nature Singapore Pte Ltd. 2021
F. Sun et al. (Eds.): ICCSIP 2020, CCIS 1397, pp. 85–93, 2021.
https://doi.org/10.1007/978-981-16-2336-3_7

the data, such as image. However, because of the differences in medical devices or the sampling method, the same category data may have the different background or camera angle. If we would like to use the trained model into a new hospital, we could not to collect the whole data each-time, due to the time-consuming. Different background or camera angle from data, we could call the domain. The DA is to learn a new model which directly generalizes to new clinical sites would be of great practical value.

Unlike domain adaption, domain generalization does not require acquisition of a large target domain set for off-line analysis to drive adaptation. A cat is a cat no matter if it is shown in the form of a photo, cartoon, painting, or a sketch. To achieve this target, several methods have been proposed, mainly including three method, one is to train the feature extractor, so that the common feature learned to apply the unseen domain. Another is to train models for each domain and which combine them in testing. Our method is orthogonal to previous work, proposing a novel and realistic method, which combined the source domain contains multiple latent domains by adversarial network with style feature and episodic training strategy that mimics train-test domain-shift training. Experiments show that our method is effective for domain generalization.

2 Related Works

Domain Generalization. Domain generalization is also related to learning to learn. That aims to learn no just specific skills, but also learning algorithms or models that improve generalization [1–3]. DG is to extract common feature from the source domain, and combined the learning model to apply to unseen target domains. Compared with few-shot learning [2, 3], DG is a zero-shot problem which could evaluated on the target domain with on further learning. Through learning a domain-invariant feature representation, and then train the classification model with them. Assume the source domain invariant feature will reflect the target domain. For this purpose, adversarial network (GAN) has been explored for generative tasks. This include two components: a generative model G and a discriminative model D, G is to capture the distribution of the training data, D is to distinguish between the instances from G and the original data. Recently, mand GAN-based algorithms are applied to the DG field. For example, MMD is employed to match the latent domain representations samples from training data and random noise [4]. Adversarial autoencoder (AAE) is to train the encoder and the decoder with an adversarial learning [5]. Our approach is different to all of these methods, we take advantage of the domain multiple latent domains to capture the discriminative feature with style transfer with episodic training.

Neural Network. It is known that the Meta-learning methods have resurged recently in few-show tasks, and learning to optimization tasks [6–9]. No matter what their motivation and methodological formalisations are, the episodic training strategy is their common feature. In few-shot learning, source tasks and data are used for training the model that closely simulates the testing procedure. And at each iteration, training episode is generated by the random subset of source tasks and instances. In this paper, our goal is to improve domain-robustness with an episodic training strategy by the adversarial domain generalization.

3   The Proposed Methodology

The DG it to learn a domain agnostic model which can apply on the unseen domain, unlike with domain adaption, we could not obtain the label from those domains to train. Unlike the general DG method which is put all the source domain data into the model to train, in this paper, aim to improve the performance, we proposed a novel training method base on the adversarial domain generalization.

Problem Setting. In the DG setting, we assume that there exist n source domains, which $\mathcal{D} = [\mathcal{D}_1, \ldots, \mathcal{D}_n]$, where $\mathcal{D}_i$ is the ith source domain including label pairs $\left(x_i^j, y_i^j\right)$. Aim to use the knowledge to learn a model $f : x \rightarrow y$ which could be generalized well to a 'unsee' domain $\mathcal{D}^*$.

3.1   Adversarial Domain Generalization

As we know. The deep learning network is used for feature extractor F_f and the classifier F_c. These models could be train through the classification loss L_{cls}.

$$L_{cls} = -\frac{1}{N_s}\sum_{i=1}^{N_s}\sum_{c=1}^{C}\mathbb{I}_{[c=y_i]}logF_c\left(F_f(x_i)\right) \tag{1}$$

Depend on these components, adversarial learning is developed, which has been used for domain adaptation, and generalization [10, 11]. In addition, a domain discriminator F_d and feature extractor F_f is introduced during the training procedure. F_d is trained to discriminator the domains of inputted feature extractor, and F_f is trained to extract features. Especially, this make it possible to extract domain-invariant feature from source and unsee target domain. Because of the target domain is unsee, pseudo domain labels $\hat{d}$ by assigning samples into $\hat{K}$ pseudo domain using clustering. Therefore, the adversarial loss L_{adv} is defined:

$$L_{adv} = -\frac{1}{N_s}\sum_{i=1}^{N_s}\sum_{k=1}^{\hat{K}}\mathbb{I}_{\left[k=\hat{K}\right]}logF_d\left(F_f(x_i)\right) \tag{2}$$

Entropy loss L_{ent} is introduced to all labeled source samples to train the discriminative model [12–14]. Compared to the general domain adaptation methods adapt it to only unlabeled target samples.

$$L_{ent} = -\frac{1}{N_s}\sum_{i=1}^{N_s} H\left(F_c\left(F_f(x_i)\right)\right) \tag{3}$$

$H(\cdot)$ refer to the entropy function, which enables us to extract discriminative features for object categories and to improve the classification performance. λ could be obtained from $\lambda = \frac{2}{1+\exp(-10 \cdot p)}$, p is linearly changed from 0 to 1 as training progresses. The training objective is as follows:

$$\min_{F_f, F_c} = L_{cls}\left(F_f, F_c\right) + \lambda\left(L_{ent}\left(F_f, F_c\right) - L_{adv}\left(F_f, F_d\right)\right)$$

$$\underset{F_d}{min} = L_{adv}\left(F_f, F_d\right) \tag{4}$$

For the domain discriminative features, style feature is introduced, to generate a stylized image [16, 17]. Style loss L_{sty} is used to align the convolutional feature between the generate image x_{gen} and the style image x_{sty} [16]:

$$L_{sty} = \sum_{m=1}^{M} \left\| \mu\left(\phi_m\left(x_{gen}\right)\right) - \mu\left(\phi_m\left(x_{xty}\right)\right)\right\|_2 + \sum_{m=1}^{M} \left\| \sigma\left(\phi_m\left(x_{gen}\right)\right) - \sigma\left(\phi_m\left(x_{xty}\right)\right)\right\|_2 \tag{5}$$

Each $\phi_m(x)$ refer to the outputs in a layer to compute the style loss, and mean $\mu(x)$ and $\sigma(x)$ could be calculated as follows:

$$\mu_c(x) = \frac{1}{HW} \sum_{h=1}^{H} \sum_{w=1}^{W} x_{chw} \tag{6}$$

$$\sigma_c(x) = \sqrt{\frac{1}{HW} \sum_{h=1}^{H} \sum_{w=1}^{W} (x_{chw} - \mu_c(x))^2 + \epsilon} \tag{7}$$

At the end, to calculated the domain-discriminative feature $Ddf(x)$ by using multiple layers' outputs $\phi_1(x), \cdots, \phi_M(x)$ as follows:

$$Ddf(x) = \{\mu(\phi_1(x)), \sigma(\phi_1(x)), \cdots, \mu(\phi_M(x)), \sigma(\phi_M(x)),\} \tag{8}$$

3.2 Episodic Training

In this section, in order to improve robustness by exposing individual modules to neighbours domain, through train domain-specific models. It is shown in Fig. 1 each domain i has its own model composed of feature extractor F_f, classifier F_c and discriminator F_d which is shown above. It means that the domain specific module it to optimize by using the corresponding data:

$$\underset{F_{f1}...F_{fn}, F_{c1}...F_{cn}}{min} = L_{cls}\left(F_{fi}, F_{ci}\right) + \lambda\left(L_{ent}\left(F_{fi}, F_{ci}\right) - L_{adv}\left(F_{fi}, F_{di}\right)\right)$$

$$\underset{F_{d1}\cdots F_{dn}}{min} = L_{adv}\left(F_f, F_d\right) \tag{9}$$

For Feature Extractor side, in order to train a robust feature extractor F_f which are robust enough that data from domain i could be processed by a classifier. To generate this criterion, we just optimize the feature extractor part from Eq. 8. Only the feature extractor F_f is penalized whenever the classifier F_c makes the wrong prediction. Similar to episodic training of classifier part, only the classifier F_c is penalized, and must be robust enough to accept data x_i that has been encoded by a naive feature extractor. For every one epoch $\left\{\widehat{d_i'}\right\}_{i=1}^{N_s}$, in order to maximize the rate of consistence between the

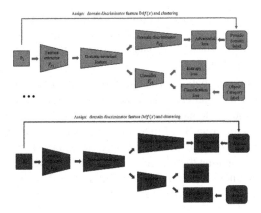

Fig. 1. An overview of our approach to domain generalization

cluster assignments $\{a_i\}_{i=1}^{N_s}$ and pseudo domain labels. We should convert the cluster assignment a_i into the pseudo domain label $\hat{d}_i$ by calculating the permutation $\hat{\pi}$ [18] as follows:

$$\hat{\pi} = \frac{\arg\max}{\pi \in \Pi} \frac{1}{N_s} \sum_{i=1}^{N_s} \sum_{c=1}^{C} \mathbb{I}_{[\widehat{d_i^c} = \pi(a_i)]} \tag{10}$$

Algorithm 1 Training algorithm.

---

1. Input: $\mathcal{D} = [\mathcal{D}_1, \ldots, \mathcal{D}_n]$
2. Initialize hyper parameters: λ
3. Initialize model parameters: $\widehat{d_i}, \widehat{d_i'}$ with zero
4. **While** not done training do
5.   Calculate $\{Ddf(x)\}_{i=1}^{N_s}$
6.   Obtain $\{a_i\}_{i=1}^{N_s}$ by clustering $\{Ddf(x)\}_{i=1}^{N_s}$
7.   Update $\widehat{d_i}$ with $\hat{\pi}(a_i)$
8.   **While** not end of minibatch do
9.   Sample a minibatch of x_i , y_i , $\widehat{d_i}$
10.   Update parameters using Eq.9
11.   **End while**
12.   Update $\widehat{d_i'}$ with $\widehat{d_i}$
13. **End while**

---

4 Experiments

In this section, we conduct several experiments on datasets to evaluate the effectiveness of our proposed method for domain generalization. The datasets are: the popular benchmark

MNIST which include the rotations for digit recognition [19]. PACS which consists of four domains: photo, art painting, cartoon and sketch as shown in Fig. 2. VLCS [20], which includes images for four famous datasets PACAL VOC2007 [21], LavelMe [22], Caltech [23] and SUN09 [24].

Then we compared out method with the following bassline methods for domain generalization in terms of classification accuracy. SVM: a linear SVM to train a classifier by directly using the source-domain labeled instances. LRE-SVM: the method is based on SVM, which trains different SVM model for each source domain [25]. DANN: the method used domain adversarial neural networks to train a feature extractor with a domain-adversarial loss among the source domains [26]. MLDG: this is a meta-learning based optimization method, which is by splitting source domain into meta-train and meta-test to improve meta-test performance.

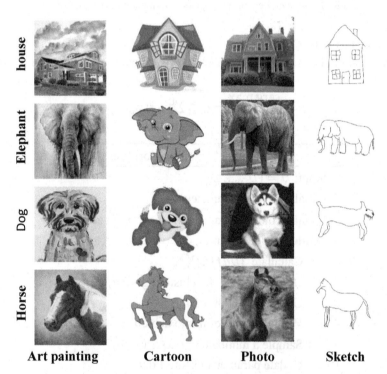

Fig. 2. Visualization of the preferred images of House, Elephant, Dog, Horse from PACS dataset.

4.1 Experiments on MNIST Dataset

MNIST dataset is the baseline dataset to prove the algorithm quality during the research field. In this paper, we randomly chose ten classes form the 1000 digital images. Then rotate the digit image in a counter-clock wise direction by $0°$, $15°$, $30°$, $45°$, respectively, to imitate the different domains. And denoted the digit images with H_0, H_{15}, H_{30}, H_{45}.

The learning rate of our method is set to be 0.01. As the feature extractor, AlexNet pre-trained on ImageNet by removing the last layer. As the classifier, we initialize one fully connected layer to have the same number of inputs. The optimize is M-SGD with learning rate 1e−3, momentum 0.9 and weight decay 5e−5.

From the results, it is obviously that our method achieved the best performance with a clear margin on 3 out of 4 domain generalization tasks (H_0, H_0, H_{30}, H_{45}). There are several possible reasons, our method is based on the adversarial network which could learn more feature information compared other methods (Table 1).

Table 1. Performance on handwritten digit recognition

Source	Target	SVM	LRE-SVM	DANN	MLDG	Ours
H_{15}, H_{30}, H_{45}	H_0	52.4	75.2	59.1	73.9	**79.2**
H_0, H_{30}, H_{45}	H_{15}	74.1	86.8	**89.6**	81.4	83.2
H_0, H_{15}, H_{45}	H_{30}	71.4	84.4	85.1	92.3	**93.6**
H_0, H_{15}, H_{30}	H_{45}	61.4	75.8	72.8	86.2	**89.4**
Average		64.825	80.55	76.65	84.2	**86.4**

4.2 Experiments on VLCS Dataset

In this experiment, we use pre-extracted DeCAF6 features and randomly split each domain into train (70%) and test (30%) and do leave-one-out evaluation. The optimize is M-SGD with learning rate 1e−3, momentum 0.9 and weight decay 5e−5.

From the results in Table 2, we could see that the MLDG is again competitive with many published algorithms, so is DANN. Our method achieves the best performance, improving on MLDG by 1.15%, also improve the classification accuracy compared to other methods.

Table 2. Performance on handwritten digit recognition

Source	Target	SVM	LRE-SVM	DANN	MLDG	Ours
L, C, S	V	58.86	60.6	66.4	**67.7**	67.1
V, C, S	L	52.9	59.7	64.0	62.6	**64.7**
V, L, S	C	77.67	88.1	92.6	92.4	**94.1**
V, L, C	S	49.09	54.9	63.6	64.4	**67.9**
Average		59.63	65.825	71.65	72.275	**73.5**

4.3   Experiments on PACS Dataset

The PACS is a recent benchmark with more severe distribution shift between domain, which is more challenging than VLCS. Following other literature training setting, we also use leave one domain out cross validation, for example, training on three domains and testing on the remaining unseen one. The optimize is M-SGD with learning rate 1e−3, momentum 0.9 and weight decay 5e−5.

From the results in Table 3, we could see that our method obtained the best performance on held out domains C and S, comparable performance on A, P domains. It is also achieves the best performance overall, with 4.7% improvement on DANN, that means using adversarial learning is effective for domain generalization.

Table 3. Performance on PACS dataset

Source	Target	SVM	LRE-SVM	DANN	MLDG	Ours
C, P, S	A	47.9	52.3	63.2	66.2	64.7
A, P, S	C	53.6	60.2	67.5	66.9	**74.3**
A, C, S	P	61.1	78.5	**88.1**	88.0	86.1
A, C, P	S	66.8	65.4	57.0	59.0	**66.2**
Average		57.35	64.1	68.95	70.0	**72.5**

5   Conclusion

In this paper, we proposed a novel framework for domain generalization, denoted by adversarial network with episodic training. The main idea is to learn the invariant-feature during the source domain by jointly adversarial network with style feature and episodic training strategy that mimics train-test domain-shift training, thus improving the trained model's robustness to novel domains. Extensive experimental results on handwritten digit recognition, PACS and VLCS that the main existing DG benchmarks, demonstrate that our proposed method without domain labels not only could be able to learn domain-invariant features, but also achieved a better performance than conventional methods that use them.

References

1. Munkhdalai, T., Yu, H.: Meta networks. In: ICML (2017)
2. Ravi, S., Larochelle, H.: Optimization as a model for fewshot learning. In: ICLR (2017)
3. Finn, C., Abbeel, P., Levine, S.: Model-agnostic metalearning for fast adaptation of deep networks. In: ICML (2017)
4. Li, Y., Swersky, K., Zemel, R.: Generative moment matching networks. In: ICML (2015)
5. Makhzani, A., Shlens, J., Jaitly, N., Goodfellow, I., Frey, B.: Adversarial autoencoders. In: ICLR Workshop (2016)

6. Finn, C., Abbeel, P., Levine, S.: Model-agnostic meta-learning for fast adaptation of deep networks. In: ICML (2017)
7. Snell, J., Swersky, K., Zemel, R.S.: Prototypical networks for few shot learning. In: NIPS (2017)
8. Mishra, N., Rohaninejad, M., Chen, X., Abbeel, P.: Meta-learning with temporal convolutions. arXiv (2017)
9. Ravi, S., Larochelle, H.: Optimization as a model for few-shot learning. In: ICLR (2017)
10. Ganin, Y., Lempitsky, V.: Unsupervised domain adaptation by backpropagation. In: ICML (2015)
11. Li, H., Jialin Pan, S., Wang, S., Kot, A.C.: Domain generalization with adversarial feature learning. In: CVPR (2018)
12. Grandvalet, Y., Bengio, Y.: Semi-supervised learning by entropy minimization. In: NIPS (2005)
13. Long, M., Zhu, H., Wang, J., Jordan, M.I.: Unsupervised domain adaptation with residual transfer networks. In: NIPS (2016)
14. Zhang, Y., Tang, H., Jia, K., Tan, M.: Domain-symmetric networks for adversarial domain adaptation. In: CVPR (2019)
15. Gatys, L.A., Ecker, A.S., Bethge, M.: Image style transfer using convolutional neural networks. In: CVPR (2016)
16. Li, Y., Wang, N., Liu, J., Hou, X.: Demystifying neural style transfer. In: IJCAI (2017)
17. Huang, X., Belongie, S.: Arbitrary style transfer in real-time with adaptive instance normalization. In: ICCV (2017)
18. Munkres, J.: Algorithms for the assignment and transportation problems. J. Soc. Ind. Appl. Math. **5**, 32–38 (1957)
19. LeCun, Y.: The MNIST database of handwritten digits (1998). https://yann.lecun.com/exdb/mnist/
20. Fang, C., Xu, Y., Rockmore, D.N.: Unbiased metric learning: on the utilization of multiple datasets and web images for softening bias. In: ICCV (2013)
21. Everingham, M., Van Gool, L., Williams, C.K.I., Winn, J., Zisserman, A.: The pascal visual object classes (VOC) challenge. IJCV **88**, 303–338 (2010)
22. Russell, B.C., Torralba, A., Murphy, K.P., Freeman, W.T.: LabelMe: a database and web-based tool for image annotation. IJCV **77**, 157–173 (2008)
23. Li, F.-F., Rob, F., Pietro, P.: Learning generative visual models from few training examples: an incremental bayesian approach tested on 101 object categories. In: CVPR Workshop on Generative-Model Based Vision (2004)
24. Choi, M.J., Lim, J., Torralba, A.: Exploiting hierarchical context on a large database of object categories. In: CVPR (2010)
25. Xu, Z., Li, W., Niu, L., Xu, D.: Exploiting low-rank structure from latent domains for domain generalization. In: Fleet, D., Pajdla, T., Schiele, B., Tuytelaars, T. (eds.) ECCV 2014. LNCS, vol. 8691, pp. 628–643. Springer, Cham (2014). https://doi.org/10.1007/978-3-319-10578-9_41
26. Ganin, Y., et al.: Domain-adversarial training of neural networks. JMLR **17**, 2096-2030 (2016)
27. Li, D., Yang, Y., Song, Y.-Z., Hospedales, T.: Learning to generalize: meta-learning for domain generalization. In: AAAI (2018)

A Novel Attitude Estimation Algorithm Based on EKF-LSTM Fusion Model

Yufan Zhuo[1], Fuchun Sun[2], Zhenkun Wen[3], Huisi Wu[3], and Haiming Huang[1(✉)]

[1] College of Electronics and Information Engineering,
Shenzhen University, Shenzhen 518060, China
[2] Department of Computer Science and Technology,
Tsinghua University, Beijing 100083, China
[3] College of Computer Science and Software Engineering,
Shenzhen University, Shenzhen 518060, China

Abstract. The application of the low-cost inertial measurement unit (IMU) in many fields is growing, but the related attitude algorithms have the problems of low precision and poor adaptability. In this paper, a novel attitude estimation algorithm based on the fusion model of extend Kalman filter (EKF) and long short-term memory (LSTM) is proposed, which is composed of two main process: the initial attitude estimation of EKF and the subsequent calibration of LSTM. In this algorithm, EKF estimates the target's attitude angles by the inputs of sensor data from IMU, then LSTM makes a calibration of each axis' estimated angles, which is weighted with KEF's result to export the optimal estimation finally. The result of simulation experiment shows that this algorithm is 50.515% lower on average than EKF under different working conditions when using mean squared error (MSE) as the evaluation indicator, which could be concluded that this novel algorithm performs better than EKF, and provides a new way for attitude estimation.

Keywords: Attitude estimation · Extend kalman filter · LSTM · Neural network

1 Introduction

The low-cost, high-integration actuators and sensors are widely used in science and engineering with the rapid progressive technology of micro electro mechanical system (MEMS) [1]. Among these devices, a large number of applications of the inertial measurement unit (IMU) [2] integrated with the gyroscope, the accelerometer and the magnetometer are adopted widely in many fields such as robotic controlling, navigation system and kinesiology. While using the low-cost IMUs for the target's attitude estimation, some flaws will show up. For example, long term use of gyroscope will generate an integral accumulation error due to its temperature drift characteristic, the accelerometer and the magnetometer are easily affected by vibration and electromagnetic perturbations. Gaining the optimal estimation of the target's posture changes with the data fusion of acceleration, angle velocity, magnetic field and other sensors' data is an important orientation of attitude algorithm [3].

© Springer Nature Singapore Pte Ltd. 2021
F. Sun et al. (Eds.): ICCSIP 2020, CCIS 1397, pp. 94–104, 2021.
https://doi.org/10.1007/978-981-16-2336-3_8

There is a great diversity of algorithms applied for attitude estimation, such as Kalman filter [4–6], complementary filter [7, 8], the fusion of these two algorithms [9, 10], and neural network [11, 12] in machine learning. Complementary filter is simply calculated but with low precision. Kalman filter has the problem of modeling deviation and the equilibrium between the accuracy and the computation of iterations. Furthermore, these traditional methods need the mathematical model of the target system which is usually a nonlinear system, and the actual ambient noise is not conformed to the condition of Gaussian distribution.

Artificial neural network (ANN) uses numbers of data processing units to simulate the neural network structure of the biological brain, which has good nonlinear mapping capability and adaptive ability [13]. As an important branch of ANN, the recurrent neural network (RNN) is widely used to semantic recognition and content recommendation due to its ability to establish a connection between current data processing and previous information with the long data sequence of time-domain sampling. However, RNN easily reaches the past best value with the problem of gradient dispersion and explosion. Long short-term memory (LSTM) network solves the problem of gradient disappearance through structural improvement [14]. LSTM takes advantage of a cell state link to transmit correlation of input's data, which has more advantages in processing longer time series data, and it is widely used combined with traditional algorithms such as self-model improvement [15], pose regularization [14].

The sensor sampling data of IMU are long time series sequences with a high temporal correlation between the front and rear frames. In this paper, an EKF-LSTM fusion model are proposed which uses LSTM to calibrate the outputs of EKF's attitude estimation, and it compensates the EKF's modeling deviation and reduces the influence of external disturbance to the optimal estimate.

The rest of the article is framed as follows: Sect. 2 explains the EKF's attitude estimation and introduces the LSTM general principle, then an EKF-LSTM fusion model for attitude estimation is described. Section 3 preforms the simulation experiment and the analysis of result. Conclusion is expounded in Sect. 4.

2   Related Background

The novel attitude estimation algorithm consisted of EKF and LSTM is a fusion algorithm, in which EKF makes the target's initial estimation based on the sensor data of IMU, then LSTM calibrates the EKF's result with the temporal context of sensor data to expert the optimal estimation of attitude angles.

2.1   Extended Kalman Filter

Extended Kalman filter is the extension of Kalman filter under the situation of nonlinear dynamic modeling. Extended Kalman filter could be considered an iterative self-feedback circulation, which principally consist of the prediction phase and the update phase [16].

In the prediction phase, extended Kalman filter base on the last time step's updated system state to predict the current state's mean $\hat{x}'_k$ and covariance $\hat{P}'_k$:

$$\hat{x}'_k = f\left(\hat{x}_{k-1}, u_k\right) \tag{1}$$

$$\hat{P}'_k = F\hat{P}_{k-1}F^T + Q \tag{2}$$

In the update phase, extended Kalman filter uses $\hat{P}'_k$ in Eq. 2 to calculate the Kalman gain K_k, and update the mean and the covariance of current state with the system current observable measurement z_k:

$$K_k = \hat{P}'_k H^T \left(H\hat{P}'_k H^T + R\right)^{-1} \tag{3}$$

$$\hat{x}_k = \hat{x}'_k + K_k\left(z_k - h\left(\hat{x}'_k\right)\right) \tag{4}$$

$$\hat{P}_k = (I - K_k H)\hat{P}'_k \tag{5}$$

For the dynamic modeling of attitude estimation, the usual way is linearizing the state transition equation f via Taylor series expansion. We adopt the quaternion q to explain rotation between the carrier coordinate system b and the geographical reference coordinate system n. The rotator from n to b could declare as:

$$q = \cos\frac{\theta}{2} + u^R \sin\frac{\theta}{2} \tag{6}$$

where u^R are the instantaneous axis and the direction of rotation, θ is the rotation angle.

In Eq. 1, the state transition equation f could be the quaternion differential equations of Picard algorithm in first approximation, and the state transition matrix F in Eq. 2 is the Jacobian matrix of f. So, the state's mean prediction function of extend Kalman filter could explained in matrix form, where $\hat{x}$ is the quaternion and u is the current state's 3-axis gyro data w_x, w_y, w_z:

$$\begin{bmatrix} q_0 \\ q_1 \\ q_2 \\ q_3 \end{bmatrix}_k = \left(I + \frac{dt}{2}\begin{bmatrix} 0 & -w_x & -w_y & -w_z \\ w_x & 0 & w_z & -w_y \\ w_y & -w_z & 0 & w_x \\ w_z & w_y & -w_x & 0 \end{bmatrix}\right) * \begin{bmatrix} q_0 \\ q_1 \\ q_2 \\ q_3 \end{bmatrix}_{k-1} \tag{7}$$

The measurement function h in Eq. 2 transform the quaternion into the dimension of z_k in b which is consisted of 3-axis accelerometer and 3-axis magnetometer. The acceleration of gravity in n always be one G of z-axis, in order to align it at the dimension of the accelerometer in b, the rotation matrix R^b_n multiplies by the optimal gravity matrix to get the projection of gravity in b. Meanwhile, magnetic field intensity in n always have the components of geographic north and verticality under the north east astronomical coordinate system, in order to get the projection of magnetic field distribution on b, the magnetic field distribution n_x, n_z on n could be calculated by the rotation matrix R^n_b and the magnetometer's 3-axis data m_x, m_y, m_z, then the projection of magnetic field distribution on b could be gained by n_x, n_z and R_n^b. So the measurement function h is given by:

$$h\left(\hat{x}_k'\right) = \begin{bmatrix} 2(q_1q_3 - q_0q_2) \\ 2(q_2q_3 + q_0q_1) \\ q_0^2 - q_1^2 - q_2^2 + q_3^2 \\ n_x\left(q_0^2 + q_1^2 - q_2^2 - q_3^2\right) + 2n_z(q_1q_3 - q_0q_2) \\ 2n_x(q_1q_2 - q_0q_3) - 2n_z(q_2q_3 + q_0q_1) \\ 2n_x(q_1q_3 + q_0q_2) + n_z\left(q_0^2 - q_1^2 - q_2^2 + q_3^2\right) \end{bmatrix} \tag{8}$$

In Eq. 3 and 5, the measurement matrix H is the Jacobian matrix of h. In order to gain the Euler angles from EKF, we use the transformation between Euler angles and quaternion that is calculated as:

$$\emptyset = \tan^{-1}\left(\frac{2(q_1q_2 + q_0q_3)}{q_0^2 + q_1^2 - q_2^2 - q_3^2} \right) \tag{9.1}$$

$$\theta = \sin^{-1}(-2(q_0q_2 + q_1q_3)) \tag{9.2}$$

$$\varphi = \tan^{-1}\left(\frac{2(q_0q_1 + q_2q_3)}{q_0^2 + q_1^2 - q_2^2 - q_3^2} \right) \tag{9.3}$$

where $\emptyset$, θ, φ are the representations of the pitch, yaw and roll [17].

2.2 Long Short-Term Memory

As the improved part of recurrent neural network (RNN), Long short-term memory neural network (LSTM NN) is superior than RNN with the solution of vanishing gradient problem. With regard to the time domain continuously sampled data from IMU, LSTM have an advantage on processing these sensor data because of its time memory function. As shown in Fig. 1, each LSTM network unit has three correlative gates and a state of cells h. The forget gate determine discarded information of the state of cells h_{t-1} by the current input x_t and the last output y_{t-1}, which activation function always is logarithmic logical curves [18]. The input gate adds new information into the state of cells h_t. The final process is the output gate, which control the structure of LSTM's output y_t. The activation functions of the input gate and output gate of units are usually hyperbolic tangent curves [19, 20]. The state of cells containing all the time node information is the crucial part of LSTM structure, which will transmit on the cells' wiring with a few linear operations.

2.3 EKF-LSTM Fusion Model for Attitude Estimation

The EKF-LSTM fusion model for attitude estimation is shown in the Fig. 2. In the scheme, the inputs of model are consisted of the IMU's sensor data (ACC, GYRO, MAG) from the current moment. Firstly EKF makes the initial attitude estimation of target's 3-axis Euler angles (roll, pitch, yaw) through the prediction phase and the update

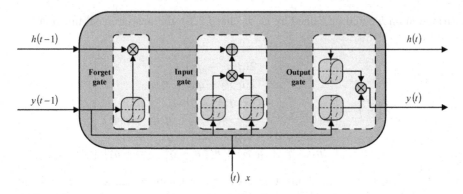

Fig. 1. The structure of the LSTM unit

phase. Then the EKF's results and the original sensor data are fitted into three LSTMs instead of one LSTM to avoid the cross coupling [21], where each LSTM adjusts EKF's attitude estimation in a small range according to the potential relationship between sensor data and the outputs of LSTM are each attitude angles' calibration. Finally, model's outputs are the calibrated attitude Angles, which are combined of the results of EKF and LSTMs. The model's framework takes EKF as the core, takes LSTM as the bias calibrator of EKF's nonlinear fitting, and its final output is the optimal estimate of 3-axis attitude angles.

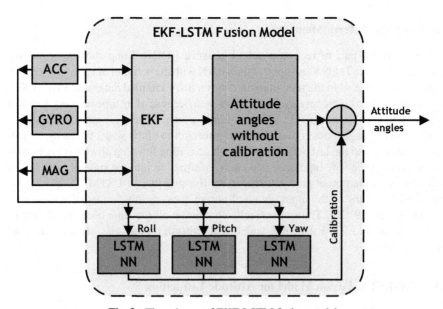

Fig. 2. The scheme of EKF-LSTM fusion model

The mean squared error (MSE) is used to evaluate model's output performance, the smaller MSE, the higher accuracy of the model, the equation of MSE as:

$$MSE = \frac{1}{N} \sum_{i=1}^{n} (\overline{m}_i - m_i)^2 \tag{10}$$

where $\overline{m}_i$ is the model's output, m_i is the true value.

3   Simulation Experiment and Analysis

In order to test the EKF-LSTM fusion model in Sect. 2, the simulation experiment bases on the deep learning framework using Python 3.6 and Keras 2.2.4. The experiment's computer is configured as: Intel Core i5 -8250U 1.60 GHz, 8 GB RAM. The experiment's IMU is JY901 which is integrated with accelerometer, gyroscope and magnetometer to obtain the sensor data and actual Euler angles in various conditions with the sampling rate of 200 Hz.

Figure 3 shows the sensor data of 3-axis gyroscope, 3-axis accelerometer, 3-axis magnetometer, which are almost 6000 training data. The first 4500 points of data are selected to train the EKF-LSTM fusion model and the LSTM as the contrast, and the rest data are selected to validate the model.

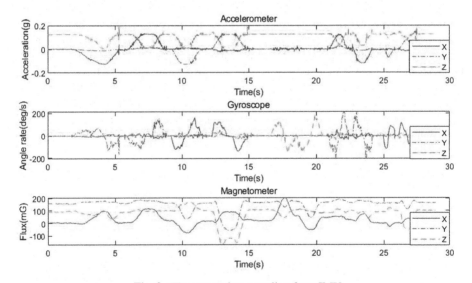

Fig. 3. The sensor data sampling from IMU

Firstly, the separate EKF is used to estimate the attitude Angle of the three axes to determine its estimated performance. In Fig. 4, the attitude estimation of EKF is closed to the true value in terms of roll and pitch, where is only a slight deviation during drastic angle changes, but the estimation of yaw has a obvious deviation because of EKF's nonlinear fitting deviation. EKF's MSE in roll, pitch and yaw are 0.00218, 0.00197 and 0.04931.

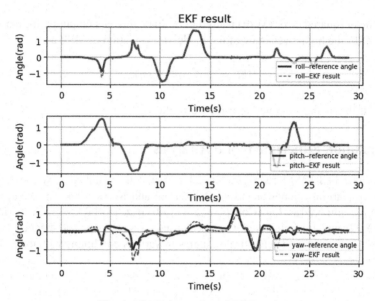

Fig. 4. The Euler angles of EKF result

Secondly, in order to achieve the optimal calibration effect of LSTM, the selecting of interior parameters should be confirmed by comparative experiment. In the LSTM parameters comparison experiment, the parameters such as the numbers of neurons in the hidden layer (HN), the timesteps (TS), the training time (TT), the MSE of roll (MSE1), the MSE of pitch (MSE2) and the MSE of yaw (MSE3) are listed in Table 1. It could be figured out that the MSEs decrease gradually as HN increases but MSEs begin to increase as HN exceeds a certain value. As TS increases, the MSEs decrease gradually but TT has a sharp increase simultaneously. Considering the accuracy and real-time performance of the algorithm, the parameters of No. 5 is adopted.

Table 1. The parameters and comparative results of LSTM parameters selecting experiment.

No	HN	TS	Epoch	TT(s)	MSE1	MSE2	MSE3
1	10	2	40	46.24	0.00082059	0.00066379	0.0077
2	10	5	40	73.57	0.00075836	0.00056065	0.0066
3	10	10	40	119.51	0.00062646	0.00050121	0.0048
4	20	2	40	46.01	0.00078448	0.00063158	0.007
5	20	5	40	76.98	0.00061906	0.00053342	0.005
6	20	10	40	120.5	0.0004358	0.00034101	0.0028
7	30	2	40	46.81	0.00084767	0.00062017	0.0072
8	30	5	40	77.31	0.00052815	0.00052687	0.0048
9	30	10	40	122.78	0.00032836	0.0002953	0.0021

Finally, as shown in Fig. 5, the validation of EKF-LSTM fusion model has better fitting quality especially in yaw comparing the EKF's result. The MSE of roll, pitch and yaw are 0.00049, 0.00119 and 0.02386.

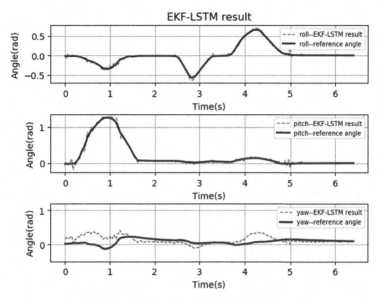

Fig. 5. The Euler angles of EKF-LSTM test result

By comparing the result of MSE between the EKF and the EKF-LSTM fusion model, EKF-LSTM has an improvement on estimation accuracy, which is 56.24% lower on average than EKF in MSE. In order to evaluate the adaption of EKF-LSTM on various working condition, the sensor data with the vibration and electromagnetic interference are collected to test its adaptive capacity.

As shown in Fig. 6 and Fig. 7, the result of EKF reflects that the fluctuation in a small range is relatively frequent in each axis. However, the result of EKF-LSTM fusion model shows that its curves are smoother with fewer destabilization.

As shown in Fig. 8, the errors of EKF-LSTM fusion model in roll and pitch are lower and more stable than EKF's, but the error between these two models in yaw are both in a great fluctuation which means that the calibration is out of work caused by the major estimation deviation of EKF. The EKF's MSE of roll, pitch and yaw are 0.00972, 0.01079 and 0.01731, correspondingly the EKF-LSTM's MSE of roll, pitch and yaw are 0.000237, 0.00095 and 0.02674, which is 44.79% lower on average than EKF.

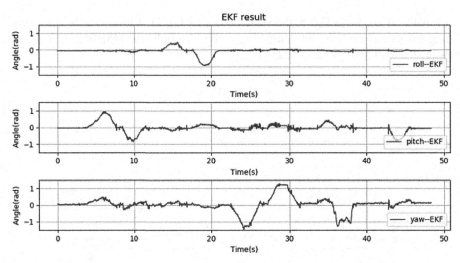

Fig. 6. The Euler angle of EKF result with electromagnetic interference

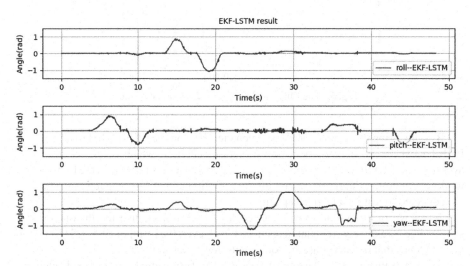

Fig. 7. The Euler angle of EKF-LSTM result with electromagnetic interference

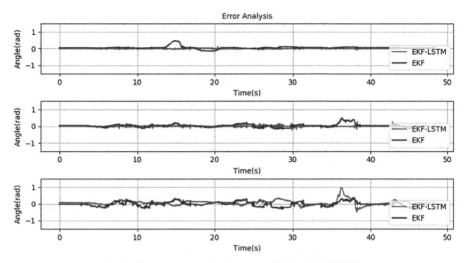

Fig. 8. The error analysis between EKF and EKF-LSTM

4 Conclusion

In this paper, a novel attitude estimation algorithm based on EKF-LSTM fusion model is proposed, which is consisted of EKF's initial attitude estimation and LSTM's Euler angles calibration. When taking MSE as the evaluation criterion, this algorithm is 50.515% lower on average than the traditional attitude estimation algorithm EKF under different working conditions, which explains that this novel algorithm has an improvement on accuracy and adaptability. The EKF-LSTM fusion model is proposed based on the LSTM's advantage of time sequential data processing and the traditional algorithm's problem of the modeling deviation and poor adaptability, which has some downsides that the algorithm verification experiment and multi-algorithm comparison experiment under different working conditions still need to be improved. In the future's research, this algorithm will be improved by using LSTM to adjust EKF internal parameters in real time to improve the adaptability, and physical verification experiments will be conducted, such as attitude calculation for unmanned aerial vehicle, manual motion acquisition and so on.

Acknowledgement. The authors are grateful for the support by the National Natural Science Foundation of China (Nos. 61803267 and 61572328), the China Postdoctoral Science Foundation (No. 2017M622757), the Beijing Science and Technology program (No. Z171100000817007), and the National Science Foundation (DFG) in the project Cross Modal Learning, NSFC 61621136008/DFG TRR-169. The authors are grateful for the support of Science and Technology Commissioned Project scheme of Shenzhen University.

References

1. Khoshnoud, F.: Recent advances in MEMS sensor technology-mechanical applications. Instrum. Measur. Mag. **15**(2), 14–24 (2012)

2. Kuang, J., Niu, X., Chen, X.: Robust pedestrian dead reckoning based on MEMS-IMU for smartphones. Sensors-Basel **18**(5), 1391 (2018)
3. Pierleoni, P., Belli, A., Palma, L., Pernini, L., Valenti, S.: An accurate device for real-time altitude estimation using data fusion algorithms. In: IEEE/ASME International Conference on Mechatronic & Embedded Systems & Applications, 2014 (2014)
4. Hajiyev, C., Conguroglu, E.S.: Integration of algebraic method and EKF for attitude determination of small information satellites. In: 7th International Conference on Recent Advances in Space Technologies (RAST), 2015 (2015)
5. Markley, F.L., Sedlak, J.E.: Kalman filter for spinning spacecraft attitude estimation. J. Guidance Control Dyn. **31**(6), 1750–1760 (2015)
6. Li, H., Tang, Q., Li, J.: Attitude/position estimation of monocular vision based on multiple model Kalman filter (2018)
7. Vlastos, P., Elkaim, G., Curry, R.: Low-cost validation for complementary filter-based AHRS. In: 2020 IEEE/ION Position, Location and Navigation Symposium (PLANS) (2020)
8. Del Rosario, M.B., Lovell, N.H., Redmond, S.J.: Quaternion-based complementary filter for attitude determination of a smartphone. IEEE Sens. J. **16**(15), 6008–6017 (2016)
9. Chen, M., Xie, Y., Chen, Y.: Attitude estimation of MEMS based on improved quaternion complementary filter. J. Electron. Measur. Instrum. **29**(9), 1391–1397 (2015)
10. Zhang, D., Jiao, S.M., Liu, Y.Q.: Fused attitude estimation algorithm based on complementary filtering and Kalman filtering. Transducer Microsyst. Technol. **36**, 62–66 (2017)
11. Du, S., Wu, H., Zhang, J., Ma, W.: Kind of improving compensation filter algorithm for AHRS. Foreign Electron. Measur. Technol. **3**, 13–18 (2015)
12. Omid, D., Mojtaba, T., Raghvendar, C.V.: IMU-based gait recognition using convolutional neural networks and multi-sensor fusion. Sensors-Basel **17**(12), 2735 (2017)
13. Jain, A., Zamir, A.R., Savarese, S., Saxena, A.: Structural-RNN: deep learning on spatio-temporal graphs. In: Computer Vision & Pattern Recognition, 2016 (2016)
14. Coskun, H., Achilles, F., Dipietro, R., Navab, N., Tombari, F.: Long short-term memory kalman filters: recurrent neural estimators for pose regularization. In: 2017 IEEE International Conference on Computer Vision (ICCV), 2017. IEEE (2017)
15. Wang, J.J., Wang, J., Sinclair, D., Watts, L.: A neural network and Kalman filter hybrid approach for GPS/INS integration. In: 12th IAIN Congress and 2006 International Symposium (2006)
16. Wang, J., Ma, J.: Research on attitude algorithm of EKF and complementary filtering fusion. Chin. J. Sens. Actuators **31**(8), 1187–1191 (2018)
17. Nonami, K., Kendoul, F., Suzuki, S., Wei, W., Nakazawa, D.: Autonomous Flying Robots. Springer, Japan (2010). https://doi.org/10.1007/978-4-431-53856-1
18. Karim, F., Majumdar, S., Darabi, H., Chen, S.: LSTM fully convolutional networks for time series classification. IEEE Access **6**(99), 1662–1669 (2018)
19. Yildirim, Z.: A novel wavelet sequences based on deep bidirectional LSTM network model for ECG signal classification. Comput. Biol. Med. **96**, 189–202 (2018)
20. Liu, J., Wang, G., Duan, L.Y., Abdiyeva, K., Kot, A.C.: Skeleton-based human action recognition with global context-aware attention LSTM networks. IEEE Trans. Image Process. **27**(99), 1586–1599 (2018)
21. Qu, D.C., Feng, Y.G., Fan, S.L., Qi, C.: Study of a fault diagnosis method based on Elman neural network and trouble dictionary (2008)

METAHACI: Meta-learning for Human Activity Classification from IMU Data

Benjakarn Leelakittisin[1]([✉]) [iD] and Fuchun Sun[2]

[1] Vidyasirimedhi Institute of Science and Technology, Rayong 21210, Thailand
benjakarn.l_S18@vistec.ac.th, benjakarn@163.com
[2] Tsinghua University, Beijing 100084, China
fcsun@mail.tsinghua.edu.cn

Abstract. In the digital era, time-series data is pervasive to various applications and domains such as robotics, healthcare, finance, sport, etc. The inertial measurement unit (IMU) sensor is one of the popular devices collecting time-series data. Together with deep neural network implementation, this results in facilitating advancement in time series data analysis. However, the classical problem for the deep neural network is that it requires a vast amount of data which causes difficulty in the development and analysis process. Thus, we hypothesize that this problem can be avoided by combining data from many subjects that perform the same common tasks to get a larger amount of data. The consequence problem is that this decreases the overall classification accuracy. To tackle this, optimization-based meta-learning algorithms were selected, which are Reptile and model-agnostic meta-learning (MAML). The differences between Reptile and MAML are they use different rules for update gradient descent and differentiating through the optimization process. Leveraging their pre-existing meta-parameter weight before fine-tuning results in preferable accuracy for the existing amount of data, the figure is 89.65% for MAML and 78.38% for Reptile. To our knowledge, this is the first time comparing joint training with the meta-learning model, specifically, Reptile, and MAML for human activity classification from IMU sensors data. Experiment results show the superiority of classification accuracy from METAHACI proposed compare to joint training and simple CNNs.

Keywords: Meta learning · Human activity classification · IMU data · The inertial measurement unit sensor · Convolutional neural network

1 Introduction

In the computerized age, numerous applications and disciplines are unavoidable from time-series information. Examples are robotic [1], healthcare [2], finance [3], sport [4], and so on. IMU sensor is one of the popular devices collecting time-series data [5]. Together with deep neural network implementation, this results

© Springer Nature Singapore Pte Ltd. 2021
F. Sun et al. (Eds.): ICCSIP 2020, CCIS 1397, pp. 105–113, 2021.
https://doi.org/10.1007/978-981-16-2336-3_9

in facilitating of advancement in time-series data analysis, such as IMU-based HAR [6].

However, the classical problem for the deep neural network is that it requires lots of data. In case we have a very little amount of labeled-data will cause difficulty in the development and analysis process.

Hence, we hypothesize that this problem can be avoided by combining data from many subjects that perform the same common tasks to get a larger amount of data. In our experiment, this is called the joint dataset.

Unfortunately, the preliminary result shows the consequence problem. The problem is the overall classification accuracy analyzed from the joint dataset is worse than the original dataset, decreased from 85.75% to 77.93%. This is due to Non-independent and identically distributed (non i.i.d.) between different subjects, different datasets, together with slightly different sensor placement positions which contains a certain amount of disparity. To tackle this, the meta-learning algorithm which is one of the popular technics in the computer vision field is selected to explore in this case.

There are many types of algorithms in meta-learning [7]. For example, learning from model evaluation, task properties, and prior model. The type selected is learning from the prior model which learns the structure and model parameters. In short, we want a meta-learner that learns how to train a (base-) learner for a new task with a small amount of data. The learner is typically defined by its model parameters or its configuration. The concept of training steps is to give similar tasks with the corresponding optimized model.

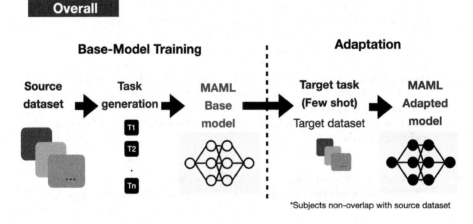

Fig. 1. Graphical summary, MAML as an example

A subtype of meta-learning technic selected is few-shot learning which mimics human-innate-ability, MAML as an example (Fig. 1). The idea is to train an accurate deep learning model using only a few training samples by prior train the model with similar tasks that we have larger training samples. In our experiments, this larger training sample refers to the joint dataset.

According to the above information, we aim to first emphasize optimization-based approaches. This is because of its superior performance on broader task distributions compare to other types of meta-learning approaches. This characteristic is suitable for the current experiment design which uses test data from unseen subjects to the model. To be precise, two different model structures in this subtype were selected to use in our experiment; specifically, Reptile, and model-agnostic meta-learning (MAML). Distinctions of Reptile [8] and MAML [9] are rules for updating parameters and the value of hyper-parameters used (more detail in method section). Moreover, popularity and computational expensiveness are also considered factors for selecting this first group candidate model too.

The major contributions of this work are i) In this work, we propose a new learner called METAHACI which is composed of specific data preprocessing part, task generation part, and meta-learning model selection. METAHACI achieves good results for classifying human activity testing with three different datasets; two benchmark datasets and one additional public dataset. ii) To our knowledge, this is the first time to compare joint training with meta-learning models–specifically, Reptile, and MAML–for human activity classification from IMU sensors data. iii) Novel design of the task generation part for meta-learning training which distinct from general meta-learning technic that utilized random task generation. The distinctive subjects experiment design can also contribute to other studies that distinguishing subject-based, for instance, study about personalized recognition, biometrics, etc.

2   Related Work

Human activity classification from sensor data is a technique that expects to learn high-level knowledge about human activities from the low-level sensor inputs [10]. One of the technics that is widely used in this case is machine learning (ML) algorithms. An example of traditional ML tools is decision trees [11]. However, they are specific to particular tasks. Therefore, traditional ML algorithms cannot handle complex scenarios.

The weakness of traditional ML-based for human activity classification methods can be remarkably alleviated by deep learning methods which can be reused for similar tasks to make human activity classification model construction more proficient. For instance, deep neural networks [12], convolutional neural networks [13], autoencoders [14], and recurrent neural networks [15].

Unlike other methods above that require large training samples, meta-learning aims to learn new tasks faster with obviously fewer training examples by learning to learn. Although meta-learning is still widely used in computer vision studies–such as metasearch [16]–the application of meta-learning in human activity classification has been much more limited. To the best of our knowledge, no studies have ever compared joint training with meta-learning–specifically, Reptile, and MAML–in the human activity classification domain. Thus, we conduct an experiment to provide a contribution to this missing area; the overall graphical summary is presented in Fig. 2.

3   Methodology

3.1   Source of Dataset

Datasets used in this work are public data. Details are as following.

PAMAP2 [17,18]: physical activity monitoring dataset. This benchmark dataset was collected with nine subjects (1 female, 8 males) aged 27.22 ± 3.31 on average. Eighteen human activities collected from these subjects are laying down, sitting, standing, walking, running, cycling, Nordic walking, watching TV, computer work, car driving, ascending stairs, descending stairs, vacuum cleaning, ironing, folding laundry, house cleaning, playing soccer, and rope jumping. The aggregated time of all activities performed by all subjects is approximately 5.5 h. The sampling rate used is 99.63 Hz. Each user was equipped with; 1. IMU wireless sensors at the wrist (dominant arm), chest, and ankle (dominant side) 2. heart rate monitor at the subject's chest.

HAR UCI [19]: human activity recognition using smartphones dataset. This benchmark dataset was collected with thirty subjects within an age bracket of 19–48 years. Twelve human activities collected from these subjects are walking, walking upstairs, walking downstairs, sitting, standing, laying down, stand to sit, sit to stand, sit to lay down, lay down to sit, stand to lay down, and lay down to stand. The sampling rate used is 50 Hz. Each user was equipped with Samsung Galaxy S II at the subject's waist.

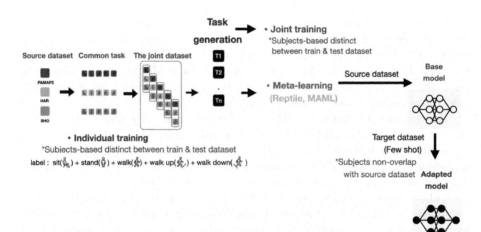

Fig. 2. Overall graphical summary

SHO [20]: sensor activity dataset. This dataset was collected with ten male subjects between the ages of 25 and 30. Eight human activities collected from these subjects are walking, running, sitting, standing, jogging, biking, walking upstairs, and walking downstairs. The sampling rate used is 50 Hz. Each user was equipped with Samsung Galaxy S II at the subject's positions as followed; one in their right jeans pocket, one in their left jeans pocket, one on the belt position towards the right leg using a belt clip, one on the right upper arm, and one on the right wrist.

3.2 Data Preprocessing

In our experiment, raw data from the accelerometer and gyroscope used is collected from the chest position (from PAMAP2 dataset), waist position (from HAR UCI dataset), and the belt position towards the right leg (from SHO dataset). Next, data of five activities were selected from these 3 datasets by criteria as follows: (1) activities are common activities for many datasets which regardless of gender and age so the discovery from our work will have potential benefits for further contribution to the wider community (2) activities selected are a mixture of static and dynamic activities that contain a certain amount of variety with reasonable sense to have potential benefits for further development into the activity-focus aspect. Due to the model will be trained with data that have sampling rate around 50 Hz, selected data from PAMAP2 was downsampled to 50 Hz before other steps of signal preprocessing. After that, all data were then sampled in fixed-width sliding windows with fifty-percent-overlapped between them before feeding to train the models.

3.3 Method

In our experiment, data were trained by different technics with the convolutional neural network (CNN) based model vice versa. Details are as followed.

3.3.1 Baseline Model This model is the CNN-based model developed and tuning hyperparameters for using as an initial model for our experiment.

3.3.2 Individual Trained Model Individually train each dataset using the K-fold technic with the baseline model. Selected labels are sitting, standing, walking, walking upstairs, and walking downstairs. After that, freeze all the models. The baseline accuracy of each dataset and activity selected is obtained from the accuracy result from this step.

3.3.3 Joint Training Model The joint dataset obtained from grouping all datasets used in the Sect. 3.3.2 by activity-label to get a big dataset. The train dataset obtained from a part of the joint dataset that will be trained with only one CNN-based baseline model. Reserved some data from the joint dataset which are unseen subjects from the train dataset to be used in the next step as the test dataset.

3.3.4   Reptile Model The Reptile structure model has simpler rules which require less computation for update gradient descent and differentiating through the optimization process compare to the model in the Sect. 3.3.5. Starting from the Reptile structure model together with the set1-value of hyper-parameters and the number of shot equal to 5, the two training steps for our specific objective are as following: (Step 1) base model training (meta-training) using source dataset which is the same as the train dataset of the joint training model in the Sect. 3.3.3, (Step 2) adaptation (meta-testing) of the model from step 1 which the weights of the meta parameter are already updated. In this step, the target dataset which is the same as the test dataset of the joint training model in the Sect. 3.3.3 will be used to fine-tune the model.

Algorithm 1: Sketch mechanism of meta-learning models

Input the joint dataset, learning rate, hyper-parameters
Output trained parameters
initilization
while *not finished* **do**

  Step 1: base-model training
  input initial parameters, the train dataset
  output trained parameters after base-model training
  substep 1.1: feed the train data from tasks assigned
  substep 1.2: evaluate via rule for update gradient descent
  substep 1.3: follow assigned differentiating rule through the process
  substep 1.4: update parameters
  Step 2: adaptation
  input trained parameters from base-model training, the test dataset
  output trained parameters after adaptation
  substep 2.1: feed the test data from tasks assigned
  substep 2.2: evaluate via rule for update gradient descent
  substep 2.3: follow assigned differentiating rule through the process
  substep 2.4: update parameters

3.3.5   Model-Agnostic Meta-Learning, MAML Model The MAML structure model compatible with any model trained with gradient descent and applicable to the classification problems. Its rules for update gradient descent and differentiating through the optimization process are famous in terms of it trains the model to be easy to fine-tune. The values of hyper-parameters of MAML are less than the set1-value of Reptile model. For example, one hyper-parameter less than Reptile by half, another less than Reptile by one-third, etc. Starting from the MAML structure model together with the set2-value hyper-parameters then continue with two training steps for our specific objective which are the same pattern as stated in the Sect. 3.3.4.

4   Result

From the experiment, accuracy results from the models mentioned above were analyzed and compared. Accuracy results from the individual trained model refer to a general baseline. Accuracy results from the joint training model demonstrate the effect of the test factor. Accuracy results from the Reptile model and MAML model illustrate the improvement of accuracy after the selected technics were employed. Please see Fig. 3.1. We can see that the result from the reptile model has a tiny improvement from the joint training model so we exclude the result of this model when further investigate class comparison. For class comparison, all classes demonstrated the improvement of accuracy (%) after using the MAML technic compare to the accuracy result from joint training. Please see Fig. 3.2.

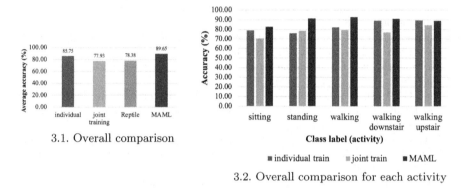

3.1. Overall comparison

3.2. Overall comparison for each activity

Fig. 3. Comparison of accuracy result from each step with different settings

5   Discussion and Conclusion

The results reveal our success in experiment design to retrieve improvement in human activities classification from IMU time series data by METAHACI learner. The METAHACI composed of; 1. particular data preprocessing process–preprocess with the fixed sampling rate and fixed-width sliding windows, 2. task generation approach–specific joint dataset from selected different datasets, slightly different sensors position and different subjects with five opted activities according to specific criteria, 3. meta-learning model choosing–MAML model was chosen in accordance with its remarkable performance among others model in the experiment and manifests satisfactory-result after testing with the test dataset comes from non-overlap subjects. It can be seen that METAHACI improves both overall classification accuracy and each class (activity) accuracy. In the future, we will further investigate more on the task generation part, other benchmark datasets, and related advanced technics especially the state of the art technics of related technics, such as prototypical networks or other small sample learning technics, and so on.

Acknowledgement. Thank you Vidyasirimedhi Institute of Science and Technology (VISTEC) for supporting. Thank you very much to the anonymous faculty member of VISTEC for supervision and intellectual discussions. Thank you very much to Dr. Stephen John Turner from the School of Information Science and Technology at VISTEC for professional-suggestions. Thank you very much to Mr. Pichayoot Ouppaphan for technical help. Also, thank you very much to Dr. Chotiluck Leelakittisin for the intellectual suggestions.

References

1. Chen, T., et al.: Unsupervised anomaly detection of industrial robots using sliding-window convolutional variational autoencoder. IEEE Access **8**, 47072–47081 (2020)
2. Kaushik, S., et al.: AI in healthcare: time-series forecasting using statistical, neural, and ensemble architectures. Front. Big Data **3**, 4 (2020)
3. Xu, Z., et al.: Prediction research of financial time series based on deep learning. Soft Comput. 1–18 (2020)
4. Rantalainen, T., et al.: Jump height from inertial recordings: a tutorial for a sports scientist. Scand. J. Med. Sci. Sports **30**(1), 38–45 (2020)
5. Mukhopadhyay, S.C.: Wearable sensors for human activity monitoring: a review. IEEE Sens. J. **15**(3), 1321–1330 (2014)
6. Hou, C.: A study on IMU-based human activity recognition using deep learning and traditional machine learning. In: 5th International Conference on Computer and Communication Systems (ICCCS) 2020, Shanghai, pp. 225–234. IEEE (2020)
7. Vanschoren, J.: Meta-learning: a survey. arXiv preprint arXiv:1810.03548 (2018)
8. Nichol, A., et al.: On first-order meta-learning algorithms. arXiv preprint arXiv:1803.02999 (2018)
9. Finn, C., et al.: Model-agnostic meta-learning for fast adaptation of deep networks. arXiv preprint arXiv:1703.03400 (2017)
10. Wang, J., et al.: Deep learning for sensor-based activity recognition: a survey. Pattern Recogn. Lett. **119**, 3–11 (2019)
11. Jatoba, L.C., et al.: Context-aware mobile health monitoring: evaluation of different pattern recognition methods for classification of physical activity. In: 30th Annual International Conference of the IEEE Engineering in Medicine and Biology Society 2008, Vancouver, pp. 5250–5253. IEEE (2008)
12. Walse, K.H., Dharaskar, R.V., Thakare, V.M.: PCA based optimal ANN classifiers for human activity recognition using mobile sensors data. In: Satapathy, S.C.C., Das, S. (eds.) Proceedings of First International Conference on Information and Communication Technology for Intelligent Systems: Volume 1. SIST, vol. 50, pp. 429–436. Springer, Cham (2016). https://doi.org/10.1007/978-3-319-30933-0_43
13. Ha, S., et al.: Multi-modal convolutional neural networks for activity recognition. In: IEEE International Conference on Systems, Man, and Cybernetics 2015, Kowloon, pp. 3017–3022. IEEE (2015)
14. Almaslukh, B., et al.: An effective deep autoencoder approach for online smartphone-based human activity recognition. Int. J. Comput. Sci. Netw. Secur. **17**(4), 160–165 (2017)
15. Inoue, M., et al.: Deep recurrent neural network for mobile human activity recognition with high throughput. Artif. Life Robot. **23**(2), 173–185 (2018)
16. Wang, Q., et al.: MetaSearch: incremental product search via deep meta-learning. IEEE Trans. Image Process. **29**, 7549–7564 (2020)

17. Reiss, A., et al.: Introducing a new benchmarked dataset for activity monitoring. In: 16th International Symposium on Wearable Computers 2012, Newcastle, pp. 108–109. IEEE (2012)

18. Reiss, A., et al.: Creating and benchmarking a new dataset for physical activity monitoring. In: Proceedings of the 5th International Conference on PErvasive Technologies Related to Assistive Environments 2012, Heraklion, pp. 1–8. PETRA (2012)

19. Anguita, D., et al.: A public domain dataset for human activity recognition using smartphones. In: ESANN 2013 Proceedings, European Symposium on Artificial Neural Networks, Computational Intelligence and Machine Learning 2013, Belgium, p. 3. ESANN (2013)

20. Shoaib, M., et al.: Fusion of smartphone motion sensors for physical activity recognition. Sensors **16**(4), 10146–10176 (2014)

Fusing Knowledge and Experience with Graph Convolutional Network for Cross-task Learning in Visual Cognitive Development

Xinyue Zhang[1(✉)], Xu Yang[1], Zhiyong Liu[1], Lu Zhang[1], Dongchun Ren[2], and Mingyu Fan[2]

[1] State Key Laboratory of Management and Control for Complex Systems, Institute of Automation, Chinese Academy of Sciences, Beijing 100190, People's Republic of China
{Zhangxinyue2020,xu.yang}@ia.ac.cn
[2] Meituan-Dianping Group, Beijing 100190, People's Republic of China
rendongchun@meituan.com

Abstract. Visual cognitive ability is important for intelligent robots in unstructured and dynamic environments. The high reliance on large amounts of data prevents prior methods to handle this task. Therefore, we propose a model called knowledge-experience fusion graph (KEFG) network for novel inference. It exploits information from both knowledge and experience. With the employment of graph convolutional network (GCN), KEFG generates the predictive classifiers of the novel classes with few labeled samples. Experiments show that KEFG can decrease the training time by the fusion of the source information and also increase the classification accuracy in cross-task learning.

Keywords: GCN · Few-shot learning · Cognitive development · Transfer learning · Image recognition · Cross-task learning

1 Introduction

Visual cognitive development is vital for intelligent robots in unstructured and dynamic environments. However, limited by the number of available labeled samples, an intelligent robot faces lots of novel categories in realistic environments. An ideal robot can transfer the knowledge and experience from the base classes to novel ones independently. The ability of predictive knowledge transferring efficiently cuts down the training cost and extends the range of cognition. Since

This work is supported partly by National Key R&D Program of China (grants 2017YFB1300202 and 2016YFC0300801), partly by National Natural Science Foundation (NSFC) of China (grants 61973301, 61972020, 61633009, and U1613213), partly by Beijing Science and Technology Plan Project (grant Z181100008918018), and partly by Meituan Open R&D Fund.

F. Sun et al. (Eds.): ICCSIP 2020, CCIS 1397, pp. 114–120, 2021.
https://doi.org/10.1007/978-981-16-2336-3_10

the robot only obtains a few labeled samples of the novel categories other than some supplementary information, few-shot learning is often used.

Previously, the basic idea of few-shot learning is to exploit the knowledge from the base classes to support the novel ones. Most existing methods can be divided into two groups: metric-learning based method [1,8,9] and meta-learning method [10–12]. However, these methods mainly focus on inter-class dissimilarity. The relationship among classes is also important for knowledge transfering. To improve the efficiency of the sample utilization, some researchers exploit the knowledge graph to make up a relation map among categories [2,3,5]. Thus the structural information is also taken into account and the propagation becomes more reasonable. However, pure knowledge information shows a deviation between semantic space and visual space. This one-sidedness of pure knowledge graph leads to an unsatisfactory accuracy. Besides, the amount of knowledge graph to support the novel classes is huge, due to the sparseness of the information. Thus a more sophisticated inference mechanism is in need.

Humans can rapidly adapt to an unfamiliar environment. This is mainly based on two parts of information: *common sense* and *visual experience*. With the common sense, they know the descriptions of the novel class and its relationship with the base ones. With the experience of learning the base classes, they quickly grasp the method to classify the novel ones. These two parts of information enable humans to develop their visual cognitive ability accurately and quickly.

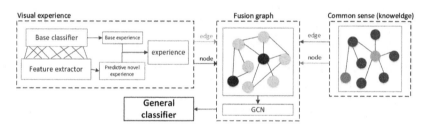

Fig. 1. We jointly explore the source information from visual experience and common sense to predict the general classifier of novel categories.

Motivated by this, we propose a model called knowledge-experience fusion graph network (KEFG) for few-shot learning. The goal of KEFG is to jointly explore the common sense (knowledge) and visual experience to accomplish the cognitive self-development of robots. For convenience and according to the daily usage, below the common sense is directly abbreviated by *knowledge*, while the visual experience is denoted by *experience*. Specifically, KEFG obtains experience from the original trained recognition model based on Convolutional Neural Network (CNN). It recalls the visual representation of the base classes and generates the predictive classifiers of the novel ones. KEFG further explores the prestored knowledge graph from WordNet [7] and builds a task-specific subgraph for efficiency. With the employment of GCN [4], novel classes generate its own classifier following the mechanism of related base classes on the fusion graph. To evaluate the effectiveness of KEFG, cross-task experiments are conducted to transfer the cognition ability from ImageNet 2012 to two typical datasets, fine-grained medium size dataset Caltech-UCSD Birds 200 (CUB) [13] and coarse-grained small size dataset miniImageNet [8]. The results show satisfactory performance.

The main contributions are as follows: (1) The knowledge graph builds a developmental map suitable for cognitive development. KEFG conducts a developmental framework to transfer the base information to specific tasks. (2) KEFG jointly explores information from the visual space and word space. It cuts down the number of nodes to support the inference and decreases the deviation. (3) The experiments show that KEFG conducts well not only on the coarse-grained small size dataset but also on the fine-grained medium size dataset.

2   Methodology

The set of all categories contains training set C_{train}, support set $C_{support}$, and testing set C_{test}. C_{train} has sufficient labeled images. $C_{support}$ and C_{test} are from the same categories called *novel classes*, while the training categories called *base classes*. If the support set contains K labeled samples for each of the N classes, we call this problem $N - way \; K - shot$ few-shot problem. KEFG is built on an undirected knowledge graph, denoted as $G = (V, E)$. V is a node set of all classes. Each node represents a class. $E = \{e_{i,j}\}$ is an edge set. The classification weights are defined as $w = \{w_i\}_{i=1}^{N}$ where N is the number of total categories.

2.1   Information Injected Module

KEFG employs the knowledge graph from WordNet. Better than taking the whole graph, KEFG adds the novel classes to the constant graph of the base classes in ImageNet 2012. If there are N classes, KEFG takes a subgraph with N nodes. To transfer the description into vectors, we use the GloVe text model and get S input features per class. The feature matrix of knowledge is $V_K \in R^{N \times S}$. KEFG only uses the hyponymy as the principle of the edge construction. The edge matrix from the knowledge space refers to $E_K \in R^{N \times N}$.

KEFG learns from the experience of the original model which is denoted as $C(F(\cdot|\theta)|w)$. It consists of feature extractor $F(\cdot|\theta)$ and category classifier $C(\cdot|w)$. θ and w indicate the classification parameters of the model. Feature extractor $F(x|\theta)$ takes an image as input and figures out the feature vector of it as z_i. The parameter w^{train} refers to the classification weights of different classes in training set. The final classification score is computed as $s = \{z^T w\}$

The feature extractor part $F(\cdot|\theta)$ can compute feature representations of the $C_{support}$. According to the rule of the template matching, the feature representation of the novel class can well represents its classification weights. Thus the initial weights can be represented as the average of the features.

$$v_i^E = \begin{cases} w_i^{train}, & x_i \in C_{train} \\ \frac{1}{P} \sum_{k=1}^{P} F(x_{i,p}|\theta), & x_i \in C_{test} \end{cases} \quad (1)$$

Where v_i^E refers to the visual feature of the ith class. $x_{i,p}$ refers to the pth image in the ith class. P is the total number of the images in the ith class.

Motivated by the denoising autoencoder network, KEFG injects the word embedding to the initial classification weights to generate a more general classifiers. The features of the ith class in the fusion graph is represented as follows

$$v_i = \alpha \frac{v_i^K}{\|v_i^K\|_2} + \beta \frac{v_i^E}{\|vi^E\|_2} \tag{2}$$

where α and β refers to the proportion of each source of information.

Except the relationship of hyponymy, KEFG also introduces cosine similarity to the graph. The edges are denoted as follows

$$e_{i,j} = \begin{cases} 1, & Simi(x_i, x_j) > S \text{ or } Hypo(x_i, x_j) \\ 0, & otherwise \end{cases} \tag{3}$$

$Simi(x_i, x_j)$ refers to the cosine similarity. S represents the similarity boundary to judge whether there is a relationship between two classes and it is a hyperparameter. $Hypo(x_i, x_j)$ refers to the mechanism to judge whether there if the relationship of hyponymy between ith class and jth class.

2.2   Information Transfer Module

With the framework of the GCN, KEFG propagates information among nodes by exploring the classes relationship. The mechanism of GCN is described as

$$H^{(l+1)} = ReLu(\hat{D}^{-\frac{1}{2}}\hat{E}\hat{D}^{-\frac{1}{2}}H^{(l)}U^{(l)}) \tag{4}$$

where $H^{(l)}$ denotes the output of the lth layer. $\hat{E} = E + I$, where $E \in R^{N \times N}$ is the symmetric adjacency matrix and $I \in R^{N \times N}$ represents identity matrix. $D_{ii} = \sum_j E_{ij}$. U^l is the weight matrix of the lth layer.

The fusion graph is trained to minimize the loss between the predicted classification weights and the ground-truth weights.

$$L = \frac{1}{M} \sum_{i=1}^{M} (w_i - w_i^{train})^2 \tag{5}$$

where w refers to the output of base classes on GCN. w^{train} denotes the ground truth obtained from the category classifier. M is the number of the base classes.

KEFG further applies the general classifiers to the original model. By computing the classification scores $s = z^T w$, KEFG distinguishes novel classes with few samples and transfers the original models to other datasets efficiently.

3   Experiments

3.1   Experimental Setting

The fundamental base classes remain the training set of ImageNet 2012. We test the developmental ability on CUB and miniImageNet. The knowledge graph is exploited from the WordNet. CUB includes 200 fine-grained classes of birds. We only take 10 classes, which are disjoint from the 1000 training classes of ImageNet 2012. MiniImageNet consists of 100 categories. For fairness, we only take 90 base classes as the training set. The remaining 10 classes in the miniImageNet consist of the novel task with few examples. The original recognition model is pre-trained on the ResNet50 [6] with base classes.

3.2   Comparision

Table 1. Comparision with prior models

Model	MiniImageNet		CUB	
Setting	1-shot	5-shot	1-shot	5-shot
Nearest neighbor [15]	44.1	55.1	52.4	66.0
Matching Nets [16]	46.6	60.0	49.3	59.3
MAML [17]	48.7	63.1	38.4	59.1
DEML+Meta-SGD [18]	58.5	71.3	66.9	77.1
Δ-encoder [14]	59.9	69.7	69.8	82.6
KEFG	61.34	77.11	73.78	84.15

The comparison between KEFG and other exiting methods is reported in Table 1, where the performance is evaluated by the average top-1 accuracy. KEFG achieves the best or competitive performance for both 10-way 1-shot and 10-way 5-shot recognition tasks. Especially, KEFG shows remarkable improvement in the fine-grained dataset. The accuracy on CUB increases almost twenty percentage the most. However, the training set in KEFG completely comes from ImageNet 2012. The relationship between the base and novel classes is weaker. We owe this excellent transferability to two aspects. First, the prestored graph knowledge provides an excellent developmental graph for the model. Second, the combination of the knowledge and the experience provides abundant information for the novel classes to refer to. Thus the transfer accuracy increases notably.

Table 2. Comparison on details

Model	Node size	Edge size	Training time
DGP [5]	32324	32538	27 min
SGCN [5]	32324	32544	20 mmin
KEFG	1010	719	7 min

In Table 2, we analyze the details. Both DGP and SGCN only exploit the knowledge graph for the inference. From the experiments, KEFG declines the amount of subgraph a lot. Furthermore, it cuts down the training time as well. SGCN and DGP only exploit the inheritance relationship in the knowledge graph. To gather abundant information, the subgraph involved in the inference should be large. On the other hand, KEFG takes visual similarity into account, which leads to a dense graph. Thus the novel nodes can gather more information with a smaller amount of graph.

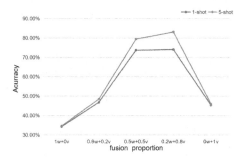

Fig. 2. In the test, w refers to the knowledge while v refers to the visual experience.

Table 3. Ablation study

Setting	1-shot	5-shot
KEFG (knowledge only)	34.33	34.67
KEFG (experience only)	45.33	48.75
KEFG (Gaussian noise+experience)	71.62	75.64
KEFG	73.78	79.47

We further test the effectiveness of the fusion idea. With different fusion proportions of knowledge and experience, the recognition accuracy changes as well. From Fig. 2, it is obviously noticed that the accuracy increases rapidly when the two sources of information are combined. After the peak accuracy of 73.78% for 1-shot and 79.47% for 5-shot, the accuracy declines as the combination becomes weak. Table 3 shows that KEFG improves the performance by almost 30% than only using knowledge or experience. Because the novel nodes gather more supplementary information from its neighbors. Both the information from word space and visual space is taken into account. Besides, not only the parent nodes and offspring nodes but also the visual similar nodes are connected to the novel ones. Furthermore, we combine the experience with Gaussian Noise to test the effectiveness of the knowledge. Table 3 shows that the combination of knowledge increases the accuracy by about 4% than Gaussian noise. Thus the knowledge information makes sense in the process of inference.

4   Conclusion

In this paper, we propose KEFG which takes advantage of information from both knowledge and experience to realize visual cognitive development. To take the interrelationship among categories into account, KEFG is based on the framework of the graph convolution network. During experiments, the ability of the proposed model outperforms previous state of art methods and obviously declines the time of training. In future work, we will devote to improving the mechanism of fusion to further improve the performance of our model.

References

1. Koch, G., Zemel, R., Salakhutdinov, R.: Siamese neural networks for one-shot image recognition. In: International Conference for Learning Representation (2017)
2. Carlson, A., Betteridge, J., Kisiel, B., Settled, B., Hruschka, E.R., Mitchell, T.M.: Toward an architecture for never ending language learning. In: AAAI (2010)
3. Wang, X.L., Ye, Y.F., Gupta, A.: Zero-shot recognition via semantic embeddings and knowledge graphs. In: CVPR (2017)
4. Kipf, T.N., Welling, M.: Semi-supervised classification with graph convolutional networks. In: ICLR (2017)
5. Kampffmeyer, M., Chen, Y., Chen, Y.: Rethinking knowledge graph propagation for zero-shot learning. In: Conference on Computer Vision and Pattern Recognition (2019)
6. Kingma, D.P., Ba, J.: Adam: a method for stochastic optimization. In: 2015 Machine Learning Research on International Conference for Learning Representations, vol. 15, no 1, pp. 3563–3593 (2014)
7. Miller, G.A.: WordNet: a lexical database for English. Commun. ACM **38**(11), 39–41 (1995)
8. Vinyals, O., Blundell, C., Lillicrap, T., Wierstra, D., et al.: Matching networks for one shot learning. In: NIPS (2016)
9. Snell, J., Swersky, K., Zemel, R.: Prototypical networks for few-shot learning. In: NIPS (2017)
10. Finn, C., Abbeel, P., Levine, S.: Model agnostic meta-learning for fast adaptation of deep networks. In: ICML (2017)
11. Mishra, N., Rohaninejad, M., Chen, X., Abbeel, P.: A simple neural attentive meta-learner. In: ICLR (2018)
12. Sung, F., Yang, Y., Zhang, L., Xiang, T., Torr, P., Hospedales, T.M.: Learning to compare: relation network for few-shot learning. In: CVPR (2018)
13. Wah, C., Branson, S., Welinder, P., Perona, P., Belongie, S.: The Caltech-UCSD Birds 200 Dataset. Technical Report CNS-TR-2011-001, California Institute of Technology (2011)
14. Schwartz, E., Kalinsky, L., Shtok, J., et al.: δ-encoder: an effective sample synthesis method for few-shot object recognition. In: NeurIPS (2018)
15. Weinberger, K.Q., Saul, L.K.: Distance metric learning for large margin nearest neighbor classification. J. Mach. Learn. Res. **10**, 207–244 (2009)
16. Ravi, S., Larochelle, H.: Optimization as a model for few-shot learning. In: International Conference on Learning Representations (ICLR), pp. 1–11 (2017)
17. Finn, C., Abbeel, P., Levine, S.: Model-agnostic meta-learning for fast adaptation of deep networks. arXiv:1703.03400 (2017)
18. Zhou, F., Wu, B., Li, Z.: Deep meta-learning: learning to learn in the concept space. arXiv:1802.03596, February 2018

Factored Trace Lasso Based Linear Regression Methods: Optimizations and Applications

Hengmin Zhang[1], Wenli Du[1(✉)], Xiaoqian Liu[2], Bob Zhang[3], and Feng Qian[1]

[1] School of Information Science and Engineering, Key Laboratory of Advanced Control and Optimization for Chemical Processes, Ministry of Education, East China University of Science and Technology, Shanghai 200237, People's Republic of China
{wldu,fqian}@ecust.edu.cn

[2] Department of Computer Information and Cyber Security, Jiangsu Police Institute, Nanjing 210031, People's Republic of China
liuxiaoqian@jspi.edu.cn

[3] Department of Computer and Information Science, University of Macau, Macau 999078, People's Republic of China
bobzhang@um.edu.mo

Abstract. Consider that matrix trace lasso regularized convex ℓ_p-norm with $p = 1, 2$ regression methods usually have the higher computational complexity due to the singular value decomposition (SVD) of larger size matrix in big data and information processing. By factoring the matrix trace lasso into the squared sum of two Frobenius-norm, this work studies the solutions of both adaptive sparse representation (ASR) and correlation adaptive subspace segmentation (CASS), respectively. Meanwhile, the derived models involve multi-variable nonconvex functions with at least two equality constraints. To solve them efficiently, we devise the nonconvex alternating direction multiplier methods (NADMM) with convergence analysis satisfying the Karush-Kuhn-Tucher (KKT) conditions. Finally, numerical experiments to the subspace clustering can show the less timing consumptions than CASS and the nearby performance of our proposed method when compared with the existing segmentation methods like SSC, LRR, LSR and CASS.

Keywords: Matrix trace lasso · Nuclear norm factorization · Convergence analysis · ADMM · KKT conditions

1 Introduction

It follows from [1] that matrix trace lasso $\|\mathbf{D}\mathrm{Diag}(\mathbf{x})\|_*$ can balance convex ℓ_1-norm and ℓ_2-norm of representation coefficient $\mathbf{x} \in \mathbb{R}^n$, i.e., $\|\mathbf{x}\|_2 \leq \|\mathbf{D}\mathrm{Diag}(\mathbf{x})\|_* \leq \|\mathbf{x}\|_1$, when the columns of matrix $\mathbf{D} \in \mathbb{R}^{m \times n}$ have the independent and corrected properties. The existing matrix trace lasso based linear regression methods have the popular applications, e.g., face recognition and subspace clustering.

© Springer Nature Singapore Pte Ltd. 2021
F. Sun et al. (Eds.): ICCSIP 2020, CCIS 1397, pp. 121–130, 2021.
https://doi.org/10.1007/978-981-16-2336-3_11

However, when the data matrix $\mathbf{D}$ and the representation coefficient $\mathbf{x}$ have the larger dimensions, the computational complexity is very higher in the optimization procedures. Then it can lead to the lower computational efficiency, which makes the optimization algorithms be challengeable for facing some of real-world applications [2,3]. Besides, different noise styles need to the proper measure criteria, e.g., ℓ_1-norm for laplace noise, ℓ_2-norm for gaussian noise and nuclear norm for matrix variate power exponential distribution of dependent noise. The related explanations can be found in the existing works as [4,5].

Based upon these statements, the matrix trace lasso related with regression models would be more general for the proper measurements of residual function and representation coefficients. Subsequently, we study the formulation of matrix trace lasso based linear regression problem

$$\min_{\mathbf{x}} \frac{1}{p}\|\mathbf{y} - \mathbf{Dx}\|_{\ell_p} + \lambda\|\mathbf{D}\mathrm{Diag}(\mathbf{x})\|_*, \tag{1}$$

where $\mathbf{D} = [\mathbf{D}_1, \mathbf{D}_2, ..., \mathbf{D}_c]$, and $\mathbf{D}_i$ is the i-th class samples and c is the total number of training classes, and the regularization parameter $\lambda > 0$, and $\mathbf{y} \in \mathbb{R}^m$ is the testing sample, and $\|\cdot\|_{\ell_p}$ measures the residual function for $p = 1, 2$, i.e., $\|\cdot\|_1$ and $\|\cdot\|^2$, and $\|\cdot\|_*$ describes the regularization term by computing the sum of singular values. It follows from some minor revisions that sparse representation based classification (SRC) [6], collaborative representation based classification (CRC) [7], sparse subspace clustering (SSC) [8] and least squares regression (LSR) [9] can be regarded as the specific examples of problem (1), and the regression methods related with trace lasso such as adaptive sparse representation (ASR) [10] and correlation adaptive subspace segmentation (CASS) [11] can be generalized to the problem (1), respectively.

To optimize problem (1) efficiently, we firstly write the augmented Lagrange function, and then updating the primal variables, the dual variables and the penalty parameters in sequence. In the process of optimizations, there exist two points to stress out: one is the closed-form solvers of subproblems related with ℓ_1/ℓ_2-norm and nuclear norm as low rank representation (LRR) [12], which need to introduce the auxiliary variables but avoiding of any inner loops; the other is the computations of singular values thresholding (SVT) operator which can lead to the higher computational complexity, i.e., $o(mn^2)$ for $m \geq n$, when processing a large-scale matrix. By factoring $\mathbf{Z} = \mathbf{D}\mathrm{Diag}(\mathbf{x}) \in \mathbf{R}^{m \times n}$ into two smaller matrices given $\mathbf{Z} = \mathbf{U}\mathbf{V}^{\mathrm{T}}$ as in [13,14], where $\mathbf{U} \in \mathbf{R}^{m \times d}$ and $\mathbf{V} \in \mathbf{R}^{n \times d}$ for $d \ll \min(m, n)$. For rank at most $r \leq d$, the nuclear norm has the following alternative non-convex formulation, given by

$$\|\mathbf{Z}\|_* = \min_{\mathbf{Z}=\mathbf{U}\mathbf{V}^{\mathrm{T}}} \frac{1}{2}\left(\|\mathbf{U}\|^2 + \|\mathbf{V}\|^2\right), \tag{2}$$

where the decomposable strategy of representation formulas (2) has the popular applications in the low-rank matrix recovery problems. It should be noted that this strategy can reduce the computational complexity and be widely used in most cases. Relying on these descriptions, we outline the main contributions and the further researches of this work as below.

1.1 Contributions

- By factoring matrix trace lasso norm through (2), we further convert problem (1) into nonconvex multi-variable problem with equality constraints. Then the derived ℓ_1/ℓ_2-norm regularization problems become more general and the computational complexity can be reduced at each of iterations. This aims to improve the computational efficiency in the process of optimizations.
- By developing efficient ADMM to solve problem (1) shown later, it not only guarantees the closed-form solvers of each subproblems but also provides the local convergence properties, i.e., the objective function has the monotonically nonincreasing and the limiting point satisfies the KKT conditions. This makes the programming easy to conduct and the theoretical analysis to support the optimization scheme.
- By conducting the experiments on the subspace clustering to face and digital databases, numerical results of our approaches can achieve less timing consumptions and/or relatively higher performance than some existing regression methods in the verifications.

1.2 Outline

Section 2 presents the model formulation of factored trace lasso regularization problem and its optimization algorithm. Section 3 provides the main results for the theoretical convergence analysis. Section 4 conducts the numerical experiments to validate the theoretical results and the computational efficiency and the superior performance. Finally, Sect. 5 concludes this work.

2 Model and Algorithm

Based upon the above statements, we introduce (2) into problem (1) for the regularization term and choose the generalized ℓ_p-norm for the loss functions, then it is easy to achieve the factored trace lasso based linear regression (FTLR) problem, denoted as

$$\min_{\mathbf{x},\mathbf{Z},\mathbf{U},\mathbf{V}} \frac{1}{p}\|\mathbf{y} - \mathbf{Dx}\|_{\ell_p} + \frac{\lambda}{2}\left(\|\mathbf{U}\|^2 + \|\mathbf{V}\|^2\right),$$
$$s.t., \quad \mathbf{Z} = \mathbf{D}\mathrm{Diag}(\mathbf{x}), \quad \mathbf{Z} = \mathbf{UV}^{\mathrm{T}}, \tag{3}$$

where model formulation (3) is provided for the cases of $p = 1$ and 2. It can be regarded as the decomposable variant of both ASR and CASS in [10,11]. Then we write the augmented Lagrange function of problem (3), represented by

$$\mathcal{L}_\mu(\mathbf{x},\mathbf{Z},\mathbf{U},\mathbf{V},\Lambda_1,\Lambda_2) = \frac{1}{p}\|\mathbf{y} - \mathbf{Dx}\|_{\ell_p} + \frac{\lambda}{2}\left(\|\mathbf{U}\|^2 + \|\mathbf{V}\|^2\right)$$
$$+ \frac{\mu}{2}\left\|\mathbf{Z} - \mathbf{D}\mathrm{Diag}(\mathbf{x}) + \frac{\Lambda_1}{\mu}\right\|^2 - \frac{1}{2\mu}\|\Lambda_1\|^2$$
$$+ \frac{\mu}{2}\left\|\mathbf{Z} - \mathbf{UV}^{\mathrm{T}} + \frac{\Lambda_2}{\mu}\right\|^2 - \frac{1}{2\mu}\|\Lambda_2\|^2 \tag{4}$$

where $\mu > 0$, Λ_1 and Λ_2 are the dual variables responded to two equality constraints in problem (3). Subsequently, we study (4) for the case of $p = 2$, and write the factorable formulation of CASS with noisy data in [11], the equality constraint $\mathbf{e} = \mathbf{y} - \mathbf{Dx}$ does not need in the process of optimization because of the differentiable property of $\|\cdot\|^2$. Naturally, there are less variables compared with $\|\cdot\|_1$, i.e., $p = 1$, combined with the factored trace lasso, when optimizing the ℓ_2-norm minimization problems. The main differences of both above cases concentrate on the model formulations, optimization algorithms and practical applications though both of them exist some slight differences but having the necessary relations. This is due to the usage of (2), and they fall into the iteration procedure of ADMM [15,16], in which the programming is very easy to be done and each of subproblems has the closed-form solver, respectively. Along this way, we focus on achieving the optimal solver, i.e., $\mathbf{x}_*$, in the given two cases, and then defining the rules of classification and clustering accordingly. Observing the similarity with the solutions, we mainly consider the case of $p = 2$. Given the initial variables, i.e., $(\mathbf{x}_0, \mathbf{e}_0, \mathbf{Z}_0, \mathbf{U}_0, \mathbf{V}_0, \Lambda_{1,0}, \Lambda_{2,0})$, this section mainly provides the iteration steps of nonconvex ADMM for solving problem (4) as follows

$$
\begin{cases}
\mathbf{x}_{k+1} = \operatorname{argmin}_{\mathbf{x}} \dfrac{1}{2}\|\mathbf{y} - \mathbf{Dx}\|^2 + \dfrac{\mu_k}{2}\left\|\mathbf{DDiag}(\mathbf{x}) - \left(\mathbf{Z}_k + \dfrac{\Lambda_{1,k}}{\mu_k}\right)\right\|^2, & (5)\\[2ex]
\mathbf{Z}_{k+1} = \operatorname{argmin}_{\mathbf{Z}} \dfrac{\mu_k}{2}\left\|\mathbf{Z} - \widehat{\mathbf{x}}_{\Lambda_{1,k}}^{k+1}\right\|^2 + \dfrac{\mu_k}{2}\left\|\mathbf{Z} - \widehat{\mathbf{UV}}_{\Lambda_{1,k}}^{k}\right\|^2 & \\[1ex]
\quad \text{with } \widehat{\mathbf{x}}_{\Lambda_k}^{1,k+1} = \mathbf{DDiag}(\mathbf{x}_{k+1}) - \dfrac{\Lambda_{1,k}}{\mu_k}, \quad \widehat{\mathbf{UV}}_{\Lambda_{2,k}}^{k} = \mathbf{U}_k\mathbf{V}_k^{\mathrm{T}} - \dfrac{\Lambda_{2,k}}{\mu_k}, & (6)\\[2ex]
\mathbf{U}_{k+1} = \operatorname{argmin}_{\mathbf{U}} \dfrac{\lambda}{2}\|\mathbf{U}\|^2 + \dfrac{\mu_k}{2}\left\|\mathbf{UV}_k^{\mathrm{T}} - \widehat{\mathbf{Z}}_{\Lambda_{2,k}}^{k+1}\right\|^2, & (7)\\[2ex]
\mathbf{V}_{k+1} = \operatorname{argmin}_{\mathbf{V}} \dfrac{\lambda}{2}\|\mathbf{V}\|^2 + \dfrac{\mu_k}{2}\left\|\mathbf{U}_{k+1}\mathbf{V}^{\mathrm{T}} - \widehat{\mathbf{Z}}_{\Lambda_{2,k}}^{k+1}\right\|^2, & (8)\\[2ex]
\Lambda_{1,k+1} = \Lambda_{1,k} + \mu_k\left(\mathbf{Z}_{k+1} - \mathbf{DDiag}(\mathbf{x}_{k+1})\right), & (9)\\[1ex]
\Lambda_{2,k+1} = \Lambda_{2,k} + \mu_k\left(\mathbf{Z}_{k+1} - \mathbf{U}_{k+1}\mathbf{V}_{k+1}^{\mathrm{T}}\right), & (10)\\[1ex]
\mu_{k+1} = \rho\mu_k, \quad \rho > 1, & (11)
\end{cases}
$$

where the choices of value ρ would influence the iteration speed and the quality of optimality solver as explained in [15,16], and $\widehat{\mathbf{Z}}_{\Lambda_{2,k}}^{k+1} = \mathbf{Z}_{k+1} + \dfrac{\Lambda_{2,k}}{\mu_k}$ can be simply represented in the subproblems of both (7) and (8). It is easy to obtain the analytic solvers of subproblems (5)-(8) by computing the derivatives of (5), (6)-(8) with $\mathbf{x}$, $\mathbf{Z}$, $\mathbf{U}$ and $\mathbf{V}$ to be $\mathbf{0}$, respectively. Instead of using the linearization strategy in [17,18], we will present the iteration scheme of nonconvx ADMM with two dual variables and penalty parameter in (9)-(11) for the proper solution of model formulation in the optimization process. The optimization algorithm converges until reaching the maximize iteration number or satisfying the stopping conditions, given as

$$
\max\left(\|\mathbf{Z}_{k+1} - \mathbf{DDiag}(\mathbf{x}_{k+1})\|_\infty, \|\mathbf{Z}_{k+1} - \mathbf{U}_{k+1}\mathbf{V}_{k+1}^{\mathrm{T}}\|_\infty\right) < 10^{-6}. \tag{12}
$$

3   Convergence Analysis

The convergence analysis for nonconvex ADMM with multi-variables mainly depends on the updating rules of involved variables in solving problem (4) though it may be challenging [19, 20]. Besides the empirical convergence verifications, we further provide the convergence guarantees, where we firstly prove the boundedness of both primal and dual variables, and then analyze the generated variable sequence satisfying the KKT conditions as well as it converges to a critical point. Follow this way, the subsequent context will present a briefly theoretical proofs[1] for the above-given optimization algorithm.

Lemma 1. *Let* $\{\mathcal{T}_k = (\mathbf{x}_k, \mathbf{Z}_k, \mathbf{U}_k, \mathbf{V}_k, \Lambda_{1,k}, \Lambda_{2,k})\}$ *be the generated sequence by (5)-(10), then the sequence* $\{\mathcal{T}_k\}$ *is bounded as long as the penalty sequence* $\{\mu_k\}$ *is non-decreasing and satisfying* $\sum\limits_{k=1}^{+\infty} \frac{\mu_k + \mu_{k-1}}{2\mu_{k-1}^2} < +\infty$, *and* $\mu_k(\mathbf{Z}_{k+1} - \mathbf{Z}_k)$, $\mu_k(\mathbf{V}_k - \mathbf{V}_{k+1})$ *and* $\mu_k \left(\mathbf{U}_{k+1}\mathbf{V}_{k+1}^{\mathrm{T}} - \mathbf{U}_k\mathbf{V}_k^{\mathrm{T}}\right)$ *are boundedness.*

Proof. *Firstly*, we prove the boundedness of sequence $\{(\Lambda_{1,k}, \Lambda_{2,k})\}$. By the updated rules in (5)-(8), we can obtain the gradient/subgradient of function (4) with each of primal variables, represented by

$$
\begin{cases}
\mathbf{0} = \mathrm{Diag}(\mathbf{x}_{k+1})\mathbf{D}^{\mathrm{T}} \left(\mu_k(\mathbf{Z}_{k+1} - \mathbf{Z}_k) - \Lambda_{1,k+1}\right) + \mathbf{D}^{\mathrm{T}} \left(\mathbf{D}\mathbf{x}_{k+1} - \mathbf{y}\right), & (13) \\
\mathbf{0} = \Lambda_{1,k+1} + \mu_k \left(\mathbf{U}_{k+1}\mathbf{V}_{k+1}^{\mathrm{T}} - \mathbf{U}_k\mathbf{V}_k^{\mathrm{T}}\right) + \Lambda_{2,k+1}, & (14) \\
\mathbf{0} = \lambda\mathbf{U}_{k+1} - \Lambda_{2,k+1}\mathbf{U}_{k+1} + \mu_k\mathbf{U}_{k+1}(\mathbf{V}_k - \mathbf{V}_{k+1})^{\mathrm{T}}\mathbf{U}_{k+1}, & (15) \\
\mathbf{0} = \lambda\mathbf{V}_{k+1} - \Lambda_{2,k+1}^{\mathrm{T}}\mathbf{V}_{k+1}, & (16)
\end{cases}
$$

where the equalites (13)-(16) are derived from the updated rules in both (9) and (10). Then, based on the given assumptions, it is easy to obtain that the sequences of both $\{\Lambda_{1,k}\}$ and $\{\Lambda_{2,k}\}$ are all boundedness.

Secondly, we prove that the boundedness of sequence $\{(\mathbf{x}_k, \mathbf{Z}_k, \mathbf{U}_k, \mathbf{V}_k)\}$. Actually, by the alternative iteration procedures in (5)-(11), we have

$$
\begin{aligned}
&\mathcal{L}_{\mu_k}(\mathbf{x}_{k+1}, \mathbf{Z}_{k+1}, \mathbf{U}_{k+1}, \mathbf{V}_{k+1}, \Lambda_{1,k}, \Lambda_{2,k}) \\
&\leq \mathcal{L}_{\mu_k}(\mathbf{x}_k, \mathbf{Z}_k, \mathbf{U}_k, \mathbf{V}_k, \Lambda_{1,k}, \Lambda_{2,k}, \Lambda_{3,k}) \\
&= \frac{\mu_k + \mu_{k-1}}{2\mu_{k-1}^2} \sum_{j=1}^{2} \|\Lambda_{j,k} - \Lambda_{j,k-1}\|^2 \\
&\quad + \mathcal{L}_{\mu_{k-1}}(\mathbf{x}_k, \mathbf{Z}_k, \mathbf{U}_k, \mathbf{V}_k, \Lambda_{1,k-1}, \Lambda_{2,k-1}, \Lambda_{3,k-1}).
\end{aligned}
\tag{17}
$$

Then iterating the inequality (17), and combining it with (4) and the above conclusions, we can reformulate the objective inequality and further achieve the boundedness of each term through the involved relationships, i.e.,

---

[1] The detailed convergence proofs of optimization algorithms for the case $p = 1$, i.e., ℓ_1FTLR, and $p = 2$, i.e., ℓ_2FTLR, of this work will be appeared in the extended manuscript.

$$\mathcal{L}_{\mu_k}(\mathbf{x}_{k+1}, \mathbf{Z}_{k+1}, \mathbf{U}_{k+1}, \mathbf{V}_{k+1}, \Lambda_{1,k}, \Lambda_{2,k})$$

$$= \frac{1}{p}\|\mathbf{y} - \mathbf{D}\mathbf{x}_{k+1}\|_{\ell_p} + \frac{\lambda}{2}\left(\|\mathbf{U}_{k+1}\|^2 + \|\mathbf{V}_{k+1}\|^2\right)$$

$$+ \frac{\mu}{2}\left\|\mathbf{Z}_{k+1} - \mathbf{D}\mathrm{Diag}(\mathbf{x}_{k+1}) + \frac{\Lambda_{1,k}}{\mu_k}\right\|^2 - \frac{1}{2\mu_k}\|\Lambda_{1,k}\|^2$$

$$+ \frac{\mu_k}{2}\left\|\mathbf{Z}_{k+1} - \mathbf{U}_{k+1}\mathbf{V}_{k+1}^{\mathrm{T}} + \frac{\Lambda_{2,k}}{\mu_k}\right\|^2 - \frac{1}{2\mu_k}\|\Lambda_{2,k}\|^2. \tag{18}$$

It follows from the nonnegative property and the boundedness of dual variables that the primal sequences $\{\mathbf{x}_k\}$, $\{\mathbf{Z}_k\}$, $\{\mathbf{U}_k\}$ and $\{\mathbf{V}_k\}$ can also guaranteed to be boundedness through (18). More further, by virtue of the Bolzano-Weierstrass theorem, it is easy to conclude that each bounded variable sequence must exist a convergent subsequence.   □

Theorem 1. *Let* $\{\mathcal{T}_k = (\mathbf{x}_k, \mathbf{Z}_k, \mathbf{U}_k, \mathbf{V}_k, \Lambda_{1,k}, \Lambda_{2,k}, \Lambda_{3,k})\}$ *be the generated sequence, and the same assumptions with **Lemma** 1.* $\mu_k(\mathbf{Z}_{k+1} - \mathbf{Z}_k) \to \mathbf{0}$, $\mu_k(\mathbf{V}_k - \mathbf{V}_{k+1}) \to \mathbf{0}$ *and* $\mu_k\left(\mathbf{U}_{k+1}\mathbf{V}_{k+1}^{\mathrm{T}} - \mathbf{U}_k\mathbf{V}_k^{\mathrm{T}}\right) \to \mathbf{0}$ *are assumed to hold. Then there exists at least one accumulation point, e.g.,* $\{\mathcal{T}_*\}$, *satisfying the KKT conditions of function (4), and* $(\mathbf{x}_*, \mathbf{Z}_*, \mathbf{U}_*, \mathbf{V}_*)$ *is a stationary point of problem (3).*

Proof. Without loss of generality, we can conclude from **Lemma** 1 that $\mathcal{T}_{k_j} \to \mathcal{T}_*$ as $j \to +\infty$. Thus it follows from (9)-(10) that, for $j \to +\infty$,

$$\mathbf{0} \leftarrow \mathbf{Z}_* - \mathbf{D}\mathrm{Diag}(\mathbf{x}_*), \quad \mathbf{0} \leftarrow \mathbf{Z}_* - \mathbf{U}_*\mathbf{V}_*^{\mathrm{T}}, \tag{19}$$

hold for the existed accumulation point $\{(\mathbf{x}_*, \mathbf{Z}_*, \mathbf{U}_*, \mathbf{V}_*)\}$ and the boundedness of subsequence $\{(\Lambda_{1,k_j}, \Lambda_{2,k_j})\}$. Obviously, this can guarantee the dual feasibility condition. Further, we prove the primal feasibility conditions by virtue of first-order optimality conditions (13)-(16) and the updated rules in (5)-(8) for setting $k = k_j$, then using $\mathcal{T}_{k_j} \to \mathcal{T}_*$ again, it is easy to obtain

$$\begin{cases} \mathbf{0} = -\mathrm{Diag}(\mathbf{x}_*)\mathbf{D}^{\mathrm{T}}\Lambda_{1,*} + \mathbf{D}^{\mathrm{T}}\left(\mathbf{D}\mathbf{x}_* - \mathbf{y}\right), & (20) \\ \mathbf{0} = \Lambda_{1,k+1} + \Lambda_{2,*}, & (21) \\ \mathbf{0} = \lambda\mathbf{U}_* - \Lambda_{2,*}\mathbf{U}_*, \ \mathbf{0} = \lambda\mathbf{V}_* - \Lambda_{2,*}^{\mathrm{T}}\mathbf{V}_*, & (22) \end{cases}$$

where we stress that the given assumptions and the updated dual variables can lead to this conclusion according to (19) and series of computations. In detail, we here consider the case of $p = 2$, i.e., ℓ_2FTLR for the theoretical convergence guarantee. Similarly, the other case, i.e., ℓ_1FTLR with $p = 1$, can also be conducted to guarantee the convergence analysis along this routine though it may be very challenging because of involving more variables. It should be special noted that the KKT optimality conditions are actually reduced to the stationary and primal feasibility ones. Thus, $\mathcal{T}_*$ satisfies the KKT conditions and $\{(\mathbf{x}_*, \mathbf{Z}_*, \mathbf{U}_*, \mathbf{V}_*)\}$ is a stationary point.   □

Table 1. The comparisons of clustering accuracy (%) and timing consumptions (in seconds) for the involved methods on three real-world databases

Clustering tasks	Evaluations	SSC	LRR	LSR	CASS	ℓ_2FTLR
Yale B	Accuracy	92.8	97.2	96.6	97.5	97.5
(30,320)	Time	0.5 s	3.6 s	<0.1 s	99.5 s	82.2 s
USPS	Accuracy	72.4	87.6	93.0	93.4	93.6
(50,500)	Time	2.1 s	8.8 s	<0.1 s	707.2 s	612.1 s
MNIST	Accuracy	73.6	80.4	87.2	88.0	89.7
(100,500)	Time	2.5 s	9.6 s	<0.1 s	981.8 s	732.3 s

4 Numerical Experiments

This section will show the superiority of proposed algorithms to the practical application for subspace clustering [11,14], in which the databases include Yale B, USPS and MNIST and the comparison methods include SSC[2], LRR[3], LSR[4] and CASS[5], we achieve the clustering accuracy by using the Normalized Cuts technique for the obtained coefficient matrix and choosing the proper value for estimating d. Note that the data matrices are respectively projected onto 30, 50 and 100-dimensional subspace for each dataset by PCA. The parameters are manually tuned for each method and we report the qualitative and quantitative comparisons as well as the timing consumptions in Table 1 and Fig. 1. All of the following experiments are performed by Matlab2016b on a personal computer with 8.0 GB of RAM and Intel Core i7-7700 CPU@3.60 GHz. Based upon the numerical results, we have the following observations:

Table 1 lists the evaluation comparisons for clustering accuracy and timing costs. The proposed ℓ_2FTLR can achieve higher clustering accuracy, i.e., 97.5%, 93.6% and 89.7%, than the compared ones like SSC, LRR and LSR, which have the fewer timing costs, i.e., less than 10 s. It also has the less timing consumptions than CASS in the experimental databases. The superiority of computational efficiency seems clear over CASS except other methods. The evaluation results further verify the advantages derived from the adaptive merits of trace lasso and the usage of decomposable strategy.

Figure 1 provides the comparisons of both plotted curves for clustering accuracy (a) and stopping values (b) and visual result for the affinity matrix (c), in which the effects of several parameters are discussed for the numerical results and the norms $\| \cdot \|_\infty$ in (12) have the non-increasing property. Besides, we verify the consistence of both theoretical results and experimental ones from the convergence curves, and also tune the values of parameters,

---

[2] https://khoury.northeastern.edu/home/eelhami/codes.htm.
[3] https://zhouchenlin.github.io/lrr(motion-face).zip.
[4] https://github.com/canyilu/LSR.
[5] https://github.com/canyilu/LibADMM.

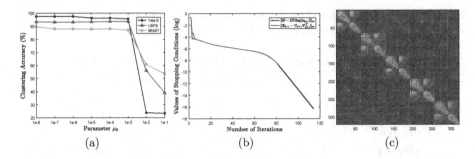

Fig. 1. The comparisons of plotted curves and visual result of ℓ_2FTLR solutions for the involved parameters and databases under various settings

e.g., $\mu_0 \in \{1e-8, 1e-7, ..., 1e-2, 1e-1\}$, $\lambda \in \{1e-5, 1e-4, ..., 1e-1, 1.0, 5.0\}$, carefully to get the best clustering accuracy as possible.

It is mentioned that the proposed iteration algorithm can achieve less time consumptions, which are slightly less than CASS, but more time-consuming than other three clustering methods. The reason is that both ℓ_2FTLR and CASS are related with the computations of SVD and the matrix inverse and multiplier, and both LSR and SSC have the higher computational efficiency. In a word, the numerical results in both Table 1 and Fig. 1 can show the quantitative and qualitative comparisons for the clustering tasks to the real-world databases.

5   Conclusions

In this paper, we provide the theoretical analysis of nonconvex ADMM with multiple variables, which aim to optimize the factored trace lasso based linear regression problems. The optimization programming does not involve the inner loops and each of subproblems can be guaranteed to have the closed-form solver. The main merits are to reduce the computational efficiency and achieve the nearly performance compared with the related methods in the numerical experiments. Finally, the numerical results on several real-world databases can show the superiority of our proposed methodology for subspace clustering.

Acknowledgment. The authors would like to the anonymous reviewers for their valuable comments. This work was supported in part by the National Natural Science Fund for Distinguished Young Scholars under Grant 61725301, in part by the National Natural Science Foundation of China (Major Program) under Grant 61590923, in part by the China Postdoctoral Science Foundation under Grant 2019M651415 and 2020T130191, in part by the National Science Fund of China under Grant 61973124, and Grant 61906067, in part by the Natural Science Foundation of the Jiangsu Higher Education Institutions of China under Grant 19KJB510022, and in part by the Research Start-up Funds for the Introduction of High-level Talents at Jiangsu Police Institute under Grant JSPIGKZ.

References

1. Grave, E., Obozinski, G., Bach, F.: Trace Lasso: a trace norm regularization for correlated designs. In: Proceeding of Neural Information Processing System (NeurIPS), pp. 2187–2195 (2011)
2. Shang, F., Cheng, J., Liu, Y., Luo, Z., Lin, Z.: Bilinear factor matrix norm minimization for robust PCA: algorithms and applications. IEEE Trans. Pattern Anal. Mach. Intell. 40(9), 2066–2080 (2018)
3. Zhang, H., Yang, J., Xie, J., Qian, J., Zhang, B.: Weighted sparse coding regularized nonconvex matrix regression for robust face recognition. Inf. Sci. 394–395, 1–17 (2017)
4. Yang, J., Luo, L., Qian, J., Tai, Y., Zhang, F., Xu, Y.: Nuclear norm based matrix regression with applications to face recognition with occlusion and illumination changes. IEEE Trans. Pattern Anal. Mach. Intell. 39(1), 156–171 (2017)
5. Bouwmans, T., Sobral, A., Javed, S., Jung, S.K., Zahzah, E.H.: Decomposition into low-rank plus additive matrices for background/foreground separation: a review for a comparative evaluation with a large-scale dataset. Comput. Sci. Rev. 23, 1–71 (2017)
6. Wright, J., Yang, A., Ganesh, A., Sastry, S., Ma, Y.: Robust face recognition via sparse representation. IEEE Trans. Pattern Anal. Mach. Intell. 31(2), 210–227 (2009)
7. Zhang, L., Yang, M., Feng, X.: Sparse representation or collaborative representation: Which helps face recognition? In: Proceeding of International Conference on Computer and Vision (ICCV), pp. 471–478 (2011)
8. Elhamifar, E., Vidal, R.: Sparse subspace clustering: algorithm, theory, and applications. IEEE Trans. Pattern Anal. Mach. Intell. 35(11), 2765–2781 (2013)
9. Lu, C.-Y., Min, H., Zhao, Z.-Q., Zhu, L., Huang, D.-S., Yan, S.: Robust and efficient subspace segmentation via least squares regression. In: Fitzgibbon, A., Lazebnik, S., Perona, P., Sato, Y., Schmid, C. (eds.) ECCV 2012. LNCS, vol. 7578, pp. 347–360. Springer, Heidelberg (2012). https://doi.org/10.1007/978-3-642-33786-4_26
10. Wang, J., Lu, C., Wang, M., Li, P., Yan, S., Hu, X.: Robust face recognition via adaptive sparse representation. IEEE Trans. Cybern. 44(12), 2368–2378 (2014)
11. Lu, C., Feng, J., Lin, Z., Yan, S.: Correlation adaptive subspace segmentation by trace lasso. In: Proceeding of International Conference Computer Vision (ICCV), pp. 1345–1352 (2013)
12. Liu, G., Lin, Z., Yan, S., Sun, J., Yu, Y., Ma, Y.: Robust recovery of subspace structures by low-rank representation. IEEE Trans. Pattern Anal. Mach. Intell. 35(1), 171–184 (2013)
13. Srebro, N., Rennie, J., Jaakkola, T.S.: Maximum-margin matrix factorization. In: Proceeding of Neural Information Processing System (NeurIPS), pp. 1329–1336 (2004)
14. Zhang, H., Yang, J., Shang, F., Gong, C., Zhang, Z.: LRR for subspace segmentation via tractable Schatten-p norm minimization and factorization. IEEE Trans. Cyber. 49(5), 1722–1734 (2019)
15. Boyd, S., Parikh, N., Chu, E., Peleato, B., Eckstein, J.: Distributed optimization and statistical learning via the alternating direction method of multipliers. Found. Trends. Mach. Learn. 3(1), 1–122 (2011)
16. Lin, Z., Chen, M., Wu, L., Ma, Y.: The augmented Lagrange multiplier method for exact recovery of corrupted low-rank matrices. arXiv preprint arXiv:1009.5055 (2010)

17. Lin, Z., Liu, R., Su, Z.: Linearized alternating direction method with adaptive penalty for low-rank representation. In: Proceeding Neural Information Processing System (NeurIPS), pp. 612–620 (2011)
18. Liu, R., Lin, Z., Su, Z.: Linearized alternating direction method with parallel splitting and adaptive penalty for separable convex programs in machine learning. In: Proceeding of Asian Conference Machine Learning (ACML), pp. 116–132 (2013)
19. Chen, C., He, B., Ye, Y., Yuan, X.: The direct extension of ADMM for multi-block convex minimization problems is not necessarily convergent. Math. Program. **155**, 57–79 (2014). https://doi.org/10.1007/s10107-014-0826-5
20. Lin, T., Ma, S., Zhang, S.: On the global linear convergence of the ADMM with multiblock variables. SIAM J. Optim. **25**(3), 1478–1497 (2015)

Path Planning and Simulation Based on Cumulative Error Estimation

Can Wang[✉], Chensheng Cheng, Dianyu Yang, Feihu Zhang, and Guang Pan

Northwestern Polytechnical University, Xi'an, China
wangcan2017@mail.nwpu.edu.cn

Abstract. Path planning plays a significant role in robot navigation applications, as path exploration ability requires the knowledge of both the kinematics and the environments. Most of the current methods consider the planning process alone instead of combining the planning results with tracking control, which leads to a significant reduction in the availability of the path, especially in complex scenarios with missing GPS and low positioning sensor accuracy. This paper proposes a reinforcement learning-based path planning algorithm, which aims to consider the errors caused by the robot's motion during the dead-reckoning process and effectively reduces the cumulative error within the optimization process. The simulation conclusion in the 2D scene verifies the effectiveness of the algorithm for reducing the cumulative error.

Keywords: Reinforcement learning · Path planning · Cumulative error estimation

1 Introduction

Motion planning is a series of tasks that enable the robot from its current position to the target position. In general, it relied on robot's geometric size and dynamic model [1], environment map [2], the initial state and target state [3]. The planning task focuses on structured scenarios to find a collision-free path from the initial state to the target state through multiple dimensions [4]. According to multi-perspective requirements, it could be divided into the shortest path, the smallest energy loss, the safest path [5], etc.

Traditional path planning includes relies on heuristic modes range from A* and D*, RRT* which depends on sampling, and polynomial method which depends on mathematics [6], etc. In real applications, it is not feasible to combine the robot's motion attributes in the province with the support of inaccurate sensors, which will cause obvious tracking errors in a long-term mission. Considering the trade-off between single and complexity, machine learning-based approaches is considerable as a promising way to perform offline learning based on the robot kinematics model and sensor error statistical parameters to achieve more precise planning and control functions. By building an experience value evaluation network and increasing dense connections, and adopting a parallel

© Springer Nature Singapore Pte Ltd. 2021
F. Sun et al. (Eds.): ICCSIP 2020, CCIS 1397, pp. 131–141, 2021.
https://doi.org/10.1007/978-981-16-2336-3_12

exploration structure when the robot is drifting, Lv et al. have achieved an increase in algorithm speed, success rate and accuracy [7]. In the Q-Learning algorithm, Peifang et al. use the combination of gravitational potential field and environmental trap search as a priori information to initialize the Q-value, eliminate the Q-value iteration of the concave trap area, and accelerate the iterative speed of the algorithm [8].

The conventional path planning process does not consider the robot's motion effect after path planning or considers the dynamic characteristics and performs maximum fault tolerance planning [9]. The task is limited to the motion planning stage, and the control strategy is not combined to optimize the planning and motion results. However, in the following process, as sensor registration and other reasons, system errors and bias deviations are generated, which are inevitable. Some people also have made similar efforts. Carlson et al. combined path planning and motion simulation, proposed and compared three different strategies for estimating the change of the robot's motion, effectively reducing the probability of collisions and avoided the source of error in industrial scenarios [10]. Eaton et al. proposed a robust Partially Observable Markov Decision Process (POMDP) formula, which is evaluated by tracking error and observation percentage and provides path planning and target tracking capabilities in the case of limited observations [11].

The proposed method bridges gaps between the systematic errors generated during the movements, and the path planning process with the reinforcement learning algorithm to address the localization problem due to cumulative errors. The key novelty is the theoretical modeling from a systematic view of reinforcement learning-based path planning problem in real scenarios. It will learn autonomously and find the optimal path according to the task requirements.

This paper is structured as follows: The second part analyzes the mathematical representation and statistical characteristics of the system error generated by the robot, and calculates its bias deviation and scale deviation. The third part is based on the calculation results, adding reward parameters to the reinforcement learning path planning process and adjusting the algorithm process. In the fourth part, simulation planning results are compared. Finally, the full text is summarized in the fifth part.

2   Related Work

Assumed the odometry sensor measurement presented in polar coordinates, and there is noise between the measurement and ground truth at each step. Hence, the robot has to correct its positions regularly. When the global positioning system is unavailable, the robot uses the attitude sensor and inertial sensor (gyro and accelerometer) to perform ranging-based localization as dead reckoning by measuring angle and speed changes robot's positioning purpose.

Although it is relatively high-precision positioning information, this problem's main challenge is the drift caused by the relative noise measurement. In general, the cumulative error non-linearly increases with distance or time has not be numerical analyzed yet. To address such issue, the proposed approach utilizes the relative noise measurement to study the cumulative error growth rate [12]. Finally, incremental error growth is applied to the reinforcement learning path planning algorithm to the cumulative errors.

The position of the robot in the process of traveling will be estimated through the accumulation of relevant measurement values (see Fig. 1). Define the measurement:

$$\theta_n^m = \bar{\theta}_n + \tilde{\theta}_n; d_n^m = \bar{d}_n + \tilde{d}_n \tag{1}$$

where n is the time index, d, θ represents relative distance and direction between consecutive frames. The pose measurement (θ_n^m, d_n^m) is consisted of ground truth $(\bar{\theta}_n, \bar{d}_n)$ and error $(\tilde{\theta}_n, \tilde{d}_n)$ with standard deviation δ_θ and δ_d.

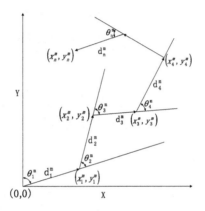

Fig. 1. Relationship between robot relative measurement and position.

Based on the dead-reckoning, the trajectory of the robot in cartesian coordinate system is then calculated as:

$$x_n^m = \sum_{i=1}^{n} \left(d_i^m \sin \sum_{j=1}^{i} \theta_j^m \right) \tag{2}$$

$$y_n^m = \sum_{i=1}^{n} \left(d_i^m \cos \sum_{j=1}^{i} \theta_j^m \right) \tag{3}$$

Due to the drift accumulation caused by noisy measurement, the position error increases infinitely. It is quite challenging to estimate the cumulative error without the ground truth; however, the corresponding statistical characteristics are feasible.

The trajectory can also be expressed as a combination of true value and cumulative error:

$$\widetilde{x_n} = \sum_{i=1}^{n} \overline{d_i} \left[\sin \sum_{j=1}^{i} \overline{\theta_j} \left(\cos \sum_{j=1}^{i} \widetilde{\theta_j} - 1 \right) + \cos \sum_{j=1}^{i} \overline{\theta_j} \sin \sum_{j=1}^{i} \widetilde{\theta_j} \right]$$
$$+ \sum_{i=1}^{n} \widetilde{d_i} \left[\sin \sum_{j=1}^{i} \overline{\theta_j} \cos \sum_{j=1}^{i} \widetilde{\theta_j} + \cos \sum_{j=1}^{i} \overline{\theta_j} \sin \sum_{j=1}^{i} \widetilde{\theta_j} \right] \tag{4}$$

Cumulative errors are correlated, and each error depends on the true value. The expected and variance of the cumulative error are estimated based on the statistical properties of the relative measurements:

$$\mu_n \left(\overline{\theta}, \overline{d} \right) = \begin{bmatrix} E\left[\widetilde{x} | \overline{\theta}, \overline{d} \right] \\ E\left[\widetilde{y} | \overline{\theta}, \overline{d} \right] \end{bmatrix} = \begin{bmatrix} \sum_{i=1}^{n} \overline{d_i} \left[\sin \sum_{j=1}^{i} \overline{\theta_j} \left(e^{-\frac{i\delta_\theta^2}{2}} - 1 \right) \right] \\ \sum_{i=1}^{n} \overline{d_i} \left[\cos \sum_{j=1}^{i} \overline{\theta_j} \left(e^{-\frac{i\delta_\theta^2}{2}} - 1 \right) \right] \end{bmatrix} \tag{5}$$

The variance in x direction is expressed as:

$$\text{var}\left(\widetilde{x} | \overline{\theta}, \overline{d} \right) = E\left[\widetilde{x} | \overline{\theta}, \overline{d} \right] - E^2 \left[\widetilde{x} | \overline{\theta}, \overline{d} \right]$$
$$= A + B + C - E^2 \left[\widetilde{x} | \overline{\theta}, \overline{d} \right] \tag{6}$$

where:

$$A = \sum_{i=1}^{n} \overline{d_i^2} \begin{bmatrix} \sin^2 \sum_{j=1}^{i} \overline{\theta_j} \left(0.5 e^{-2i\delta_\theta^2} + 1.5 - 2e^{-\frac{i\delta_\theta^2}{2}} \right) \\ +0.5\cos^2 \sum_{j=1}^{i} \overline{\theta_j} \left(e^{-2i\delta_\theta^2} + 1 \right) \end{bmatrix} \tag{7}$$

$$B = 2\sum_{i=1}^{n-1} \sum_{p=1+i}^{n} \overline{d_i d_p}$$
$$\left\{ \begin{array}{l} \sin^2 \sum_{j=1}^{i} \overline{\theta_j} \cos \Delta\overline{\theta} \begin{bmatrix} 1 + 0.5 \left(1 + e^{-2i\delta_\theta^2} \right) e^{-0.5(p-i)\delta_\theta^2} \\ e^{-0.5i\delta_\theta^2} - e^{-0.5i\delta_\theta^2} e^{-0.5(p-i)\delta_\theta^2} \end{bmatrix} \\ + \sin \sum_{j=1}^{i} \overline{\theta_j} \sin \Delta\overline{\theta} \cos \sum_{j=1}^{i} \overline{\theta_j} \begin{bmatrix} 1 + 0.5 \left(1 + e^{-2i\delta_\theta^2} \right) e^{-0.5(p-i)\delta_\theta^2} + 1 \\ -e^{-0.5i\delta_\theta^2} - e^{-0.5i\delta_\theta^2} e^{-0.5(p-i)\delta_\theta^2} \\ -0.5 \left(1 - e^{-2i\delta_\theta^2} \right) e^{-0.5(p-i)\delta_\theta^2} \end{bmatrix} \\ + \cos^2 \sum_{j=1}^{i} \overline{\theta_j} \cos \Delta\overline{\theta} \cdot 0.5 \left(1 - e^{-2i\delta_\theta^2} \right) e^{-0.5(p-i)\delta_\theta^2} \end{array} \right\} \tag{8}$$

$$C = \sum_{i=1}^{n} \left[0.5\sin^2 \sum_{j=1}^{i} \overline{\theta_j} \left(e^{-2i\delta_\theta^2} + 1 \right) + 0.5\cos^2 \sum_{j=1}^{i} \overline{\theta_j} \left(1 - e^{-2i\delta_\theta^2} \right) \right] \tag{9}$$

3   Path Planning Method Based on Reinforcement Learning

3.1   Q-Learning Path Planning Algorithm

The Q-Learning algorithm is an off-policy strategy evaluation method based on reinforcement learning, which uses Q-estimation to make decisions and

Q-reality to perform update learning. It assumes that the interaction between the agent and the environment can be viewed as a Markov decision process, that is, the current state and selected actions of agent determine a fixed state transition probability distribution, the next state, and get an immediate reward. The update of the Q-value is realized through the Q-table, and its state-action value function is expressed as:

$$q^T(s,a) = q^{T-1}(s,a) + \frac{1}{N}\left[r(s') + \lambda max_{a'}q^{T-1}(s,a) - q^{T-1}(s,a)\right] \quad (10)$$

where N is the cumulative quantity, r is the return sequence, λ is the attenuation factor, a and $a\prime$ represent the current and next selected actions.

In view of the fact that each decision is executed according to the maximum reward value estimated by Q, it will be easy to reach the problem of local optimal solution. The $\varepsilon - greedy$ method is introduced. This paper has passed multiple tests and finally used $\varepsilon = 0.95$ for simulation.

3.2   Path Planning Strategy

Whereas the Q-Learning algorithm does not need to follow the interaction sequence, it only needs to choose the behavior that optimizes the value at the next moment. In the path planning process, the Q-Learning algorithm is embodied in each discrete area, selecting the action to make the robot reach the destination. This action maximizes its value in the reward and punishment function [13]. This paper uses the Q-Learning method as a learning method for reinforcement learning, and performs the discrete learning reinforcement process in a rasterized environment.

In reinforcement learning, the Q-table is first established and initialized according to the action space and the state space. In each iteration process, the robot reaches the obstacle area, or the robot reaches the end state, the iteration ends, that is, the "trial and error" process of the agent. After each iteration, the robot updates the corresponding grid and corresponding action values in the Q-table according to the selection of each step of the action and the reward and punishment strategy. After multiple iterations, the agent's action choices will tend to a fixed sequence, the path planning result. According to the idea of the Q-Learning algorithm, we need to design a reward and punishment function strategy that enables the agent to reach the destination quickly and smoothly. Simultaneously, in strengthening the reward and punishment, it is required to achieve the robot's ability to reduce accumulated errors.

According to the qualitative and quantitative analysis results of the robot's cumulative error, the fewer turning movements the robot performs during the movement, the smaller the robot's cumulative error. Therefore, we innovatively change the reward strategy to reward the robot's movement along a straight line during the learning process, but not reward the robot's turning action. After several iterative processes, the agent will always strengthen the action that tends to the target point and fewer turns according to the reward and

Table 1. Reward/penalty settings for robots

	Reward/penalty	Value
Reaching the obstacle area	Penalty	−1
Reaching the end	Reward	100
Action does not travel in a straight line	Penalty	−0.0001

punishment strategy to achieve the desired result. See Table 1 for the effects of setting specific rewards and penalties during path planning. The flowchart of the entire reinforcement learning path planning strategy is shown in Fig. 2.

4   Simulation

In the process of reinforcement learning global path planning, the path passes near the edge of the obstacle area, and there are many turns as the randomness is too high. The robot is likely to hit obstacles during the actual tracking with the cumulative error increase. As the number of iterations increases, the algorithm can find the destination more easily and quickly, and the path becomes better and better. Simultaneously, with a probability of ε for random action selection, the convergence time and the number of reinforcement learning will not be a particular value. According to multiple simulation experiments, the reinforcement learning algorithm can find the best path after more than 8,000 learnings. Since each feasible path found by the algorithm may differ, we choose a typical path for analysis.

We first assume that the initial global map size is 100×100 m and the minimum resolution of the map is 0.02 m, that is, each grid represents an area of 0.02×0.02 m, with a total of 5000×5000 pixels see Fig. 3. Given the discrete nature of reinforcement learning and the timeliness of data processing, we perform smooth processing through a cost function that includes kinematics and curvature constraints [14]. The final map after raster processing is shown in Fig. 4.

Let's first assume that the initial state of the robot itself is toward the right by default, the initial position is at (0.5, 0.5), the posture of the target point is by default to the right, and the target position is at (97.5, 97.5). In the general planning results, the robot path can reach the endpoint in a relatively normal path. Considering the cumulative error of the robot odometer, we performed the actual path analysis under the cumulative error, and set the sensor angular error and positioning error to meet N (0,1) and N (0,0.1). In the path planning results, the paths affected by the cumulative error under the results of the traditional reinforcement learning planning algorithm are shown in Fig. 5, where the green path is the initial planned path and the red is the path affected by the odometer cumulative error (similarly hereinafter). We can find that the robot's cumulative error is still large, especially in paths with many turns, if the robot

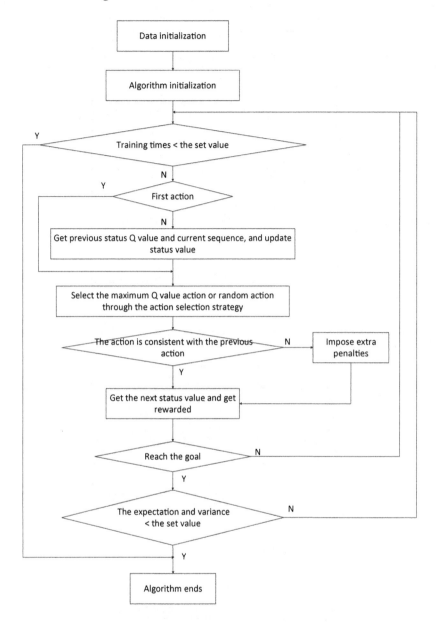

Fig. 2. Reinforcement learning path planning flowchart considering cumulative errors.

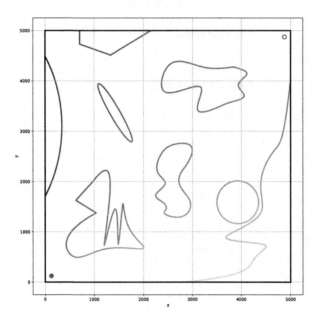

Fig. 3. Initial global map

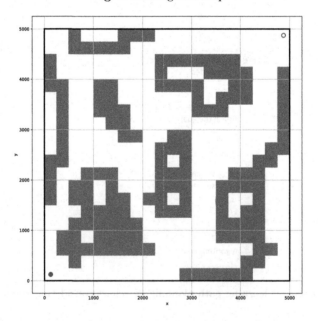

Fig. 4. Rasterized map after convex target processing

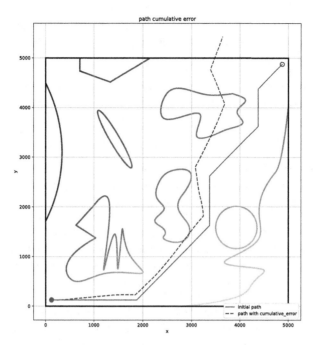

Fig. 5. General reinforcement learning path planning results and cumulative error estimation

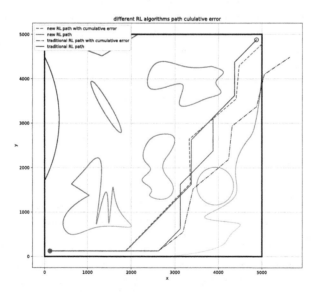

Fig. 6. Comparison of planning effects of the two algorithms

only relies on its inertial navigation for positioning, it will easily deviate from the predetermined path.

We adopt the proposed algorithm to obtain new planning results (see Fig. 6). And found that the number of rotations of the path planned by the proposed algorithm is reduced, the cumulative error is relatively small, and the path looks simpler. Although the robot's path has a certain deviation under the influence of the cumulative error, as the qualitative control of the planning process, the error is within a certain range, which does not affect the robot's navigation safety.

5   Conclusion

Aiming at the problem of path planning for robots in the absence of a global positioning environment, a reinforcement learning path planning algorithm based on robot motion characteristics is proposed. First, the pre-processing under the robot motion planning is performed on the prior map to prevent the robot from entering the smaller concave area and falling into the local closed area. Secondly, the reinforcement learning algorithm is improved, considering the cumulative error caused by the robot sensor and the robot's positioning error during the tracking process. In the algorithm learning process, dynamic constraints are creatively added to enable the robot to track the planned path's navigation path. By improving the original method, the cumulative error estimation of the path planning process is significantly reduced. The simulation experiments verify that the strategy proposed in this paper can effectively reduce the robot's cumulative error under the premise of meeting the robot's global planning requirements in a complex environment, which will reflect the advantages of the algorithm in the process of robot tracking.

The movement of the robot is a continuous process, which is also our future consideration. The robot's action selection and angle change are used as the primary data source and optimization goal of cumulative error analysis. Finally, the robot path planning simulation and experimental research for the specific GPS lack are realized in the 2/3D scenario.

Acknowledgments. This work was supported by the National Natural Science Foundation of China (NSFC) under Grans 61703335.

References

1. Bidot, J., Karlsson, L., Lagriffoul, F., Saffiotti, A.: Geometric backtracking for combined task and motion planning in robotic systems. Artif. Intell. **247**(Jun.), 229–265 (2013)
2. Peng, Y., Green, P.N.: Environment mapping, map constructing, and path planning for underwater navigation of a low-cost μAUV in a cluttered nuclear storage pond. IAES Int. J. Robot. Autom. **8**(4), 277–292 (2019)
3. Choset, H., Lynch, K., Hutchinson, S., Kantor, G., Burgard, W., Kavraki, L., et al.: Principles of robot motion: theory, algorithms, and implementation ERRATA!!!!, p. 1 (2003)
4. Zeng, J., Qin, L., Hu, Y., Yin, Q., Hu, C.: Integrating a path planner and an adaptive motion controller for navigation in dynamic environments. Appl. Sci. **9**(7), 1384 (2019)

5. Ibraheem, I. K., Ajeil, F. H., Khan, Z. H.: Path planning of an autonomous mobile robot in a dynamic environment using modified bat swarm optimization. arXiv preprint arXiv:1807.05352 (2018)
6. Yilmaz, N.K., Evangelinos, C., Lermusiaux, P.F., Patrikalakis, N.M.: Path planning of autonomous underwater vehicles for adaptive sampling using mixed integer linear programming. IEEE J. Oceanic Eng. 33(4), 522–537 (2008)
7. Lv, L., Zhang, S., Ding, D., Wang, Y.: Path planning via an improved DQN-based learning policy. IEEE Access PP(99), 1 (2019)
8. Peifang, D., Zhian, Z., Xinhu, M., Shuo, Z.: Reinforcement learning path planning algorithm based on gravitational potential field and trap search. Comput. Eng. Appl. (2018)
9. Rolland, L.: Path planning kinematics simulation of CNC machine tools based on parallel manipulators. Mech. Mach. Sci. 29, 147–192 (2015). https://doi.org/10. 1007/978-3-319-14705-5-6
10. Carlson, J., Spensieri, D., Soderberg, R., Bohlin, R., Lindkvist, L.: Non-nominal path planning for robust robotic assembly. J. Manuf. Syst. 32, 429–435 (2013). https://doi.org/10.1016/j.jmsy.2013
11. Eaton, C.M., Chong, E.K.P., Maciejewski, A.A.: Robust UAV path planning using POMDP with limited FOV sensor. In: 2017 IEEE Conference on Control Technology and Applications (CCTA), pp. 1530–1535 (2017)
12. Zhang, F., Simon, C., Chen, G., Buckl, C., Knoll, A.: Cumulative error estimation from noisy relative measurements, pp. 1422–1429 (2013). https://doi.org/10.1109/ ITSC.2013.6728430
13. Su, M.-C., Huang, D.-Y., Chou, C.-H., Hsieh, C.-C.: A reinforcement-learning approach to robot navigation, vol. 1, pp. 665–669 (2004). https://doi.org/10.1109/ ICNSC.2004.1297519
14. Hernandez, J. D., Vidal, E., Vallicrosa, G., Galceran, E., Carreras, M.: Online path planning for autonomous underwater vehicles in unknown environments. In: IEEE International Conference on Robotics and Automation, pp. 1152–1157. IEEE (2015)

MIMF: Mutual Information-Driven Multimodal Fusion

Zhenhong Zou[1,2], Linhao Zhao[1,2], Xinyu Zhang[1,2(✉)], Zhiwei Li[1,2], Dafeng Jin[1,2], and Tao Luo[3]

[1] State Key Laboratory of Automotive Safety and Energy, Tsinghua University, Beijing 100084, China
xyzhang@tsinghua.edu.cn
[2] School of Vehicle and Mobility, Tsinghua University, Beijing 100084, China
[3] China North Vehicle Research Institute, Beijing 100072, China

Abstract. In this paper, we propose a novel adaptive multimodal fusion network MIMF that is driven by the mutual information between the input data and the target recognition pattern. Due to the variant weather and road conditions, the real scenes can be far more complicated than those in the training dataset. That constructs a non-ignorable challenge for multimodal fusion models that obey fixed fusion modes, especially for autonomous driving. To address the problem, we leverage mutual information for adaptive modal selection in fusion, which measures the relation between the input and target output. We therefore design a weight-fusion module based on MI, and integrate it into our feature fusion lane line segmentation network. We evaluate it with the KITTI and A2D2 datasets, in which we simulate the extreme malfunction of sensors like modality loss problem. The result demonstrates the benefit of our method in practical application, and informs the future research into development of multimodal fusion as well.

Keywords: Multimodal fusion · Mutual information · Dynamic algorithm · Autonomous driving

1 Introduction

Autonomous driving requires robust models to sense the environment with multiple sensors and generate the perception accordingly, however, though existing multimodal methods can perform well in most scenes, their fusion strategies may fail severely in some abnormal scenarios [1, 2]. For instance, bad weather like rainy and foggy days can put obstacles in the way of camera's work [3]. The sensors themselves also contain potential perception deviations such as the noise in the LiDAR point clouds intensity [4]. In addition to these external and internal problems, there is another common but disturbing trouble in practice, data streams from different sensors do not always match in time due to the hardware limitation [5]. As the result, these problems lead to the uncertainty in data, hence widen the model performance gap between the datasets and real conditions and prevent the application of multimodal fusion methods.

© Springer Nature Singapore Pte Ltd. 2021
F. Sun et al. (Eds.): ICCSIP 2020, CCIS 1397, pp. 142–150, 2021.
https://doi.org/10.1007/978-981-16-2336-3_13

In order to overcome the obstacles, researchers have proposed several approaches to enhance the robustness of models. Some research proposed to select a main modality like images, to guide the fusion detection [5, 6] depending on the prior knowledge of sensors under different conditions, but did not solve the problem yet. Others' work was about specific problems such as foggy [3] and illumination changes [7], which may not be universal for other cases. These methods either focused on a specific issue, or were not real robust models. Instead, Caltagirone et al. proposed to learn an adaptive fusion weight in the LiDAR-camera network [2]. Mario et al. [3] and Yang et al. [8] applied dropout to build adaptive models, while Kim et al. [9] used gate to decide which data to fuse. These solution focus on the balance in multimodal fusion. That is, how to select the proper sensor or feature dynamically, rather than using mixing them in a fixed way?

Inspired by the mutual information (MI) [10, 11], that measures the relation between two variables, people refer to the amount of information in models [11–15]. A network is supposed to reach its best during information acquisition. Therefore, the information maximization equals to the fusion efficiency maximization to some extent. To address efficient usage of MI, some research contributes to the MI estimation in neural network [12, 13]. Based on the previous work Deep InfoMax (DIM) [13], we proposed a novel MI-based data fusion that figures the weight for feature fusion dynamically. The key idea of our work is real-time calculation on the MI value of multimodal features and recognition targets, which further generalize the fusion tendentiousness on them. We build an end-to-end model and examine it on LiDAR-camera fusion lane line segmentation task on the KITTI and A2D2 datasets [16–18].

The rest of the article is organized as follows. In the Sect. 2, we provide the definition the adaptive multimodal fusion problem. In the Sect. 3, we first present the backbone of our LiDAR-camera fusion network, then illustrate the integration of DIM. In the Sect. 4, we present the experiment procedure, the results and discussion.

2 Problem Statement

Let $X = [X_1, \ldots, X_n]^T$ denotes the data of different modalities, W presents the weight matrix in neural networks, and Y denotes the target to be recognized. In deep learning, we train the model with the optimization goal

$$\widehat{W} := \mathrm{argmin}_W \|Y - WX\| + \|W\| \tag{1}$$

where the multiplication contains normal matrix multiplication and Hadamard product. Suppose $\{X_1, \ldots, X_n\}$ are coherent information source for recognition, for example, the LiDAR point clouds X_1 and camera images X_2 provide relative measurements of the same objects, although they are in different domains. For the common and basic fusion, weighted-sum as feature fusion, it can be formulated as,

$$Z(X) = AW_0[X_1, X_2]^T = W_0[\alpha_1 X_1, \alpha_2 X_2]^T \tag{2}$$

where $A = [\alpha_1 I, \alpha_2 I]^T$ and $W = W_1 A W_0$. Notice that $W_0 = [W_{01}, W_{02}]^T$ is individual for different modalities, that means for $W_0 X$ we use Hadamard product, but for $W_{0_i} X_i$ we use both matrix product and Hadamard product.

Then, Eq. 1 is written as,

$$\hat{W} := \operatorname{argmin}_W Y - W_1 Z(X) + W = \operatorname{argmin}_W Y - W_1 A W_0 X + W \qquad (3)$$

Now we consider the computation of A. Usually, A is an empirical preset coefficient matrix or is learned from the training data. However, in practical usage, the real-time collected $\hat{X}$ is different from the training set, that indicates the domain-gap between $A W_0 X$ and $A W_0 \hat{X}$, and constructs a severe bias in fusion. Therefore, the key is to figure out a dynamic adjustment algorithm for A. In the following section, we will present how to apply the mutual information to obtain it by $A \sim \mathrm{MI} := \mathrm{I}(X; Y)$.

3   MIMF Network

3.1   Multimodal Feature Fusion Network

In this paper, we select the common middle feature fusion (MF) as backbone network, which presents robustness in general tests and is regarded as the balance among early fusion, middle fusion, and late fusion [1]. We use an encoder-decoder architecture, in this way, the network can be easy to modify and compare the performance change. The network comprises two pipelines in the encoder for point clouds and images, with 3 convolutional blocks in both branches. To process more complex features in the images, we replace the convolutional blocks with ResNet-34 blocks except the first one. We fuse the features of two modalities by concatenation when two pipelines merge as shown in the Eq. 2. The information will be mix up in the following convolutional layers. Each convolutional block includes a convolution layer, a batch normalization layer, and a ReLU activation layer. The blocks in decoder distinguish the ones in the encoder for they use transposed convolution to recover the feature maps. In order to better utilize the raw information, we add skip-connection between the encoder layers and decoder layers. In MF, we do not assign a fusion weight, instead, the network learns the adaptive weight. But in MIMF, we embed the DIM module to provide a prior weight that can not only work as regularization, but also avoid influence of bad observations.

3.2   DIM Module for MI Estimation

DIM was proposed by Hjelm et al. [13]. Based on MINE [12], which is regarded as an efficient estimator for mutual information of two feature maps in neural networks. in this paper, we modify the DIM to fit our fusion network. For two variables X, Y, their mutual information $I(X; Y)$ is,

$$I(X; Y) = \Sigma_{x \in X} \Sigma_{y \in Y} p(x, y) \log \frac{p(x,y)}{p(x)p(y)} \qquad (4)$$

$$I(X; Y) = D_{KL}(P_{XY} \| P_X \otimes P_Y) \qquad (5)$$

where D_{KL} is the KL-divergence. It is defined as:

$$D_{KL}(P \| Q) := E_P \left[\log \frac{dP}{dQ} \right] \qquad (6)$$

We mark P_{XY} as J, and $P_X \otimes P_Y$ as M. By using the DV-distribution form and nature of KL-divergence, we obtain the lower bound $\hat{I}$ of $I(X; Y)$:

$$I(X; Y) \geq \hat{I}(X; Y) = E_J\left[T_\omega(x, y)\right] - \log E_M\left[e^{T_\omega(x,y)}\right] \tag{7}$$

where $T_\omega : x \times y \to \mathbb{R}$ is a function parameterized by ω that can be used in the Eq. 7 to approximate $I(X; Y)$. We simply present a sample of T_ω and consider it enough to the expected function [13]. Provided that the multimodal features X_1, X_2 have the same dimension, which can be achieved by feature alignment, and the size is (C, H, M, N). C is the number of channels in convolutional layers, and (H, M, N) is the size of a channel. We note the map in each channel as X_{i_n}, $n \in [1, C]$. Therefore, we rewrite the Eq. 7 as:

$$I\left(X_{i_n}; Y\right) \doteq \hat{I}\left(X_{i_n}; Y\right) = \log\left(\Sigma S e^{u-u_{max}}\right) + u_{max} - \log(\Sigma S) - \frac{\Sigma\left(u_{avg} \cdot S\right)}{\Sigma S} \tag{8}$$

where $S = 1 - \overline{S}$, and $\overline{S} = H \times H$ is a diagonal matrix. Besides, $U = X_n \times Y$, and u_{max} is the maximum value in matrix U, while u_{avg} is the average value. Therefore, the mutual information is represented as below, $C \in \{1, 2\}$ in our model:

$$I(X_i; Y) = \frac{1}{C} \sum_{n=1}^{C} I\left(X_{i_n}; Y\right) \tag{9}$$

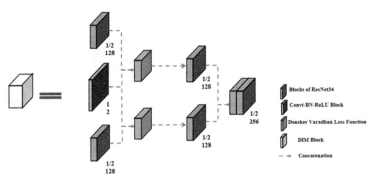

Fig. 1. The structure of DIM block in our fusion network. It adopts features from two modalities, the images and point clouds respectively, as X_1 and X_2, while taking the features from the last convolution layer as $\hat{Y}$. Then, DIM block figures out the mutual information $I\left(X_i, \hat{Y}\right)$.

3.3 Mutual Information-Driven Multimodal Fusion

Recurrent Training Process. In the Sect. 3.2, we present how to compute the MI. To apply it in the weighted-fusion model, we integrate it into the network and training-testing procedure as well. As shown in Fig. 1, we take two branches in the DIM block, which are for two data. DIM block computes the mutual information between them and the expected feature Y respectively. However, we cannot obtain Y ahead of the network computation. Instead, we make the time-continuity assumption: for each i, X_i is a given stable time sequence, that means $X_i^t \approx X_i^{t-1}$ and $Y^t \approx Y^{t-1}$. In autonomous driving, that indicates two frames of a sensor observations are similar because of the continuity of scenarios and events. With this assumption, when we acquire a well-trained model in test, we can treat the recognition of last frame as an approximation of the target at current time, especially in a sequence model. Obviously, the fault rate of the last recognition will be enlarged. But when DIM is integrated into a robust backbone, we can ignore it in most time, and use a reset strategy to reduce the cumulative error. However, we have only implemented a single-frame recognition model and lack enough time-series data, thus we simply use compute the current data cyclically. Specifically, we compute on it for the first time to simulate the 'last frame result', and use it in the second computation. Therefore, we finish a DIM process approximately in testing. The Fig. 2 presents the overall structure of MIMF. The yellow block is the DIM module, and the rest is the MF baseline. The RGB images and point clouds are processed in two separated pipelines in the encoder, and get fused in the DIM module. The sizes of feature maps are not changed in DIM. That means DIM is flexible for most models. When DIM outputs the $I\left(X_i, \hat{Y}\right)$ as above, we normalize them by

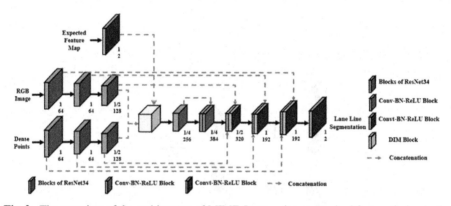

Fig. 2. The overview of the architecture of MIMF. It comprises a standard feature fusion in the middle of an encoder-decoder network, and the DIM block during fusion. Before fusion, MIMF has two individual pipelines to process different modal data.

$$\alpha_i = \frac{I\left(X_i, \hat{Y}\right)}{\Sigma I\left(X_i, \hat{Y}\right)} \tag{10}$$

MI as Fusion and Regularization. With Eq. 10 we obtain the fusion weight A in Eq. 2. As a prior knowledge of the target of the tasks, MIMF pre-fetches data with a bias. It further forces the fusion models to focus on more relevant information in testing. The bias makes it unwilling to get affected by the fault measurements or information loss data in complex scenes in practice. In addition, we observe that MIMF performs better on the normal data. We explain the result with the random regularization effect which is similar with the dropout. As MI is independent to the network or data, instead, it is determined by both the data and target simultaneously, it will be treated as a random process under a distribution different from those of the noised data. Therefore, by learning the data-independent input, the network avoids over-fitting the data. Notice our method can only operate the case when as least one modality has good observation. Otherwise, the dominated data will lead to serious problem.

4 Experiment

4.1 Dataset and Metrics

To evaluate our models, we select pictures by ignoring the roads with intersections or without forward lines. Finally, we pick up around 400 data pairs from the KITTI road detection track [17], and around 1000 pairs from the A2D2 dataset [18]. We use 60% of the data as the training set, 10% for validation and rest for testing. The image resolution is 1242×375 in KITTI, and 1920×1208 in A2D2. KITTI uses a 64-line Velodyne to generate point clouds, but A2D2 combines one 8-line and two 16-line LiDARs. The difference in LiDARs causes the gap in performance, but it would not matter in the evaluation of the adaptive fusion. Because KITTI dataset has no lane line labels, we add pixel-level annotation to it by hand. Labeled lines are supposed to be not only parallel to the driving direction but also on the driving area. To reduce noise in the annotation, we do not estimate any markings, behind obstacles like vehicles and poles on the roadside. Different from KITTI, A2D2 provides similar lane line labels but they ignore the intervals in dash lines.

We focus more on the recall of lane line and compute it as the lane accuracy. We also consider the F2-score to balance in case the network over fits any class, and count the mean recall on both class as the *mAcc*.

Implementation and Training. To integrate LiDAR point clouds and RGB images in the same network, projection and value normalization are essential in preprocess. To project the point clouds onto the image plane, given a point $P_v = \begin{pmatrix} x_v; & y_v; & z_v \end{pmatrix}^T$, we calculate:

$$Pv = K_v[R_v; T_v]P_v \tag{11}$$

where Kv; Rv; Tv refer to the camera calibration matrix, rotation matrix and translation matrix respectively. Then the projected front-view point cloud reflectance map will be cropped to the same size of RGB images at 128×256. After that, the value of both reflectance map and the RGB images will be normalize to [0, 1] interval. After data preprocessing, we train our model for 250 epochs on two datasets respectively. As shown in the Sect. 3, we generate the simulated ground truth of target features in the first round of training, in which we also get the result of original MF model. Then in the second round, we train the MIMF with the features. In testing, we use the pre-trained MF, just as the procedure in training, to get target features, and test MF and MIMF.

Result and Analysis. We present the training record in the Fig. 3, and the result of testing in the Fig. 4. Note that we only put the training record of the last 50 epochs in the figures, in which we can see the MIMF performs worse than MF at first, but they converge together at last, that indicates the random disturbance from the independent mutual information. However, in testing, we observe that MIMF performs better than MF by 1–2%, which indicates the potential regularization function of MI-driven models on the small training data. Note that due to the unknown unstable calculation in MIMF, we have different output in testing, for which we process it tenth and count the average value. Though the result is not deterministic, the DIM in MIMF output the stable fusion weight, which is 1.25 : 0.75 for images and point clouds fusion in normal data in KITTI. For A2D2, the ratio is 1.35 : 0.65, and that meats the prior in dataset when we declare that the LiDARs in A2D2 is not so suitable for segmentation tasks. We further complete the modality loss on the KITTI dataset. With a prior knowledge of the MI of each sensor, MIMF can keep the performance elimination in an acceptable range, while MF only recall 50.29% of the lane pixels, far less than the result on normal data.

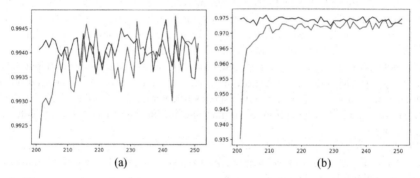

(a)   (b)

Fig. 3. The comparison of training process between the baseline and MIMF on the KITTI and A2D2 datasets. The blue lines are the MF baseline and the red are the MIMF. The lines present the accuracy during training, which finally converge together. The X-axis indicates the epochs. (Color figure online)

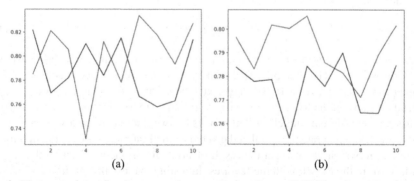

(a)   (b)

Fig. 4. The comparison of testing process between the baseline and MIMF on the testing datasets. The blue lines are the MF baseline and the red are the MIMF. The X-axis indicates the epochs. (Color figure online)

5   Conclusion

In this paper, we propose a novel adaptive multimodal fusion network named MIMF. It is driven by the mutual information between the input data and the target recognition patterns. By leveraging the mutual information in fusion, our weight-fusion module is able to perform adaptively based on the variant data. We further observe the regularization effect of our MI-driven method. The evaluation result on the KITTI and A2D2 datasets demonstrates the benefit of our method in practical application. In the following research, we will complete the experiments on more complex segmentation tasks and integrate a more flexible MI-estimator will better real-time processing procedure.

Acknowledgements. This work was supported by the National High Technology Research and Development Program of China under Grant No. 2018YFE0204300, the Beijing Science and Technology Plan Project No. Z191100007419008, the Guoqiang Research Institute Project No. 2019GQG1010, and the National Natural Science Foundation of China under Grant No. U1964203.

References

1. Feng, D., et al.: Deep multi-modal object detection and semantic segmentation for autonomous driving: datasets, methods, and challenges. IEEE Trans. Intell. Transport. Syst (2019)
2. Caltagirone, L., Bellone, M., Svensson, L., Wahde, M.: LIDAR-camera fusion for road detection using fully convolutional neural networks. Robot. Autonom. Syst. **111**, 125–131 (2019)
3. Mario, B., et al.: Seeing through fog without seeing fog: deep multimodal sensor fusion in unseen adverse weather. In: CVPR (2020)
4. Carballo, A. et al.: LIBRE: The multiple 3D LiDAR dataset. ArXiv, abs/2003.06129
5. Vora, S., Lang, A., Helou, B., Beijbom, O.: PointPainting: sequential fusion for 3D object detection. In: CVPR (2020)
6. Qi, C.R., Liu, W., Wu, C., Su, H., Guibas, L.: Frustum PointNets for 3D object detection from RGB-D data. In: CVPR (2018)
7. Su, Y., Gao, Y., Zhang, Y., Álvarez, J.M., Yang, J., Kong, H.: An illumination-invariant nonparametric model for urban road detection. IEEE Trans. Intell. Vehicles **4**, 14–23 (2019)
8. Yang, B., Liang, M., Urtasun, R.: HDNET: exploiting HD maps for 3D object detection. In: CoRL (2018)
9. Kim, J., Koh, J., Kim, Y., Choi, J., Hwang, Y., Choi, J.W.: Robust deep multi-modal learning based on gated information fusion network. In: ACCV (2018)
10. Shannon, C.E.: A mathematical theory of communication. Bell Syst. Tech. J. **27**(3), 379–423 (1948)
11. Gabrié, M., et al.: Entropy and mutual information in models of deep neural networks. In: NeurIPS (2018)
12. Belghazi, M.I., et al.: Mutual information neural estimation. In: ICML (2018)
13. Hjelm, R.D., Fedorov, A., Lavoie-Marchildon, S., Grewal, K., Trischler, A., Bengio, Y.: Learning deep representations by mutual information estimation and maximization (2019)
14. Bramon, R., et al.: Multimodal data fusion based on mutual information. IEEE Trans. Visual. Comput. Graph. **18**, 1574–1587 (2012)
15. Yousef, A., Iftekharuddin, K.: Shoreline extraction from the fusion of LiDAR DEM data and aerial images using mutual information and genetic algorithms. In: IJCNN (2014)

16. Pan, X., Shi, J., Luo, P., Wang, X., Tang, X.: Spatial as deep: spatial CNN for traffic scene understanding. In: AAAI (2018)
17. Geiger, A., Lenz, P., Urtasun, R.: Are we ready for autonomous driving? The KITTI vision benchmark suite. In: CVPR (2012)
18. Geyer, J., et al.: A2D2: Audi autonomous driving dataset. ArXiv, abs/2004.06320

Application

Application

Spatial Information Extraction of *Panax Notoginseng* Fields Using Multi-algorithm and Multi-sample Strategy-Based Remote Sensing Techniques

Shengliang Pu(✉), Yining Song, Yingyao Chen, Yating Li, Lingxin Luo, Guangyu Xu, Xiaowei Xie, and Yunju Nie

Faculty of Geomatics, East China University of Technology, Nanchang 330013, China

Abstract. *Panax notoginseng* has been regarded as one of raw materials in Chinese medicinal products which have been recommended as a common recommendation for the treatment of the novel coronavirus patients. Accordingly, in this study, a variety of supervised intelligent algorithms based on multi-algorithm and multi-sample strategy (MAMS) are used to implement spatial distribution information extraction for distinctive landscape types under unique environmental conditions. The experimental results demonstrate that the presented MAMS method is more effective than an individual classifier only with limited samples. The confidential interval of the planting area of *Panax notoginseng* is evaluated between 32.47 and 35.45^2 km, and the most likely area is determined nearby 34.04^2 km. Moreover, this presented study provides a practical foundation for land cover change detection under special observation conditions serving the government for a decision. There still needs further study, however, if this method could be applied to the fields of high-precision dynamic monitoring and change detection as a great contribution to precision agriculture.

Keywords: *Panax notoginseng* · Geoherbs · Precision agriculture · Information extraction · Remote sensing

1 Introduction

Traditional Chinese medicine (TCM) has played an important role in the treatment of the novel coronavirus patients [1], related studies have proved that TCM can coexist with Western medicine [2, 3]. TCM is originated in ancient China [4] and has evolved over thousands of years as the only health care and disease healing. *Panax notoginseng* is a rare medicinal plant (see Fig. 1), which has been a highly regarded traditional Chinese medicine resource in China for hundreds of years and has scarcely been observed and monitored from space until now. Besides, it is a typical shaded herbal plant or crop is grown under the protection of shade-net, particularly as geographical identification products with a specific spatial distribution pattern. Machine learning-based remote-sensing techniques have been widely used for the production of specific land cover

© Springer Nature Singapore Pte Ltd. 2021
F. Sun et al. (Eds.): ICCSIP 2020, CCIS 1397, pp. 153–163, 2021.
https://doi.org/10.1007/978-981-16-2336-3_14

maps at a fine scale. Remote sensing of natural resources provides us new insights into the resource inventory of Chinese materia medica resources, particularly of *Panax notoginseng*. The geographical identification products such as a certain medicinal herb cultivated under the protection of shade-net, which could be recognized as a special type of terrestrial eco-environment remote sensing. However, as for the specific land cover of cultivating geoherbs, their spatial distribution information has rarely been studied by the scientific community [5].

Land cover data sets are crucial for the modeling of earth observing system and the research of human-nature interaction at local, regional and global scales in the case of the integration of multi-sources data [6]. The improvement of spatial, spectral and radiometric resolution of satellite remote sensing brings high-quality and high-resolution information to the ability to recognize various landscape types towards the dynamic trends of development. At the same time, the spatial distribution information extraction of special land cover using remote sensing images facilitates to characterize complex landscape details, and a wide range of landscape types could be accurately extracted based on feature extraction and image classification. As a result, the accurate land cover and land use map produced by remote sensing techniques at fine spatial resolution become an essential part of remote sensing applications.

Fig. 1. The product cycle of *Panax notoginseng* in different stages. *Panax notoginseng* is a well-known geoherb, which has acquired a very favorable reputation for the treatment of blood disorders, including blood stasis, bleeding, and blood deficiency. Its root can be turned to powder as a medicinal material, and the shade-net cover can be observed from space utilizing satellite images.

Panax notoginseng is a cultivated ginseng species highly valued for its various pharmacological activities [7], as a specific geographical identification product, accordingly the harshly cultivated conditions of which in concentrated geography also under the protection of laws. The cultivated land of *Panax notoginseng* under shade-net forms a special type of land cover, which could be used for dynamic monitoring and remote sensing analysis quantitatively. By the way, this kind of distinctive land cover mainly distributes in Yunnan, Guangxi and Guizhou province of Southwest China, and the Wenshan city of Yunnan province is chosen as the study area. For the reason of standardized planting with shade-net, so apt for collecting training samples and extracting spatial distribution information of *Panax notoginseng* fields.

The intelligent computing theory promotes remote sensing image classification towards intellectualization gradually, many intelligent classification approaches, such as Support Vector Machine (SVM), Neural Network (NN) and automatic Classification and Regression Tree (CART), have been used to realize the comprehensive utilization of spectral and auxiliary information to improve the classification accuracy [8]. When it comes to the extraction of spatial distribution and planting area of *Panax notoginseng* fields, various integrated or combined algorithms could consider the advantages and disadvantages comprehensively, which could strengthen the abilities to extract land cover types precisely, also make the estimated results as accurate as possible. In this study, the iterative self-organizing data analysis technique (ISODATA) and K-means are used as unsupervised classification algorithms, while SVM and NN as supervised classification algorithms. Moreover, the unsupervised classification results of ISODATA and normalized difference vegetation index (NDVI) data sets derived from multi-spectral images are further introduced into the procedure of CART. In this case, the decision tree (DT) of expert knowledge would be generated automatically. Finally, the results of unsupervised and supervised machine learning-based remote sensing classification are brought together to be checked mutually and analyzed comprehensively.

The reason why the multi-algorithm and multi-sample strategy (MAMS) has been adopted lies in there are no auxiliary and validated data sets as referenced data for recognizing the distinctive landscape types—*Panax notoginseng* fields in this study. When using the supervised classification methods (e.g., DT algorithm) to conduct land cover classification, the quality of samples would determine the classification accuracy. As a result, it is necessary to adopt multiple algorithms and multiple sample sets to conduct the mutual check and comparable analysis to guarantee and improve the final classification accuracy. From the above, the intrinsic aim of this study is to integrate a variety of traditional algorithms, namely unsupervised and supervised algorithms (i.e., ISODATA, K-means, SVM, NN, DT and so forth), to construct new strategies or stable classifiers, further to realize better efficiency and good performance in comparison with the individual classifiers, even only having instantly labeled samples with the expert experiences while lacking ground-truth data. At last, the extraction results of spatial information of *Panax notoginseng* fields (e.g., distribution, area and density) could be provided to the government in time for policy-making.

The remainder of this paper is structured as follows. In Sect. 2, the employed data sets in the study area are delineated. The methodology is presented in Sect. 3, and Sect. 4 describes the experimental results and analysis. Finally, conclusions and an outlook are given in Sect. 5.

2 Materials

The study area is located in Wenshan city of Yunnan Province in southwest China, whose eastern longitude from 103.71 to 104.46°, and northern latitude from 23.07 to 23.73° (see Fig. 2). There contains complex terrain, rolling hills, crossing valleys, and ravines. The multi-spectral images of the study area acquired by Landsat-8 OLI land imager, whose spatial resolution is 30 m, and including nine bands. Particularly, the eighth band of Landsat-8 OLI as a panchromatic band, its spatial resolution is up to 15 m. Google Earth high-resolution images could be used as referenced data for collecting ground-truth samples. Note that, the time-nodes of Google Earth history images utilized in this study should keep consistency with the captured time of multi-spectral images approximately. In addition to the mentioned data above, the digital elevation model (DEM) could be used as auxiliary data sets or referenced data sets for CART classification. The spatial resolution of Landsat 8 OLI multi-spectral images means that a single pixel is equal to 900^2 m on the ground, about 0.22 acres. Despite the standardized planting of *Panax notoginseng* has been widely promoted, as Wenshan city appears relatively complex terrain. the contiguous planting zones remain small and fragmented.

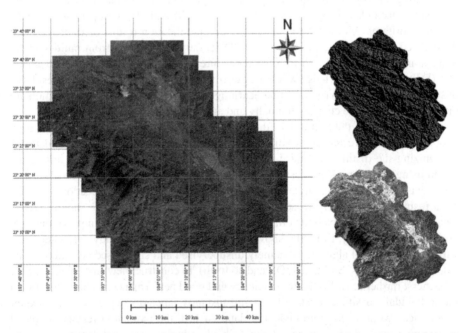

Fig. 2. Google Earth high-resolution image (left), Landsat multi-spectral image (lower-right) and DEM (upper-right).

The training samples are collected from field surveys or referenced data sets. If we would yield sufficient samples or ensure the reliability of samples, then we require visual interpretation to distinguish different land cover types. In the case of Landsat-8 imagery, the fifth, fourth and third bands are assigned to R, G and B channels, then the pseudo-color image could be got. Due to this kind of color is the same as natural color, to collect visual samples. Additionally, the procedure of visual interpretation might be influenced by a variety of subjective factors when collecting samples. Thereby, the *in-situ* way is always time-consuming and labor-intensive, and hard to ignore the importance of experience and the limitation of transportation.

As a lack of high-resolution satellite images and land cover products except Google Earth historical images archived in the study area. In this case, we have to employ the pseudo-color image generated from the band composition of multi-spectral images to collect training samples. Furthermore, there still needs to utilize necessary auxiliary data such as Google Earth historical images to ensure the quality of visual samples. Therefore, the Sample-T and Sample-V samples derived from the pseudo-color composition (see Fig. 3 (a)-(b)) are compared with the Sample-B and Sample-S samples in reference with Google Earth historical images (see Fig. 3 (c)-(d)). Here, different postfixes mean different samples, T means that designed as training samples, V means validating samples. Similarly, B means a large scale on the average size of samples, while the meaning of S is on the contrary.

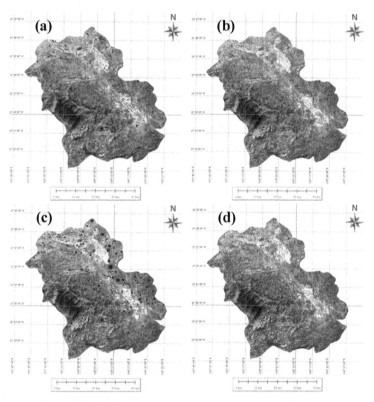

Fig. 3. Spatial distribution of different sample sets: (a) Sample-T; (b) Sample-V; (c) Sample-B; (d) Sample-S. Blue color means "Other" class, red color means "Panax" class. (Color figure online)

During the procedure of image classification, two basic sets of samples (i.e., Sample-T and Sample-V) derived from a pseudo-color image are directly used as training samples or employed as evaluating samples for each other, to facilitate statistical analysis. Similarly, another two control sets of samples (i.e., Sample-B and Sample-S) derived from Google Earth historical images corresponding to ground-truth data, which are used to further examine the reliability of two basic sets. Herein, the Sample-T and Sample-B sets hold a large scale but little number relatively.

3   Methodology

The approaches of remote sensing image classification consist of unsupervised and supervised algorithms based on the statistical analysis of spectral characteristics [9]. In this study, the typical unsupervised algorithms (e.g., ISODATA and K-means) and the canonical supervised algorithms such as SVM, NN, and CART (see Table 1) are chosen as the efficient classifiers [10, 11]. The clustering results could be used as validating results to facilitate the comprehensive analysis of results of multiple supervised classifiers [12]. As the grow-cells scattered in spatial distribution [13], it might not be suitable for the object-oriented and multi-scale classification approaches [14], consequently excluded in this study.

Table 1. Comparison of various classification algorithms.

Alg./No.	Characteristics	Advantages	Shortcomings
SVM	Automatic search for the support vector with large discrimination capacity	High accuracy	Hard to collect marginal samples
NN	Based on the principle of neural networks	Self-learning	Low efficiency
CART	Using samples without orders and rules to generate binary trees	For high-dimensional data with high accuracy	Avoiding "over-fitting" phenomena

Generally, basic geographic data such as public or authoritative data sets and topographic maps should be gathered in the first place, merely keep necessary coverage relative to the study area. Above all, it is of importance to prevent the samples of the "Panax" class from mixing with the samples of remaining classes to get rid of impurities.

Similar to evenly random sampling, the visually collected samples are expected to be spatially uniform with a certain quality. As for the evaluation metrics of sample quality, it has to present the separability of classes in general, which comprise of Transformed Divergence (TD_{ij}) and Jeffries-Matusita Distance ($J\text{-}M_{ij}$). Herein, the corresponding formulas for calculating TD_{ij} as shown in the following:

$$D_{ij} = \frac{1}{2}tr\left[(V_i - V_j)\left(V_j^{-1} - V_i^{-1}\right)\right] + \frac{1}{2}tr\left[\left(V_i^{-1} + V_j^{-1}\right)(M_i - M_j)(M_i - M_j)^T\right],$$

(1)

$$TD_{ij} = c\left[1 - e^{\frac{-D_{ij}}{8}}\right],$$
(2)

Where, tr [.] as the sum of diagonal elements of the matrix; V_i and V_j are the covariance matrix of category i and j, respectively; M_i and M_j as the corresponding mean matrix; c is a constant, which defined as the scope of separability, its concrete value might be 100, 1000 or 2000. Similarly, the corresponding formulas for computing J-M_{ij} as shown below:

$$B_{ij} = \frac{1}{8}(M_i - M_j)^T\left[\frac{V_i + V_j}{2}\right]^{-1}(M_i - M_j) + \frac{1}{2}\ln\frac{\left|\frac{V_i + V_j}{2}\right|}{\sqrt{||V_i||V_j|}},$$
(3)

$$J - M_{ij} = \sqrt{2(1 - e^{-B_{ij}})}.$$
(4)

When it comes to inter-class proportion, a ratio is presented to discriminate inter-class variances of pixels, which can be expressed as follows:

$$R_{r/o} = \frac{P_r^n}{P_o^n},$$
(5)

Where, $R_{r/o}$ as the ratio between the remaining and target classes, P_r^n and P_o^n represents the number of pixels corresponding to the remaining and target classes, respectively.

Several widely used accuracy metrics, i.e., the overall accuracy (O) and Kappa index (K), which are used to assess the final classification results. These metrics are derived from the site-specific confusion matrix. Particularly, the tiny changes of pixels of categories would bring about significant changes regarding accuracies. By the way, there are two kinds of confusion matrix which are pixel- and percentage-based forms.

4   Experiments

The four sets of samples acquired by visual interpretation could be assessed by separability metrics such as TD_{ij} and J-M_{ij} exactly. The statistical results of class separability for four sets of samples summarized below. As per the literature investigation, the TD_{ij} and J-M_{ij} values range from 0.0 to 2.0. If the class separability is greater than 1.9 that means good separability. On the contrary, if less than 1.8 that might be on account of poor separability. Note that, the class separability would significantly influence the final classification accuracy.

As Fig. 4(a) illustrated, the separability of Sample-T and Sample-V looks quite good, while the separability of Sample-B and Sample-S appears poor. On one side, the poor situation ascribes multi-sources, or there might be inconsistencies with spatial reference and geometric scale, resulting in the heterogeneous pixels mixed into the wrong category. On the other side, the archived Google Earth historical images regarding the time-span have been over about a year. The ratio between the remaining and target classes as shown in Fig. 4(b)-(c), whose tendency is supposed to go down.

The MAMS method is used for spatial information extraction of *Panax notoginseng* fields as a special crop in this study, its outcomes as shown in the following (see Fig. 5). Thereby, the K-means algorithm in terms of two unsupervised algorithms, which has apparent misclassification in the southwestern area.

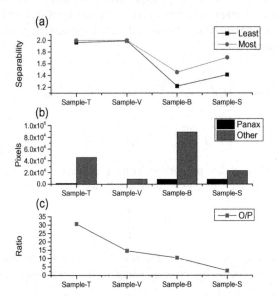

Fig. 4. Statistical analysis of different sets of samples: (a) The separability values; (b) The number of pixels; (c) The ratio of the number of pixels between the "Other" and "Panax" classes.

Table 2. Accuracy statistics of the presented MAMS method.

Alg./Acc./No.		T-V	T-B	T-S	V-T	V-B	V-S
SVM	O	1.00	0.95	0.84	0.99	0.94	0.84
	K	0.97	0.57	0.52	0.89	0.54	0.49
NN	O	0.99	0.94	0.83	0.99	0.94	0.83
	K	0.96	0.54	0.48	0.89	0.54	0.48
CART	O	0.95	0.85	0.99	0.95	0.84	0.95
	K	0.59	0.54	0.90	0.57	0.52	0.59

The accuracy statistics of the presented MAMS method as shown in Table 2. Due to the good quality of samples would reduce the commission and omission errors, however, the actual combinations of training and validation sets, i.e., SVM-T-B, SVM-T-S, SVM-V-B, and SVM-V-S, which show greater omission errors and worst Producer's accuracies. Herein, the first letter denotes the sample set involved in training, the second letter represents the sample set for validation. Moreover, the focused "Panax" class

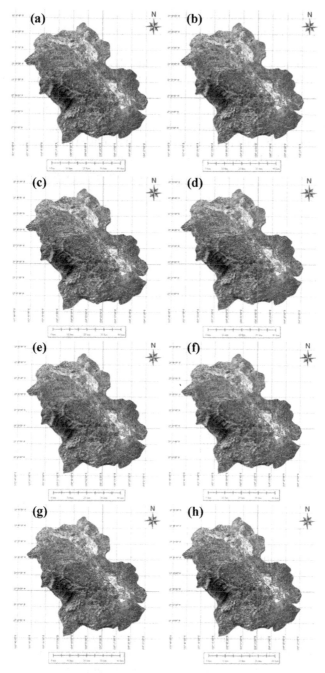

Fig. 5. Multi-algorithm and multi-sample strategy-based classification results: (a) ISODATA result (class 7/10); (b) K-means result (class 6/10); (c) SVM result (Sample-T); (d) SVM result (Sample-V); (e) NN result Sample-T; (f) NN result (Sample-V); (g) CART result (Sample-T); (h) CART result (Sample-V).

is particularly sensitive to changes in different classes of samples, while the "Other" category would enclose most of the remaining classes that might lead to relatively low sensitivity.

Apart from mapping *Panax notoginseng* fields, the planting area of *Panax notoginseng* fields could be estimated between 32.47 and 35.45^2 km using the MAMS method. Here, we get rid of the outliers, the maximum and the minimum to determine the changeable interval as $\sim3.0^2$ km eventually, whilst most likely value would be $\sim34.04^2$ km as an average. Also, a comparative analysis demonstrates that the most likely maximum nearby 0.279^2 km. As shown in Fig. 6, the statistical results of the planting area indicate that the results of SVM-T-V and CART-T-V turn out to be abnormal (see Fig. 6). The possible reason might be caused by the poor training samples containing heterogeneous pixels.

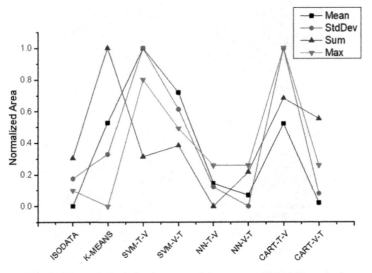

Fig. 6. The statistical planting area of the presented MAMS method.

5   Conclusions

As the fight against the novel coronavirus continues, TCM has been widely used, and a combined treatment of TCM and Western medicine has proven to be effective. In this study, the machine learning-based remote-sensing techniques have been used for the production of Panax notoginseng maps at a fine scale, a variety of supervised intelligent algorithms based on multi-algorithm and multi-sample strategy (MAMS) is used to implement spatial distribution information extraction for distinctive landscape types— *Panax notoginseng* fields. The presented study would provide a practical foundation for land cover change detection under special observation conditions serving the government for a decision.

Acknowledgment. This research was financially supported by the Research Fund of East China University of Technology (DHBK2019192).

References

1. Maxmen, A.: More than 80 clinical trials launch to test coronavirus treatments. Nature **578**(7795), 347 (2020)
2. Stone, R.: Lifting the veil on traditional Chinese medicine. Science **319**, 709–710 (2008)
3. Xue, T., Roy, R.: Studying traditional Chinese medicine. Science **300**, 740–741 (2003)
4. Tsai, C.: A brief introduction to traditional Chinese medicine. In: 30 Years' Review of China's Science and Technology, World Scientific, Singapore, pp. 125–138 (1981)
5. Deng, F., Pu, S.: Single-class data descriptors for mapping *Panax notoginseng* through p-learning. Appl. Sci. **8**(9), 1448 (2018)
6. Chen, Y.Y., Wang, Q.F., Wang, Y.L., et al.: A spectral signature shape-based algorithm for Landsat image classification. ISPRS Int. J. Geo-Inf. **5**(9), 154 (2016)
7. Wang, D., Hong, D., Koh, H., et al.: Biodiversity in cultivated *Panax notoginseng* populations. Acta Pharmacol. Sin. **29**(9), 1137–1140 (2008)
8. Kotsiantis, S.B., Zaharakis, I.D., Pintelas, P.E.: Machine learning: a review of classification and combining techniques. Artif. Intell. Rev. **26**(3), 159–190 (2006)
9. Patil, P.D., Gude, V.G., Mannarswamy, A., et al.: Land cover classification and information extraction of multi-temporal high-resolution images. Energy Procedia. **11**(22), 4248–4255 (2011)
10. Burges, C.J.C.: A tutorial on support vector machines for pattern recognition. Data Min. Knowl. Disc. **2**(2), 121–167 (1998)
11. Bhadeshia, H.K.D.H.: Neural networks in materials science. ISIJ Int. **39**(10), 966–979 (1999)
12. Breiman, L., Friedman, J.H., Olshen, R.A., et al.: Classification and Regression Trees. Wadsworth International Group, Monterey (1984)
13. Tsitsimpelis, I., Wolfenden, I., Taylor, C.J.: Development of a grow-cell test facility for research into sustainable controlled-environment agriculture. Biosyst. Eng. **150**, 40–53 (2016)
14. Wang, L.: Adaptive regional feature extraction for very high spatial resolution image classification. J. Appl. Remote Sens. **6**(1), 339–355 (2012)

Application of Convolution BLS in AI Face-Changing Problem

Junxi Wang[1], Xiaoqiang Li[2], Wenfeng Wang[3(✉)], and Jian Huang[4]

[1] YanBian University Institute of Tech, Hainan, China
[2] Fudan University, Shanghai, China
xiaoqiangl19@foxmail.com
[3] Sino-Indian Joint Research Center of Artificial Intelligence and Robotics, Interscience IIMT,
Bhubaneswar 752054, India
wangwenfeng@iimtcair.edu.in
[4] Nanchang University, Nanchang, China

Abstract. AI face-changing is a new technology that is developing in recent years, and its appearance may bring unnecessary trouble to certain fields of human society. On special occasions, there is an urgent need for a model that can autonomously determine whether an image has undergone AI face-exchanging processing.Proposed two convolutional structures based on the braod learning system (BLS), and give the specific algorithm flow. Using the convolution method for the basic BLS structure, try to directly convolve the feature mapping layer and the input data. The experimental results show that the BLS with convolutional structure performs well on small face data sets, and a very simple structure can achieve satisfactory accuracy and training time on the data set. It reflects the simplicity and reliability of the BLS-Convolution structure.

Keywords: Face change · Broad learning system · Convolution · Small dataset · COVID-19

1 Introduction

Since the outbreak of Severe Acute Respiratory Syndrome Coronavirus 2 (SARS-CoV-2), which caused coronavirus disease in 2019 (COVID-19), people using masks have spread all over the world [1]. The popularity of face masks has challenged existing face recognition methods. The occlusion of the face poses a significant obstacle to face recognition.

However, there are currently some AI face-changing technologies. They can synthesize fake faces through artificial intelligence, which makes the recognition of face wearing masks more difficult. Therefore, constructing a model to identify the face data of wearing a mask has become one of the primary tasks. In order to achieve this goal, we need to start research from existing face recognition algorithms.

The traditional face recognition algorithms are mostly based on deep network structure, and the performance of the model can be improved to a certain extent by increasing the number of deep network layers [2]. However, due to the huge number of hyperparameters in the network, and the increase in depth will also cause the structure to become

© Springer Nature Singapore Pte Ltd. 2021
F. Sun et al. (Eds.): ICCSIP 2020, CCIS 1397, pp. 164–173, 2021.
https://doi.org/10.1007/978-981-16-2336-3_15

more complicated, so most networks with deep structures have the disadvantage of too long training time. Not only that, the complexity of the deep structure also increases the difficulty of analysis. In order to achieve high precision, the performance requirements of computing equipment are also increasing. In addition, some problems that may arise in the deepening of the model are that some shallow learning capabilities are reduced, thereby limiting the learning of deep networks [3].

Broad learning is proposed as an alternative method for Deep Learning. It is a horizontally extended and efficient learning system, uses random vector functions to connect neural networks as mapping features. It is based on a single hidden layer neural network and is directly connected through neural enhancement nodes to the output.

Compared with Deep Learning, the obvious advantage of Broad Learning is that its simple single hidden layer structure and small amounts of parameters solve the problems of long training time and high device performance requirements for deep learning. But its randomness and pseudo-inverse calculations determine that the accuracy of the network when using large-scale data is often lower than network with deep structures.

This article is organized as follows. The second part briefly introduces the principle of the basic BLS model. The third part attempts to use the convolution method to adjust the mapping structure of the basic BLS. The fourth part is to convolutional the input data of the BLS model. In the fifth part, we show the performance on the face dataset with using basic BLS and Conv-BLS. In the conclusion part of the paper, some model application suggestions on prevention and control of COVID-19 are given. Finally, the potential problems are discussed.

2 Related Work

A major challenge in the face recognition process is: when the amount of data input and data dimensions continue to increase, due to the sparseness of high-dimensional data, the data processing methods in high-dimensional space and the low-dimensional space has more obvious differences. Many mature algorithms in low-dimensional space cannot achieve the desired effect in high-dimensional space, even cannot run.

The common solutions are as follows: [4–6].

The purpose of the width learning system is to solve the problem of high-dimensional data in the face recognition field due to the increase in data volume and dimension. Its excellent operation speed and simple structure are a good advantage.

The system takes the feature mapping as input and gradually updates the entire system. Input-data into the system, generate feature mapping, and form feature nodes. In basic BLS, part of the feature nodes are enhanced to enhancement nodes with random weights [7, 8].

Both the feature node and the enhancement node are input, so the input of the output-layer is equal to the set of all the feature nodes and the enhancement nodes connected. The required connection weights are obtained by solving pseudo-inverse ridge regression.

Suppose that we have a data set X with dimension M and sample size N. This data set will be used as the input of BLS, and feature node group generated after entering the system is as follows

$$Z_i = \emptyset\left(XW_{e_i} + \beta_{e_i}\right), i = 1, \ldots, n \tag{1}$$

where, W_{e_i} represents a randomly generated connection weight, and β_{e_i} represents a bias term. And $Z^i \equiv [Z_1, \ldots, Z_i]$ represents all the feature nodes from the 1st to the ith.

Enhancement node generation process is similar to feature node, as follows

$$H_m \equiv \xi\left(Z^n W_{h_m} + \beta_{h_m}\right), m = 1, 2, .. \tag{2}$$

where, W_{h_m} represents a randomly generated connection weight, and β_{h_m} represents a bias term.

Based on the above two Eqs. (1) and (2), the output layer Y can be expressed as follows

$$Y = [Z_1, \ldots, Z_n]|H_1, \ldots, H_m]W^m = [Z_n|H_m]W^m \tag{3}$$

which means, the connection weights as follows

$$W^m = \left[Z^n|H^m\right]^+ Y \tag{4}$$

Connection weights can be obtained by solving pseudo-inverse ridge regression[9, 10], as follows (Fig. 1)

$$A^+ = \lim_{\lambda \to 0}\left(\lambda I + AA^T\right)^{-1} A^T \tag{5}$$

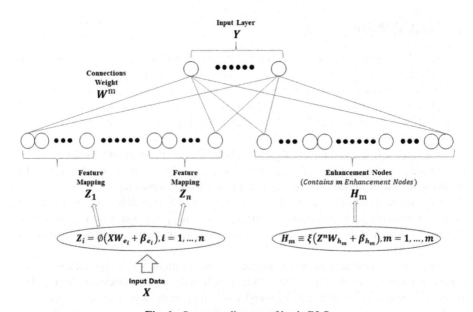

Fig. 1. Structure diagram of basic BLS

3   Model Adjustment

3.1   Feature Mapping to Convolution in BLS

In this part, we cancel the feature mapping layer in the basic BLS model structure and use convolution and pooling layers instead (collectively called convolution layer).

First, input the data set into the BLS system, and use the previously defined kernel to perform convolution processing on each picture. The number of windows generated during the convolution process can be artificially adjusted according to the training (test) time and accuracy of subsequent output.

Suppose we set up i windows during the convolution process, then the convolution layer formed by all the windows is finally represented by C_i (shown in the Fig. 2).

Second, select a part of the window in the convolution layer, add a bias term, connect to the input of the feature mapping layer, and use this part of the window with bias as the input of the enhancement layer.

The weights of the enhancement layer are still randomly generated. The enhancement layer input and the randomly generated weights are subjected to a dot product operation, and the result obtained is the temporary output of the enhancement layer. The result of maximizing compression on this output is the final output of the enhancement layer.

Finally, combine the respective outputs of the convolutional layer and the enhancement layer to get the output layer.

It also provides the specific algorithm implementation scheme of the model in Table 1, and expects that the algorithm can be applied to face recognition of masks during COVID-19 epidemic prevention and control.

The model using this algorithm can quickly identify whether the face of the person wearing the mask has undergone AI face change processing with high accuracy.

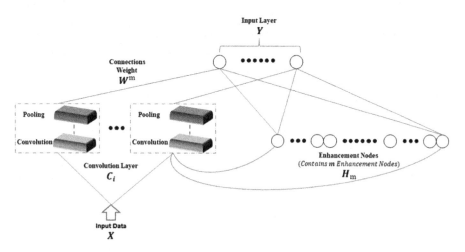

Fig. 2. BLS-feature mapping layer to convolution layer

Table 1. BLS-feature mapping layer to convolution layer.

Algorithm 1
Input : training data train_x and testing data test_x; basic BLS with given parameters : s, C, N1, N2, N2, N3.

Output: BLS for AI exchange face recognition with most suitable parameters in accuracy and training(testing) time
1 Sparse coding of **train_x** and **test_x**;
2 Start timing, define **time_strart**;
3 Training data train_x input, define convolution kernel and randomly generate weights;
4 Generate the results of each convolution window and store;
5 The convolution result with **4** as input to the enhancement layer;
6 Generate enhancement layer weights;
7 Combine the convolutional layer and the enhancement layer as the output layer;
8 Solve the pseudo-inverse to get the connection weight;
9 Connection weight multiplication output layer to get the training output: **OutputOfTrain**;
10 End timing, define **time_end**;
11 **Accuracy = (OutputOfTrain / train_x)**;
12 The same method applies to the test dataset: **test_x**;
13 **end**
14 Choose appropriate parameters based on training (test) time and accuracy.

3.2 Input Data with Convolution in BLS

In this part, we first perform convolution preprocessing on the input data set, and then the convolutional data is used as the input of the basic BLS to enter the entire learning system.

In the feature mapping layer, the weights are generated randomly, the input data after the convolution process and the random weights are dot product. The result obtained is the feature generated for each feature mapping window.

Store the result of sparse calculation of window features, and the result is the final weight of each feature mapping window. Let this part of the weights be dot-multiplied with the input data added with the bias term, and the result of sparseness is the output of each window.

The output of the feature mapping layer is the output of all the windows after merging. Select a part of it as the input of the enhancement layer.

The process of generating the enhancement layer and the output layer is exactly the same as the second half of Algorithm 1, so it will not be repeated.

The algorithm details of this model are still provided in Table 2 (Fig. 3).

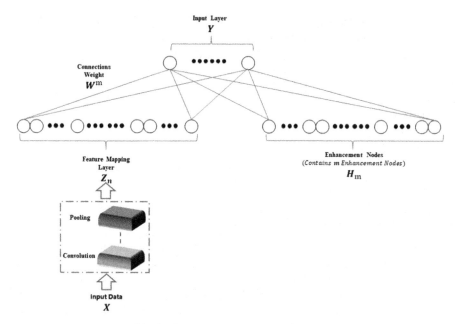

Fig. 3. BLS-Input data with convolution

Table 2. BLS-input data with convolution.

Algorithm 2
Input : training data train_x and testing data test_x; basic BLS with given parameters : s, C, N1, N2, N2, N3.
Output: BLS for AI exchange face recognition with most suitable parameters in accuracy and training(testing) time
1 Sparse coding of **train_x** and **test_x**;
2 Start timing, define **time_start**;
3 Define the convolution kernel, make the convolution kernel slide and multiply on all training pictures;
4 Store the new training set after convolution as input;
5 Randomly generate mapping layer weights and generate features for each window;
6 The output of the storage mapping layer is used as the input of the enhancement layer;
7 Generate enhancement layer weights;
8 Combine the convolutional layer and the enhancement layer as the output layer;
9 Solve the pseudo-inverse to get the connection weight;
10 Connection weight multiplication output layer to get the training output: **OutputOfTrain**;
11 End timing, define **time_end**;
12 Accuracy = (OutputOfTrain / train_x);
13 The same method applies to the test dataset: **test_x**;
14 end
15 Choose appropriate parameters based on training (test) time and accuracy.

4 Experiment and Result

In order to show the reliability of the two modified structures on the AI face exchange discrimination problem (the real face output is '1' and the fake face output is '0'), experiments were conducted on two data sets, *Labled Faces in the Wild* and *FaceForensics++*. The data of the real face comes from *Labled Faces in the Wild*, and the data of the fake face comes from *FaceForensics++*. In order to allow the model to be used normally on the face data set of the mask, we collected smaples from RMFD(*Real-World Masked Face Dataset*) conducted by WuHan University.

All experiments were run in the following laptop environment:

- Intel-8265U
- MX150
- 8 GB Memories
- 512GB SSD
- Spyder 3.3.6
- Python 3.7.3
- WINDOWS 10

4.1 Labled Faces in the Wild Data Set

Labled Faces in the Wild (LFW) is a commonly used training and testing set for face recognition (shown in Fig. 4). The face pictures provided are all from natural scenes in real life, so the recognition difficulty will increase, due to its various poses, lighting, expression, age, occlusion and other factors, it will cause even the photos of the same person to vary greatly. The complete data set contains a total of 13233 face images, with 1000 randomly selected as real face data. The ratio of the training set and the test set is 3:1. And add a considerable part of the face pictures wearing masks in the data set.

Fig. 4. LFW Data set and RealFace with Mask

4.2 FaceForensics++ Data Set

FaceForensics++ (FF++) is a face-forged dynamic image dataset (shown in Fig. 5). The creation process of the dataset uses four most advanced AI face-exchanging methods: Face2Face、FaceSwap、DeepFake and NeuralTextures [12]. The complete data set contains more than 1 million GIF images, and randomly intercepts 2,500 images as fake face data. The ratio of the training set and the test set is 3:2. Corresponding to the real face data set, some face pictures wearing masks are also added to the fake face data set, too.

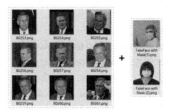

Fig. 5. FF++ Data set and FakeFace with mask

4.3   Experiment

In this part, we get the comparison result of Convolution-BLS and basic BLS by changing the number of convolution nodes (feature nodes) and enhancement nodes.

We found that the model performs very well on small data sets in BLS-Input Data with convolution.

The experimental steps are as follows: First, the convolutional layer and the feature mapping layer are defined as Layer 1, the enhancement layer is defined as Layer 2, the initial number of nodes of Layer 1 is set to 2, and Layer 2 is 2, too.

In each experiment, the number of nodes in Layer 1 and Layer 2 increases according to Table 3. A total of 7 experiments were conducted.

After the experiment, we can find that for the *basic BLS*, although the training speed is very fast, there is still room for improvement in terms of accuracy. In the *BLS-Feature mapping layer to convolution*, we observe that as the number of nodes increases, the accuracy on the training set gradually improves, but the performance on the test set is not good. It is speculated that there is overfitting. The experimental results show that *BLS-Input data with convolution* has a better performance in accuracy, so we also compared other deep learning methods based on convolutional neural networks [14], and found that their method has a higher accuracy, speculated that due to the increase in depth, the expressive ability of the model is improved. Therefore, it can be considered to further improve the accuracy by increasing the complexity of our model.

Table 3. Output result in basic BLS & BLS-feature mapping layer to convolution layer & BLS-input data with convolution (M1: Basic BLS M2: Conv-Mapping M3: Conv-Input)

Layer		Train effect (%)			Test effect (%)			Training time (s)			Testing time (s)		
L1	L2	M1	M2	M3	M1	M2	M3	M1	M2	M3	M1	M2	M3
2	2	66.67	75.11	66.67	80.00	85.04	80.00	0.000	0.170	0.150	0.000	0.080	0.090
4	4	66.67	75.07	66.62	80.16	84.96	80.16	0.012	0.192	0.140	0.002	0.100	0.080
10	10	68.00	78.53	67.33	82.24	81.68	82.24	0.030	0.350	0.290	0.000	0.180	0.170
20	20	68.76	87.16	69.69	83.12	75.60	85.60	0.040	0.750	0.590	0.000	0.350	0.340
40	40	70.44	92.93	71.20	87.52	68.72	88.32	0.070	0.362	0.982	0.001	0.456	0.430
80	80	73.11	92.93	72.84	88.96	68.56	87.12	0.120	1.000	0.743	0.010	0.450	0.420
160	160	75.42	91.11	86.80	86.80	71.12	88.08	0.260	0.860	0.790	0.020	0.500	0.450

5   Conclusion

This paper made some structural changes to the basic BLS model, and used the convolution method to process the original feature mapping layer and the input data. From the experimental results of Table 3, it can be seen that the modified model not only retains the characteristics of the basic BLS rapid training, but also performs very well on small data sets. Since the number of nodes in each layer we set in the experiment is not large, it is reasonable to believe that we can use very simple models to achieve good results on a variety of small face data sets.

Based on the excellent performance of this experiment on the face data set (including mask face data), we believe that the BLS-Convolution model can adapt to the current environment of the new coronavirus pneumonia and provide a feasible plan for possible public safety event management in the future.

Propose some environments that may be used during the prevention and control of the COVID-19 epidemic by Conv-BLS: entry and exit control of personnel when the community is closed, face recognition gates at stations and airports, and upgrades to face access control and attendance equipment.

However, the actual problem is that the large face database is not used in this experiment. When the amount of input data is too large, we are not sure whether the performance of the model can still be kept good.

References

1. Feng, S., Shen, C., Xia, N., Song, W., Fan, M., Cowling, B.J.: Rational use of face masks in the COVID-19 pandemic. LANCET-2600(20)30134-X (2020)
2. Sun, Y., Liang, D., Wang, X., Tang, X.: Face recognition with very deep neural networks. arXiv:1502.00873 [cs.CV] (2015)
3. Grm, K., Struc, V., Artiges, A., Caron, M., Ekenel, H.K.: Strengths and weaknesses of deep learning models for face recognition against image degradations, vol. 7, no. 1, pp. 81–89, January 2018
4. Song, Q., Ni, J., Wang, G.: A fast clustering-based feature subset selection algorithm for high-dimensional data. IEEE Trans. Knowl. Data Eng. 25(1), 1–14 (2013)
5. Esmin, A., Coelho, R., Matwin, S.: A review on particle swarm optimization algorithm and its variants to clustering high-dimensional data. Artif. Intell. Rev. 44(1), 23–45 (2013). https://doi.org/10.1007/s10462-013-9400-4
6. Aggarwal, C.C., Yu, P.S.: An effective and efficient algorithm for high-dimensional outlier detection. VLDB J. 14, 211–221 (2005). https://doi.org/10.1007/s00778-004-0125-5
7. Chen, C.L.P., Liu, Z.: Broad learning system: an effective and efficient incremental learning system without the need for deep architecture. IEEE Trans. Neural Netw. Learn. Syst. 29(1), 10–24 (2018)
8. Wang, W., Xiao, Q., Bao, C., Yu, Z.: GA-BLS-GNN: a broad extension of graph neural network. Supported by the National Natural Science Foundation of China (41571299)
9. Greville, T.N.E.: Some Applications of the Pseudoinverse of a Matrix. SLAM Rev. 2(1), 15–22 (1960)
10. Marquardt, D., Snee, R.: Ridge regression in practice. Am. Stat. 29(1), 3–20 (1975). https://doi.org/10.1080/00031305.1975.10479105
11. Parkhi, O.M., Vedaldi, A., Zisserman, A.: Deep face recognition. In: British Machine Vision Association, pp. 1–12 (2015)

12. Rössler, A., Cozzolino, D., Verdoliva, L., Riess, C., Thies, J., Nießner, M.: FaceForensics: a large-scale video dataset for forgery detection in human faces. arXiv:1803.09179 [cs.CV] (2018)
13. Ma, J., Yu, M., Fong, S., et al.: Using deep learning to model the hierarchical structure and function of a cell. Nat. Methods **15**, 290–298 (2018)
14. Jia, S., Lansdall-Welfare, T., Cristianini, N.: Gender classification by deep learning on millions of weakly labelled images. In: 2016 IEEE 16th International Conference on Data Mining Workshops (ICDMW), Barcelona, pp. 462–467 (2016). https://doi.org/10.1109/ICDMW.2016.0072

Cognitive Calculation Studied for Smart System to Lead Water Resources Management

Xiaohui Zou[1,2,4(✉)] ⓘ, Huajian Gou[3], Qiang Yang[4], and Jian Li[4]

[1] Interdisciplinary Knowledge Center, Sino-US Searle Research Center, Berkeley, CU, USA
[2] Zhuhai Fudan Innovation Research Institute, IoT Smart City Innovation Platform,
Room 106, Building 21C, Hengqin-Macau Youth Entrepreneur
Valley, Zhuhai 519000, Guangdong, China
[3] Chengdu China Railway Automation System Research Institute, Sichuan, China
[4] Sichuan Technology and Business College, Chengdu, Sichuan, China

Abstract. This article aims to explore cognitive calculation studied for smart system to lead the innovative path of social development in the field of water resources management from an interdisciplinary perspective. The basic method steps are: first, the specific entry point of target management is defined as water resources information management; second, the water resources knowledge management is emphasized, and in particular, the eight kinds of knowledge system synergy management is emphasized; third, through software-assisted Cognitive Calculation Studied for Smart System to Lead Water Resources Management engineering practice for interpersonal and human-computer collaboration. Its significance lies in: taking advantage of the new opportunity of the second leap in human cognition, from a new perspective to explore how to apply the smart system studied ideas namely cognitive calculation studied for smart system to lead the innovative road of social development in the specific field of water resources management.

Keywords: Cognitive sciences and technology · Cognitive metrics · Information presentation and metrics · Multi-modal information interaction and fusion · Multi-modal cognitive mechanism · Cognitive computing · Intelligent carrier · Smart transportation · Smart city

1 Introduction

This article aims to explore how to apply smart system studied ideas namely cognitive calculation studied for smart system to lead the innovative path of social development in the field of water resources management from an interdisciplinary perspective. After reviewing past practical experience and research papers, we found a series of problems: Why should we only pay attention to the issues of water resources management after a health emergency [1]? Why only realize the importance of water resources management when it comes to an economic crisis in water supply [2]? Why did you go early [3]? Interpersonal and human-computer mutual assistance should have been systematically put on the agenda for a long time, but it has not really been done yet [4]. We found that

© Springer Nature Singapore Pte Ltd. 2021
F. Sun et al. (Eds.): ICCSIP 2020, CCIS 1397, pp. 174–183, 2021.
https://doi.org/10.1007/978-981-16-2336-3_16

Rongzhixue already had a good idea [5], but in the field of water resources management, it has not yet been promoted and applied. In recent years, Rongzhixue idea has made great progress, and the ecological characteristics of information and scientific research [6] and how to eliminate ambiguity [7] and natural language understanding [8] and even the construction of interdisciplinary knowledge centers [9], etc. In many ways, there have been breakthrough research results. Even in big data and education [10], smart tourism [11] and its education [12] and food knowledge ontology [13], there are specific practices that can be implemented. Therefore, the goal of applying the smart system studied idea to lead the water resources management was naturally put forward.

2   The Methods

The basic methods are: first, the specific entry point of target management is defined as water resources information management; second, the management of water resources knowledge is emphasized, and in particular, the eight knowledge system synergy integrated management is emphasized; third, through software-assisted promoting the self-management to new heights.

2.1   Information Management Model: ($I_U = I_D - I_K$)

First, the specific entry point of target management is defined as water resources information management. This study found that there is a large amount of research data at home and abroad to be systematically digested and absorbed. Since water resources management is a very difficult comprehensive governance problem both at home and abroad, why don't we first learn how to stand on the shoulders of giants on the premise of understanding current affairs? Since predecessors and others have accumulated a lot of experience and lessons, why don't we digest them quickly and absorb them first? Since we are in an era with three major technologies: information processing, big data and artificial intelligence, why are we not using them? In view of such investigation and research and rational thinking, we should make great efforts in water resources management information to ensure the effectiveness of target management-more focused, more accurate and more efficient.

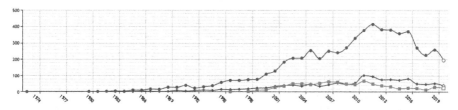

Fig. 1. Trends of comparative research on the correlation between water resources management and utilization and sustainable development.

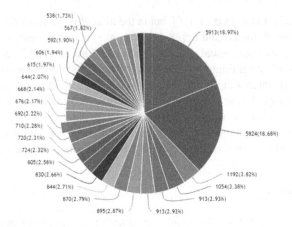

538(1.73%)
567(1.82%)
592(1.90%)
606(1.94%)
615(1.97%)
644(2.07%)
668(2.14%)
676(2.17%)
692(2.22%)
710(2.28%)
720(2.31%)
724(2.32%)
805(2.58%)
830(2.66%)
844(2.71%)
870(2.79%)
895(2.87%)
913(2.93%)
913(2.93%)
1054(3.38%)
1192(3.82%)
5824(18.68%)
5913(18.97%)

Fig. 2. Graph of the distribution of statistical results of various related research related to water resources management.

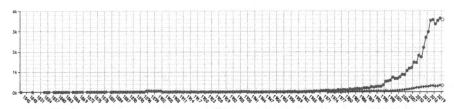

Fig. 3. A comparison trend chart of research papers published in English and Chinese on rainfall.

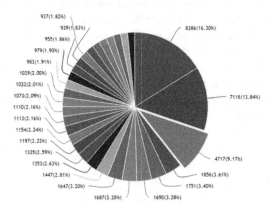

937(1.82%)
939(1.83%)
955(1.86%)
979(1.90%)
983(1.91%)
1029(2.00%)
1032(2.01%)
1073(2.09%)
1110(2.16%)
1113(2.16%)
1154(2.24%)
1197(2.33%)
1335(2.59%)
1353(2.63%)
1447(2.81%)
1647(3.20%)
1687(3.28%)
1690(3.28%)
1751(3.40%)
1856(3.61%)
4717(9.17%)
7118(13.84%)
8386(16.30%)

Fig. 4. Graphical illustration of the proportion of water resources management and related rainfall and related research statistics.

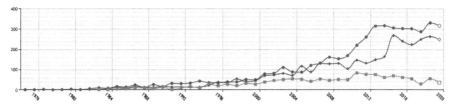

Fig. 5. Trend graph of the relationship between water quality testing, water pollution prevention and water resources protection research.

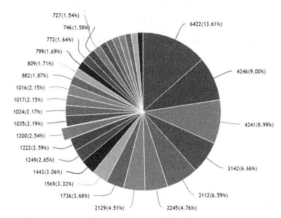

Fig. 6. Graphical illustration of the proportion of water resources pollution and related research statistics that are crucial in water resources management.

Figures 1, 2, 3, 4, 5 and 6 is the survey data we did. Comparison of three major trends in water resources management and protection and sustainable use, the trend map of comparative research on the relevance of water resources management and utilization and sustainable development can remind us of the focus of attention. The distribution ratio map of various related research statistical results related to water resources management is beneficial to our rational distribution to further study the key directions of water resources information management. Comparative trend graphs of rainfall research papers published in English and Chinese, and graphical illustrations of the proportion of water resources management and related rainfall and related research statistics, prompt us to note the natural information change of water resources information management. The trend graph of the relationship between water quality detection, water pollution prevention and water resource protection research, and the graphic illustration of the proportion of water resource pollution and related research statistics that are crucial in water resource management, warning us to pay more attention to water resource information management Key target management information in.

$$I_U = I_D - I_K \qquad (1)$$

water resource information management model can remind us of the focus of attention on it.

2.2 Knowledge Management Model: $I_K = I_D - I_U$

$$I_K = I_D - I_U \tag{2}$$

To draw a good blueprint for water resources management, not only need to have sufficient water resources information management, but also need comprehensive and accurate water resources knowledge management. Of course, they must be guided by corresponding theoretical models in order to do better. (1) To ensure complete recall rate,
(2) To ensure accurate recall rate. Both are indispensable. The unity of knowledge and
action is inseparable from information and knowledge, otherwise, it is not only difficult
to achieve the unity of knowledge and action, but also, it may lead to wrong decisions
or inappropriate behavior and habits due to cognitive errors, thus making it difficult to
achieve the ideal goal of water resources management. Draw a Good and Sustainable
Comprehensive Management Blueprint: As the saying goes, a picture is worth a thousand
words.

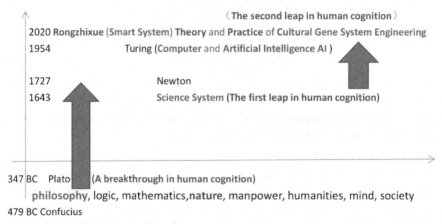

Fig. 7. Schematic diagram of the relationship between the eight university question system and
the two great leaps in human cognition.

Figure 7 is a schematic diagram of the relationship between the eight university
question system and the second great leap of mankind. From this we emphasize that
the management of water resources knowledge is emphasized, and in particular, the
integrated management of the eight knowledge system synergy is emphasized. The
following discussion can be made from Figs. 1, 2, 3, 4, 5 and 6 in conjunction with
Fig. 7: Water resources management essentially involves disciplines such as philosophy,
logic, and mathematics. Precipitation mainly involves the field of natural sciences. Water
pollution also involves social, artificial, humanistic, and mental disciplines.. It can be
seen that not only is the eight university questioning system to be used in its entirety,
but also further in-depth refinement to many specific subject areas and industries. This
is far from being limited to philosophical reflection and scientific prediction in the past.
This necessarily involves: the problem of the second leap in human cognition (see the

arrow from Newton's scientific system to Turing computers and artificial intelligence in Fig. 7). Water resource management awareness, systems and specific measures, etc., are inseparable from accurate knowledge management of water resources. Otherwise, we will lose our goal. Its work efficiency involves a computer-aided self-management model.

2.3 Computer-Aided Self-management Model: ID = IK + IU

$$I_D = I_K + I_U \tag{3}$$

Just as, education is for not to be educated, and management is also for not to be managed. This is the highest state of education and management. This requires creating conditions to give full play to the advantages of human nature, and at the same time, strictly restrict the shortcomings of human nature. People in society are developed from natural people. Human civilization is at the threshold of the second leap in human cognition. All kinds of smart systems contribute to the continuous improvement and optimization of human self-management. The most pragmatic way is to implement computer-aided

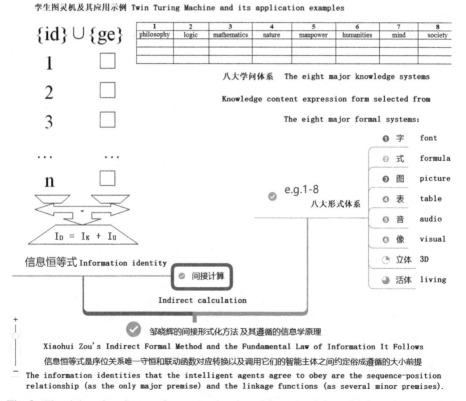

Fig. 8. The eight university question system is selected from the eight major formal systems and presented.

self-management mechanism. Character = person + thing. Among them, the biggest advantage of people is the ability to acquire knowledge. This is a half-knowledge person who can gradually approach the omnipotent God (although this is only ideal) under the condition of computer-aided self-management.

Figure 8 is a schematic diagram of the relationship between the eight formal systems and the eight university question systems and their indirect calculation. The information identity reveals that the data information (total) is equal to the sum of the known knowledge information and the unknown semantic information. Within the scope of the popular existing direct calculation theory, it is both simple (only involving the numerical calculation of lattice points or natural numbers) and complex (covering all kinds of phenomena information and cannot be explained completely in both philosophy and science). The eight university question system and any of its contents must be selected and presented from the eight major formal systems and any methods. Therefore, they are all indirectly calculated by software that expressed by Rongzhixue.

Fig. 9. A mind map of the complete system from the computer to the learning machine and then to the understanding machine.

Moreover, we have constructed a complete system from computer to learning machine to understanding machine, see Fig. 9.

3   The Validation of the Model

All three models can be calculated and verified on the double matrix grid of numbers and characters.

Figure 10 is an actual specific example of the verification method: An example of language chessboard software based on double matrix and its scientific schematic diagram. In this way, any text data can be quickly checked. Everyone's thoughts, words and deeds manage their data and can be automatically verified at any time. The overall data (covering information and knowledge) of whether humans use water resources reasonably can also be verified. Although Fig. 10 only uses the first natural paragraph of Tao Te Ching as a practical example, it shows how a natural language text can be quickly and automatically converted from unstructured data to semi-structured data (Chinese character chessboard) and structured data (digital chessboard) with the software

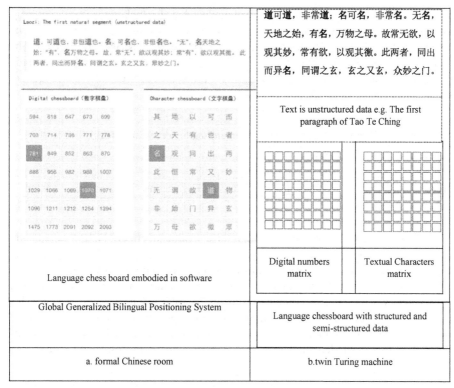

Fig. 10. An example of language chessboard software based on double matrix and its scientific schematic diagram.

and principles, but it is enough to explain that any piece of text in broad sense (not only text, but also any of the eight major form systems) can be used in this way to achieve information extraction and knowledge acquisition, not just data processing. The scientific principles can be better understood in conjunction with Fig. 8. Target management, information management, knowledge management, self-management, and various management data can be automatically recorded at the first time. Moreover, the combination of personalization (privacy is protected) and standardization (water resources management for best results) is organically combined. Planning, execution (doing), inspection (checking) and actions, and the overall quality management process of water resources are also guaranteed.

4   Result and Discussion

The result is: highlight the three technical advantages of information processing, big data and artificial intelligence, make up for the insufficiency of human brain intelligence, and give full play to the advantages of smart system theory and cultural gene system engineering practice for interpersonal and human-computer collaboration. Water resources information and knowledge management models not only give the constraints for the practical application of scientific theoretical models, but also lock in specific target management scopes (such as the nature and engineering aspects related to rainfall, and the manpower, humanities and society, etc. to water pollution) are also conducive to the establishment of scientific indicators of self-management of various units. With the help of computer-aided comprehensive management tools, the requirements of total quality management can be achieved (Table 1).

Table 1. Single subject and interdisciplinary research field.

1	2	3	4	5	6	7
Philosophy	Logic	Mathematics	Nature	Engineering	Humanities	Mind

The results show that these three models have significant effects. First, it can quickly narrow the scope. Second, it can accurately target the management direction. Third, it can respond quickly, efficiently and sustainably. Popularizing and applying them can form a long-span long-term cooperation between multi-disciplinary experts and corresponding units to deal with a series of complex problems in water resources management. This was lacking in the past, which was limited to philosophical talks or specific scientific and technological applications. The combination of the eight major knowledge systems is not only a useful supplement, but also a development of vision, especially a huge leap in cognition.

5   Conclusion

Its significance lies in: taking advantage of the new opportunity of the second leap in human cognition, from a new perspective to explore how to apply the smart system ideas to lead the innovative road of social development in the specific field of water management.

Natural resources, especially water resources, are enduring resources on which human beings depend. The shortage or pollution leads to serious survival threats or economic losses. The water resources management infrastructure is not only closely related to natural resources such as groundwater, rivers, lakes and oceans, but also It is also inseparable from artificial facilities such as ditches, reservoirs and dams, and humans and biodiversity are inseparable from water resources. This article discusses the characteristics of water resources management, the application and development of the content information processing model of the eight university question systems of nature, manpower, humanities, mind, society, logic, mathematics, and philosophy, especially the characteristics of the eight formal systems that respond to it., And simulated the characteristics of this type of water resources management model. From December 26, 2000 to June 26, 2020, basic academic exchanges at several first-class research universities at home and abroad. The intelligent system model developed by Rongzhixue Research is used to simulate the characteristics of various types of comprehensive management, and the observational experimental features located in relevant places are used for model verification. From the blueprints and models, the maximum simulation effective model is observed, and the maximum simulation effective result observed in the related field is close to the ideal expectation.

References

1. Al-Jawad, J.Y., Alsaffar, H.M., Bertram, D.F., Kalin, R.M.: A comprehensive optimum integrated water resources management approach for multidisciplinary water resources management problems. J. Environ. Manage. **239**, 211–224 (2019)
2. Koop, S., van Leeuwen, C.: Assessment of the sustainability of water resources management: a critical review of the city blueprint approach. Water Resour. Manage. **29**(15), 5649–5670 (2015). https://doi.org/10.1007/s11269-015-1139-z
3. Singh, V.P., Yadav, S., Yadava, R.N. (eds.): Water Resources Management. WSTL, vol. 78. Springer, Singapore (2018). https://doi.org/10.1007/978-981-10-5711-3
4. Basco-Carrera, L., Warren, A., Beek, E.V., Jonoski, A., Giardino, A.: Collaborative modelling or participatory modelling? A framework for water resources management. Environ. Model. Softw. **91**, 95–110 (2017)
5. Zou, X.: Intelligence means information processing. In: VII International Ontology Congress: Real or Virtual: from Plato's Cave to Internet, Spain (2006)
6. Zou, S., Zou, X.: Ecological characteristics of information and its scientific research. In: IS4SI 2017 Summit Digitalisation for a Sustainable Society, Gothenburg, Sweden (2017)
7. Zou, S., Zou, X.: Understanding: how to resolve ambiguity. In: Shi, Z., Goertzel, B., Feng, J. (eds.) ICIS 2017. IAICT, vol. 510, pp. 333–343. Springer, Cham (2017). https://doi.org/10.1007/978-3-319-68121-4_36
8. Zou, X., Zou, S., Wang, X.: Smart system studied: new approaches to natural language understanding. In: Proceedings of the 2019 International Conference on Artificial Intelligence and Computer Science (2019)
9. Zou, X., Zou, S., Wang, X.: The strategy of constructing an interdisciplinary knowledge center. In: Liu, Y., Wang, L., Zhao, L., Yu, Z. (eds.) ICNC-FSKD 2019. AISC, vol. 1075, pp. 1024–1036. Springer, Cham (2020). https://doi.org/10.1007/978-3-030-32591-6_112
10. Zou, X., Zou, S., Wang, X.: New approach of big data and education: any term must be in the characters chessboard as a super matrix. In: ICBDE 2019: Proceedings of the 2019 International Conference on Big Data and Education March 2019, pp. 129–134 (2019)
11. Yang, Q., Li, J., Zou, X.: Big data and higher vocational and technical education: green tourism curriculum. In: ICBDE 2019: Proceedings of the 2019 International Conference on Big Data and Education March 2019, pp. 108–112 (2019)
12. Yang, Q., Li, J., Zou, X.: Green tourism courses customized with digital maps. In: Series: Advances in Social Science, Education and Humanities Research. Proceedings of the International Academic Conference on Frontiers in Social Sciences and Management Innovation (IAFSM 2019) (2020)
13. Li, J., Yang, Q., Zou, X.: Big data and higher vocational and technical education: green food and its industry orientation. In: ICBDE 2019: Proceedings of the 2019 International Conference on Big Data and Education, March 2019, pp. 118–123 (2019)

A Robotic Arm Aided Writing Learning Companion for Children

Minghao Yang[1,2(✉)] and Yangchang Sun[1,2]

[1] Research Center for Brain-Inspired Intelligence (BII), Institute of Automation, Chinese Academy of Sciences (CASIA), Beijing, China
mhyang@nlpr.ia.ac.cn, yangchang.sun@ia.ac.cn
[2] School of Artificial Intelligence, University of Chinese Academy of Sciences, Beijing, China

Abstract. It was reported that robot aided learning techniques helped children to learn knowledge and improve their confidence on skill practice. Because of the children' communication abilities in interaction, traditional robot aided writing learning companions were often designed and at the same time were limited in the following two points: (1) machines dominated the interactions mostly on screen inter-action; and (2) unreal feels exist when robot write characters without real pen in hands. In this work, we construct a writing learning companion, which is able to write the character indicated by children and learn the writing orders demonstrated by children and potentially reinforce their knowledge. Besides the ability of physically writing, the proposed companion enable children to interact more freely by the following two points: (1) an information fusion model which enables children' audio-visual behaviors and system inner states to fit together; (2) depended on the information fusion model, a multi-modal dialog management organizes children' audio-visual behaviors, image based drawing order recovery (DOR), video based drawing order learning (DOL) techniques and robotic arm' physically writing into a whole cowriter. The proposed writing learning companion is evaluated in real interaction environment by over 150 children aged 5–10 during one and a half year. The objective and subjective evaluation results validate the performance of the information fusion model and dialog management. The positive feedbacks from children indicate that socially engaged as a role of teacher to the learning companion is a way to make the kids be glad to learn writing knowledge themselves.

Keywords: Human computer interaction · Multi-modal fusion · Robot companion

1 Introduction

Learning to write characters using the standardized shapes and the official stroke orders has long an important and established place in the periods of pre-school and school education. In this period, they are demanded to write neatly and orderly. In traditional pre-school character writing learning phases, even nowadays, the children are asked to repeat the writing process on writing book tens or hundreds of times for a character.

F. Sun et al. (Eds.): ICCSIP 2020, CCIS 1397, pp. 184–193, 2021.
https://doi.org/10.1007/978-981-16-2336-3_17

These repetition practices are necessary but they are actually tedious not only for children but also for parents, because a considerable proportion of little kids need their parent to accompany in their early study period.

It was reported that robot-aided learning techniques helped children to learn knowledge, improve their confidence on skill learning, as well as to ease parents' burden on keeping their attention on kids all time [1, 2]. In history, various robot-aided and agent-aided learning companions have been proposed to play roles as learning partners with Children. For instances, an English letters' writing companion proposed by [3, 4] introduced a NAO robot, which shows deformed letters and asks the children to demonstrate their regular writing instead. There were other kinds of companions such as reading humanoid robot [1], virtual agent aided language learning companion [5], schools telepresence experiences robot [2], etc. In spite of their effectiveness, these traditional robots and virtual agent aided companions were limited in the interaction and physically participation. For example in the English letters' writing companion [3, 4], the children were limited and dominated by screen interaction with system and the NAO robot's writing possibly past to unreal feels to children since there wasn't a real pen in NAO's hands.

Different from the traditional companions, the new robot aided companions are hoped to have the abilities that: (1) children' audio-visual behaviors could be well understood so that they can interaction with companion more freely with speech commands, image and video presentations; (2) different from traditional gesture writing in the air or simulated writing in screen, physically writing are adopted both in children' teaching and robot's writing phases. To this end, we construct a robotic arm aided writing companion in this work, which is able to learn and write the character on the paper according to the shapes and orders demonstrated by children, and conversely reinforce children' knowledge on characters' writing.

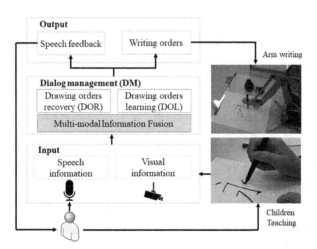

Fig. 1. The high level of interaction workflow and system architecture of the proposed robot arm writing companion.

2 System Structure

The interaction workflow between children and companion mainly contains four steps: (1) children present a card or ask the system to write a character; (2) the robot arm write the character on paper according to learned experiences or orders recovered form static image; (3) When the robotic arm makes mistakes on the writing orders or children are not satisfied with the robot writing, children teach the arm by writing the characters on drawing board; (4) the robot arm records the children' writing orders, match them to the previous written skeleton, and write again according to the writing order taught by kids. These steps loop until the children are satisfied with the robot's writing.

Table 1. Dialog states

Index	State description	Index	State description
S_{Start}	Dialog new turn start	S_1^{CA}	Children ask robot to write a character using speech command through microphone
S_2^{CV}	Children ask robot to write by showing a card before camera	S_2^{CV}	Children ask robot to write by showing a card before camera
S_3^{RA}	Robot query the character's information using synthesized speech	S_4^{CA}	Children tell robot the character information using microphone
S_5^{RV}	Robot retrieves or recovers drawing orders from learned characters' information	S_6^{RA}	Robot announces to write using voice prompt
S_7^{RV}	Robot writes the characters on paper using retrieved or recovered orders	S_8^{RA}	Robot asks children whether they are satisfied with the writing using voice prompt
S_9^{CA}	Children tell the robot current writing is good using speech command	S_{10}^{CA}	Children tell the robot current writing needed to be improved using speech command
S_{11}^{RA}	Robot announces thanks to children' teaching with using voice prompt	S_{12}^{RA}	Robot asks children to show the character's correct writing order using voice prompt
S_{13}^{CV}	Children demonstrate the character's correct writing order on drawing board	S_{14}^{RV}	Robot detect whether children finished the demonstration
S_{15}^{RV}	Robot match the orders taught by children to the characters' skeleton written in previous turn	S_{16}^{RV}	Robot write the characters on paper using learned orders
S_{End}	End of current dialog turn		

The system architecture is given in Fig. 1, which contains three components: system input (SI), dialog management (DM), and system output (SO). SI is mainly related to information process of children' audio-visual behaviors. A wireless microphone is used to obtain children' speech command and an open Chinese automatic speech recognition (ASR) engine is used to obtain the text information from speech command [6]. Sequentially, the text information is fused with visual information before they are inputted into DM. SO is used to control the robotic and provides children audio-visual responses. In audio output channel, system plays the response sentences generated by DM through a speaker using text to speech (TTS) technique [7]. At the same time in vision channel, system sends instructions to robot arm, and controls the arm to write characters on paper with a pen in its clamp.

There are mainly four techniques in the DM component: multi-modal information fusion, image based drawing order recovery (DOR), video based drawing order learning (DOL), dialog state tracking (DST) and sentences prediction (SP). We will introduce the four techniques used in this work in next section.

3 Method

3.1 Dialog State Definition

According to the interaction demands of writing learning companion, we design 18 dialog states in DM and Table 1 lists all these dialog states. In these states, 16 states are related to interactions, which are denoted as S_i^X ($i \in [1, 16]$) and $X = (CA, CV, RA, RV, T)$. The states labeled by "C" and "R" mean that these states are related to children behaviors and root operation respectively. The states labeled by "A" and "V" mean that these states are related to audio interaction channel and visual interaction channel respectively. "T" means dialog start and end states.

3.2 Multi-modal Dialog States Tracking

Given current state S_i^t as time t, then the probability of DM states at $t + 1$ could be written as Eq. (1) according to Bayes' theorem [8].

$$p\left(S_j^{t+1}\right) = \forall_i \arg\max_j \left(f(i,j) * p\left(S_j^{t+1}|Slt_i^t, A_i^t, V_i^t, S_i^t\right) * p\left(Slt_i^t|A_i^t, V_i^t, S_i^t\right) * p\left(A_i^t, V_i^t|S_i^t\right) * p\left(S_i^t\right)\right)$$

$$\text{where } f(i,j) = \begin{cases} 1 \text{ if } i \rightarrow j \\ 0 \text{ if } i \nrightarrow j \end{cases}$$

$$(1)$$

In Eq. (1), $Slt_i^t, A_i^t, V_i^t, S_i^t, S_i^{t+1}$ present dialog inner slots' values, audio features, visual features, state location at time t and the predicted state at time $t + 1$ respectively. The arrow sign $i \rightarrow j$ and $i \nrightarrow j$ in $f(i,j)$ means the j-th state are connected to the i-th state or not. $p\left(A_i^t, V_i^t | S_i^t\right)$ is the condition probability for children' audio-visual behaviors at state S_i^t. $p\left(Slt_i^t | A_i^t, V_i^t, S_i^t\right)$ is the possible three inner slots' values which are jointly decided by the users' behaviors, DOR and DOL techniques, and $p\left(Slt_i^t | A_i^t, V_i^t, S_i^t\right)$ could be written as Eq. (2).

$$p\left(Slt_i^t | A_i^t, V_i^t, S_i^t\right) = p(Slt_i^t, A_i^t, V_i^t) * p\left(S_i^t\right) / p\left(A_i^t, V_i^t, S_i^t\right)$$
$$= p(Slt_{i-1}^t, A_i^t) * p\left(Slt_{i-2,3}^t, V_i^t\right) * p\left(S_i^t\right) / p\left(A_i^t, V_i^t, S_i^t\right) \quad (2)$$

Take Eq. (2) to Eq. (1), then we obtain Eq. (3).

$$p\left(S_j^{t+1}\right) = \forall_i \arg\max_j \left(f(i,j) * p\left(S_j^{t+1} | Slt_i^t, A_i^t, V_i^t, S_i^t\right) * p\left(Slt_{i-1}^t, A_i^t\right) * p\left(Slt_{i-2,3}^t, V_i^t\right) * p\left(S_i^t\right)\right) \quad (3)$$

In Eq. (3), $f(i,j), p\left(S_i^t\right)$ are known and $p(Slt_{i-1}^t, A_i^t), p\left(Slt_{i-2,3}^t, V_i^t\right)$ could be obtained from children' audio/visual behaviors, DOR and DOL techniques. In this way, the DM states transition is determined by the conditional probability $p\left(S_j^{t+1} | Slt_i^t, A_i^t, V_i^t, S_i^t\right)$. We denote it as $P_{i \rightarrow j}^{t+1}$ in this work for simplification. Inspired by the CSLTM (Contextual LSTM) method proposed by [9], we modify CSLTM a multi-modal DM model to select the response sentences from candidates in this work. For simplification, we name the proposed multi-modal CLSTM as MM-CLSTM.

3.3 Drawing Order Recovery (DOR)

In the cases that the system starts from state S_2^{CV} where the children show a card and ask robot to write a character unknown before, the system first confirms the character index in dictionary, and then recover the drawing order from the static image. In this work, we first detect junction points and segment the skeleton into stroke components [10]. Then we use the pen tip motion prediction CNN (SDE-NN) proposed in [11] to predict the junction points one by one from start to end.

3.4 Drawing Order Learning (DOL)

When the system are in the states between S_{13}^{CV} and S_{14}^{RV}, system records and learns the writing orders demonstrated on the writing board by children. In these methods, the CGE method [12] was originally proposed for character selection matching and it was reported that CGE could obtain 94% accuracy for the characters which junction points are less than 20 on Chinese handwriting database HWDB 1.1 [13]. In this work, we use the CGE algorithm for DOL task.

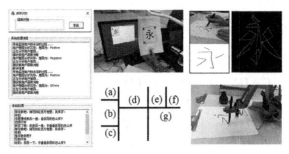

Fig. 2. User interfaces for system operation, dialog history records, image and video displaying and robotic arm physically writing.

4 Experiments

4.1 Interaction Environment

Hardware. The system runs on a notebook computer (Dell i7–4720) with 2.6G CPU, 8G RAM, built-in wireless microphone and speaker. A robotic arm UArmSwift [14] is connected with notebook computer, receives the junction points' orders from computer and write them on paper with a soft-head pen in its clip.

User Interface. Figure 2 lists the system's user interfaces, including ASR interface shown as Fig. 2(a), the recording and visualization panels for DST and sentences selection shown as Fig. 2(b) and Fig. 2(c), the panels for card displaying and drawing order demonstration shown as Fig. 2(d) and Fig. 2(e), DOR and DOL panels shown as Fig. 2(f) and the robotic arm physically writing area shown as Fig. 2(g). In these interfaces, only Fig. 2(a), Fig. 2(d) and Fig. 2(e) are provided to children in interactions as system inputs.

4.2 Data Preparation and Experiment Setting

There are total 16 interaction dialog states in the system. In these states, the speech commands in dialog are varying and flexible for different children. Since there is no existing dialog corpus before, we first adopt user simulator [15] and build a corpus for MM-CSLTM training. At the beginning, we invited 20 volunteers aged between 20 and 30, and introduced them the system in details. Then we asked them to simulate the roles of children and robot in conversation. We recorded their questions or responses and removed the duplicate sentences. About 57 and 30 sentences for children and robot are obtained respectively.

Table 2. DST and sentences selection accuracies for traditional LSTM, CSLTM and the propose MM-CLSTM for different values of m and n.

(m, n)	DST			Sentence selection		
	SLTM	CSLTM	Proposed	SLTM	CSLTM	Proposed
(3,3)	85.19	93.19	**96.23**	69.49	71.31	75.49
(3,4)	82.57	90.57	93.93	73.23	84.56	88.23
(3,5)	80.58	87.58	91.70	82.13	89.74	**91.13**
(4,3)	85.23	93.23	**97.95**	61.65	72.59	76.56
(4,4)	84.93	90.93	95.18	81.40	85.51	89.40
(4,5)	79.70	88.70	92.32	85.58	87.43	**92.58**
(5,3)	84.70	86.70	88.70	62.55	75.37	79.55
(5,4)	79.34	82.34	83.34	83.69	82.15	86.75
(5,5)	76.78	79.78	80.78	89.69	85.66	90.69

*Numbers in the table are prediction accuracy and measurement is percentage (%).

4.3   Performance

DST and Sentence Selection. We first train the MM-CSLTM sentence model on a large scale Chinese short text summarization dataset [16]. Being similar to the structure presented in CSLTM, the hidden layer with 1024 units is used for sentences model, and the length of input and output units in training is given by m. In the third step, we train the MM-CSLTM sentence selection model using the expanded dialog sentences. As what we have introduced before, there are about $16 \times K^n$ samples used for next sentences selection task since each sentence is related to the previous $n - 1$ states. We denote the model as $MM\text{-}CSLTM_{m,n}$ according to the different values of m and n. Table 3 lists the DST and next sentences selection accuracies for the proposed $MM\text{-}CSLTM_{m,n}$, CSLTM and traditional SLTM respectively on the same network structure.

Table 2 reveals that $MM\text{-}CSLTM_{3,3}$ and $MM\text{-}CSLTM_{4,3}$ obtain the top 2 performances on the task of DST, and they are better than those results of CSLTM and SLTM. It because that dialog states in this work are not only related to text information, but also the inner states of DOR, DOL and interactive drawing order learning from visual channel.

For the task of next sentences selection, it is obvious that MM-CSLTM$_{3,5}$ and MM-CSLTM$_{4,5}$ obtain the highest values among the results. Being similar to DST task, MM-CSLTM obtain higher performance than those of CSLTM and LSTM, it is because that the multi-modal information not only help to improve the DST accuracy, but also the performance of sentence selection in interactions.

Table 3. Four questions used for system subjective evaluation

Id	Question	TP
Q1	Is the robot arm clever to understand you?	DST
Q2	Are you satisfied with the robot arm's answers?	FSS
Q3	Does the robot arm write well?	RW
Q4	Do you like to be a teacher for the robot arm in writing?	SYS

Social Companionship Evaluation. As what we introduced in the second paragraph of Sect. 4.2, 120 and 30 children took part in the experience to teach the robot writing in short and long duration interaction respectively. In these children, there are 57 girls and 93 boys. To validate the performance of the MM-CSLTM and the whole companion system, the children were asked to score ten questions themselves after their experiences. The ranges of the scores are from 0 to 5. The higher scores the better. Because of limited space, we only list four questions among these ten questions in Table 3. Figure 3(a) presents the mean opinion score (MOS) for 120 children' short duration interactions (denoted as *Short*), 30 children' long duration interactions (denoted as *Long*) and the average values of MOS for all children (denoted as *Mean*). Figure 3(b) presents the MOS for 57 girls, 93 boys and mean values respectively.

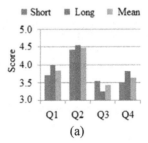 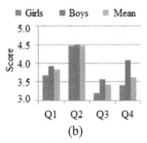

(a)   (b)

Fig. 3. MOS of the four questions on: (a) different tasks (short versus long interaction); (b) different gender (girls versus boys).

We can see from Fig. 3 that most children are satisfied with the DM feedback sentences (Q2) with score at 4.5 points. With longer duration interaction, children are more likely to be used to the interaction with robotic arm, and the scores increase nearly 0.5 points, shown as Q1 and Q4 in Fig. 3(a). Secondly, Fig. 3(b) shows that the scores from boys are obviously higher than those of girls, including Q1, Q3 and Q4. It indicates that the boys are more interesting in the robotic arm writing companion than girls. However, with longer duration interactions, children became more fastidious about the appearance of physically writing of robotic arm, shown as Q3 in Fig. 3(a).

5   Conclusions

In this work, we construct a robotic arm aided writing learning companion. Different from the traditional screen interaction and unreal writing companions, the children could interact with the proposed companion more freely with their audio-visual behaviors and physically writing. The statistic results from 150 children experiences prove the social companionship of the proposed companion and the effectiveness of the proposed fusion and multi-modal DM model. The future work includes more accuracies of DST and sentences selection, appearance improvement of physically writing by robotic arm and operation safety for children in interaction.

Acknowledgement. This work is supported by the National Key Research & Development Program of China (No. 2018AAA0102902), the National Natural Science Foundation of China (NSFC) (No. 61873269), the Beijing Natural Science Foundation (No: L192005), the CAAI-Huawei MindSpore Open Fund (CAAIXSJLJJ-20202-027A), the Guangxi Key Research and Development Program (AB18126053, AB18126063, AD18281002, AD19110001, AB18221011), the Natural Science Foundation of Guangxi of China (2019GXNSFDA185007, 2019GXNSFDA185006), Guangxi Key Laboratory of Intelligent Processing of Computer Images and Graphics (No GIIP201702), Guangxi Key Laboratory of Trusted Software (No kx201621, kx201715), and Guangxi Science and Technology Planning Project (No. AD19110137).

References

1. Michaelis, J.E., Mutlu, B.: Someone to read with design of and experiences with an in-home learning companion robot for reading. In: Presented at the ACM CHI Conference is the World's Premiere Conference on Human Factors in Computing Systems (2017)
2. Newhart, V.A., Olson, J.S.: My student is a robot: how schools manage telepresence experiences for students. In: Presented at the CHI Conference on Human Factors in Computing Systems. ACM (2017)
3. Hood, D., Lemaignan, S., Dillenbour, P.: When children teach a robot to write: an autonomous teachable humanoid which uses simulated handwriting. In: Presented at the Tenth ACM/IEEE International Conference on Human-Robot Interaction (2015)
4. Lemaignan, S., Jacq, A., Hood, D., Garcia, F., Paiva, A., Dillenbourg, P.: Learning by teaching a robot: the case of handwriting. IEEE Robot. Autom. Mag. **23**(2), 56–66 (2016)
5. Cheng, A., Yang, L., Andersen, E.: Teaching language and culture with a virtual reality game. In: Presented at the the ACM CHI Conference is the World's Premiere Conference on Human Factors in Computing Systems (2017)
6. YuyinBaiduAsr (2020). https://yuyin.baidu.com/asr
7. YuyinBaiduTTS, 11 September 2020. https://ai.baidu.com/sdk#tts
8. Lee, P.M.: Bayesian Statistics: An Introduction, 4th edn. Wiley, Hoboken (2012). (No. ISBN 978-1-118-33257-3)
9. Ghosh, S., Vinyals, O., Strope, B., Roy, S., Dean, T., Heck, L.: Contextual LSTM (CLSTM) models for Large scale NLP tasks (2016)
10. Hen, S., Wiering, M., Schomaker, L.: Junction detection in handwritten documents and its application to writer identification. Pattern Recogn. **48**(12), 4036–4048 (2015)
11. Zhao, B., Yang, M., Tao, J.: Drawing order recovery for handwriting Chinese characters. In: Presented at the International Conference on Acoustic, Speech, and Signal Processing, Brighton, United Kingdom, 12–17 May 2019 (2019)

12. Zhao, B., Yang, M., Pan, H., Zhu, Q., Tao, J.: Nonrigid point matching of chinese characters for robot writing. In: Presented at the IEEE International Conference on Robotics and Biomimetics, Macao, 5–8 December 2017 (2017)
13. Liu, C.-L., Yin, F., Wang, D.-H., Wang, Q.-F.: CASIA online and offline Chinese handwriting databases. In: Presented at the 2011 International Conference on Document Analysis and Recognition, Beijing, China, 18 September 2011–21 September 2011 (2011)
14. uArmSwift, 28 February. https://www.ufactory.cc/#/en/uarmswift
15. Li, X., Lipton, Z.C., Dhingra, B., Li, L., Gao, J., Chen, Y.-N.: A user simulator for task-completion dialogues. arXiv preprint arXiv:1612.05688 (2016)
16. Hu, B., Chen, Q., Zhu, F.: LCSTS: a large scale chinese short text summarization dataset. In: Presented at the Proceedings of the 2015 Conference on Empirical Methods in Natural Language Processing, Lisbon, Portugal, 17–21 September 2015 (2015)

Design of Omnidirectional Mobile Robot Platform Controlled by Remote Visualization

Kunhua Li[1], Xiaotao Liang[1], Ming Xu[1], Zhouyang Hong[1], Heng Li[1], Fuchun Sun[1,2,3], and Haiming Huang[1,2(✉)]

[1] College of Electronic and Information Engineering,
Shenzhen University, Shenzhen 518060, China
[2] Peng Cheng Lab, Shenzhen 518055, GD, China
[3] Department of Computer Science and Technology,
Tsinghua University, Beijing 100084, China

Abstract. Mobile Robot can realize non-contact operation of medical and rehabilitation services in the outbreak of CoVID-19, and Mobile Robot Platform (MRP) is the key component in Mobile Robots. By using Mecanum wheels, the omnidirectional MRP (OMRP) of four-wheel layout is realized. Combined with raspberry PI and STM32 micro-controller, the OMRP is driven by motion control algorithm to moves and rotates in all directions. The remote visual control link is built through 4G data transmission and 4G diagram transmission to realize the 4G visual control mode. Also, combined with the digital control mode of RS-485 data transmission and the Bluetooth controller, the multi-mode control of OMRP is realized. Finally, a prototype of OMRP is made. Experiments of the prototype verify the feasibility of OMRP, and the effectiveness of the 4G remote visual control. Overall, this paper provides a new way of robot remote control in wireless communication for the upcoming 5G era.

Keywords: Mobile robot platform · Mecanum wheel · Motion control · Remote visual control

1 Introduction

Mobile Robot Platform (MRP) is an important carrier for material transport or equipment in the industrial field [1, 2]. The MRP of traditional gear train is difficult to meet the increasing demand of maneuverability. At the same time, different working environments also put forward new requirements for the remote-control mode of MRP [3]. In 1973, the Mecanum wheel was first designed by Bengbllon, a Swedish, and became the patent of Mecanum Company. After continuous improvement, the Mecanum wheel system became a mature method for mobile robot platform to realize omnidirectional mobile function [4, 5]. Therefore, in view of the omnidirectional movement demand, this paper designs a set of omnidirectional MRP (OMRP) based on the Mecanum gear train, and realizes the OMRP motion control algorithm [6] based on the STM32 bottom control panel. On the other hand, the traditional wired data transmission has been difficult to

© Springer Nature Singapore Pte Ltd. 2021
F. Sun et al. (Eds.): ICCSIP 2020, CCIS 1397, pp. 194–205, 2021.
https://doi.org/10.1007/978-981-16-2336-3_18

meet the remote-control demand [7] for OMRP under the huge production scale in the industrial environment. Considering the mature application of RS-485 in the industrial environment, the security guarantee of Bluetooth operation, and the remote transmission capability of 4G technology, multi-mode control methods such as RS-485, Bluetooth control [8, 9], 4G remote visual control [10] are implemented in this paper to improve the control performance of OMRP and meet the requirements of robot operation and control under complex conditions.

The rest of the article is framed as follows: Sect. 2 explains the OMRP movement principle and algorithm, Sect. 3 describes the OMRP software system constitution, and Sect. 4 explains the multi-mode control system in OMRP. Prototype test experiment is preforming in Sect. 5. Conclusion is expounded in Sect. 6.

2 Related Background

The driving mode of OMRP is the chassis system composed of Mecanum wheel, which can move freely in the limited space by using the omnidirectional movement principle of Mecanum wheel and the corresponding control algorithm.

2.1 Mecanum Structure

The Mecanum wheel (see Fig. 1) is composed of several rollers, hubs, supporting cores, bearings, bolts, nuts, etc. When the motor drives the wheel to rotate around the wheel axis, on the one hand, longitudinal movement perpendicular to the direction of the wheel axis will occur; on the other hand, transverse movement parallel to the direction of the wheel axis will occur due to the free rotation of the roller [11].

Fig. 1. Mecanum wheel and its exploded view

2.2 Mecanum Wheels Layout

The Mecanum wheel layout consists of a three-wheel layout (see Fig. 2(a)) and a four-wheel layout (see Fig. 2(b)). A single wheel has two moving directions. Therefore, in theory, the three-wheel layout can realize OMRP's omnidirectional movement function [12]. However, the asymmetry of the three-wheel layout will lead to the difficulty of algorithm design, while the four-wheel layout can better avoid the difficulty of algorithm and the instability of OMRP. Therefore, this paper implements OMRP based on four-wheel layout design [13].

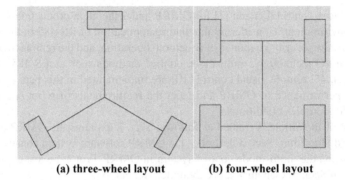

(a) three-wheel layout   (b) four-wheel layout

Fig. 2. Two Mecanum wheel layouts

2.3   Mecanum Wheel Motion Mechanism

As shown in Fig. 3, set parallel to the axle direction for x is to the right direction, upward for the y axis is perpendicular to the shaft direction. OMRP axial length for D, axial spacing for E, the horizontal distance of the center of each wheel and platform center for d, longitudinal distance to e, the wheel center and the platform of the connection with the horizontal Angle for the β, the included angle γ of the roll axis and the wheel axis is 45°, wheel radius for R, the roller radius for r.

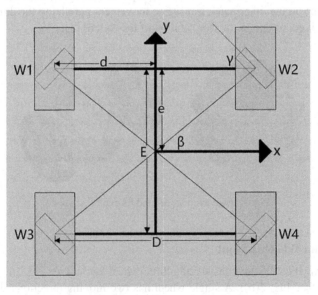

Fig. 3. OMRP mechanical parameter

$W_i (i = 1, 2, 3, 4)$ represent four Mecanum wheels. $V_r = \begin{bmatrix} v_{Rx} & v_{Ry} & \omega_R \end{bmatrix}^T$ represent platform velocity vectors, where v_{Rx} represents horizontal velocity for platform, v_{Ry} represents vertical velocity for platform, and ω_R represents rate of angular velocity for platform. $\omega_i = \begin{bmatrix} \omega_{iw} & \omega_{ir} & \omega_{iz} \end{bmatrix}^T$ represents angular velocity vector for wheel W_i, where ω_{iw} represents angular velocity of a wheel around its axis, ω_{ir} represents angular velocity of a roller around its axis, and ω_{iz} represents the angular velocity of a wheel around a perpendicular line of the ground at the point of contact.

The Jacobian matrix, which is established by each velocity component of wheel W_1 and each velocity component of platform, is written as formula (1).

$$v_R = \begin{bmatrix} v_{Rx} \\ v_{Ry} \\ \omega_R \end{bmatrix} = \begin{bmatrix} 0 & -r \sin \gamma & -e \\ R & r \cos \gamma & -d \\ 0 & 0 & 1 \end{bmatrix} \begin{bmatrix} \omega_{1w} \\ \omega_{1r} \\ \omega_{1z} \end{bmatrix} = J_1 \omega_1 \tag{1}$$

Similarly, the Jacobian matrix J_2, J_3, J_4 of wheels W_2, W_3, W_4 can be obtained, and OMRP composite velocity model (2) is obtained by combing these four formulas.

$$\begin{bmatrix} v_R \\ v_R \\ v_R \\ v_R \end{bmatrix} = \begin{bmatrix} J_1 & & & \\ & J_2 & & \\ & & J_3 & \\ & & & J_4 \end{bmatrix} \begin{bmatrix} \omega_1 \\ \omega_2 \\ \omega_3 \\ \omega_4 \end{bmatrix} \tag{2}$$

Further, the relation between velocity components and external manipulators can be obtained as formula (3).

$$\begin{bmatrix} v_{Rx} \\ v_{Ry} \\ \omega_R \end{bmatrix} = \frac{R}{4} \begin{bmatrix} \tan \gamma & -\tan \gamma & -\tan \gamma & \tan \gamma \\ 1 & 1 & 1 & 1 \\ \frac{tan\gamma}{e+dtan\gamma} & \frac{-tan\gamma}{e+dtan\gamma} & \frac{tan\gamma}{e+dtan\gamma} & \frac{-tan\gamma}{e+dtan\gamma} \end{bmatrix} \begin{bmatrix} \omega_{1w} \\ \omega_{2w} \\ \omega_{3w} \\ \omega_{4w} \end{bmatrix} = J_b \omega_b \tag{3}$$

The inverse solution of OMRP kinematics is formula (4).

$$\begin{bmatrix} \omega_{1w} \\ \omega_{2w} \\ \omega_{3w} \\ \omega_{4w} \end{bmatrix} = \frac{1}{R} \begin{bmatrix} \cot \gamma & 1 & d + e \cot \gamma \\ -\cot \gamma & 1 & -(d + e \cot \gamma) \\ -\cot \gamma & 1 & d + e \cot \gamma \\ \cot \gamma & 1 & -(d + e \cot \gamma) \end{bmatrix} \begin{bmatrix} v_{Rx} \\ v_{Ry} \\ \omega_R \end{bmatrix} \tag{4}$$

According to formula (4), STM32 can realize the conversion of external manipulators including X axis velocity, Y axis velocity and angular velocity around Z axis to the driving data of each motor.

3 Software System Design

The software systems of OMRP include remote-control part and bottom control part. The inner control loop by using STM32 can be responsible for the motor control, which can complete movement automatically. A Raspberry PI is used to be responsible for the connection between remote-control module and STM32.

3.1 Overall System Design

The overall system design of OMRP (see Fig. 4) includes hardware control system, remote-control system, functional hardware system, mechanical structures, etc.

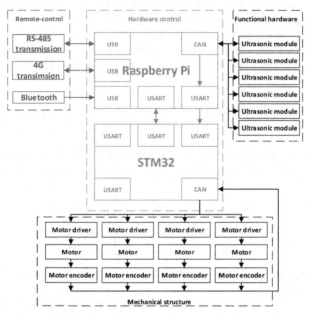

Fig. 4. OMRP overall system design

3.2 Raspberry PI Data Transceiver

As the upper computer of OMRP system, raspberry PI is responsible for data receiving, processing and distribution under multi-mode control (see Fig. 5). The corresponding data communication link is selected for different operation modes. In digital operation mode, through RS-485 data transmission, USB serial port 1 into the raspberry PI system; In Bluetooth control mode, data is sent from PS controller to raspberry PI system through USB serial port 3. In the 4G visual control mode, the remote control data in the control center is transmitted to the 4G network communication card on the robot system by the server through the 4G network, and data communication is carried out through USB serial port 2 to realize data interaction with raspberry PI. After the control instruction data under different control modes enter into raspberry PI through the corresponding communication link, the control data is processed and repackaged, and data communication is conducted between the USART serial port and the STM32 control board of the lower computer, and the control instruction is transmitted to the underlying control system.

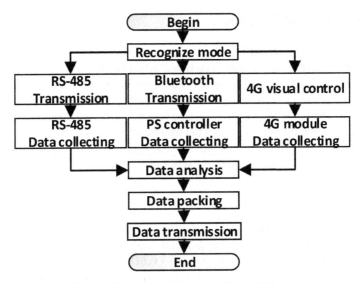

Fig. 5. Flow chart of raspberry PI data delivery

3.3 Bottom Control Based on STM32

STM32 connected Raspberries PI system and executive components. STM32 via a serial port will be treated as raspberries PI receive and decode the good control instruction and access speed and winding speed x axis and y axis z axis angular velocity control capacity. According to the algorithm formula, STM32 will control the amount into the motor drive data, through CAN bus of the motor drive for identification and distribution, to control the speed of the four motors, achieve control of the OMRP (see Fig. 6).

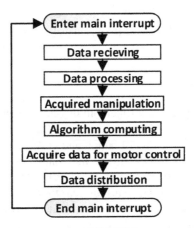

Fig. 6. Flow chart of STM32 bottom control.

4   Multi-mode Control System

The multi-mode control of OMRP includes: digital control mode based on RS-485 data transmission, PS2 gamepad control mode based on Bluetooth transmission, and remote visual control mode based on 4G communication. Remote visual control mode includes control instruction transmission (digital transmission) and image transmission (image transmission). The key to realize the 4G-based visual control is to obtain and encode the control data, and use the cloud server as the data transfer station to forward the data. At the same time, both the driver and OMRP serve as the terminals of signals to receive or send data to the cloud server from the cloud server.

4.1   Digital Control Mode

The data communication link of the digital control mode is shown in Fig. 7. The RS-485 data transmission module is connected on the upper computer (laptop or industrial control computer), and the Raspberry PI on the OMRP is connected to another RS-485 data transmission module. A communication link is formed through the antenna through a pair of data transmission modules matched. When OMRP is working, the upper computer uses the serial port assistant to send data to the RS-485 module through USB serial port, and the data is transmitted wirelessly to the RS-485 module on raspberry PI and enters the raspberry PI system. After raspberry PI receives, processes, and encapsulates the data, it sends the data to STM32. STM32 decoding the data through USART3 serial port and controls the motor driver through CAN bus to achieve the control of OMRP.

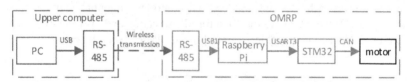

Fig. 7. Flow chart of RS-485 digital remote-control.

4.2   Bluetooth Control Mode

The PS2 controller is equipped with Bluetooth module, which is paired with the Bluetooth receiver on the raspberry PI to connect to the Raspberry PI. The corresponding control instructions of PS2 (see Fig. 8) button and OMRP system respectively realize the control of X and Y axes of OMRP and the control of Z axis rotation. The specific communication link is shown in Fig. 9. After the PS controller is connected to the Raspberry PI through Bluetooth transmission, the raspberry PI receives the data, processes, and encapsulates the data, and transfers it to STM32. OMRP is controlled through algorithmic operation.

Fig. 8. Remote-control button of PS2 controller.

Fig. 9. PS2 controller control link

4.3 4G Remote Visual Control Mode

The 4G remote visual control mode includes the data link of the control instruction and the graph link of the image signal.

The data transmission link realizes the control of OMRP by connecting to the server and receiving control instructions. The OMRP driver is equipped with 4G module, control box and upper computer control software as shown in Fig. 10. The control software of PC processes and encodes the data from the control box or keyboard, and then transmits it to OMRP through cloud server and 4G data transmission module, realizing the control of OMRP by the operator.

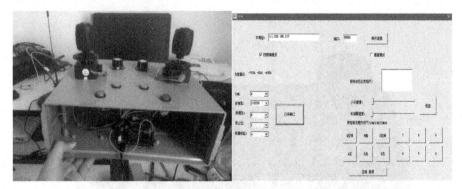

Fig. 10. Control box and control software based on 4G transmission

The image transmission link mainly realizes the transmission of real-time images of the surrounding environment from OMRP to the operator. The CAMERA and 4G image transmission module of OMRP (see Fig. 11) are responsible for the collection and transmission of image data. The cloud server completes data sending and receiving (see Fig. 12), and realizes real-time image monitoring through remote visualization software (see Fig. 13).

Fig. 11. Camera and 4G image transmission module

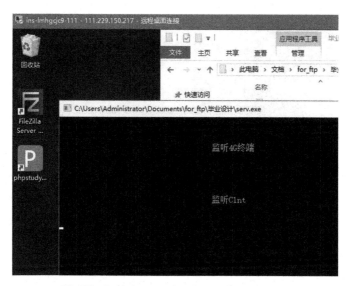

Fig. 12. Real-time monitoring on cloud services

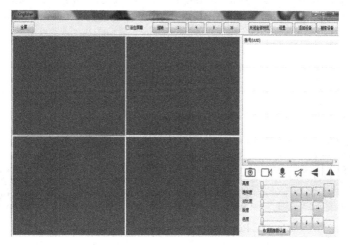

Fig. 13. Remote visualization software

5 Experimental Result

In this paper, an OMRP prototype based on Mecanum wheel is completed as shown in Fig. 14. In the actual production process, an emergency stop switch and a 220 V charging head are added to the prototype. In the performance tests of the prototype, it was able to achieve a maximum forward speed of 1 m/s and undertake a task load of 50 KG.

Fig. 14. Omni-directional mobile robot platform prototype

As shown in Fig. 15, through 4G remote communication, the operator can observe the surrounding environment of OMRP in real time at the control terminal and realize visual control of OMRP.

Fig. 15. Real-time scene and observation images.

Prototype test experiment and remote image transmission experiment have verified the reliability of OMRP's design and the feasibility of 4G communication application. Subsequent experiment will realize the transplantation of image recognition system on OMRP, making OMRP more intelligent and reliable.

6   Conclusion

According to the characteristics of Mecanum wheel, this paper realizes the OMRP prototype of four-wheel system and the underlying control system of OMRP through raspberry PI and STM32. On this basis, combined with 4G communication technology, the visual remote-control mode of 4G is realized. Combined with the software digital control and Bluetooth controller, the multi-mode control of OMRP is realized. The experiment verifies the remote visual control ability of OMRP and provides a feasible scheme for the remote visual control of the robot. In addition, the installation flange of UR manipulator is reserved on the top of OMRP to meet the requirement of carrying industrial manipulator. Therefore, it provides a new idea for 5G to combine with robots in the coming 5G era, and provides a reference for remote mobile operation robots based on 5G communication.

Acknowledgement. The authors are grateful for the support by the National Natural Science Foundation of China (Nos. 61803267 and 61572328), the China Postdoctoral Science Foundation (No. 2017M622757), the Beijing Science and Technology program (No. Z171100000817007), and the National Science Foundation (DFG) in the project Cross Modal Learning, NSFC 61621136008/DFG TRR-169. The authors are grateful for the support of Science and Technology Commissioned Project scheme of Shenzhen University.

References

1. Lee, K., Lee, J., Woo, B.: Modeling and control of a articulated robot arm with embedded joint actuators, pp. 1–4. IEEE (2018)
2. Zhang, K., Liu, L., Tao, C.: Doppler frequency trajectories of the mechanical robot arm and automated guided vehicle in industrial scenarios. In: 2019 IEEE 89th Vehicular Technology Conference (2019)
3. Tian, J.F.: Explore the status quo and development trend of key technologies of AGV. Auto Time (06), 42–43 (2019)
4. Jiang, R.J., Mu, P.G.: Omnidirectional AGV control based on Mecanum wheel. Electron. Measur. Technol. **41**(08), 74–78 (2018)
5. Wang, W.J., Yang, G.L., Zhang, C.: Design of four-wheel omnidirectional mobile robot. Chin. J. Constr. Mach. **14**(04), 327–331 (2016)
6. Wu, X.X.: Research on the belt platform system of patrol rescue robot. Beijing University of Aeronautics and Astronautics (2014)
7. Zhang, J., Li, S.: Application of wireless communication technology in industrial automation. China Chlor-Alkali (01), 28–31 (2020)
8. Zhang, Q., Yang, X., Zhang, Z.Y.: Design and Implementation of Bluetooth module serial port communication. Res. Explor. Lab. **31**(03), 79–82 (2012)
9. Rao, M., Wang, Y.-N., Ma, G.Q.: The electronic piano design based on FPGA and PS2 Interface, pp. 1442–1444. IEEE (2013)
10. Wang, H., Kondi, L., Luthra, A.: 4G Wireless Video Communications (2009)
11. Shi, W.L., Wang, X.S., Jia, Q.: Development of omnidirectional mobile robot based on Mecanum wheel. Mech. Eng. (09), 18–21 (2007)
12. Cao, D., Wang, J.F.: Design and implementation of a three-wheeled omnidirectional mobile robot. J. Beijing Inf. Sci. Technol. Univ. **34**(02), 75–80 (2019)
13. Wang, S.: The chassis and power system design of the omni-directional moving platform. Dalian University of Technology (2016)

AG-DPSO: Landing Position Planning Method for Multi-node Deep Space Explorer

Yongquan Chen[1], Qingjie Zhao[1(✉)], and Rui Xu[2]

[1] Beijing Laboratory of Intelligent Information Technology, School of Computer Science, Beijing Institute of Technology, Beijing 100081, China
{3220190782,zhaoqj}@bit.edu.cn

[2] Institute of Deep Space Exploration Technology, School of Aerospace Engineering, Beijing Institute of Technology, Beijing 100081, China
xurui@bit.edu.cn

Abstract. Explorer landing is a key stage in the deep space exploration mission for small celestial body. Traditional single-node deep space explorers are difficult to land on small celestial body with complex conditions. This paper analyzes the characteristics and difficulties of deep space exploration missions for small celestial body and proposes a new paradigm of multi-node deep space explorers, then analyzes the constraints of the multi-node explorer system and proposes a method for multi-node landing position selection named Adaptive Genetic Discrete Particle Swarm Optimization (AG-DPSO). AG-DPSO inherits GA's global search capability and PSO's fast convergence quality. Through adaptive genetic factors to control the mutation behavior of particle swarms, the landing position of multi-node deep space explorer can be obtained. Experiments demonstrate that the proposed approach is effective in dealing with the multi-node landing position planning issue.

Keywords: Autonomous landing · Position plan · AG-DPSO

1 Introduction

The aerospace field is one of the main areas of autonomous intelligent technology development in the 21st century. For small celestial body, deep space exploration missions generally have the characteristics of being far away from the earth, large communication delays, weak surface gravity and uncertain environment [1], which lead to huge challenges in the operation and control of the explorer. The use of artificial intelligence technology to improve the on-board autonomous capability of the explorer is an important direction to overcome the above challenges.

The landing mission is a key stage in the deep space exploration mission for small body, which is related to the success of the mission. At the beginning of the explorer's landing process, the landing position needs to be selected, then the explorer can plan and execute the landing actions. Small body has a small size and lacks a large flat area on

The work is supported by National Key R&D Program of China (No. 2019YFA0706500).

F. Sun et al. (Eds.): ICCSIP 2020, CCIS 1397, pp. 206–218, 2021.
https://doi.org/10.1007/978-981-16-2336-3_19

the surface. It is prone to rebound when landing under weak gravity [2]. Therefore, the local topography of the landing area, including obstacles such as slopes, pits and rocks, has an important impact on landing safely and maintaining the stable attitude [3].

Traditional single-node explorers are prone to rebound, roll and overturn when actually executing landing missions for small body, such as Hayabusa (Japan) [4, 5], Rosetta (ESA) [6, 7] et al. In response to this issue, we propose a novel multi-node deep space explorer landing system whose nodes can be maneuvered individually. There are flexible physical connections between nodes (see Fig. 1) and each node interacts with others through the physical connection to reduce the probability of rebound, roll and overturn when landing. This is a novel research issue in the field of landing mission planning for deep space explorer. Unlike traditional single-node explorers, multi-node explorer landing systems need to tackle the issue of how to choose the landing position of each node effectively to ensure the efficient landing while satisfying the constraints between nodes and avoiding obstacles on the surface of small body.

Therefore, this paper focuses on the selection issue of the landing position of multi-node deep space explorer, utilizes a grid map to model the landing area map and proposes a method named Adaptive Genetic Discrete Particle Swarm Optimization (AG-DPSO), which enhances global search capability and realizes efficient search in problem space.

Our contributions mainly include the following points:

- We propose a novel deep space explorer system paradigm, analyze and model the constraints of the multi-node system.
- Focusing on the issue of landing position planning, we propose an Adaptive Genetic Discrete Particle Swarm Optimization (AG-DPSO) method to obtain final landing position.
- Through experiments, which demonstrates that the proposed approach can obtain planning solution efficiently.

Fig. 1. Illustration of multi-node explorer.

2 Our Method

At the beginning of the landing process, the multi-node deep space explorer faces a technical issue of landing position selection. In this section, we propose a constraint modeling and processing method and a landing position planning method named AG-DPSO in detail, which based on discrete particle swarm algorithm fused adaptive genetic mechanism to efficiently calculate the optimal landing position of each node. Particle swarm optimization (PSO) [8] operates according to the fitness value of individual particles, abstracts each individual into a particle with no weight and volume in the search space and flies at a certain speed. The flight speed is dynamically adjusted by the flight experience of individual and group. The basic PSO algorithm is used to settle the continuous optimization issues as the variables and functions are continuous, it is easier to fall into the local optimum as well [9]. However, the landing position is represented by coordinate with discrete values for the issue of landing position plan. Therefore, we discretize the PSO algorithm and introduce an adaptive genetic mechanism by encoding the particles discretely, imitating the crossover and mutation behavior of chromosomes [10] and adaptively controlling the probability of crossover and mutation behavior. When the particle swarm is more likely to fall into the local optimum, our approach increases the probability of mutation behavior to maintain a strong convergence rate and enhance the capability to jump out from the local optimum, which can efficiently obtain the planning solution of the multi-node landing position for deep space explorer.

2.1 Constraint Modeling Among Deep Space Explorer Nodes

The landing node of the deep space explorer has a certain size, and there may be flexible physical connections among multiple landing nodes (see Fig. 2). The nodes of the deep space explorer have anti-collision constraint and connection constraint.

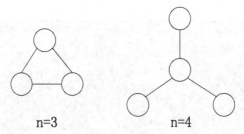

Fig. 2. Illustrations of the connection modes among nodes. Left: a connection mode of 3 nodes. Right: a connection mode of 4 nodes.

Anti-collision Constraint. Anti-collision constraint means that the node cannot collide with the obstacle area and other nodes. The idea to tackle this constraint is twofold. First, the landing node is abstracted into a point, on which a circular area with radius r centered is the smallest area that can accommodate the actual size of the landing node. Second, the edges of the obstacles on the landing area map are expanded with the width r. It can be guaranteed that the landing node will not collide with obstacles on the surface of the small body as long as the abstract point does not fall into the obstacle area after the expansion process. Figure 3 shows a 32×32 grid map of the landing area. The black grids are obstacles and the white grids are flat ground. After expansion processing, the gray and black grids are both new obstacles area.

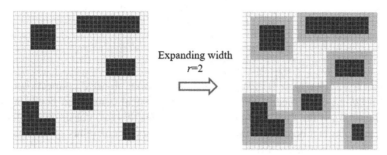

Fig. 3. Expand the edges of the obstacles on the grid map of landing area with the width $r = 2$. The white grids are flat ground, the black are obstacles. After expanding, the gray grids are also seen as obstacle area.

The anti-collision constraint of the deep space explorer nodes is also reflected in the issue of anti-collision among nodes. Two nodes will collide if they are too close, so the minimum threshold d_{min} is set to avoid this collision. While the distance between nodes is greater than the minimum threshold d_{min}, the node collision won't happen.

Connection Constraint. Connection constraint means that the distance between nodes which have flexible physical connections cannot exceed the physical length limit of the connection. In order to deal with this constraint, the maximum threshold d_{max} is set for the nodes with flexible physical connection.

Assuming that the deep space explorer has n landing nodes, the distance between the nodes can be represented by a matrix D, as in Eq. (1):

$$D = \begin{bmatrix} 0 & d_{12} & d_{13} & \dots & d_{1n} \\ d_{21} & 0 & d_{23} & \dots & d_{2n} \\ \vdots & \ddots & \ddots & \ddots & \vdots \\ \vdots & \ddots & \ddots & 0 & d_{n-1,n} \\ d_{n1} & d_{n2} & \dots & \dots & 0 \end{bmatrix} \tag{1}$$

Where d_{pq} is the distance between node p and q. Whether there is a flexible physical connection between two nodes can be represented by a matrix C, as in Eq. (2):

$$C = \begin{bmatrix} 0 & c_{12} & c_{13} & \cdots & c_{1n} \\ c_{21} & 0 & c_{23} & \cdots & c_{2n} \\ \vdots & \ddots & \ddots & \ddots & \vdots \\ \vdots & \ddots & \ddots & 0 & c_{n-1,n} \\ c_{n1} & c_{n2} & \cdots & \cdots & 0 \end{bmatrix} \quad (2)$$

Where $c_{pq} \in \{0, 1\}$, $c_{pq} = 0$ means there is no flexible physical connection between node p and q. $c_{pq} = 1$ means there is a flexible physical connection between node p and q. Therefore, if the final landing position satisfies this two constraints at the same time, we can obtain a qualified solution. The multi-node constraints of the deep space explorer can be expressed as Eq. (3):

$$\begin{cases} d_{min} \le d_{pq} \le d_{max}, \, p < q \le n \; and \; c_{pq} = 1 \\ d_{min} \le d_{pq}, \qquad else \end{cases} \quad (3)$$

2.2 Basic PSO Algorithm

The PSO algorithm is an evolutionary algorithm proposed by Kennedy and Eberhart in 1995 [8]. It is inspired by a social behavior model that imitates a flock of birds or fish in nature [11]. PSO utilizes information sharing and collaboration between individuals in a group to guide the entire group to move towards possible solutions and gradually finds better solutions in the process. A flock of birds or fish is abstracted into particles without mass and volume in the PSO algorithm, the movement speed and direction of each particle are affected by its own historical optimal position and the group's historical optimal position, so as to organically complete the search for the optimal solution of the entire particle swarm in the search space.

The principle of the basic PSO algorithm is as follows [12]: Each particle has a position and velocity in the search space, usually x_i represents the current position of the particle i. v_i represents the current speed of the particle i. $f(x_i)$ represents the fitness function value of the particle i at the current position, which is used to measure the pros and cons of the particle position. p_{best_i} represents the best position in history experienced by the particle i (that is, the position corresponding to the best fitness of the particle), also called the local extremum. g_{best} represents the best historical position experienced by all particles in the entire group, called the global extremum as well.

All historical optimal position information in the particle swarm guides the flight of the entire particle swarm. In each iteration, the velocity and position of the particle i are updated by the local extremum p_{best_i} and the global extremum g_{best} as in Eq. (4, 5):

$$v_i^{t+1} = wv_i^t + c_1 r_1 \left(p_{best_i} - x_i^t \right) + c_2 r_2 \left(g_{best} - x_i^t \right) \quad (4)$$

$$x_i^{t+1} = x_i^t + v_i^{t+1} \quad (5)$$

where w is the inertia factor, which represents the influence weight of the current velocity on the velocity of the next generation particles. c_1 and c_2 are learning factors, which represent the acceleration changes of particles approaching the corresponding positions of p_{best_i} and g_{best}. r_1 and r_2 are uniformly distributed random numbers between 0 and 1. After obtaining the new position of the particle, the corresponding fitness function value $f(x_i)$ can be calculated, p_{best_i} and g_{best} can be updated. The initial position and velocity of the particle swarm are randomly generated and then iterate according to the update formula until a satisfactory solution is found.

2.3 Adaptive Genetic Discrete PSO (AG-DPSO)

The basic PSO algorithm is used to solve the continuous optimization problem and is easier to fall into the local optimum [9]. Thus we propose Adaptive Genetic Discrete Particle Swarm Optimization (AG-DPSO) algorithm, which discretizes the PSO algorithm and introduces an adaptive genetic mechanism for improvement by encoding the particles discretely, imitating the crossover and mutation behavior of chromosomes [10] and adaptively controlling the probability of mutation behavior (see Fig. 4).

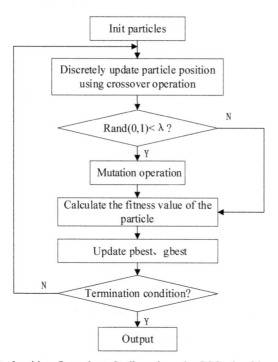

Fig. 4. AG-DPSO algorithm flow chart. It discretizes the PSO algorithm and introduces an adaptive genetic mechanism for improvement by encoding the particles discretely, imitating the crossover and mutation behavior of chromosomes and adaptively controlling the probability of mutation behavior.

Particle Encoding Scheme. The basic PSO algorithm is discretely modeled, which combining with the parameters of the multi-node landing system of the deep space explorer. The particles are discretely encoded according to the number of landing nodes. Assuming that the deep space explorer has n landing nodes and the landing node label is set to $\{1, 2, \ldots, n\}$, then a particle can be expressed as a $2n$-dimensional row vector, which means the current position of the particle i is $X_i = (x_{i1}, y_{i1}, x_{i2}, y_{i2}, \ldots, x_{in}, y_{in})$, where x_{ij} and y_{ij} respectively represent the abscissa and ordinate of the landing position of node j in the particle i.

Fitness Function Design. The fitness function is related to whether the multi-node deep space explorer can efficiently satisfy the constraints and ensure the safety and stability of the landing or not. After landing on the surface of small body, it can play the role of mutual restraint between nodes better if the distance and distribution among the nodes are more balanced. Therefore, the fitness function of the particle is defined as: If the landing position distribution satisfies the connection and anti-collision constraints of the explorer, the fitness is the reciprocal of the distance variance between nodes with flexible physical connections; if not, the fitness is 0. Therefore, the higher the fitness, the better the particles, that is, the more balanced the distribution of nodes with flexible connections, the more stable the explorer will be after landing. The fitness function can be calculated by Eq. (6):

$$f(x_i) = \begin{cases} \dfrac{1}{\sum_{p,q}^{n} c_{pq} \times \left(d_{pq} - \bar{d}\right)^2}, & p < q \text{ and } d_{pq} \geq d_{min} \text{ and } 0 < c_{pq} \times d_{pq} \leq d_{max} \\ 0, & else \end{cases} \tag{6}$$

Where $c_{pq} \in \{0, 1\}$, $c_{pq} = 0$ means there is no flexible physical connection between node p and q. $c_{pq} = 1$ means there is a flexible physical connection between node p and q. d_{pq} is the distance between node p and q. $\bar{d}$ indicates the average distance between nodes with flexible physical connections. $d_{pq} \geq d_{min}$ means that the distance between nodes must be greater than the minimum threshold. $0 < c_{pq} \times d_{pq} \leq d_{max}$ means that the distance between nodes with flexible physical connections should be less than the maximum threshold.

Particle Update Strategy. Genetic algorithm is designed and proposed according to the evolutionary laws of organisms in nature. Genetic operations include three basic genetic operators: selection, crossover and mutation [13]. We discretize the update strategy of particle i and introduce a genetic mechanism, which treats each particle as a chromosome. The proposed approach's update operations are crossover and mutation.

Particle Update Formula. The discretized position update formula is as Eq. (7):

$$x_i^{t+1} = \lambda \otimes mutation\left(c_2 \otimes cross\left(c_1 \otimes cross\left(w \otimes f_{a,b}\left(x_i^t\right), p_{best_i}\right), g_{best}\right)\right) \tag{7}$$

Where w, c_1, c_2 are constants between 0 and 1, λ is the adaptive genetic factor. Binary operator $\otimes$ defines the operation rule of a constant and a function: $constant \otimes function()$ means to generate a random number ρ between 0 and 1, only if $\rho < constant, function()$ will be executed. $f_{a,b}\left(x_i^t\right)$ represents the swap operation of the segment a and b in x_i^t. $cross\left(x_i^t, p_{best_i}\right)$ represents the cross operation x_i^t and p_{best_i}, same goes for $cross\left(x_i^t, g_{best}\right)$. $mutation\left(x_i^t\right)$ represents the mutation operation of the random segment in x_i^t.

Crossover Operation. As shown in Fig. 5, this operation selects two particles first, then selects a segment in the sequence and swaps the values of the two particles in this segment. There are three situations in the crossover operation of particle i: (i) Particle i crosses with itself, (ii) particle i crosses with the local optimal particle p_{best_i}, (iii) particle i crosses with the global optimal particle g_{best}. Since p_{best_i} and g_{best} are better particles, choosing to cross with them will help to obtain better particles, but it is also easier to fall into the local optimum on the other hand.

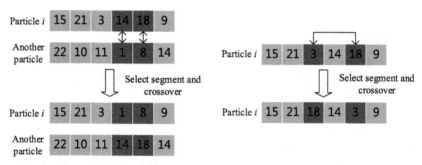

Fig. 5. Chromosome's crossover operation. Left: segment {14, 8} in particle i crosses with segment {1, 8} in another particle. Right: segment {3} in particle i crosses with segment {18}.

Mutation Operation. As shown in Fig. 6, some segments of particle i are mutated, that is, the values of one or several segments are randomly reset. The introduction of mutation operation can effectively jump out from the local optimal limit and have a greater probability of obtaining better global particles.

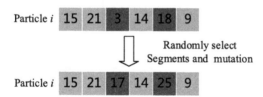

Fig. 6. Chromosome's mutation operation. Segments {3}{18} in particle i are randomly reset to {17}{25}.

Adaptive Genetic Factor. At the beginning of the iteration of particle swarm, it will hardly fall into the local optimum. As the iteration progresses, the possibility of the particle swarm falling into the local optimum increases. It can be analyzed that the mutation operation which can help the particle swarm jump out from the local optimum has little effect in the early stage of the iteration, but the influence becomes stronger in the latter stage. Therefore, we design an adaptive factor to affect the mutation operation, so the probability of the mutation operation can be adjusted according to the iteration situation to achieve the purpose of optimizing the genetic operation. Assuming that the adaptive factor is λ, the maximum iteration number of the swarm is T_{max} and the current iteration number is t, the formula of the adaptive factor can be expressed as Eq. (8):

$$\lambda = \frac{t}{T_{max}} \tag{8}$$

As the iteration number increases, λ gradually approaches 1. By adding an adaptive factor, the particles are more likely to undergo more drastic mutations as the iteration number increases. It can improve the efficiency of the algorithm while ensuring a high probability of jumping out from the local optimum.

3   Experiments

We use a grid map data to conduct a validity experiment on the AG-DPSO algorithm, then use the other two algorithms to test under the same environment and parameters, and finally compare the performance of the three algorithms.

3.1   Configuration

The hardware platform used in the experiment is a Windows10 64bit notebook with an AMD Ryzen5 3550H 2.10 GHz CPU and 8 GB RAM. The language used is Pyhon 3.7.7 and the programming environment is Visual Studio Code (version 1.46).

3.2   Parameters Settings

System Parameters Setting. We initialize the explorer system parameters in our experiments first. As the Table 1 shows, we set the number of nodes $n = 3$, the node radius $r = 2$, the minimum distance between nodes $d_{min} = 10$ and the maximum distance between nodes with flexible physical connections $d_{max} = 20$, we also set the node connection mode of the explorer to $C = \begin{bmatrix} 0 & 1 & 1 \\ 1 & 0 & 1 \\ 1 & 1 & 0 \end{bmatrix}$.

Table 1. System parameters setting.

System parameters	Value
Nodes number n	3
Node radius r	2
Minimum distance d_{min}	10
Maximum distance d_{max}	20

Algorithm Parameters Setting. As shown in Table 2, we initialize the algorithm parameters by setting particle swarm size $p\_n = 50$, the maximum iteration number $T_{max} = 1000$, inertia factor $\omega = 0.5$, learning factor of crossover operation with p_{best_i} $c_1 = 0.6$, learning factor of crossover operation with g_{best} $c_2 = 0.6$.

3.3 Results and Analysis

Verification Experiment. After the iterative operation in one experiment, the global optimal particle is obtained $g_{best} = \{17, 22, 14, 11, 25, 14\}$, that is, the coordinates of three landing positons are $(17, 22)$, $(14, 11)$, $(25, 14)$, the distance matrix between nodes

is $D = \begin{bmatrix} 0 & 11.4 & 11.3 \\ 11.4 & 0 & 11.4 \\ 11.3 & 11.4 & 0 \end{bmatrix}$.

As shown in Fig. 7, through visualizing the grid map data and the planning solution, it can be seen intuitively that the landing positions avoid the collision with obstacle area and other nodes.

Table 2. Algorithm parameters setting.

System parameters	Value
Swarm size p_n	50
Iteration number T_{max}	1000
Inertia factor ω	0.5
Learning factor c_1	0.6
Learning factor c_2	0.6

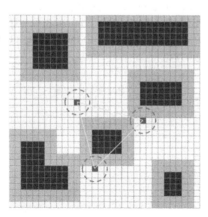

Fig. 7. Landing position planning results of multi-node explorer

Comparative Experiment. We compare the AG-DPSO algorithm with G-DPSO algorithm and DPSO algorithm in this experiment. the G-DPSO algorithm does not introduce an adaptive genetic operator and the DPSO algorithm does not have mutation operation or adaptive genetic operator. In the case of same environment and parameters settings, we conduct multiple experiments. In order to display the results more intuitively, the optimal fitness and average optimal fitness are converted to their reciprocal, as in Eq. (9, 10).

The experimental results are shown in Table 3, after adding mutation operation, the algorithm's global search ability is improved and better solutions can be obtained. The introduction of an adaptive genetic operator to dynamically control the mutation behavior reduces the running time while maintaining the performance of the algorithm, which shows the efficiency of the AG-DPSO algorithm.

$$F = \frac{1}{optimal\ fitness} \tag{9}$$

$$\overline{F} = \frac{1}{average\ optimal\ fitness} \tag{10}$$

Table 3. Comparison of experimental results of 3 algorithms.

Algorithm	F	$\overline{F}$	Average time
AG-DPSO (proposed)	**6**	**26.53**	2.72 s
G-DPSO	8.67	28.27	3.19 s
DPSO	24	59.6	**2.26 s**

The convergence curves of the three algorithms are shown in Fig. 8. The DPSO algorithm starts to converge after 200 iterations and falls into the local optimum while the AG-DPSO algorithm and the G-DPSO algorithm have stronger ability to jump out from the local optimum. Based on the indicators of global search capability, solution quality, convergence speed and running time, AG-DPSO algorithm is better than G-DPSO algorithm and DPSO algorithm. The comparative experiment reveals that the AG-DPSO algorithm is efficient in dealing with the landing position planning issue for multi-node deep space explorer.

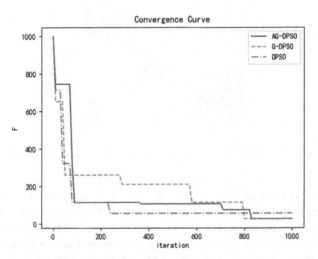

Fig. 8. Convergence curves of 3 algorithms.

4 Conclusions

Aiming at the landing position planning issue for the multi-node deep space explorer, this paper analyzes and models the system constraint information, proposes Adaptive Genetic Discrete Particle Swarm Optimization (AG-DPSO) by discretizing the particle swarm algorithm, fusing the crossover and mutation operation in the genetic mechanism and adding an adaptive genetic factor to control the probability of mutation operation to enhance global search ability and improve algorithm efficiency. AG-DPSO can effectively deal with the anti-collision constraint and connection constraint of the multi-node deep space explorer, generate landing positions that satisfy the distance constraint, prevent collisions with ground obstacles and other nodes, maintain a balanced distribution of nodes with flexible physical connections and increase the stability and safety of the explorer after landing.

This is a small step in the study of multi-node deep space explorer landing mission planning. In future work, we are going to study the issue of multi-node landing position allocation and dynamic planning of multi-node deep space explorer landing position in a dynamic environment. Then, we will study the action planning during the landing process after obtaining the landing position.

References

1. Gomez, M.: A typical spacecraft autonomy system. In: IMCL Workshop on Machine Learning for Autonomous Space Applications (2003)
2. Cui, P., Yuan, X., Zhu, S., Qiao, D.: Research progress of small body autonomous landing techniques. J. Astronaut. **37**(07), 759–767 (2016). (in Chinese with English abstract)
3. Sun, Z., Meng, L., Zhang, H., Jia, Y., Peng, J., et al.: Technology of Deep Space Exploration. Beijing Institute of Technology Press, Beijing (2018). (in Chinese)
4. Abe, S., Mukai, T., Hirata, N., Barnouin, O.S., et al.: Mass and local topography measurements of Itokawa by Hayabusa. Science **312**(5778), 1344–1347 (2006)
5. Barnouin-Jha, O.S., Cheng, A.F., Mukai, T., et al.: Small-scale topography of 25143 Itokawa from the Hayabusa laser altimeter. Icarus **198**(1), 108–124 (2008)
6. Biele, J., Ulamec, S., Maibaum, M., Roll, R., Witte, L., et al.: The landing(s) of Philae and inferences about comet surface mechanical properties. Science **349**(6247), aaa9816 (2015)
7. Accomazzo, A., Lodiot, S., Companys, V.: Rosetta mission operations for landing. Acta Astronaut. **125**, 30–40 (2016)
8. Kennedy, J., Eberhart, R.: Particle swarm optimization. In: Proceedings of the IEEE International Joint Conference on Neural Networks, Perth, Australia, vol. 4, pp. 1942–1948 (1995)
9. Shi, Y., Eberhart, R.: A modified particle swarm optimizer. In: IEEE International Conference on Evolutionary Computation, Anchorage, pp. 69–73 (1998)
10. Holland, J.H.: Adaptation in Natural and Artificial Systems: An Introductory Analysis with Applications to Biology, Control, and Artificial Intelligence, 2nd edn. MIT Press, Cambridge (1992)

11. Reynolds, C.W.: Flocks, herds and schools: a distributed behavioral model. Comput. Graph. **21**(4), 25–34 (1987)
12. Shi, Y., Eberhart, R.: Particle swarm optimization: developments, applications and resources. In: Proceedings of the 2001 Congress on Evolutionary Computation, vol. 1, pp. 81–86. IEEE Press, Seoul (2001)
13. Li, M., Kou, J., Lin, D., et al.: Basic Theories and Applications of Genetic Algorithms. Science Press, Beijing (2002). (in Chinese)

A New Paralleled Semi-supervised Deep Learning Method for Remaining Useful Life Prediction

Tiancheng Wang[1,2](✉) 🆔, Di Guo[1,2] 🆔, and Ximing Sun[1,2] 🆔

[1] School of Control Science and Engineering, Dalian University of Technology,
Dalian 116024, China
wangtc@mail.dlut.edu.cn, sunxm@dlut.edu.cn
[2] Key Laboratory of Intelligent Control and Optimization for Industrial Equipment
of Ministry of Education, Dalian University of Technology, Dalian 116024, China

Abstract. As a complex and expensive system, the aero-engine is confronted with many problems that are difficult to be handled by traditional methods, especially in the remaining useful life (RUL) estimation field. In recent studies, the accuracy and stability of remaining useful life prediction are still defective. In this paper, a new paralleled semi-supervised network is proposed to predict the remaining useful life of the turbofan engine to improve the stability of the predicted results. To demonstrate the effectiveness of the system, experimental verification is carried out by using the popular commercial modular aero propulsion system simulation (C-MAPSS) data set which is published by the national aeronautics and space administration (NASA). Moreover, the superiority of this method is proved by comparing with the other semi-supervised learning methods. The results of this study suggest that this paralleled semi-supervised training model is a new and promising approach.

Keywords: Aero-engine · Prognostics and health management ·
Remaining useful life · C-MAPSS · Paralleled semi-supervised

1 Introduction

During the past few decades, the prosperous evolution of artificial intelligence is significant in promoting the progress of industries, computers, and other areas. Meanwhile, prognostics and health management (PHM) is one of the products of industrial intelligence [1]. Moreover, PHM has attracted enormous attention, especially in aerospace equipment and large industrial devices which has security-related components or systems with expensive downtime and maintenance costs [2,3]. It is used for maintenance before system/facility failure by assessing system

Supported by the National Natural Science Foundation of China under Grant Nos 61890920 & 61890921 and LiaoNing Revitalization Talents Program XLYC1808015.

status which includes operating environment, real-time risk, or remaining useful life (RUL) based on historical trajectory data [4]. As a result, these make the importance of RUL prediction exceed CBM and PHM according to the increasing problems of global warming [5]. However, when faced with extremely complex data, traditional prognosis algorithms cannot achieve good results [6]. In recent years, deep learning (DL) has become a vigoroso field for processing highly non-linear and changing sequential data in the PHM domain with minimal human input [7].

In general, RUL prediction methods can divide into model-based, data-driven, and hybrid systems. Although several articles utilized the model or traditional machine learning approach to estimate the turbofan engines remaining useful life. Because of the complexity of modeling with this data set, and even the RUL can hardly be accurately assessed by human beings, thus most of the research is related to deep learning. Therefore, the method based on the neural network is promising in the RUL estimating. Recently, more and more articles started to focus on the combination of two different networks [5, 10, 11].

In this article, the popular publicly available NASA C-MAPSS dataset [8] is used to verify the effectiveness of the proposed approach. This studys main contributions are as follows:

- Application of a self-gated activation function Swish, and discussion on loss function and evaluation criteria.
- The paralleled semi-supervised learning improves the accuracy and stability of RUL estimation compared to the related works in multivariate time series data.
- Substantial comparative reproduction experiments are carried out to verify the method.

This paper starts with introducing the structure of proposed method in Sect. 2. The superiority and effectiveness of the method are verified by numerous of experiments and compared in Sect. 3. We conclude the paper with conclusions in Sect. 4.

2   Architecture

In this section, the proposed architecture for estimation is presented with its key components, i.e. variational auto encoder and the proposed method.

2.1   Variational Auto Encoder (VAE)

Variational auto-encoder (VAE) is proposed by Kingma and Welling [12] as an improved version of auto-encoder (AE), and Doersch [13] made a detailed introduction and tutorial about VAE. VAE has a wide range of applications in data generation and has been proved to be extremely effective in generating complex data. In this research, a VAE model is utilized for reducing the data dimension, and its structure is shown in Fig. 1.

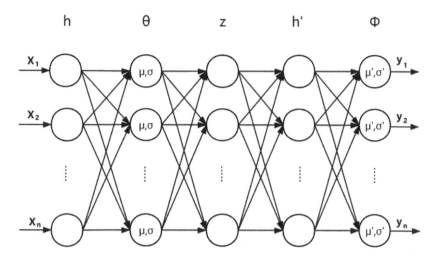

Fig. 1. The difference between VAE and AE

The input sequential data is $x_t (t = 1, 2, 3 \cdots, n)$ where n denotes the sequence length. The layer h is the hidden layer of the encoder part, and θ is the mean vectors and standard deviation vectors, which can be expressed as Eq. (1) and Eq. (2).

$$\mu = W_\mu h + b_\mu \tag{1}$$

$$\sigma = W_\sigma h + b_\sigma \tag{2}$$

The layer z is the output of the encoder layers, i.e. in this research, its outputs are the data after dimension reduction.

The layers h′ and ϕ is the counterpart of the layers h and n in the decoder layers. The outputs of the VAE model is $y_t (t = 1, 2, 3 \cdots, n)$ which is used to compare with the inputs for unsupervised learning.

2.2   The Proposed Model Architecture

The paralleled semi-supervised architecture is shown in Fig. 2. In the first stage, trained encoder layers will be utilized as an unsupervised pretraining part in order to learn abstract features and reduce dimension from the unlabeled input data. In the second stage, a paralleled LSTM and CNN layers are used to learn the dimensionality reduction data at the same time. In the last stage, deep neural networks (DNN) layers are used to concentrate the results of the second stage and estimate the remaining useful life.

3   Experiments

In this section, the results of the proposed semi-supervised architecture will be compared to recent studies, and several works have been reproduced. Experiments are performed on the four subsets provided in the C-MAPSS dataset.

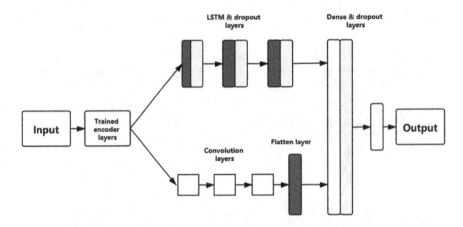

Fig. 2. The structure of the proposed model architecture

All experiments are run on Intel(R) Core(TM) i5-9400 CPU @ 2.90 GHz and the Microsoft Windows 10 operating system. The programming language is python 3.8 under the TensorFlow 2.2.0 frame, and all the results in this section are based on the average value of 10 times.

The training process can be divided into four steps. First, extracting the useful data from the C-MAPSS dataset and processing the data. Secondly, establishing a variational auto-encoder model and training variational auto-encoder model with training data, and output the untrainable encoder layers. Next, building the entire model with the trained encoder layers. Finally, using testing data to verify results.

3.1 Experimental Setup

C-MAPSS Dataset. The Commercial Modular Aero Propulsion System Simulation (C-MAPSS) dataset had been wildly used in the turbofan engines RUL research. It is released by NASA [8] contains 4 different data-sets including 3 operational setting parameters, combined with 21 sensor measurement parameters. It includes 4 subsets, shown in Table 1. Each subset contains a training set and a testing set.

Table 1. The C-MAPSS dataset

Dataset	FD001	FD002	FD003	FD004
Time series training set	100	260	100	249
Time series testing set	100	259	100	248
Operating conditions	1	6	1	6
Fault conditions	1	1	2	2

Performance Assessment. In recent research, two functions are used for performance assessment: score function and root mean square error (RMSE). The RMSE is one of the parameters used to evaluate a prediction problem in normally, and score function is proposed by NASA [8] which is more valuable, and shown in Eq. (3).

$$score = \sum_{i=1}^{n} s_i \tag{3a}$$

$$s_i = \begin{cases} e^{-\frac{d_i}{13}}, & for \quad d_i < 0 \\ e^{\frac{d_i}{10}}, & for \quad d_i \geq 0 \end{cases} \tag{3b}$$

$$d_i = RUL_{pred} - RUL_{true} \tag{3c}$$

For engine degradation, an early prediction is preferred than a late prediction, predicting engine failure in advance can effectively avoid huge economic losses. Furthermore, predictions that deviate far from the actual value are meaningless. The scoring algorithm proposed by NASA is asymmetric in terms of the true time of failure, late predictions are penalized more severely than early predictions, and the penalty increases exponentially with the increase in error [8]. And the difference between the two values shown in Fig. 3. Therefore, this study chooses the score function as the main evaluation criteria.

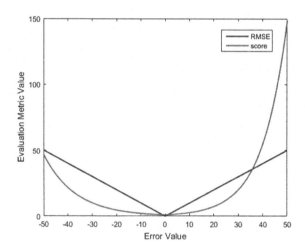

Fig. 3. The difference between RMSE and score

3.2 Data Processing

Zhang et al. [14] indicated some sensors records are essentially unchanged, i.e. they cannot provide valuable information for RUL prediction. Therefore, the sensor measurements involved in the training can be reduced to 14, which including 2, 3, 4, 7, 8, 9, 11, 12, 13, 14, 15, 17, 20 and 21.

In general, data should be normalized before machine learning. This study utilized Minmax standardization. For the residual useful life prediction problem, it is impossible to accurately evaluate the RUL of the system at each time step without a precise model. According to the research in literature [15], RUL constant R_{early} was used as the target tag of early data points. Li et al. [9] had verified the effectiveness of R_{early}, and it was set as 125 in this paper.

3.3 Loss Function and Activation Function

In this study, RMSE and score are found cannot be an ideal value at the same time. As shown in the picture, there are remarkable differences between score and RMSE, mainly including gradients and symmetry. Moreover, this papers assessment is mainly according to the score function. Thus, this study selects the score function as the loss function.

The selection of activation function also has a great influence on deep learning. In recent research, Relu and Sigmoid is a standard choice. In this paper, a self-gated activation called Swish will be proposed, which can be expressed as (4).

$$f(x) = x \cdot sigmoid(\beta x) \tag{4}$$

The parameter β can be a constant or trainable parameter. Swish is more derivable, continuous and smooth compared to other functions. Therefore, this study proposed Swish as the activation function.

3.4 Experimental Performance

VAE Performance. The VAE model in this study played a role in dimension reduction and feature extraction, and the effect of feature extraction had a decisive impact on the predicted results. Figure 4 shows the effect of the number of hidden layers and the feature dimensionality in the VAE model on the network prognostic performance. According to the figure, more hidden layers of VAE lead to higher score values. That indicates the shallow ones is able to capture more useful information than the deep ones.

Comparing with Other Architectures. In this study, some of the methods with better effects were selected for comparison. The comparison results of the RUL estimation only with sequence data using different methods are presented in Table 2. Compared with other semi-supervised deep learning method, the paralleled systems has higher accuracy, especially in FD002 and FD004.

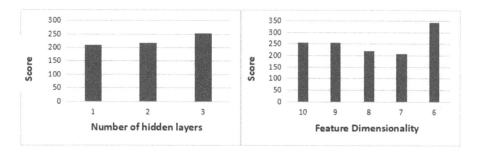

Fig. 4. The effect of the number of hidden layers and the feature dimensionality in VAE model based on FD001

Table 2. The comparison with other methods

		VAE+LSTM	VAE+CNN	Proposed model
RMSE	RMSE	12.14	12.98	12.19
	Score	214.3	215.7	**208.11**
RMSE	RMSE	22.15	21.09	18.71
	Score	3576.52	3412.38	**2079.27**
RMSE	RMSE	12.97	13.49	12.95
	Score	263.0	287.5	**246.75**
RMSE	RMSE	24.19	23.57	22.67
	Score	3581.40	3697.45	**2619.20**

4 Conclusions and Discussion

In this paper, a deep learning prediction method with paralleled semi-supervised structure is proposed. Moreover, a new activation function is applied to alleviate the over-fitting problem. Furthermore, comparing with the related works, the paralleled semi-supervised structure has higher stability and accuracy.

Different from previous articles, this paper makes a discussion on loss function and evaluation criteria. According to the uniqueness of aero-engines, this paper proposed the score function as the main evaluation criteria. What's more, experiments show that a self-gated activation function Swish is more effective.

Furthermore, this research proposed a new paralleled semi-supervised structure for RUL estimation. The un-supervised part was used to reduce the dimension of the original data and improve the accuracy of the results effectively. Moreover, a paralleled network structure is utilized to increase the stability of the predicted results. The experiments on popular C-MAPSS data sets demonstrate the effectiveness of the proposed method.

References

1. Benkedjouh, T., Medjaher, K., Zerhouni, N., et al.: Remaining useful life estimation based on nonlinear feature reduction and support vector regression. Eng. Appl. Artif. Intell. **26**, 1751–1760 (2016)
2. Zaidan, M.A., Mills, A.R., Harrison, R.F., et al.: Gas turbine engine prognostics using Bayesian hierarchical models: a variational approach. Mech. Syst. Sign. Process. **70**, 120–140 (2016)
3. Kan, M.S., Tan, A.C., Mathew, J.: A review on prognostic techniques for non-stationary and non-linear rotating systems. Mech. Syst. Sign. Process. **62**, 1–20 (2015)
4. Shin, J.H., Jun, H.B.: On condition based maintenance policy. J. Comput. Des. Eng. **2**, 119–127 (2015)
5. Si, X.S., Wang, W., Hu, C.H., et al.: Remaining useful life estimation – a review on the statistical data driven approaches. Eur. J. Oper. Res. **213**, 1–14 (2011)
6. Ellefsen, A.L., Bjørlykhaug, E., Æsøy, V., et al.: Remaining useful life predictions for turbofan engine degradation using semi-supervised deep architecture. Reliab. Eng. Syst. Saf. **183**, 240–251 (2019)
7. Zhao, G., Zhang, G., Ge, Q., et al.: Research advances in fault diagnosis and prognostic based on deep learning. In: (PHM-Chengdu) 2016, PSHMC, Heidelberg, pp. 1–6. IEEE (2016). https://doi.org/10.1109/PHM.2016.7819786
8. Damage Propagation Modeling for Aircraft Engine Run-to-Failure Simulation. https://ti.arc.nasa.gov/project/prognostic-data-repository. Accessed 12 Dec 2008
9. Li, X., Ding, Q., Sun, J.: Remaining useful life estimation in prognostics using deep convolution neural networks. Reliab. Eng. Syst. Saf. **172**, 1–11 (2018)
10. Li, J., Li, X., He, D.: A directed acyclic graph network combined with CNN and LSTM for remaining useful life prediction. IEEE Access **7**, 75464–75475 (2019)
11. Yu, W., Kim, Y., Mechefske, C.: An improved similarity-based prognostic algorithm for RUL estimation using an RNN autoencoder scheme. Reliab. Eng. Syst. Saf. **199**, 1–12 (2020)
12. Kingma, D.P., Welling, M.: Auto-encoding variational bayes, pp. 1–14. arXiv:1312.6114v10 [stat.ML] (2014)
13. Doersch, C.: Auto-encoding variational bayes, pp. 1–23. arXiv:1606.05908 [stat.ML] (2016)
14. Zhang, C., Lim, P., Qin, A.K., et al.: Multiobjective deep belief networks ensemble for remaining useful life estimation in prognostics. IEEE Trans. Neural Netw. Learn. Syst. **99**, 1–13 (2016)
15. Ramasso, E.: Investigating computational geometry for failure prognostics. Int. J. Prognostics Health Manage. **5**, 1–13 (2014)

Balancing Task Allocation in Multi-robot Systems Using adpK-Means Clustering Algorithm

Ling Chong, Qingjie Zhao$^{(\boxtimes)}$, and Kairen Fang

Beijing Laboratory of Intelligent Information Technology, School of Computer Science,
Beijing Institute of Technology, Beijing 100081, China
{chongling,zhaoqj,3220180793}@bit.edu.cn

Abstract. Multi-robot systems are becoming more and more significant in industrial, where allocating tasks for every robot in a reasonable way is a tedious process. The current research mainly focused on reducing the distance between robots and tasks while ignoring the balance of workloads between robots. To address the aforementioned issues, this paper proposes an adaptive K-means clustering algorithm (adpK-means) in order to control a team of robots to accomplish all tasks with a good balance and at a minimal cost. Compared with the K-means clustering algorithm, our proposed algorithm has better performance, where through adaptive dynamic scaling of the clustering space in the iterative process, multiple robots can complete missions with well-distributed workloads. The experimental results show that the algorithm effectively reduces the total energy consumption of the entire robot system and ensures that the tasks of robots are comparative.

Keywords: Multi-robot · Task allocation · adpK-means clustering algorithm

1 Introduction

With the development of modern industry and manufacturing, industrial robots are widely used in automobiles, electronics, logistics, metals, food, and chemicals [1]. In recent years, with the highly coupled and coordinated development of multiple disciplines such as computer technology, electronic communication, automation control, artificial intelligence, chips, robots have almost replaced highly repetitive and dangerous tasks [2]. However, the single-robot system cannot undertake the complex task requirements of industry and manufacturing because of its weak individual perception and processing information ability and single task execution ability, and the multi-robot system has emerged as the times require [3]. The multi-robot system is composed of multiple intelligent robots that can perceive the environment and perform different tasks. The collaborative work of multi-robots can make full use of the advantages of multi-machine collaboration and carry out industrial production more efficiently and stably,

This work was supported by the National Key R&D Program of China (No. 2017YFB1303300 and 2019YFA0706500).

but it also brings scholars [4]. Here comes a huge challenge, that is, how to allocate tasks for the multi-robot system.

The core problem of the multi-robot system's task allocation is to make the task allocation of different robots more balanced as much as possible to minimize the overall consumption of the multi-robot system. The collaborative work of multi-robot systems usually has two stages [5]. The first link is multi-robot task allocation, and the second link is multi-robot path planning. Usually, the task allocation result of the first stage directly affects whether the second stage can be solved to obtain the lowest cost work path. If the distribution is unreasonable or unbalanced, it isn't easy to find an efficient path planning sequence in the second stage of planning [6]. Multiple Traveling Salesman Problem [7] (Multiple Traveling Salesman Problem, MTSP) is a way to model this problem. This modelling method compares each robot to a travelling salesman, and the waypoint represents the city location that the traveling salesman needs to visit. The goal of optimization is to meet the constraint conditions; all path points will be called, and optimize the objective function [8].

Many types of research on task allocation for multi-robots system have been performed. For instance, these studies include combinatorial auction algorithm [9], genetic algorithm [10], agent-based algorithm [11], pattern formation algorithm [12], the graph matching algorithm [13] and so on. For example, Xu et al. [14] proposed a two-stage MTSP solution method, which clustered all cities through the K-means clustering method. The number of clusters is the number of traveling salesmen. During the clustering, the workload of a different travelling salesman is guaranteed to be as balanced as possible. The upper limit is set for the number of cities allocated by each travelling salesman after clustering to make the distribution result more reasonable. In the second stage, a genetic algorithm is used to plan and solve the results after clustering. Xie [15] uses the multi-knapsack algorithm to allocate the welding path points and improves the genetic algorithm to realize the path planning of a single robot. Shi Dechao [16] also used the multi-knapsack algorithm to learn the distribution of welding points and added the limit of the number of welding points so that the workload of each robot could be balanced, which solved the problem of welding point path distribution in white body welding. In the planning stage, detailed parameter analysis and adjustment are carried out according to the actual scene to realize welding path planning. Burger et al. [17] proposed a dichotomous variable method based on 2-index. Each time the next path point is selected, the selection is based on the current path point, which reduces the complexity of running time and improves the efficiency of the algorithm. Kitjacharoenchai et al. [18] used K-means clustering pre-allocation for the logistics and distribution of trucks to obtain the set of goods that each car needs to be responsible for. In planning, the idea of a greedy strategy is adopted, and the cargo location with the shortest distance from the current location is selected as the next route point.

However, the current attempts made by the researchers concentrate only on minimizing the distance between the robots and the tasks, and not much importance is given to the utilization of the robots. In industrial production, multi-robot systems mostly work in an assembly-line manner. Uneven distribution of tasks among multiple robots will result in higher system consumption. The K-means algorithm can divide all vectors in the clustering space into K clusters. Formally, because of this, the clustering algorithm can be used to solve the multi-robot task allocation problem. However, it has limitations. The algorithm is relatively affected by initialization and is more susceptible to outliers. Therefore, it cannot guarantee the balance of multi-robot task allocation. To overcome these deficiencies, this paper proposes an adpK-means clustering algorithm through adaptive dynamic scaling of the clustering space in the iterative process.

2 Problem Statement

The multi-traveling salesman problem means that multiple traveling salesmen traverse all cities under the condition of satisfying the constraints, and solve the planning path of each traveling salesman when the objective function is optimized [19]. The path planning problem of multi-robots is that n robots are responsible for executing m task points. After completing the task, each robot returns to its starting position to ensure that each task point will be executed by the robot and cannot be performed repeatedly. In this article, we define it as a multi-source closed-loop multi-traveling salesman problem. The traveling salesman can be abstracted as a robot, and the task point is abstracted as the city that the traveling salesman wants to visit. The following will conduct mathematical modeling and research on this problem.

There are two commonly used evaluation methods in the multi-source closed-loop multi-traveling salesman problem: minimizing the maximum cost $maxspan$ and minimizing the total cost $mincost$. Suppose there are a total of n traveling salesmen, and the cost of the i-th traveling salesman is $cost_i$ ∘ The description of $maxspan$ is shown in formula (1), and the description of $mincost$ is shown in formula (2).

$$maxspan = max\{cost_1, cost_2, \cdots, cost_n\} \tag{1}$$

$$mincost = \sum\nolimits_{i=1}^{n} cost_i \tag{2}$$

Because the engineering problem faced by this article is a multi-robot collaborative operation problem, in the actual operation process, only when all the robots complete the operation can the operation of the next workpiece be successfully carried out. Considering that multi-robot systems are commonly oriented to industries, the robot's working time is based on the robot with the longest working time, so we use the minimized maximum cost $maxspan$ as the objective function.

The specific mathematical definition of the multi-source closed-loop multi-traveling salesman problem is given here: Given a set of n cities, the number of traveling salesmen is t, and the distance between city i and city j is defined as $d(i, j)$. The number of cities allocated by the k-th traveling salesman is $count_k$, and the sequence of cities visited is $Tout_k = (c_1^k, c_2^k, \cdots, c_{count_k}^k)$, where $\sum_{k=1}^{t} count_k = n$, each city will be Traverse and only traverse once, according to formula (3), calculate the path length $cost_k$ of the k-th traveling salesman as shown in formula (3), and the objective function calculation is shown in formula (2).

$$cost_k = \sum\nolimits_{i=j}^{count_k - 1} d\left(c_j^k, c_{j+1}^k\right) + d\left(c_1^k, c_{count_k}^k\right) \tag{3}$$

Task allocation is to allocate tasks to the corresponding traveling salesman for planning, simplifying complex problems, and turning them into general traveling salesman problems, which can significantly reduce the complexity of the problem and improve calculation efficiency. The path point allocation process will have different restrictions according to actual application scenarios. The scenario in this article is the collaborative work of multiple robots, and it is stipulated that each robot has the same structure and the same type of task point. Therefore, any task point can be assigned to any robot, and there is no upper limit on the number of task points for each robot. In this paper, our objective function metric is to minimize the maximum cost *maxspan*, which is also out of consideration for practical problems. The multi-robot execution operation process is an assembly line operation process in an industrial environment. Therefore, optimizing the robot with the longest working time and reducing its running time can improve the efficiency of industrial production.

3   AdpK-Means Clustering Algorithm

3.1   K-Means Clustering Algorithm

Researchers related to task allocation algorithm used K-means clustering or other clustering algorithms [20] to solve the problem, and achieved good results. The clustering algorithm is an unsupervised algorithm used for sample classification problems in machine learning [21]. K-means clustering algorithm (K-means) is the most common, most commonly used, and most effective clustering algorithm. The K-means clustering result divides all vectors in the clustering space into K clusters [22]. It is precisely because of this characteristic that the clustering algorithm can solve the path point allocation problem in multi-robot path planning. Suppose the number of robots is K, then the goal of clustering is to divide the path points into K sets, and one robot is responsible for planning the path points in each group. The specific calculation process of K-means is described in detail in Algorithm 1.

Algorithm 1: K-means clustering algorithm

---
1 Set the number of cluster center points K, select K points as the initial points

2 **while** The category of all points remains unchanged **do**

3   Calculate the Euclidean distance from all points to K cluster center points

4   Return points: the attribution category of each store is the closest cluster center point

5   Recalculate the new cluster center point for each cluster set: take the average

6 **end while**

Euclidean distance is commonly used in K-means clustering algorithm to estimate the similarity between different samples [23]. Also, there are Manhattan distance [24], cosine distance [25], etc. The distance measurement methods used for different types of data and tasks are other. In this article, we plan the optimal path of the robot in the geometric space. The length of the way of the robot between different path points is calculated using Euclidean distance. Therefore, in this article, we also use Euclidean distance to estimate the similarity between different samples.

The K-means algorithm also has some limitations. The algorithm is more affected by initialization, different initialization will bring different results, and it is more susceptible to outliers [26], Although the subsequent improved K-means++ algorithm [27] improves this deficiency by selecting the initial point based on probability, the influence of initialization still exists. Moreover, the distribution result obtained by K-means cannot guarantee the balance of tasks between robots. During the operation of the algorithm, which set the waypoint belongs to is determined by the distance from the waypoint to the central point of the set, which cannot directly reflect different groups. Whether the workload is balanced, especially when there is a long tail effect of outliers in the data distribution, the imbalance of distribution is more serious. On this point, related experiments have also been carried out in this article, which proves that the distribution results obtained by the K-means clustering algorithm have room for improvement in the distribution balance. However, it has particular applicability as a waypoint allocation scheme in the multiple traveling salesman problem. It is necessary to avoid collisions as much as possible when multi-robots work together. The different path point sets resulting from K-means clustering are relatively independent, and there is no overlap. This can make the planned paths of other robots fewer collision problems, which is very beneficial for the subsequent collision detection optimization steps. Therefore, this paper proposes an adpK-means clustering algorithm, which achieves the balanced distribution of path points by adaptively scaling the clustering space in the iterative process, and proves the effectiveness of the algorithm through experiments.

3.2   AdpK-Means Clustering Algorithm Task Allocation

The adpK-means algorithm is an iterative optimization algorithm, and the running process is shown in Fig. 1. The adpK-means algorithm will count the current clustering results during each iteration and dynamically scale the clustering space according to the products until the termination condition is met. The optimal outcome is output. This way of dynamic scaling and iterative optimization can make the distribution of path points more balanced.

In order to describe the operation process of the algorithm more clearly, this article will define the implementation steps and details of the adpK-means clustering algorithm in a two-dimensional space. The algorithm operation flow in the three-dimensional space is the same as that in the two-dimensional space, and only one dimension parameter needs to be added. The specific operation flow is described in detail in Algorithm 1. The number of clustering categories K is the number of robots, and the workload of the robots is estimated as the length of the path sequence estimated by the greedy strategy. From the description of the algorithm, it can be seen that in each iteration, the algorithm shrinks the path points in the set with the smallest workload and enlarges the points in the group with the most massive workload. After shrinking and zooming in, the distribution of path points in the clustering space changes, and the results will also change after K-means clustering. More path points will be allocated in the set with the smallest workload, and the number of path points in the set with the largest workload will be reduced. This is how the adaptive zoom operation makes the workload of different robots more balanced.

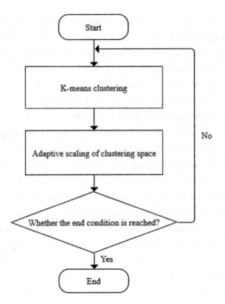

Fig. 1. Flow chart of adpK-means clustering algorithm.

Algorithm 2: AdpK-means clustering algorithm

---

1 Set the maximum number of iterations $Kmeans\_max\_iter$, adaptive scaling $Scale$, the number of categories is K

2 **while** Maximum number of iterations not reached **do**

3   Use K-means algorithm to cluster all path points into K sets

4   Calculate the planned path obtained according to the greedy strategy in each set, and record the path length as l_i, where $i = \{1,2,\cdots,K\}$

5   In the set l_i, the set corresponding to the maximum value is the set with the largest workload. Calculate the center point of all path points in the set as $P_{center} = (X_c - Y_c)$, and perform the zoom operation on the path points in the set:

$$P_x^i = (P_x^i - X_c) \times Scale + X_c$$
$$P_y^i = (P_y^i - Y_c) \times Scale + Y_c$$

6   In the set l_i, the set corresponding to the minimum value is the set with the smallest workload. Calculate the center point of all path points in the set as $P_{center} = (X_c - Y_c)$, and perform the reduction operation on the path points in the set:

$$P_x^i = (P_x^i - X_c) \div Scale + X_c$$
$$P_y^i = (P_y^i - Y_c) \div Scale + Y_c$$

7 **end while**

8 Output the final classification result

To better illustrate the effect of adaptive scaling on the change of clustering space and the balanced distribution of path points, this paper visualizes the scaling adjustment process of the algorithm in the experiment of the TSPLIB dataset [28] pr76.tsp in Fig. 2. In this data set, we set the number of robots to 4. After a K-means clustering, four point sets are obtained, marked with different colors in the figure. As described in Algorithm 2, a greedy strategy is used to find a path for other sets, and the workload of the robots in the set is estimated according to the length of the path. The light red set is the set with the largest amount of work path, and the light black set is the set with the smallest amount of work. Algorithm 2 describes a scaling process. In the example, the center point is calculated for the light red point group, and all points in the set are spread out with the scaling factor of *Scale*. In Fig. 2. the spread point set is marked in dark red. The light black point set also calculates the position of the center point, and all points in the set are contracted inward by the scaling factor of *Scale*. The dark black point set in the figure is the result of the contraction.

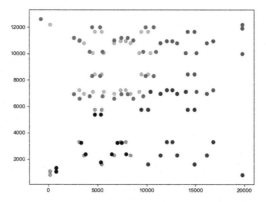

Fig. 2. Schematic diagram of the change process of task points in adpK-means clustering.

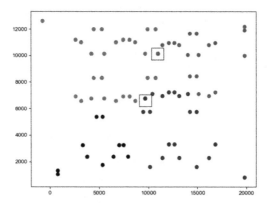

Fig. 3. Clustering result graph after change.

The points in Fig. 3 are the positions of all path points after dynamic shrinkage. The K-means algorithm is used to cluster again on the new data distribution, and you can see that the clustering results have changed. One of the path points in the red set is allocated to the green set, and one is assigned to the blue group. In Fig. 3, the waypoints where the attribution category changes are marked with boxes. The red waypoint set is the set with the most massive workload estimated in the previous iteration. After one adjustment, the samples in the red waypoint set are allocated to other robots, and the workload of the robots in this set will be reduced. The robot workload will increase. From the example, we can intuitively see the change of adaptive clustering to the clustering results. Among them, the scaling factor *Scale* plays a vital role. Adaptive scaling does not guarantee that you can get better than the last time. As a result, setting an appropriate *Scale* value can make the algorithm search for clustering results with a balanced workload faster.

3.3   Path Planning

To verify that the task allocation algorithm proposed in this paper can reduce the overall consumption of the system after the task allocation is completed, the same path planning algorithm is used, namely the discrete multi-group fruit fly algorithm (GA-DMFOA) fused with genetic operators, Carry out path planning. Path planning is to transform the problem into a general traveling salesman problem to solve it according to the distribution result. The GA-DMFOA algorithm [29, 30] is used to complete the path planning of each robot. As shown in Fig. 4, taking ten path points {1,2,3,4,5,6,7,8,9,10} as an example, and three robots as an example, the distribution result is {1,2,3},{4,5,6,7},{8,9,10} three sets, each robot is responsible for planning a group, and the intended path of each robot is obtained through the GA-DMFOA algorithm. To verify that the task allocation algorithm proposed in this paper can reduce the overall consumption of the system after the task allocation is completed, the same path planning algorithm is used, namely the discrete multi-group fruit fly algorithm (GA-DMFOA) fused with genetic operators, Carry out path planning.

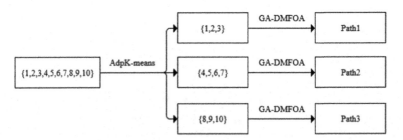

Fig. 4.   Schematic diagram of path planning example.

3.4   Algorithm Overall Steps

This paper introduces the relevant steps and implementation details of the adpK-means clustering algorithm and completes the balanced allocation of path points. The multi-traveling salesman problem is decomposed into a single traveling salesman problem in a two-stage manner. The improved fruit fly optimization algorithm GA-DMFOA is used to plan the path of each robot, and an effective solution to the multi-robot path planning problem is proposed. The parameters used in the multi-robot path planning algorithm are shown in Table 1, where Algorithm 3 describes the solution process of the multi-robot path planning problem. Figures 5(a) and 5(b) show the comparison of the results before and after optimization using the delayed wait strategy when the distance between robots is less than the safe distance l_safe.

Table 1. Multi-robot path planning parameter description table.

Parameter	Description
Kmeans_max_iter	Maximum iteration times of adpK-means clustering
Scale	Adaptive scaling
K	Number of robots
l_{safe}	Safe distance between multiple robots
v	The speed of the robot
M	Number of individuals in the population
MaxIter	The maximum number of iterations
Group	Population size in multi-species co-evolution
P_{mutate}	Mutation probability in genetic operators

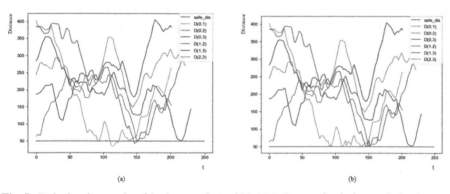

Fig. 5. Path planning results of 4 robots on the tsp225. (a) Robot spacing before optimization. (b) The distance between the robots after optimization.

Algorithm 3: Multi-robot path planning algorithm flow

---

1   The related parameters of initial adpK-means clustering and GA-DMFOA are described in
      detail in Table 1

2   Use adpK-means clustering algorithm for task allocation

3   Each data set after allocation is planned by a robot, and the GA-DMFOA algorithm is used
      for each robot to find the optimal path

4   Use collision detection algorithm 6 to optimize the planned path

5   **if** Collision **then**

6   Adopt a delayed wait strategy

7   **end if**

8   Output the optimal solution for path planning of all robots

---

4 Experiments

4.1 Parameter Analysis Experiment

A key parameter of the adpK-means clustering algorithm is the scaling factor *Scale*, which is used to dynamically adjust the clustering space. This parameter directly affects the degree of change of the path points in the clustering space in each iteration and has a certain impact on the results of the algorithm. So this article debugs this parameter and tests it in pr76.tsp, kroA100.tsp and tsp225. The value set of the parameter *Scale* is $\{1.05, 1.10.1.15, \cdots, 1.5\}$, for these 10 different values conduct experiment. The number of robots is set to $K = 4$, and the maximum number of iterations is *Kmeans*_max_*iter* $= 100$. In order to ensure the accuracy of the experiment, this paper runs the algorithm 20 times independently. It takes the average value of the maximum path length *maxspan* estimated by the greedy strategy as the final evaluation result.

Figure 6(a) is the data distribution diagram of pr76, and the experimental results of the *Scale* parameter are shown in Fig. 6(b). Among them, the resulting curve obtained by K-means clustering only once is marked as K-means, and the result obtained by the adpK-means clustering algorithm is marked as adpK-means. It can be seen from Fig. 6(b) that the experimental results of adpK-means are better than those of K-means under ten sets of *Scale* parameter values, which can prove that the process of the adaptive clustering algorithm is effective. Let's analyze its experimental curve again. As the *Scale* parameter increases, *maxspan* also tends to increase overall. This phenomenon is because the more extensive the *Scale*, the greater the degree of displacement of the points in the clustering space. The clustering results will also experience severe jitter. From the experimental results log in the middle, we also observed that the larger the *Scale*, the larger the clustering results will be in the iterative process. The *maxspan* fluctuates violently into a broader data range. From the experimental results of pr76, the *maxspan* obtained when *Scale* is 1.15 is the minimum value.

The parameter verification on a single data set is difficult to be convincing. This paper conducted the same experiment on the larger-scale data set kroA100 and the ultra-large-scale data set tsp225. The experimental results are shown in Fig. 7(b) and

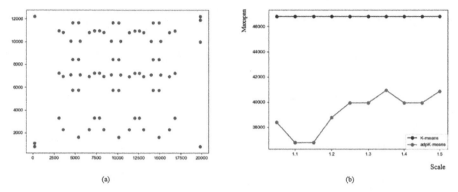

Fig. 6. The experimental results of the scaling factor Scale in the pr76 dataset. (a) pr76 data distribution. (b) pr76 AdpK-means clustering allocation result

Fig. 8(b). In the experimental results, it can still be seen that after the *Scale* gradually increases, the overall *maxspan* is also increasing. However, in the experimental results of these two large-scale data sets, it can be seen that the larger the data scale, the greater the difference in results caused by the changes in *Scale*. Because adpK-means is an algorithm that dynamically adjusts the clustering space, when the data scale is large and the point sets are denser, the *Scale* is too large, which will cause a large number of sample categories to shift, and the results become of difficult to control. The iterative process in adpK-means is to adjust the categories of samples at the edge of each point concentration, and the category of a small number of samples should be changed during each adjustment. Only in this way can we find a better solution, and the algorithm will converge faster. In kroA100 and tsp225, *Scale* = 1.1 obtained the optimal solution in the experiment. From the experimental results of the three data sets, it can be seen that *Scale* = {1.05, 1.1, 1.15} is the three best solutions in the experimental results. Based on this result, this paper uses *Scale* = 1.1 as a benchmark value, and dynamically adjusts it on this basis when experimenting on different datasets.

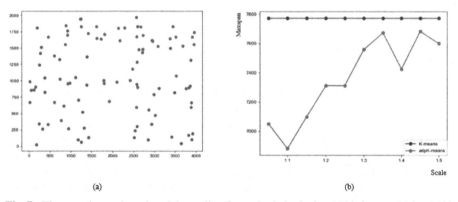

Fig. 7. The experimental results of the scaling factor Scale in the kroA100 dataset. (a) kroA100 data distribution. (b) kroA100 AdpK-means clustering allocation result

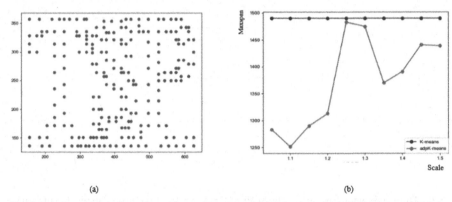

(a)

(b)

Fig. 8. The experimental results of the scaling factor Scale in the tsp225 dataset. (a) tsp225 data distribution. (b) tsp225 AdpK-means clustering allocation result

4.2 Comparison with Basic K-Means Experiment

In order to verify the effectiveness of the algorithm, this paper compares the adpK-means clustering algorithm (adpK-means) with the basic K-means clustering algorithm (K-means) on different data sets. The path planning part adopts GA-DMFOA algorithm, and the control parameters are consistent. Set the number of robots to $K = 4$, the adaptive clustering scaling factor is $Scale = 1.05$, the number of adaptive clustering iterations is $Kmeans\_max\_iter = 100$, the maximum number of iterations in the GA-DMFOA algorithm is $MaxIter = 500$, and there are fruit flies in the population The number of individuals is $K = 60$, the number of multi-group cooperation is $Group = 3$, and the probability of mutation in the genetic operator is $Pmuate = 0.05$. In order to avoid accidental interference, the algorithm was independently run 20 times in the experiment, and the optimal value, average value, and worst value of the 20 results were compared. The experimental results are shown in Table 2. From the experimental results, it can be seen that on all the tested data sets, the experimental results obtained by the adpK-means algorithm are better than the K-means regardless of the optimal value, average value, or worst value. The development of the algorithm shows that the effectiveness and applicability of the adpK-means algorithm are very high.

This paper visualizes the running results of the tsp225 data set and analyzes and discusses the intermediate results of its running. Figure 9(a) shows the effect of path allocation after using K-means clustering. In the figure, four different colors are used to represent the results of varying robot allocation, and the path obtained under the greedy strategy is drawn. Figure 9(b) shows the visualization of adpK-means results. It can be seen from the figure that the clustering results of adpK-means and K-means are inconsistent. According to the calculation process of the adaptive clustering algorithm, it can be seen that the adpK-means clustering has found a better solution in the iterative process. Observing the path curve drawn in the figure, it can be seen that the path is still staggered, which further proves that the path planned under the greedy strategy is not the optimal solution, and the GA-DMFOA algorithm is needed to prepare the path further.

Table 2. Comparison of experimental results of adpK-means clustering algorithm.

Dataset	Method		Optimal	Average	Worst
St70	GA-MDFOA	+K-means	199.87	200.10	228.56
		Adp K-means	**197.56**	**199.28**	**223.67**
rat99	GA-MDFOA	+K-means	376.57	388.10	414.36
		Adp K-means	**340.41**	**363.08**	**366.78**
ch150	GA-MDFOA	+K-means	2070.66	2082.37	2131.75
		Adp K-means	**2009.63**	**2056.08**	**2122.88**
tsp225	GA-MDFOA	+K-means	1237.29	1270.57	1298.11
		Adp K-means	**1180.17**	**1228.48**	**1263.70**
tsp442	GA-MDFOA	+K-means	16024.63	16362.57	16716.76
		Adp K-means	**15988.97**	**16316.12**	**16716.27**

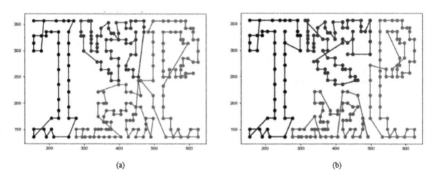

(a)   (b)

Fig. 9. On the tsp225 dataset, the path initialized after apdK-means is allocated. (a) K-means. (b) apdK-means.

Table 3 shows the path length of each robot according to the greedy strategy. The robot corresponds to the four colors of red, green, blue and black in Fig. 9(a) according to the serial number. Directly from the maximum path length *maxspan*, adpK-means obtains better results. Observing the data of each robot in the table, we can see that the K-means distribution results are not balanced. The maximum and minimum values are 1358.25 and 965.48, respectively, while the maximum and minimum values are 1188.67 and 1047.10 in the results of adpK-means. It can be seen that adpK-means is deployed between different robots, which makes the workload of each robot more balanced.

Table 3. The path length of each robot in the clustering result of tsp225.

Method	Maxspan	Robot1	Robot2	Robot3	Robot4
K-means	1358.25	1358.25	1182.47	**1042.91**	**965.48**
AdpK-means	**1188.67**	**1188.67**	**1092.34**	1047.10	1161.31

In the second stage, the path planning needs to be redone after the path point allocation. Table 4 shows the results of GA-DMFOA path planning. It can be seen from the results that compared to Table 3, *maxspan* has been optimized slightly, which proves the effectiveness of GA-DMFOA in the path planning stage, and also reflects that the path obtained by the greedy strategy is closer to the optimal solution. Therefore, it is reasonable to use the path length obtained by the greedy strategy as the workload of the robot. The path planning results after K-means and adpK-means are allocated shown in Fig. 10(a) and Fig. 10(b).

Table 4. Comparison of results after path planning.

Method	Maxspan	Robot1	Robot2	Robot3	Robot4
K-means	1237.29	1237.29	1049.92	966.37	**920.74**
AdpK-means	**1180.17**	**1154.30**	**1016.58**	**946.59**	1180.17

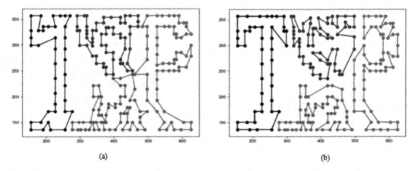

(a)   (b)

Fig. 10. On the tsp225 dataset, the effect of different allocation strategies on path planning. (a) K-means. (b) apdK-means.

5   Conclusions and Future Work

Multi-robot systems are becoming an intensively investigated area of modern robotics in the last few years. The key to using multi-robot systems is coordination. This paper proposes an adaptive K-means clustering algorithm. Through experimental verification, the algorithm improves the balance of multi-robot system task allocation, and reduces the overall consumption of the multi-robot system, and improves the traditional K-means algorithm from being initialized. And the influence of outliers. In the future, it is necessary to consider how to allocate tasks when there are multiple tasks of different types in a multi-robot system, that is, the task allocation of a heterogeneous multi-robot system.

References

1. Ahmadi, M., Stone, P.: A multi-robot system for continuous area sweeping tasks. In: Proceedings 2006 IEEE International Conference on Robotics and Automation, 2006. ICRA 2006, pp. 1724–1729. IEEE (2006)
2. Kumar, V., Michael, N.: Opportunities and challenges with autonomous micro aerial vehicles. Int. J. Robot. Res. **31**(11), 1279–1291 (2012)
3. Freund, E.: Fast nonlinear control with arbitrary pole-placement for industrial robots and manipulators. Int. J. Robot. Res. **1**(1), 65–78 (1982)
4. Burgard, W., Moors, M., Stachniss, C., et al.: Coordinated multi-robot exploration. IEEE Trans. Rob. **21**(3), 376–386 (2005)
5. Fong, T., Thorpe, C., Baur, C.: Multi-robot remote driving with collaborative control. IEEE Trans. Industr. Electron. **50**(4), 699–704 (2003)
6. Gerkey, B.P., Matarić, M.J.: A formal analysis and taxonomy of task allocation in multi-robot systems. Int. J. Robot. Res. **23**(9), 939–954 (2004)
7. Bektas, T.: The multiple traveling salesman problem: an overview of formulations and solution procedures. Omega **34**(3), 209–219 (2006)
8. Wagner, G., Choset, H.M.: A complete multirobot path planning algorithm with performance bounds. In: 2011 IEEE/RSJ International Conference on Intelligent Robots and Systems, pp. 3260–3267. IEEE (2011)
9. Berhault, M., Huang, H., Keskinocak, P., et al.: Robot exploration with combinatorial auctions. In: Proceedings 2003 IEEE/RSJ International Conference on Intelligent Robots and Systems (IROS 2003) (Cat. No. 03CH37453), vol. 2, pp. 1957–1962. IEEE (2003)
10. Chu, P.C., Beasley, J.E.: A genetic algorithm for the generalised assignment problem. Comput. Oper. Res. **24**(1), 17–23 (1997)
11. Akkiraju, R., Keskinocak, P., Murthy, S., et al.: An agent-based approach for scheduling multiple machines. Appl. Intell. **14**(2), 135–144 (2001)
12. Starke, J., Schanz, M., Haken, H.: Self-organized behaviour of distributed autonomous mobile robotic systems by pattern formation principles. In: Distributed Autonomous Robotic Systems, vol. 3, pp. 89–100. Springer, Berlin, Heidelberg (1998)
13. Kwok, K., Driessen, B.J., Phillips, C.A., et al.: Analyzing the multiple-target-multiple-agent scenario using optimal assignment algorithms. Journal of Intelligent and Robotic Systems (2002)
14. Xu, X., Yuan, H., Liptrott, M., et al.: Two phase heuristic algorithm for the multiple-travelling salesman problem. Soft. Comput. **22**(19), 6567–6581 (2018)
15. Xie, P.: Research on Welding Path Planning of Automobile Interior and Exterior Parts Based on Multi-Robot Collaboration. South China University of Technology, Guangdong (2018)
16. Shi, D.: Research on the Path Planning of the Body-in-White Welding Robot Based on the Secondary Development of ROBCAD. Hefei University of Technology, Hefei (2014). In Chinese
17. Burger, M., Su, Z., De Schutter, B.: A node current-based 2-index formulation for the fixed-destination multi-depot travelling salesman problem. Eur. J. Oper. Res. **265**(2), 463–477 (2018)
18. Kitjacharoenchai, P., Ventresca, M., Moshref-Javadi, M., et al.: Multiple traveling salesman problem with drones: mathematical model and heuristic approach. Comput. Ind. Eng. **129**, 14–30 (2019)
19. Qu, H., Yi, Z., Tang, H.J.: A columnar competitive model for solving multi-traveling salesman problem. Chaos, Solitons Fractals **31**(4), 1009–1019 (2007)
20. Kanungo, T., Mount, D.M., Netanyahu, N.S., et al.: An efficient k-means clustering algorithm: analysis and implementation. IEEE Trans. Pattern Anal. Mach. Intell. **24**(7), 881–892 (2002)

21. Hartigan, J.A., Wong, M.A.: Algorithm AS 136: a k-means clustering algorithm. J. Roy. Stat. Soc. Ser. c (Appl. Stat.) **28**(1), 100–108 (1979)
22. Loohach, R., Garg, K.: Effect of distance functions on k-means clustering algorithm. Int. J. Comput. Appl. **49**(6), 7–9 (2012)
23. Sinwar, D., Kaushik, R.: Study of euclidean and manhattan distance metrics using simple k-means clustering. Int. J. Res. Appl. Sci. Eng. Technol. **2**(5), 270–274 (2014)
24. Sahu, L., Mohan, B.R.: An improved K-means algorithm using modified cosine distance measure for document clustering using Mahout with Hadoop. In: 2014 9th International Conference on Industrial and Information Systems (ICIIS), pp. 1–5. IEEE (2014)
25. Celebi, M.E., Kingravi, H.A., Vela, P.A.: A comparative study of efficient initialization methods for the k-means clustering algorithm. Expert Syst. Appl. **40**(1), 200–210 (2013)
26. Kivelevitch, E., Cohen, K., Kumar, M.: A market-based solution to the multiple traveling salesmen problem. J. Intell. Robot. Syst. **72**(1), 21–40 (2013)
27. Arthur, D., Vassilvitskii, S.: k-means++: the advantages of careful seeding. Stanford (2006)
28. Reinelt, G.: TSPLIB—a traveling salesman problem library. ORSA J. Comput. **3**(4), 376–384 (1991)
29. Wu, L., Zuo, C., Zhang, H.: A cloud model based fruit fly optimization algorithm. Knowl.-Based Syst. **89**, 603–617 (2015)
30. Mousavi, S.M., Alikar, N., Niaki, S.T.A., et al.: Optimizing a location allocation-inventory problem in a two-echelon supply chain network: a modified fruit fly optimization algorithm. Comput. Ind. Eng. **87**, 543–560 (2015)

Reinforcement Learning for Extreme Multi-label Text Classification

Hui Teng[1,2(✉)], Yulei Li[1,2], Fei Long[1,2,3], Meixia Xu[1,2], and Qiang Ling[4]

[1] Chinaso Inc., Beijing 100077, China
tenghui@chinaso.com
[2] State Key Laboratory of Media Convergence Production Technology and Systems,
Xinhua News Agency, Beijing, China
[3] Department of Computer Science, Northeast University, Shenyang 110819, China
[4] Department of Automation, University of Science and Technology of China,
Hefei 230027, China

Abstract. Extreme multi-label text classification (XMC) is an important yet challenging problem in the NLP community, which refers to the problem of assigning to each document its most relevant subset of class labels from an extremely large label collection. For example, the input text could be a story document on chinastory.cn and the labels could be story categories that implies the potential meaning. However, naively applying normal neural network models to the XMC problem leads to sub-optimal performance due to the large output space and the label sparsity issue. In this paper, we presents the first attempt at applying reinforcement learning to XMC. Experimental results on public and our own engineering datasets demonstrate that our approach achieves expecting performance compared with the evaluation of the state-of-the-art methods.

Keywords: Extreme multi-label text classification · Reinforcement learning

1 Introduction

There has been a lot of interests in extreme multi-label text classification (XMC) problem: given an input text instance, return the most relevant labels from an enormous label collection, where the number of labels could be in the millions or more, which becomes increasingly important due to the fast growing of internet contents and the urgent needs for organizational views of big data. Multi-label classification is fundamentally different from the traditional binary classification problems which have been intensively studied in the machine learning literature. Binary classifiers treat class labels as independent target variables, which is clearly sub-optimal for multi-label classification as the dependencies among class

---

H. Teng and Y. Li—Contributed equally.

F. Sun et al. (Eds.): ICCSIP 2020, CCIS 1397, pp. 243–250, 2021.
https://doi.org/10.1007/978-981-16-2336-3_22

labels cannot be leveraged. Of the many related tasks, discovering relevant labels from document is of considerable practical importance.

In Ref. [1], XML-CNN is first adopted for XMC task which modifies the traditional TextCNN [2] architecture by using a dynamic max pooling scheme and adding a hidden bottleneck layer that captures richer information from different regions of the document. However, such a method admits the following disadvantages: (1) CNN model is unable to discover the dependency patterns due to the sparsity issue of the XMC datasets which typically exhibit a power-law distribution of labels, and the substantial proportion of the labels have very few training instances associated with them. (2) The computational costs in both training and testing of mutually independent classifiers would be practically prohibiting when the number of labels reaches hundreds of thousands or even millions.

In Ref. [5,6], interactive methods are proposed for topic discovery in order to incorporate with user's intention. However such interactive algorithms are for clustering, which introduces the uncertainty and randomness.

Specifically, representation learning is a fundamental problem in natural language processing and how to learn a structured representation for text classification is still challengeable. Unlike most existing representation models that either use no structure or rely on pre-specified structures, the reinforcement learning (RL) method that we apply is able to learn sentence representation by discovering optimized structures automatically [10]. However, there are few attempts to apply RL method into XMC tasks due to the intractable issues of XMC datasets.

The main contributions are summarized as follows:

1. We apply a reinforcement learning method and make a optimization for extreme multi-label text classification.
2. We re-examine the state of the art of XMC by conducting a comparative experimental evaluation of 5 methods which are most representative in text classification.
3. We develop a practical CMS online system for editors and perform extensive experimental validations for the proposed method.

The rest of this paper is organized as follows: Sect. 2 gives the related works and background of XMC. In Sect. 3 we give a detailed introduction about the RL method and Sect. 4 presents our extensive experiments and results, followed by conclusion and future work in Sect. 5.

2   Related Works and Background

2.1   Methods for Text Classification

Methods for comparison are outlined, including the most representative methods in XMC and some successful deep learning methods which are designed for mutliclass text classification but also applicable to XMC with minor adaptations.

a. FastText. FastText [7] is a simple yet effective baseline method for text classification, which is inspired by the recent work on efficient word representation learning, such as skip-gram and CBOW [8]. The representation of text is constructed by averaging the embeddings of the words, upon which a softmax layer is applied to map the document representation to class labels. This simplicity makes FastText very efficient to train and achieves state-of-the-art performances on both precision and time consuming. However, simply averaging input word embeddings with the shallow architecture for document-to-label mapping might limits its success in XMC. In XMC task, document presentations need to capture more high dimensional information for predicting multiple correlated labels and discriminating them from enormous numbers of irrelevant labels.

b. FastXML. FastXML [9] aims to develop an extreme multi-label classifier that is faster to train and more accurate at prediction and is considered as the state-of-the-art tree-based method for XMC. It learns a hierarchy of training instances and optimizes an NDCG-based objective at each node of the hierarchy. Specifically, a hyperplane parameterized by $w \in \mathbb{R}^D$ is induced at each node, which splits the set of documents in the current node into two subsets; the ranking of the labels in each of the two subsets are jointly learned. The key idea is to have the documents in each subset sharing similar label distribution, and to characterize the distribution using a set-specific ranked list of labels. This is achieved by jointly maximizing NDCG scores of the ranked label lists in the two sibling subsets. In practice, an ensemble of multiple induced trees are learned to improve the robustness of predictions. At prediction time, each test document is passed from the root to a leaf node in each induced tree, and the label distributions in all the reached leaves are aggregated for the test document.

c. TextCNN. TextCNN [2] applys convolutional neural networks to text classification for the first time. TextCNN depicts three filter region sizes in the convolutional layer, each of which has two filters. Filters perform convolutions on the sentence matrix and generate feature maps which are fed to a max-pooling layer. By concatenating the outputs that generated from all six maps, a feature vector is generated. The final fully-connected layer with L softmax outputs corresponding to L labels uses it as inputs to classify the sentence representation. TextCNN obtains excellent performance in text classification, and is considered as a strong baseline comparative method. Considering the two distinct type of words embedding inputs, we distinguish TextCNN into two categories: Bow-CNN [3] and XML-CNN [1], which take bag of words feature and word vector as input respectively.

d. SLEEC. SLEEC [4] is most representative for target-embedding methods in XMC which extends embedding methods in multiple ways and uses KNN for classification stage.

2.2   Chinaso Application

The database "China Story" [12] is built by Chinaso of Xinhua News Agency with the aim of "telling China's stories well, and making the voice of China heard". A challenging problem at the database amounts to discovering relevant labels from an enormous output space of potential candidates for one story document: for example, suggesting keywords to editors labeling new stories, as well as to internet users starting new campaign on Chinaso website. Normally, this task was accomplished manually, which consumes a large amount of manpower and time.

3   Reinforcement Learning

In the RL [10] method, three components are interleaved together. The policy network adopts a stochastic policy and uses a delayed reward from the final classification network to guide the policy learning for structure discovery. While the state representation of policy network is derived from the representation models which contains two models: Information Distilled LSTM which selects important, task-relevant words to build sentence representation, and Hierarchical Structured LSTM which discovers phrase structures and builds sentence representation with a two-level LSTM. The final classification network makes prediction on top of structured sentence representation and facilitates reward computation for the policy network. Figure 1 gives the detailed illustration of the overall framework.

Generally, the most straightforward adaptation from the multi-class classification problems to multi-label ones would be to extend the traditional cross-entropy loss as follows:

$$\mathcal{L} = -\frac{1}{n}\sum_{i=1}^{n}\sum_{j=1}^{L} y_{ij}\log\left(\hat{p}_{ij}\right) \tag{1}$$

where Θ denotes classification model parameters, $\hat{p}_{ij}$ is the model prediction for instance i on label j via a softmax activation. Specifically, in our RL method, we modify the loss function and introduce binary cross-entropy objective as a substitute which can be formulated as follows:

$$\min_{\Theta} -\frac{1}{n}\sum_{i=1}^{n}\sum_{j=1}^{L} \left[y_{ij}\log\left(\sigma\left(f_{ij}\right)\right) + \left(1 - y_{ij}\right)\log\left(1 - \sigma\left(f_{ij}\right)\right)\right] \tag{2}$$

where σ is the sigmoid function $\sigma\left(x\right) = 1/1 + e^{-x}$.

4   Performance Evaluation

4.1   Datasets

We first use the well-known RCV1 [11] datasets to evaluate the above method, which contains manually categorized newswire stories made available by Reuters, Ltd.

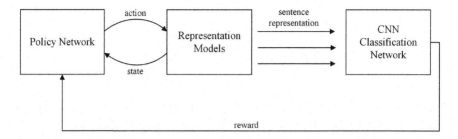

Fig. 1. Overview of the overall RL network. The policy network (PNet) samples an action at each state. The structured representation model offers state representation to PNet and outputs the final sentence representation to the classification network (CNet). CNet performs text classification and provides reward to PNet.

Table 1. Datasets statistics of RCV1

Datasets	Train instances	Test instances	Labels	Labels/document	Documents/label
RCV1	23149	781265	103	3.18	729.67
ChinaStory	8668	963	118	6.19	81.62

In addition, based on the consideration of actual needs for online application and demand for evaluating the practical performance of XMC methods, we build our own practical Chinese datasets as well. The statistical details of the two datasets are displayed in Table 1.

4.2   Experimental Validation Results

a. Evaluation Metrics. To test the performance of different methods in XMC, we introduce several evaluation metrics. In XMC datasets, each instance only has very few relevant labels which means that how to present a short ranked list of potentially relevant labels for each test instance and evaluate the quality of such ranked lists with an emphasis on the relevance of the top portion of each list is far more important. As a result rank-based evaluation metrics have been commonly used for comparing XMC methods, including the precision at top K (P@K) and the Normalized Discounted Cummulated Gains (NDCG@K) [9]. We follow such convention and use these two metrics in our evaluation in this paper, with $k = 1, 3, 5$. Denoting by $\mathbf{y} \in \{0, 1\}^L$ as the vector of true labels of an document, and $\hat{\mathbf{y}} \in \mathbb{R}^L$ as the system-predicted score vector for the same document, the metrics are defined as:

$$P@k = \frac{1}{k} \sum_{l \in r_k(\hat{\mathbf{y}})} y_l \tag{3}$$

$$DCG@k = \sum_{l \in r_k(\hat{\mathbf{y}})} \frac{y_l}{\log(l+1)} \tag{4}$$

$$NDCG@k = \frac{DCG@k}{\sum_{l=1}^{\min(k, \|\mathbf{y}\|_0)} \frac{1}{\log(l+1)}} \tag{5}$$

where $r_k(\hat{\mathbf{y}})$ is the set of rank indices of the truly relevant labels among the top-k portion of the system-predicted ranked list for a document, and $\|\mathbf{y}\|_0$ counts the number of relevant labels in the ground truth label vector $\mathbf{y}$. P@K and NDCG@K are calculated for each test document and then averaged over all the documents.

b. Evaluation Results. Using these specific evaluation metrics, we conduct extensive experiments on the two datasets. Table 2 and 3 demonstrates the P@K and G@K results of the methods on RCV1 respectively, showing that RL method achieved competitive performance which consistently produced the best or the second best results on the datasets no matter when $k = 1, 3$ or 5. Note that the RCV1 datasets have a higher number of training instances per class and the RL method is capable to learn accurate sentence representation, especially when $k = 5$. Meanwhile, based on the actual needs for online application Fig. 2 displays the results on our Chinese datasets compared with other 5 state-of-the-art method. Note that owing to the small scale of practical datasets, all the methods obtained close performance, which strongly indicates that our RL method is able to discover the representation in small datasets and can be easily scaled to the larger datasets. However, due to the very limit manual scale of China Story database, all data-driven representation learning methods are hardly capable to capture the complete feature, while FastText works better under this circumstance on account of its simplify.

Table 2. Evaluation results in P@K on datasets RCV1

Metrics	FastXML	SLEEC	FastText	Bow-CNN	XML-CNN	Ours
P@1	94.62	95.35	95.40	96.40	**96.86**	**96.54**
P@3	78.40	79.51	79.96	**81.17**	81.11	**81.13**
P@5	54.82	55.06	55.64	56.74	56.07	**56.89**

Table 3. Evaluation results in G@K on datasets RCV1

Metrics	FastXML	SLEEC	FastText	Bow-CNN	XML-CNN	Ours
G@1	94.62	95.35	95.40	96.40	**96.86**	**96.54**
G@3	89.21	90.45	90.95	92.04	**92.22**	91.89
G@5	90.27	90.97	91.68	92.89	92.63	**92.96**

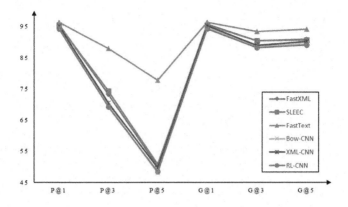

Fig. 2. Evaluation results on our ChinaStory datasets

5 Conclusion and Future Work

In this paper, we present reinforcement learning approach to discover the structured document representation for extreme multi-label text classification. Experimental validation in comparison with other state-of-the-art methods on datasets is conducted, demonstrating that on both public and practical datasets, expecting results have been obtained. However, There still exists a lot work to be further investigated. Firstly, we wish to discover more relevant label patterns from document for the end editors; Secondly, we hope to develop a more flexible graphic user interface (GUI) and integrate more high-level knowledge of the human's intention as a feedback information into the model. Finally, we wish to discover more hierarchical structure of the label in the document in a coarse-to-fine manner.

References

1. Liu, J., Chang, W. C., Wu, Y., Yang, Y.: Deep learning for extreme multi-label text classification. In: International ACM SIGIR Conference on Research and Development in Information Retrieval, pp. 115–124 (2017)
2. Kim, Y.: Convolutional neural networks for sentence classification. arXiv preprint arXiv:1408.5882 (2014)
3. Johnson, R., Zhang, T.: Effective use of word order for text categorization with convolutional neural networks. arXiv preprint arXiv:1412.1058 (2014)
4. Bhatia, K., Jain, H., Kar, P., Varma, M., Jain, P.: Sparse local embeddings for extreme multi-label classification. In: Advances in Neural Information Processing Systems, pp. 730–738 (2015)
5. Choo, J., Lee, C., Reddy, C.K., Park, H.: UTOPIAN: user-driven topic modeling based on interactive nonnegative matrix factorization. IEEE Trans. Vis. Comput. Graph. **19**(12), 1992–2001 (2013)

6. Teng, H., Liu, H., Yu, L., Sun, F.: Representative video action discovery using inter-active non-negative matrix factorization. In: Hu, X., Xia, Y., Zhang, Y., Zhao, D. (eds.) ISNN 2015. LNCS, vol. 9377, pp. 205–212. Springer, Cham (2015). https://doi.org/10.1007/978-3-319-25393-0_23

7. Joulin, A., Grave, E., Bojanowski, P., Mikolov, T.: Bag of tricks for efficient text classification. arXiv preprint arXiv:1607.01759 (2016)

8. Mikolov, T., Chen, K., Corrado, G., Dean, J.: Efficient estimation of word repre-sentations in vector space. arXiv preprint arXiv:1301.3781 (2013)

9. Prabhu, Y., Varma, M.: FastXML: a fast, accurate and stable tree-classifier for extreme multi-label learning. In: Proceedings of the 20th ACM SIGKDD Interna-tional Conference on Knowledge Discovery and Data Mining, pp. 263–272 (2014)

10. Zhang, T., Huang, M., Zhao, L.: Learning structured representation for text clas-sification via reinforcement learning. In: Proceedings of the Thirty-Second AAAI Conference on Artificial Intelligence (2018)

11. Lewis, D.D., Yang, Y., Rose, T.G., Li, F.: RCV1: a new benchmark collection for text categorization research. J. Mach. Learn. Res. **5**, 361–397 (2004)

12. Chinastory. https://www.chinastory.cn/english/index.html

Manipulation

Multimodal Object Analysis with Auditory and Tactile Sensing Using Recurrent Neural Networks

Yannick Jonetzko[1(✉)], Niklas Fiedler[1], Manfred Eppe[2], and Jianwei Zhang[1]

[1] Technical Aspects of Multimodal Systems, Universität Hamburg, Vogt-Kölln-Straße 30, 22527 Hamburg, Germany
{jonetzko,5fiedler,zhang}@informatik.uni-hamburg.de
[2] Knowledge Technology, Universität Hamburg, Vogt-Kölln-Straße 30, 22527 Hamburg, Germany
eppe@informatik.uni-hamburg.de

Abstract. Robots are usually equipped with many different sensors that need to be integrated. While most research is focused on the integration of vision with other senses, we successfully integrate tactile and auditory sensor data from a complex robotic system. Herein, we train and evaluate a neural network for the classification of the content of eight optically identical medicine containers. To investigate the relevance of the tactile modality in classification under realistic conditions, we apply different noise levels to the audio data. Our results show significantly higher robustness to acoustic noise with the combined multimodal network than with the unimodal audio based counterpart.

Keywords: Multimodal · Neural network · Tactile · Audio · Object analysis

1 Introduction

In a domestic environment designed by and for humans, robots have to overcome similar challenges and conditions. Therefore, the employed sensors are often inspired by humanoid senses, mimicking their form and functionality. For successful interaction and exploration, it is essential for the robot to rely on the quality and accuracy of its perception. Nevertheless, in diverse natural scenarios, not all senses are reliable or can be used at all, due to environmental conditions, such as ambient light or acoustic noise. To overcome these handicaps, humans use several senses combined. In the field of robotics, the advantages of using multimodal input are extensively explored. However, the majority of the work focuses

This research was funded by the German Research Foundation (DFG) and the National Science Foundation of China in project Crossmodal Learning, TRR-169. It is also partially financed by the H2020-MSCA-RISE Project ULTRACEPT. Manfred Eppe acknowledges support via the DFG-funded IDEAS (EP 143/2-1) and LeCAREbot (EP 143/4-1) projects.

F. Sun et al. (Eds.): ICCSIP 2020, CCIS 1397, pp. 253–265, 2021.
https://doi.org/10.1007/978-981-16-2336-3_23

on combining visual information with other modalities (e.g., [1–5]). In contrast, our work is focused on the integration of acoustic and tactile data. In Sect. 2 of this article, we describe existing unimodal auditory and tactile approaches for object analysis and classification. We also describe multimodal approaches that use vision in combination with additional sensors. However, to the best of our knowledge, there exists no approach that systematically investigates in how far acoustic noise can be addressed by integrating auditory and tactile information. To address this gap, we present a novel approach that performs well in a scenario where i) visual data is not useful, ii) the audio signal is noisy, and iii) tactile data is available but not as accurate as the other senses. This motivates our following research question:

To what extent can the multimodal analysis of noisy audio data and tactile information lead to a significant improvement of the classification accuracy of bulk materials in visually indistinguishable objects?

To address this question, we perform experiments with an anthropomorphic robotic hand. The hand is equipped with bio-inspired tactile sensors and shakes multiple visually indistinguishable objects in front of a microphone [1]. Each object contains different pills which the robot classifies using audio and tactile information (see Sect. 3). We preprocess the signals using Mel coefficients (see Sect. 4) and perform classification with recurrent neural networks (see Sect. 5). Our evaluative comparison of the multimodal network with the individual counterparts (see Sect. 6) provides details on the performance gain when combining auditory and tactile data. Section 7 concludes the results.

2   Related Work

Our multimodal approach builds on audio and tactile measurements to classify pills in identical containers. The following approaches explore related problems.

2.1   Tactile Object Analysis and Classification

Tactile measurements are applied in various applications, such as braille reading [6] or fall detection of elderly people based on vibration measurements on the ground [7]. We use the BioTac sensor for tactile measurements. This sensor was initially presented by Wettels et al. [8] and has since been used for various tasks including tumor localization [9], force estimation, and slip detection [10].

We use the sensor to measure vibrations that result from exploratory movements. Fishel and Loeb [11] demonstrate that the device "exceeds human performance in detecting sustained vibrations". Xu et al. [12] elaborate on active tactile perception by proposing six exploratory movements that cause tactile sensations: pressure, lateral sliding, static contact, enclosure, hefting, and contour following. The first three are supposed to generate sensory information with

---

[1] To enable control over the acoustic noise, we used a high-quality external microphone and added separately recorded noise of the robot to the signal during the evaluation.

a BioTac sensor, while the others rely on joint positions and forces of the robot. Specifically, lateral sliding was used to generate vibration data as one modality for object classification. Another approach that focuses explicitly on texture classification by lateral sliding is the work by Kerzel et al. [13], who achieve more than 99 % classification accuracy for 32 different materials.

In the field of classifying container contents based on tactile data with machine learning, the work of Chen et al. [14] is probably most related to our approach. The authors perform multiple experiments based on the vibration signatures, which they acquire while shaking containers filled with various objects. In their object classification experiments, the authors were able to classify shaken objects into one of 12 classes with an accuracy of $93.8 \pm 4\%$ using a Support Vector Machine. In contrast to our approach, they used a custom shaking mechanism that involves a contact microphone mounted at the container. Therefore, the resolution of the measurements is higher, and the signal is most likely less noisy than in our work. Additionally, the object types are more diverse than the ones classified in this work (e.g., ball bearing, acrylic piece, rubber ball).

2.2 Acoustic Object Analysis and Classification

Durst and Krotkov [15] classify objects based on the sound resulting from an impact between an aluminum cane and the object itself. A Fourier transform was applied for preprocessing. The performance of a minimum-distance classifier was compared to a decision-map classifier, which combines a minimum-distance with a decision-tree classifier. They reached comparable results for classifying objects into five different classes with an accuracy of 94.2% and 93.8%, respectively. Luo et al. [16] also use the sound of an impact between the object and a marker pen to classify the object. They create a dataset by knocking 120 times with the pen on 30 different objects. Similar to our work, they feed the resulting signal into a Deep Neural Network. Therefore, the authors use stacked denoising autoencoders to train the network and reach a classification accuracy of 91.50%.

Our presented audio processing is inspired by the work of Eppe et al. [17]. The authors present an approach where the content of visually indistinguishable plastic capsules is determined by a robot that analyzes an audio signal resulting from shaking the capsules. The material type is classified and the weight estimated using the resulting audio samples. More diverse object classes are used in their work, while our approach distinguishes a range of pill types. In their case, the shaking movement is faster, so that the produced sound is generated from the material hitting the capsule walls. In contrast, because of hardware constraints, we slowly rotate the container, which produces sliding and rattling sounds when the pills slowly slide down the container wall.

Liang et al. [18] use audio signals to analyze robotic pouring and estimate the liquid height in several containers. In this scenario, it is hard to estimate the height with visual sensors because of the transparency of liquids.

2.3   Multimodal Object Analysis and Classification

The multimodal object categorization approach proposed by Nakamura et al. [1] investigates unsupervised learning of object categories using visual, audio, and tactile measurements fed into an adaption of probabilistic Latent Semantic Analysis (pLSA). Though the authors consider unsupervised categorization, whereas our work concerns supervised object classification, their findings are very relevant to ours, as they demonstrate that combining audio and tactile data leads to improved categorization results.

Sinapov et al. [19] present another example of object categorization based on multimodal perception. The authors categorize 36 unique containers (three container colors, four content types, and three content weights) with a robot by learning their features while performing ten exploratory movements. In addition to the categorization of objects into groups, their approach is able to learn relations of object pairs and groups. Parts of their results show that shake and rattle movements are well suited for content and weight detection via audio and proprioception measurements.

Pieropan et al. [2] propose a "method for audio-visual recognition of human manipulation actions". In their work, the authors classify human manipulation actions (e. g., opening a milk bottle or pouring cereal) based on visual and audio data. For the classification, audio features, orientations, and positions of manipulated objects are fed into a Hidden Markov Model (HMM). Similar to our work, the audio features are extracted by a Mel Frequency Cepstral Coefficients (MFCC) analysis of the raw signal. The authors are able to classify the actions with an average accuracy of 73% over seven classes (including the class *no action*).

3   Experiment Setup

In the experimental setup, a PR2 robot [20] shakes eight 3D printed medicine containers that are visually indistinguishable. Container contents that the robot is supposed to classify are listed in Table 1. The robot holds a container with

Table 1. Pill classes included in the data set and used in the experiment

		Magnesium	Calcium	B-Complex	Big Mints	Chew	Small Mints	Vitamin B	Candy
	Weight per pill	1.27g	2.2g	0.31g	1.2g	1.13g	0.5g	0.55g	0.6g
Sample count	One pill	166	99	104	110	118	137	126	137
	Small amount	228	405	222	212	299	218	260	391
	Half full	239	407	232	413	251	293	290	336
	Full	237	184	242	215	243	296	304	174
	Overall	820	1095	800	950	911	944	980	1008

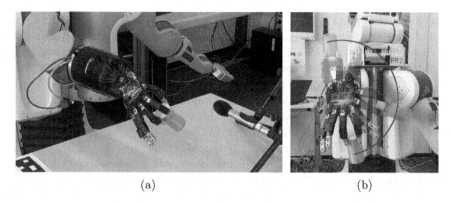

(a)   (b)

Fig. 1. Overview of the experiment setup. **(a)** The Shadow Dexterous Hand holds a medicine container filled with pills to classify with three fingers. BioTac sensors are mounted at each fingertip of the hand. An external microphone is placed in front of the hand to record the resulting noise. **(b)** Depiction of the applied shake motion. Each container was rotated up- and downwards again along the red line with a rotation velocity of 0.8 and 1 radian per second.

a tripod grasp, using three tactile-sensitive fingertips. The content is classified based on auditory and tactile measurements acquired while shaking the container in front of a microphone (see Fig. 1a).

3.1 Sensors

For the experiment, the PR2 robot is equipped with a five-finger 19° of freedom Shadow Dexterous Hand [21] (see Fig. 1a). Each of the five fingers is fitted with a tactile BioTac sensor [22] at the last phalanx. The sensor mimics the human fingertip and its sensory modalities, as depicted in the cross-section of the sensor in Fig. 2.

The bone-like rigid core is surrounded by a flexible silicone hull filled with a conductive liquid. With its various embedded sensors, it is capable of measuring multiple modalities, like pressure, temperature, and the deformation of the silicon hull. A hydroacoustic pressure sensor at the end of a small tube inside the rigid core of the BioTac measures the pressure of the liquid, which changes during contacts. To gather the absolute fluid pressure (DC), the transducer output is amplified with a gain of 10 and low-pass filtered with 1040 Hz.

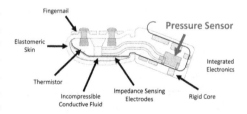

Fig. 2. A cross-section of the BioTac sensor used for the acquisition of vibration measurements. The pressure sensor used in this work is marked in **blue** [11]. (Color figure online)

Afterward, the signal is band-pass filtered between 10 and 1040 Hz with a gain of 99.1 and produces the dynamic fluid pressure (AC) value, also referred to as vibrations. 19 electrodes, distributed over the rigid core, measure changes in impedance due to the dispersion of the conductive liquid. Based on this information, the deformation of the hull can be inferred. The resulting spacial tactile information is not useful for the classification of the bottle's ingredients as the containers are physically similar. The liquid inside the BioTac is indistinguishable from water regarding the vibration properties [11]. For the classification evaluated in this work, we consider only the AC value because neither the temperature nor the hull deformation provides any meaningful information to classify the pills. Since no direct contact with the pills is made, we also do not consider thermal conductivity, as proposed by Xu et al. [12]. In addition to the tactile information, an audio signal is used for the classification. As shown in Fig. 1a, a microphone is pointing to the sound source of the rattling pills. We record a single 44.1 kHz acoustic signal, which is later downsampled, as described in Sect. 4.

3.2   Pill Container

In our considered scenario, the robot can only rely on its tactile and audio perception because the containers are visually equal. To ensure the same preconditions for each type, the containers were 3D printed in a typical medicine container optic, with an FDM printer and PLA plastic. We chose the size of the can in a way that it is easy to grasp for the robot, with an inner height of 80 mm, a radius of 20 mm, and a wall thickness of 2.5 mm.

3.3   Dataset Recording

We recorded the dataset in a robot laboratory with ordinary environmental noise (e.g., computers running, nearby airport). The robot's fans, motors, and gears produce most of the noise. To achieve comparable auditory and tactile data, the robot arm is straightened out, pointing forward to the microphone and rotates around the rotatory joint between elbow and forearm. Before the shaking movement, an experimenter hands over the medicine container and firmly places it inside a tripod grasp with the thumb, the fore- and the middle finger. Only the tactile fingertips touch the object to reduce vibration noise produced by the robot in the tactile readings. In each iteration, the force applied to the object, as well as the finger poses, remain constant to produce homogeneous data. The actual shaking motion is shown in Fig. 1b. One shake is either a lifting or lowering 180° rotation around the middle axis of the forearm. Each of the 8 pill classes is recorded with 2 different velocities (0.8 and 1.0 radian per second) and 4 different amounts of pills, with 12 shaking motions a time. This results in an overall number of 768 shaking movements in the dataset. Each sample includes information about the pill class, the number of pills, the number of shaking movements, and the angular velocity. Besides the audio and tactile data, the joint position of the forearm is recorded.

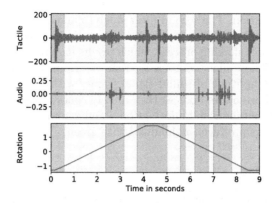

Fig. 3. Exemplary data stream from 10 Big Mint pills shaken at an angular velocity of 0.8 radian per second. The tactile and audio signals and the applied rotation of two shaking processes are shown. Parts of the stream which are used for training and testing are marked in **green**. Areas marked in **red** are excluded from the data set based on the rotation of the hand, while those marked in **yellow** are removed because the audio signal did not surpass a threshold defining a minimum signal strength. (Color figure online)

4 Data Preprocessing

To maximize the amount of relevant information in the data, we extract the samples with features of particular interest. That is, we cut samples from the auditory and tactile data stream based on the rotation angle and the maximal audio signal amplitude, as described in Sect. 4.1 and Fig. 3.

The preprocessing of the selected samples involves *Mel Frequency Cepstral Coefficents* (MFCC) [23], a common method to preprocess human speech and other auditory data. MFCC have been successfully applied among others in the field of music synthesis [24] and acoustic classification [17,25]. Since tactile data can also be decomposed into different frequencies, we apply MFCC to both tactile and audio data (see Sect. 4.2 and Sect. 4.3). Preliminary experiments have demonstrated that applying MFCC to tactile information provide a significant performance gain.

4.1 Sample Selection

The realistic experiment setup leads to much noise and unusable samples in the dataset, due to ego noises of the robot, in particular, the fans and the motors. Figure 3 depicts the raw data stream of two shaking motions, starting with a lifting movement that ends after 4.5 s, followed by a returning motion (see Fig. 1b). To select those samples of the signal that contain useful information about the container contents, we apply two filter stages consecutively. The first filter stage (marked red in Fig. 3) removes the samples close to the direction change outside the joint position range of -1 to 1.5 radians. Due to the jerk (see Rotation in Fig. 3), especially the tactile signal is very noisy in that region and consequently useless for classification. The second filter stage (marked yellow in the diagram) considers that the pills inside the container do not produce sounds and vibrations throughout the whole shaking process, which results in many samples without significant features. These silent samples are removed from the dataset by considering the maximal amplitude of sound signal frames with a size of 0.2 s. Samples below a threshold are filtered out as they merely contain noise. We assume that all other samples contain useful information about sound and vibration, the pills inside the containers produce (highlighted with green).

4.2 Auditory Data

The MFCC feature extraction process can be split into multiple stages. After a Fourier transformation is applied to sequences of the audio signal, the resulting power spectrum is mapped onto the Mel scale. First, logarithm activation is applied to the frequency energies, and second, a discrete cosine transformation is used, which results in a spectrum of the amplitudes, the MFCC.

Multiple parameters are important for the calculation of MFCC. In our experiments, we considered the following: window size, step size, and amount of Mel coefficients. All of these parameters were determined with Tree-Parzen-based hyperparameter optimization [26], using a hyperparameter space similar to that of Eppe et al. [17]. We achieved the best results with a window size of 0.03, a step size of 0.02, and 21 Mel coefficients.

4.3 Tactile Data

The tactile data for each finger was recorded at a rate of 1000 Hz. Due to the high frequency, it is possible to use methods from audio processing for the tactile signal. Similar to the auditory data, we applied MFCC to the normalized tactile signal, further explained in the previous paragraph. Experiments showed improvements using the MFCC over feeding the raw tactile signals directly into the neural network. Since the sample rate of the tactile sensor is significantly lower compared to a microphone, the range of the analyzed frequency spectrum has to be adapted accordingly. Again, the same parameters as for the audio data, as well as the frequency range, were tested with hyperparameter optimization. We achieved the best results with a window size of 0.04, a step size of 0.04, 9 Mel coefficients, and a frequency range from 4 Hz to 440 Hz.

5 Neural Network Architecture

The architecture of the neural networks is based on the system proposed by Eppe et al. [17], but extended with the tactile modality. To this end, we define two separate neural networks, one for the classification of tactile measurements and another one for auditory data. While the general architecture of both networks is similar (see Fig. 4a), they differ mainly in the MFCC parameters, as mentioned before, and parameters of the specific layers.

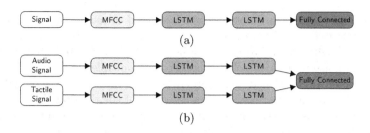

Fig. 4. Schematic view of the **(a)** unimodal and multimodal **(b)** neural network architectures used in this work.

We feed features extracted by the MFCC into two consecutive *Long Short-Term Memory* (LSTM) layers [27] which use a RELU activation function. The last hidden LSTM state of each data sequence is piped into a fully connected layer with dropout. Then, to perform the classification, we apply a softmax activation. Through hyperparameter optimization [26], the parameters of the layers were optimized for each modality separately. For the audio-based classifier, we achieved the best results with 400 units in the first LSTM, 90 units in the second one, and a dropout rate of 0.34. In the tactile version, 180 and 90 units worked best in the first and second LSTM, respectively. A dropout of 0.7 leads to the highest classification accuracy. The usage of *Gated Recurrent Units* (GRU) [28] instead of LSTMs was evaluated but did not impact the classification accuracy of the architectures.

To use multimodal input in the classifier, the developed architecture had to be adapted for two input sequences with differing sample rates and signal frequency range. Therefore, the multimodal version of the architecture concatenates the unimodal networks by feeding the results of the recurrent layers into one fully connected layer with eight neurons (see Fig. 4b). Due to sampling rates and MFCC parameters, the sequence sizes differ. The fully connected layer for the multimodal case is configured similarly to the one in the unimodal architecture. We trained the resulting architecture with an Adam optimizer [29] at a learning rate of $lr = 0.001$ and the default momentum parameters provided by the Keras deep learning framework, i.e., $\beta_1 = 0.9$, $\beta_2 = 0.99$. In preliminary tests, we also considered variations of our architecture, in particular, the application of adding a second dense layer for both modalities combined as well as one additional dense layer for each. However, we have not observed any significant effect on the classification results.

6   Results

For the training and evaluation of our system, we split the dataset into 80% training and 20% testing samples. An overview of the classification results is provided in Table 2. The best classification accuracy on the testing split of the dataset was 56.06% for tactile only data, 89.1% on audio only data, and 91.23% with multimodal input. To have optimal control over the amount of noise, the microphone was placed at a position which allowed to record the audio signal as clearly as possible (see Fig. 1a). In practical applications, where the microphone is mounted directly to the robot, more noise is to be expected. To explore the effect of ego-noise under controllable conditions, multiple training and test runs were conducted in which the prerecorded noise of the robot was added to the original audio signal. The classification accuracy of the developed networks was evaluated with regard to the noise ratio by training and testing individual audio and multimodal networks in 21 different noise conditions with a noise ratio between 0 and 1. Noise in the audio signal does not affect the results of the network designed for the tactile input signal. Therefore, only one evaluation step was carried out with the tactile architecture. In each evaluation step, ten iterations of training and testing were conducted. Figure 5 shows the results of the study as a plot of the mean accuracy of each network, as well as a depiction of the 25- and 75-percentiles.

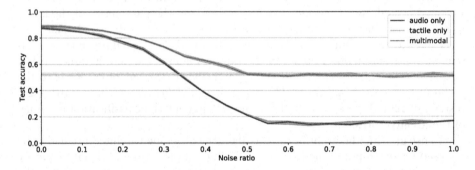

Fig. 5. Comparison of the classification accuracy of both unimodal and the multimodal approaches with increasing noise ratio in the audio signal. trained and tested ten times. The mean of the results of each step consisting of ten train and test iterations is drawn as a solid line as well as the 25- and 75-percentiles are indicated translucently.

For a noise ratio of 0.3, the confusion matrices for the three models are given in Table 2. The matrices link the actual pill type (rows) and the classified ones (columns), with the corresponding success rate. In Table 2a the performance of the unimodal audio network is visualized, the accuracy of this sample is 58.75%. The overall classification accuracy of the given median tactile model is 51.25% (see Table 2b). While segment (a) shows distributed weaknesses in the detection independently of the pill type, matrix (b) indicates a clear accumulation of detection insecurities. In contrast, the multimodal-based network shows a significantly better accuracy of 71.63% compared to the unimodal counterparts (see Table 2c). None of the confusion matrices indicate a strong within-pair confusion, meaning that none of the models performed particularly badly in distinguishing one class from another.

Table 2. Confusion matrices for all three models at a noise ratio of 0.3

	Magnesium	Calcium	B-Complex	Big Mints	Chew	Small Mints	Vitamin B	Candy	Magnesium	Calcium	B-Complex	Big Mints	Chew	Small Mints	Vitamin B	Candy	Magnesium	Calcium	B-Complex	Big Mints	Chew	Small Mints	Vitamin B	Candy
	(a) Audio only ⌀ 58.75%								(b) Tactile only ⌀ 51.25%								(c) Multimodal ⌀ 71.63%							
Magnesium	0.42	0.21	0.02	0.19	0.03	0.01	0.05	0.07	0.49	0.07	0.13	0.09	0.05	0.14	0.0	0.01	0.73	0.08	0.09	0.07	0.04	0.0	0.01	0.02
Calcium	0.1	0.68	0.0	0.06	0.0	0.01	0.03	0.12	0.12	0.46	0.02	0.15	0.1	0.06	0.01	0.09	0.15	0.73	0.01	0.02	0.0	0.0	0.01	0.09
B-Complex	0.07	0.02	0.61	0.01	0.0	0.18	0.09	0.01	0.03	0.0	0.66	0.03	0.03	0.24	0.02	0.0	0.08	0.01	0.42	0.05	0.03	0.12	0.09	0.0
Big Mints	0.11	0.05	0.1	0.5	0.05	0.03	0.05	0.11	0.02	0.05	0.03	0.44	0.08	0.23	0.09	0.08	0.05	0.06	0.04	0.56	0.12	0.05	0.09	0.04
Chew	0.14	0.05	0.0	0.14	0.51	0.0	0.06	0.09	0.08	0.11	0.04	0.12	0.35	0.18	0.07	0.05	0.07	0.03	0.02	0.1	0.68	0.02	0.02	0.07
Small Mints	0.01	0.02	0.07	0.02	0.01	0.53	0.02	0.03	0.05	0.02	0.12	0.07	0.06	0.63	0.03	0.02	0.0	0.01	0.02	0.01	0.01	0.9	0.03	0.01
Vitamin B	0.08	0.09	0.05	0.06	0.0	0.07	0.47	0.18	0.0	0.0	0.05	0.05	0.05	0.19	0.63	0.01	0.0	0.0	0.04	0.08	0.06	0.01	0.74	0.08
Candy	0.06	0.11	0.02	0.05	0.02	0.03	0.04	0.68	0.02	0.04	0.02	0.19	0.17	0.11	0.01	0.44	0.0	0.03	0.0	0.04	0.03	0.02	0.09	0.79

7   Conclusion

We successfully combined the tactile information with noisy audio data to improve the accuracy compared to approaches regarding the individual signals. The effect of combining different modalities in a single network is distinctly visible in Table 2. The classification errors of the unimodal approaches could be reduced significantly by fusing the single modalities. While the advantage of multimodal classification over unimodal audio-based classification is insignificant without noise in the signal, even so, it could be an improvement for noisy environments. By considering tactile information, our work extends the approach by Eppe et al. [17] who classify materials in optically identical capsules just by considering audio data. Specifically, we show that taking tactile signals into account improves the robustness of neural network-based classification, even if the accuracy resulting from only the tactile modality is significantly lower than the accuracy of the audio network without noise. The neural network architecture used in this work was deliberately chosen to be simple as the main goal was to highlight the effect of multi sensor fusion of the audio and tactile modalities.

The overall classification accuracy of our approach without acoustic noise is slightly lower than the results provided by Eppe et al. [17] and Chen et al. [14]. However, the focus of our work was to show to what extend tactile data can improve the auditory classification performance under noisy conditions, and not to obtain a good absolute performance value. Furthermore, both approaches collected more data than we do and used more diverse materials.

Currently, the amount of pills in the container is not considered by the proposed approach. Potential future work involves the extension of our neural architecture to also estimate the filling state of the medicine containers. Furthermore, we will consider *interactive sensing* in the future. Specifically, we would like to investigate how we can actively modulate the shaking motion on-line during the classification process to further optimize the classification. A potential method to realize this is reinforcement learning [30,31].

References

1. Nakamura, T., Nagai, T., Iwahashi, N.: Multimodal object categorization by a robot. In: 2007 IEEE/RSJ International Conference on Intelligent Robots and Systems, pp. 2415–2420 (2007)
2. Pieropan, A., Salvi, G., Pauwels, K., Kjellström, H.: Audio-visual classification and detection of human manipulation actions. In: 2014 IEEE/RSJ International Conference on Intelligent Robots and Systems, pp. 3045–3052 (2014)
3. Sun, F., Liu, C., Huang, W., Zhang, J.: Object classification and grasp planning using visual and tactile sensing. IEEE Trans. Syst. Man Cybern. Syst. **46**(7), 969–979 (2016)
4. Eppe, M., Kerzel, M., Griffiths, S., Ng, H.G., Wermter, S.: Combining deep learning for visuo-motor coordination with object detection and tracking to realize a high-level interface for robot object-picking. In: IEEE RAS International Conference on Humanoid Robots (Humanoids), pp. 612–617 (2017)
5. Kerzel, M., Eppe, M., Heinrich, S., Abawi, F., Wermter, S.: Neurocognitive shared visuomotor network for end-to-end learning of object identification, localization and grasping on a humanoid. In: IEEE Conference on Development and Learning and Epigenetic Robotics (ICDL-EpiRob), pp. 19–24 (2019)
6. Alfadhel, A., Khan, M.A., Cardoso de Freitas, S., Kosel, J.: Magnetic tactile sensor for braille reading. IEEE Sens. J. **16**(24), 8700–8705 (2016)
7. Litvak, D., Zigel, Y., Gannot, I.: Fall detection of elderly through floor vibrations and sound. In: 30th Annual International Conference of the IEEE Engineering in Medicine and Biology Society, vol. 2008, pp. 4632–4635. IEEE (2008)
8. Wettels, N., Santos, V.J., Johansson, R.S., Loeb, G.E.: Biomimetic tactile sensor array. Adv. Robot. **22**(8), 829–849 (2008)
9. Arian, M.S., Blaine, C.A., Loeb, G.E., Fishel, J.A.: Using the BioTac as a tumor localization tool. In: IEEE Haptics Symposium (HAPTICS), pp. 443–448. IEEE (2014)
10. Su, Z., Hausman, K., Chebotar, Y., Molchanov, A., Loeb, G.E., Sukhatme, G.S., Schaal, S.: Force estimation and slip detection/classification for grip control using a biomimetic tactile sensor. In: 2015 IEEE-RAS 15th International Conference on Humanoid Robots (Humanoids), pp. 297–303 (2015)
11. Fishel, J.A., Loeb, G.E.: Sensing tactile microvibrations with the BioTac - comparison with human sensitivity. In: 2012 4th IEEE RAS EMBS International Conference on Biomedical Robotics and Biomechatronics (BioRob), pp. 1122–1127 (2012)
12. Xu, D., Loeb, G.E., Fishel, J.A.: Tactile identification of objects using Bayesian exploration. In: 2013 IEEE International Conference on Robotics and Automation, pp. 3056–3061. IEEE (2013)
13. Kerzel, M., Ali, M., Ng, H.G., Wermter, S.: Haptic material classification with a multi-channel neural network. In: International Joint Conference on Neural Networks (IJCNN), pp. 439–446 (2017)
14. Chen, C.L., Snyder, J.O., Ramadge, P.J.: Learning to identify container contents through tactile vibration signatures. In: 2016 IEEE International Conference on Simulation, Modeling, and Programming for Autonomous Robots (SIMPAR), pp. 43–48. IEEE (2016)
15. Durst, R.S., Krotkov, E.P.: Object classification from analysis of impact acoustics. In: Proceedings 1995 IEEE/RSJ International Conference on Intelligent Robots and Systems. Human Robot Interaction and Cooperative Robots, vol. 1, pp. 90–95 (1995)

16. Luo, S., Zhu, L., Althoefer, K., Liu, H.: Knock-Knock: acoustic object recognition by using stacked denoising autoencoders. Neurocomputing **267**, 18–24 (2017)
17. Eppe, M., Kerzel, M., Strahl, E., Wermter, S.: Deep neural object analysis by inter-active auditory exploration with a humanoid robot. In: 2018 IEEE/RSJ International Conference on Intelligent Robots and Systems (IROS), pp. 284–289. IEEE (2018)
18. Liang, H., Li, S., Ma, X., Hendrich, N., Gerkmann, T., Zhang, J.: Making Sense of Audio Vibration for Liquid Height Estimation in Robotic Pouring. arXiv preprint arXiv:1903.00650 (2019)
19. Sinapov, J., Schenck, C., Stoytchev, A.: Learning Relational Object Categories using Behavioral Exploration and Multimodal Perception. In: 2014 IEEE International Conference on Robotics and Automation (ICRA), IEEE (2014) 5691–5698
20. Meeussen, W., et al.: Autonomous door opening and plugging in with a personal robot. In: 2010 IEEE International Conference on Robotics and Automation, pp. 729–736. IEEE (2010)
21. The Shadow Robot Company: The Shadow Dexterous Hand. https://www.shadowrobot.com/products/dexterous-hand/. Accessed 6 Oct 2020
22. Wettels, N., Fishel, J.A., Loeb, G.E.: Multimodal tactile sensor. In: Balasubrama-nian, R., Santos, V.J. (eds.) The Human Hand as an Inspiration for Robot Hand Development. STAR, vol. 95, pp. 405–429. Springer, Cham (2014). https://doi.org/10.1007/978-3-319-03017-3_19
23. Davis, S., Mermelstein, P.: Comparison of parametric representations for monosyl-labic word recognition in continuously spoken sentences. IEEE Trans. Acoustics Speech Sig. Process. **28**(4), 357–366 (1980)
24. Eppe, M., Alpay, T., Wermter, S.: Towards end-to-end raw audio music synthesis. In: International Conference on Artificial Neural Networks (ICANN), pp. 137–146 (2018)
25. Strahl, E., Kerzel, M., Eppe, M., Griffiths, S.: Hear the egg - demonstrating robotic interactive auditory perception. In: International Conference on Intelligent Robots and Systems (IROS), p. 5041 (2018)
26. Bergstra, J., Yamins, D., Cox, D.D.: Making a Science of Model Search: Hyperpa-rameter Optimization in Hundreds of Dimensions for Vision Architectures (2013)
27. Hochreiter, S., Schmidhuber, J.: Long short-term memory. Neural Comput. **9**(8), 1735–1780 (1997)
28. Cho, K., et al.: Learning Phrase Representations using RNN Encoder-Decoder for Statistical Machine Translation. arXiv preprint arXiv:1406.1078 (2014)
29. Kingma, D.P., Ba, J.L.: Adam: a method for stochastic optimization. In: Interna-tional Conference on Learning Representations (ICLR) (2015)
30. Eppe, M., Magg, S., Wermter, S.: Curriculum goal masking for continuous deep reinforcement learning. In: International Conference on Development and Learning and Epigenetic Robotics (ICDL-EpiRob), pp. 183–188 (2019)
31. Eppe, M., Nguyen, P.D.H., Wermter, S.: From semantics to execution: integrating action planning with reinforcement learning for robotic causal problem-solving. Front. Robot. AI **6**, 123 (2019)

A Novel Pose Estimation Method of Object in Robotic Manipulation Using Vision-Based Tactile Sensor

Dan Zhao[1]([⊠]), Fuchun Sun[1], Quan Zhou[2], and Zongtao Wang[3]

[1] Beijing National Research Center for Information Science and Technology,
Department of Computer Science and Technology, Tsinghua University, Beijing 100083, China
fcsun@mail.tsinghua.edu.cn
[2] AnHui Province Key Laboratory of Special Heavy Load Robot,
Anhui University of Technology, Ma Anshan, China
[3] Key Lab of Industrial Computer Control Engineering of Hebei Province,
Yanshan University, Qinhuangdao 066000, China

Abstract. The computer vision techniques have been widely used in the robotic manipulation for perception and positioning. However, duo to the inaccuracy of camera calibration and measurement, there is a greatly need for more accurate method to estimate the object pose especially for robotic precise manipulation. In this paper, we propose a novel pose estimation method of object in robotic manipulation using a vision-based tactile sensor. The structure of the tactile sensor and the proposed model are introduced in detail, and verification experiments have been performed. The results show the advantages and better performance of the proposed method.

Keywords: Tactile sensor · Pose estimation · Orientation prediction · Robotic manipulation

1 Introduction

After robots were introduced into the manufacturing industry, great progress has been made which have largely improved the working conditions, efficiency and quality. With the development of the robotic techniques, more and more different kinds of robots have come into our lives which bring new blood of freshness, modernity and technology [1–3].

As senses are important to people which can provide great conveniences for our daily work and life, perception is similarly one of the most important capabilities of an intelligent robotic system, which is essential for a robot to interact with the environment. There are many research on perception such as computer vision, tactile sensors, force sensors, laser displacement sensors, and so on [4–6]. Among them, computer vision has been greatly developed in recent years which is widely adopted for object recognition, positioning and tracking. Researchers have made great efforts and many attempts over the past few years. Zhu et al. analyzed the measurement error to improve the accuracy

© Springer Nature Singapore Pte Ltd. 2021
F. Sun et al. (Eds.): ICCSIP 2020, CCIS 1397, pp. 266–275, 2021.
https://doi.org/10.1007/978-981-16-2336-3_24

of 2D vision system for robotic drilling [7]. Liu et al. published a series of papers to research on the pose measurement and visual servoing methods for positioning in aircraft digital assembly [8, 9].

It is known that there are many errors in the measurement with camera. On the one hand, the accuracy of depth measurement is limited which depends on the distance between camera and target object [10]. Besides, the errors introduced in camera calibration process will also lead to the deviations of the visual measurement results. Therefore, a novel pose estimation method using a vision-based tactile sensor is proposed in this paper to improve the positioning accuracy of the target object for the robotic manipulation.

2   Related Works

Tactile Sensors. Tactile sensors have been focused by the researchers in the robotic fields in recent years. Most of the tactile sensors are used in the application of multi-finger robotic hand. There are great challenges for the tactile information capturing, efficient processing and effective applications. Fang et al. designed a cross-modal tactile sensor for measuring the robotic grasping forces [11, 12]. Sun et al. developed a novel multi-modal sensor using thermochromic material to measure the contact temperature, and described the fabrication method of proposed sensor [13]. Liu et al. proposed several kernel sparse coding methods to address the tactile data representation and classification problem in object recognition using tactile measurements of the Barrett Hand [14]. Ma et al. studied a method for dense tactile force estimation using GelSlim and inverse FEM [15], and Dong et al. studied the tactile-based insertion for dense box-packing with two GelSlim fingers in which the error direction and magnitude of the grasped object were estimated based on the neural networks [16]. The methods have been verified in the robotic manipulation experiments. However, the focused dimension of the error space is small which only consider translation errors in axis x and rotation errors in yaw θ. They set $T\theta = 5°$ as the threshold of rotation errors and $Tx = 2.5$ mm as the threshold of translation errors in the experiments, which means the errors within the thresholds cannot estimate effectively with the method.

Convolutional Neural Networks. With the development of computer hardware and the improvement of data volume, deep learning ushered in a vigorous development. Convolutional Neural Networks (CNN) is an important deep learning method which is widely used to solve problems about images in computer vision field. Compared with the traditional methods, deep learning methods can extract more robust and complex features. In recent years, there are many papers published in this fields and make great contribution for research and applications [17–20].

3   The Proposed Methodology

To improve the positioning accuracy of the target object in robotic manipulation, we propose an orientation prediction method using a vision-based tactile sensors, which will be introduced in detail in this section.

3.1 Tactile Sensor

To realize the tactile perception of the robot, a vision-based tactile sensor was developed in our research team. The structure of tactile sensor and the principle of its tactile perception will be introduced in detail in this part. As shown in Fig. 1 the tactile sensor is mainly composed of support component, a camera, light sources, acrylic board, an elastomer and surface attachment.

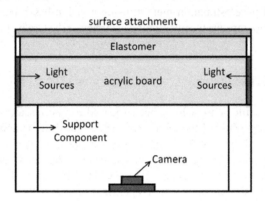

Fig. 1. The structure of the tactile sensor.

The camera is the key part which should be paid more attention to in the design, and a custom miniature ultra-short focal length camera is used in the tactile sensor. The LED unit provides the light sources for the camera with LEDs and flexible circuit board. The acrylic board is used to support the elastomer above and dissipate the light from the LEDs. The elastomer is another critical part of the sensor, and its hardness, thickness and transmittance can directly affect the sensor performance. The elastomer should have good elasticity, low viscosity, and as transparent as possible. The tactile information is obtained by analyzing the deformation of the elastomer. The material used here is polydimethylsiloxane (PDMS). Above the elastomer, there is a surface attachment to protect the elastomer.

When the tactile sensor contact with the object, the elastomer and surface attachment will be deformed which reflect the features of the object's contact surface. Then, the micro camera in the sensor can capture the images of these deformations. Besides, the surface properties like temperature and texture of the object can also be measured with the appropriate materials of the sensor's surface attachment. In this paper, we aim to predict the orientation of target object in robotic manipulation, and will not focus its temperature and texture of the surface.

3.2 Pose Estimation with Vision-Based Tactile Sensor

As the skins of a robot, touch perception plays an important role for robotic systems, especially in precise manipulation fields. In this paper, we propose an orientation prediction method using a vision-based tactile sensors for the robotic manipulation, which will be introduced in this part.

The orientation deviations between the target object and robot end in the tactile coordinate system can be predicted by the tactile image and described as:

$$\Delta_{ori} = (\Delta\alpha, \Delta\beta, \Delta\gamma) = f(I_{touch}) \tag{1}$$

where $\Delta\alpha, \Delta\beta, \Delta\gamma$ are the angle deviations between the target object and robot end around X-, Y- and Z-axes of the tactile coordinate system, I_{touch} represents the tactile image captured by the tactile sensor, and $f(\cdot)$ represents the mapping relationship between the angle deviations and the tactile image which can be modeled as an end-to-end model by deep learning method.

Convolutional Neural Networks (CNN) is an important deep learning method which is widely used to solve problems about images in the computer vision field. In this paper, a CNN-based model is proposed to predict the relative orientation deviations between the target object and robot end based on tactile sensor. The architecture of the proposed model is shown in Fig. 2 which describes the mapping relationship between the angle deviations and the captured tactile images.

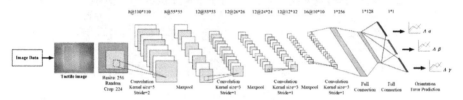

Fig. 2. The structure of the tactile sensor.

Convolution layer is the core of convolution neural network. Because of the existence of convolution layer, convolution neural network has a strong ability to extract features. At the same time, convolution neural network can process data in parallel, which greatly improves the computing speed of the model. The calculation formula for the convolutional layer is as follows:

$$x_j^n = F\left(\sum_{i\in M_j} x_i^{n-1} * k_{ij}^n + b_j^n\right) \tag{2}$$

where x_j^n is the output feature map, x_i^{n-1} is the input feature map, M_j is the selected area in the $n-1$ layer, k_{ij}^n is the weight parameter, b_j^n is the bias, and $F(\cdot)$ is the activation function.

After the convolution layer, the full connection layer are added to achieve the regression of the orientation deviations $(\Delta\alpha, \Delta\beta, \Delta\gamma)$. The calculation formula for the fully connected layer is:

$$y_j = F\left(\sum_{i=1}^{N} x_i * w_{i,j} + b_j\right) \tag{3}$$

where x is the input layer, N is number of input layer nodes, w_{ij} is the weight between the links x_i and y_j, b_j is the bias, and $F(\cdot)$ is the activation function.

4 Experiments and Results

To validate the method and algorithm proposed in the paper, experiments have been performed in the real application. The experimental platform is shown in Fig. 3, which mainly includes the UR5 robot, the Kinect DK camera, the tactile sensor, the target objects and the control computer. The robot is set on the one side of the table whose arm can cover the space above the target object. Then, the tactile sensor is connected at the end of the robot.

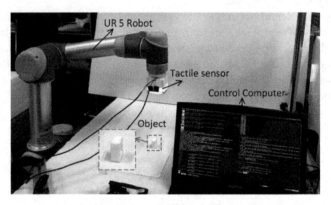

Fig. 3. Experimental platform.

In the experiment, the target object is firstly set on the table at a certain position and orientation. Secondly, the robot takes the tactile sensor to move above the target object and keep a safe distance with the target object. Then, the robot keep the same orientation and press on the target object until the tactile sensor touch the target object and the force reach the given threshold. In this process, the pose of the robot can be controlled and the values of roll, pitch and yaw (RPY) angles can be recorded. At the same time, the tactile sensor can capture the image when it contact with the target object. With the different pose deviations between the tactile sensor and target robot, the tactile images will be different. The tactile images with the corresponding labels of angle deviations will form the fundamental data set for the pose estimation of the target object.

We separate all of the captured data set into training data and test data, which are used for model training and performance testing. The performance of the training model are shown in the results listed below. In the Fig. 4, we can see that the predicted values are similar with the true values of the pose deviations of the target object. The Fig. 5 shows losses in the training and testing stages. These results show the proposed model is correct and effective.

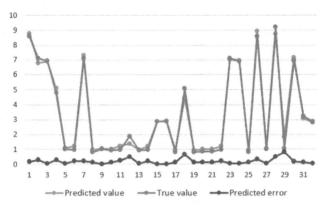

Fig. 4. The predicted performance with the proposed method. The ordinate unit is millimeter.

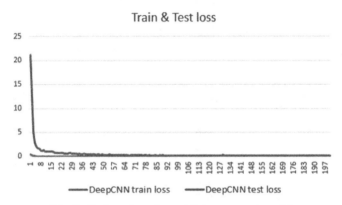

Fig. 5. Train and test loss with the proposed model.

To better verify the proposed model and algorithm in the paper, we also perform the comparison experiments. BP modeling method is selected as the comparison method. With the different models, we can obtain the different results which are shown in the following figures and tables. Figure 6 shows the error distribution of pose estimation which reflect the deviations between predicted and true values. In this figure, we can see that the results with the proposed method in column A have more concentrative distribution especially in the error distribution of $\Delta\alpha$ in the first row. In the Table 1, we can see the whole circumstance of the predicted error, and the average and standard deviation of predicted errors in three directions with the proposed method are all lower than that of comparison method which show the validation and advantages of the proposed method.

In the Fig. 7 and Fig. 8, we can see that the training loss and test loss of different methods. From these figures, the change tendency of the loss are clearly shown. The training loss and test loss of the proposed method decrease more smoothly and with little large-magnitude up and downs. The training loss of two methods are almost same in the end, while the final test loss with the proposed method is smaller than that of the

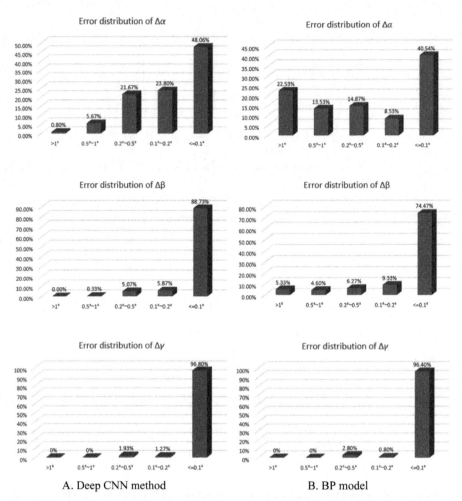

A. Deep CNN method   B. BP model

Fig. 6. The error distribution of pose estimation with different methods.

Table 1. The predicted errors of pose estimation with different methods.

Method	Deep CNN model			BP model		
Error(°)	abs($\Delta\alpha$)	abs($\Delta\beta$)	abs($\Delta\gamma$)	abs($\Delta\alpha$)	abs($\Delta\beta$)	abs($\Delta\gamma$)
Mean	0.24187	0.060328	0.023558	0.921979	0.275116	0.033392
Std.	0.21537	0.084081	0.05859	1.04168	0.627638	0.063863

comparison method. All of the above results of experiments show the effectiveness and efficiency of the proposed model and algorithms.

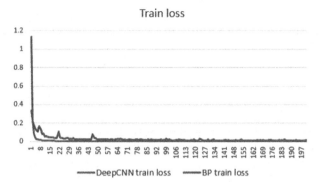

Fig. 7. The training loss with different methods.

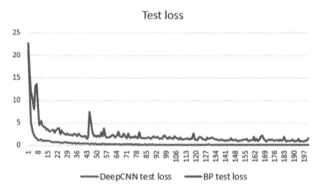

Fig. 8. The test loss with different methods.

5   Conclusion

To improve the accuracy of the object pose estimation in robotic manipulation, we propose a novel pose estimation method of object in robotic manipulation using a vision-based tactile sensor. Firstly, the research background and related works are introduced. Secondly, the proposed methodology is described in detail which includes the structure of the tactile sensor and architecture of the proposed model. Finally, experiments have been performed to verify the effectiveness of the proposed method. The comparison method has also been performed to show the advantages and better performance of the proposed method. The experimental results show that the average and standard deviations of predicted errors with the proposed method are smaller and the loss in training and testing stage are more stable and smaller than the comparison method. With the proposed method in the paper, the pose estimation of object in robotic manipulation has successfully been improved. In the future works, the application of this method can be extended into the manipulation with robotic hands in which the tactile sensor can be combined with the present robotic hands.

Acknowledgement. This research was sponsored by the Major Project of the New Generation of Artificial Intelligence (No. 2018AAA0102900) and the China Postdoctoral Science Foundation Grant (No. 2019TQ0170).

References

1. Fazeli, N., Oller, M., Wu, J., Wu, Z., Tenenbaum, J., Rodriguez, A.: See, feel, act: hierarchical learning for complex manipulation skills with multisensory fusion. Sci. Robot. **4**(26), eaav3123 (2019)
2. Lars, K., Nick, H., Tom, D., Marc, H., Tomas, K.: Artificial intelligence for long-term robot autonomy: a survey. IEEE Robot. Autom. Lett. **3**, 4023–4030 (2018)
3. Hansen, E., Andersen, R., Madsen, S., Bøgh, S.: Transferring human manipulation knowledge to robots with inverse reinforcement learning. In: Proceedings of the 2020 IEEE/SICE International Symposium on System Integration, SII 2020, pp. 933–937. Hawaii Convention Center, Honolulu, United States (2020)
4. Park, H., Park, J., Lee, D., Park, J., Baeg, M., Bae, J.: Compliance-based robotic peg-in-hole assembly strategy without force feedback. IEEE Trans. Industr. Electron. **64**(8), 6299–6309 (2017)
5. Chan, Y., Yu, H., Khurshid, R.: Effects of force-torque and tactile haptic modalities on classifying the success of robot manipulation tasks. In: 2019 IEEE World Haptics Conference, pp. 586–591. IEEE, Tokyo, Japan (2019)
6. Zhu, W., Liu, H., Ke, Y.: Sensor-based control using an image point and distance features for rivet-in-hole insertion. IEEE Trans. Industr. Electron. **67**(6), 4692–4699 (2020)
7. Zhu, W., Mei, B., Yan, G., Ke, Y.: Measurement error analysis and accuracy enhancement of 2D vision system for robotic drilling. Robot. Comput. Integr. Manuf. **30**(2), 160–171 (2014)
8. Liu, H., Zhu, W., Ke, Y.: Pose alignment of aircraft structures with distance sensors and CCD cameras. Robot. Comput. Integr. Manuf. **48**, 30–38 (2017)
9. Liu, H., Zhu, W., Dong, H., Ke, Y.: An adaptive ball-head positioning visual servoing method for aircraft digital assembly. Assembly Autom. **39**(2), 287–296 (2019)
10. Poggi, M., Aleotti, F., Tosi, F., Mattoccia, S.: On the uncertainty of self-supervised monocular depth estimation. In: 2020 IEEE Conference on Computer Vision and Pattern Recognition, pp. 1–26. IEEE, China (2020)
11. Fang, B., Sun, F., Yang, C., Xue, H., Liu, H.: A dual-modal vision-based tactile sensor for robotic hand grasping. In: 2018 IEEE International Conference on Robotics and Automation, pp. 4740–4745. IEEE, Brisbane, Australia (2018)
12. Fang, B., Xue, H., Sun, F., Yang, Y., Zhu, R.: A cross-modal tactile sensor design for measuring robotic grasping forces. Ind. Robot **46**(3), 337–344 (2019)
13. Sun, F., Fang, B., Xue, H., Liu, H., Huang, H.: A novel multi-modal tactile sensor design using thermochromic material. Sci. Chin. **62**(11), 185–187 (2019)
14. Liu, H., Guo, D., Sun, F.: Object recognition using tactile measurements: kernel sparse coding methods. IEEE Trans. Instrum. Meas. **65**(3), 656–665 (2016)
15. Ma, D., Donlon, E., Dong, S., Rodriguez, A.: Dense tactile force estimation using GelSlim and inverse FEM. In: 2019 IEEE International Conference on Robotics and Automation, pp. 1–7. IEEE, Montreal, Canada (2019)
16. Dong, S., Rodriguez, A.: Tactile-based insertion for dense box-packing. In: 2019 IEEE/RSJ International Conference on Intelligent Robots and Systems, pp. 1–8. IEEE, Macau, China (2020)

17. Du, G., Wang, K., Lian, S., Zhao, K.: Vision-based robotic grasp detection from object localization, object pose estimation to grasp estimation: a review. Artificial Intelligence Review, pp. 1–36 (2020)
18. Sünderhauf, N., et al.: The limits and potentials of deep learning for robotics. Int. J. Robot. Res. **37**(4–5), 405–420 (2018)
19. Caldera, S., Rassau, A., Chai, D.: Review of deep learning methods in robotic grasp detection. Multimodal Technol. Interact. **2**(3), 57 (2018)
20. Han, X., Liu, H., Sun, F., Zhang, X.: Active object detection with multi-step action prediction using deep q-network. IEEE Trans. Industr. Inf. **15**(6), 3723–3731 (2019)

Design and Implementation of Pneumatic Soft Gripper with Suction and Grasp Composite Structure

Haiming Huang[1,2(✉)], Xiaotao Liang[1], Yufan Zhuo[1], Linyuan Wu[1], Zhenkun Wen[3], and Fuchun Sun[1,2,4]

[1] College of Electronic and Information Engineering,
Shenzhen University, Shenzhen 518060, China
[2] Peng Cheng Lab, Shenzhen 518055, GD, China
[3] College of Computer Science and Software Engineering,
Shenzhen University, Shenzhen 518060, China
[4] Department of Computer Science and Technology, Tsinghua University,
Beijing 100084, China

Abstract. Robot gripper is used in many different places at present, but traditional gripper is difficult to grasp and sort soft and fragile fruits and vegetables effectively. Based on manipulator technology, this paper presents a design scheme of pneumatic multi-fingered gripper. This design combines the vacuum chunk and soft fingers to make the gripper precisely grasp the target object without damaging the surface of the object. The flexible fingers can be made quickly by using a compound injection molding method. Combined with the STM32 microcontroller and the Universal Robots 5 (UR Arm), the operation system of the soft gripper is realized, and the man-machine interaction presents a good performance. Through the grasping experiment, it is proved that the prototype can grasp, transport, and place soft and fragile objects stably and accurately. Overall, this design implements the combination of pneumatic unit and soft gripper, and provides a new orientation to the research of soft robot.

Keywords: Soft gripper · Flexible material · Pneumatic drive · Non-destructive grasp · Robot operation

1 Introduction

As a new device in intelligent manufacturing, the manipulator can complete the corresponding action according to the set instruction and meet the requirements of modern industrial production [1]. However, due to the limitation of metal manufacturing materials, traditional manipulator has disadvantages such as low degree of freedom, big self-weight, poor adaptability, and low safety, which makes it difficult to meet the requirements of fragile products production [2].

With the development of 3D printing technology and hyperelastic materials, soft gripper hands made of soft materials show obvious advantages in freedom, flexibility, safety,

© Springer Nature Singapore Pte Ltd. 2021
F. Sun et al. (Eds.): ICCSIP 2020, CCIS 1397, pp. 276–286, 2021.
https://doi.org/10.1007/978-981-16-2336-3_25

and force control [3]. In this paper, according to the requirements in the field of fragile products production and processing, a set of suction and grasp composite structure soft gripper based on soft materials is designed. The designed pneumatic unit can reach into a narrow space and draw out the target object, which improves the weakness of soft gripper hand working in a narrow space and has the advantage of not damaging the object surface. The fingers of soft gripper is designed to hold the object stably and the soft material can also protect the object's surface well. Combined with Universal Robots 5 robot arm, the soft gripper forms a whole robot with the higher flexibility and working range.

The rest of the article is framed as follows: Sect. 2 explains the composite structure of the gripper and its manufacturing processes, Sect. 3 describes control system of the gripper, and Sect. 4 explains combination between soft gripper and UR arm. Prototype test experiment is performed in Sect. 5. Conclusion is expounded in Sect. 6.

2 Design of Soft Gripper with Suction and Grasp Composite Structure

Traditional rigid manipulator has complex structure, numerous sensors, great difficulty in operation and high maintenance cost. Compared with the traditional rigid manipulator, the soft gripper hand is made of silica gel for the fingers and has a simple structure design. It can bend the fingers of the gripper hand and accurately and reliably grasp the target object through simple and continuous pressure inflation.

2.1 Suction and Grasp Composite Structure Design

Pneumatic multi-finger soft gripper hand (see Fig. 1) includes vacuum adsorption device and four soft fingers, wherein the vacuum adsorption device includes vacuum chuck and cylinder piston rod, etc., to complete the work of sucking objects [4, 5]. Soft fingers made of liquid silica gel [6] by 3D printing technology [7], accomplish the task of grasping objects.

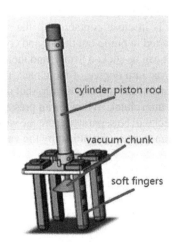

Fig. 1. Design drawing of soft gripper structure

2.2 Soft Gripper

The soft finger is made of silica gel, and the inside of the finger is inflated by continuous pressure, making the soft finger bend, accurately and reliably grasping the target object, and ensuring that the target object does not fall off, and the surface of the target object is not damaged.

Soft fingers adopt pneumatic driving mode, pneumatic has more output force than EAP drive, faster response speed than SMA drive, better interactivity than cable drive, lower price than other drives [8].

Software finger size and body shape can close, made of silica gel inside and outside walls and do not stretch the bondage of layer structure, the lining inside a chamber designed for semicircle, middle bound layer is composed of Kevlar thread and nylon fiber cloth, the outer wall silicone outer array groove of the grain, easy to make software fingers to inflate bending in specific directions [9], as shown in Fig. 2(a).

When the soft finger cavity is inflated and pressurized, the wound Kevlar line can make the finger not expand laterally but longitudinally. The inner side of the nylon fiber cloth is not extensible, and the silicone wall with grain on the other side expands and expands, so "differential strain" will make the finger bend to grasp the object [10].

The processing of soft fingers uses the compound injection molding method, that is, through curing the hydraulic material into shape, the hydraulic material uses liquid silica gel with good ductility and high softness. Firstly, the Solidworks 3D design software makes the mold design (see Fig. 2(b)), then the 3D printer prints out the mold, finally the first round of finger inner wall, strain limiting layer and second round of finger outer wall are generated. The Kevlar wire was wound and nylon fiber cloth was used to form the strain limiting layer (see Fig. 2(c)). The nylon fiber cloth was attached to the inner wall plane, and the Kevlar wire was wound around the inner wall and outer wall of the finger in the way of cross winding. The finished soft finger is shown in Fig. 2(d).

2.3 Vacuum Adsorption Unit

The vacuum chuck is connected to the vacuum generator through the pneumatic hose, and then the vacuum chuck is in close contact with the surface of the target object. Then the vacuum chuck is started to pump out the air and create negative pressure in the suction cup, so that the object can be sucked firmly, and then the object can be lifted and transported. The greater the vacuum degree of the chuck, the closer the chuck and the object fit. When the object reaches the target position, shut down the vacuum generating device and inflate into the vacuum chuck. When the air pressure inside the vacuum chuck is no longer negative, the object will be separated from the vacuum chuck, thus achieving the function of lifting, and transporting the object by the vacuum chuck [11].

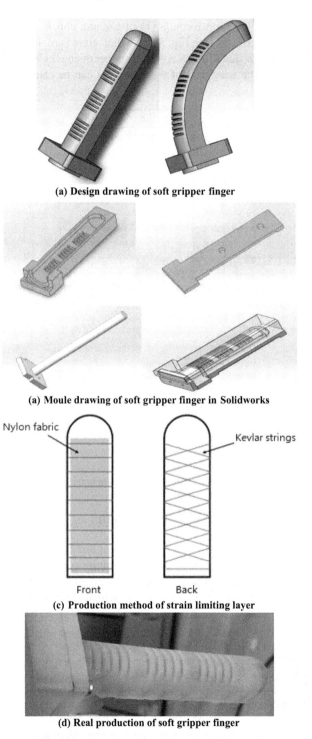

(a) Design drawing of soft gripper finger

(a) Moule drawing of soft gripper finger in Solidworks

(c) Production method of strain limiting layer

(d) Real production of soft gripper finger

Fig. 2. Procedures for making soft gripper finger

According to the calculation formula (1) of vacuum chuck diameter, the vacuum chucks used in this experiment (see Fig. 3) have diameters D of 40, 35, 30 and 25 mm. The safety factor of horizontal lifting S is 4, the number of chucks N is 1, and the vacuum pressure P is 70 kPa. The weight M of the adsorbent can be calculated as 0.87, 1.26, 1.72, and 2.24 kg

$$D = 2\sqrt{\frac{M \times 9.8 \times S \times 1000}{\pi \times N \times P}} \tag{1}$$

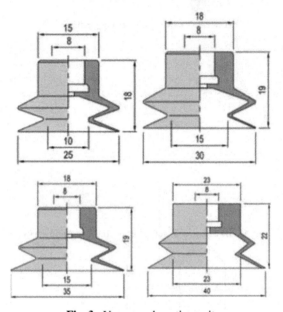

Fig. 3. Vacuum adsorption unit

3   Design of Soft Gripper Control System

The control system includes software control system and hardware control system, in which the software control system includes the operating system of the upper computer and the control program of the lower computer, and the hardware control system includes the controller and pneumatic network execution system. Its control link is shown in Fig. 4.

Fig. 4. Link diagram of soft gripper control system

3.1 Hardware Control System

The designed pneumatic network execution system [12, 13] is mainly composed of high-pressure air pump, solenoid valve, proportional valve, pneumatic hose, air nozzle and pneumatic interface. The high-pressure air pump supplies air to the cylinder piston rod and soft fingers, and the solenoid valve is used to control the expansion of the cylinder piston rod and the ventilation, retention, and bleed of the soft fingers. The proportional valve controls the aperture of the gas flow channel to adjust the air pressure of the soft finger to prevent the soft finger from expanding and bursting due to too much air pressure. The structure diagram of its gas path is shown in Fig. 5.

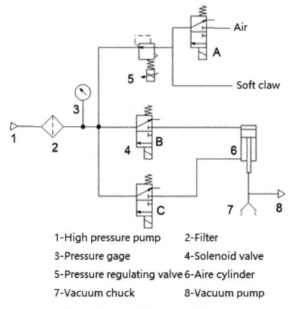

1-High pressure pump   2-Filter
3-Pressure gage   4-Solenoid valve
5-Pressure regulating valve 6-Aire cylinder
7-Vacuum chuck   8-Vacuum pump

Fig. 5. Structure diagram of air path

3.2 Software Control System

Carry on the STM32 micro-controller the control program of single-chip processor system through multiple electromagnetic valve on-off control, fingers and vacuum adsorption device, further control software to complete object handling action and action process for programming specific include: cylinder piston rod drives the vacuum chuck, chuck adsorption after objects, the piston rod back to drive objects up and software compression bending finger hold objects, lose vacuum suction cups away from the object and reach the designated position software finger deflated to restore the initial state after placing objects, action flow diagram as shown in Fig. 6.

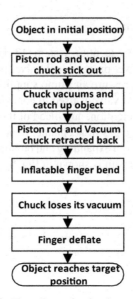

Fig. 6. Flow chart of soft gripper action

4   The Soft Gripper Is Combined with the UR Arm

The UR arm is characterized by easy programming, fast installation, high security, and human cooperation, which can make up for the disadvantages of small working range of the soft gripper and expand the usage scenario of the whole device.

On the mechanical level, the soft gripper and UR arm are connected through flange connectors, and four supporting rods are used to enhance the stability of the connection. The assembly drawing is shown in Fig. 7(a).

At the software level, the teaching box with UR arm can control the robot arm and control box by using the graphical user interface PolyScope (see Fig. 7(b)) to execute program instructions, which has the advantage of easy programming.

At the hardware level, the UR arm control box has multiple electrical interfaces. The opening and closing of STM32 and micro vacuum pump are controlled through the control box's digital output control mode, to further realize a series of actions such as grasping, moving, and preventing targets by the soft gripper and the UR arm. The connection mode of the control box is shown in Fig. 7(c).

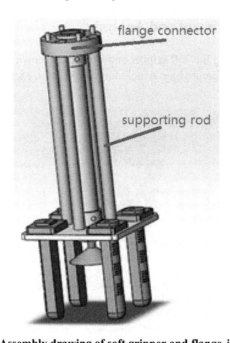

(a) Assembly drawing of soft gripper and flange joint

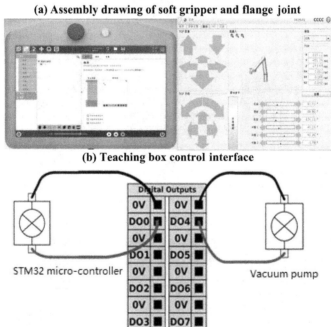

(b) Teaching box control interface

(c) Digital output control connection

Fig. 7. The articulation of the soft gripper and the UR arm at all levels

5   Grasping Experiment and Analysis

The prototype combining the soft gripper and UR arm is shown in Fig. 8(a). The prototype test captures six different objects, including a box cutter, vacuum generator, Vitasoy,

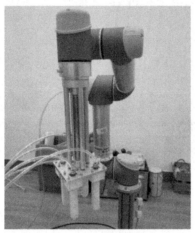

(a) Prototype of soft gripper and UR arm

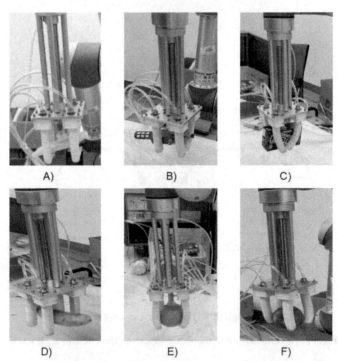

A)   B)   C)

D)   E)   F)

(b) Grasping experiment for six different objects

Fig. 8. a) Prototype of soft gripper and UR arm and experiments, b) Grasping experiment for six different objects, c) Transportation experiment

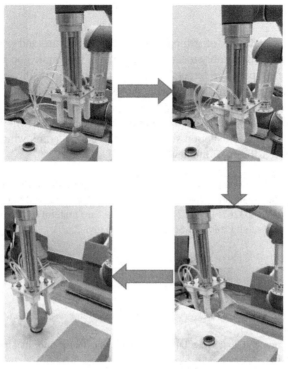

(c) Transportation experiment

Fig. 8. (*continued*)

banana, orange, and apple. In the experiment, soft gripper hands show high adaptability and stability when grasping different objects. Meanwhile, soft gripper hands show the advantage of not damaging easily objects when grasping target objects, especially bananas, oranges, and apples, as shown in Fig. 8(b).

In the transportation experiment (see Fig. 8(c)), the soft gripper reaches out the chuck to absorb the target, retract the chuck and control the soft finger to grasp the target, move the UR arm to the target position, loosen the finger and reach out the chuck, and place the target precisely to the target position. The experimental process shows that the prototype's composite structure of suction and grasp and the UR arm have good cooperation ability. During the process of placing objects at the same time, the structure of suction cup is very good to improve the working accuracy of the soft gripper.

The multi-object grasping experiment and object handling experiment show that the soft grasping device with suction cup has good object adaptability and grasping accuracy. This structure can passively fit with the grabbed object through the flexible grippers and absorb the specified object through the scalable function suction cup, which shows that the design has a good practical value.

6 Conclusion

In this paper, a new design of gripper with suction structure and grasp structure is pro- posed, which can preferably meet the requirement for fragile goods transportation. In the manufacturing part, the fingers which is made of liquid silica gel by using 3D printing technology is put into use, which shows the further advantage in preventing abrasion on the fragile goods. In the experiment part, by combining the soft gripper and UR arm, the prototype has a large working space. And the experiments also show a good collaboration between suction structure and grasp structure, which can prove the effectiveness and feasibility of the new idea.

Acknowledgement. The authors are grateful for the support by the Major Project of the New Generation of Artificial Intelligence (No. 2018AAA0102900), the National Natural Science Foundation of China (No. 61803267, U1613212). The authors are grateful for the support of Young Teachers Scientific Research Project of Shenzhen University.

References

1. Zhang, J., Wang, T., Hong, J.: Overview of soft manipulator research. J. Mech. Eng. **13**(53), 19–28 (2017)
2. Xiao, Y.: Design and experimental research of pneumatic soft manipulator. Southeast University (2016)
3. Zhang, L., Bao, G.J., Yang, Y.: Research progress of soft manipulator claw in fruit and vegetable picking. Trans. Chinese Soc. Agric. Eng. **09**(34), 11–20 (2018)
4. Krahn, J., Fabbro, F., Menon, C.: A soft-touch gripper for grasping delicate objects. IEEE/ASME Trans. Mechatron. **22**, 1276 (2017)
5. Xu, M.X.: Research on pneumatic drive software clamping device. Nanjing University of Science and Technology (2015)
6. Diemel, R., Brock, O.: A novel type of compliant and underactuated robotic hand for dexterous grasping. Int. J. Robot. Res. **1-3**(35), 161–185 (2016)
7. Zhang, X.J., Tang, S.Y., Jiang, H.: Research status and key technologies of 3D printing technology. J. Mater. Eng. **02**(44), 122–128 (2016)
8. Cianchetti, M., Ranzani, T., Gerboni, G.: Soft robotics technologies to address shortcomings in today's minimally invasive surgery: the STIFF-FLOP approach. Soft Robot. **2**(1), 122–131 (2014)
9. Connolly, F., Walsh, C.J., Bertoldi, K.: Automatic design of fiber-reinforced soft actuators for trajectory matching. In: Proceedings of the National Academy of Sciences of the United States of America, vol. 1, no. 114, pp. 224–228 (2017)
10. Wei, S.J., Wang, T.Y., Gu, G.Y.: Design of pneumatic soft grip based on fiber reinforced actuator. J. Mech. Eng. **13**(53), 29–38 (2017)
11. Miao, D.Y., Zhou, X., Zhang, Z.W.: Design of vacuum sucker type multi-function grab device. Packaging Food Mach. **06**(34), 39–42 (2016)
12. Mosadegh, B., Polygerinos, P., Keplinger, C.: Pneumatic networks for soft robotics that actuate rapidly. Adv. Func. Mater. **15**(24), 45–48 (2014)
13. Rus, D., Tolley, M.T.: Design, fabrication, and control of soft robots. Nature **7553**(521), 453–457 (2015)

Movement Primitive Libraries Learning for Industrial Manipulation Tasks

Ailin Xue, Xiaoli Li$^{(\boxtimes)}$, Chunfang Liu, and Xiaoyue Cao

Department of Information, Beijing University of Technology, Beijing, China
{xueailin,caoxiaoyue}@emails.bjut.edu.cn, lixiaolibjut@bjut.edu.cn

Abstract. Task Primitive Library (TPLib) consists of task primitives which places dynamic or probabilistic movement primitives in chronological order. A teaching and learning system is formed with TPLib, from which task trajectories can be saved with less parameters and generated in a new situation. TPLib is built by learning from a industrial task dataset which contains 8 tasks from simple to complex in this work. The dataset is collected by Kinect2.0 depth camera with visual motion capture algorithm. To reduce error, Savizkg-Golag smoothing algorithm is utilized after the collection. To test the performance of our TPLib, we simulated on ROS platform. The result shows that specific task trajectories can be finished through this library. The property of temporal modification is also proved in simulation. In the purpose of modifying a exact trajectory in a task without removing all the knowledge learned before, a correlation update rule is proposed. It also can meet the expectation in the simulation on ROS platform.

Keywords: Teaching and learning · Movement primitives · Mechanical arm · Industrial task

1 Introduction

With the developing of technology and industrial process, the requirement of industrial productivity grows rapidly. To adapt for the rapidly growing demand, more mechanics have been used in production in order to replace human beings, e.g., mechanical arm.

Mechanical arms have been used in many kinds of industrial operations, such as handling, welding, spraying, assembling and sorting, etc. [1]. It can greatly improve production efficiency, meanwhile, decrease the probability that a worker get injured during operation. At present, most of mechanical arms only have the ability to perform single, repetitive and regular tasks [2]. However, many more complicated and sophisticated productive processes are required to be finished [3], hence mechanical arms need to have adaptability and learning ability. To possess the learning ability, several methods have been proposed and developed, among which machine learning and imitation learning occupy the mainstream.

© Springer Nature Singapore Pte Ltd. 2021
F. Sun et al. (Eds.): ICCSIP 2020, CCIS 1397, pp. 287–300, 2021.
https://doi.org/10.1007/978-981-16-2336-3_26

Machine learning has two main branches, deep learning and reinforcement learning. They are mostly employed in the motion and trajectories planning and executing in a robot's control system. In addition, they have the problem of rewarding sparsity in the learning procedure [4], which makes machine learning not effective.

Teaching and learning or imitation learning describes the process that human or other creatures learn by observing, understanding and imitating [5]. It has been widely applied in the learning of robots. According to the concept of teaching and learning, its system can be separated into perception system, learning mechanism, knowledge library, etc. The demonstration provided by teacher can be in different patterns. Some are given in the form of data, while others may be given in image format, depending on the type of tasks. Movement Primitives is a study about creating complex and discrete movements [14], which is suitable for reproducing demonstrations in teaching and learning system.

In our paper, a kind of task primitive library for teaching and learning system to guide the movement trajectories of a mechanical arm is proposed. Firstly, we build a industrial task dataset that a mechanical arm needs to learn as the teaching or demonstrating trajectories for getting movement primitives. The trajectories are collected by visual sensor, Kinect2.0 depth camera, which is briefly introduced in Sect. 2. To reduce the influence of error in the acquisition environment, the Savizkg-Golag smoothing algorithm is applied to optimize the collected trajectories.

Afterwards, a type of Task Primitive Library (TPLib) with updating ability is introduced for the dataset we built. To construct the initial TPLib, we applied Dynamic Movement Primitives (DMPs) and Probabilistic Movement Primitives (ProMPs) respectively to obtain the movement primitives (MPs) for every single action sequence in a task, Sect. 4.

On the basis of the front, one task primitive is built by placing the foregoing movement primitives in chronological order. Considering some trajectories generated from the TPlib in a task can't reach our expectation in the simulation or reality, the renewability of the TPlib without losing previous knowledge becomes necessary. A Correlation update rule is raised to realize this property, Sect. 5.

The trajectories generated by task primitive library are simulated on the ROS platform to show the effect of our work. A AUBO-i5 robot is used to finish the tasks included in industrial task dataset using TPLib, also the update function of TPLib according to our correlation update rule is also proved, Sect. 6.

2 Related Work

In this section, some related works are presented about teaching and learning system and movement primitives.

Teaching and learning system was proposed by Bandera [6], which consists of input, perception system, learning mechanism, knowledge library, movement mechanism and output [7]. Some common teaching and learning methods are briefly introduced. Supervised learning is a basic imitation learning method, but it's generalization ability is not ideal [8]. Feed forward training [9] was proposed by Ross in 2010, whose accuracy is better but learning efficiency is not good enough. SEARN algorithm came out in 2009, it can learn on the basic of previous strategy [10].

Movement Primitives is also designed to learn by imitation [11]. In 2010, Kruger decomposed and learned movement primitives by hidden Markov model and regrouped the learned primitives to finish grab motion [12], enhanced the adaptability of MPs. A support vector machine and Gaussian mixture model based changing rule is raised by Manschitz in 2014 [13]. It can autonomously learn switching action but not adaptable enough in different situations.

DMPs and ProMPs are two kinds of Movement Primitives that are already used in the control of mechanical arms by many scholars.

DMPs was firstly proposed to solve the problem of trajectory discontinuity by Schaal, in 2012 [14]. In next year, this method is improved by jointly adjusting the starting position, target position and time of nonlinear function [15]. Some works focused on how to reach a expected final velocity through DMPs [16–18], but how to reach a desired point in the motion space is still a difficulty. Mulling trained a mechanical arm to complete a hitting ball task with DMPs, and built a DMPs' library for this task [17]. However, it's still just a single and repeating movement which means it's not representative enough.

As for ProMPs, Paraschos raised this method by utilizing the probability information of data so that robot can generate more adaptable trajectories [19]. It can generate trajectories in a new situation better and allows combine and sequence that DMPs can't. Paraschos improved ProMPs to reproduce trajectories without modeling the system dynamics [20]. Guiherme applied ProMPs in the coordination of multiple human-robot collaborative tasks [21], but it's sensitive to variability of speed. Besides, a kind of primitive library to segment unlabeled demonstrations into a representative set is proposed by Lioutikov in 2017 [22].

3   Establishment of Industrial Task Dataset

3.1   Vision Sensor

In this work, the Kinect2.0 is used as the vision sensor, showed in Fig. 1. Kinect2.0 contains a RGB and an IR camera. The depth information is calculated by ToF principle [23]. It should be noted that the coordinate system of Kinect is different from the world coordinate system. The Z-axis represents the depth of the area and the Y-axis represents the longitudinal height.

3.2   Visual Motion Capture Algorithm

The visual motion capture algorithm is used to obtain the 3d position of teacher's joints. It matches 25 human joints or points with 25 skeleton points, like Fig. 2 presents. Since the purpose of our work is to control a mechanical arm, only the

Fig. 1. A figure of Kinect2.0

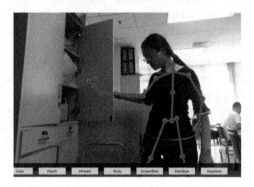

Fig. 2. 25 skeleton points of visual motion capture algorithm

right wrist and right elbow joints are useful. The algorithm collects the joints' position at a frequency of 30 fps.

However, affected by environment and light also the joints may overlap, the trajectories may have comparatively obvious noises. To reduce these noises to a acceptable limitation, Savizkg-Golag (S-G) smoothing algorithm is employed. The main idea of S-G filter is making use of various polynomial order to match the given data [24]. The equation of S-G filter is showed below.

$$X_i^* = \frac{\sum_{j=-T}^{T} X_{i+j} W_j}{\sum_{j=-T}^{T}} \tag{1}$$

where X_i is the original data and X_i^* is the optimized data. W_j represents optimizing weight factor of moving window smoothing, while the length of the moving window is $2r + 1$. The effect of S-G is showed in Fig. 3.

3.3   Dataset Establishment

A set of tasks is designed in this work, which consists of eight industrial action tasks: (a) circle; (b) write words (e.g., A, C); (c) pull drawer; (d) open cupboard; (e) hit hammer; (f) move things; (g) put thing on shelf; (h) assemble parts. These tasks are arranged from simple to complicated, the schematic diagram of these tasks is shown in Fig. 4.

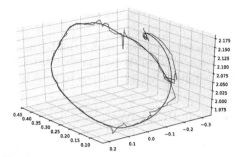

Fig. 3. The effect of S-G filter when the length of window is 59 and the order of polynomial fitting is four. This is a trajectory of task circle, the optimized curve (blue) is smoother than the original one (green). (Color figure online)

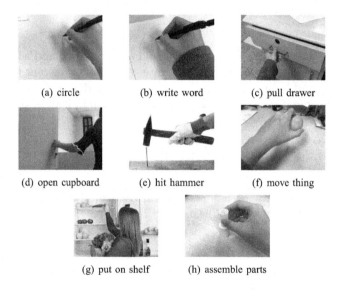

Fig. 4. Industrail tasks dataset

For each task, the teacher repeats the action for 20 times, so we can record 20 task's trajectories of arm's joints. Some tasks are simple, like (a), just need one movement, while some are a little complex, like (b) to (f), each task has two movements. As for (c), (g) and (h), they are composed by three or more movements. We collect the trajectories for each movement in each task.

4   Task Primitives

To better describe a task, we proposed task primitives. Task primitives is on the basic of dynamic movement primitives or probabilistic movement primitives, and put the movement primitives as a sequence in time order.

4.1   Dynamic Movement Primitives

Dynamic Movement Primitives is derived from second order spring damping model. It's basic concept is to use a group of Nonlinear differential equations which contain nonlinear terms that own the ability of autonomous learning to converge the motion state to the target position [14]. Using mathematics to express it is:

$$\tau \ddot{y} = a_y(b_y(y^* - y) - \hat{y} + f) \tag{2}$$

$$\tau \hat{x} = -a_x x \tag{3}$$

where y is the motion state of a system, $\hat{y}$ and $\ddot{y}$ is the speed and acceleration of motion. y^* represents the target motion state. τ is a time constant to adjust the decay rate, a_y and b_y are coefficients. x can be regarded as a phase variable, the goal is to converge it to zero. f in Eq. 2 is the key term in DMPs, the expression is showed in Eq. 4.

$$f(x, y^*) = \frac{\sum_{i=1}^{N} \psi_i(x)\omega_i}{\sum_{i=1}^{N} \psi_i(x)} x(y^* - y_0) \tag{4}$$

where $\psi(x)$ represents the basis function, and Gaussian Basis function is usually chose, Eq. 5. N is the number of basis functions and y_0 is the original state of a system.

$$\psi_i = e^{-h_i(x-c_i)^2} \tag{5}$$

Using DMPs method, a set of exact weights W can be obtained for each trajectory, W is known as a dynamic MP. This trajectory can be represented with this MP in a new place. In this way, a trajectory can be expressed precisely with fewer parameters.

4.2   Probabilistic Movement Primitives

Probabilistic Movement Primitives presents the probability distribution of a trajectory [19]. Assume a trajectory $\lambda = \{y_0, y_1, ..., y_T\}$, where T is the number of collecting points. Each y_t in λ can be expressed by ω_t:

$$y_t = \psi_t \omega_t + \epsilon_y \tag{6}$$

Hence, the probability of the trajectory λ on the premise of one ω is showed in Eq. 7.

$$p(\lambda|\omega) = \prod_t N(y_t|\psi_t\omega_t, \Sigma_y) \tag{7}$$

In order to get the probability distribution of trajectories $p(\lambda; \theta)$, we also need to know the distribution of ω and θ, that is $p(\omega, \theta)$. Noted that $\theta = \mu_\omega, \Sigma_\omega$. To simplify the problem, $p(\omega, \theta)$ is regarded Gaussian, Eq. 8.

$$p(\omega; \theta) = N(\omega|\mu_\omega, \Sigma_\omega) \tag{8}$$

then $p(\lambda; \theta)$ can be calculated as Eq. 9 shows.

$$p(\lambda; \theta) = \int p(\lambda|\omega)p(\omega; \theta)d\omega \tag{9}$$

The ProMPs absorbs information from several trajectories for one movement not just learn from one demonstration. So it has the ability to deliver a more suitable fitting trajectory for different situations. It also allows some properties come true that DMPs doesn't have, e.g., temporal modulation illustrated in Fig. 5.

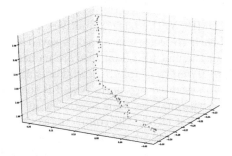

Fig. 5. Temporal modulation of ProMPs. Using the first movement in task(c) for example, the speed of the blue, green and orange lines are 0.5:1:2. It can be observed that the intensity of these colors dots are different, the sparser it is, the faster it means. (Color figure online)

4.3   Task Primitives

It has been noted in dataset part that one task trajectory is formed by several movements' trajectories. Therefore, one movement trajectory can correspond to one MP, and a task primitive Υ is a set of these movements' MPs W_k. We can use a sequence to present a task primitive in Eq. 10.

$$\Upsilon = \{W_1, W_2, ..., W_K\} \tag{10}$$

where K is the number of movements in a task and W_k is the MP of the k_th movement. Attention, W_k must be placed follow the ascending order of k as k illustrates the time sequence of movements.

In the situation of our dataset, Υ of task (a) has one MP, of task (b) to (f) has two MPs, of task (c) and (g) has three MPs and of task (h) has six MPs.

5   Establishment of Task Primitive Library

We build a task primitive library for the industrial tasks dataset. To compare the difference between DMPs and ProMPs, TPLib is established on the basic of these two kinds of movement primitives respectively. A correlation update rule is introduced in this section for modifying the performance of task primitives more reasonable and convenient without losing the knowledge that has been learned.

5.1   Dynamic Task Primitive Library

Dynamic TPLib uses DMPs as the basic primitives. For task (a) to (h) in the dataset, the weight of each trajectory in a task is saved as a mat file, and each task has a folder to save the mat files. Mat files are named as follows in order of occurrence, from $weight\_0.mat$ to $weight\_K.mat$. For example, task (h) describes a series of movements to assemble two parts A and B together. In light of when machining the part A, there may be some waste left in the groove, so the arm needs to tip it back to make it clean. The complete task trajectory of right hand can be separated into six actions' trajectories: (1) reach to A; (2) tip back; (3) move A to target place; (4) back to initial position; (5) reach to B; (6) move B to target place and assemble them together. DMPs can use weights to fit these six trajectories like Fig. 6 displays. For the task primitive of this task, the fitting trajectory is illustrated in (h) of Fig. 7.

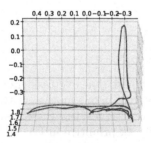

Fig. 6. The dynamic TPLib effect for task (h). Noted the blue lines are original and red lines are generated through dynamic TPLib

The reproduction effect of each task trajectory can be indicated by Fig. 7.

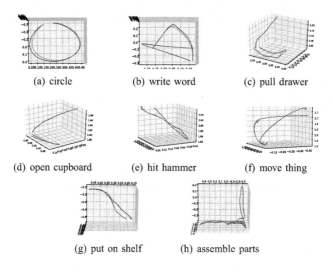

(a) circle   (b) write word   (c) pull drawer

(d) open cupboard   (e) hit hammer   (f) move thing

(g) put on shelf   (h) assemble parts

Fig. 7. The trajectories generated from DMPs

5.2 Probabilistic Task Primitive Library

As for the probabilistic TPLib, it shares the same saving rules as the dynamic TPlib, but is based on ProMPs. The teacher teaches each task for 20 times. Also using task (h) for example, each action's trajectory generated from the ProMPs are showed in Fig. 8.

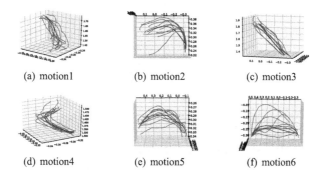

(a) motion1   (b) motion2   (c) motion3

(d) motion4   (e) motion5   (f) motion6

Fig. 8. Task (h)'s each motion's trajectory generated form probabilistic TPLib. Green lines are the original ones and blue lines are generated. (Color figure online)

5.3 Correlation Update Rule

Considering in real industrial tasks, there may be many movements in a task. Sometimes, we may want to modify only one movement in a task. It will be very inconvenient to teach the mechanical arm the whole task again. Furthermore, if in this way, it can't access to prior knowledge. Therefore, a correlation update rule is raised here. This rule makes use of correlation between matrices to help the robot determine which movement it belongs to if a new trajectory is provided. Then, the weight will combine with this new trajectory's weight, and this MP will be replaced by the new weight. The correlation between matrix X_{mn} and Y_{mn} can be calculated by Eq. 11.

$$r = \frac{\sum_m \sum_n (X_{mn} - \bar{X})(Y_{mn} - \bar{Y})}{\sqrt{(\sum_m \sum_n (X_{mn} - \bar{X})^2)(\sum_m \sum_n (Y_{mn} - \bar{Y})^2)}} \qquad (11)$$

The movement in a task with highest correlation will be chose to execute a modulation. A new weight W^* will be computed by Eq. 12.

$$W^* = \alpha W_{new} + (1 - \alpha)W \qquad (12)$$

where α is a modification coefficient for the modified trajectory, with a value between 0 and 1.

Using task (c) as example, there are 3 movements in this task, and only the first movement needs modification. It is hoped to start from a higher place so that it can perform better. The original trajectory of this movement is illustrated as the blue lines in Fig. 9(a), and its desired trajectory is the yellow line.

First, obtain the MP, i.e. W_d, of the desired trajectory. Then, calculate the correlations r between W_d and W_1 to W_3 stored in TPLib in task (c) respectively: $r_{d1} = 2.9219$, $r_{d2} = -0.0804$ and $r_{d3} = 0.7774$. As a result, modify W_1 with Eq. 11 for r_{d1} is largest. Use this new W_1, the modified trajectory is like the red line in Fig. 9(b).

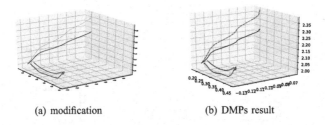

(a) modification   (b) DMPs result

Fig. 9. Modification of a movement in a task.

6 Simulation on ROS

In this part, an AUBO mechanical arm model is applied to simulate the learning from TPLib on ROS platform. In the coming simulations, we plan and execute the movement of end-effector-link of AUBO-i5, follows the trajectories generated by TPLib.

Fig. 10. A figure of AUBO-i5 on ROS

AUBO-i5 is a mechanical arm with 6 free degrees. The arm span is 1008 mm, which can meet the working task within 886.5 mm. The model of AUBO on the ROS platform is showed in Fig. 10, and it's end-effector-link is pointed in red.

We let AUBO-i5 executes each task in industrial task dataset. The eight tasks' trajectories generated from TPLib are illustrated in Fig. 11. These results shows that AUBO-i5's endpoint can move according to the trajectories of teaching, thus completing the specified tasks.

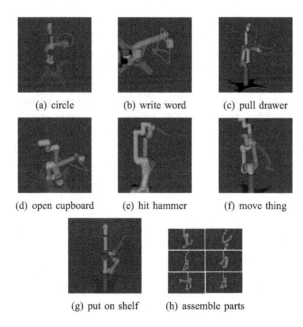

(a) circle   (b) write word   (c) pull drawer

(d) open cupboard   (e) hit hammer   (f) move thing

(g) put on shelf   (h) assemble parts

Fig. 11. DMPs effect on ROS simulation

Now, we simulate the effect of trajectories' update based on correlation update rule.

The simulation comparison about the task(c)'s example is showed in Fig. 12. Among three movements in this task, only motion one is different from the original one. Obviously, the simulated trajectory after modification is higher than the original for motion one, which is consistent with our prediction.

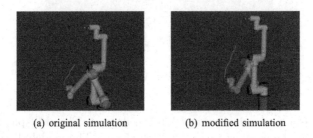

(a) original simulation   (b) modified simulation

Fig. 12. Comparison between the original and modified simulations.

7 Conclusion

Task Primitives are series of dynamic movement primitives or probabilistic movement primitives arranged in chronological order. By organizing task primitives learned from the task trajectories in industrial task dataset, a Task Primitive Library can be produced. This TPLib is updatable with the correlation update rule.

Trajectories can be generated from TPLib in a new situation. Mechanical arm plans and executes its movements following the generated trajectories.

Simulations on the ROS platform shows that using TPLib, AUBO-i5 can finish the tasks that it learned. Moreover, with probabilistic TPLib, temporal modulation is realized. The TPLib of can also be updated to correct its movement in a task.

However, only one joint's information is employed in this work. There's a waste of information because we collected the 3d information of more joints. In the future, a map between two arm joints and the AUBO-i5 will be produced to direct the robot better, and to complete more complicated tasks.

Acknowledgment. The work was jointly supported by National Key Research and Development Project (2018YFC1602704, 2018YFB1702704), and in part by the National Natural Science Foundation of China under Grant 61703230, Grant 61873006, and Grant 61673053.

References

1. Xu, K.: Research on positioning and grasping technology of manipulator based on binocular vision. Zhejiang University (2018)
2. Duan, J.B.: Teaching learning and intelligent control method for robot operation. University of Chinese Academy of Sciences (Shenzhen advanced technology research institute of Chinese Academy of Sciences) (2020)
3. Hui, Y., Saiyan, W., Gang, H.: Fuzzy neural network control for mechanical arm based on adaptive friction compensation. J. Vibroeng. **22**(5), 1099–1112 (2020)
4. Zhu, Y.Z., Li, J., Hu, Y.: Application progress of imitative learning in robot field. Guangdong Commun. Technol. **40**(9), 44–47 (2020)
5. He, J.Y., Zhou, H.J.: Demonstration learning: an end-to-end imitation learning method for robot behavior recognition and generation. In: The 36th China Control Conference, Dalian, Liaoning, China (2017)
6. Bandera, J.P., Molina-Tanco, L., Rodriguez, J.A., Bandera, A.: Architecture for a robot learning by imitation system. In: IEEE Mediterranean Electrotechnical Conference (2010)
7. Jin, S.K.: Research on robot demonstration learning based on dynamic scene understanding. University of Chinese Academy of Sciences (Shenzhen Institute of advanced technology, Chinese Academy of Sciences) (2020)
8. Zheng, J.T.: Trajectory planning simulation of manipulator based on deep reinforcement learning. University of Electronic Science and technology (2020)
9. Ross, S., Bagnell, D.: Efficient reductions for imitation learning. In: Proceedings of the Thirtieth International Conference on Artificial Intelligence and Statistics, pp. 661–668 (2010)
10. Daumé, H., Langford, J., Marcu, D.: Search-based structured prediction. Mach. Learn. **75**(3), 297–325 (2009)
11. Wang, N.Y., Gong, J.W., Zhang, R.Z., Chen, H.Y.: Motion primitives extraction and regeneration based on real driving data. J. Mech. Eng. **56**, 1–11 (2020)
12. Kruger, V., Herzog, D.L., Baby, S., Ude, A., Kragic, D.: Learning actions from observations. IEEE Robot. Autom. Mag. **17**(2), 30–43 (2010)
13. Manschitz, S., Kober, J., Gienger, M.: Learning to sequence movement primitives from demonstrations. In: 2014 IEEE/RSJ International Conference on Intelligent Robots and Systems, pp. 4414–4421. IEEE (2014)
14. Schaal, S.: Dynamical movement primitives - a framework for motor control in humans and humanoid robotics. In: Kimura, H., Tsuchiya, K., Ishiguro, A., Witte, H. (eds.) Adaptive Motion of Animals and Machine. Springer, Tokyo (2006). https://doi.org/10.1007/4-431-31381-8_23
15. Ijspeert, J., Nakanishi, J., Homann, H., Pastor, P., Schaal, S.: Dynamical movement primitives: learning attractor models for motor behaviors. Neural Comput. **25**(2), 328–373 (2013)
16. Kober, J., Muelling, K., Kroemer, O., Lampert, C.H., Scholkopf, B., Peters, J.: Movement templates for learning of hitting and batting. In: International Conference on Robotics and Automation, pp. 853–858 (2010)
17. Mülling, K., Kober, J., Kroemer, O., Peters, J.: Learning to select and generalize striking movements in robot table tennis. Int. J. Rob. Res. **32**(3), 263–279 (2013)
18. Pastor, P., Hoffmann, H., Asfour, T., Schaal, S.: Learning and generalization of motor skills by learning from demonstration. In: International Conference on Robotics and Automation (ICRA), pp. 763–768 (2009)

19. Paraschos, A., Daniel, C., Peters, J., Neumann, G.: Using probabilistic movement primitives in robotics. Auton. Robots **42**, 529–551 (2018)
20. Paraschos, A., Rueckert, E., Peters, J., Neumann, G.: Probabilistic movement primitives under unknown system dynamics. Adv. Robot. **32**(6), 297–310 (2018)
21. Maeda, G., Neumann, G., Ewerton, M., Lioutikov, R., Kroemer, O., Peters, J.: Probabilistic movement primitives for coordination of multiple human-robot collaborative tasks. Auton. Robots **41**, 593–612 (2017)
22. Lioutikov, R., Neumann, G., Maeda, G., Peters, J.: Learning movement primitive libraries through probabilistic segmentation. Int. J. Robot. Res. **36**(8), 879–894 (2017)
23. Amadeus, J., Victor, O., Arnd, G., Markus, C., Urs, G., Bert, A.: Evaluation of the pose tracking performance of the azure kinect and kinect v2 for gait analysis in comparison with a gold standard. Pilot Study **20**(18), 5104 (2020)
24. Rahman, A., Rashid, A., Ahmad, M.: Selecting the optimal conditions of Savitzky-Golay filter for fNIRS signal. Biocybern. Biomed. Eng. **39**(3), 624–637 (2019)

Guided Deep Reinforcement Learning for Path Planning of Robotic Manipulators

Yue Shen[✉], Qingxuan Jia, Zeyuan Huang, Ruiquan Wang, and Gang Chen

Beijing University of Posts and Telecommunications, Beijing, China
yuefei@bupt.edu.cn

Abstract. To improve the efficiency of deep reinforcement learning (DRL)-based methods for robotic path planning in the unstructured environment with obstacles, we propose a Guided Deep Reinforcement Learning (GDRL) for path planning of robotic manipulators. Firstly, we introduce guided path planning to accelerate approaching process. Secondly, we design a brand-new dense reward function in DRL-based path planning. To further improve learning efficiency, the DRL agent is only trained for collision avoidance, rather than for the whole path planning process. Many useless explorations in RL process can be eliminated with these three ideas. In order to evaluate the proposal, a Franka Emika robot with 7 joints has been considered in simulator V-Rep. The simulation results show the effectiveness of the proposed GDRL method. Compared to the pure DRL method, the GDRL method has much fewer training episodes, and converges $4\times$ faster.

Keywords: Deep reinforcement learning · Path planning · Soft Actor-Critic · Reward function

1 Introduction

Nowadays robotic manipulators are widely used in the field of industrial automation. Generally, they are used to execute pre-programmed tasks in a structured environment like production line. When the working environment changes, tedious reprogramming work is required, leading to low efficiency and poor generalization. In order to improve the autonomous movement ability and reduce the application cost of robotic manipulators, autonomous path planning technology is essential, which aims to find a collision-free path for the given start and goal configurations [1].

Path planning is one of the core research problems for robotic manipulators, and decades of research have produced many significant milestones. Conventional path planning methods like A* [2], Artificial Potential Field [3], Probabilistic Road Maps [4] algorithm are usually appropriate for the structured environment. However, these methods have poor dynamic planning, low intelligence and no self-learning ability when the working environment changes. With the progress of artificial intelligence, DRL [5] provides a new idea for path planning of robotic manipulators in recent years [6–8]. RL in the context of robotics, in general, is often represented with continuous high-dimensional action and state space. Deep Q-learning Network (DQN) [9] with action

© Springer Nature Singapore Pte Ltd. 2021
F. Sun et al. (Eds.): ICCSIP 2020, CCIS 1397, pp. 301–308, 2021.
https://doi.org/10.1007/978-981-16-2336-3_27

discretization is first introduced to solve robotic path planning. Normalized Advantage Function (NAF) [10] is a method that allows one to enable Q-learning in continuous action space with deep neural networks. And then, Deep Deterministic Policy Gradient (DDPG) [11], Asynchronous Advantage Actor-Critic (A3C) [12], Proximal Policy Optimization (PPO) [13], Trust Region Policy Optimization (TRPO) [14], Twin Delayed Deep Deterministic Policy Gradient (TD3) [15] and Soft Actor-Critic (SAC) [16] have been proposed one by one, which can be applied to the tasks with continuous action space. It can make the robotic manipulator learn autonomously and plan an optimal path in unstructured environment. Nevertheless, randomness and blindness are still the problems in DRL methods due to large exploration space.

To cope with the problems in DRL-based path planning, recent researches focus on designing reward function. The reward function in [17] consists of three terms: the distance between the end-effector and the target point, the magnitude of the actions, and the distance of the obstacle from the robot. [18] proposed two brand-new dense reward functions containing azimuth reward and subtask-level reward. [19] introduced the manipulability index into the reward function. However, since reward function is a scalar function, it's not clear to identify which term contributes to useful movement, where some useless explorations still exist. In this paper, we propose a Guided Deep Reinforcement Learning (GDRL) method for path planning of robotic manipulators. The primary contributions of this paper are summarized as follows: 1) Guided path planning is proposed to accelerate approaching process. 2) A brand-new dense reward function is designed in DRL-based path planning. 3) The DRL agent is only trained for collision avoidance, rather than for the whole path planning process. Overall, the GDRL method can guide a robotic manipulator reach the target fast without collision.

2   Basics on Reinforcement Learning

2.1   Reinforcement Learning

Reinforcement learning refers to the idea that an agent constantly gets information from the environment and takes actions to adapt to the environment. RL framework shown in Fig. 1 is based on Markov Decision Process (MDP), which is usually represented by five tuples (S, A, R, P, γ), where S, A and R represents the state, action and reward space respectively, P represents the probability of state transition, $\gamma \in [0, 1]$ is the discount rate for cumulative reward.

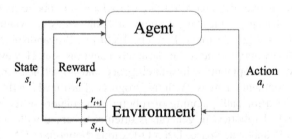

Fig. 1. Reinforcement learning framework

At each time step t, the agent is in the state $s_t \in S$, then takes an action $a_t \in A$ according to a policy π mapping from states to actions. Each action affects the environment and hence changes its state to s_{t+1}. The agent receives a reward $r_{t+1} \in R$ at time step $t + 1$. The goal of the agent is to find the optimal policy π^* that maximizes the total expected reward G_t.

$$G_t = r_{t+1} + \gamma r_{t+2} + \gamma^2 r_{t+3} + \ldots = \sum_{k=0}^{\infty} \gamma^k r_{t+k+1} \tag{1}$$

$$\pi^* = \arg\max_{\pi} \mathbb{E}\left[\sum_t \gamma^t r(s_t, a_t)\right] \tag{2}$$

Depending on the task, the policy can either be deterministic or stochastic. The expected cumulative reward following the policy π has two forms: state value function $V_\pi(s)$ and state-action value function $Q_\pi(s, a)$.

$$V_\pi(s) = \mathbb{E}[G_t | s_t = s] \tag{3}$$

$$Q_\pi(s, a) = \mathbb{E}[G_t | s_t = s, \ a_t = a] \tag{4}$$

2.2 Soft Actor-Critic Algorithm

The SAC algorithm is one of state-of-art model-free DRL algorithms for continuous action space. Instead of maximizing the discounted cumulative reward, the optimal policy aims to maximize entropy regularized reward.

$$\pi^* = \arg\max_{\pi_\theta} \mathbb{E}\left[\sum_t \gamma^t (r(s_t, a_t) + \alpha \mathcal{H}(\pi_\theta(\cdot|s_t)))\right] \tag{5}$$

where α is the regularization coefficient, $\mathcal{H}$ represents the entropy.

Soft policy iteration is a general algorithm for learning the optimal maximum entropy policy with provable guarantees. SAC extends soft policy iteration to approximate Q function $Q_\phi(s, a)$ and policy π_θ. The Q function can be learned by minimizing the soft Bellman residual,

$$J_Q(\phi) = \mathbb{E}\left[\left(Q(s_t, a_t) - r(s_t, a_t) - \gamma \mathbb{E}_{s_{t+1}}[V_{\tilde{\phi}}(s_{t+1})]\right)^2\right] \tag{6}$$

where $V_{\tilde{\phi}}(s) = \mathbb{E}_{\pi_\theta}[Q_{\tilde{\phi}}(s, a) - \alpha \log \pi_\theta(a|s)]$, and $Q_{\tilde{\phi}}$ is a target Q network, whose parameter $\tilde{\phi}$ is obtained as an exponentially moving average of ϕ. Moreover, the policy π_θ can be learned by minimizing the expected KL-divergence.

$$J_\pi(\theta) = \mathbb{E}_{s \sim \mathcal{D}}\left[\mathbb{E}_{a \sim \pi_\theta}[\alpha \log \pi_\theta(a|s) - Q_\phi(s, a)]\right] \tag{7}$$

Finally, SAC also provides an automatic way to update the regularization coefficient α by minimizing the loss below:

$$J(\alpha) = \mathbb{E}_{a \sim \pi_\theta}[-\alpha \log \pi_\theta(a|s) - \alpha \kappa] \tag{8}$$

where κ is a hyperparameter interpreted as the target entropy.

SAC algorithm is summarized in Algorithm 1.

Algorithm 1 Soft Actor-Critic (SAC)

Hyperparameters: target entropy κ, step size $\lambda_Q, \lambda_\pi, \lambda_\alpha$, exponentially moving average coefficient τ

Input: initial policy parameters θ, initial Q value function parameters ϕ_1 and ϕ_2

$\mathcal{D}=\varnothing$, $\bar{\phi}_i=\phi_i$, for $i \in \{1,2\}$

for each iteration **do**

  for each environment step **do**

    Sample a_t from $\pi_\theta(\cdot \mid s_t)$, collect (r_t, s_{t+1})

    $\mathcal{D}=\mathcal{D} \cup \{s_t, a_t, r_t, s_{t+1}\}$

  end for

  for each gradient step **do**

    $\phi_i = \phi_i - \lambda_Q \nabla J_Q(\phi_i)$, for $i \in \{1,2\}$

    $\theta = \theta - \lambda_\pi \nabla J_\pi(\theta)$

    $\alpha = \alpha - \lambda_\alpha \nabla J(\alpha)$

    $\bar{\phi}_i = (1-\tau)\phi_i + \tau\bar{\phi}_i$; for $i \in \{1,2\}$

  end for

end for

Output: θ, ϕ_1, ϕ_2

---

3 Guided Deep Reinforcement Learning for Path Planning

In this section, the proposed guided reinforcement learning method for path planning is discussed in detail. Path planning of robotic manipulators consists of two parts: guided planning and collision avoidance planning. Guided planning leads a robotic manipulator reach the target in Cartesian space, while collision avoidance planning based on SAC avoids obstacles in configuration space. The GDRL method aims to guide a robotic manipulator reach the target fast without collision.

3.1 Guided Planning

Guided planning is focused on reaching the target without considering obstacles in environment. It leverages traditional path planning method to reach the target directly. For simplicity, we use a position-based servo method to complement the guided planning.

Given the current joint positions q, we can get the end-effector position p_e using forward kinematics. Based on the distance between the end-effector p_e and the target p_t, the guided planning is represented as below:

$$\Delta q_g = \eta J^+ (p_t - p_e) \tag{9}$$

where η is the speed ratio, $J^+ = J^T(JJ^T)^{-1}$ represents the pseudo-inverse of Jacobian matrix.

3.2   Collision Avoidance Planning

Collision avoidance planning is modeled as a RL process. The robotic manipulator starts at a virtual collision state, and it aims to be collision free with trail-and-error based on SAC algorithm.

State Space. The observation for the robotic manipulator contains joint positions q. As for the obstacle position p_o, it is assumed known and provided by cameras or other sensors located in the workspace. The state space S is hence defined as

$$S = \{q,\ p_o\} \tag{10}$$

Action Space. The action space A is defined as

$$A = \{\dot{q}\} \tag{11}$$

where $\dot{q}$ is rotational velocity at each joint.

Reward Function. The reward function is a scalar function defined by the collision state and the distance between each joint and obstacles.

$$r = -\sum_{i=1}^{N} c_i R_i \tag{12}$$

where N is the degrees of freedom of a manipulator, $c_i = 0$ if link i dosen't collide with obstacles, otherwise $c_i = 1$. R_i referred to distance is defined as

$$R_i = \begin{cases} ||p_i - p_o||, & \text{for } i = 1 \text{ or } N \\ ||p_{i-1} - p_o|| + ||p_i - p_o||, & \text{otherwise} \end{cases} \tag{13}$$

where p_i is the distance between joint i and obstacles.

In an episode of training process, the robotic manipulator starts at a virtual collision state, and ends when it is collision-free or exceeds the maximum timestep.

3.3   Guided Deep Reinforcement Learning for Path Planning

Combining guided planning and collision avoidance planning, we propose the guided deep reinforcement learning method for path planning of robotic manipulators. The pipeline of GDRL method is shown in Fig. 2.

The SAC agent learns how to avoid collision in the training process. Then the robotic manipulator tries to move to the target based on guided planning. When potential collision is detected, SAC agent will adjust the joints to a safe state. Otherwise the robotic manipulator will reach the target directly. Before executing joint command, joint velocity limits should be checked. GDRL for path planning is summarized in Algorithm 2.

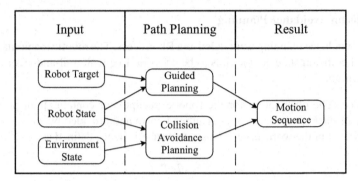

Fig. 2. Pipeline of GDRL method

Algorithm 2 Guided Deep Reinforcement Learning(GDRL) for Path Planning

---

Input: robot target p_t, robot state $\{q, p_e\}$, environment state p_o

while $Dist(p_e, p_t) > \varepsilon$, **do**

$\quad J^+ = J^T (JJ^T)^{-1}$

$\quad \Delta q_g = \eta J^+ (p_t - p_e)$

$\quad q_{tmp} = q + \Delta q_g$

$\quad$ **while** CollisionDetection (q_{tmp}, p_o) ==True, **do**

$\quad\quad \Delta q_c = SAC(q_{tmp}, p_o)$

$\quad\quad q_{tmp} = q_{tmp} + \Delta q_c$

$\quad\quad q_{tmp} = \mathrm{clip}(q_{tmp}, q_{min}, q_{max})$

$\quad$ **end while**

$\quad q = q_{tmp}$

end while

---

4   Simulation

In this section, we design a reach target task for a Franka Emika robot with 7 joints. In order to evaluate the proposed method, the scene is built in simulator V-Rep. The simulator is interfaced using PyRep [20] and GDRL method is implemented with Python and PyTorch. The target point is represented as a sphere with radius ε. The obstacle is represented as a cuboid in the workspace. The scene setting is shown in Fig. 3.

All the training sessions have been carried out on a workstation mounting a 8x Intel(R) Xeon(R) CPU E5-1620 v3 @ 3.50 GHz with a 16 GB RAM and a Nvidia Quadro K2200 GPU. Given the same state and target, we compare the SAC algorithm and our GDRL algorithm. The SAC algorithm is implemented with a dense reward function for the whole path planning process as a baseline. As shown in Fig. 4, the GDRL method has much fewer training episodes, and converges 4× faster.

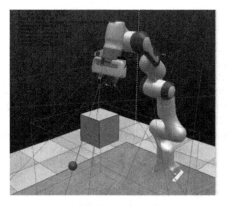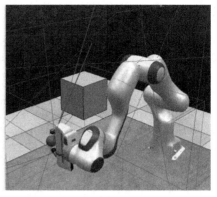

Fig. 3. Reach target task from given state(left) to target(right)

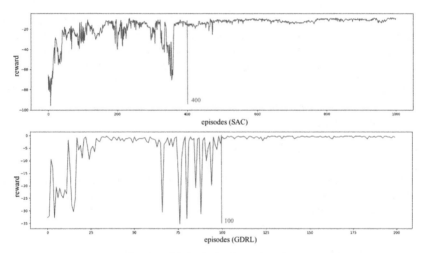

Fig. 4. Training episodes comparison

5   Conclusion

To cope with the inefficiency and blindness of DRL-based methods for robotic path planning, we propose a Guided Deep Reinforcement Learning (GDRL) for path planning of robotic manipulators. The method mainly consists of guided planning and SAC-based collision avoidance planning, enabling the robotic manipulator to reach the target quickly without collision in a much efficient way. The simulation results show the effectiveness of the proposed GDRL method. Compared to the pure DRL method, the GDRL method has much fewer training episodes, and converges $4 \times$ faster. In the future, we are intended to expand the method to adapt to moving target and obstacles. Experiment with real robotic manipulator will also be performed.

Acknowledgement. This work was supported by Major Project of the New Generation of Artificial Intelligence (No. 2018AAA0102900).

References

1. LaValle, S.M.: Planning Algorithms. Cambridge University Press, Cambridge (2006)
2. Jia, Q., Chen, G., et al.: Path planning for space manipulator to avoid obstacle based on A* algorithm. J. Mech. Eng. **46**(13), 109–115 (2010)
3. Li, H., Wang, Z., Ou, Y.: Obstacle avoidance of manipulators based on improved artificial potential field method. In: 2019 IEEE International Conference on Robotics and Biomimetics (ROBIO), Dali, China, pp. 564–569. IEEE (2019)
4. Al-Hmouz, R., Gulrez, T., Al-Jumaily, A.: Probabilistic road maps with obstacle avoidance in cluttered dynamic environment. In: Proceedings of IEEE International Conference on Intelligent Sensors, Sensor Networks and Information Processing Conference (ISSNIP), Melbourne, AUS, pp. 241–245. IEEE (2004)
5. Sutton, R.S., Barto, A.G.: Reinforcement Learning: An Introduction. MIT Press, MA (2018)
6. Katyal, K., Wang, I., Burlina, P.: Leveraging deep reinforcement learning for reaching robotic tasks. In: 2017 IEEE Conference on Computer Vision and Pattern Recognition Workshops (CVPRW), Honolulu, HI, pp. 490–491. IEEE (2017)
7. Kamali, K., Bonev, I.A., Desrosiers, C.: Real-time motion planning for robotic teleoperation using dynamic-goal deep reinforcement learning. In: 2020 17th Conference on Computer and Robot Vision (CRV), Ottawa, Canada, pp. 182–189. IEEE (2020)
8. Li, Z., Ma, H., et al.: Motion planning of six-dof arm robot based on improved DDPG algorithm. In: 2020 39th Chinese Control Conference (CCC), Shenyang, China, pp. 3954–3959. IEEE (2020)
9. Mnih, V., Kavukcuoglu, K., et al.: Human-level control through deep reinforcement learning. Nature **518**(7540), 529–533 (2015)
10. Gu, S., Lillicrap, T.P., et al.: Continuous deep q-learning with model-based acceleration. In: Proceedings of the 33rd International Conference on Machine Learning, New York, USA, pp. 2829–2838 (2016)
11. Lillicrap, T.P., Hunt, J.J., et al.: Continuous control with deep reinforcement learning. arXiv preprint arXiv:1509.02971 (2015)
12. Mnih, V., Badia, A.P., et al.: Asynchronous methods for deep reinforcement learning. In: Proceedings of the 33rd International Conference on Machine Learning, New York, USA, pp. 1928–1937 (2016)
13. Schulman, J., Wolski, F., et al.: Proximal Policy Optimization Algorithms. arXiv preprint arXiv:1707.06347 (2017)
14. Schulman, J., Levine, S., et al.: Trust region policy optimization. In: Proceedings of the 31st International Conference on Machine Learning, Lille, France, pp. 1889–1897 (2015)
15. Fujimoto, S., Hoof, H.V., et al.: Addressing function approximation error in actor-critic methods. arXiv preprint arXiv:1802.09477 (2018)
16. Haarnoja, T., Zhou, A., et al.: Soft Actor-Critic: Off-Policy Maximum Entropy Deep Reinforcement Learning with a Stochastic Actor. arXiv preprint arXiv:1801.01290 (2018)
17. Sangiovanni, B., Rendiniello, A., et al.: Deep reinforcement learning for collision avoidance of robotic manipulators. In: 2018 European Control Conference (ECC), Limassol, Cyprus, pp. 2063–2068. IEEE (2018)
18. Xie, J., Shao, Z., et al.: Deep reinforcement learning with optimized reward functions for robotic trajectory planning. IEEE Access **2019**(7), 105669–105679 (2019)
19. Zeng, R., Liu, M., et al.: Manipulator control method based on deep reinforcement learning. In: 2020 Chinese Control and Decision Conference (CCDC), Hefei, China, pp. 415–420. IEEE (2020)
20. James, S., Freese, M., Davison, A.J.: PyRep: Bringing V-REP to Deep Robot Learning. arXiv preprint arXiv:1906.11176 (2019)

Large-Scale Multi-agent Reinforcement Learning Based on Weighted Mean Field

Baofu Fang[1](✉), Bin Wu[1], Zaijun Wang[2], and Hao Wang[1]

[1] Hefei University of Technology, Hefei, Anhui, China
fangbf@hfut.edu.cn
[2] Civil Aviation Flight University of China, Guanghan, Sichuan, China

Abstract. Deep reinforcement learning is an emerging approach to solve the decision making of multi-agent systems in recent years, and currently has achieved good results in small-scale decision problems. However, when the number of agents increases, the dynamic of the other agent strategies and the proportional enlargement of information between the agent lead to "non-stationarity", "dimensional catastrophe" and many other problems. In order to solve Multi-Agent Deep Deterministic Policy Gradient (MADDPG) are difficult to converge when the size of multi-agent systems exceeds a certain number, a deep reinforcement learning collaboration algorithm for multi-agent systems based on weighted mean field is proposed. The mean field is used to reconstruct the dynamic decision action of other agent involved in the decision making, while assigning different weights to each agent action based on the set of relevant attributes, transforming the joint action of the agent into the mean action of the other agent formed through the weighted mean field, and serving as an update function of the actor network and state function in the multi-agent deep deterministic policy gradient algorithm parameters to simplify the scale of interaction. In this paper, the effectiveness of the algorithm is validated by Battle game scenarios from convergence, win rates at different scenario sizes, win rates of different algorithms, and other game performance.

Keywords: Multi-agent system · Reinforcement learning · Weighted mean field

1 Introduction

A multi-agent system is a collection of multiple autonomous, interacting agent, which is an important branch of distributed artificial intelligence. Such problems are significantly more difficult than those of single agent [1].

Reinforcement learning (RL) search for the optimal policy in a Markov process by obtaining as many rewards as possible. Articles [2] extends the Tit-for-tat policy with deep Q learning to maintain two agent cooperation even in the face of a prisoner's dilemma in order to achieve an optimal policy. Articles [3] investigates the performance of deep reinforcement learning. It is ultimately shown that deep reinforcement learning can achieve high performance. Articles [4] investigates the problem of cooperation in

© Springer Nature Singapore Pte Ltd. 2021
F. Sun et al. (Eds.): ICCSIP 2020, CCIS 1397, pp. 309–316, 2021.
https://doi.org/10.1007/978-981-16-2336-3_28

simple scenarios in a discrete structure for each agent that learns independently using the Q learning algorithm. The problem sizes studied above are typically a few agents, however, in real life, a large number of agents are indeed required to interact strategically with each other, such as fleet dispatch management problems [5], online role-playing games [6] or online advertising bidding auctions [7]. Existing multi-agent reinforcement learning solutions are effective, but they can only solve the problems of small-sized agent. In an environment where "an infinite number of agents are approached and imprecise probabilistic models are assumed to operate", existing methods for deep reinforcement learning are not realistic [8]. Articles [9] designed an actor-critic algorithm to train a very large-scale taxi dispatching problem regionally. Articles [10] uses a centralized approach to learn distributed execution, learning to consider the Q-value function simultaneously. The team's Q-value functions are decomposed into sums of their respective Q-value functions through a value decomposition network. Articles [11] uses a mixing network to combine local values, but this network is very difficult to train.

Learning between agents promotes each other: the learning of a single agent is based on the state of cluster agents [12].This paper proposes a multi-agent reinforcement learning algorithm based on a weighted mean field, using the Multi-Agent Deep Deterministic Policy Gradient (MADDPG) [13] as the framework in order to highlight the importance of different agents, the algorithm Based on related attribute sets, different weights are assigned to each agent action, and the weighted mean field is used to simplify the interactive information, which improves the performance of multi-agent reinforcement learning algorithms under large-scale multi-agents.

2 Weighted Mean Field Reinforcement Learning

2.1 Mean Field Theory

The mean field theory is a method of collectively processing the effects of the environment on individuals, and replacing the accumulation of multiple effects with mean effects. The strategic decision-making relationship between individuals and the whole and the relationship between joint strategy $\pi(s, a)$ and single agent strategy $\pi(s, a_i)$ in a multi-agent system.

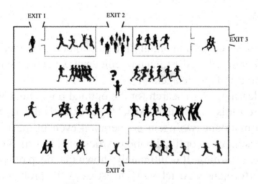

Fig. 1. Evacuation diagram

For example, many people do not know all the information about the surrounding environment, such as exit locations and routes, when people need to be evacuated urgently in Fig. 1. Each person does not need to observe the evacuation status of all people, but only needs to observe the status of the people around him. Based on the evacuation of the surrounding people, he can follow the people to different exits.

Wang [15] proposed the concept of mean field reinforcement learning (MFRL), but the use of mean field is simply to mean the action states of the surrounding agents of each agent and then import the critic network. But according to the multi-agent system consistency idea, the state information of different agents has different reference value to the central agent. Since exit 4 has the most people and may have the greatest impact on the evacuees, evacuees are directed to exit 4, in fact exit 2 is the best select. At this time, the surrounding people have different weights due to distance and other attributes. Those who are closer to the evacuees have a higher weight, and the evacuees are guided to choose the exit 2 which may be smaller but closer. At this time, the different distance or intimacy between each person forms a weight, and the relationship with the evacuees and the closest person. The weight distribution of the mean field is carried out through the influence of related factors, when applied to multi-agent reinforcement learning, it can better reflect the cluster effect of the mean field idea.

2.2 Weighted Mean Field

The size of the joint action increases exponentially with the size of the agent. All agents take their own strategy actions dynamically, which makes the reward function $Q(s, a)$ unable to converge effectively. In order to solve this problem, the reward function is reconstructed, and the local joint action using weighted mean field is used as the parameter added value function.

$$Q_\mu^i(s, a) = \frac{1}{\omega(x_i)} \sum_{j \in N(i)} \omega\left(x_i^j\right) Q^i\left(s, a_i, a_j\right) \tag{1}$$

Where $N(i)$ is the collection of agents around the agent i, $N^i = |N(i)|$ represents the number of agents around the agent i, $\omega(x_i) = \sum_{j \in N(i)} \omega\left(x_i^j\right)$, and $\omega\left(x_i^j\right)$ is the weight coefficient function of the corresponding central agent i to the agent j. The weight parameters $x_i^j = f(Parameter1, Parameter2, \cdots)$ are determined by the relevant agent attribute set, such as position, importance, intimacy, etc., which can be flexibly defined according to the scene and reward.

$$
\begin{aligned}
Q_\mu^i(s, a) &= \frac{1}{\omega(x_i)} \sum_j \omega\left(x_i^j\right) Q_\mu^i\left(s, a_i, a_j\right) \\
&= \frac{1}{\omega(x_i)} \sum_j \omega\left(x_i^j\right) \left[Q_\mu^i(s, a_i, \bar{a}_i) + \nabla_{\bar{a}_i} Q_\mu^i(s, a_i, \bar{a}_i) * \delta \alpha_{i,j} \right. \\
&\quad + \frac{1}{2} \delta \alpha_{i,j} * \nabla_{\bar{a}_{i,j}}^2 Q_\mu^i s, a_i, \bar{a}_i * \delta \alpha_{i,j}] \\
&= Q_\mu^i(s, a_i, \bar{a}_i) + \nabla_{\bar{a}\bar{a}_i} Q_\mu^i(s, a_i, \bar{a}_i) * \left[\frac{1}{\omega(x_i)} \sum_j \delta \omega\left(x_i^j\right) \alpha_{i,j}\right]
\end{aligned}
$$

$$+ \frac{1}{2\omega(x_i)} \sum_j \left[\delta\omega\left(x_i^j\right)\alpha_{i,j} * \nabla_{\bar{a}_{i,j}}^2 Q_\mu^i s, a_i, \bar{a}_i * \delta\alpha_{i,j} \right]$$
$$\approx Q_\mu^i \left(s, a_i, a_j\right) \tag{2}$$

For the $Q_\mu^i \left(s, a_i, a_j\right)$ according to Eq. (1), we approximate it by mean field theory, and the agent i action adopts a_i. For example, Eq. (2) is used to calculate the mean weighted actions $\bar{a}_i$ of the agents around the agent i, and the actions a_j of the neighboring agent j are converted into $\bar{a}_i$ and a margin $\delta\alpha_{i,j}$.

$$\begin{cases} \bar{a}_i = \frac{1}{\omega(x_i)} \sum_j \omega\left(x_i^j\right)a_j \\ a_j = \bar{a}_i + \delta\alpha_{i,j} \end{cases}, \ j \in N(i) \tag{3}$$

2.3 Weighted Mean Field Multi-agent Deep Deterministic Policy Gradient (WMPG)

The decision-making behavior between multiple agents is transformed into the weighted behavior of central agent and adjacent agent by mean field theory, so as to modify the reward function and state value function of Multi-Agent Reinforcement Learning (MARL). By means of mean field theory, for example, the original critic network of multi-agent depth deterministic strategy gradient algorithm is simplified to the weighted mean of adjacent agent actions, which simplifies the calculation of other agent information, so that it can be applied to large-scale agent scenarios, and introduces weight information. The algorithm framework is shown in Fig. 2.

When calculating the loss function L and the strategy gradient, where $Q_\varphi^i(s, a_1, \cdots, a_n)$ is approximately transformed into $Q_\varphi^i(s, a_i, \bar{a}_i)$. The calculation of $\bar{a}_i$ is as shown in Eq. (3), which simplifies the iteration of value function and state value function in critic network.

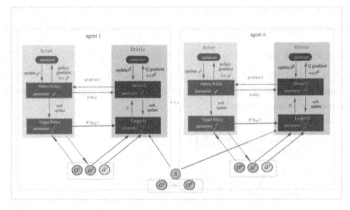

Fig. 2. Weighted Mean Field Multi-Agent Deep Deterministic Policy Gradient, WMPG

The update mode of the critic network is changed to, φ is the weight parameter of the critic network

$$L(\varphi_i) = \frac{1}{S} \sum_j \left(y_j - Q_{\varphi_j}^i \left(s, a_j, \bar{a}_j \right) \right)^2 \tag{4}$$

Where S is the number of training samples θ is actor network parameter, the gradient equation of actor network strategy can be written.

$$\nabla_{\theta_j} J(\theta_i) \approx \frac{1}{S} \sum_j \nabla_{\theta_j} \log \pi_{\theta_j}^j (s) Q_{\varphi_j}^i \left(s, a_j, \bar{a}_j \right) \Bigg|_{a_j = \pi_{\theta_j}(s)} \tag{5}$$

3   Experiment Results and Analysis

In order to verify the effectiveness of the algorithm, the performance of weighted mean field in large-scale Multi-Agent Reinforcement Learning is explored by using the Battle environment. Battle is a mixed combat multi-agent combat scenario of the open-source MAgent [16] framework. In Fig. 3, the blue side is the algorithm of this paper, and the red side is MFAC. It can be seen from the course of the battle that when an agent chooses to encircle, the nearby agents will be affected by the decision of the agent, thus forming a trend of encircling the red side by the blue side.

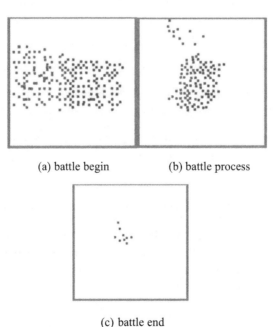

(a) battle begin   (b) battle process

(c) battle end

Fig. 3. Confrontation graph between WMPG and MFAC under Battle (Color figure online)

3.1 Convergence Experiment

In order to show the training performance of the algorithm under different scale agents, this paper conducts experiments on the algorithm convergence of MADDPG which only uses mean field and weighted mean field. It can be seen that in a large scale, the convergence speed of this algorithm is obviously better than the other two. The multi-agent depth deterministic strategy gradient algorithm has been difficult to converge at the scale of 400. The weighted mean field algorithm proposed in this paper can reduce the difficulty of convergence to a certain extent (Fig. 4).

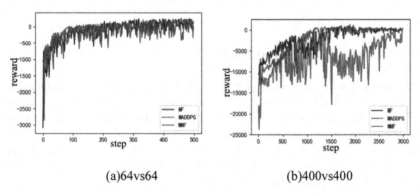

(a)64vs64   (b)400vs400

Fig. 4. Analysis of algorithm convergence under different agent scale

3.2 Cross-Contrast

In order to prevent contingency, in the Battle environment, set the size of both agents to 200vs200.WMPG performed 200 rounds of cross-comparison with traditional reinforcement learning algorithm actor-critic AC, multi-agent deep reinforcement learning algorithm MADDPG, and mean field algorithm MFQ and MFAC [15] algorithm to verify the performance of this algorithm. Table 1 and Table 2 show the experimental results of the win rate and total return in the comparative experiment. It can be seen from the results in Table 1 that the WMPG algorithm is significantly better than other algorithms when experimenting with different types of algorithms, and from Table 2, it can be seen that the total return can also be higher, which also reflects the effectiveness of our algorithm. The poor performance of the multi-agent deep deterministic strategy gradient algorithm and the actor-critic algorithm also reflects the current traditional deep reinforcement learning algorithms mentioned in this article facing the problems of large-scale multi-agent systems. The research value of this article.

Table 1. The win rate of different algorithms

Algorithm	AC	MADDPG	MFQ	MFAC	WMPG
AC VS	–	0.34	0.15	0.29	0.0
MADDPG VS	0.66	–	0.44	0.38	0.17
MFQ VS	0.85	0.56	–	0.0	0.0
MFAC VS	0.71	0.62	1.0	–	0.285
WMPG VS	**1.0**	**0.830**	**1.0**	**0.715**	–

Table 2. The total reward of different algorithms

Algorithm	AC	MADDPG	MFQ	MFAC	WMPG
AC VS	–	13773	4645	3716	5712
MADDPG VS	18920	–	17053	17560	12845
MFQ VS	13040	14729	–	7959	12617
MFAC VS	22510	17471	16894	–	19759
WMPG VS	**21918**	**22265**	**22575**	**19758**	–

4 Conclusion

Based on the idea of mean field, this paper proposes a deep reinforcement learning algorithm of mean field multi-agent with weight information. Aiming at the problem that when the number of larger multi-agent systems exceeds a certain scale, the complex interactive information between agents will make the original reinforcement learning algorithm difficult to converge, and the weighted mean field is used to simplify the interactive information and transform the multi-agent information It is two-body information, used to simulate the interaction in the multi-agent system. The algorithm in this paper reduces the instability and difficulty of convergence of the combat environment in the open-source MAgent framework. In addition to giving certain proofs in theory, the experimental results also verify the rationality and effectiveness of this algorithm. In the follow-up, we need to consider the combination of large-scale multi-agent and mean field in heterogeneous scenarios.

References

1. Hernandez-Leal, P., Kartal, B., Taylor, M.E.: A survey and critique of multiagent deep reinforcement learning. Autonom. Agents Multi Agent Syst. **33**, 750–797 (2019)

2. Peysakhovich, A., Lerer, A.: Maintaining cooperation in complex social dilemmas using deep reinforcement learning. arXiv: Artificial Intelligence (2018)
3. Raghu, M., Irpan, A., Andreas, J., et al.: Can deep reinforcement learning solve Erdos-Selfridge-Spencer games? arXiv: Artificial Intelligence (2017)
4. Foerster, J.N., Nardelli, N., Farquhar, G., Afouras, T., Torr, P.H.S., Kohli, P., Whiteson, S.: Stabilising experience replay for deep multi-agent reinforcement learning. In: International Conference on Machine Learning (2017).
5. Lin, K., Zhao, R., Xu, Z., et al.: Efficient large-scale fleet management via multi-agent deep reinforcement learning. In: Knowledge Discovery And Data Mining, pp. 1774–1783 (2018)
6. Peng, P., Wen, Y., Yang, Y., et al.: Multiagent bidirectionally-coordinated nets for learning to play starcraft combat games (2017)
7. Jin, J., Song, C., Li, H., et al.: Real-time bidding with multi-agent reinforcement learning in display advertising (2018).
8. Hernandez-Leal, P., Kartal, B., Taylor, M.E.: Is multiagent deep reinforcement learning the answer or the question? A brief survey. Learning **21**, 22 (2018)
9. Thien, N., Kumar, A., Lau, H.: Policy gradient with value function approximation for collective multiagent planning (2017)
10. Sunehag, P., Lever, G., Gruslys, A., et al.: Value-decomposition networks for cooperative multi-agent learning (2017)
11. Rashid, T., Samvelyan, M., De Witt, C.S., et al.: Monotonic value function factorisation for deep multi-agent reinforcement learning (2020)
12. Sharma, M.K., Zappone, A., Assaad, M., et al.: Distributed power control for large energy harvesting networks: a multi-agent deep reinforcement learning approach. IEEE Trans. Cogn. Commun. Network. **5**(4), 1140–1154 (2019)
13. Lowe, R., Wu, Y., Tamar, A., et al.: Multi-agent actor-critic for mixed cooperative-competitive environments. In: Neural Information Processing Systems, pp. 6379–6390 (2017)
14. Zhang, K., Yang, Z., Basar, T., et al.: Multi-agent reinforcement learning: a selective overview of theories and algorithms. arXiv: Learning (2019)
15. Yang, Y., Luo, R., Li, M., et al.: Mean field multi-agent reinforcement learning. In: International Conference on Machine Learning, pp. 5567–5576 (2018)
16. Zheng, L., Yang, J., Cai, H., et al.: MAgent: a many-agent reinforcement learning platform for artificial collective intelligence (2017)

Selective Transition Collection in Experience Replay

Feng Liu[1]([✉]), Shuling Dai[1,2], and Yongjia Zhao[1]

[1] State Key Laboratory of VR Technology and Systems, Beihang University (BUAA), Beijing 100191, China
by1503101@buaa.edu.cn
[2] Jiangxi Research Institute, Beihang University (BUAA), Beijing 100191, China

Abstract. Experience replay method is often used in off-policy reinforcement learning. As the training progresses, the distribution of the collected transitions becomes more and more concentrated, and this will lead to catastrophic forgetting and a low rate of convergence. In this paper, we present selective transition collection algorithm which is a new design to address the concentrated distribution by selectively collection the transitions. We propose a method to estimate the similarity between transitions, and a probability function to reduce the chance of transitions with high similarity to the experience memory being collected. We test our method on familiar reinforcement learning tasks and the experimental results demonstrate that selective transition collection can not only speed up the learning but also prevent catastrophic forgetting effectively.

Keywords: Experience replay · Selective transition collection · Reinforcement learning

1 Introduction

When it comes to the way of transition usage, reinforcement learning can be classified into on-policy method and off-policy method. In the on-policy method, the policy for generating experience transitions is the same policy as when updating the network parameters. SARSA [1] and PPO [2] are classic on-policy algorithms. However, only learning recent transitions, the on-policy method is easy to forget the previous valuable experience and it is easy to converge to a local optimum. Excessive variance is also an issue for on-policy method. Distributed training is an efficient approach to addresses both of these issues [3, 4], but it needs more simulation environments, and it is difficult to achieve on the real tasks, because building a mass of real learning environments is much more difficult than building some virtual environments.

The issues of on-policy method will not happen on the off-policy method, because it uses the experience replay method [5], which can make the learning review the previous experience persistently. In a general off-policy reinforcement learning algorithm, it often has an experience memory which is used to store the collected transitions, and randomly selects transitions from the memory to train the agent. The off-policy method uses the

F. Sun et al. (Eds.): ICCSIP 2020, CCIS 1397, pp. 317–324, 2021.
https://doi.org/10.1007/978-981-16-2336-3_29

transitions generated by the previous policy indiscriminately, which can make it has a more stable training and easy to converge to the position which is closer to the global optimum.

Although the off-policy method can overcome some issues of the on-policy method, it still has its own problems: low efficiency on transitions utilization and catastrophic forgetting with a small experience memory [6]. In 2016, Google DeepMind proposed prioritized experience replay [7] which is a method to increase the sampling probability of transitions with a large TD-error [8], and experiments proved that this method can speed up the convergence of learning. Although prioritized experience replay can improve learning efficiency of off-policy to some extent, the issues are still there.

In our recent research, we found that the transitions distribution in the experience memory of off-policy reinforcement learning will change slowly with the progress of learning. Because of the greedy learning rules [9, 10], at the stage of mid-learning, more similar states and actions will appear and a large number of similar or repetitive state-action transitions will be stored in the memory sequentially. In most off-policy reinforcement learning algorithms, the experience memory is a large sliding window which overwrites the previous transitions with new transitions when the memory is full. If the capacity of the experience memory is not sufficient (actually, it is difficult to determine whether an experience memory is large enough, this is also a hard work of tuning a hyperparameter), the transitions of some high frequency states will overwrite the transitions of low frequency states. For example, in a bipedal walking control task, when the robot gets the ability of walking upright, there will generate a large number of transitions walking upright and the space of transitions standing up from tumble will become smaller and smaller in spite of these are essential for the learning. In this paper, we propose an algorithm to estimate the similarity between a new transition and the transitions in the experience memory, and the transition which has a higher similarity to the memory has the bigger chance not to be collected.

The remainder of the paper is organized as follows. Section 2 introduces the background of this article. In Sect. 3, we detail the selective transition collection algorithm. In Sect. 4, we describe detailed experimental settings, results and discussions. Finally, we draw a conclusion for our research in Sect. 5.

2 Background

There are many works on optimizing sampling algorithm and tuning transition distribution in the field of reinforcement learning [11–13]. Prioritized experience replay is a member of the importance sampling field and has been shown to be effective in improving learning speed. In this work, the authors inspired by the recent neuroscience studies that sequences of prior experience are replayed in the hippocampus of rodents and experiences with high magnitude TD error also appear to be replayed more often.

In Prioritized experience replay, TD error is used to be the priority of a transition, and a sum-tree is used to store the transitions and priorities. The TD error is defined as

$$\delta_t = R_{t+1} + \gamma V(s_{t+1}) - V(s_t) \tag{1}$$

here γ is the discounted reward coefficient.

In order to avoid transitions with large TD errors from being replayed too much and leading to overfitting. The authors combine random sampling method with prioritized sampling method to ensure that transitions with smaller errors also have a chance to be selected. The chance of a transition be selected is defined as

$$P(i) = \frac{p_i^\alpha}{\sum_k p_k^\alpha} \tag{2}$$

where p_i is the priority of transition i. The exponent α determines the weight of prioritized sampling. If $\alpha = 0$, it is corresponding to the uniform case.

The authors defined 2 type of p_i. One is $p_i = |\delta_i| + \epsilon$, where ϵ is a small positive constant. And another one is $p_i = \frac{1}{rank(i)}$, where $rank(i)$ is the rank of transition i when the replay memory is sorted according to $|\delta_i|$. The second variant is more robust and less sensitive to outliers.

Episodic memory is a method to optimize the transition distribution of the experience memory and stores the specific experiences in different memories to prevent some important experiences from being overwritten [14–16]. Usually, these specific experiences help to preserve past performance and constrains the network to find an optimum that respects both the past and present tasks [17].

In this paper we attempt to optimize the experience memory of off-policy reinforcement learning in another way. We focus on reducing the numbers of similar transitions in the experience memory. There are many ways to calculate the deference between two vectors, such as norms, angle between them, Euclidean distance, Standardized Euclidean distance, etc. Because the scales of each component with big disparity, we used Standardized Euclidean distance to denote the discrepancy between transitions which is defined as

$$d = \sqrt{\sum_{k=1}^n \left(\frac{x_{1k} - x_{2k}}{sd_k}\right)^2} \tag{3}$$

where sd_k is the standard deviation of the component k.

We experiment our method on some simulated environments that are from OPENAI-GYM [18] which is a library containing numbers of reinforcement learning environments, such as classic control tasks, Atari games, 3D simulated physical tasks, etc. Many reinforcement learning researchers have been used environments in this library to test whether their algorithms work [19, 20], and more information about OPENAI-GYM can be seen at its official website https://gym.openai.com.

3   Selective Transition Collection Algorithm

3.1   Estimating Similarity Between Transitions

In reinforcement learning, at the step i, a training transition is a vector which is usually composed of $state_i$, $action_i$, $reward_i$ and $state_{i+1}$. In this paper, we describe the transition vector at step i as $T_i = [s_i, a_i, r_i, s_{i+1}]$. We use Standardized Euclidean distance to measure the discrepancy between 2 transition vectors, and it is defined as

$$d = \sqrt{\sum_{k=1}^n \left(\frac{t_{1k} - t_{2k}}{sd_k}\right)^2} \tag{4}$$

where k is the dimension index of the transition vector, and sd_k is the standard deviation of the component k of all the transition vectors in the experience memory. Since the transitions in the memory keep changing with the training process, the sd_k should be calculated in each training step. Under normal circumstances, the experience memory contains hundreds of thousands of transitions, and using traditional method to calculate standard deviation will bring a prodigious computation cost. So, we use a recurrent way to calculate sd_k in each step. The recurrence formula is

$$sd_{k_i} = \sqrt{\frac{i-2}{i-1}sd_{k_{i-1}} + \frac{\left(t_{k_i}-\bar{t}_{k_{i-1}}\right)^2}{i}} \tag{5}$$

where $\bar{t}_k$ is the average of component k which is also calculated in a recurrent way

$$\bar{t}_{k_i} = \frac{(i-1)\bar{t}_{k_{i-1}}+t_{k_i}}{i} \tag{6}$$

3.2 Selective Collection

In this paper, we optimize the distribution of transitions in the collection stage. In the experience memory, transitions have different distributions. Because of the greedy learning method, the distribution will become more and more concentrated as the training goes on and this change is very likely to lead to catastrophic forgetting. So, as the Fig. 1 shows, our intention is reducing the proportion of similar distributions so as to insure the diversity of experiences in the memory.

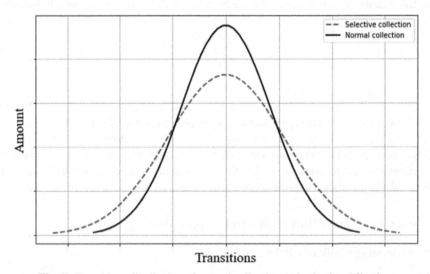

Fig. 1. Transitions distribution of normal collection and selective collection.

To prevent too much similar transitions from being collected in the experience memory, we define the probability of collecting transition i as

$$P(i) = \mu \sin\left(\frac{\pi d_i}{2d_{max}}\right) \ (\textit{if } P > 1 : P = 1) \tag{7}$$

where μ is the proportion factor, with $\mu > 0$. To get the similarity between the new transition T_i and the transitions memory, we randomly select N transitions in the memory and calculate the Standardized Euclidean distance between each transition and T_i, and $d_i = min(d_{i1}, d_{i2}, \ldots d_{iN})$. d_{max} is the current maximum d which constantly changing as training progresses.

We combine selective transition collection algorithm into a full-scale reinforcement learning agent, based on the state-of-the-art Deep Deterministic Policy Gradient (DDPG) [21]. Our principal modification is to replace the uniform collection method used by DDPG with our selective collection method (see Algorithm 1).

Algorithm 1 DDPG with selective transition collection

1: **Input:** proportion factor μ, comparing number N

2: Randomly initialize critic network $Q(s, a|\theta^Q)$ and actor $\mu(s|\theta^\mu)$ with weights θ^Q and θ^μ.

3: Initialize target network Q' and μ' with weights $\theta^{Q'} \leftarrow \theta^Q$, $\theta^{\mu'} \leftarrow \theta^\mu$

4: Initialize experience memory H

5: for episode = 1 to M do

6:    Initialize a random process $\mathcal{N}$ for action exploration

7:    Receive initial observation state S_1

8:    for i = 1 to T do

9:       Select action $a_i = \mu(s_i|\theta^\mu) + \mathcal{N}_i$ according to the current policy and exploration noise.

10:      Execute action a_i and observe reward r_i and observe new state s_{i+1} and observe new transition

$$T_i = [s_i, a_i, r_i, s_{i+1}]$$

11:      Compute the standard deviation of each component:

$$sd_{k_i} = \sqrt{\frac{i-2}{i-1} sd_{k_{i-1}} + \frac{\left(t_{k_i} - \bar{t}_{k_{i-1}}\right)^2}{i}}$$

12:      Select N transitions randomly from the experience memory and compute Standardized Euclidean distances between each of them and T_i:

$$d_{in} = \sqrt{\sum_{k=1}^{n} \left(\frac{t_{1k} - t_{2k}}{sd_k}\right)^2}$$

13:      Update d_{max} and get $d_i = min(d_{i1}, d_{i2}, \ldots d_{iN})$

14:      Compute the probability of collecting the current transition T_i:

$$P(i) = \mu \sin\left(\frac{\pi d_i}{2 d_{max}}\right) \quad (if\ P > 1: P = 1)$$

15:      Collect T_i in H according to $P(i)$

16:      Sample a random minibatch from H and update $\theta^{Q'}$, θ^Q, $\theta^{\mu'}$, θ^μ according to DDPG [21].

17:   end for

18: end for

---

4 Experiments

To verify whether our method is effective, we integrated selective transition collection algorithm into DDPG which has been introduced in Algorithm 1 and performed trials in 2 classic reinforcement learning tasks. In these experiments, we compared selective collection method, normal collection method and prioritized sampling with DDPG in the speed and stability of learning.

Environments: As Fig. 2 shows, BipedalWalker-v2 is a bipedal walking control task from OPENAI-GYM. The goal of this task is to learn to make the robot walk on the uneven ground by driving four joints of the legs. Pendulum-v0 is a classic continuous control task and it also from OPENAI-GYM. The goal is to make a pole stand up by applying a torque. Figure 3 shows the motion sequences of a successful operation for Pendulum-v0.

Fig. 2. The motion sequences of BipedalWalker-v2.

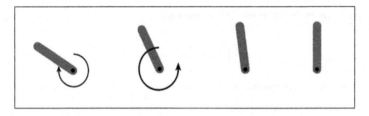

Fig. 3. The motion sequences of Pendulum-v0.

Experiment Details: In the BipedalWalker-v2 task, the actor network has 2 hidden layers with 500 * 200 units, and the critic network has one hidden layer with 700 units. In Pendulum-v0 task, the actor network has 2 hidden layers with 64 * 32 units, and the critic network has one hidden layer with 128 units. All the trials used a soft update factor $\tau = 0.9$ for updating target networks. Table 1 shows more details of the experiments.

Results and Discussion: From the results demonstrated by Fig. 4, compared with normal collection method, both selective collection and prioritized sampling lead to speed-ups, and the prioritized sampling has the faster learning speed. However, the performance of selective collection is more stable, especially in the middle and later stages of training. In other words, the selective collection can prevent catastrophic forgetting to a certain extent.

Table 1. Detailed configurations for BipedalWalker-v2 and Pendulum-v0 tasks.

	BipedalWalker-v2	Pendulum-v0
Actor network	500, 200 (relu, relu)	64, 32 (relu, relu)
Critic network	700 (relu)	128 (relu)
Learning rate (actor)	5^{-4}	1^{-3}
Learning rate (critic)	5^{-4}	2^{-3}
Optimization method	Adam	Adam
τ	0.9	0.9
Batch size	32	32
N	200	100
Memory Capacity	100000	50000
μ	2	2

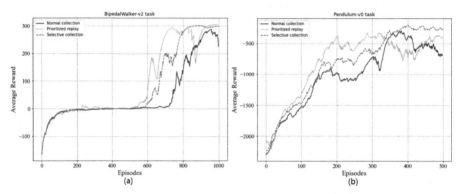

Fig. 4. Learning curves of DDPG with different transitions management methods. (a): experiments on BipedalWalker-v2 task, (b): experiments on Pendulum-v0 task.

5   Conclusion

In this work we have proposed selective transition collection algorithm for experience replay in off-policy reinforcement learning. Our method estimates the similarity between every new transition and the transitions in the experience memory, and it selectively collect transitions based on the similarity to reduce the distribution of similar transitions. To the best of our knowledge, we are the first to propose this method. Selective transition collection is easy to integrated into the existing algorithms. In our experiments, we integrated selective collection into DDPG which is a classic RL algorithm and performed testing in simulated physical environments. The results demonstrate that with our method the learning can improve its convergence speed and the training process becomes more stable. We hope selective transition collection could become a useful component for experience replay.

Funding. This work was supported by Major Project of the New Generation of Artificial Intelligence, China (No. 2018AAA0102900).

References

1. Sutton, R.S., Barto, A.G.: Reinforcement Learning: An Introduction. MIT Press, Cambridge (2018)
2. Schulman, J., Wolski, F., Dhariwal, P., et al.: Proximal policy optimization algorithms. arXiv preprint arXiv:1707.06347 (2017)
3. Mnih, V., Badia, A.P., Mirza, M., et al.: Asynchronous methods for deep reinforcement learning. In: International Conference on Machine Learning, pp. 1928–1937 (2016)
4. Heess, N., Dhruva, T.B., Sriram, S., et al.: Emergence of locomotion behaviours in rich environments. arXiv preprint arXiv:1707.02286 (2017)
5. Mnih, V., Kavukcuoglu, K., Silver, D., et al.: Playing Atari with deep reinforcement learning. arXiv preprint arXiv:1312.5602 (2013)
6. Arulkumaran, K., Deisenroth, M.P., Brundage, M., et al.: Deep reinforcement learning: a brief survey. IEEE Signal Process. Mag. **34**(6), 26–38 (2017)
7. Schaul, T., et al.: Prioritized experience replay. arXiv preprint arXiv:1511.05952 (2015)
8. Tesauro, G.: Temporal difference learning and TD-Gammon. Commun. ACM **38**(3), 58–68 (1995)
9. Bellman, R.: Dynamic programming and stochastic control processes. Inf. Control **1**(3), 228–239 (1958)
10. Watkins, C.J.C.H., Dayan, P.: Q-learning. Mach. Learn. **8**(3–4), 279–292 (1992)
11. Shelton, C.R.: Importance sampling for reinforcement learning with multiple objectives. Dissertation, Massachusetts Institute of Technology (2001)
12. Hachiya, H, et al.: Adaptive importance sampling for value function approximation in off-policy reinforcement learning. Neural Netw. **22**(10), 1399–1410 (2009)
13. Uchibe, E., Doya, K.: Competitive-cooperative-concurrent reinforcement learning with importance sampling. In: Proceedings of International Conference on Simulation of Adaptive Behavior: From Animals and Animats (2004)
14. Lopez-Paz, D., Ranzato, M.A.: Gradient episodic memory for continual learning. In: Advances in Neural Information Processing Systems (2017)
15. Lin, Z., et al.: Episodic memory deep Q-networks. arXiv preprint arXiv:1805.07603 (2018)
16. Fortunato, M., et al.: Generalization of reinforcement learners with working and episodic memory. In: Advances in Neural Information Processing Systems (2019)
17. Isele, D., Cosgun, A.: Selective experience replay for lifelong learning. In: AAAI Conference on Artificial Intelligence 2018. Association for the Advancement of Artificial Intelligence (AAAI) (2018)
18. Brockman, G., et al.: Openai gym. arXiv preprint arXiv:1606.01540 (2016)
19. Zamora, I., et al.: Extending the OpenAI gym for robotics: a toolkit for reinforcement learning using ROS and Gazebo. arXiv preprint arXiv:1608.05742 (2016)
20. Vázquez-Canteli, J.R., et al.: Citylearn v1. 0: an OpenAI gym environment for demand response with deep reinforcement learning. In: Proceedings of the 6th ACM International Conference on Systems for Energy-Efficient Buildings, Cities, and Transportation (2019)
21. Lillicrap, T.P., Hunt, J.J., Pritzel, A., et al.: Continuous control with deep reinforcement learning. arXiv preprint arXiv:1509.02971 (2015)

Design and Grasping Experiments of Soft Humanoid Hand with Variable Stiffness

Shulin Du[1], Qingchao Wang[1], Yan Zhao[3], Fuchun Sun[2(✉)], Xiao Lu[1(✉)], Bin Fang[2], and Shoucheng Hou[4]

[1] College of Electrical Engineering and Automation, Shandong University of Science and Technology, Qingdao, Shandong, People's Republic of China
[2] Department of Computer Science and Technology, Tsinghua National Laboratory for Information Science and Technology, Tsinghua University, Beijing, People's Republic of China
fcsun@tsinghua.edu.cn
[3] Shanghai Institute of Satellite Engineering, Shanghai, China
[4] China University of Geosciences, Beijing, China

Abstract. To improve the safety and adaptability of the human–machine and environment–machine interactions, the research of soft grippers has attracted much attention. In this study a novel Soft Humanoid Hand with Variable Stiffness (SHH-VS) is presented. The SHH-VS has 6 degrees of freedom, and the design of the soft finger with variable stiffness adopts the principle of layer jamming. The SHH-VS can complete grasping, pinching, holding, lifting and other multi-skill grasping operations, using the tendon-driven mechanism. Tactile sensors are installed at the fingertips, which can realize real-time feedback of tactile information. The SHH-VS has better flexibility, greater grasping power, and multi-skill grasping ability. Through a number of grasping experiments, it has been verified that the SHH-VS has greater reliability and safety, and can be used in various daily situations.

Keywords: Soft humanoid hand · Variable stiffness · Multi-skill grasping · Tactile sensor · Grasping experiments

1 Introduction

As an important end effector of the robot, the manipulator plays a very important role in the filed of the robot, it can accomplish various operations like grasping, pinching, holding and lifting. Robots equipped with the manipulator are able to complete tasks such as item classification and assembly. The main components of traditional manipulators are rigid connecting rods, while the working space is limited, the safety is difficult to guarantee when interacting with people. Moreover, It is hard to grasp the objects without causing damage in the picking and sorting of objects with soft and fragile surfaces. Therefore, complex force closed-loop control algorithms and expensive sensing devices are indispensable, for rigid manipulators, to achieve compliant operation.

S. Du, Q. Wang and Y. Zhao—The same contributions.

© Springer Nature Singapore Pte Ltd. 2021
F. Sun et al. (Eds.): ICCSIP 2020, CCIS 1397, pp. 325–336, 2021.
https://doi.org/10.1007/978-981-16-2336-3_30

In this paper, a novel Soft Humanoid Hand with Variable Stiffness(SHH-VS) is presented [1, 2]. The SHH-VS has 6 degrees of freedom, of which the thumb has two and each of the other fingers has one. The design ensures it can grasp objects of various sizes, and is able to complete more complex tasks. We achieve the variable stiffness performance of the SHH-VS by the layer jamming principle, and adopt the tendon-driven mechanism to control the soft fingers, which makes the heavy objects grasped. Moreover, the SHH-VS can also increase the possibility for human-robot communication based on the gestures.

2 Related Works

In recent years, to improve the safety and adaptability of the human–machine and environment–machine interactions, the research of soft grippers has attracted much attention. Mechanical Engineering Department of Korea Advanced Institute of Science and Technology (KAIST) has proposed a novel variable-stiffness mechanism inspired from the connected ossicle structure of an echinoderms body wall which can overcome the limitations of the existing methods. The structure of the echinoderms body wall can induce a change of stiffness, and based on this feature, they developed a structure-based vacuum driven mechanism applicable to soft robot with elastomerfoam and ossicles [1]. Computer Science and Artificial Intelligence Laboratory of Massachusetts Institute of Technology has proposed a soft hand capable of robustly grasping and identifying objects based on internal state measurements along with a combined system which autonomously performs grasps

A highly compliant soft hand allows for intrinsic robustness to grasping uncertainties;the addition of internal sensing allows the configuration of the hand and object to be detected [4]. The Soft Robot Laboratory at the Robotics Department of Ritsumeikan University in Japan has proposed a dual-mode soft gripper that integrates a suction pad on the tip of each pneumatic actuator. By combining the advantages of both grasping and suction, the proposed gripper can handle a wide variety of objects [5]. The School of Mechanical Engineering and Automation, Beihang University incorporated vacuum-actuated suckers into the actuators for the production of a fully integrated octopus arm-inspired gripper [6].

The driven methods of manipulators is also the focus of research in the field of manipulators, and remarkable achievements have been made in recent years, such as pneumatic actuators [7, 8], chemical reaction [9], the tendon-driven mechanism [10, 11], shape memory alloy actuators [12] and so on. Compared with other driven methods, tendon line driven has better response efficiency and frequency [13]. The soft manipulator is made of flexible material with shape adaptability, which can realize the smooth operation and is suitable for grasping operation tasks. In recent years, more and more scientists have participated in the research of soft humanoid hand [7, 14–16]. Compared with traditional manipulators, soft humanoid hands are light in weight, low in cost, simple to drive, and easy to manufacture. Both in collaboration and interaction, they have higher security.

3   Design of the Soft Humanoid Hand with Variable Stiffness

3.1   Principle of the Variable Stiffness

In this paper the layer jamming principle is used to realize the variable stiffness performance of the SHH-VS. There is a sealed cavity along the length of the finger inside it. A blocking component (multi-pieces of layer jamming structure) for adjusting the stiffness is placed in the cavity. And there is a certain deformation space between the blocking component and the accommodating cavity, which is communicated with the negative pressure device through the tube. Before the cavity is in a non-negative pressure state, the layers of the layer jamming structure are relatively loose, and can move relative to each other when the soft fingers deformed. At this time, the fingers, remain soft, are easily bent with a small driving power. If the tension is removed, the fingers will immediately return to the upright state. When the cavity is in the negative pressure state, the multi-pieces of layer jamming structure is squeezed and rubbed against each other in the longitudinal and transverse directions, forming a thicker integrated structure, thus the rigidity of the soft finger becomes larger, and more force is needed to deform the fingers. At the same time, no matter what shape the finger is, if the driving force is removed, the shape can be locked under the action of the layer jamming structure and a certain supporting force can be obtained Fig. 1 shows the prototype of the soft finger with variable stiffness.

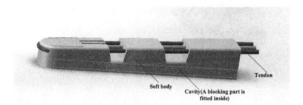

Fig. 1. Prototype of the soft finger with variable stiffness

3.2   Design of the SHH-VS

The overall design of the SHH-VS copied the shape of the human hand(Fig. 2), and adopts the method of tendon line driven. The motors that provide power are assembled in the palm (Fig. 3) to control the transmission of the tendon line, thereby controlling the fingers. The SHH-VS has 6 degrees of freedom, including two for the thumb and four for the other fingers,which can accomplish under-actuation and coupling of the finger. Thus the SHH-VS has good adaptability. The stiffness of the finger can be changed, making the SHH-VS adapted to grasp heavy objects. The fingertip is equipped with a tactile sensor, which can obtain the grasping force in real time, so that the SHH-VS can accomplish a variety of grasping operations with high precision.

The soft fingers are made of soft material. In order to fully simulate the human hand and simplify the structure, the fingers are designed in three segments, which are

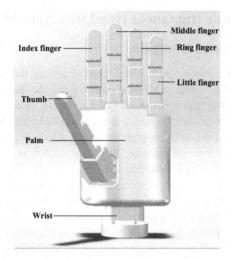

Fig. 2. Prototype of the SHH-VS assembled with five soft fingers

Fig. 3. The internal structure of the palm

jointly controlled by a shared tendon line. This design can accomplish under-actuation and coupling of the finger. The structure of the index, middle, ring and little finger is the same in this paper. Take the index finger as an example, it has 3 phalanges, and they are proximal phalanx, middle phalanx, and end phalanx (Fig. 4). The line routing adopts a "U-shape" instead of the straight, mainly to make it easier to pull the soft finger to bend. At the same time, there is a plastic hose in the tendon cavity to reduce the friction between the tendon line and the cavity to ensure the service life.

There is a thin-film tactile sensor at the phalanx of the index finger (Fig. 5), which is encapsulated by a layer of transparent silica gel. The wire of the sensor embedded in the plastic hose of the cavity, and extends to the interface module of control board to acquire tactile signals. The sensor consists of two very thin polyester films with conductors and semiconductors laid on the inner surface of the two films, which can measure the pressure of any contact surface statically and dynamically. The sensor converts the pressure applied to the sensing area into a resistance signal, and then obtains the change information of the external pressure according to the force-resistance calibration curve. The greater the pressure, the smaller the resistance output by the sensor.

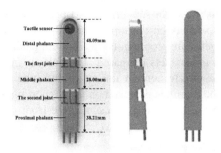

Fig. 4. Prototype of the index finger

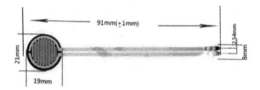

Fig. 5. The Tactile sensor

The thumb (Fig. 6) is the most important of the human hands. Almost all grasping operations require the cooperation of the thumb. Common actions of human hands, such as grasping, pinching, holding, and lifting, all require complete force closure and geometric closure to hold the target stably. The design of the thumb determines the working space, operation and gripping stability of the entire system. Similar to the index finger, the thumb is also composed of 3 phalanges. One more base joint is added. The thumb has 2 degrees of freedom, namely the flexion/extension of the finger and the rotation of the base joint. The base joint can be rotated within 0–90° and reach the position between the index and the middle finger.

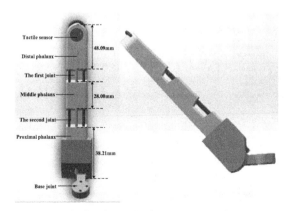

Fig. 6. Prototype of the thumb finger

The palm (Fig. 7), as the main supporting part of the soft finger, is made by 3D printing. There are four sockets on the top of the palm for fixing the soft fingers. It is packaged with silica gel. After cooling, the fixing strength and sealing performance between the fingers and the sockets increased. The palm is mainly used to place the transmission devices, air nozzle, tendon line, wire and tube. At the same time, the transmission device of the thumb is designed on the support plate which assembled on the palm. For the beauty of the palm, we designed the front and back of the palm to make it smooth.

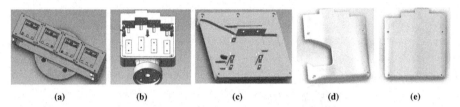

(a)   (b)   (c)   (d)   (e)

Fig. 7. The structure of the palm. (a) The rabbet of the distal phalanx. (b) The internal structure of the palm. (c) The support plate of the thumb. (d) The front of the palm. (e) The back of the palm.

3.3   The Control System of the SHH-VS

The control system of the SHH-VS is an embedded system (Fig. 8), and the model of the main chip is STM32F103RCT6. The SHH-VS system consists of two parts: the software system(Host computer) and the Hardware system, and uses UART for real-time communication. The hardware system mainly receives control commands from the software system to output PWM digital signal, which are used to control the work of each steering gear, stepper motor, vacuum pump and electromagnetic valve, and upload the data of each tactile sensor to the host computer.

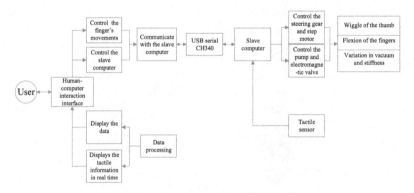

Fig. 8. Control strategy of the SHH-VS system

The hardware system mainly includes four parts: control circuit, drive circuit, signal acquisition circuit and power supply circuit. The whole system is integrated on a control board. The control circuit is used to generate control commands. The drive circuit is used to drive the devices. The acquisition circuit is used to acquire the tactile data and feed back changes in the grasping force during the grasping process. The power supply circuit provides sufficient power for some actuators and the minimum system of the main controller.

The hardware connection of the SHH-VS is shown in Fig. 11. There are 8 interface modules: (1) STM32 Virtual COM Port module, which is connected to the host computer. The interface receives control instructions and query instructions sent by the host computer, and feeds back the current tactile data. (2) USB Serial CH340 module, which is connected to host computer, providing download interface of the control program. (3) The 12 V power supply module, which is connected to the switching power supply. The 12 V voltage is divided into two functions. One is supplied to the stepper motor drive modules, and the other is reduced to 5 V and 3.3 V supplied to chip after stepping down. (4) 24 V power supply module, which is used to supply power for vacuum pump and electromagnetic valve. (5) The control module for vacuum pump and electromagnetic valve, which is used to switch them to realize the variable-stiffness operation of the fingers. (6) The driver module of stepper motors, which is connected with stepper motors to control the flexion/extension of the fingers. (7) The control module of steering gear, which provides power and control commands for the steering gear. (8) The tactile-data acquisition module, which is connected with the tactile sensors of the the SHH-VS to acquire five-channel tactile data (Fig. 9).

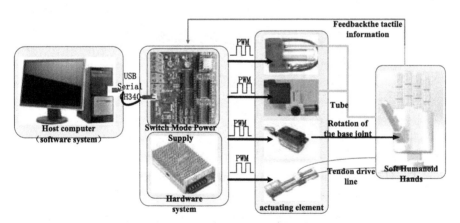

Fig. 9. Hardware connection of the SHH-VS control system

4 Experiment

4.1 Gesture Experiment of the SHH-VS

The SHH-VS can make a variety of common gestures (Fig. 10), such as number gesture "0", "1", "2", "3", "4", "5", "6", "8" as well as gesture "OK".

Fig. 10. Experiments of the common gesture

4.2 Grasping Experiment of the SHH-VS

SHH-VS has a certain limitation when making gestures because of the under-actuated structure, but outstanding performance in the grasping experiments. When grasping an object, the under-actuated structure and the compliance of the finger make SHH-VS have self-adaptability, so that it can achieve compliant operation, especially it can grasp the fragile object without damage (Fig. 11(a), (b) grabbing the egg and balloon). The main function of the SHH-VS is to accomplish the multi-skill operations such as grasping, pinching, holding and lifting, at the same time it can acquire the tactile data (Fig. 12). Table 1. shows the parameters of the items used in the experiments. When grasping, set the swing angle of the thumb according to the shape and size of the target object to match the other four fingers, then the SHH-VS can accomplish the grasping of cuboid, cylinder, sphere, hemisphere and irregular objects (Fig. 11).

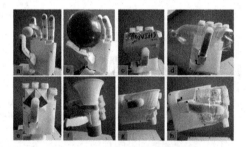

Fig. 11. Experiments of grasping a variety of objects with two or five fingers

Fig. 12. Experiments of acquiring the tactile information

Table 1. Grab item parameter table

Item	Quality/g	Size/mm	Item	Quality/g	Size/mm
Folding megaphone	900	$d_{max} = 146, d_{min} = 73, h = 240$	Egg	65	$d = 43, h = 62$
Card	5.40	$V = 85 * 55 * 1$	Balloon	1.8	$d = 170$
Wallet	125.44	$V = 115 * 90 * 20$	Cuboid	119	$V = 120 * 90 * 70$
Cookies	29.25	$V = 90 * 45 * 20$	Bottle	500	$d = 55, h = 220$
Bread	26.61	$V = 100 * 70 * 35$	Glass Cup	291	$d = 75, h = 90$
Handbag	1500	$V = 220 * 90 * 160$	Irregular Toy	80	$d = 100$
Kettle	1500	kettle handle: $V = 140 * 30 * 15$	Ball	30	$d = 60$
Bowl	31.20	$d_{max} = 115, d_{min} = 55, h = 40$			

When pinching, because of the effective cooperation of the thumb, index finger and middle finger, a force seal is formed between the fingertip and the objects, which makes the SHH-VS can complete pinching objects with two or three fingers (Fig. 13). The results of the experiments show that the SHH-VS acts flexibly, has good adaptability to the shape of different objects, and can smoothly grasp a variety of objects.

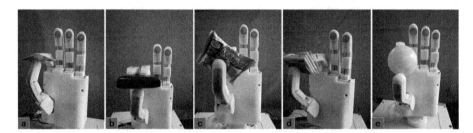

Fig. 13. Experiments of pinching different objects

4.3 Application Experiment of the SHH-VS

In the grasping experiments, the SHH-VS shows its stable and flexible grasping ability. Moreover, it can also accomplish some operations similar to the human hand, which is not available in ordinary soft grippers. Figure 14 demonstrates the process of a bowl (500 g) being held in the palm. Because the fingers are made of soft materials, in this operation, the finger part as the main stress point will undergo severe deformation and cause the operation to fail. Variable stiffness can solve this problem well. The rigidity of the fingers is increased by vacuuming, which can improve the load-bearing capacity of the fingers to heavy objects, thereby ensuring stable operation. That is a process of human-machine interaction. Figure 15 demonstrates the process of a handbag being lifted Fig. 16 and Fig. 17 respectively shows the process of picking up the kettle and pouring water. The above experiments have again verified the good grasping performance of the SHH-VS and its advantages in structure.

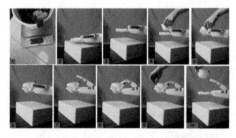

Fig. 14. Demonstration of bowl (500 g) being held in the palm

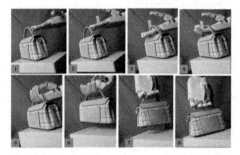

Fig. 15. Demonstration of the handbag being lifted

Fig. 16. Demonstration of the kettle being picked up

Fig. 17. Demonstration of pouring water

5 Conclusion

This paper designed a novel Soft Humanoid Hand with Variable Stiffness (SHH-VS) that capable of multi-skill grasping. The SHH-VS has 6 degrees of freedom, of which the thumb has two and each of the other fingers has one. The layer jamming principle is used to realize the variable stiffness performance, and the tendon-driven is used to realize the movement of the fingers. One servo controls the rotation of the thumb, and five stepper motors control the transmission of the tendon line to achieve the flexion of fingers. It can complete grasping, pinching, holding, lifting and other operations. The results of the experiments show that it can grasp various objects well, and the soft material ensures that the surface of the grasped objects is completely undamaged. The fingertip is equipped with a tactile sensor, which can display real-time tactile information through the interface of the host computer. Moreover, the SHH-VS can make a variety of common gestures, which improves the human–machine interaction.

References

1. Ham, K.B., Han, J., Park, Y.J.: Soft gripper using variable stiffness mechanism and its application. Int. J. Precis. Eng. Manufact. **19**(4), 487–494 (2018)
2. Feng, N., Shi, Q., Wang, H., et al.: A soft robotic hand: design, analysis, sEMG control, and experiment. Int. J. Adv. Manufact. Technol. **97**(1–4), 319–333 (2018)
3. Jeong, H., Kim, J.: Echinoderm inspired variable stiffness soft actuator with connected ossicle structure. In: 2019 International Conference on Robotics and Automation (ICRA), Montreal, QC, Canada, 2019, pp. 7389–7394
4. Homberg, B.S., Katzschmann, R.K., et al.: Robust proprioceptive grasping with a soft robot hand. Auton. Robots **43**(3), 681–696 (2019)
5. Wang, Z., Or, K., Hirai, S.: A dual-mode soft gripper for food packaging. Robotics Auton. Syst. **125**, (2020)
6. Xie, Z., et al.: Octopus arm-inspired tapered soft actuators with suckers for improved grasping. Soft Robot. (2020)
7. Zhong, G., Hou, Y., Dou, W.: A soft pneumatic dexterous gripper with convertible grasping modes. Int. J. Mech. Sci. **153**, 445–456 (2019)
8. Polygerinos, P., et al.: Modeling of soft fiber-reinforced bending actuators. IEEE Trans. Rob. **31**(3), 778–789 (2015). https://doi.org/10.1109/TRO.2015.2428504
9. Michael, W., et al.: An integrated design and fabrication strategy for entirely soft, autonomous robots. Nature **536**(7617), 451–455 (2016)
10. Mishra, A.K., Del Dottore, E., Sadeghi, A., et al.: SIMBA: tendon-driven modular continuum arm with soft reconfigurable gripper. Front. Robot AI. **4**, 4 (2017)
11. AI Abeach, L., Nefti-Meziani, S., Theodoridis, T., et al.: A variable stiffness soft gripper using granular jamming and biologically inspired pneumatic muscles. J. Bionic Eng **15**(2), pp. 236–246 (2018)
12. Kim, J.S., Lee, J.-Y., Lee, K.-T., Kim, H.-S., Ahn, S.-H.: Fabrication of 3D soft morphing structure using shape memory alloy (SMA) wire/polymer skeleton composite. J. Mech. Sci. Tech. **27**(10), 3123–3129 (2013)
13. Mizushima, K., Oku, T., Suzuki, Y., Tsuji, T., Watanabe, T.: Multi-fingered robotic hand based on hybrid mechanism of tendon-driven and jamming transition. In: 2018 IEEE International Conference on Soft Robotics (RoboSoft), Livorno, pp. 376–381 (2018). https://doi.org/10.1109/robosoft.2018.8404948

14. Zhao, H., Huang, R., Shepherd, R.F.: Curvature control of soft robotics via low cost solid-state optics. In: International Conference on Robotics and Automation, Stockholm, pp. 4008–4013. IEEE (2016)
15. Zhao, H., Jalving, J., Huang, R., et al.: A helping hand: Soft orthosis with integrated optical strain sensors and EMG control. IEEE Robot. Autom. Mag. **23**(3), 55–64 (2016)
16. Al-Rubaiai, M., Pinto, T., Qian, C., et al.: Soft actuators with stiffness and shape modulation using 3D printed conductive polylactic acid material. Soft Robot. **6**(3), 318–332 (2019)

Bioinformatics

Prediction the Age of Human Brains from Gene Expression

Wei Liu, Jian Qin, Lingli Zeng, Hui Shen, and Dewen Hu[✉]

College of Intelligence Science and Technology, National University of Defense Technology, Changsha 410073, Hunan, People's Republic of China
dwhu@nudt.edu.cn

Abstract. Understanding temporal characteristics of gene expression in normal human brain can help explain the neurodevelopment, working mechanism and functional diversity. Based on the gene expression dataset of developing human brains from the Allen Brain Atlas, we accurately predicted the age of human brains using support vector machine and identified 9,934 age related genes. Significant changes occur in gene expression of human brains before and after birth, thus we establish support vector machine (SVM) models for the subjects before birth and after birth, respectively. In general, the age of subjects can be well predicted by the SVM models, with the Pearson correlation coefficient of predicted age and the labeled age of all subjects is 0.9397 with P-value < 0.001 (before birth: r = 0.9465, P-value < 0.001; after birth: r = 0.9121, P-value < 0.001). For the total subjects, mean absolute error (MAE) of age prediction is 2.82 years with standard error (SE) is 0.15 years (before birth: MAE = 1.03 post-conceptual weeks (pcws), SE = 0.08 pcws; after birth: MAE = 4.70 years, SE = 0.20 years). This investigation reveal the bulk of temporal regulation occurred during prenatal development. By analyzing the functional annotations of age related genes, we found expression differences of genes before and after birth may be related to their functions. Finally, we found the prediction accuracy of each period can reflect its specificity of gene expression, which is negatively correlated to the gene expression similarity across periods. This study provides new insights into temporal dynamic pattern of gene expression in human brains and its relationship with functions.

Keywords: Age prediction · Support vector machine · Functional annotation

1 Introduction

Brain is the most complex organ of human body, each brain region has more than 10,000 gene expressions [1]. With the development of human brain, molecular activities in the brain change with time [2]. Analyzing temporal dynamic pattern of gene expression in human brain is essential for a comprehensive understanding of neurodevelopment, working mechanism of brains, and our susceptibility to neuropsychiatric diseases [3–5].

Gene expression technology provides useful information related to the state of brain by measuring gene expression in human brain samples [6–8]. It is an important means to study the temporal dynamic characteristics of gene expression in brain. In recent

© Springer Nature Singapore Pte Ltd. 2021
F. Sun et al. (Eds.): ICCSIP 2020, CCIS 1397, pp. 339–347, 2021.
https://doi.org/10.1007/978-981-16-2336-3_31

years, researchers have made great progress in this field, not only building a variety of mammalian brain genome-wide expression datasets, but also for the temporal expression of genes in the brain has been further understood [9–13]. However, the dynamic characteristics of gene expression across time and the relationship between temporal characteristics of genes and their functions have not been fully studied.

The work described here had two major objectives. The first aim was to develop an approach for analyzing temporal expression characteristics of single gene and the overall expression trend of genes in periods. The second aim was to know the temporal expression specificity of genes and the relationship with their functions.

2 Result

2.1 Classification of the Age of Samples Based on Gene Expression

To investigate the temporal dynamics of the human brain transcriptome, we downloaded the gene expression dataset of developing human brains from the Allen Brain Atlas (https://www.brainspan.org). Only brains from clinically unremarkable donors with no signs of large-scale genomic abnormalities were included in the study (N = 41; age, 8 pcws to 40 years; sex, 22 males and 19 females). We created an 8-period system spanning from embryonic development to adulthood (Table 1) and used 547 transcriptome samples in 16 brain regions for investigation, including the cerebellar cortex, mediodorsal nucleus of the thalamus, striatum, amygdala, hippocampus, and 11 neocortex areas.

Table 1. Periods of human development and adulthood as defined in this study.

Period	Description	Age	Sample number
1	Early fetal	Age < 14 pcw	8
2	Middle fetal	14 pcw ≤ Age < 24 pcw	7
3	Late fetal	24 pcw ≤ Age < Birth	3
4	Infancy	Birth ≤ Age < 1 yrs	4
5	Early childhood	1 yrs ≤ Age < 6 yrs	5
6	Middle and late childhood	6 yrs ≤ Age < 12 yrs	3
7	Adolescence	12 yrs ≤ Age < 20 yrs	4
8	Adulthood	20 yrs ≤ Age	7

Significant changes occur in gene expression of human brains before and after birth, as shown in the correlation heatmap of gene expression samples (Fig. 1). Thus, we establish SVM models for the subjects before birth and after birth, respectively. Feature selection or dimensionality reduction of the predictors is an essential step in machine learning when the number of predictors is large. We used Pearson correlation to identify the feature genes which are significant correlated between the expression level and

labeled age of subjects in training dataset. To measure the performance of the SVM prediction model, we used the leave-one-out cross-validation (LOOCV) method to evaluate
the performance of all predictors. We took the expression data of each subject as the test
and the others as the training to establish the models of age prediction. The P-values of
the correlation coefficients of predicted results and labeled ages were varied for feature
selection and mean accuracy of test samples are taken as evaluation indicators for age
prediction.

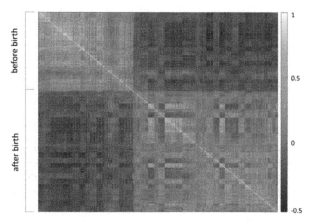

Fig. 1. The correlation heatmap of gene expression samples. The correlations within the samples
before/after birth are obviously higher than those between samples before/after birth.

In general, the age of subjects can be well predicted by the SVM models, with the
Pearson correlation coefficient of predicted age and the labeled age of all subjects is
0.9397 with P-value < 0.001 (before birth: $r = 0.9465$, P-value < 0.001; after birth:
$r = 0.9121$, P-value < 0.001), as shown in Fig. 2. For the total subjects, MAE of age
prediction is 2.82 years with SE is 0.15 years (before birth: MAE $= 1.03$ pcws, SE $=$
0.08 pcws; after birth: MAE $= 4.70$ years, SE $= 0.20$ years). Although the prediction
accuracy of this model is similar to that based on functional connectivity of human
brains for postnatal individuals [14, 15], prediction accuracy based on gene expression
is possible to further improve when the sample size is increased and the time interval is
reduced to a level similar to the functional connection experiment.

Our analysis revealed the bulk of temporal regulation occurred during prenatal development, in accord with the previous report [7]. We need 8,924 feature genes in the
classifier to predict age of subjects before birth, far more than 752 feature genes in the
classifier after birth. Because the gene expression changes more rapidly and dramatically
during the prenatal development than that in the process from children to adults, it is
reasonable to obtain a better prediction result from the model before birth than that after
birth.

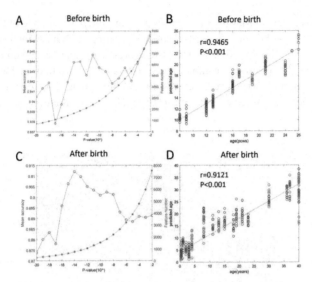

Fig. 2. The age prediction results of brain samples based on SVM models. (A) The prediction accuracy varied with the P-value of correlation of predicted age and the labeled age of individuals before birth; (B) The cross-validation results for age prediction before birth; (C) The prediction accuracy varied with the P-value of correlation of predicted age and the labeled age of individuals after birth; (D) The cross-validation results for age prediction after birth.

2.2 Significance Testing of Classification Accuracy

The statistical significance of all LOOCV results was assessed using permutation testing as proposed by Golland et al. [31]. Using this approach, we estimated the empirical cumulative distribution of the predictor accuracies under the null hypothesis. For each SVM classification described in this paper, the class labels are randomly permuted 1,000 times, and the entire classification process including feature selection is carried out with each one of the sets of randomized class labels. The P-values reported for accuracy represent the probability of observing the reported accuracy by chance ((number of permutation errors < observed error) + 1)/(number of permutations + 1). The reported P-values for the age prediction correlation coefficients represent the probability of observing the reported correlation coefficients by chance. The results of permutation test are given in Fig. 3. All the results of age prediction are significant, with the P-values for permutation test are smaller than 0.001.

2.3 Analysis of the Specificity and Similarity of Gene Expression in Different Periods

Furthermore, we subdivided the human lifespan to 8 periods and established the classification model based on SVM models. As shown in Fig. 4A, classification accuracy reaches the highest in the early fetal period and goes down in the prenatal stage, then reach a high point in infancy and go to bottom in adolescence, finally reach another high point in adulthood. The classification accuracy of each period can reflect its specificity of

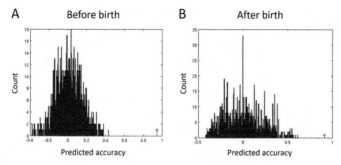

Fig. 3. The prediction accuracies of permutation testing and real prediction in age (A) before birth and (B) after birth. The results of permutation testing are represented as bars, while the results of real classification are represented as circles.

gene expression, which is negatively correlated to the gene expression similarity across periods (Fig. 4B). In 8 periods, early fetal period, infancy and adulthood has the highest expression specificity in the embryo, growing period and adulthood, respectively. As expected, we found there are significant differences between the periods before birth and after birth. Similarly, previous developmental functional magnetic resonance imaging (fMRI) studies have shown reliable differences between children and adults [26–28]. Especially, high similarity of gene expression exists between adolescence and adulthood, with their correlation coefficient is as high as 0.9341 (P-value < 0.001). This can explain why the classification accuracy for adolescence subjects is the lowest throughout human lifespan, the reason of which may lie in the gene expression in adolescence is already very close with that in adulthood subjects.

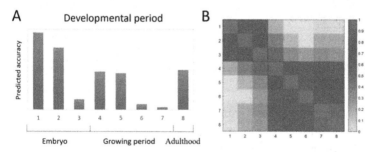

Fig. 4. The prediction accuracies of periods are negatively correlated to the gene expression similarity across periods. (A) Accuracy for 8 period classification of cross-validation. (B) The correlation of gene expression in different periods.

2.4 Functional Analyses of Age Related Genes

A predictable prediction model can not only provide valuable information about unknown subjects, but also indicate significant and reliable age-dependent pattern. By averaging the weights of each gene above 0 in multiple classifiers based on the training data of the LOOCV method, we extracted the mean weight of feature genes in SVM classifiers. The greater the weight of a feature gene, the greater its contribution to prediction. In 21,935 genes expressed in at least one sample of human brains, 9,934 genes (45.29%) are found useful for age prediction, including 8,924 and 752 genes contribute to age prediction before birth and after birth.

To investigate the relation of temporal expression characteristics of age related genes with their functions, we extracted 752 age related genes (after birth) and top 1,000 feature genes with largest weight in age prediction (before birth), then analyzed their function annotations and biological pathways using the Functional Annotation Bioinformatics Microarray Analysis (DAVID) tools [18]. The top 5 enriched functional annotation terms of age related genes are given in Table 2.

Table 2. The most enriched GO terms of molecular function and biological process in age related genes. MF: molecular function, BP: biological process.

Category	GO terms in MF	P-values of MF terms	GO terms in BP	P-values of BP terms
Age related (before birth)	GO:0008083 ~ growth factor activity	2.29×10^{-5}	GO:0007218 ~ neuropeptide signaling pathway	6.70×10^{-5}
	GO:0019838 ~ growth factor binding	0.0013	GO:0007399 ~ nervous system development	1.92×10^{-4}
	GO:0003700 ~ transcription factor activity, sequence-specific DNA binding	0.0043	GO:0010862 ~ positive regulation of pathway-restricted SMAD protein phosphorylation	3.28×10^{-4}
	GO:0001601 ~ peptide YY receptor activity	0.0064	GO:0032570 ~ response to progesterone	3.69×10^{-4}
	GO:0004983 ~ neuropeptide Y receptor activity	0.0070	GO:0060021 ~ palate development	0.0027
Age related (after birth)	GO:0003824 ~ catalytic activity	1.26×10^{-5}	GO:0051592 ~ response to calcium ion	0.0041
	GO:0017137 ~ Rab GTPase binding	0.0030	GO:0030036 ~ actin cytoskeleton organization	0.0062
	GO:0005089 ~ Rho guanyl-nucleotide exchange factor activity	0.0059	GO:0010044 ~ response to aluminum ion	0.0071
	GO:0008017 ~ microtubule binding	0.0076	GO:0035023 ~ regulation of Rho protein signal transduction	0.0076
	GO:0048306 ~ calcium-dependent protein binding	0.0166	GO:0071805 ~ potassium ion transmembrane transport	0.0104

There are significant differences in the functions of genes related with age before birth and after birth. The most enriched molecular functions of age related genes before birth are growth factor activity, growth factor binding, transcription factor activity, sequence-specific DNA binding. The most enriched biological processes of age related genes before birth are neuropeptide signaling pathway, nervous system development and positive regulation of pathway-restricted SMAD protein phosphorylation. The gene with the largest feature weight in the age regression before birth is cathepsin G (CTSG), whose function include serine-type endopeptidase activity, protein binding, heparin binding and peptidase activity.

The most enriched molecular functions of age related genes after birth are catalytic activity, Rab GTPase binding and Rho guanyl-nucleotide exchange factor activity. The most enriched biological processes of age related genes after birth are response to calcium ion, actin cytoskeleton organization, and response to aluminum ion. The gene with the largest feature weight in the age regression after birth is nuclear receptor subfamily 0 group B member 1 (NR0B1), which plays role in DNA binding, steroid hormone receptor activity, transcription corepressor activity and RNA binding. NR0B1 is involved in multiple biological pathways, including CARM1 and regulation of the estrogen receptor, 46XY sex reversal, and congenital Adrenal hypoplasia with hypogonadotropic hypogonadism. It specifically highly expresses in period 4–6.

There is only a small amount of cross between age related genes before and after birth, with 45.48% (342/752) age related genes after birth contributing to age prediction after birth. Based on functional annotations of age related genes, we may be significant differences between the functions of genes before and after birth, which can explain expression differences of genes before and after birth to some extent.

3   Discussion

The human brain is highly dynamic, reflected in the great changes of gene expression in different time stages. It is an important task in brain science to recognize the temporal expression patterns of genes, to understand the temporal expression characteristics and their corresponding functions. It can illuminate the typical development process of human brains and provide a prerequisite for studying developmental disorders and neuropsychiatric diseases.

In this paper, we revealed several important aspects of the human brain transcriptome. Firstly, we established age prediction models and identified feature genes with temporal specific expression. Consistent with many previous studies in other species [10, 30], we found that gene expression has complex dynamically regulated patterns across time. We obtained a better prediction result from the model before birth than that after birth, since the gene expression changes more rapidly and dramatically during the prenatal development than that in the process from children to adults. Secondly, we analyzed the functional annotations of genes, and found significant differences in the functions of genes related with age before birth and after birth. The most enriched molecular functions of age related genes before birth are growth factor activity, growth factor binding, transcription factor activity, sequence-specific DNA binding; while the most enriched molecular functions of age related genes after birth are catalytic activity, Rab GTPase binding and Rho guanyl-nucleotide exchange factor activity. Finally, we investigated the specificity of gene expression in different periods, as well as the correlation of gene expression across periods. We identified the change trend of gene expression specificity over time, and found that was negatively correlated with the expression similarity of different periods. These can explain why the different periods have different prediction accuracy from gene expression. These findings can promote the understanding of the temporal development of gene expression in human brains and its relationship with functions.

Acknowledgements. This study was supported by the National Science Foundation of China (61722313, 61503397, 61420106001, and 61773391) and the Fok Ying Tung Education Foundation (161057).

References

1. Salzberg, S.L.: Open questions: how many genes do we have? BMC Biol. **16**, 94 (2018)
2. Wang, W., Wang, G.Z.: Understanding molecular mechanisms of the brain through transcriptomics. Front Physiol. **10**, 214 (2019)
3. Colantuoni, C., Lipska, B.K., Ye, T., et al.: Temporal dynamics and genetic control of transcription in the human prefrontal cortex. Nature **478**, 519–523 (2011)
4. Hawrylycz, M., Miller, J.A., Menon, V., et al.: Canonical genetic signatures of the adult human brain. Nature Neurosci. **18**(12), 1832–1846 (2015)
5. Li, M., Santpere, G., Imamura Kawasawa, Y., et al.: Integrative functional genomic analysis of human brain development and neuropsychiatric risks. Science **362**(6420), eaat7615 (2018)
6. Hawrylycz, M.J., Lein, E.S., Guillozet-Bongaarts, A.L., et al.: An anatomically comprehensive atlas of the adult human brain transcriptome. Nature **489**(7416), 391–399 (2012)
7. Kang, H.J., Kawasawa, Y.I., Cheng, F., et al.: Spatio-temporal transcriptome of the human brain. Nature **478**(7370), 483–489 (2011)
8. Miller, J.A., Ding, S.L., Sunkin, S.M., et al.: Transcriptional landscape of the prenatal human brain. Nature **508**(7495), 199–206 (2014)
9. Bakken, T.E., Miller, J.A., Ding, S.L., et al.: A comprehensive transcriptional map of primate brain development. Nature **535**(7612), 367–375 (2016)
10. Thompson, C.L., Ng, L., Menon, V., et al.: A high-resolution temporal-spatial atlas of gene expression of the developing mouse brain. Neuron **83**, 309–323 (2014)
11. Zhu, Y., Sousa, A.M.M., Gao, T., et al.: Temporal-spatial transcriptomic divergence across human and macaque brain development. Science **362**(6420), eaat8077 (2018)
12. Wang, D., Liu, S., Warrell, J., et al.: Comprehensive functional genomic resource and integrative model for the human brain. Science **362**(6420), eaat8464 (2018)
13. Amiri, A., Coppola, G., Scuderi, S., et al.: Transcriptome and epigenome landscape of human cortical development modeled in organoids. Science **362**(6420), eaat6720 (2018)
14. Dosenbach, N.U.F., et al.: Prediction of individual brain maturity using fMRI. Science **329**, 1358 (2010)
15. Qin, J., et al.: Predicting individual brain maturity using dynamic functional connectivity. Front. Hum. Neurosci. **9**, 418 (2015)
16. Pan, J.B., Hu, S.C., Wang, H., Zou, Q., Ji, Z.L.: PaGeFinder: quantitative identification of temporal-spatial pattern genes. Bioinformatics **28**(11), 1544–5 (2012)

17. Hoshiba, Y., Toda, T., Ebisu, H., et al.: Sox11 balances dendritic morphogenesis with neuronal migration in the developing cerebral cortex. J. Neurosci. **36**(21), 5775–84 (2016)
18. Huang, D.W., Sherman, B.T., Lempicki, R.A.: Systematic and integrative analysis of large gene lists using DAVID bioinformatics resources. Nature Protoc. **4**(1), 44–57 (2009)
19. Noordermeer, S.D.S., Luman, M., Greven, C.U., et al.: Structural brain abnormalities of attention-deficit/hyperactivity disorder with oppositional defiant disorder. Biol. Psychiatry **82**(9), 642–650 (2017)
20. Beitz, J.M.: Parkinson's disease: a review. Front. Biosci. (Schol. Ed.) **6**, 65-74 (2014)
21. Mao, N.N., Zheng, H.N., Long, Z.Y., et al.: Gender differences in dynamic functional connectivity based on resting-state fMRI. Conf. Proc. IEEE Eng. Med. Biol. Soc. **2017**, 2940–2943 (2017)
22. Zhang, C., Dougherty, C.C., Baum, S.A., White, T., Michael, A.M.: Functional connectivity predicts gender: evidence for gender differences in resting brain connectivity. Hum. Brain Mapp. **39**(4), 1765–1776 (2018)
23. Weis, S., Patil, K.R., Hoffstaedter, F., Nostro, A., Yeo, B.T.T., Eickhoff, S.B.: Sex classification by resting state brain connectivity. Cereb Cortex **pii**, bhz129 (2019)
24. Curtis, C.E., D'Esposito, M.: Persistent activity in the prefrontal cortex during working memory. Trends Cogn. Sci. **7**(9), 415–423 (2003)
25. Eckert, U., Metzger, C.D., Buchmann, J.E., et al.: Preferential networks of the mediodorsal nucleus and centromedian-parafascicular complex of the thalamus–a DTI tractography study. Hum. Brain Mapp. **33**(11), 2627–37 (2012)
26. Marusak, H.A., Calhoun, V.D., Brown, S., et al.: Dynamic functional connectivity of neurocognitive networks in children. Hum. Brain Mapp. **38**(1), 97–108 (2017)
27. Mak, L.E., Minuzzi, L., MacQueen, G., Hall, G., Kennedy, S.H., Milev, R.: The default mode network in healthy individuals: a systematic review and meta-analysis. Brain Connect. **7**(1), 25–33 (2017)
28. Chen, Y., Zhao, X., Zhang, X., et al.: Age related early/late variations of functional connectivity across the human lifespan. Neuroradiology **60**(4), 403–412 (2018)
29. Richiardi, J., et al.: Correlated gene expression supports synchronous activity in brain networks. Science **348**(6240), 1241–1244 (2015)
30. Bakken, T.E., Miller, J.A., Luo, R., et al.: Temporal-spatial dynamics of the postnatal developing primate brain transcriptome. Hum. Mol. Genet. **24**(15), 4327–4339 (2015)
31. Golland, P., Fischl, B.: Information Processing in Medical Imaging. Taylor, C.J., Noble, J.A. (eds.), vol. 2732, pp. 330–41. Springer, Heidelberg (2003). https://doi.org/10.1007/b11820
32. Craddock, R.C., James, G.A., Holtzheimer, P.E., Hu, X.P., Mayberg, H.S.: A whole brain fMRI atlas generated via spatially constrained spectral clustering. Hum. Brain Mapp. **33**, 1914–1928 (2012)
33. Zeng, L.L., et al.: Neurobiological basis of head motion in brain imaging. PNAS **111**(16), 6058–6062 (2014)
34. Tzourio-Mazoyer, N., et al.: Automated anatomical labeling of activations in SPM using a macroscopic anatomical parcellation of the MNI MRI single-subject brain. Neuroimage **15**, 273–289 (2012)

Deep LSTM Transfer Learning for Personalized ECG Anomaly Detection on Wearable Devices

Xin Deng[1], Jianqiao Zhou[1(✉)], Bin Xiao[2], Xiaohong Xiang[1], and Yi Yuan[1]

[1] Key Laboratory of Data Engineering and Visual Computing, Chongqing University of Posts and Telecommunication, Chongqing 400065, China
[2] Chongqing Key Laboratory of Image Recognition, Chongqing University of Posts and Telecommunication, Chongqing 400065, China

Abstract. Cardiovascular diseases are the main cause of global non-communicable deaths, accounting for about one-third of the total deaths in the world. Wearable devices are used for early monitoring and early prevention of cardiovascular diseases. Aimed at the low configuration, low power consumption and personalized characteristics of the wearable ECG equipment, a transfer learned with deep LSTM model is proposed in this work. The model is computational efficient and serves as the patient-specific ECG anomaly detector that can be used on the wearable devices. Based on the MIT-BIH open dataset, the experiment results show that the transfer learning model produces superior weighted F2 scores compared to the general model and the naive model for detecting ECG anomalies, such as the premature ventricular contractions and atrial premature beats. The transfer learning model proposed here provides a sensitive, personalized ECG anomaly detection mechanism that has the added benefit of light, quick and robust learning process to be used on wearable devices, which can meet the requirement of ECG monitoring for patients by wearable devices.

Keywords: Wearable devices · ECG anomaly detection · Patient monitoring · LSTM

1 Introduction

Cardiovascular diseases (CVDs) are one of the major causes of death globally and there is an estimation that about 17.9 million people died from CVDs in 2018 alone [1]. Cardiac arrhythmias are among the most fatal CVDs, and are most easily identified by electrocardiograms. The Electrocardiograms (ECGs) are representations of electrical activity in the heart. They can be used to detect beat abnormalities and arrhythmias that can be crucial to the health and well-being of a patient. There is a challenge that the detecting of an arrhythmia or beat abnormality in someone is not currently under observation. Recently, the wearable industry has begun to correct for that challenge through the widespread development of commercially available wearable ECGs. There has been an increasing availability of consumer wearables capable of reading single-lead ECGs. One estimate for the global single-lead ECG market in 2024 is over 487 million

© Springer Nature Singapore Pte Ltd. 2021
F. Sun et al. (Eds.): ICCSIP 2020, CCIS 1397, pp. 348–357, 2021.
https://doi.org/10.1007/978-981-16-2336-3_32

USD [2]. AliveCor, a company offering commercially available, wearable ECGs, has collected over 25 million ECG samples alone [3]. As the amount of ECG data available continues to exceed the amount of professionals capable of reading ECGs, there will exist a need for an automated algorithm to screen ECGs for anomalies. This algorithm will need to be lightweight in order to be used on wearable devices with limited computing power, sensitive to changes specific for a given patient, and easily scalable in order to be commercially successful. In this paper, an adaptive transfer-learned deep LSTM model for personalized ECG anomaly detection is proposed to meet these needs.

2 Related Works

Two broad types of ECG analysis coexist in the literature. One is the detection of the anomalies in general (a sensitive test), and the other is to identify the anomalies (a specific test). By combining the two, we can arrive at a classic screening test a highly sensitive test followed by a highly specific, typically costlier one. A great deal of work has been done in the identification of specific heart arrhythmias and beat abnormalities [4–10]. Less work has been in the area of developing a test that favors detection of sensitive changes in a patient's ECG. The proposed transfer learning model focuses on modeling normal ECG behavior and detecting anomalous behavior as a real-time, sensitive screening test.

Convolutional neural networks, or convolutional/recurrent hybrid neural networks have set the gold standard for accuracy in classification models. Limam et al. [11] and Zihlmann et al. [12] have proposed hybrid CNN/RNN models for ECG classification with excellent accuracy. Notably, CNNs can take much longer to run than RNNs, require snapshots of data in time versus streaming data in real-time, and in general are used for the purpose of classification and diagnosis as opposed to generalized anomaly detection. LSTM models were found to be more accurate and sensitive than either the classic RNN or GRU cells, while GRU cells were found to be most specific [13]. Chauhan et al. demonstrated the efficacy of using a pure LSTM model for anomaly detection in ECGs [14]. They demonstrated a significant difference in prediction error on anomalies versus normal sinus data. A transfer learning, or specifically personalized, model was not addressed.

In 2019, Saadatnejad et al. described a lightweight, fast algorithm using stacked LSTMs for anomaly detection in ECGs. Their method trained a naive LSTM model from an individual patient's data and augmented it with general data from a database. However, they used 5 min of ECG training data from that individual patient. While this is per AAMI standards [15], it also would be a barrier for implementation on wearable devices with limited storage and computational power. Additionally, they didn't use a true transfer learning model instead of using all the available data for training at once. Their model doesn't allow for the iterative improvements over time and is considerably slower than the transfer learning model. Thus, a continuous transfer learning model is demonstrated here to have more rapid convergence and requires much less training data than existing methods. In addition, the proposed transfer learning model in this paper can be continually updated to improve performance.

3 Methods

3.1 Deep LSTM

Traditional recurrent neural networks suffer from a decaying error during recurrent backpropagation, which causes error signals flowing backwards in time to either "blow up" or "vanish". A modern LSTM mitigate this issue by altering the cell state C_t, removing or adding information deemed to be relevant by the "gates" – the "forget gate" f_t (Eq. (1)), "input gate" i_t (Eq. (2)), and "candidate update gate" $\tilde{C}_t$ (Eq. (3)) layers. It should be noted that the cell state C_t is persistent, allowing the network to reach back in the sequence. Just as the "forget gate" is combined with the previous cell state C_{t-1}, the "input" and "candidate update" gate's values combine with each other. After cross multiplication, both are added together to form a vector of update values for the new cell state C_t (Eq. (4)). The "output gate" O_t provides a filtered version of the cell state, where a sigmoid layer determines the important aspects of the cell state (Eq. (5)). A *tanh* layer places the cell state values between and –1 and 1, and then is multiplied by the output of the sigmoid gate (Eq. (6)). The end result from an individual cell is an output h_t of what the network deems relevant components of the input h_{t-1}, x_t. The following is an overall representation of this process (Eqs. (1–6)).

$$f_t = \sigma(W_f \cdot [h_{t-1}, \ x_t] + b_f \tag{1}$$

$$i_t = \sigma(W_i \cdot [h_{t-1}, \ x_t] + b_i \tag{2}$$

$$\tilde{C}_t = tanh(W_C \cdot [h_{t-1}, \ x_t] + b_C \tag{3}$$

$$C_t = f_t * C_{t-1} + i_t * \tilde{C}_t \tag{4}$$

$$O_t = \sigma(W_o[h_{t-1}, \ x_x] + b_o \tag{5}$$

$$h_t = O_t * tanh(C_t) \tag{6}$$

The Deep LSTM RNNs are built by stacking several LSTM layers on top of one another (Fig. 1), possibly allowing for RNNs to learn at different time scales across the input. Each LSTM layer's output is used as the adjacent LSTM layer's input, meaning that each recurrent layer may be unfolded in time to an equivalent feed forward network whose layers share the same parameters. This yields a superior temporal analysis [16].

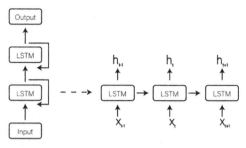

Fig. 1. A deep LSTM network (Left) and unrolled LSTM layer (Right)

3.2 Data and Pre-processing

The popular MIT-BIH Arrhythmia and MIT-BIH Normal Sinus Rhythm databases were utilized for this study [17]. The baseline wander is a low frequency component of ECG distortion caused by normal contributors of noise in ambulatory ECGs (such as respiration, body movements, or poor electrode contact) [18]. In order to fix the baseline wander, a 2 median filter technique similar to the method described in Zhang et al. was used [19]. A 200 ms width median filter removes the P wave and QRS complex, and then a 600 ms width median filter removes T waves. The fitted baseline is then subtracted from the signal, resulting in a removal of the baseline wander (Fig. 2, Raw Data - Baseline Fixed). In addition, in order to produce a robust and generalized model, it is a good practice to normalize data prior to using a neural network. A simple standard scaling method was used to normalize input data (Fig. 2 Baseline Fixed - Standardized).

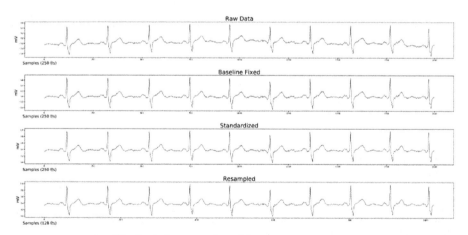

Fig. 2. A demonstration of the pre-processing steps

The commercial mobile devices tend to have different sampling rates for electrocardiograms, and even may alter their sampling rates based on battery power or memory availability. To account for this, resampling was implemented in the preprocessing algorithm. The training set was sampled at 128 samples per second, and the personalized retraining/testing sets were sampled at 360 samples per second. The testing group was down-sampled to 128 samples per second to match the training set (Fig. 2, Standardized - Resampled).

Naturally, we are equally interested in accurately detecting normal sinus rhythm in a given patient as we are in detecting anomalous behavior. The dataset was split into three parts, a normal sinus sample set (V_N) for training and parameter tuning, a validation set (V_{N+A}) for optimization of an anomaly threshold that included normal sinus and labeled anomalous samples, and a testing set (T_{N+A}). It should be noted that we seek to develop a sensitive test for abnormality, and not necessarily one with a high degree of specificity for a particular anomaly.

3.3   Model Training

A simple test was conducted to determine how well the best model could predict the normal sinus rhythm. The general model is seeded with an array of n zeros ($window = [s_1, ..., s_n]$). By predicting the next value p_{n+1} and sliding the window forward, we get this value ($window = [s_2, ..., s_n; p_{n+1}]$). Then performing this action iteratively, results from this process are demonstrated below. As expected, the model produced a normal-appearing sinus rhythm after recovering from being given just an array of zeros (Fig. 3, General Model (Synthetic Data)). This demonstrates that the base model successfully learned normal sinus rhythm from the training database.

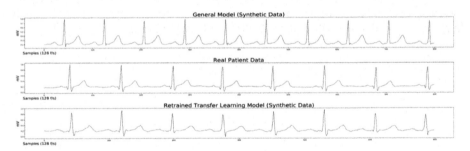

Fig. 3. A demonstration of the transfer learning model.

Employing a transfer learning method is expected to result in a rapid convergence of a personalized model. In order to retrain the incremental depth layers of the general model, we use preserved normal sinus data (~10 s of ECG data for training, ~10 s of ECG data for validation) from individual patients. The assumption is that the early layers of the general model contain important structural information regarding the p waves, QRS complexes and t waves. The last layers of the general model contain nuances in distances, orientations and widths of the waves specific to individual patients.

The discriminate learning rates are utilized for retraining. By training late layers more quickly than early layers, this helps the preserve features in the first few layers being learned early, while quickly re-train for the nuances in the patient data. This transfer learning method has been thoroughly explored in the context of convolutional neural networks and computer vision [20], and specifically discriminates the learning rates.

In an effort to visualize this process, noisy signals and outliers in the MIT-BIH database are kept and reported. This was done to demonstrate the power of the transfer learning model, and the statistically significant performance increase between populations despite poor signal. As can be seen from Fig. 3, the newly retrained and personalized patient model was seeded with an array of zeros and the results were compared to the general model.

The impact of the length of time in the ECG sample used for retraining is explored to determine a minimum threshold for a patient-specific and sensitive model. As discussed earlier, Saadatnejad et al. trained their naive models on up to five minutes of ECG data [15]. The proposed transfer learning model requires a small fraction of that training time, only about 10 s for training data and 10 s for validation data for early stopping.

3.4 Anomaly Detection

After dividing the individual patients in the dataset into normal sinus (V_n), normal sinus + anomaly validation set (V_{N+A}), and normal sinus + anomaly testing set (T_{N+A}), each model (General, Transfer-learned, and Naive) is run on each ECG segment, and an anomaly detection algorithm is implemented. Figure 4 is a demonstration of anomaly detection using single-scalar probabilities.

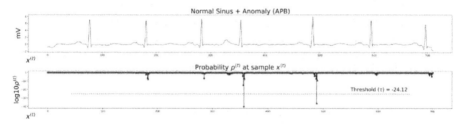

Fig. 4. A demonstration of anomaly detection using single-scalar probabilities

A modified version of time-series anomaly detection described by Malhotra et al. [21] is used to detect anomalous behavior in the ECG segments. With a prediction length of l, each of the selected d dimensions of $x(t) \in x$ for $l < t \le n - l$ is predicted l times. The error vector $e^{(t)}$ for point $x^{(t)}$ as $e^{(t)} = [e_{11}^{(t)}, ..., e_{1l}^{(t)}, ..., e_{d1}^{(t)}, ..., e_{dl}^{(t)}]$ is computed, where $e_{ij}^{(t)}$ is the difference between $x_i^{(t)}$ and its value as predicted at time $t - j$. The error vectors from their V_N were used to fit a multivariate Gaussian distribution, where $N = N(\mu_{VN}, \Sigma_{VN})$. The likelihood $\rho^{(t)}$ for observing an error vector $e^{(t)}$ is given by the value of N at $e^{(t)}$.

For the purpose of ECG detection, two key modifications are made to this error generation algorithm. First, the error vectors assume the equal value for each time point predicted at the time point $t - j$. However, as the model approaches a given point $x^{(t)}$, it can be assumed that the model has more information for a reliable prediction of $x^{(t)}$. Therefore, the weighted scalar average of the error vector $e^{(t)}$, where the closest values of the error vector are weighted 5 times as heavily as the furthest values, is calculated to be more representative than an equal value vector $e^{(t)}$ of length (l). This also means a univariate Gaussian distribution is calculated where $N = N (\mu_{VN}, \sigma_{VN})$ in place of a multivariate Gaussian distribution. Second, due to the nature of an RNN, the anomalies affect not only the time point $x^{(t)}$, but also a range of n time points after $x^{(t)}$ ($x^{(t)} \ldots x^{(t+n)}$). To help account for this, as well as mitigating the issue of outlier values, the average sliding window of the error scalar's probability is found to be particularly effective in setting a threshold.

By using this modified method, the prediction model is used to compute the error scalars $e^{(t)}$ for V_N, V_{N+A}, and T_{N+A}. The first half of the $V_{N\,errors}$ are fit to a univariate Gaussian distribution ($N = N (\mu_{VN}, \sigma_{VN})$). Using the probability density function from this distribution, a likelihood $\rho^{(t)}$ for each $e^{(t)}$ scalar in $V_{N\,errors}$ (the second half), $V_{N+A\,errors}$ and $T_{N+A\,errors}$ are generated to produce $V_{N\,probs}$, $V_{N+A\,probs}$, and $T_{N+A\,probs}$.

Using differential evolution optimization, the optimum threshold was found with each model to separate the normal sinus rhythm from the anomaly with a mixture of $V_{N\,probs}$ and $V_{N+A\,probs}$, maximizing F2 score to classify anomalous behavior where $\frac{1}{n} \sum_{t=1}^{n} \rho^{(t)} < \tau s$. This threshold τ is then used for the preserved testing set of a mixture of $V_{N\,probs}$ and $T_{N+A\,probs}$ for generation of the final metrics.

4 Results

4.1 Performance Metrics

An F-score is the weighted average of precision and recall. When the β is set to 2, it becomes an F2 score. A β of 2 indicates that recall is more heavily weighted than precision. F2 scores were determined for both the optimized validation set (F2$_{val}$) and testing set (F2$_{test}$). The scores were weighted based on the number of testing samples per patient.

$$F_\beta = (1 + \beta^2) \cdot \frac{precision \cdot recall}{(\beta^2 \cdot precision) + recall} \tag{7}$$

$$Recall = \frac{TruePositive}{TruePositive + FalseNegative} \tag{8}$$

For a sensitive anomaly detection system, a high true positive rate (TPR) to false positive rate (FPR) ratio is desirable. A weighted TPR/FPR for each model was calculated.

$$TPR = \frac{TruePositive}{TruePositive + FalseNegative} \tag{9}$$

$$FPR = \frac{FalsePositive}{FalsePositive + TrueNegative} \tag{10}$$

The threshold (τ) for given window $\frac{1}{n} \sum_{t=1}^{n} \rho^{(t)}$ is optimized on the validation set and used on the testing set. A low weighted average threshold indicates that the anomalies are considered more "anomalous" or "improbable" than the retrained model. This may be due to minimizing error scalars on normal data, maximizing error scalars on anomalous data, or some combination of the two.

4.2 Results

As shown in Tables 1 and 2, the transfer learning model (TLM) outperforms the general model with an F2 increase in detecting PVC's (weighted F2 score increased by .065, n = 20, $p = .002$) and APB's (weighted F2 score increased by 0.256, n = 8, $p = .018$). The TPR/FPR ratio was over 13 times higher in the transfer learning model than the general model (GM) for detecting APB's. The optimum threshold generated from the validation set also has a lower weighted average (−7.4 versus −4.7 for PVC detection and −21.5 versus −7.7 for APB detection).

The naive model (NM) does not outperform the general model significantly, and performs significantly worse than the transfer learning model for detecting PVC's (weighted F2 score lower by .081, n = 20, $p = .001$) and APB's (weighted F2 score lower by .252, n = 8, $p = .012$). The TPR/FPR is nearly identical to the general model, and 12 times lower than the transfer learning model for detecting APB's. The optimum threshold found for the transfer learning model is lower on average than the naive model (−7.4 versus −4.6 for PVC detection and −21.5 versus −7.2 for APB detection).

Table 1. Comparing F2 scores and other metrics for detecting PVC's between the general model, transfer learning model, and naive model.

Methods	F2$test$	F2val	TPR	FPR	TPR/FPR	Threshold
GM	0.798	0.855	0.885	0.422	2.094	−4.7
TLM	**0.863**	**0.906**	**0.921**	**0.302**	**3.053**	**−7.4**
NM	0.782	0.841	0.858	0.434	1.978	−4.6

Table 2. Comparing F2 scores and other metrics for detecting APB's between the general model, transfer learning model, and naive model

Methods	F2$test$	F2val	TPR	FPR	TPR/FPR	Threshold
GM	0.662	0.789	0.666	0.476	1.399	−7.7
TLM	**0.918**	**0.936**	**0.817**	**0.044**	**18.655**	**−21.5**
NM	0.666	0.774	0.559	0.364	1.537	−7.2

5   Conclusions

In this paper, we proposed an efficient deep LSTM mode for the personalized anomaly detection in wearable ECG. We first perform the data preprocessing, and then train the transfer learning model based on the deep LSTM network. Finally, we use this model to detect abnormal ECG beats. In contrast to a general model, the experiment results show that the combined transfer learning model is faster and more scalable, with a significant increase in performance for the detection of premature ventricular contractions and atrial premature beats. Nevertheless, there is a large amount of unlabeled ECG data in the mobile medical industry, and the existing methods cannot achieve fast unsupervised learning. In contrast to the existing methods, the proposed model helps mitigating this issue by rapidly learning in an unsupervised way. This sensitive and lightweight model for the real-time ECG anomaly detection, when compared with a specific and more computationally heavy model for classification and diagnosis, could be an effective means for outpatient ECG analysis. Overall, it shows that transfer learning has a role in personalized anomaly detection in wearable ECG technology. In the future, we will also include demonstrating efficacy for other anomalies, such as paced beats or QT prolongation.

Acknowledgments. This work was financially supported by the National Nature Science Foundation of China (No. 61806033, 61703065), the National Natural Science Foundation of Chongqing(cstc2020jcyj-msxm1555), the Scientific and Technological Research Program of Chongqing Municipal Education Commission (No. KJ202000646472197), the Key Industry Core Technology Innovation Project of CQ (cstc2017zdcy-zdyfX0012).

References

1. Sinha, A., Gopinathan, P., Chung, Y.D.: An aptamer based sandwich assay for simultaneous detection of multiple cardiovascular biomarkers on a multilayered integrated microfluidic system. In: IEEE 20th International Conference on Solid-State, pp. 1075–1077 (2019)
2. Research and Markets Authors: Single lead ECG equipment market size, share trends analysis report by end use (hospitals clinics, homecare, ascs), by indication (arrhythmia, syncope) (2019). https://www.researchandmarkets.com/reports/4751811/single-lead-ecg-equipment-market-size-share-and. Accessed 28 Apr 2019
3. Han, X., Hu, Y., Foschini, L.: Deep learning models for electrocardiograms are susceptible to adversarial attack. Nat. Med. **26**(3), 360–363 (2020)
4. Acharya, U.R., Fujita, H., Lih, O.S., Hagiwara, Y., Tan, J.H., Adam, M.: Automated detection of arrhythmias using different intervals of tachycardia ECG segments with convolutional neural network. Inf. Sci. **405**, 81–90 (2017)
5. Oh, S.L., Ng, E.Y., San Tan, R.: Automated diagnosis of arrhythmia using combination of CNN and LSTM techniques with variable length heart beats. Comput. Biol. Med. **102**, 278–287 (2018)
6. Warrick, P., Homsi, M.N.: Cardiac arrhythmia detection from ECG combining convolutional and long short-term memory networks. In: IEEE Computing in Cardiology (CinC), pp. 202–206 (2017)
7. Hannun, A.Y., Rajpurkar, P., Haghpanahi, M.: Cardiologist-level arrhythmia detection and classification in ambulatory electrocardiograms using a deep neural network. Nat. Med. **25**(1), 65 (2019)
8. Kiranyaz, S., Ince, T., Gabbouj, M.: Real-time patient-specific ECG classification by 1-D convolutional neural networks. IEEE Trans. Biomed. Eng. **63**(3), 664–675 (2015)
9. Kachuee, M., Fazeli, S., Sarrafzadeh, M.: ECG heartbeat classification: a deep transferable representation. In: IEEE International Conference on Healthcare Informatics (ICHI), pp. 443–444 (2018)
10. Jun, T.J., Nguyen, H.M., Kang, D.: ECG arrhythmia classification using a 2-D convolutional neural network. arXiv preprint arXiv:1804.06812 (2018)

11. Limam, M., Precioso, F.: Atrial fibrillation detection and ECG classification based on convolutional recurrent neural network. In: IEEE Computing in Cardiology (CinC), pp. 1–4 (2017)
12. Zihlmann, M., Perekrestenko, D., Tschannen, M.: Convolutional recurrent neural networks for electrocardiogram classification. In: IEEE Computing in Cardiology (CinC), pp. 12–16 (2017)
13. Singh, S., Pandey, S.K., Pawar, U., et al.: Classification of ECG arrhythmia using recurrent neural networks. Procedia Comput. Sci. **132**, 1290–1297 (2018)
14. Chauhan, S., Vig, L.: Anomaly detection in ECG time signals via deep long short-term memory networks. In: IEEE International Conference on Data Science and Advanced Analytics (DSAA), pp. 1–7 (2015)
15. Saadatnejad, S., Oveisi, M., Hashemi, M.: LSTM-based ECG classification for continuous monitoring on personal wearable devices. IEEE J. Biomed. Health Inf. **24**(2), 515–523 (2019)
16. Keogh, K., Lin, J., Fu, A.: Hot sax: efficiently finding the most unusual time series subsequence. In: Fifth IEEE International Conference on Data Mining (ICDM 2005), pp. 8–10 (2005)
17. Moody, G.B., Mark, R.G.: The impact of the MIT-BIH arrhythmia database. IEEE Eng. Med. Biol. Mag. **20**(3), 45–50 (2001)
18. Joshi, S.L., Vatti, R.A., Tornekar, R.V.: A survey on ECG signal denoising techniques. In: IEEE 2013 International Conference on Communication Systems and Network Technologies, pp. 60–64 (2013)
19. Zhang, C., Wang, G., Zhao, J.: Patient-specific ECG classification based on recurrent neural networks and clustering technique. In: IEEE 13th IASTED International Conference on Biomedical Engineering (BioMed), pp. 63–67 (2017)
20. Yosinski, J., Clune, J., Bengio, Y., et al.: How transferable are features in deep neural networks? Adv. Neural Inf. Process. Syst. **8**(6), 3320–3328 (2014)
21. Malhotra, P., Vig, L., Shroff, G., et al.: Long short term memory networks for anomaly detection in time series. In: Proceedings, vol. 89, pp. 89–94. Presses universitaires de Louvain, Belgium (2015)

Reflection on AI: The Cognitive Difference Between Libraries and Scientists

Xiaohui Zou[1,2,3](✉) ⓘ, Xueqiu Wu[3], Baoping Zhang[4], Qiang Yang[5], and Jian Li[5]

[1] Sino-American Searle Research Center, UC Berkeley, Berkeley, USA
[2] Zhuhai Hengqin Macau Youth Entrepreneur Valley 21C Zhuhai Fudan Innovation Research Institute Room 106 IoT Smart City Innovation Platform, Room D623, Building 13, Macau Youth Entrepreneur Valley Talent Apartment, Hengqin, Zhuhai 519000, China
[3] Shuangyashan Radio and Television University, Shuangyashan, Heilongjiang, China
[4] Shenzhen Zhongzhi Autolink Pansystems IoT Research Institute, Shenzhen, Guangdong, China
[5] Sichuan Technology and Business College, Chengdu, China

Abstract. The aim is to make appropriate reflections on artificial intelligence AI through the differences in cognitive systems between intelligent digital libraries and well-trained experts, especially scientists. The method is: first, compare the difference and connection between data structure and knowledge reserve, then compare the difference and connection between query, retrieval or search algorithm path, finally, compare the difference and connection between cognitive computing and cognitive ability. Its characteristics are: data query or search algorithm and logical reasoning or cognitive computing, knowledge graph and cognitive graph are all conducive to the construction of intelligent digital library. The result is: it is found that whether it is based on rules or statistics or a combination of the two cognitive systems, there are limitations in cognitive computing and cognitive ability or intelligence. Its significance lies in: from this we can at least reflect on the theoretical limits of AI and some worthy questions, such as the calculability problem and Turing test problem and the Chinese Room Argument of the intelligent digital library. The problem of isomorphism with the information processing mode of the intelligent digital computer, and why can't the intelligent digital library become a well-trained expert or even a scientist, and so on are worthy of the philosophy of logic and mind with Cognitive Science.

Keywords: Cognitive system · Cognitive computing · Information processing

1 Introduction

The aim is to make appropriate reflections on artificial intelligence AI through the differences in cognitive systems between intelligent digital libraries and well-trained experts, especially scientists. In short, the digital library is a digital information resource with multiple media content, which can provide users especially scientists with convenient, fast and high-level information service mechanism.

© Springer Nature Singapore Pte Ltd. 2021
F. Sun et al. (Eds.): ICCSIP 2020, CCIS 1397, pp. 358–369, 2021.
https://doi.org/10.1007/978-981-16-2336-3_33

It can be seen from Fig. 1 that the digital library is not only a brand-new technology, but also a brand-new social undertaking; it is not only a digital information resource, but also a kind of information service mechanism. It will be discussed the hubs of digital libraries and interdisciplinary knowledge centers, including: intelligent text analysis and finishing knowledge modules, which are characterized by several aspects of language, information, knowledge, intelligence and data in the human-computer collaborative processing environment. The generalized translation can be understood as the product or process for the combination of philosophical knowledge fusion theory and cultural genetic system engineering (intelligence or smart) practice.

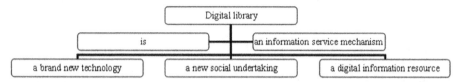

Fig. 1. A mind map for the definition or interpretation of the digital library

2 The Main Text

2.1 Reviews

The Digital Library is a library that uses especially scientists use digital technology to process and store a variety of graphic and textual documents. It is essentially a distributed cognitive system for multimedia production. It stores various information resources of different carriers and geographical locations in digital technology to facilitate cross-regional, object-oriented network query and dissemination. It involves the processing, storing, retrieving, transmitting and utilizing information resources. In layman's terms, the digital library is a virtual, unenclosed library. It is a scalable knowledge network system built and shared based on the network environment. It is ultra-large-scale, distributed, easy to use, and has no time and space restrictions as a knowledge center that enables seamless linking and retrieval across libraries.

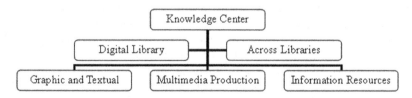

Fig. 2. Mind map from digital library development to knowledge center

It can be seen from Fig. 2 that the knowledge center is the target of development of the digital library further. From the mind map shown in Fig. 2, you can see the leopard, that is, see it. The digital libraries development is not limited to the library disciplines development, but also faces major challenges in the development of the internet and mobile networks, especially data centers and even knowledge centers. From the technical point of view, the development of information processing, AI artificial intelligence and big data technology provides a strong technical support for our research; the theoretical discussion of language, information, knowledge, intelligence and data is beneficial to our research in-depth development also more from the scientific level; from the application level, focusing on generalized text analysis and generalized translation reuse provides a more targeted implementation of our research for method of finding problems by reviewing the digital library [1–11].

2.2 The Method

The method is: first, compare the difference and connection between data structure and knowledge reserve, then compare the difference and connection between query, retrieval or search algorithm path, finally, compare the difference and connection between cognitive computing and cognitive ability. Its characteristics are: data query or search algorithm and logical reasoning or cognitive computing, knowledge graph and cognitive graph are all conducive to the construction of intelligent digital library. Through the review of the digital library and data center and its information processing, artificial intelligence and big data, explore the characteristics of the dual formal approach. The problem of digital libraries: Due to the lack of unified planning and coordination, digital library standards are different, relevant legislation has not been formulated and implemented, and the interests of various units are difficult to find a balance point that they all agree with each other. At the same time, some units hold with the idea of "quickness and quick success" and one-sided pursuit of the amount of digital resources, some units ignore the characteristics of their collections and the actual situation of school teaching, which has caused many universities in China to blindly build digital libraries, with less cooperation. The phenomenon of individual politics is not uncommon. The user search interface, search language and management system of each digital library are quite different. The databases of different libraries are incompatible, and it is difficult for each system to communicate and apply with each other. A large amount of financial and human resources are available. Material resources are wasted at a low level of redundant construction. Based on the above phenomena, this paper puts forward the substantive issues: man-machine cooperation in the era of globalization necessarily requires the establishment of a linkage mechanism between law and standards. The issue of "law and standards" has been put on our agenda here. Dual formalization came into being: On the one hand, the standardized form of technology is that computers are easy to calculate, count and compare; on the other hand, the individualized form of art is easy to use, judge and make decisions. This is the focus of strong AI and weak artificial intelligence: how to divide and cooperate between the human brain and the computer. The general development trend of information processing, artificial intelligence and big data technologies and the milestones behind the programming language play a role in helping us find out why the double-chessboard of human-computer dual-brain collaboration is compatible with two formal strategies. The scientific principle on which it is based (the three basic laws of information).

Fig. 3. Trends in intelligence processing, information processing, AI, and big data

As can be seen from Fig. 3, intelligence processing and information processing are almost always intertwined before 2016. From 2016 to 2019, the trend of intelligence processing is falling, and the trends of the three technologies of information processing, artificial intelligence (AI) and big data are gradually convergence. The reasons for this are interesting.

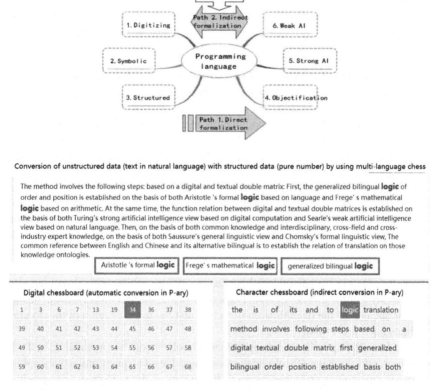

Fig. 4. Seven milestones and a double-chessboard that reflects the second path

From Fig. 4, it can be seen that several milestones in the programming language and two chess boards compatible with human-computer dual-brain collaboration are two major formal strategies. Among them, the formation of the first path has gone through four stages of development, and currently encounters great difficulties in the fifth stage of development, while in the sixth stage of development it is found that the second path can be combined with the first stage to form a unique highlight. The seven stages, a new strategy combining the dual path of human intelligence (HI) and artificial intelligence (AI) can be called: "the third type of formal strategy" combined with the two major type of formal strategy.

Both digital books and knowledge graphs or mind maps all will demonstrate a new paradigm (high efficiency) of rational division of labor and high collaboration between humans and machines in the process of this new dual formalization strategy. The problems of standards and law will also be gradually resolved in it. Imagine: the language (and thus the generalized broad text) in every paragraph, every article, each book (or journal) is just that people make it on a certain group, some even the only double chessboard. A series of choices (the selected object and the record of the selection activity itself belong to big data, the selection process is the information processing process, why and how to choose, etc. requires God's wisdom, human brain intelligence or artificial intelligence), it will be what is the situation? The information carried by all books and their processing methods will undergo tremendous changes. Data center hardware will also be redefined by Knowledge Center software.

Method of Analyzing Problems by Reviewing Generalized Translation

Through the reviewing the generalized translation techniques of language, information, knowledge and intelligence and data in the context of human-computer collaborative processing, exploring the specific application characteristics of formal understanding models.

First, analyze the core problem of natural language understanding: the ambiguity of any language text (the meaning of the words and the choice of the author's intention). Natural language processing techniques in Computer Science can be broken down into five areas: classification, matching, translation, prediction and decision making. Not to mention the technical details of each direction, involving a variety of issues that require user choice, just focusing only on the most fundamental issue of the classification of digital books. We know that the internal structure of any discipline (discipline construction) is a matter of great concern to all departments of the university. Linguistics, informatics, psychology, education, artificial intelligence, etc. all have philosophical problems, and there are many technical details, and the task of scientific discussion is arduous (the most important one is how the discipline construction and the research team of the dominant disciplines form problems).

Then, from the early literature (grammar school), medicine (medical school), law (law school) and theology (theological school) and its subsequent philosophy (philosophy) basic curriculum knowledge system framework in the university, then gradually formed the humanities art, the natural sciences and engineering technology, the social sciences and psychology, the logic and mathematics and the philosophy, the basic framework of the human knowledge system and the basic structure of its methods have been initially established. Such a macroscopic model and a later microscopic model can be linked by three basic types of attribute coordinates. This can form a series of judgment basis for the classification of digital book content.

Further, it can be seen from Fig. 5 that the macroscopic model of the five stages of cognitive development (left side) can show the three-dimensional range covered by human thinking through the three-dimensional coordinates, that is, the mesoscopic model (middle) of the three types of thinking attribute coordinates, straight through the microscopic formal understanding model (right side). The combination of the three, expresses the bit-list structure of macro-micro-through and the logic and mathematics and the scientific principles of translation: First, the true-basic information embodied by the bit-list structure has the unique conservation property in the system; The direct or indirect type of data refers to the ontology information that satisfies the synonymous parallel conversion rule; thirdly, the phenomenon information can be mutually in the human brain and the computer under the constraint of agreeing to be juxtaposed passing follows the corresponding conversion rules. They are the three basic rules that must be followed in the construction of virtual super digital libraries. Because any data can be automatically processed according to the three basic laws and can be reused in a targeted manner. It should be the critical point D (L, T, W) of the world physics P (W) and the meaning of thought M (T) and the grammar of language G (L) at the critical point D (L, T, W) Tao function Tao (G, M, P) changes can be played in the two aspects of the human brain and computer formalization strategy, that is, three types of formal understanding models can play an important role.

Therefore, in knowledge ocean, conditional can be done, with the aid of the knowledge navigation device, the task of finding a needle in a haystack. With the digital library, the task of finding a needle in a haystack in the sea of knowledge is the goal we set for the unified digital library of human beings. This is the key to the question of whether the law and standards can be satisfactorily resolved.

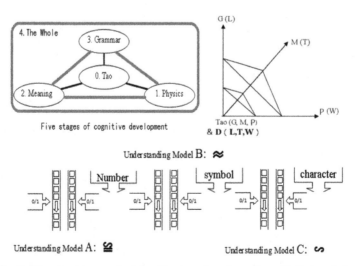

Fig. 5. The structure or principle of logic and mathematics with its translation

Finally, the author found that formal understanding models (theories) and intelligent generalized translations (practices) are complementary.

Way of Solving the Problem by Using the Two Technologies
Through the review of the two technologies of intelligent text analysis and knowledge module finishing of interdisciplinary knowledge centers, combined with the previous review and exploration, further explores the hub of digital libraries and interdisciplinary knowledge centers. Intelligent text analysis (formal information processing) and knowledge module finishing (content information processing) are two basic ways for human-computer bi-brain-integrated information processing (building a digital library and better reusing it). How to further extract the knowledge modules of various disciplines (at least: Complete "seven times through" with "understanding - operation - skilled - smart - applied or practiced") from the big data (generalized text: language, knowledge and software) stored in the data center (hardware) rather than just digital books and knowledge maps or graphs? This is a challenging issue. The knowledge center we are talking about is based on the large-scale production of knowledge modules in interdisciplinary and multidisciplinary. It is characterized by its clear processing specifications to follow. Therefore, the processing of knowledge modules based on disciplines is the key to this study.

Table 1. The big production of knowledge module processing

知识中心 Knowledge Center						
知识模块加工(七遍通) Knowledge Module Processing (Seven steps passes)						
整体把握 Overall	宏观掌控 Macro Control			微观操作 Micro Operation		
原材料 Material	粗加工 Rough Processing			精加工 Finishing Processing		
图书 Book	简纲 Outline	主线 Main line	大块 Big Block	概念 Concept	例题 Example	重点 Key Point
图谱 Graph	详纲 Detailed	辅线 Guide	小块 Small Block	原理 Principle	习题 Exercise	盲点 Blind Spot
				方法 Method	试题 Test Question	难点 Difficulty

It can be seen from Table 1 how to use the intelligence ability from human brain and computer, combined with the knowledge module processing (seven steps passes) as generalized translation, to create a knowledge navigation instrument? Among them, the basic norms that must be followed in the processing of knowledge modules are the laws and standards that must be followed in the big production of knowledge.

2.3 Experiments

Experiment 1: Digital Library

The intelligent text analysis and knowledge module finishing for the definition or interpretation of the digital library is carried out through the following steps: first, importing the text on definition or interpretation of the digital library; and, in turn, the repeated word form in the unstructured text is de-duplicated by not representing, generating a digital chessboard with a unique number and a text chessboard that records non-repeating words forms, the digital chessboard is purely structured, and the textual chessboard is semi-structured; finally, finds the basic knowledge points and implements software modeling from the unstructured text "Digital Library Definition", where it draws its structured mind map or knowledge graph, by using the person and machine interaction system. The definition or interpretation of other concepts, principles, and methods can also be used the way to perform intelligent text analysis and knowledge module finishing.

Four typical rendering styles for unstructured, semi-structured, pure structured and structured text are seen in Fig. 6. From this reader can imagine: a variety of large and small double-character chessboards, language and speech both for human brain and computer are best adapted to show the way. It is characterized by that the law of mutual transformation between unstructured, semi-structured and pure structured and structured texts should be highlighted with. They are the unique conservation characteristics of the true-basic information contained in the bit-list structure, the highlighting of the direct and indirect linkage function between various hexadecimal numbers (synonymous juxtaposition), and the conventions followed by the generalized translation (consent juxtaposition). There are the three basics laws.

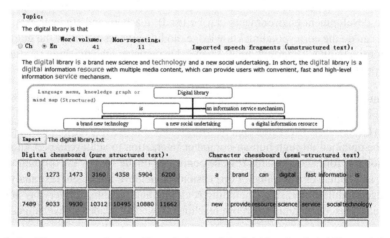

Fig. 6. Intelligent text analysis and knowledge module finishing for digital library definition

Experiment 2: How to process the knowledge module processing of the classic texts of the pre-Qin philosophers at the hub of the digital library and the interdisciplinary knowledge center?

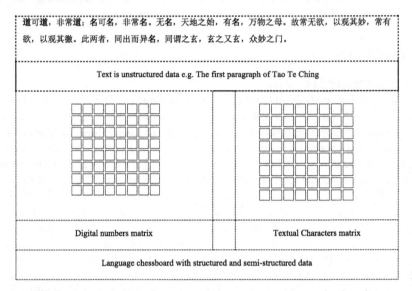

道可道，非常道；名可名，非常名。无名，天地之始，有名，万物之母。故常无欲，以观其妙，常有欲，以观其徼。此两者，同出而异名，同谓之玄，玄之又玄，众妙之门。

Text is unstructured data e.g. The first paragraph of Tao Te Ching

Digital numbers matrix   Textual Characters matrix

Language chessboard with structured and semi-structured data

Fig. 7. A section of Laozi presents a human-computer interaction interface

It can be seen from Fig. 7 that each of the natural sections of Laozi's Tao Te Ching presents a human-computer interaction interface that can be reused by the user one by one. It is characterized in that the combination of a digital chessboard and a Chinese chessboard constitutes a system for sequencing and locating each symbol of a language text. Any user's choice can be automatically recorded: not only is the data acquisition method very straightforward, but the knowledge module processing and its results can also be fully documented. It is relatively easy for teachers and students to be able to make similar chessboard software under the guidance of the author (different programming language development environments can be used); teachers and students who do not program can do the corresponding knowledge module processing under the guidance of the author (including: The roughing of knowledge menu and the finishing of mind map) are also popular.

Experiment 3: How to reflect the processing of knowledge modules on original texts in the digital library and the interdisciplinary knowledge center?

It can be seen from Fig. 8 that anyone's original words (text) in the process of processing can be obtained through human-computer interaction to achieve expert knowledge acquisition and formal expression (can be confirmed on the spot by the originator). That is to say, any course or discipline or discussion can achieve intelligent text analysis and knowledge module processing (including roughing and finishing). Everyday activities such as daily discourse and classroom teaching as well as academic exchanges can be

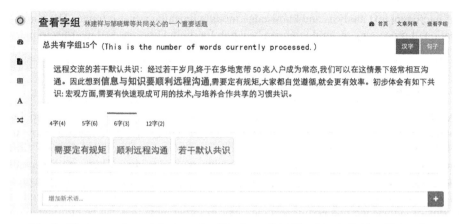

Fig. 8. The processing original words of Professor Lin Jianxiang in Peking University

carried out in such a way (the process is repeatable and the results are easy to verify and reuse).

As we all know, in the era of network information, not only the explosion of data, but also the explosion of knowledge, its cost is huge on obtaining accurate information and knowledge that is really needed. Therefore, the quality of life, the efficiency and quality of learning or work (including teaching and research) are all serious impact. The most important key minority or even unique information or knowledge cannot be obtained in time. Not to mention the integration of knowledge and the continuous construction of cultural genetic systems engineering.

All that must be addressed for smart interdisciplinary knowledge centers (it is difficult to solve the above problems in digital libraries or knowledge bases or data centers where different standards belong), so we have chosen from a few peers (many times only quasi-peers and even laymen) commented on the multi-pronged approach of teaching evaluation and research evaluation.

Furthermore, from the three levels of calculation, statistics and similarity, we should consider the auxiliary role of computer batch processing that can be used to make up for the lack of human-computer interaction, and at the same time to make up for the lack of interpersonal communication.

3   Conclusion

3.1   Result

The result is: it is found that whether it is based on rules or statistics or a combination of the two cognitive systems, there are limitations in cognitive computing and cognitive ability or intelligence. The result is that not only the interpersonal and human-machinery of generalized translation, but also the new requirements of formal technology in many aspects of the inter-machinery are found. Moreover, the two human-machine synergies of intelligent text analysis and knowledge module finishing are also found. The combination of processing technologies can be a hub for digital libraries and interdisciplinary knowledge centers.

3.2 Discussion

Although the electronic version as picture or pdf to the digital version as word for books, journals, or magazines have enriched the inventory of digital libraries, how to efficiently obtain the expert knowledge and public experience recorded therein? Still need to dig, extract, acquire and even redevelop multiple times. These are the small production methods that have been going on for a long time and have to be done again. Therefore, the era calls for the large production methods can be quickly promoted in terms of knowledge processing accuracy. For example, how that can be eliminated on the ambiguity of authors with the same name? How that can be fully automatically determined on the interpretations or texts belong to the same term or topic and its set of specific constraints? How that can be optimized on the various explanations of the same concepts, principles, methods and their typical examples (how to choose one from two or more that is there any best)?

3.3 Conclusion

Its significance lies in: from this we can at least reflect on the theoretical limits of AI and some worthy questions, such as the calculability problem and Turing test problem and the Chinese Room Argument of the intelligent digital library.

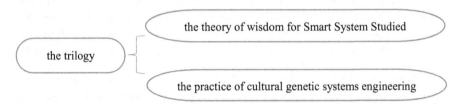

Fig. 9. The theory of wisdom and the practice of cultural genetic systems engineering

The social system engineering of education, management, learning and application highlighted. At the same time, the formal system engineering of language, knowledge, software and hardware has also been highlighted. Moreover, it is a pivotal role, value and significance for the hub of digital libraries and interdisciplinary knowledge centers with the combination of the two engineering systems. It can be seen from Fig. 9 that the basic content of understanding the world (knowledge) and transforming the world (action) are: the trilogy of theory, engineering and application; the trilogy of intelligence, formalization and socialization. It is characterized in that the philosophical theory and the practice of cultural genetic system engineering are mutually exclusive. The former is a philosophical theory based on philosophy and science; the latter is a cultural gene system engineering practice based on art and technology. The big data involved can be incorporated into the new generation of digital libraries and the hub of the interdisciplinary or multidisciplinary knowledge center. The Twin Turing Machine is the memory or storage system of collaborative intelligent computing systems with formal understanding capabilities. And that can be reused at any time and any place. The system memorizes or stores the wisdom module of the result of the theory of wisdom and the practice of cultural genetic system engineering, and can repeatedly use every specific detail on intelligent text analysis (precision rate and recall rate all are first class). The problem of isomorphism with the information processing mode of the intelligent digital computer, and why can't the intelligent digital library become a well-trained expert or even a scientist, and so on are worthy of the philosophy of logic and mind with Cognitive Science. The hub of digital libraries and interdisciplinary knowledge centers is based on the philosophical theory and cultural genetic systems engineering practice. The following figure is a schematic diagram on the relationship between the theory and the practice.

References

1. Chomsky, N.: Three models for the description of language. IRE Trans. Inf. Theory **2**(3), 113–124 (1956)
2. Gruber, T.R.: A translation approach to portable ontology specifications. Knowl. Acquis. **5**(2), 199–220 (1993)
3. Saracevic, T.: Digital library evaluation: toward an evolution of concepts. Libr. Trends **49**(2), 350–369 (2000)
4. Witten, I.H., Bainbridge, D.: How to Build a Digital Library. Elsevier Science Inc., Amsterdam (2003)
5. Sliger Krause, R., Langhurst Eickholt, A., Otto, J.L.: Creative collaboration: student creative works in the institutional repository. Digit. Libr. Perspect. **34**, 20–31 (2017)
6. Mary, W., Kostelecky, S.R.: Respecting the language: digitizing Native American language materials. Digit. Libr. Perspect. **34**, 200–214 (2018). https://doi.org/10.1108/DLP-02-2018-0006
7. Weig, E.C., Slone, M.: SPOKEdb: open-source information management system for oral history. Digit. Libr. Perspect. **34**(2), 101–116 (2018)
8. Hahn, J., Mcdonald, C.: Account-based recommenders in open discovery environments. Digit. Libr. Perspect. **34**(1), 70–76 (2018)
9. Fox, R.: Information economy. Digit. Libr. Perspect. **34**(1), 78–83 (2018)
10. Newman, J., Bonefas, S., Trenthem, W.: Creating capacity for digital projects. Digit. Libr. Perspect. **34**, 9–19 (2017). https://doi.org/10.1108/DLP-08-2017-0026
11. Zou, X., Zou, S., Wang, X.: The strategy of constructing an interdisciplinary knowledge center. In: Liu, Y., Wang, L., Zhao, L., Yu, Z. (eds.) ICNC-FSKD 2019. AISC, vol. 1075, pp. 1024–1036. Springer, Cham (2020). https://doi.org/10.1007/978-3-030-32591-6_112
12. Zou, S., Zou, X.: Understanding: how to resolve ambiguity. In: Shi, Z., Goertzel, B., Feng, J. (eds.) ICIS 2017. IAICT, vol. 510, pp. 333–343. Springer, Cham (2017). https://doi.org/10.1007/978-3-319-68121-4_36
13. Zou, S., Zou, X., Wang, X.: How to do knowledge module finishing. In: Shi, Z., Pennartz, C., Huang, T. (eds.) ICIS 2018. IAICT, vol. 539, pp. 134–145. Springer, Cham (2018). https://doi.org/10.1007/978-3-030-01313-4_14

A Review of Research on Brain-Computer Interface Based on Imagined Speech

Chengyin Wang[1], Wenlong Ding[1], Jianhua Shan[1], and Bin Fang[2(✉)]

[1] Anhui University of Technology, Maanshan 243032, Anhui, China
[2] Tsinghua University, Beijing 100085, China
fangbin@tsinghua.edu.cn

Abstract. Brain-computer interface is currently a rapidly developing technology. In recent years, it has received extensive attention and high expectations in the fields of biomedical engineering and rehabilitation medicine engineering. Brain-computer interfaces can enable patients with communication skills or physical disabilities to communicate with machines and equipment, and brain-computer interfaces based on imagined speech can provide patients with normal and effective language communication. At present, its related research has achieved certain results. This article introduces the principles, advantages and disadvantages of several common BCI systems, as well as the two most widely used brain signals EEG and EcoG, and then studies some related feature extraction and data classification algorithms used in current research. Finally, the current problems and future development trends of brain-computer interfaces based on imagined speech are discussed.

Keywords: BCI · Imagined speech · EEG · EcoG

1 Introduction

The brain-computer interface (BCI, hereinafter referred to as BCI) is a direct connection channel created between the human or animal brain and external equipment. The BCI is divided into one-way BCI and two-way BCI; one-way BCI technology means that the computer only accepts information from the brain or transmits information to the brain. The two-way BCI allows two-way information exchange between the brain and external devices. The emergence of BCI has provided great convenience to patients with speech and physical impairments. Nowadays, patients can realize cursor movement through the BCI system, control wheelchairs, letter input and prosthetic movements [1–3].

BCI system includes BCI system based on External Stimulation (Visual P300, SSVEP) and Motor Imagery (SMR, IBK) system. First, the P300 component refers to the positive waveform generated by the EEG signal about 220 to 500 ms after the target stimulus occurs in a stimulation sequence with a small proportion of target stimuli [4]. The P300 paradigm includes auditory P300 and visual P300. At present, the

This work was supported by National Natural Science Foundation of China with Grant No. 91848206 and Natural Science Foundation of university in Anhui Province (No. KJ2019A0086).

visual P300 paradigm is more widely used [5, 6]. The advantage of P300-BCI is that it is non-invasive, requires less training times, provides communication and control functions, and is a stable and reliable BCI system. So, P300-BCI is the most suitable BCI system for severely disabled patients to independently use in the home environment for a long time. Second, the Steady State Visual Evoked Potential (SSVEP) is another popular visual component used in BCI, SSVEP is also called an optical drive because the generator of this response is located in the visual cortex. The subject must look away and pay attention to the flickering stimulus, not the movement execution or imaginary movement, which requires highly precise eye control, common stimulus sources include flash, light-emitting diodes and a checkerboard pattern of displays. The advantage of SSVEP-BCI is that it has high information transmission rate and many output commands. The subjects only need relatively little training to use it. The disadvantage is that it needs to rely on a stimulus source. However, long-term use of flicker (mainly low frequency) stimulation may cause subject fatigue [7–10]. Then, the SMR paradigm is the most widely used Imagined Motor paradigms. Imagined Motor refers to the imagination of the kinesthetic movement of larger parts of the body such as the hands, feet, and tongue, which can lead to the regulation of brain activity. Specifically, it is the electrophysiological phenomenon of Event-related Desynchronization (ERD/Event-related Synchronization, ERS) to control the device [11]. Finally, Imaginary Body kinematics (IBK) is a motor imagery paradigm derived from invasive BCI techniques [12, 13]. However, non-invasive research pointed out that this mode of information is extracted from low-frequency SMR signals (less than 2 Hz) [14]. Although IBK belongs to SMR, it is classified into a separate category due to its different training and analysis methods from the SMR paradigm. The biggest advantage of MI-BCI is that the BCI control signal generated by the brain action intention is an endogenously induced EEG, so it does not require external stimulation; but it requires multiple training, and the classification accuracy rate is not high, and individual differences cannot be resolved. Imagined speech is similar to motor imagery, and we often use it in our lives, such as silently reading magazines, books, the process of thinking about something in the brain, and recalling conversations with others. The BCI system based on imagined speech extracts the brain signals of the subjects when they imagine pronunciation, and then through a series of data processing, it is finally converted into speech. In order to remove noise, the subjects will be asked not to make a sound when imagining the pronunciation and try not to change their expressions. The BCI system based on imagined speech and the BCI system based on motor imagination are similar in that they both extract the brain signals of the participant during the imagination and convert them into desired actions, such as body movements or voice output, and neither need external stimuli. The BCI system based on P300 and SSVEP requires external stimuli, such as light flicker. The BCI system based on imagined speech also has great prospects in application. It can help patients with language barriers, muscle atrophy, locked-in syndrome and other diseases to communicate and communicate effectively with the outside world. Input letters, cursor selection, etc. are more efficient and more convenient. However, compared with other BCI systems, the technology of the BCI system based on imagined speech is not mature enough, and there are still shortcomings in hardware and brain signal decoding, but the BCI system based on imagined speech has great potential and research significance. It is worth our continued in-depth study.

2 Brain Sensor

The common methods of brain-computer connection can be divided into two types: invasive and non-invasive. Non-invasive methods do not require surgery, mainly including electroencephalography (EEG), magnetoencephalography (MEG), functional magnetic resonance imaging (fMRI), near infrared spectroscopy (NIRS), etc. In addition, it also includes many invasive methods, which may cause certain harm to the human body, including neuron firing signals (spikes), laminar potentials (electrocortex, ECoG), etc. Most brain-computer interfaces have selected EEG signals as the input, which has become the most important part of the brain-computer interface.

2.1 EEG Device

Electroencephalography (EEG) is a widely used non-invasive method for monitoring the brain. It is based on the function of placing conductive electrodes on the scalp, which can measure small electric potentials generated outside the head due to the action of neurons in the brain. The original EEG acquisition device was: a user wore a cap with holes and placed several electrodes next to the scalp. Each electrode had a long wire connected to the recording instrument, the wires are tangled together, which is troublesome to install, and the movement of the unshielded EEG wire will have a great impact on the quality of the collected signal. At present, EEG collection equipment is very advanced, Ahn JW [30] has developed a new wearable device that can measure both electrocardiogram (ECG) and EEG at the same time to realize continuous pressure monitoring in daily life, the developed system is easy to hang on two ears, is light in weight (ie 42.5 g), and has excellent noise performance of 0.12 μVrms. [31] studied a wearable in-ear EEG for emotion monitoring. The device is a low-cost, single-channel, dry contact, in-ear EEG, suitable for non-invasive monitoring, based on the valence and arousal Emotion model, the device can classify basic emotions with 71.07% accuracy, 72.89% accuracy (awakening) and 53.72% (all four emotions). [32] studied the hat-shaped EEG device EEG-Hat with candle-shaped dry microneedle electrodes. The current wearable EEG device has two main problems: 1) it is not adaptable to each participant, 2) in EEG cannot be measured on the hair area. The device can adjust the electrodes according to the size of the subject's head and can be used by multiple people. The device has a louver-like structure to separate hair. After experiments, it was found that the EEG cap successfully measured the EEG of 3 hair parts without manual separation. Currently, the most widely used commercial products are: mBrainTrain Smarting, Brain Products LiveAmp, g.tec g.Nautilus, Cognionics Mobile-128, Emotiv Epoc Flex.

2.2 EcoG Device

Cortical ECoG is used clinically for the detection of epileptic foci, ECoG electrodes are very common and mature clinically, and neurosurgeons need to perform craniotomy or craniotomy to insert them. The electrode disk is inlaid on a silicon rubber sheet, during the operation, the doctor covers the silicon rubber sheet on the patient's cerebral cortex and subdura, which can collect cortical EEG signals. Generally, the clinical detection of epileptic foci ranges from 1–2 weeks, experiments on mice and monkeys have proved that the signals collected by EcoG can remain stable for up to 5 months. [34] designed a novel spiral electric cortex (ECoG) electrode, which consists of three parts: recording electrode, insulator and nut, compared with electroencephalogram (EEG), it has a higher SNR and a wider frequency band, with higher sensitivity, and can capture different responses to various stimuli. [33] et al. studied a flexible EcoG electrode for studying spatiotemporal epilepsy morphological activity and multimodal neural encoding/decoding. The flexible electrode has very little damage to patients and is of great significance for clinical treatment and research. [35] studied a novel flexible and bioabsorbable ECoG device integrated with an intracortical pressure sensor to monitor cortical swelling during operation. The flat and flexible ECoG electrode can minimize the risk of infection and severe inflammation. Its good shape adaptability enables the device to adapt to complex cortical shapes and structures to record brain signals with high spatiotemporal resolution.

3   Research Status

In the experiment of [16], some native speakers were asked to tell a story, and the subjects were asked to listen to the story carefully. After the story was told, the subjects were asked some related questions to ensure that the subjects listened carefully. The classification accuracy of Chinese phoneme clusters according to the pronunciation position and pronunciation mode was tested by using the small Wave sign and support vector machine classifier, with the accuracy of about 60%. In the experiment of [25], RNN and DBN were used to classify and recognize five vowels respectively, and it was found that DBN had a better effect, 8% higher than RNN. In the experiment [19], subjects were asked not to perform any movements or activities, especially lips, tongue and chin, and then brain signals were used to decode whether they were thinking "yes" or "no" with an average accuracy of 69.3%. The subjects will be asked ten questions with answers of "yes" or "no", such as: Are you hungry? The subjects answered "yes" or "no", and the decoding of the brain signal was accurate 92 percent of the time compared to the real thing [22]. In Dash [18]'s experiment, the screen went blank for the first second, then text appeared. The subjects imagined it for one second, then read it aloud for two seconds. They trained on five commonly used phrases and analyzed MEG using CNN with 93% accuracy. Tottrup L [24] use of EMG signal to improve the training effect, every action is secrecy speech or MI (interior), six seconds, then repeat openly talking or ME (external), corresponds to a clock cycle time in front of the subjects had a clock, subjects first imagine some action, such as stopping or walking, bending the left arm, after 6 s, they repeat these movements overtly, the highest with 76% accuracy. At present, many researches are based on monosyllables or monosyllables. It is still difficult to carry out experiments on words or sentences, but some achievements have been made. In the experiments of [26], using the same algorithm, the accuracy rate of the experimental results was 57.4%/57CV, 61.2%/19cons, 88.2%/3VOWels, proving that

Table1. Research status

Signal	Area	Subject	Feature extraction	Classification	Accuracy	Author
EcoG	vSMC	5 epliepsy patients	Hilbert	LSTM	Almost 70%	Anumanchipalli [17]
EcoG	Posterior temporal lobe and inferior parietal cortex	5 epliepsy patients	Wavelet transform	SVM	Mean 60.47%	Song C [16]
MEG	All	8 healthy adults	Wavelet transform	CNN	93%	Dash D [18]
SUA/LFP/ EcoG	vSMC	6 epilepsy patients	Construct feature vector	Sparse Logistic Regression classifier	Mean 59%	Ibayashi [15]
EEG	All	12 healthy adults	Wavelet transform, Autoregressive model	SVM	Mean 69.3%	Sereshkeh [19]
EcoG	Frontal and temporal areas	4 epilepsy patients	FFT	Linear classifier	63% for single phoneme	Mugler [20]
EcoG	Frontal, parietal and temporal regions	8 epliepsy patients	Power Spectral Density	Naive Bayes classifier	Vowel-mean 37.5% Consonant-mean 36.3%	Pei [21]
EEG	Brocas, Geshwind-Wernicke's area	5 healthy adults	PCA	ANN	Best 92.18%	Balaji [22]
EEG	All	6 healthy adults	Wavelet transform	Extreme Learning Machine	Multi-category 49.77%/Two categories 85.57%	Pawar [23]

(continued)

Table1. (*continued*)

Signal	Area	Subject	Feature extraction	Classification	Accuracy	Author
EEG	Frontal, central, parietal areas	7 healthy adults	The temporal and spectral features	Random forest classifier	Best 76%	Tottrup [24]
EEG	All	6 healthy subjects	Power Spectral Density	DBN/RNN	DBN80%/RNN72%	Chenggaiyan [25]
EcoG	vSMC	4 epilepsy patients	Deep network	Deep network	Bset: 57.4%/57CV, 61.2%/19 cons, 88.2%/3 vowels	Livezey [26]
EcoG	Left Brain	2 epilepsy patients	Hilbert transform	Linear decoder	81%	Bouchard [27]

the more difficult the task, the lower the accuracy rate. Subjects were asked to read and read the story silently, then to convert the brain signals they collected into speech, and to listen to the final synthetic sentence to complete the test. After hearing 101 sentences, the accuracy rate was about 70% [17]. Anumanchipalli [17] and other experiments also found that reading aloud was more effective than silent reading because sounds were added to aid training. The accuracy of reading aloud was 3% higher in the experiment than in silent reading training. MFCCS features are generally extracted from speech to facilitate training, such as [28] and [17]. Makin JG [28] also used MOCHATIMIT data set to decode and synthesize sentences, and they achieved 97% decoding accuracy by using EcoG signal, and achieved certain results in transfer learning. Pre-training participant A's data improved participant B's performance. For the least effective participant D, there was no improvement, and all individual differences remained difficult to eliminate. See Table 1 for more research status.

4   Conclusion

The brain-computer interface system based on imagined speech has achieved certain results, but there is still a lot to go. At present, it is possible to improve the training effect and improve the test accuracy by extracting the characteristics of the speech signal and fusing the brain signal. Our application target is those who can't speak, so we can only use brain signals for training. Therefore, the brain-computer interface system based on imagined speech has a good development prospect, but further research is needed.

References

1. Kübler, A., Kotchoubey, B., Hinterberger, T., et al.: The thought translation device: a neuro-physiological approach to communication in total motor paralysis. Exp. Brain Res. **124**(2), 223–232 (1999)
2. Yahud, S., Abu Osman, N. A.: Prosthetic hand for the brain-computer interface system. In: Ibrahim, F., Osman, N.A.A., Usman, J., Kadri, N.A. (eds.) 3rd Kuala Lumpur International Conference on Biomedical Engineering 2006. IP, vol. 15, pp. 643–646. Springer, Heidelberg (2007). https://doi.org/10.1007/978-3-540-68017-8_162
3. Rebsamen, B., Burdet, E., Guan, C., et al.: Controlling a wheelchair indoors using thought. IEEE Intell. Syst. **22**(2), 18–24 (2007)
4. Abiri, R., Borhani, S., Sellers, E.W., Jiang, Y., Zhao, X.: A comprehensive review of EEG-based brain-computer interface paradigms. J. Neural Eng. **16**(1), 011001 (2019). https://doi.org/10.1088/1741-2552/aaf12e
5. Fabiani, M., Gratton, G., Karis, D., Donchin, E.: Definition, identification, and reliability of measurement of the P300 component of the event-related brain potential. Adv. Psychophysiol. **2**(S 1), 78 (1987).
6. Polich, J.: Updating P300: an integrative theory of P3a and P3b. Clin. Neurophysiol. **118**(10), 2128–2148 (2007)
7. Chang, M.H., Baek, H.J., Lee, S.M., Park, K.S.: An amplitude-modulated visual stimulation for reducing eye fatigue in SSVEP-based brain–computer interfaces. Clin. Neurophysiol. **125**(7), 1380–1391 (2014)

8. Molina, G.G., Mihajlovic, V.: Spatial filters to detect steady-state visual evoked potentials elicited by high frequency stimulation: BCI application. Biomedizinische Technik/Biomed. Eng. **55**(3), 173–182 (2010)
9. Müller, S.M.T., Diez, P.F., Bastos-Filho, T.F., Sarcinelli-Filho, M., Mut, V., Laciar, E.: SSVEP-BCI implementation for 37–40 Hz frequency range. In: Engineering in Medicine and Biology Society, EMBC, 2011 Annual International Conference of the IEEE, pp. 6352–6355: IEEE (2011)
10. Volosyak, I., Valbuena, D., Luth, T., Malechka, T., Graser, A.: BCI demographics II: how many (and what kinds of) people can use a high-frequency SSVEP BCI? IEEE Trans. Neural Syst. Rehabil. Eng. **19**(3), 232–239 (2011)
11. Morash, V., Bai, O., Furlani, S., Lin, P., Hallett, M.: Classifying EEG signals preceding right hand, left hand, tongue, and right foot movements and motor imageries. Clin. Neurophysiol. **119**(11), 2570–2578 (2008)
12. Hochberg, L.R., et al.: Neuronal ensemble control of prosthetic devices by a human with tetraplegia. Nature **442**(7099), 164–171 (2006)
13. Kim, S.-P., Simeral, J.D., Hochberg, L.R., Donoghue, J.P., Black, M.J.: Neural control of computer cursor velocity by decoding motor cortical spiking activity in humans with tetraplegia. J. Neural Eng. **5**(4), 455 (2008)
14. Yuan, H., He, B.: Brain-computer interfaces using sensorimotor rhythms: current state and future perspectives. IEEE Trans. Biomed. Eng. **61**(5), 1425–1435 (2014)
15. Ibayashi, K., Kunii, N., Matsuo, T., et al.: Decoding speech with integrated hybrid signals recorded from the human ventral motor cortex. Front. Neurosci. **12,** 221 (2018). https://doi.org/10.3389/fnins.2018.00221
16. Song, C., Xu, R., Hong, B.: Decoding of Chinese phoneme clusters using ECoG. In: Conference Proceedings-IEEE Engineering in Medicine and Biology Society 2014, pp. 1278–1281 (2014). https://doi.org/10.1109/EMBC.2014.6943831
17. Anumanchipalli, G.K., Chartier, J., Chang, E.F.: Speech synthesis from neural decoding of spoken sentences. Nature **568**(7753), 493–498 (2019). https://doi.org/10.1038/s41586-019-1119-1
18. Dash, D., Ferrari, P., Wang, J.: Decoding Imagined and spoken phrases from non-invasive neural (MEG) signals. Front. Neurosci. **14**, 290 (2020). https://doi.org/10.3389/fnins.2020.00290
19. Sereshkeh, A.R., Trott, R., Bricout, A., Chau, T.: Online EEG classification of covert speech for brain-computer interfacing. Int. J. Neural Syst. **27**(8), 1750033 (2017). https://doi.org/10.1142/S0129065717500332
20. Mugler, E.M., Patton, J.L., Flint, R.D., et al.: Direct classification of all American English phonemes using signals from functional speech motor cortex. J. Neural Eng. **11**(3), 035015 (2014). https://doi.org/10.1088/1741-2560/11/3/035015
21. Pei, X., Barbour, D.L., Leuthardt, E.C., Schalk, G.: Decoding vowels and consonants in spoken and imagined words using electrocorticographic signals in humans. J. Neural Eng. **8**(4), 046028 (2011). https://doi.org/10.1088/1741-2560/8/4/046028
22. Balaji, A., Haldar, A., Patil, K., et al.: EEG-based classification of bilingual unspoken speech using ANN. In: Conference Proceedings-IEEE Engineering in Medicine and Biology Society 2017, pp. 1022–1025 (2017). https://doi.org/10.1109/EMBC.2017.8037000
23. Pawar, D., Dhage, S.: Multiclass covert speech classification using extreme learning machine. Biomed. Eng. Lett. **10**(2), 217–226 (2020). https://doi.org/10.1007/s13534-020-00152-x
24. Tottrup, L., Leerskov, K., Hadsund, J.T., Kamavuako, E.N., Kaseler, R.L., Jochumsen, M.: Decoding covert speech for intuitive control of brain-computer interfaces based on single-trial EEG: a feasibility study. In: IEEE International Conference on Rehabilitation Robotics 2019, pp. 689–693 (2019). https://doi.org/10.1109/ICORR.2019.8779499

25. Chengaiyan, S., Retnapandian, A., Anandan, K.: Identification of vowels in consonant–vowel–consonant words from speech imagery based EEG signals. Cogn. Neurodyn. **14**(1), 1–19 (2019). https://doi.org/10.1007/s11571-019-09558-5

26. Livezey, J.A., Bouchard, K.E., Chang, E.F.: Deep learning as a tool for neural data analysis: speech classification and cross-frequency coupling in human sensorimotor cortex. PLoS Comput. Biol. **15**(9), e1007091 (2019). https://doi.org/10.1371/journal.pcbi.1007091

27. Bouchard, K.E., Chang, E.F.: Neural decoding of spoken vowels from human sensory-motor cortex with high-density electrocorticography. In: Conference Proceedings-IEEE Engineering in Medicine and Biology Society 2014, pp. 6782–6785 (2014). https://doi.org/10.1109/EMBC.2014.6945185

28. Makin, J.G., Moses, D.A., Chang, E.F.: Machine translation of cortical activity to text with an encoder-decoder framework. Nat. Neurosci. **23**(4), 575–582 (2020). https://doi.org/10.1038/s41593-020-0608-8

29. Akbari, H., Khalighinejad, B., Herrero, J.L., Mehta, A.D., Mesgarani, N.: Towards reconstructing intelligible speech from the human auditory cortex. Sci. Rep. **9**(1), 874 (2019). https://doi.org/10.1038/s41598-018-37359-z

30. Ahn, J.W., Ku, Y., Kim, H.C.: A novel wearable EEG and ECG recording system for stress assessment. Sensors (Basel) **19**(9), 1991 (2019). https://doi.org/10.3390/s19091991

31. Athavipach, C., Pan-Ngum, S., Israsena, P.: A wearable in-ear EEG device for emotion monitoring. Sensors (Basel). **19**(18), 4014 (2019). https://doi.org/10.3390/s19184014

32. Kawana, T., Yoshida, Y., Kudo, Y., Miki, N.: In: EEG-hat with candle-like microneedle electrode. In: Conference Proceedings-IEEE Engineering in Medicine and Biology Society 2019; pp. 1111–1114 (2019). https://doi.org/10.1109/EMBC.2019.8857477

33. Shi, Z., Zheng, F., Zhou, Z., et al.: Silk-enabled conformal multifunctional bioelectronics for investigation of spatiotemporal epileptiform activities and multimodal neural encoding/decoding. Adv. Sci. (Weinh) **6**(9):1801617 (2019). https://doi.org/10.1002/advs.201801617

34. Choi, H., Lee, S., Lee, J., et al.: Long-term evaluation and feasibility study of the insulated screw electrode for ECoG recording. J. Neurosci. Methods. **308**, 261–268 (2018). https://doi.org/10.1016/j.jneumeth.2018.06.027

35. Xu, K., Li, S., Dong, S., et al.: Bioresorbable electrode array for electrophysiological and pressure signal recording in the brain. Adv. Healthc. Mater. **8**(15), e1801649 (2019). https://doi.org/10.1002/adhm.201801649

36. Brumberg, J.S., Pitt, K.M., Burnison, J.D.: A noninvasive brain-computer interface for real-time speech synthesis: the importance of multimodal feedback. IEEE Trans. Neural Syst. Rehabil. Eng. **26**(4), 874–881 (2018). https://doi.org/10.1109/TNSRE.2018.2808425

A Survey of Multimodal Human-Machine Interface

Wenlong Ding[1], Chengyin Wang[1], Bin Fang[2], Fuchun Sun[2],
and Jianhua Shan[1(✉)]

[1] Anhui University of Technology, Maanshan 243032, Anhui, China
[2] Tsinghua University, Beijing 100085, China
fangbin@tsinghua.edu.cn

Abstract. Human-machine interface (HMI) has become an indispensable part of human life. The signal generated by human body is a kind of Physiological signal. There are many devices can recognize this signal, which has great potential as the input signal of HMI. Sometimes the HMI based on single-modality can not achieve the expected goal, more and more people begin to study multimodal HMI. In the past, many researchers have studied how to use these signals to control machine equipment, especially in the field of medical rehabilitation for the disabled, many achievements have been made, so that patients can exchange information with the outside world through HMI, and improve the quality of patients' life. In this paper, the HMI and several physiological signals are introduced, and the research based on single modal HMI and multimodal HMI are investigated and analyzed. Finally, some problems existing in multimodal HMI are pointed out, and the future avenues of research in multimodal HMI is prospected.

Keywords: Multimodal · HMI · Physiological signal · Medical rehabilitation

1 Introduction

In our life, we have been interacting with a variety of machine equipment, such as watching TV with remote control and checking mobile phones by touching the touch screen. In these interactions, remote control and touch screen play a role of transmitting information between human and machine equipment. Through them, people's intention can be transformed into control command or to provide people with machine equipment request. Such a kind of equipment to realize the information exchange between human and machine equipment is called human-machine interface [1].

Supported by Natural Science Foundation of university in Anhui Province (No. KJ2019A0086) and National Natural Science Foundation of China with Grant No. 91848206.

F. Sun et al. (Eds.): ICCSIP 2020, CCIS 1397, pp. 379–386, 2021.
https://doi.org/10.1007/978-981-16-2336-3_35

These HMI mentioned above are all developed for healthy people, so it is difficult for the disabled to use them. Some patients have difficulty in pronunciation and limb movement, so they can't use the HMI developed for healthy people. But these patients can still produce physiological signals that can be detected and recognized through the brain or the residual neuromuscular of limbs. HMI based on physiological signals can help patients communicate with the outside world, improve their quality of life and reduce the burden of patients' families. Common physiological signals include electroencephalogram (EEG) [2], electrooculogram (EOG) [3] and electromyography (EMG) [4].

EEG is obtained by noninvasive brain-computer interface [5], which does not need craniotomy, it can be obtained by sticking the electrode on the scalp. EEG signal quality is relatively poor [6], but compared with the signal obtained by the invasive brain computer interface (BCI), its operation is simple, there is no medical risk, and the detection signal is more convenient. So, the EEG obtained by non-invasive BCI has better practical value.

EMG is produced in the following way: action potential is generated by the motor cortex of the brain, which reaches the muscle fiber through the spinal cord and peripheral nervous system, through the low-pass filtering of the skin, and finally forms an electric potential field on the surface of the skin. According to the different detection positions, EMG is divided into internal EMG and surface EMG [7]. Intramuscular EMG needs to penetrate the surface skin and insert probes into the deep muscle tissue. Generally, the signal quality of intramuscular EMG is very high. Surface EMG records muscle activity by sticking electrodes on the skin of the target muscle position. The signal quality measured by this method is low, but the operation is simple, and it will not cause trauma to the human body [8]. Therefore, surface EMG (sEMG) is more practical.

EOG is the most widely used eye movement detection method. EOG is a method to measure the potential difference between the anterior part of the eyeball (the positive electrode of corneal formation) and the posterior part (the negative electrode of retinal formation), which can be used to detect eye movement and blink. Compared with EEG, EOG has higher signal-to-noise ratio, lower detection difficulty, fast time response and simple operation, and the individual difference of EOG signal is not large [9]. Therefore, EOG is suitable as the input signal of HMI to achieve communicate and control function.

The above introduces the HMI based on various physiological signals, but each physiological signal has its own advantages and limitations. And the HMI using a certain single signal often fails to obtain good prediction results. For example, in the BCI, it is difficult to obtain a relatively high prediction accuracy rate using only EEG in motor imagery (MI) [10]. In order to overcome the limitation of a single signal, a new trend has emerged in recent years, which is to combine multiple signals, supplemented by other intelligent technologies, to achieve multimodal HMI intelligent technology to complete complex tasks. For example, Duke University's "Walk Again Project" project personnel [11] developed a new exoskeleton HMI system that integrates multiple modalities such as EEG, EMG, and eye tracking, and successfully helped a person physically disabled patients completed the kick-off action at the World Cup in Brazil; Witkowski et al. [12] developed a hybrid HMI to control an exoskeleton glove, which converts the user's MI signal into a continuous grasping action of the glove , and then determine whether to stop crawling by detecting the user's EOG signal. This strategy improves the overall reliability and safety of the system.

The structure of this article is as follows. The first section introduces the HMI, three physiological signals of the HMI, and the multimodal HMI. The second section introduces the research of EEG, EMG and EOG. In the third section, several researches on multimodal HMI are introduced. The fourth section summarizes the main research content of this article, points out the problems in this field and future research directions.

2   Research on Various Physiological Signals

2.1   Research on BCI Based on EEG

In recent years, a large number of results have been achieved in the application of EEG. However, EEG still has many shortcomings. For example, the EEG signal-to-noise ratio is relatively low, there is a lot of noise, and the amount of EEG data is relatively small. Therefore, various methods are needed to improve the accuracy of prediction.

In view of the large amount of noise existing in the EEG, noise can be removed by some methods such as filtering. In [13], it is mentioned that "a lot of preprocessing is required" to improve the work of deep learning. More specifically, it is necessary to trim the EEG, reduce the data 512 Hz and 64 electrodes, manually remove channels with poor signal quality, and perform high-pass filtering on the data.

In view of the relatively small amount of EEG data, data enhancement can be used to increase the amount of data. Data enhancement is to generate new data on the basis of existing data. In [14], conditional deep convolutional generative adversarial network (CDCGAN) is used to generate artificial EEG signals on the BCI competition MI dataset. The results show that data enhancement helps to improve accuracy, from around 83% to 86%, to classify MI.

Although many people have preprocessed the data, in some respects, using completely original data as input will get better results than preprocessing. For example, for the classification of epilepsy, recently proposed models use raw EEG data as input [15] to achieve better performance than classic baseline methods, such as SVMs with frequency-domain features. For this particular task, we believe that following the current trend of using raw EEG data is the best way to start exploring new methods.

In the field of EEG-based deep learning, most use CNN networks and a few use RNN, but in recent years, the use of RNN has been on the rise.

2.2 Research on HMI Based on EMG

In recent years, people have done a lot of research on the task of recognizing actions based on EMG.

In 2000, Alsayegh [16] proposed a signal based on electromyography, using arm muscles, medial deltoid (MD), anterior deltoid (AD), and biceps (BB) to recognize 12 arm movements. EMG signal processing is based on arm gestures and has unique time coordination. The classification techniques used are context-dependent classification and Bayes' theorem.

In 2011, Ishii [17] studied electromyographic prosthesis. The recognition and differentiation of gestures obtained by arms or hands is based on surface electromyography. Motion recognition uses neural networks. This shows that the researchers have conducted in-depth research on the surface EMG signal and achieved a good result.

In 2019, Dwivedi et al. [18] studied the role of different muscles in performing these tasks, and the effect of gender and hand size on the overall decoding accuracy. In this article, it uses electromyographic signals from 16 muscle parts (8 hands and 8 forearms) from 11 different subjects and an optical motion capture system to record the movement of objects. The random forest method is used to express the target motion decoding as a regression problem. The decoding accuracy of the subject-specific and object-specific model is as high as 83.61%. The subject-specific and object-common model has an accuracy of 73.82%, and the subject-common and object-common decoding model has an accuracy of 67.58%. Therefore, it can be concluded that a more specific decoding model can get better decoding accuracy. The study also shows that for the general model of subjects, if the subjects are trained in groups according to the length of the hands, better accuracy can be obtained.

2.3 Research on HMI Based on EOG

Compared with EEG, EOG has a higher signal-to-noise ratio, and most of the studies on EOG in the literature are related to eye movement and blinking.

Hande et al. [19] proposed a new intelligent detection model based on EOG signal. In this study, we used artificial neural networks to define eye movements. In addition to literature research, this research also includes twitch perception and blinking. Extract features from the EOG signal as the input of the feedforward neural network. The accuracy of this study is 94.19%.

Banerjee et al. [20] designed a human-computer interface system that uses K-NN and feedforward neural network classifiers to detect different types of eye movements (straight, up, down, right, left, blinking). They use automatic regression parameters, power spectral density (PSD) and wavelet coefficients.

Aungskan et al. [21] obtained the first derivative technique using the EOG signal and proposed a human-machine interface system. The system uses a classification algorithm consisting of threshold classification, initial analysis and feature extraction to detect eight different eye movements. This method achieves 100% accuracy in the three-disciplinary test.

3   Research on Multimodal HMI

Each source or form of information can be called a modality. For example, one of EEG, EMG and EOG can be called a modality. Sometimes a single modality can not be used to predict the target well. At this time, multimodal HMI can be considered. Multimodal HMI combines the information of multiple modalities, that is, simultaneously uses multiple signals to predict the target. The human cognitive process is multi-modal. When individuals perceive a scene, they can often quickly receive visual, auditory, olfactory, and tactile signals, And then perform fusion processing and semantic understanding on them. Therefore, the use of multimodal lHMI is more close to the form of human understanding of the world.

This article mainly introduces two multimodal HMI. The first is the multi-modal-fusion HMI: multiple modalities are used to identify one task mode of the HMI. The second is a multi-modal-combine HMI: one modality recognizes the mode of one task, and these tasks are combined to form a complete HMI task.

3.1   Multi-modal-fusion HMI

This article mainly introduces the human-machine interface based on multi-modal fusion deep learning [22]. According to the processing of different modal signals at different stages, it can be divided into early fusion (based on features), late fusion (based on decision) and hybrid fusion [23]. Early fusion integrates the features immediately after extracting the features (usually just connect the representation of each modal feature), late fusion performs integration after each mode output (such as output classification or regression results), hybrid fusion combines early fusion methods and late fusion method.

In 2020, Gordleeva et al. [10] introduced a rehabilitation technology based on lower extremity exoskeleton integrated with HMI. The HMI records and processes the foot motor imagery (EEG) based on the BCI and records the multi-channel electromyography signal (EMG) of the leg muscles. The original EEG and EMG data are filtered by band-pass filters in the frequency range of 8–15 and 10–300, respectively. The notch filter is also used to eliminate the interference 50 Hz power supply voltage. In terms of feature extraction, EMG uses root mean square (RMS) to extract features, and EEG uses common space pattern (CSP) to extract features. Both EMG based and EEG based classification are based on linear discriminant analysis (LDA). In this paper, two multimodal fusion schemes based on EEG and EMG are proposed: the first scheme is based on the HMI of early fusion; the second is based on the HMI of late fusion, and the results of each modal classification are combined by the logical operators "and" and "or". In this paper, two classification based on EEG and EMG are used (1: no distinction between left and right foot movements; 2: rest). The accuracy rate of the first scheme is 80%, which can be regarded as an "average" of EEG classification results (secondary classification: 78.13%) and EMG classification results (second classification: 89%). For the second scheme, various situations are discussed. For example, they found that single EMG signal and "or" combination are the best signal types in exercise test classification. It can be seen from this that sometimes the results of early fusion are not necessarily better than that of single-modality, while decision fusion can obtain ideal results under specified conditions.

3.2 Multi-modal-combine HMI

For a complex HMI task, such as controlling a robotic arm to grab a small ball, it is difficult to use single signal to simultaneously complete link selection, link rotation and error correction. At this time, consider dividing this complex task into Several small tasks, each of which is controlled by a signal, will make this complex task easier to complete.

In 2020, Arnab et al. [24] proposed a new method for the position control of the end effector of the robot, that is, to reasonably control the linkage of each position of the arm. Three kinds of signals, SSVEP, ERD/ERS and P300, are involved in the article and decoded respectively. Take ERD/ERS as an example here to briefly explain the decoding process. The collected EEG data is spatially filtered using Common Average Reference (CAR) to remove common mode noise evenly distributed on all EEG electrodes, including thermal noise, power line interference, and unwanted physiological signals. The EEG data after CAR spatial filtering is filtered by a band-pass filter with a pass band of 8–24. It adopts a sixth-order elliptic filter with a passband ripple of 1db and a stopband attenuation of 60db. Then using the Common Space Model (CSP) to extract features, the author here proposes two improved versions of CSP: FBCSP and MPCSP. Finally, a two-level radial basis function kernelized support vector machine (RBF-SVM) classifier is used to classify. The first stage is to classify the feature vector with or without motor imagery in the EEG test. In the second stage, the feature vector containing motor imagery is further divided into left-handed motor imagery and right-hand motor imagery. In this paper, these three signals are used to control three tasks. First, different links on the robot arm are connected with LEDs with different flashing frequencies. The experimenter generates different SSVEP signals by observing the LEDs with different flashing frequencies on the robot arm, by identifying these SSVEP signals, determine which link the experimenter wants to choose for movement. Afterwards, the ERD/ERS signal generated by the experimenter is used to determine whether the experimenter wants to rotate the connecting rod clockwise or counterclockwise, so that the connecting rod moves to the target point. Determine whether the connecting rod has passed through the target point by detecting the P300 signal. If the P300 signal is detected, the connecting rod will stop moving, then reverse the direction and move to the target point at a lower speed. This process is repeated many times, and the connecting rod will eventually stop at the target point. The comprehensive modeling and analysis of the controller performance in this paper show that the proposed brain-computer interface-based control is stable, with low steady-state error, low peak overshoot.

4   Conclusion

This article introduces the multimodal HMI and several physiological signals of the HMI, including EEG, EMG and EOG. We introduces the research of several physiological signals, and explains the concept of multimodal HMI and the research on the multimodal HMI.

There are still many problems in the field of multimodal HMI. (1) The data is relatively small. First, there are relatively few public data sets. Secondly, there are not many samples in the data set, because the collection of physiological signals is a complicated process that requires a lot of time, requires a lot of manpower and material resources, and it is generally difficult to collect a lot of useful data. (2) The quality of the data collected by one of the modalities is not good, which causes the effect of using multi-modality to be inferior to that of single-modality. For example, when performing action recognition, it is difficult to ensure that the subjects can always keep their attention during the experiment. That is to say, it is difficult to guarantee that good quality EEG is collected, which makes the effect of both EEG and EMG not as good as using only EMG. (3) Real-time acquisition of multi-source information.

There are many research directions in the field of multimodal HMI. For the problem of small amount of data, adversarial learning method is one of the feasible solutions. At present, the multi-modal database we see is still offline analysis. In reality, the real-time and natural HMI system is more realistic. Therefore, how to construct a HMI system containing real-time physiological signals will be an important challenge for multimodal HMI, and it is also a problem that researchers need to focus on in the future.

References

1. Andreoni, G., Parini, S., Maggi, L., Piccini, L., Panfili, G., Torricelli, A.: Human machine interface for healthcare and rehabilitation. In: Vaidya, S., Jain, L.C., Yoshida, H. (eds.) Advanced Computational Intelligence Paradigms in Healthcare-2. Studies in Computational Intelligence, vol. 67, pp. 131–150. Springer, Heidelberg (2007). https://doi.org/10.1007/978-3-540-72375-2_7
2. Vogel, F.: The genetic basis of the normal human electroencephalogram (EEG). Humangenetik **10**(2), 91–114 (1970)
3. Usakli, A.B., Gurkan, S., Aloise, F., et al.: On the use of electrooculogram for efficient human computer interfaces. Comput. Intell. Neurosci. **2010**(4), 1 (2009)
4. Clancy, E.A., Hogan, N.: Single site electromyograph amplitude estimation. IEEE Trans. Biomed. Eng. **41**(2), 159–167 (1994)
5. Dornhege, G., Millán, J.D.R., Hinterberger, T., et al.: Invasive BCI Approaches (2007)
6. Cunningham, J.P., Paul, N., Vikash, G., et al.: A closed-loop human simulator for investigating the role of feedback control in brain-machine interfaces. J. Neurophysiol. **105**(4), 1932–1949 (2011)
7. Moritani, T., Muro, M., Kijima, A., et al.: Electromechanical changes during electrically induced and maximal voluntary contractions: surface and intramuscular EMG responses during sustained maximal voluntary contraction. Experimental Neurol. **88**(3), 484–499 (1985)

8. Farina, D., Merletti, R., Enoka, R.M.: The extraction of neural strategies from the surface EMG an update. J. Appl. Physiol. **96**(4), 1486–1495 (2004)
9. Tomita, Y., Igarashi, Y., Honda, S., et al.: Electro-oculography mouse for amyotrophic lateral sclerosis patients. In: International Conference of the IEEE Engineering in Medicine and Biology Society, vol. 5, pp. 1780–1781. IEEE
10. Gordleeva, S., et al.: Real-time EEG-EMG human-machine interface-based control system for a lower-limb exoskeleton. IEEE Access 1 (2020). https://doi.org/10.1109/ACCESS.2020.2991812
11. Lin, A., Schwarz, D., Sellaouti, R., et al.: The walk again project: Brain-controlled exoskeleton locomotion. Neuroscience Meeting (2014)
12. Witkowski, M., Cortese, M., Cempini, M., et al.: Enhancing brain-machine interface (BMI) control of a hand exoskeleton using electrooculography (EOG). J. NeuroEngineering Rehab. **11**, 165 (2014)
13. Hefron, R., Borghetti, B., Schubert Kabban, C., Christensen, J., Estepp, J.: Cross participant EEG-based assessment of cognitive workload using multi-path convolutional recurrent neural networks. Sensors **18**(5), 1339 (2018)
14. Zhang, Q., Liu, Y.: Improving brain computer interface performance by data augmentation with conditional Deep Convolutional Generative Adversarial Networks. arXiv preprint (2018)
15. Shea, A.O., Lightbody, G., Boylan, G., Temko, A.: Investigating the Impact of CNN Depth on Neonatal Seizure Detection Performance. arXiv 15–18 (2018)
16. Alsayegh, O.A.: EMG-based signal processing system for interpreting arm gestures. In: 10th European Signal Processing Conference, pp. 1–4. IEEE (2000)
17. Ishii, C.: Recognition of finger motions for myoelectric prosthetic hand via surface EMG. INTECH Open Access Publisher (2011)
18. Dwivedi, A., Kwon, Y., Mcdaid, A., Liarokapis, M.: A learning scheme for EMG based decoding of dexterous, in-hand manipulation motions. IEEE Trans. Neural Syst. Rehab. 1 (2019). https://doi.org/10.1109/TNSRE.2019.2936622
19. Erkaymaz, H., Ozer, M., Orak, İ. M.: Detection of directional eye movements based on the electrooculogram signals through an artificial neural network. In: Chaos, Solitons and Fractals, vol. 77, pp. 225–229 (2015)
20. Banerjee, A., Datta, S., Pal, M., Konar, A., Tibarewala, D.N., Janarthanan, R.: Classifying electrooculogram to detect directional eye movements. Procedia Technol. **10**, 6775 (2013)
21. Aungsakun, S., Phinyomark, A., Phukpattaranont, P., Limsakul, C.: Robust eye movement recognition using EOG signal for human-computer interface. In: Zain, J.M., Wan Mohd, W.M., El-Qawasmeh, E. (eds.) ICSECS 2011. CCIS, vol. 180, pp. 714–723. Springer, Heidelberg (2011). https://doi.org/10.1007/978-3-642-22191-0_63
22. Ramachandram, D., Taylor, G.W.: Deep multimodal learning: a survey on recent advances and trend. IEEE Signal Process. Mag. **34**(6), 96–108 (2017)
23. Lecun, Y., Bengio, Y., Hinton, G.: Deep learning. Nature **521**(7553), 436–451 (2015)
24. Rakshit, A., Konar, A., Nagar, A.: A hybrid brain-computer interface for closed-loop position control of a robot arm. IEEE/CAA J. Automatica Sinica. **7**, 1344–1360 (2020). https://doi.org/10.1109/JAS.2020.1003336

A Logistic Regression Based Framework for Spatio-Temporal Feature Representation and Classification of Single-Trial EEG

Feifei Qi[1], Wei Wu[2,3(✉)], Ke Liu[4(✉)], Tianyou Yu[5], and Yang Cao[1]

[1] School of Internet Finance and Information Engineering,
Guangdong University of Finance, Guangzhou 510521, China
[2] Department of Psychiatry and Behavioral Sciences, Stanford University,
Stanford, CA 94304, USA
[3] Wu Tsai Neurosciences Institute, Stanford University, Stanford, CA 94304, USA
[4] Chongqing Key Laboratory of Computational Intelligence,
Chongqing University of Posts and Telecommunications, Chongqing 400065, China
liuke@cqupt.edu.cn
[5] School of Automation Science and Engineering,
South China University of Technology, Guangzhou 510640, China

Abstract. The classic motor imagery EEG signal analysis pipelines are implemented by two separate supervised stages (normally CSP+FLDA), note that the optimal solution is difficult to guarantee. Moreover, CSP only utilizes the spatial information os EEG signal, while neglecting the underlying temporal information. In this work, an alternative approach to CSP+FLDA is proposed (named LRSTC), in which only a single supervised learning stage is needed. By LRSTC, the feature extraction and classification can be tackled conveniently under a regularized empirical risk minimization problem. The input signal the whitened spatial covariance matrices, and we use a linear model to simultaneously learn the spatio-temporal filters and the weights of classifier. To address the potential over-fitting issue, an nuclear norm is added in our objective function as the regularization term. One motor imagery EEG data set from past BCI competitions is used to evaluate the performance of our algorithm. Compared with the CSP+FLDA, FBCSP+FLDA, the algorithm proposed by Tomioka (termed as LRC in this paper), and CSSSP+FLDA, our algorithm shows significant classification performance except for FBCSP+FLDA.

Keywords: EEG · BCI · Spatio-temporal filtering · Logistic regression · Sparse regularization · Nuclear norm

This work was supported in part by the National Natural Science Foundation of China (No. 61906048, No. 61703065, and No. 61876064) and Guangdong Basic and Applied Basic Research Foundation (No. 2020A1515010350).

F. Sun et al. (Eds.): ICCSIP 2020, CCIS 1397, pp. 387–394, 2021.
https://doi.org/10.1007/978-981-16-2336-3_36

1 Introduction

Brain-computer interface (BCI) could translate the brain signals to external commands [1–3]. The motor imagery based BCI is the commonly used paradigm, which could effectively decodes the brain signals from the imagination of movements [4]. EEG signal processing is very challenging due to the following aspects: first, EEG signal is very easily contaminated by noises and artefacts, therefore the signal-to-noise ratio (SNR) is very low; second, the spatial resolution of EEG is very low due to volume conduction; third, EEG signal is intrinsically nonstationary [5]. Generally, some preprocessing steps (manually or automatically) are applied in advance to remove the artifacts or noises, then the preprocessed EEG signals spatially or spatio-temporally filtered for feature extraction to further improve the signal-to-noise ratio, and finally the extracted features after filtering are feed into a classification model or regression model [6]. In summary, feature extraction and classification/regression is the core steps of EEG signal analysis.

In recent years, common spatial patterns (CSP) has gained a surge of popularity for the feature extraction of motor imagery based BCI system [1,2,6,7]. CSP is a supervised algorithm for learning spatial filters, which aims at seeking the optimal spatial filters to maximize the power of one state while minimize another state's. The optimization for CSP can be casted as a Rayleigh quotient maximization problem, which can be efficiently solved. Note that CSP only exploits the spatial information of EEG signal, while neglecting the underlying temporal information, which could lead to suboptimal solution. Many works extend CSP to implement spatial filtering and temporal filtering, such as CSSP [8], CSSSP [9], DFBCSP[10], FBCSP [11] and its variants[12,13], BSSFO [14], SPECCSP [15] and ISSPL [16]. In our previous work, the regularized spatio-temporal filtering and classification (RSTFC) algorithm [17] is proposed as a new EEG analysis framework.

Beside spatio-temporal filtering for feature extraction, how to design a sophisticated classification model to provide good generalization ability is another considerable important issue [2,7]. In recent years, FLDA, SVM, and RVM are popular classification models in EEG classification domain [2,20]. Fisher's Linear Discriminant Analysis (FLDA) [18] generally provides good performance for classification under a hypothesis that the features are Gaussian distributed, and has proven to be a highly effective in single-trial EEG classification [2]. Support Vector Machine (SVM) is another well-known classification algorithm, which adopts a soft margin regularization for obtaining a well generalization ability [19]. The relevance vector machine (RVM) is a sparse kernel technique for classification and regression that shares many characteristics of SVM. Compared to SVM, RVM typically can lead to more sparser models while maintain comparable generalization error [19]. Logistic regression is another popular model for binary decision setting, of which the output is the probability of a label given a feature vector [3]. In [17], a Sparse Fisher Linear Discriminant Analysis (SFLDA) is proposed to simultaneously select and classify the band power features form the spatial or spatio-temporal filtered EEG signals.

Note that the potential problem of the previous algorithms is that the feature extraction by spatial/spato-temporal filtering and classification stages are applied separately, therefore the optimality is difficult to be guaranteed [5]. In [21] and [3], the symmetric logit transform of the posterior class probability is modeled to be a linear function with respect to the second-order statistics of the EEG signal, and the negative log-likelihood with a nuclear norm penalization term for regularization. By this way, the spatial filtering, feature selection and classification of the motor imagery EEG signals can be implemented under a single objective function. However, the discriminative information of temporal domain is not taken into consideration, which may further improve the model's classification performance.

In this paper, we propose a framework that based on logistic regression that integrates the following two steps: feature extraction step based on spatio-temporal filtering, and the classification step. Under a single convex minimization problem and a well controlled nuclear norm regularization, the objective problem is convenient to be optimized. One motor imagery EEG data set (from past BCI competitions) from 9 subjects is used to evaluate the performance of our algorithm. Compared with the classic algorithms: CSP+FLDA, FBCSP+FLDA, the algorithm proposed in [21] (termed as LRC in this paper), and CSSSP+FLDA, our algorithm shows significant classification performance.

2 Methodology

In this section, we explain the computational steps of our algorithm (termed LRSTC). We will show how the spatio-temporal filters and the classifier are learned under a unified objective function, with a regularization term embedded in the function to ameliorate over-fitting.

2.1 Spatio-Temporal Filtering

Under the hypothesis that the discriminative frequency bands of each channel are distinct, we optimize different temporal filters for them. A spatial filter and the channel-specific temporal filters can be formulated as a unique vector, as presented below.

Let $\mathbf{X} \in \mathbb{R}^{C \times T}$ be a single-trial EEG data, where C denotes the number of channels and T denotes the number of sample points. Let $\mathbf{s} = [s(1), s(2), \cdots, s(C)]^{\top} \in \mathbb{R}^{C \times 1}$ be a spatial filter, and $\mathbf{a}_j \in \mathbb{R}^{N \times 1}$ be the j-th temporal filter for corresponding channel with order N. Based on our earlier work [17], the signal that $\mathbf{X}$ spatially filtered by $\mathbf{s}$ and temporally filtered by the temporal filters $\mathbf{a}_j$'s can be presented as: $\mathbf{z} = \mathbf{w}^{\top} \widetilde{\mathbf{X}}$, where $\mathbf{A} \in \mathbb{R}^{N \times C}$ is composed of the C temporal filters: $\mathbf{A} = [\mathbf{a}_1, \mathbf{a}_2, \cdots, \mathbf{a}_C]$, $\mathbf{w} \in \mathbb{R}^{NC \times 1}$ is the spatio-temporal filter:

$$\mathbf{w} = \text{vec}((\mathbf{s}^{\top} \odot \mathbf{A})^{\top}) = [s(1) \cdot \mathbf{a}_1^{\top}, s(2) \cdot \mathbf{a}_2^{\top}, \cdots, s(C) \cdot \mathbf{a}_C^{\top}]^{\top}, \tag{1}$$

and $\widetilde{\mathbf{X}}$ denotes the augmented data matrix:

$$\widetilde{\mathbf{X}} = \begin{pmatrix} \mathbf{X} \\ \mathbf{X}^{(1)} \\ \vdots \\ \mathbf{X}^{(N-1)} \end{pmatrix}, \tag{2}$$

here $\mathbf{X}^{(n)}$, $n \in \{1, 2, \cdots, N-1\}$ is the data matrix delayed n time steps by $\mathbf{X}$. The training data is whitened before applying LRSTC: $\hat{\mathbf{X}} = \Sigma_p^{-\frac{1}{2}}\widetilde{\mathbf{X}}$, where $\Sigma_p = \frac{1}{K}\sum_{i=1}^{K}\frac{\widetilde{\mathbf{X}}\widetilde{\mathbf{X}}^\top}{\mathrm{tr}(\widetilde{\mathbf{X}}\mathbf{X})}$, K is the number of trials for the training data set.

By this way, the temporal filters and the spatial filter can be formulated as a single vector, therefore we can optimize $\mathbf{w}$ and then decompose it into a spatial filter and channel-specific temporal filters.

2.2   Matrix Optimization for Filtering and Classification

Generally, a set of power features (term the number of features as r) are constructed by the spatio-temporal filters for classification. We model the label by weighting the power features of the spatio-temporally by $\mathbf{u}$ with a bias term b added:

$$y = \sum_{j=1}^{r} u_j \mathbf{w}_j^\top \hat{\mathbf{X}}\hat{\mathbf{X}}^\top \mathbf{w}_j + b = f(\hat{\mathbf{X}}; \theta) = \mathrm{tr}[\mathbf{W}\hat{\mathbf{X}}\hat{\mathbf{X}}^\top] + b, \tag{3}$$

where $\theta := (\mathbf{W}, b)$, tr denotes the trace operator, $\top$ demotes the transpose operator, and the rank of $\mathbf{W} = \sum_{j=1}^{r} u_j \mathbf{w}_j \mathbf{w}_j^\top$ is r. We further model the symmetric logit transform of the posterior class probability to be the linear function [3]:

$$\log \frac{P(y = +1|\hat{\mathbf{X}})}{P(y = -1|\hat{\mathbf{X}})} = \mathrm{tr}[\mathbf{W}\hat{\mathbf{X}}\hat{\mathbf{X}}^\top] + b. \tag{4}$$

Then the logistic loss for the overall K trials can be written as follows:

$$\min_{\theta} \sum_{k=1}^{K} \log(1 + \exp(-y_k \cdot (\mathrm{tr}[\mathbf{W}\hat{\mathbf{X}}_k\hat{\mathbf{X}}_k^\top] + b))) \tag{5}$$

2.3   Nuclear Norm for Sparse Constraint

Because of the volume conduction effect, it is likely that most brain sources may not contain classification-relevant information. Thus, the classifier should need only a few spatio-temporal filters to achieve high performance [23]. To address this issue, the rank of $\mathbf{W}$ is added as a penalty term: $\|\mathbf{W}\|_0$. However, the rank penalty is non-smooth, we replace it with nuclear norm, which is a well convex surrogate: $\|\mathbf{W}\|_* = \sum_{j=1}^{r} \lambda_j$, where $\lambda_j, j \in \{1, 2, \cdots, r\}$ are the singular values of $\mathbf{W}$. Consequently, the following convex optimization problem with respect to $\mathbf{W}$ and b is yielded:

$$\min_{\theta} \sum_{k=1}^{K} \log(1 + \exp(-y_k \cdot (\text{tr}[\mathbf{W}\hat{\mathbf{X}}_k\hat{\mathbf{X}}_k^{\top}] + b))) + \rho \cdot \|\mathbf{W}\|_*, \tag{6}$$

where ρ is the regularization parameter.

Therefore, $\mathbf{W}$ and b can be obtained by solving problem (6), and spatio-temporal filters $\mathbf{w}_i$'s and weights of the classifier can be obtained by implementing singular value decomposition on $\mathbf{W}$. The way we choose to decompose $\mathbf{w}$ into a spatial filter s and temporal filters $\mathbf{a}_i, i \in \{1, 2, \cdots, C\}$ is as follows. Suppose $\mathbf{w}^{\top} = [w_{11}, \cdots, w_{1C}, w_{21}, \cdots, w_{2C}, \cdots, w_{N1}, \cdots, w_{NC}]$, we partition $\mathbf{w}$ into C groups: $\mathbf{w}_c^{\top} = [w_{1c}, w_{2c}, \cdots, w_{NC}], c \in \{1, 2, \cdots, C\}$. Then c-th coefficient of the spatial filter is $s_c = \text{sgn}(w_{1c}) \cdot \|\mathbf{w}_c\|_2$, and the temporal filter for the c-th channel is $\mathbf{a}_c = \mathbf{w}_c/s_c$.

In summary, the spatio-temporal filters and the classifier can be optimized jointly by solving a convex optimization problem, which can be tackled conveniently.

3   Experimental Evaluation

In this section, the classification performance of LRSTC is evaluated on one motor imagery EEG data set. The data set is publicly available from past BCI competitions, i.e. Data Set IIa [25] form BCI Competition IV. The performance of LRSTC is compared with four classic algorithms: CSP+FLDA, FBCSP+FLDA, the algorithm proposed in [21] (termed as LRC in this paper), and CSSSP+FLDA.

3.1   Data Set Description

The data set is comprised of 22-channel EEG signals from 9 subjects (subjects $A01$–$A09$) that perform left-hand, right-hand, foot, and tongue motor imagery tasks, with the sampling rate 250 Hz. Both the training and testing sets contain 72 trials per class for each subject. As our aim is to evaluate the algorithm's performance on binary classification, the four category data of each subject is slit into $C_4^2 = 6$ data subsets, therefore we obtain $6 \times 9 = 54$ data subsets. The proposed and competing algorithms are run on each data subset for classification, with some processing details provided below.

3.2   Analysis Pipilines

The processing steps of the considered algorithms are described as follows.

(1) *Preprocessing.* The following steps are applied to the 54 data subsets:
   a) all channels are used.
   b) 7–30 Hz band-pass filtering using 6-th order Butterworth filter.
   c) 0.5–3.5 s time segments, with 0 indicates the time of cue ends.

For FBCSP, we filter the EEG signals into six sub-band components by six 6-th order Butterworth filters (7–11 Hz, 11–15 Hz, 15–19 Hz, 19–23 Hz, 23–27 Hz, 27–30 Hz).

(2) *Feature Extraction.* Multiple spatial/spatio-temporal filters are optimized by each algorithm. We choose the filters corresponding to the 3 largest eigenvalues for each class [6]. The log-variance of the spatially/spatio-temporally filtered signals with respect to each filter are determined as the features.

For CSSSP, the order of temporal filter is determined as $N = 16$, as in [9].

(3) *Classification.* The features are feed into a classification model to obtain the predicted label. FLDA is used as the classifier for CSP, FBCSP, and CSSSP.

For LRC and LRSTC, the spatial/spatio-temporal filters and the classifier are optimized jointly. The training data is also whitened before applying LRC. Considering the computational complexity, we constrain the order of temporal filter in LRSTC as $N = 2$, with the delay tap $n \in \{1, 2, 3, 4\}$. The candidate set of the regularization parameter for LRC and LRSTC is $\rho = 10^{\alpha}, \alpha \in \{-2, -1.8, \cdots, 0, \cdots, 1.8, 2\}$. n and ρ are determined by 10-fold cross-validation.

The models are determined on the training data set, and we use the testing classification accuracies to evaluate the performance of the compared algorithms.

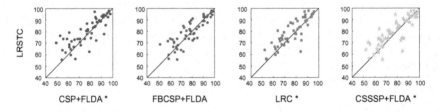

Fig. 1. Classification performance (%) of the compared algorithms on the 54 data subsets. The ∗ beneath each sub-figure shows the significance of the classification results between the two compared algorithm at 0.05 level.

Table 1. Mean classification performance of each algorithm.

	CSP+FLDA	FBCSP+FLDA	LRC	CSSSP+FLDA	LRSTC
mean ± std (%)	77.07 ± 13.70	78.24 ± 12.51	77.01 ± 12.19	77.52 ± 13.14	**79.69 ± 11.66**
p values	0.0087	0.1924	0.0007	0.0068	–

3.3   Performance Comparisons

The mean classification accuracies ± standard deviations of the compared algorithms are summarized in Table 1, the p values are obtained based on the Bonferroni-corrected Wilcoxon signed-rank tests. The testing classification accuracies for the 54 data subsets are displayed in Fig. 1. The points above the diagonals indicate the superiority of LRSTC, and the * beneath each sub-figure denotes the significance of the results between the compared algorithms at 0.05 level. The classification performance of LRSTC is significantly better than other compared algorithms except for FBCSP+FLDA.

4 Conclusions

In this paper, a new algorithm termed LRSTC is proposed, under which the spatio-temporal filters and classifier are optimized jointly. Moreover, a nuclear norm is added to ameliorate overfitting. The optimization problem is convex and thus can be efficiently optimized. LRSTC is applied to one motor imagery EEG data set with 54 data subsets. The testing classification results demonstrate that LRSTC significantly outperforms the classic CSP+FLDA, CSSSP+FLDA, and LRC algorithms. In our future work, more data sets should be added to evaluate the performance of our algorithms.

References

1. Lotte, F., Guan, C.: Regularizing common spatial patterns to improve BCI designs: unified theory and new algorithms. IEEE Trans. Biomed. Eng. **58**(2), 355–362 (2011)
2. Lotte, F., et al.: A review of classification algorithms for EEG-based brain-computer interfaces: a 10 year update. J. Neural Eng. **15**(3), 031005 (2015)
3. Tomioka, R., Müller, K.-R.: A regularized discriminative framework for EEG analysis with application to brain-computer interface. Neuroimage **49**(1), 415–432 (2010)
4. Wu, W., Chen, Z., Gao, X., Li, Y., Gao, S.: Probabilistic common spatial patterns for multichannel EEG analysis. IEEE Trans. Pattern Anal. Mach. Intell. **37**(3), 639–653 (2015)
5. Zeng, H., Song, A.: Optimizing single-trial EEG classification by stationary matrix logistic regression in brain-computer interface. IEEE Trans. Neural Netw. Learn. Syst. **27**(11), 2301–2313 (2016)
6. Blankertz, B., Tomioka, R., Lemm, S., Kawanabe, M., Müller, K.-R.: Optimizing spatial filters for robust EEG single-trial analysis. IEEE Sig. Process. Mag. **25**(1), 41–56 (2008)
7. Lemm, S., Blankertz, B., Dickhaus, T., Müller, K.-R.: Introduction to machine learning for brain imaging. Neuroimage **56**(2), 387–399 (2013)
8. Lemm, S., Blankertz, B., Curio, G., Müller, K.-R.: Spatio-spectral filters for improved classification of single trial EEG. IEEE Trans. Biomed. Eng. **52**(9), 1541–1548 (2005)
9. Dornhege, G., Blankertz, B., Krauledat, M., Losch, F., Curio, G., Müller, K.-R.: Combined optimization of spatial and temporal filters for improving brain-computer interfacing. IEEE Trans. Biomed. Eng. **53**(11), 2274–2281 (2006)
10. Higashi, H., Tanaka, T.: Simultaneous design of FIR filter banks and spatial patterns for EEG signal classification. IEEE Trans. Biomed. Eng. **60**(4), 1100–1110 (2013)

11. Ang, K.-K., Chin, Z.-Y., Zhang, H., Guan, C.: Filter bank common spatial pattern (FBCSP) in brain-computer interface. In: 2008 IEEE International Joint Conference on Neural Networks (IEEE World Congress on Computational Intelligence), pp. 2390–2397. IEEE, Hong Kong (2008)
12. Novi, Q., Guan, C., Dat, T.-H., Xue, P.: Sub-band common spatial pattern (SBCSP) for brain-computer interface. In: Proceedings of the 3rd International IEEE/EMBS Conference on Neural Engineering, pp. 204–207. IEEE, Kohala Coast (2010)
13. Kavitha, P.-T., Guan, C., Lau, C.-T., Vinod, A.-P.: An adaptive filter bank for motor imagery based brain computer interface. In: Annual International Conference of the IEEE Engineering in Medicine and Biology Society, pp. 1104–1107. IEEE Engineering in Medicine and Biology Society, Vancouver (2008)
14. Suk, H., Lee, S.: A novel Bayesian framework for discriminative feature extraction in brain-computer interfaces. IEEE Trans. Pattern Anal. Mach. Intell. **35**(2), 286–299 (2013)
15. Tomioka, R., Dornhege, G., Nolte, G., Blankertz, B., Aihara, K., Müller, K.-R.: Spectrally weighted common spatial pattern algorithm for single trial EEG classification. Technical report, Department of Mathematical Engineering, The University of Tokyo, 40 (2006)
16. Wu, W., Gao, X., Hong, B., Gao, S.: Classifying single-trial EEG during motor imagery by iterative spatio-spectral patterns learning (ISSPL). IEEE Trans. Biomed. Eng. **55**(6), 1733–1743 (2008)
17. Qi, F., Li, Y., Wu, W.: RSTFC: a novel algorithm for spatio-temporal filtering and classification of single-trial EEG. IEEE Trans. Neural Netw. Learn. Syst. **26**(12), 3070–3082 (2015)
18. Bishop, C.: Pattern Recognition and Machine Learning. Springer, Singopore (2007)
19. Murphy, K.-P.: Machine Learning: A Probabilistic Perspective. The MIT Press, Cambridge (2012)
20. Dong, E., Zhu, G., Chen, C., Tong, J., Jiao, Y., Du, S.: Introducing chaos behavior to kernel relevance vector machine (RVM) for four-class EEG classification. PLoS ONE **13**(6), e0198786 (2018)
21. Tomioka, R., Aihara, K.: Classifying matrices with a spectral regularization. In: Proceedings of 24th International Conference on Machine Learning, Corvallis, OR, USA, pp. 895–902 (2008)
22. McFarland, D.-J., Miner, L.-A., Vaughan, T.-M., Wolpaw, J.-R.: Mu and beta rhythm topographies during motor imagery and actual movements. Brain Topogr. **12**(3), 177–186 (2000). https://doi.org/10.1023/A:1023437823106
23. Farquhar, J.: A linear feature space for simultaneous learning of spatio-spectral filters in BCI. Neural Netw. **22**(9), 1278–1285 (2009)
24. Tangermann, M., Müller, K.-R., et al.: Review of the BCI competition IV. Front. Neurosci. **6**(55), 55 (2012)
25. Naeem, M., Brunner, C., Leeb, R., Graimann, B., Pfurtscheller, G.: Seperability of four-class motor imagery data using independent components analysis. J. Neural Eng. **3**(1), 208–216 (2006)

Biometric Traits Share Patterns

Zhengwen Shen, Jun Wang[(⊠)], Guoqing Wang[(⊠)], and Zaiyu Pan

School of Information Control and Engineering, China University of Mining and Technology,
Xuzhou 221000, China

Abstract. Large-scale data-driven DNN models have been proven to achieve great performance in various computer vision challenges, and transfer learning is proposed recently to take advantage of pre-trained DNN on a small database. Under such a framework, an innovative classification model for both identity and gender classification with hand vein information is proposed in this paper. By adopting pre-trained VGG and AlexNet model with ImageNet database and the corresponding fine-tuned ones with PolyU fingerprint and palmprint database, state-of-the-art classification results are obtained with the fine-tuned ones, which indicates that domain-specific model performs better than a generic one, and similar experimental results with faces further indicate that biometric traits share latent patterns. On the other hand, to evaluate the distribution of shared patterns, a quantized shared-index calculated as the number of correlated dictionary atoms is realized based on a sparse representation model.

Keywords: Biometric traits · Pre-trained DNN · Biometric patterns

1 Introduction

Vein recognition, as an emerging and prosperous branch of biometric identification, has attracted numerous research attention due to its outperformed characteristics of being unique, permanent, and live recognition [1, 2], and state of the art recognition rate has been obtained with different models on the vein. However, to the best of our knowledge, there have been no such reports regarding gender classification with analysis on vein information because it seems impossible from visual observation in terms of low-level representation. Today, deep convolutional neural network (DNN) has improved various computer vision task performances due to its ability to learn high-level representation. As a result, DNN-based gender classification with vein information is researched in this paper, and transfer learning strategy with pre-trained models on PolyU palmprint and fingerprint images [3] is introduced for high-level feature extraction followed by linear SVM for classification to obtain the state-of-the-art gender classification result. However, the classification result with the original DNN models trained on ImageNet turns out unsatisfactory, which is against the theory that a larger training dataset could generate a DNN model with better representation ability. To further evaluate the generality of such phenomenon, two different experiment sets with both vein images and face images for identification are carried out and similar results are obtained, which further demonstrate that biometric traits share patterns and the fine-tuned DNN models could well find the

F. Sun et al. (Eds.): ICCSIP 2020, CCIS 1397, pp. 395–401, 2021.
https://doi.org/10.1007/978-981-16-2336-3_37

latent shared representation even with less training images than ImageNet. On the other hand, to better understand how the patterns are shared, a quantized index calculated as the number of common dictionary atoms based on sparse representation model is designed, and the distribution of the index with the same database prove the conclusion.

2 Databases for Model Fine-Tuning

To take advantage of the transferability of the existing model for high-level hand vein feature extraction task, a similar but large-scale database is necessary for model fine-tuning, and the 7752 PolyU palmprint and 3170 fingerprint database [3] are adopted to train new high-level vein feature extraction model with the original one. The additional face recognition experiments are carried out both with the 2.6M VGG face database [4] and the 13233 LFW databases [5]. Besides, the lab-made 1000 database for both identification and gender classification experiments is included as shown in Fig. 1. Apart from keeping gender as 1:1, diversified samples differ in ages; hand thickness as well as capturing session is included in the database. Both the samples for males and females are 50 with 10 images per sample. What's more, it should be noted that the original models are also experimented with the vein images and face images.

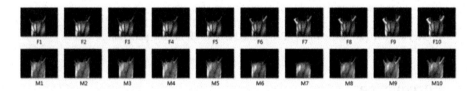

Fig. 1. Samples of the lab-made database (F: female, M: male)

VGG-16 [6] and AlexNet [7] models are selected for direct feature extraction and fine-tuning for their great performance on large-scale ILSVRC recognition challenge [7–9], and the second fully connected layer (FC7) is used for feature extraction, and both networks generate high-level 4096-dimensional feature vector. Apart from re-training the model with the selected databases, the parameters configuration of the two models are both assigned with a weight decay of 0.0005, a momentum of 0.9, a γ of 0.1 with the initial learning rate of 0.001. Besides, the fine-tuning iterations for VGG and AlexNet are 30000 and 50000 respectively.

After obtaining robust feature representation with both the original and fine-tuning DNN models, the simple but effective linear-SVM is adopted as a basis for robust classifier design, and the entire framework of the proposed strategy is illustrated in Fig. 2.

In the gender classification with hand vein information experiment, the linear-SVM is adopted directly as a bi-class classifier, and a multi-class classifier by combining numbers of bi-class linear-SVM training within grouped samples is realized for vein and face recognition. The distribution of the dataset for different task share the same ratio (train: validation: test = 0.67:0.08:0.25). The classifier training is realized in a

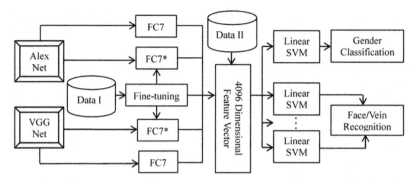

Fig. 2. Proposed recognition framework with AlexNet and VGG-16 Net

grid-search manner with five-fold cross-validation, and the corresponding cost values for linear kernel is set as C = {0.001, 0.01, 0.1, 1, 10, 100, 1000}, and the corresponding classification results under specific experiment setup with different modes could be referenced from Table 1.

Table 1. Average recognition accuracy with different models (The final accuracy are the best ones among all results with different C and folds)

Task	DNN	Model training database	Mode	Accuracy
Vein-based biometric recognition				
Gender classification	VGG	ILSVRC	VGG (I-VG)	26.8%
		PolyU palmprint	VGG (P-VG)	**93.5%**
		PolyU fingerprint	VGG (F-VG)	89.6%
	AlexNet	ILSVRC	Alex (I-VG)	19.3%
		PolyU palmprint	Alex (P-VG)	**92.4%**
		PolyU fingerprint	Alex (F-VG)	90.3%
Identification	VGG	ILSVRC	VGG (I-VI)	28.3%
		PolyU palmprint	VGG (P-VI)	**95.4%**
		PolyU fingerprint	VGG (F-VI)	86.3%
	AlexNet	ILSVRC	Alex (I-VI)	31.5%
		PolyU palmprint	Alex (P-VI)	**92.4%**
		PolyU fingerprint	Alex (F-VI)	90.8%
Face recognition				
VGG face database	VGG	ILSVRC	VGG (I-VFR)	42.6%
		LFW database	VGG (L-VFR)	**96.3%**
	AlexNet	ILSVRC	Alex (I-VFR)	39.4%
		LFW database	Alex (L-VFR)	**94.5%**
LFW face database	VGG	ILSVRC	VGG (I-LFR)	40.7%
		VGG database	VGG (V-LFR)	**92.3%**
	AlexNet	ILSVRC	Alex (I-LFR)	48.3%
		VGG database	Alex (V-LFR)	**93.6%**

Judging from the accuracy distribution from Table 1, it could be concluded that whatever the biometric recognition task is (vein based gender classification or identity recognition, face recognition), all the average classification results share similar trends: the model trained or fine-tuned from the biometrical database perform far better than those with large-scale ILSVRC database, which seems against the common theory that larger database with would generate a better model with greater representation ability. By analyzing the results, a reasonable conclusion could be drawn that biometric share patterns and model trained or fine-tuned on similar biometrical database enable it represents the new biometrical images well, and it is also applicable that larger training database could generate better model under the condition that the original database are biometrical images.

3   Quantized Evaluation on Shared Patterns

In this part, the sparse representation, which involves generating a common dictionary with training images by optimizing a pre-defined objective function followed by reconstructing testing images with the dictionary, is introduced for figuring out the shared patterns by designing a new sparse dictionary, where the atoms representing the similarity of input images are obtained, and the number of the shared atoms is the quantized index for evaluating the shared patterns between input images.

Note that the defined dictionary model is not used for image reconstruction or classification, and all the images are gathered for dictionary generation denoted as evaluated samples. Let $E_i \in \mathbb{R}^{d \times M_i}$, $i = 1, \cdots, N$, represent a group of evaluation samples of class i, and $D_i \in \mathbb{R}^{d \times A_i}$ as the corresponding dictionary, and d is the dimension of evaluated sample, M_i is the number of evaluated samples belonging to ith class, and A_i represent the number of atoms of dictionary D_i. Assuming that there must exist shared patterns between input, the learned dictionary could be divided into two constitute parts: (1) a group of shared atoms denoted as $D_s \in \mathbb{R}^{d \times A_s}$ and (2) remaining group of atoms denoted as $D_r \in \mathbb{R}^{d \times (A_i - A_s)}$. Given that $D_i = [D_s, D_r]$, $C_i = [C_s, C_r]$ the learning algorithm for generating specific dictionary with N categories could be figured out by minimizing a pre-defined objective function as expressed in (1):

$$\min_{\{D_s, D_r, C_i\}_{i=1}^N} \sum_{i=1}^{N} \left[\|E_i - [D_s, D_r][C_s, C_r]\|_F^2 + \lambda \|C_i\|_1 \right] \tag{1}$$

$$\text{And } C_i = \left[c_{i1}, \cdots, c_{iM_i}\right] \in \mathbb{R}^{A_i \times M_i} \tag{2}$$

Where C_i is defined as the corresponding sparse coefficient matrix of sample E_i over learned dictionary D_i, λ is defined as sparsity constraint coefficients with scalar value. The TwIST [8] algorithm is adopted to solve the optimization problem, and extra threshold τ is added during optimization to evaluate the similarities between iteratively optimized dictionary matrix column by column, and the specific solving procedure could be referenced from Table 2.

$$\min_{D_i} \|E_i - D_s C_s - D_r C_r\|_F^2 \text{ s.t. } \|d_r\|_2^2 \leq 1, \forall r = 1, \cdots, A_i \tag{3}$$

Table 2. Shared dictionary learning algorithm

Input: Sample data matrix $\{E_i\}_{i=1}^N$, size of learned dictionary $A_i, i = 1, \cdots, N$, sparsity constraint parameter λ and similarity threshold τ

1. Initialization of D_i and A_i

(a). Initializing the element of $\{D_i\}_{i=1}^N$ and $\{C_i\}_{i=1}^N$ according to the size of input image and database

(b). Fix D_i and update A_i class by class by solving

$\min_{A_i} \|E_i - D_i C_i\|_F^2 + \lambda \|C_i\|_1$

(c). Similarly, fix C_i and update D_i class by class by solving

$\min_{D_i} \|E_i - D_i C_i\|_F^2$ using the Lagrange dual of (1)

Repeat step (a-c) until convergence.

2. Initial Shared-Dictionary Generation

For each dictionary $\{D_i\}_{i=1}^N$, calculate the inner product column by column, and stack those vectors whose inner product is bigger than the predefined threshold τ to form the initial D_s.

3. Optimized and Complete Shared-Dictionary Generation

(d). Compute the initial D_r corresponding to the initial D_s

(e). Forming $D_i=[D_s, D_r]$ and fix it, update A_i class by class by solving equation (1) using TwIST

(f). Fix A_i and update D_r by solving the dual of equation (3)

(g). Similarly, solving the dual of (4) to update D_s

Repeat step (d-g) until convergence to obtain the optimized and complete shared dictionary.

$$\min_{D_s} \|E_s - D_s C_i^s\|_F^2 \text{ s.t. } \|d_i\|_2^2 \leq 1, \forall i = 1, \cdots, A_0 \qquad (4)$$

Where $C_i^s \overset{def}{\Rightarrow} [C_1^s, \cdots, C_N^s]$ and $E_s \overset{def}{\Rightarrow} [E_1 - C_1^s D_1^s; \cdots; E_s - C_N^s D_N^s]$.

Based on the procedure described in Table 2, we design experiments to generate a shared dictionary with all databases in Sect. 2. Before feeding the mixture mode of images into the model, the input of each input is normalized as 256 * 256. Besides, we set the dictionary size of each mode to be equal for simplicity, and the parameters setup are "$\lambda = 0.2$" and "$\tau = 0.9$". For simplicity, only some representative experiments are conducted and the samples randomly selected from VGG face, LFW and ILSVRC are 50 respectively. The number of shared-atoms for those modes could be referenced from Table 3, and it should be noted that each result is the one after convergence.

Judging from the quantized shared-atoms distribution in terms of the selected and representative experiments setup, the conclusion of the first experiment that "biometric

Table 3. Quantized results of shared pattern analysis

Database setup	Number of shared-atoms	Shared ratio
Palmprint + Vein	125	48%
Fingerprint + Vein	132	**56%**
Palmprint + ILSVRC	32	7%
Vein + ILSVRC	16	**4%**
VGG Face + LFW	168	38%
VGG Face + ILSVRC	39	12%

share patterns" are fully validated, and we also argue that the proposed quantized model is also applicable for other similar pattern analysis.

4 Conclusions

To design an appropriate model for realizing gender classification task with hand vein information, a transfer learning strategy with two representative DNN models is adopted to generate high-level feature representation followed by linear SVM for final classification, and state of the art results demonstrate the effectiveness of the proposed model. What's more, an interesting result that domain-specific model fine-tuned with PolyU palmprint and fingerprint database performs far better than the original model trained with large-scale ImageNet database indicates that biometric share patterns which could be found with DNN. On the other hand, to further validate the assumption of shared-pattern, we design a quantized model based on sparse representation to define an index for estimating the distribution of shared patterns between biometric traits, and experimental results fully demonstrate the feasibility of the assumption.

References

1. Wang, G., Sun, C., Sowmya, A.: Multi-weighted co-occurrence descriptor encoding for vein recognition. IEEE Trans. Inf. Forensics Secur. **15**, 375–390 (2020)
2. Huang, D., Tang, Y., Wang, Y., et al.: Hand-dorsa vein recognition by matching local features of multisource keypoints. EEE Trans. Cybern. **45**(9), 1823–1837 (2014)
3. http://www.comp.polyu.edu.hk/~biometrics/
4. Parkhi, O.M., Vedaldi, A., Zisserman, A.: Deep face recognition. In: British Machine Vision Conference (2015)
5. Gary, B.H., Erik, L.M.: Labeled faces in the wild: updates and new reporting procedures. Technical report UM-CS-2014-003, University of Massachusetts, Amherst, May (2014)
6. Karen, S., Andrew, Z.: Very deep convolutional networks for large-scale image recognition. ArXiv e-prints, September (2014)
7. Krizhevsky, A., Sutskever, I., Hinton, G.E.: ImageNet classification with deep convolutional neural networks. In: NIPS, Lake Tahoe, Nevada, December (2012)

8. Bioucas-Dias, J.M., Figueiredo, M.A.T.: A new twist: two-step iterative shrinkage/thresholding algorithm for image restoration. IEEE Trans. Image Process. **54**(11), 4311–4322 (2007)
9. Wang, G., Sun, C., Sowmya, A.: Learning a compact vein discrimination model with GANerated samples. IEEE Trans. Inf. Forensics Secur. **15**, 635–650 (2020)

Cervical Cell Detection Benchmark with Effective Feature Representation

Menglu Zhang$^{(\boxtimes)}$ and Linlin Shen$^{(\boxtimes)}$

Computer Vision Institute, College of Computer Science and Software Engineering of Shenzhen University, Shenzhen, China
zhangmenglu2018@email.szu.edu.cn, llshen@szu.edu.cn

Abstract. As deep convolutional neural networks have shown promising performance in medical image analysis, a number of deep learning based cervical cytology diagnosis methods were developed in recent years. Most studies have achieved available performance in cell classification or segmentation, however, there still exists some challenges for effective screening. Cervical cell detection is a more significant task in cytology diagnosis for cancers. In this paper, we propose a detection framework with effective feature representation for automatic cervical cytology analysis. We employ elastic transformation and a channel and spacial attention module to obtain a more powerful feature extractor. The experimental results demonstrate the efficiency and accuracy improved by our effective feature representation.

Keywords: Cervical cytology diagnosis · Detection framework · Feature representation

1 Introduction

Cervical cancer is one of the fastest evolving and dangerous cancers for women and is most frequently occurred in developing countries [29]. According to the reports of World Health Organization (WHO), cervical cancer is the fourth most common cancer in women. In 2018, an estimated 570,000 women were diagnosed with cervical cancer worldwide and about 311,000 women died from the disease. Nevertheless, cervical cancer is completely preventable and curable if detected and treated in the early stage. Cytological diagnosis is demonstrated to be an effective screening method for cervical cancer mortality reduction [15]. However, manual screening of microscope images is time consuming and labor intensive. Given the limited numbers of experienced pathologists available, population wide screening of cervical cancer is not realistic. Therefore, there is a strong clinical need for the automatic and accurate diagnosis of pre-cancerous changes in the uterine cervix, including cervical cell classification, segmentation and detection.

Thanks to the advent of high-resolution whole slide image (WSI) with Hematoxylin and Eosin (H&E) staining [36], the automated recognition in digital pathology has the potential to provide pathologist with valuable assistance.

© Springer Nature Singapore Pte Ltd. 2021
F. Sun et al. (Eds.): ICCSIP 2020, CCIS 1397, pp. 402–413, 2021.
https://doi.org/10.1007/978-981-16-2336-3_38

Current automation-assisted technologies for screening cervical cancer mainly rely on automated thinprep cytology test (TCT) method, which is widely used to process gynecologic specimens. Most of these studies have achieved reasonable performance in cell classification or segmentation, however, there still exists some challenges for effective screening. First, the majority of existing research in classification were tested using the Herlve dataset [11], which only contains single-cell images with a size of 200 × 100 pixels. Images from Herlve dataset are so clean (with no overlapping and impurity) that the approaches developed on Herlve data are difficult to handle the complex cellular situation in WSI. Second, the segmentation of nuclei and cytoplasm cannot distinguish different instances. Third, it is worth considering that how to extract feature to improve the network representation ability.

In this paper, we propose to utilize both one-stage and two-stage object detectors to develop automatic cervical cytology analysis models. In order to improve the robustness towards various kinds of cells, we introduce elastic transformation [23] to expand the training set by adding a more flexible form of distorted data. Given that cytology images diagnosis mainly depends on an analysis of the lesion cervical cell, on which the clinical interest is focused, the acquired microscope images comprise extra irrelevant details in large area. We apply an attention module [30] on the feed-forward convolution network to increase the network's attention to the relevant features and suppress the unnecessary features.

Our contribution summarized as follows: (1) We provide benchmark performance by leveraging various state-of-the-art detectors on cervical cell detection. (2) We employ elastic transformation to obtain a more powerful feature representation. (3) We introduce a channel and spacial attention module to guide the network to better recognize the cervical cells.

2   Related Work

2.1   Cervical Cell Recognition

Traditional machine learning techniques detect precancerous changes in cervical cells based on color and shape properties of the nuclei and cytoplasms. The extraction of hand-crafted features is difficult to represent the complexities of cell structures [8]. Most existing methods adopt two-phase approach for the segmentation and classification of cervical cells. The first phase involves automatic segmenting cell regions from the background by a multi-scale hierarchical segmentation algorithm, including thresholding [8], morphology operation [2,24], K-means [27], Hough transform [3] and watershed [17]. The second phase aims to classify the regions obtained from the segmentation process using spectral and shape features [7,8,22]. Although these methods work well for the recognition of cervical cells, it is complicated that all stages should be designed carefully. Furthermore, accurate segmentation of cytoplasm and nucleus for the cervical cell is still particularly challenging due to the complexities of cell structures and image characteristics. Therefore, the recognition of cervical cell based on automatic learning is preferred.

Recent years, along with the development of deep learning, many automatic methods have been developed for cervical cytology screening. Zhang *et al.* [37] applied convolutional neural networks to directly classify cervical cells without prior segmentation, which automatically extracts deep hierarchical features. Sornapudi *et al.* [25] proposed a deep learning based nuclei segmentation approach by considering local features, instead of features from the whole image. This CNN is trained to extract local information to classify whether a given region contains nuclei or background. Most existing works have been done for cell classification, as well as nuclei and cytoplasm segmentation [1,6,12].

As the CNN-based object detection achieves significant successes in various computer vision applications, cell detection has been viewed as a more valuable and challenging task. Zhang *et al.* [35] introduced by far the largest cervical cytology dataset and generated the baseline performance for lesion cell detection on it. Xiang *et al.* [31] used YOLOv3 for cervical cells recognition on multi-cell images. However, due to the highly-variable appearances, heterogeneous textures and similar structures, the aforementioned methods could not provide efficient performance for cancer cell detection.

2.2   CNN-Based Object Detection

In deep learning era, object detection can be grouped into two categories: two-stage detection and one-stage detection, the former frames the detection as a "coarse to-fine" process while the later frames it as to "complete in one step".

One-Stage Detector. One-stage detectors are applied over a regular, dense sampling of proposal locations with different scales and aspect ratios to generate the final classification and localization results in one step. Recent works, such as YOLO [18], SSD [14], and RetinaNet [13], have demonstrated promising performance. YOLO divided the image into regions and predicts bounding boxes and probabilities for each region simultaneously. It was the first one-stage detector in deep learning era and a series of improvements have been proposed based on the basic YOLO frame [4,19,20]. SSD combined predictions from multiple feature maps with different resolutions to better handle objects of various sizes. Discovering the foreground-background class imbalance problem, RetinaNet designed focal loss to address such an issue.

Two-Stage Detector. Though faster and simpler, one-stage detectors are generally less accurate than two-stage detectors. Current state-of-the-art detectors are based on a two-stage, proposal-driven mechanism. In a two-stage approach, a sparse set of candidate object proposals are generated first, and then classified and regressed from coarse to fine. Faster R-CNN introduced a Region Proposal Network (RPN) into Fast R-CNN to generate high-quality region proposals [21]. Motivated by the observation that detection performance tends to degrade with increasing intersection over union (IoU), Cascade R-CNN proposed a multi-stage architecture to address this problem [5]. To mitigate the adverse effects caused by imbalance, Libra R-CNN integrated three novel components: IoU-balanced sampling, balanced feature pyramid, and balanced L1 loss, respectively, for reducing the imbalance at sample, feature, and objective level [16].

2.3   Feature Representation

Learning generic and robust feature representations from data is of great value, especially for multi-category classification problem, with insufficient training data. Traditional methods utilized prior knowledges related to morphological characteristics to generate more informative features.

With the development of deep learning, some well-designed networks ensured remarkable performance improvement in various applications for effective feature extracting. ResNet [9] proposed a simple identity skip-connection to ease the optimization issues of deep networks and get more deeper architecture for better feature representation. Based on the ResNet architecture, various models such as WideResNet [33], Inception-ResNet [26], and ResNeXt [32] have been developed. WideResNet proposed to decrease depth and increase width of residual networks and outperformed all previous deep residual network in accuracy and efficiency. ResNeXt suggested to aggregate grouped convolutions and showed that increasing the cardinality led to better performance.

While most of recent networks mainly targeted on three factors: depth, width, and cardinality, attention is a sensible attempt to increase relevant features and suppress the unnecessary features. Wang et al. [28] proposed residual attention network by stacking encoder-decoder style attention modules and generating attention-aware features. Hu et al. [10] adaptively recalibrated channel-wise, instead of space-wise feature responses by explicitly modelling interdependencies between channels. Woo et al. [30] exploited both spatial and channel-wise attention based on an efficient architecture and empirically verified that exploiting both was superior to using only the channel-wise attention.

3   Methods

3.1   System Framework

Motivated by the development of object detection algorithms, we explore how recent successful and widely used detectors can be used for cervical cell detection. For one-stage detection, SSD, YOLO and RetinaNet are adopted as our detection network. While for two-stage detection, Faster R-CNN, Cascade R-CNN and Libra R-CNN are applied for comparison and analysis. The pipeline of cervical cell detection framework based on aforementioned methods is shown in Fig. 1.

3.2   Elastic Transformation

Automatic detection of the cytological image is a very challenging problem. The cytology characteristics such as subtle differences between inter-class, large

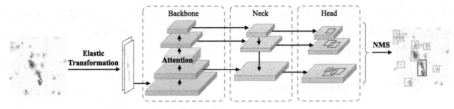

Backbone: VGG16, DarkNet53, ResNet50
Neck: FPN
Head: SSD, YOLO, RetinaNet, Faster R-CNN, Cascade R-CNN, Libra R-CNN

Fig. 1. Pipeline of different detectors for cervical cell detection. An ordinary detector is composed of several parts: Backbone, Neck and Head.

variances within intra-class and cell overlapping, etc., often bring great difficulty to detection. It is vital to improve the representation ability of handling different morphological characteristics. Therefore, we employ elastic transformation [23] to capture more invariant information by generating additional distortions.

Compared with ordinary affine transformations(*e.g.*, translation, rotation, scaling, flip, etc.), elastic deformation is done by computing a new target location, named affine displacement fields, for every pixel(x, y) with respect to the original location. The offset $\Delta x(x, y) = rand(-1, 1)$, $\Delta y(x, y) = rand(-1, 1)$ are generated randomly between -1 and 1 with uniform distribution and filtered with a Gaussian of standard deviation σ (in pixels), where σ is the elasticity coefficient to decide the distortion direction. To control the intensity of the deformation, the displacement fields are multiplied by a scaling factor α. The value of final offset position (x', y') is calculated by bilinear interpolation and used to replace the original value at position (x, y). Figure 2 illustrates how to compute new values for each pixel in a displacement field.

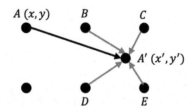

Fig. 2. Compute new value according to the values of corresponding rectangle vertexes using bilinear interpolation in a displacement image, where A indicates the original position, and A' is the target. The value of the A' is computed by the values of B, C, D, E using bilinear interpolation.

Generally speaking, the smaller the α, the smaller the deviation and the closer to the original image. Figure 3 shows examples of distortion with different α.

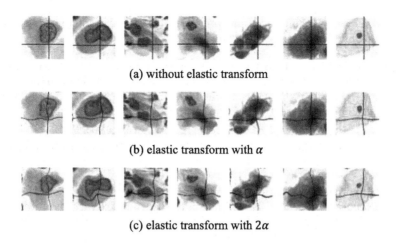

(a) without elastic transform

(b) elastic transform with α

(c) elastic transform with 2α

Fig. 3. Examples of distortion with different α

3.3 Channel and Spacial Attention

In cervical cell detection, relationship with surrounding cell morphology is one of the important cues for accurate diagnosis. As the convolution operator only has a relatively local receptive field, we introduce a channel and spacial attention module [30] during feature extraction, which could sequentially infer attention maps along two separate dimensions, channel and spatial, and compute the interactions adaptively.

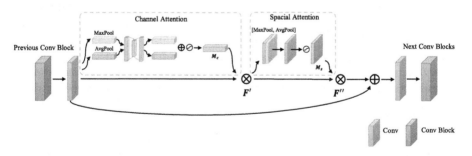

Fig. 4. Attention module introduced in the feature extractor of different backbone, where M_c is channel attention map and M_s is spacial attention map.

Taking an intermediate feature map $F \in \mathbb{R}^{C \times H \times W}$ as input, the attention module sequentially infers a 1D channel attention map $M_c \in \mathbb{R}^{C \times 1 \times 1}$ and a 2D spatial attention map $M_s \in \mathbb{R}^{1 \times H \times W}$ as depicted in Fig. 4. The overall process can be summarized as:

$$F' = M_c(F) \otimes F$$
$$F'' = M_s(F') \otimes F' \tag{1}$$

where $\otimes$ denotes element-wise multiplication. Afterwards, the output attention map is multiplied to the input feature map for adaptive feature refinement.

Channel Attention Module. Considering each channel of a feature map as a feature detector [34], channel attention focuses on 'what' is meaningful in an given image to exploit the inter-channel relationship of features. As illustrated in Fig. 4, the channel attention is computed as:

$$M_c(F) = \sigma(MLP(AvgPool(F)) + MLP(MaxPool(F))) \tag{2}$$

where σ denotes the sigmoid function and MLP represents multi-layer perceptron.

Spacial Attention Module. Different from the channel attention, the spatial attention focuses on 'where' is an informative part to extract the inter-spatial relationship of features, which is complementary to the channel attention. As illustrated in Fig. 4, the spacial attention is computed as:

$$M_s(F) = \sigma(f^{7 \times 7}([AugPool(F); MaxPool(F)])) \tag{3}$$

where σ denotes the sigmoid function and $f^{7 \times 7}$ represents a convolution operation with the filter size of 7×7.

4   Experiments and Results

4.1   Dataset

As there is no standard clinical cervical cell dataset with multi cells publicly available, we establish our own dataset captured by whole-slice scanning machine. The specimens are prepared by Thinprep cytology with H&E staining [36]. Those microscope images are of high resolution, *i.e.*, about 80000×60000 pixels. Figure 5 shows an example image of the dataset, where the region within the green rectangle has been enlarged for better visual display.

We crop each slide image to obtain regions of interest (RoI), where the size of rectangular areas is 1024×1024 pixels. Generally, a slide is converted to around $100-200$ patches. The dataset used in this paper is composed of about 6000 image patches from 7 categories, *i.e.*, Cervical Intraepithelial Neoplasia stage I(CIN_I), CIN_II, CIN_III, Atypical Squamous Cells of Undetermined Significance(ASC_US), Atypical Squamous Cells which cannot exclude High-grade squamous intraepithelial lesions(ASC_H), Squamous Cell Carcinoma(SCC) and normal.

4.2   Evaluation Metrics

We follow the evaluation metric used for Pascal VOC, *i.e.*, mean average precision (mAP). First, AP for each category is calculated at a constant IoU threshold of 0.5. Second, since cervical cell detection is a multiple classification task, we aggregate AP to evaluate the overall performance.

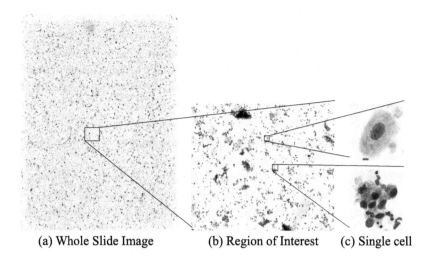

(a) Whole Slide Image   (b) Region of Interest   (c) Single cell

Fig. 5. Example of gigapixel TCT image

4.3   Implementation Details

All experiments are performed on an NVIDIA Tesla V100 GPU with 32 GB of memory. Pytorch is employed as the deep learning framework. Different optimizer, initial rates and training epochs are set for each detector. The detailed experimental settings are listed in Table 1.

Table 1. Implementation details of different detectors

Methods	Backbone	Optimizer	lr	bsz	Epoch
SSD	VGG16	SGD	2e−3	16	24
YOLO	DarkNet53	SGD	1e−2	16	24
RetinaNet	ResNet50	SGD	1e−2	16	12
Faster R-CNN	ResNet50	SGD	2e−2	16	12
Cascade R-CNN	ResNet50	SGD	2e−2	16	12
Libra R-CNN	ResNet50	SGD	2e−2	16	12

4.4   Results and Analysis

In order to validate the effectiveness of different methods for cervical cell detection, we compare the performance in term of accuracy and speed. Table 2 illustrates the results for cervical cell detection based on aforementioned networks and Table 3 shows the comparison of speed among different methods. For one-stage detection, from Table 3 we can see that SSD and YOLO have more advantage in speed. RetinaNet performs better to distinguish different cells, due to the use of focal loss function, which even catches up the results of two-stage detectors for categories like ASC_US and SCC. But in general, two-stage approaches have higher precision. Cascade R-CNN achieves promising performance by progressively increasing IoU thresholds, leveraging the observation that the resampling guarantees a better distribution during training and reduces the overfitting problem, especially for the small dataset.

Table 2. Detection performance comparison among different methods on test set

Methods	CIN_I	CIN_II	CIN_III	ASC_US	ASC_H	SCC	Normal	mAP
SSD	31.73	8.03	10.45	24.74	4.20	18.60	83.06	20.16
YOLO	32.25	8.17	9.97	25.14	4.80	19.80	84.05	20.67
RetinaNet	34.21	10.14	11.97	31.83	5.86	21.23	85.86	23.52
Faster R-CNN	36.37	11.27	12.76	29.94	6.93	20.87	86.28	24.28
Cascade R-CNN	37.14	12.51	12.99	33.63	7.40	22.66	87.19	25.56
Libra R-CNN	36.84	11.96	13.10	32.79	7.54	22.39	87.35	25.14

Table 3. Trade-off on accuracy and efficiency

Methods	mAP	FPS	bsz	Resolution
SSD	20.16	24.7	1	300×300
YOLO	20.67	31.5	1	640×640
RetinaNet	23.52	14.3	1	$\sim 1000 \times 600$
Faster R-CNN	24.28	14.6	1	$\sim 1000 \times 600$
Cascade R-CNN	25.56	13.1	1	$\sim 1000 \times 600$
Libra R-CNN	25.14	10.9	1	$\sim 1000 \times 600$

For ablation studies, we evaluate the contributions of the effective feature extracting methods, including elastic transformation and attention module. We use RetinaNet and Faster R-CNN to represent one-stage and two-stage detectors, respectively. Table 4 demonstrates the results with the improved feature representations. From the results, we can find that elastic transformation improves the accuracy compared with two baselines. It implies that more flexible augmentation on morphology can reduce the overfitting and achieve better performance. In addition, attention module performs slightly better than elastic distortion. It shows that attention module has greater representation ability to enhance relevant features and suppress the unnecessary features.

Table 4. Feature representation ablation on detection

Method	Elastic trans	Attention	mAP
RetinaNet			23.52
	✓		24.36
		✓	24.63
	✓	✓	**24.87**
Faster R-CNN			24.28
	✓		24.91
		✓	25.02
	✓	✓	**25.43**

5   Conclusion

In this paper, we utilize object detection method to achieve the automatic cervical cell detection system. We provide benchmark performance by leveraging various state-of-the-art detectors on cervical cell detection. In order to improve the robustness towards various kinds of cells, we introduce elastic transformation to expand the training set by adding a more flexible form of distorted data. In addition, We employ a channel and spacial attention module to enhance the relevant features and suppress the unnecessary features. The results indicate that better feature representation can detect the cervical cell much more efficiently and accurately. The experiments show that there is still large development space for the detection task. A better approach to analyze cervical cytology remains an open problem for future research.

References

1. Alom, M.Z., Yakopcic, C., Taha, T., Asari, V.: Microscopic nuclei classification, segmentation and detection with improved deep convolutional neural network (DCNN) approaches, November 2018
2. Bamford, P., Lovell, B.: A water immersion algorithm for cytological image segmentation, March 1998
3. Bergmeir, C., Garcia-Silvente, M., Benítez, J.: Segmentation of cervical cell nuclei in high-resolution microscopic images: a new algorithm and a web-based software framework. Comput. Methods Programs Biomed. **107**, 497–512 (2012). https://doi.org/10.1016/j.cmpb.2011.09.017
4. Bochkovskiy, A., Wang, C.Y., Liao, H.Y.M.: YOLOv4: optimal speed and accuracy of object detection. arXiv preprint arXiv:2004.10934 (2020)
5. Cai, Z., Vasconcelos, N.: Cascade R-CNN: delving into high quality object detection. CoRR abs/1712.00726 (2017). http://arxiv.org/abs/1712.00726
6. Chen, K., Zhang, N., Powers, L., Roveda, J.: Cell nuclei detection and segmentation for computational pathology using deep learning, p. 12, April 2019. https://doi.org/10.22360/springsim.2019.msm.012

7. Genctav, A., Aksoy, S.: Segmentation of cervical cell images, pp. 2399–2402, August 2010. https://doi.org/10.1109/ICPR.2010.587
8. Genctav, A., Aksoy, S., Onder, S.: Unsupervised segmentation and classification of cervical cell images. Pattern Recogn. **45**, 4151–4168 (2012). https://doi.org/10.1016/j.patcog.2012.05.006
9. He, K., Zhang, X., Ren, S., Sun, J.: Deep residual learning for image recognition. CoRR abs/1512.03385 (2015). http://arxiv.org/abs/1512.03385
10. Hu, J., Shen, L., Sun, G.: Squeeze-and-excitation networks. CoRR abs/1709.01507 (2017). http://arxiv.org/abs/1709.01507
11. Jantzen, J., Norup, J., Dounias, G., Bjerregaard, B.: Pap-smear benchmark data for pattern classification. In: Nature inspired Smart Information Systems (NiSIS 2005), pp. 1–9 (2005)
12. Khamparia, A., Gupta, D., de Albuquerque, V.H.C., Sangaiah, A.K., Jhaveri, R.H.: Internet of health things-driven deep learning system for detection and classification of cervical cells using transfer learning. J. Supercomput. **76**(11), 8590–8608 (2020). https://doi.org/10.1007/s11227-020-03159-4
13. Lin, T., Goyal, P., Girshick, R.B., He, K., Dollár, P.: Focal loss for dense object detection. CoRR abs/1708.02002 (2017). http://arxiv.org/abs/1708.02002
14. Liu, W., et al.: SSD: single shot multibox detector. CoRR abs/1512.02325 (2015). http://arxiv.org/abs/1512.02325
15. Mishra, G., Pimple, S., Shastri, S.: An overview of prevention and early detection of cervical cancers. Indian J. Med. Paediatr. Oncol. **32**(3), 125–132 (2011). https://doi.org/10.4103/0971-5851.92808
16. Pang, J., Chen, K., Shi, J., Feng, H., Ouyang, W., Lin, D.: Libra R-CNN: towards balanced learning for object detection. CoRR abs/1904.02701 (2019). http://arxiv.org/abs/1904.02701
17. Plissiti, M., Nikou, C., Charchanti, A.: Automated detection of cell nuclei in pap smear images using morphological reconstruction and clustering. IEEE Trans. Inf. Technol. Biomed. **15**, 233–241 (2010). https://doi.org/10.1109/TITB.2010.2087030. A publication of the IEEE Engineering in Medicine and Biology Society
18. Redmon, J., Divvala, S.K., Girshick, R.B., Farhadi, A.: You only look once: unified, real-time object detection. CoRR abs/1506.02640 (2015). http://arxiv.org/abs/1506.02640
19. Redmon, J., Farhadi, A.: YOLO9000: better, faster, stronger. CoRR abs/1612.08242 (2016). http://arxiv.org/abs/1612.08242
20. Redmon, J., Farhadi, A.: YOLOv3: an incremental improvement. CoRR abs/1804.02767 (2018). http://arxiv.org/abs/1804.02767
21. Ren, S., He, K., Girshick, R.B., Sun, J.: Faster R-CNN: towards real-time object detection with region proposal networks. CoRR abs/1506.01497 (2015). http://arxiv.org/abs/1506.01497
22. Sharma, B., Mangat, K.K.: Various techniques for classification and segmentation of cervical cell images - a review. Int. J. Comput. Appl. **147**, 16–20 (2016)
23. Simard, P.Y., Steinkraus, D., Platt, J.C.: Best practices for convolutional neural networks applied to visual document analysis. In: Seventh International Conference on Document Analysis and Recognition. Proceedings, pp. 958–963 (2003)
24. Sivaprakasam, A.S., Ealai Rengasari, N.: Segmentation and classification of cervical cytology images using morphological and statistical operations. ICTACT J. Image Video Process. **07**, 1445–1455 (2017). https://doi.org/10.21917/ijivp.2017.0208
25. Sornapudi, S., et al.: Deep learning nuclei detection in digitized histology images by superpixels. J. Pathol. Inf. **9**, 5 (2018)

26. Szegedy, C., Ioffe, S., Vanhoucke, V.: Inception-v4, inception-ResNet and the impact of residual connections on learning. CoRR abs/1602.07261 (2016). http://arxiv.org/abs/1602.07261
27. Tsai, M.H., Chan, Y.K., Lin, Z.Z., Yang Mao, S.F., Huang, P.C.: Nucleus and cytoplast contour detector of cervical smear image. Pattern Recogn. Lett. **29**, 1441–1453 (2008). https://doi.org/10.1016/j.patrec.2008.02.024
28. Wang, F., et al.: Residual attention network for image classification. CoRR abs/1704.06904 (2017). http://arxiv.org/abs/1704.06904
29. William, W., Ware, J., Habinka, A., Obungoloch, J.: A review of image analysis and machine learning techniques for automated cervical cancer screening from pap-smear images. Comput. Methods Programs Biomed. **164** (2018). https://doi.org/10.1016/j.cmpb.2018.05.034
30. Woo, S., Park, J., Lee, J.Y., So Kweon, I.: CBAM: convolutional block attention module. In: Proceedings of the European Conference on Computer Vision (ECCV), pp. 3–19 (2018)
31. Xiang, Y., Sun, W., Pan, C., Yan, M., Yin, Z., Liang, Y.: A novel automation-assisted cervical cancer reading method based on convolutional neural network. Biocybern. Biomed. Eng. **40**(2), 611–623 (2020)
32. Xie, S., Girshick, R.B., Dollár, P., Tu, Z., He, K.: Aggregated residual transformations for deep neural networks. CoRR abs/1611.05431 (2016). http://arxiv.org/abs/1611.05431
33. Zagoruyko, S., Komodakis, N.: Wide residual networks. CoRR abs/1605.07146 (2016). http://arxiv.org/abs/1605.07146
34. Zeiler, M.D., Fergus, R.: Visualizing and understanding convolutional networks. In: Fleet, D., Pajdla, T., Schiele, B., Tuytelaars, T. (eds.) ECCV 2014. LNCS, vol. 8689, pp. 818–833. Springer, Cham (2014). https://doi.org/10.1007/978-3-319-10590-1_53
35. Zhang, C., et al.: DCCL: a benchmark for cervical cytology analysis. In: Suk, H.-I., Liu, M., Yan, P., Lian, C. (eds.) MLMI 2019. LNCS, vol. 11861, pp. 63–72. Springer, Cham (2019). https://doi.org/10.1007/978-3-030-32692-0_8
36. Zhang, L., et al.: Automation-assisted cervical cancer screening in manual liquid-based cytology with hematoxylin and eosin staining. Cytometry Part A J. Int. Soc. Anal. Cytol. **85** (2014). https://doi.org/10.1002/cyto.a.22407
37. Zhang, L., Lu, L., Nogues, I., Summers, R.M., Liu, S., Yao, J.: DeepPap: deep convolutional networks for cervical cell classification. IEEE J. Biomed. Health Inf. **21**(6), 1633–1643 (2017)

Vision A

Image Fusion for Improving Thermal Human Face Image Recognition

Chu Wang[1], Xiaoqiang Li[2], and Wenfeng Wang[3](✉)

[1] Dongbei University of Finance and Economics, Dalian, China
[2] Fudan University, Shanghai, China
xiaoqiangli16@fudan.edu.cn
[3] Sino-Indian Joint research center of artificial intelligence and robotics, Interscience IIMT,
Bhubaneswar 752054, India
wangwenfeng@iimtcair.edu.in

Abstract. Image fusion is widely used in many fields, such as medical research and remote sensing nowadays. To better address thermal human face image recognition problem in surveillance field, extensive research is done using advanced fusion techniques such as Gabor Filtering and Genetic Algorithm. While traditional fusion techniques are often neglected in most cases. For efficient industrial usage, we compared the recognition rates of six conventional image fusion techniques using the benchmark Tufts Face Databases as data source and using recent iteratively reweighted regularized robust coding (IR^3C) algorithm as evaluation method. Final results showed a great improvement in thermal image recognition rates even compared with advanced methods. Especially the Weighted Average technique and Principal Component Analysis (PCA) shows 99.488% and 98.721% recognition accuracy with a stable performance in relatively small-scale dataset. Discrete Wavelet Transform (DWT), Pyramid Fusion and Select Maximum technique also maintained over 93% recognition rates. Discussions of those high-performance fusion techniques for particular conditions in surveillance field and certain limitations of our work are proposed.

Keywords: Image fusion · Face recognition · Principal Component Analysis · Weighted Average · Discrete Wavelet Transform · Pyramid Fusion

1 Introduction

Image fusion refers to combining multiple images into one image by preserving maximum details and enhancing the performance compared with original ones. A number of leading fusion techniques can be classified into three main levels: pixel-level, feature-level and decision-level [1]. Recently, pixel-level image fusion is widely used in remote sensing [2, 3], medical diagnosis [4] as well as surveillance [5]. However, research conducted in surveillance applications mainly focus on enhancing object or human identification in the field of military, navigation and transportation [6–8]. There is still lack of research in surveillance by fusing thermal and visual human face to enhance recognition

© Springer Nature Singapore Pte Ltd. 2021
F. Sun et al. (Eds.): ICCSIP 2020, CCIS 1397, pp. 417–427, 2021.
https://doi.org/10.1007/978-981-16-2336-3_39

rates in certain conditions. Though some scholars have already done experiments in similar field using more advanced fusion techniques such as Gabor filtering [9] and Genetic Algorithms (GAs) [10] to improve face recognition and resolve face occlusion, traditional fusion approaches are neglected in most cases. However, conventional approaches may also yield good results and are effective to be implemented for the purpose of widely industrial use. Besides, given the thermal image capturing is widely used in surveillance field, improving face recognition accuracy of thermal image will contribute to military and transportation use in foreseeable future. In this paper, we apply several conventional fusion techniques to fuse thermal and visual image of certain people, calculate the accuracy of each technique using IR^3C algorithm, then compare the results with using thermal image alone as well as some more advanced methods.

2   Methods

2.1   Data Resources

In this experiment, we use Tufts Face Databases [11], which contains 74 males and 38 males ranging from 4 to 70 years old. It contains 7 image modalities: visible, near-infrared, thermal, computerized sketch, LYTRO, recorded video and 3D images. We use the TD*IR*E (thermal) and TD*RGB*E (visible) for experiments. Each set has 112 participants and each one has five images taken in (1) a neutral expression, (2) a smile, (3) eyes closed, (4) exaggerated shocked expression, (5) sunglasses. The original resolution of each thermal and visible image is $256 \times 336, 3072 \times 4608$ respectively. After resizing all images to 128×128, we conducted face cutting using CascadeClassifier from Opencv and acquired 391 high-quality pictures in each set. Figure 1 show some thermal and visible images randomly selected after preprocessing.

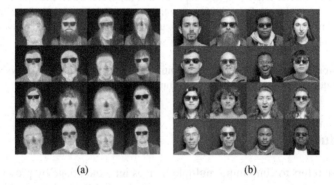

(a)   (b)

Fig. 1.   Sample thermal and visible images. (a) Thermal face image. (b) Visible face image

2.2   Research Designs

We converted thermal and visible images into gray images and conducted image fusion using several techniques (Select Maximum, Select Minimum, Weighted Average, Pyramid Fusion, PCA and DWT) to the thermal image and each corresponding visible image.

Next we evaluated the fusion result by using the original RGB image (converted to gray) as the reference image. The accuracy score is calculated using IR^3C algorithm [12]. Then we compared the accuracy of using thermal image alone with that of using various fusion techniques and evaluated results in light of practical use. Figure 2 briefly shows the whole work flow of our experiments. All the experiments are done in Anaconda-4.7.12 (Python 3.7.0) and CPU condition is Intel(R) Core (TM) i7-7500U CPU @ 2.70 GHz.

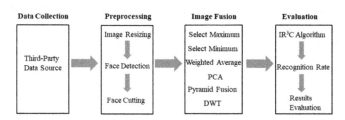

Fig. 2. Experiment work flow

2.3 Image Fusion Techniques

Select Maximum. This method chooses the greatest value pixel from corresponding position in each input image, resulting in the highly-focused fused image.

$$F(i,j) = \sum_{i=0}^{m} \sum_{j=0}^{n} \max A(i,j)B(i,j) \tag{1}$$

For Eq. (1), A(i, j) is the thermal image and B(i, j) is the corresponding visible image.

Select Minimum. Under this technique, the pixel of fused image is determined by the corresponding pixel of input images having the least intensity value.

$$F(i,j) = \sum_{i=0}^{m} \sum_{j=0}^{n} \min A(i,j)B(i,j) \tag{2}$$

For Eq. (2), A(i, j) is the thermal image and B(i, j) is the corresponding visible image.

Weighted Average. Under this technique, pixel of fused image is determined by weighted average intensity of corresponding pixels from the two input images with an added fixed scalar gamma.

$$F(i,j) = \frac{\sum_{i=0}^{m} \sum_{j=0}^{n} W1 * A(i,j) + W2 * B(i,j)}{W1 + W2} + gamma \tag{3}$$

For Eq. (3), A(i, j) is the thermal image and B(i, j) is the corresponding visible image. W1 and W2 are the weights allocated to A(i, j) and B(i, j) respectively. Gamma is the scalar added to each sum. In our experiment, we specified the W1, W2 and gamma equal to 0.4, 0.6 and 10 accordingly.

Principal Component Analysis (PCA). Principal component analysis is widely used in dealing with large amounts of data for dimension reduction. High-dimensional data are projected to eigenspace to minimize covariance and enlarge variance. PCA transforms the correlated data into a set of totally uncorrelated data. The first component is considered as the one has the largest variance, thus more informative. The second component lies in the subspace perpendicular to the first. Thus, PCA keeps important information by retaining the first few components and discarding others.

For PCA image fusion in our experiment as shown in Fig. 3, we first applied PCA to transform each input image to a new set of uncorrelated components without discarding any components. Then we replaced the first component of visible image using that of thermal image and inversely transformed to get the fused image.

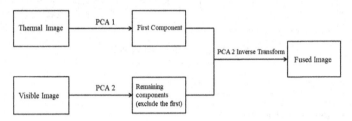

Fig. 3. PCA image fusion work flow

Pyramid Fusion. In our experiment, we applied two pyramid fusion techniques (Laplacian Pyramid and Gaussian Pyramid). As shown in Fig. 4, we first built 5-level Gaussian pyramids for both visible and thermal images. During this process, Gaussian blur and down sampling are repeated to produce the lower level images. Then we used the lowest level visible image to build 5-level Laplacian pyramids. During this process, lower level image is processed by up sampling with Gaussian blur and subtracted by the higher level image. Then the lowest level thermal image will be added to the corresponding higher level Laplacian pyramid image to acquire the first level fused image until the highest level fused image is acquired.

Discrete Wavelet Transform (DWT)
DWT decomposes the input image in different frequencies in terms of approximation component (LL) and detail components (LH, HL, HH). A family of wavelets can be generated by dilating and translating the mother wavelet (y) as shown in Eq. (4).

$$\Psi_{a,b}(y) = \frac{1}{\sqrt{a}} \Psi\left(\frac{y-b}{a}\right), \ (a, b \in R), \ a > 0 \tag{4}$$

Here, a is the scale parameter and b is the shift parameter.

In our experiment, we first conducted 5-level 'db2' wavelet decomposition and resulted in the coefficients list [LL^5, (LH^5, HL^5, HH^5) ... (LH^1, HL^1, HH^1)] for each input image. The fusion decision is to select the maximum absolute value for high frequency images and use simple average technique for low frequency images. Then we

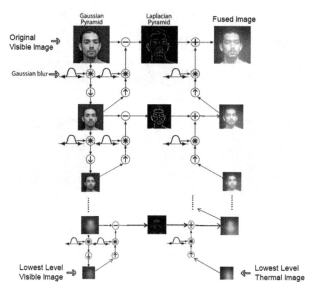

Fig. 4. Five-level pyramid fusion work flow

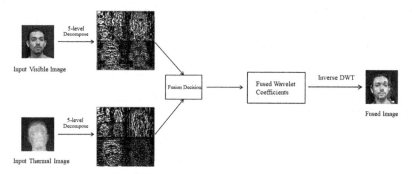

Fig. 5. Five-level db2 wavelet based image fusion

retrieved the fused wavelets coefficients and inversely transformed to get the fused image (as shown in Fig. 5).

In the end of this section, we displayed sample fused images of these six fusion techniques from Fig. 6(a) to (f) as shown in Fig. 6.

2.4 Evaluation Method

To evaluate the fusion result of different techniques, we applied iteratively reweighted regularized robust coding (IR^{3}C) algorithm [12], which is a state-of-art algorithm for face recognition and shows great robustness in various conditions (occlusion, corruption and expression) [12]. By adaptively assigning the weights to pixels iteratively given their coding residuals, IR^{3}C algorithm could reduce the effect of outliers in face recognition

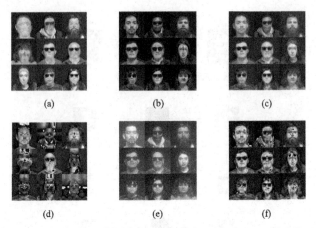

Fig. 6. Sample images of six fusion techniques. (a) Select Maximum. (b) Select Minimum. (c) Weighted Average. (d) PCA. (e) Pyramid Fusion. (f) DWT

process. We made some changes to the algorithm for our experiment needs. The input is L2-Normalized query image datasets Y $(y_1, y_2...y_n, n$ is the total number of queried images) with labels $(l_1, l_2...l_p, p$ is the number of people) and train image datasets D $(D = [r_1, r_2...r_m]$, each column of D represents a face and has unit-l2-norm) with labels $(L_1, L_2...L_p)$. We first set the vector of coding coefficients x equals to $[\frac{1}{m}; \frac{1}{m}; \ldots ; \frac{1}{m}]$. We started from y_1, l_1 and computed the residual value $e^{(t)}$ as Eq. (5):

$$e^{(t)} = y - Dx^{(t)} \tag{5}$$

Here, t is the number of iteration and starts from 1.

Then estimate weight is computed in Eq. (6):

$$\omega_\theta\left(e_i^{(t)}\right) = \frac{1}{\exp\left(\beta\left(e_i^{(t)}\right)^2 - \beta\varepsilon\right)} + 1 \tag{6}$$

Where ε is the parameter of demarcation point and β controls the decreasing rate of weight from 0 to 1, we set initial ε as 0.6 and initial β as 8. Then they will be estimated in each iteration.

The new x for next iteration is computed through weighted regularized robust coding in Eq. (7):

$$x^* = \arg min_x\left\{\frac{1}{2}\left(W^{(t)}\right)^{\frac{1}{2}}(y - Dx)_2^2 + \sum_{j=1}^{m} \rho_0(x_j)\right\} \tag{7}$$

Here $W^{(t)}$ is the estimated diagonal matrix and initial λ as 0.0001.

$$W_{i,i}^{(t)} = \omega_\theta\left(e_i^{(t)}\right), \rho_0(\alpha_j) = \lambda|x_j|^1 + b_{x0} \tag{8}$$

Next we updated the sparse coding coefficients:

$$x^t = x^* \tag{9}$$

Then, we calculated the new residual value using renewed x in Eq. (5), then compared the difference between the new ω and previous one, when the difference is less than 0.05 then stop the iteration. Retrieving the train image label having the minimum difference and recording whether the query image is classified correctly by comparing L with input query image label l. Then processing next query image by resetting t = 1 until all images in query set have been processed. We calculate the recognition rate as Eq. (10)

$$\text{Recognition Rate} = \frac{correct\ classified\ number}{total\ number\ of\ query\ images\ (n)} \tag{10}$$

3   Experiment Results

3.1   Recognition Rates

The recognition rates of six fusion techniques as well as using thermal images are shown in Table 1.

Table 1. Recognition rates of each fusion technique and thermal images

Image fusion techniques	Number of total images processed	Number of successful recognized images	Recognition rates for 128×128 images
Thermal Images	391	18	4.604%
Select Maximum	391	365	93.350%
Select Minimum	391	227	58.056%
Weighted Average	391	389	99.488%
PCA	391	386	98.721%
Pyramid Fusion	391	376	96.164%
DWT	391	375	95.908%

In summary, recognition rate of thermal images is relatively low compared with that of fused images. Among six fusion techniques, recognition rates of PCA and Weighted Average are extremely high by achieving approximately 99%. For Pyramid Fusion, DWT and Select Maximum, recognition results are still over 90%. Though Select Minimum shows lowest performances among them, the recognized pictures are still over half. From Fig. 7(a) to (b), we displayed sample successful recognized faces of thermal image and each fusion technique.

3.2   Further Analysis

According to the recognition rates results, we could find that directly using thermal images for face recognition will result in low performance. However, we could retrieve

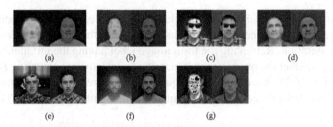

Fig. 7. Sample images of successful recognized thermal images and each fusion technique. (a) Thermal images. (b) Select Maximum. (c) Select Minimum. (d) Weighted Average. (e) PCA. (f) Pyramid Fusion. (g) DWT

a fairly good result while fusing the thermal image with visible image. To justify the robustness of the fusion techniques and minimize the possibility of fluctuant results brought by limited source images, we did another experiment by dividing the each fusion datasets into cumulative and sequential 8 subsets (50, 100, 150, 200…350, 391) and recorded recognition rates of each subset. Table 2 shows the recognition rates in cumulative datasets for each fusion technique.

Table 2. Recognition rates (%) for cumulative query sets of six fusion techniques

Techniques	Sample size of query set							
	50	100	150	200	250	300	350	391
Select Maximum	94.0	90.0	90.7	92.0	92.8	91.7	92.6	93.3
Select Minimum	58.0	51.0	52.0	50.5	53.6	55.0	55.4	58.0
Weighted Average	100.0	99.0	99.3	99.5	99.6	99.3	99.4	99.5
PCA	96.0	98.0	97.3	97.5	98.0	98.3	98.6	98.7
Pyramid	98.0	92.0	94.0	95.0	96.0	96.7	96.3	96.2
DWT	100.0	90.0	93.3	94.5	95.6	95.0	95.4	95.9

Figure 8(a) shows the relationship between recognition rate of each fusion technique and the size of query set. Figure 8(b) shows the zoomed in version. In Fig. 8(a), each plot tends to smooth without obvious fluctuations in general. Such results justified that our data volume is enough for making effective judgements among those fusion techniques and minimized the possibility of disbursements or noise. Select Minimum technique showed the lowest performance among them. Pyramid Fusion, DWT and Select Maximum showed fairly good results from around 90% to 96%. The results of Weighted Average and PCA techniques are approximately 98%–99.5%. From Fig. 8(b), the PCA and weighted Average method did not undergo severe fluctuations like DWT and Pyramid Fusion but achieved higher accuracy and smoother trend. Such findings suggest that PCA and Weighted Average technique may achieve better results compared with other image fusion techniques.

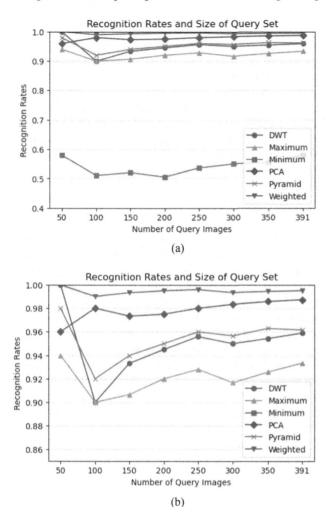

Fig. 8. Relationship between recognition rate of each fusion technique and the cumulative query sets (a) Full version. (b) Zoomed in version.

4 Discussion

The observations from previous section underlie the great enhancement of thermal image face recognition rates using several fusion techniques. Even compared with 95.84% recognition rate of proposed optimized image fusion with Gabor Filter technique [9], PCA and Weighted Average fusion methods yield great results of over 98.5% with stable performance even in small scale datasets. Such results could even compete with Genetic Algorithm fusion technique [10] with recognition rates of 96.8%–99.6%. Though there are still slight differences between recognition rates among those high-performance methods, appropriately choosing methods according to practical conditions should be taken into consideration. For particular, weighted average technique provides a way to adjust the weights allocated to two input images, which could be used when one input image is blurred or corrupted. Weights could be tuned to acquire more accurate fused image and improve the recognition rates for surveillance usage. PCA transformed the data into uncorrelated form and kept most important information of the image by retaining the first few components. For practical use, such technique provides an efficient way to process large image datasets with corruption or occlusion by retaining a reduced set of variables (principal components). Also, Select Maximum technique will produce highly focused fused image for better recognition especially input images are showing low intensity. Even wisely combining PCA and DWT will produce high spatial resolution with high quality spectral content image [13].

5 Conclusion

In this paper, we evaluated results of six image fusion techniques for better thermal image recognition. All fusion techniques show much better performance than directly using thermal image for recognition. Among them, we found that PCA and Weighted Average technique not only showed great results but also maintained stable recognition rates in relatively small scale datasets. The robust feature of these two methods can efficiently minimize noise in small dataset but still show good performance. Other fusion techniques also have particular use in certain conditions, though they have slightly lower performance compare with PCA and Weighted Average.

Certain limitations also existed in our current work. One is that human faces we used are in good illumination conditions, basically registered and free of corruption. Though it still provides a solid conclusion, real conditions are more complex and need further considerations. Another limitation is that fusion techniques are still limited. Though we acquired fairly good results, there is still some space for further optimization using more advanced methods. Thus, there should be more research in optimizing fusion results using more techniques in different illumination conditions, miss registration and severe corruption.

References

1. Blum, R.S., Liu, Z.: Multi-Sensor Image Fusion and Its Applications. Taylor & Francis, Boca Raton (2005)
2. Thomas, C., Ranchin, T., Wald, L., et al.: Synthesis of multispectral images to high spatial resolution: a critical review of fusion methods based on remote sensing physics. IEEE Trans. Geosci. Remote Sens. **46**(5), 1301–1312 (2008)
3. Simone, G., Farina, A., Morabito, F.C., et al.: Image fusion techniques for remote sensing applications. Inf. Fusion **3**(1), 3–15 (2002)
4. James, A.P., Dasarathy, B.V.: Medical image fusion: a survey of the state of the art. Inf. Fusion **19**, 4–19 (2014)
5. Zhou, Z.Q., Wang, B., Li, S., et al.: Perceptual fusion of infrared and visible images through a hybrid multi-scale decomposition with Gaussian and bilateral filters. Inf. Fusion **30**, 15–26 (2016)
6. Kao, W.C., Hsu, C.C., Kao, C.C., et al.: Adaptive exposure control and real-time image fusion for surveillance systems. In: 2006 IEEE International Symposium on Circuits and Systems (2006)

7. Sadhasivam, S.K., Keerthivasan, M.B., Muttan, S.: Implementation of max principle with PCA in image fusion for surveillance and navigation application. ELCVIA: Electron. Lett. Comput. Vis. Image Anal. **10**, 1–10 (2011)
8. Cai, Y., Huang, K., Tan, T., et al.: Context enhancement of nighttime surveillance by image fusion. In: 18th International Conference on Pattern Recognition (ICPR 2006), vol. 1, no. 1 (2006)
9. Hanif, M., Ali, U.: Optimized visual and thermal image fusion for efficient face recognition. In: 2006 9th International Conference on Information Fusion. IEEE (2006)
10. Singh, S., Gyaourova, A., Bebis, G., et al.: Infrared and visible image fusion for face recognition. In: Biometric Technology for Human Identification, vol. 54, no. 4 (2004)
11. Panetta, K., Wan, Q.W., Agaian, S., et al.: A comprehensive database for benchmarking imaging systems. IEEE Trans. Pattern Anal. Mach. Intell. **42**, 509–520 (2018)
12. Yang, M., Zhang, L., Yang, J., et al.: Regularized robust coding for face recognition. IEEE Trans. Image Process. **22**(5), 1753–1766 (2012)
13. Sahu, D.K., Parsai, M.P.: Different image fusion techniques–a critical review. Int. J. Mod. Eng. Res. (IJMER) **2**(5), 4298–4301 (2012)

Automatic Leaf Recognition Based on Attention DenseNet

Huisi Wu[1], Zhouan Shi[1], Haiming Huang[2], Zhenkun Wen[1(✉)],
and Fuchun Sun[3(✉)]

[1] College of Computer Science and Software Engineering, Shenzhen University,
Shenzhen 518060, China
wenzk@szu.edu.cn
[2] College of Electronics and Information Engineering, Shenzhen University,
Shenzhen 518060, China
[3] Department of Computer Science and Technology, Tsinghua University,
Beijing 100083, China
fcsun@tsinghua.edu.cn

Abstract. Automatic leaf recognition algorithm is widely used in plant taxonomy, horticulture teaching, traditional Chinese medicine research and plant protection, which is one of the research hotspots in information science. Due to the diversity of plant leaves, the variety of leaf forms, and the susceptibility to seasonal and other external factors, there is often a small inter-class variance and a large intra-class variance, which brings great challenges to the task of automatic leaf recognition. To solve this problem, we propose a leaf recognition algorithm base on the attention mechanism and dense connection. Firstly, base on dense connection, DenseNet is applied to realize the cross-layer learning of our model, which effectively improves the generalization ability of the network to the intra-class variance. At the same time, the learning ability of our model to the discriminative features such as the veins and textures of plant leaves is also improved. Secondly, we also employ the attention mechanism to further enhance the ability of our network in learning discriminative features of plant leaves. The experimental results show that our Attention DenseNet achieves a high accuracy of leaf recognition in our plant leaf database, including the challenging cases. Visual and statistical comparisons with state-of-the-art methods also demonstrate its effectiveness.

Keywords: Plant leaf recognition · Deep learning · DenseNet · Attention mechanism

1 Introduction

Plants are one of the most important forms of life on Earth, and they are widely distributed and diverse. At present, there are about 300,000 species [13] of plants in nature. Plant taxonomy has a variety of recognition methods such as plant

© Springer Nature Singapore Pte Ltd. 2021
F. Sun et al. (Eds.): ICCSIP 2020, CCIS 1397, pp. 428–436, 2021.
https://doi.org/10.1007/978-981-16-2336-3_40

cell classification, plant genetic recognition, plant serum recognition, and plant chemical recognition. For most non-research professionals, these classification methods are difficult to master, difficult to operate, poor in practicality, and the traditional method of plant classification identification requires the recognition personnel to have rich taxonomic knowledge and long-term practical experience. Even for completing the accurate recognition, sometimes we need to refer to the corresponding search table. The recognition of plants has important value and significance. Among them, plant leaves, as one of the important organs of higher plants, have ubiquitous and easy-to-observe characteristics and are often used by experienced botanists as an important basis for plant recognition [17].

In recent years, research institutions have carried out extensive research on plant recognition based on image processing technology. At present, there are two main methods for leaf recognition based on image processing. One is based on texture, contour, color, vein, shape and other traditional feature extraction methods [2]. The other one is end-to-end deep learning based feature extraction and recognition methods [7]. Recently, with the wide application of deep learning in the field of computer vision [11], the automatic recognition methods of leaf data based on deep learning [4,15] has developed rapidly. The automatic recognition of plant leaf images has two difficulties: one is the large intra-calss variance and the other one is the small inter-calss variance among leaf database. Furthermore, the recognition result of most current automatic plant leaf recognition methods are still lower than behave of most botanists [10]. Therefore, how to train an effective deep learning network, which can enhance the ability to automatically recognize plant leaf images, is still a major challenge.

In this paper, we propose a deep learning model base on the attention mechanism and dense connection. We employ DenseNet [8] to enhance the cross-layer learning ability of the network, thus improving the adaptability of our method to data with large intra-class variance and strengthening the learning ability of the network to discriminative features such as context and texture. Moreover, inspired by SENet [6], we combine the attention mechanism into our model to further enhance the network's learning ability of discriminative features in plant leaf data, enabling the model to have better recognition ability for data with small inter-class variance. We design our model to address these above challenges, while the data may be particularly difficult to recognize by human eyes. Visual and statistical comparisons with state-of-the-art methods on our leaf database also verifies its advantages.

2 Methodology

The framework of our proposed network is shown in Fig. 1. We summarize the architecture of our proposed method into three parts, includes model input, deep features learning and recognition. We employ DenseNet and AM (Attention Mechanism) for obtaining the strongly learning ability of discriminative characteristics in this fine-grained recognition task. Next, the trained model are used to recognize the test image and output the accuracy of the top 5 similar images, which is mainly achieved by using the softmax classifier and the operation of global average pooling. Through these three parts, we achieve a competitive result on leaf database which includes large intra-class variance and small inter-class variance.

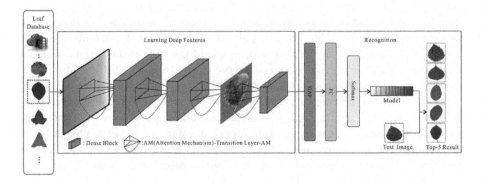

Fig. 1. The framework of our method.

2.1 DenseNet

According to the design concept of DenseNet [8], Attention DeseNet is designed for addressing the challenges of plant leaf recognition task which can partly solve the problem of insufficient learning of important plant leaf features like veins. Similarly, Attention DenseNet also use the Dense Block (DB) module and the Transition Layers as its basic module. Each layer in DB is directly connected so that the output of it in the network can be used as an input to the latter layer to ensure maximum information transmission between layers. This makes the transfer of features and gradients in the network more efficient, and the feature map can be fully utilized. The layer in the DB is a combined structure of BN-ReLU-Conv [14]. The input of each layer in the DB comes from the output of all the previous layers (Fig. 2). Each Transition Layer (TL) consists of a combined structure of BN-ReLU-Conv and a average pooling layer [9]. Specifically, TL can control the number of the output channels by the compression factor (0.5 in our paper). It can optimization the parameters of the model. In this paper, we employ the DenseNet-121 to our model. Similarly, the DenseNet-169 and DenseNet-201 also can be used as the backbone of the our model.

Compared with traditional CNNs [5], DenseNet further solve the insufficient learning problem and can also achieve a deep layer model. Its connectivity pattern can be written as following:

$$\mathbf{x}_\ell = H_\ell([\mathbf{x}_0, \mathbf{x}_1, ..., \mathbf{x}_{\ell-1}]) \tag{1}$$

where $[\mathbf{x}_0, \mathbf{x}_1, ..., \mathbf{x}_{\ell-1}]$ represent a single tensor constructed by concatenation of the previous layers output feature maps. The ℓth layer receives the feature maps of all previous layers as inputs. Therefore, even for the last layer we can still access the input information of the first layer. And all layers receive direct supervision through the shortcut connections.

In our method, the Attention DenseNet contains four dense blocks. Among the dense blocks, there are TLs consisted of a 1×1 convolution followed by a 2×2 average pooling.

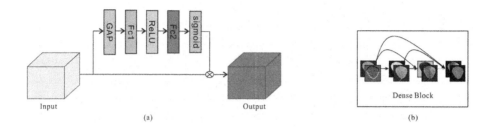

Fig. 2. (a) Attention mechanism; (b) Dense block.

2.2 Attention Module

The attention module for leaf recognition is a computing unit which is designed based on SeNet [6], as shown in Fig. 2(a), in order to enhance the learning weight of important features in plant leaves during the training process of convolutional neural network (CNN), our attention module which is designed by applying the technique of convolution channel weighting is combined to our Attention DenseNet.

Our attention module mainly includes three parts. In detail, we first through the global average pooling (GAP) operation to squeeze the previous feature maps, and the feature compression is performed along the spatial dimension. Meanwhile, each feature channel is converted into a real weight number with global receptive field, while the output dimensions is matching the number of input feature channels. It characterizes the global distribution of the response on feature channels, and allows the layer close to the input for obtaining a global receptive field. Moreover, this characteristic allows the network training to fully learn the global feature information of leaves; Then, we employ a module similar to the gate in recurrent neural network [1]. Moreover, the two fully connected layers form a bottleneck structure to model the correlation between feature channels. The weight of fully connected layers is generated for each feature maps by the parameter w, where the parameter w is learned to explicitly model the correlation between feature channels and output the same number of weights as the input features. The output weight of the two fully connected layers represent the importance of each feature channels; Finally, each channel is weighted to the preceding feature channels by multiplication, and the original feature in channel dimension is re-weighting.

3   Experiment

In our experiment, the PyTorch framework is used for training and model test. All the experiments in this paper are running on the Nvidia GeForce TITANRTX (24 GB RAM) graphics card server. We choose ImageNet database to train from scratch, so that our network can obtain better initialization weights. The training configure follows the standard set in DenseNet [8]. The parameter w in our attention module is set to 16.

Table 1. The detail of our leaf database.

Dataset	Train		Test		All	
	classes	cases	classes	cases	classes	cases
Ours	300	15000	300	3000	300	18000

3.1   Database and Metrics

Our plant leaf database contains 18000 image data of 300 categories, of which 3000 are test data (as shown in Table 1). The leaf database covers single-leaf and compound-leaf plants, which contains the same kind of leaf data and the same compound-leaf category plants with different numbers of compound leaves in different seasons and plant leaves that have been affected by diseases and insect pests and slightly damaged. We use accuracy and MRR (Mean Reciprocal Rank) [3] as the main evaluation indexes in our experiment. In addition, we further evaluates the calculation power, number of parameters and infer time of the model.

3.2   Visual Results

We use the data of plant leaves trained the Attention Densenet. The trained model is then tested on the test set. The final output is most top5 similar recognition results to the test cases. The visualization results of our method on the test cases is shown in Fig. 3.

From the first line of Fig. 3, we can observe that our method can still achieve good recognition result even on complex compound leaves. This mainly benefit from the large depth of our network and the learning ability of cross layer features. As we employ the attention mechanism in our network to enhance the learning ability on discriminative features, we can clearly observe that our method obtains a good recognition result on two categories with high similarity which is shown in the second line and third line of Fig. 3. It can be seen from the visualization results in the fourth line of Fig. 3 that our method can still achieve good recognition result on the test case with smooth surface, no prominent texture and vein features. This is due to the employ of dense connected network which has strong cross-layer learning ability and attention mechanism, which

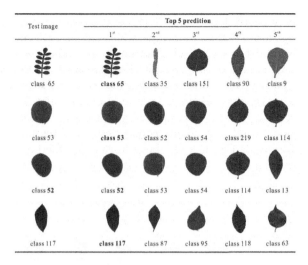

Fig. 3. Visualization of leaf recognition results on our leaf database.

enables our model to fully learn and utilize the characteristics of each layer in the network, so there are good results in identifying such more difficult data. Visual result shows that our model can still achieves good recognition results on challenging samples with large intra-class variance, small inter-class variance and non-prominent veins and texture features.

3.3 Comparison with State-of-the-Art Methods

In order to further evaluate the performance of our method on test cases, three state-of-the-art leaf recognition methods were selected for comparison. Similarly, we use the same experimental environment configuration on these methods, and the test results are visualized as shown in Fig. 4. The fourth line in Fig. 4 represents the test results of our method. From the first line to the third line of Fig. 4 respectively represents the test results of Lee et al. [12], Resnet-26 [16] and Wu et al. [18]. As the deep feature extraction network used by Wu et al. [18] is relatively simple with only contains five layers, the generalization ability among cases with large intra-class is weak. By observing the third line of Fig. 4, it can be seen that the sample cannot be recognition correctly. There is a small inter-class variance between the top1 result which was mistaken by the method of Wu et al. [18] and the correct result. Compared with Wu et al. [18], Lee et al. [12] enhanced the model's ability to recognize the vein characteristics of plant leaves through a strong transformation. Although the sample image is not completely and accurately identified, it obtains a second rank of the recognition probability for the correct sample (as shown in the first line of Fig. 4). Specifically, this strong transformation has a large limitation, and it can not perform well on the leaf data with petioles. Resnet-26 [16] also obtains a second place of the recognition probability for correct sample, which is shown in the second line of Fig. 4. This is due to its deeper network than Wu et al. [18] and a residual structure which can learn identity transformation relationships, which enhances the model's ability to learn depth characteristics and to adapt to intra-class variances. However, while increasing the number of network layers, it also increases the network parameters greatly. Compared with the above three state-of-the-art methods, our method can not only realize the network cross-layer learning and high feature reuse, but also has a strong ability to recognize discriminative features. This mainly benefit from that our model employ the dense connection and attention mechanisms to our model. By observing Fig. 4, it can be seen that our method can still obtain accurately recognition results on the case with small inter-class variance.

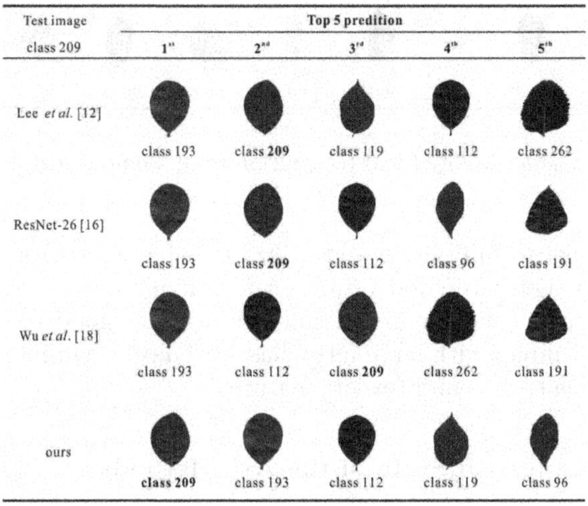

Fig. 4. Comparisons with state-of-the-art methods on our leaf database.

Table 2. Statistical results of comparisons with state-of-the-art methods.

Method	Our Leaf Database				
	Acc.(%)	infer(ms)	MRR(%)	params(M)	flops(G)
Lee et al.[12]	96.9	109	97.5	86.5	0.730
ResNet-26[16]	96.8	29	97.7	13.72	2.41
Wu et al.[18]	96.7	101	97.3	233	0.724
Ours	**97.7**	**26**	**98.6**	**7.52**	**2.88**

The performance of four methods in our database was further compared and analyzed with five metrics which include accuracy rate, MRR, infer time, parameters and flops. It can be seen from Table 2 that compared with the other three state-of-the-art methods, we obtain a higher accuracy rate, which benefit from the deeper layers of our network and stronger discriminative feature learning ability. Furthermore, as the high characteristic reuse of our model, we obtain a better performance on infer time and params. Because our method uses a large depth feature extraction network, it is not superior to the other three methods in calculating power consumption. However, the infer time of our method is shorter than others under the same configuration.

4 Conclusion

In this paper, we present a plant leaf recognition network based on dense connect and attention mechanism. To improve the model's adaptability to intra-class variances, we employ DenseNet as the backbone of our feature extraction network. By employing skip connections and transition layers in DenseNet, our method achieves high feature reuse and strong model generalization capabilities. Furthermore, in order to solve the difficult point of the recognition for data with small variance, we employ the attention mechanism to our model, which effectively enhances the learning ability of discriminatory features on leaf database, meanwhile, only a few model parameters and computational consumption are increased. Visual and statistical results demonstrate its effectiveness. Comparison results with state-of-the-art methods also conducted to verify its advantages.

Acknowledgement. This work was supported in part by grants from the National Natural Science Foundation of China (No. 61973221), the Natural Science Foundation of Guangdong Province, China (Nos. 2018A030313381 and 2019A1515011165), the Major Project or Key Lab of Shenzhen Research Foundation, China (Nos. JCYJ2016060 8173051207, ZDSYS2017073 11550233, KJYY201807031540021294 and JSGG201 805081520220065), the COVID-19 Prevention Project of Guangdong Province, China (No. 2020KZDZX1174), the Major Project of the New Generation of Artificial Intelligence (No. 2018AAA0102900) and the Hong Kong Research Grants Council (Project No. PolyU 152035/17E and 15205919).

References

1. Bahdanau, D., Cho, K., Bengio, Y.: Neural machine translation by jointly learning to align and translate. arXiv preprint arXiv:1409.0473 (2014)
2. Chaki, J., Parekh, R., Bhattacharya, S.: Plant leaf recognition using texture and shape features with neural classifiers. Pattern Recogn. Lett. **58**, 61–68 (2015)
3. Goeau, H., Bonnet, P., Joly, A.: Plant identification based on noisy web data: the amazing performance of deep learning (LifeCLEF 2017) (2017)
4. Gong, D., Cao, C.: Plant leaf classification based on CNN. Comput. Modernization **4**, 12–15 (2014)
5. He, K., Zhang, X., Ren, S., Sun, J.: Deep residual learning for image recognition. In: Proceedings of the IEEE Conference on Computer Vision and Pattern Recognition, pp. 770–778 (2016)
6. Hu, J., Shen, L., Sun, G.: Squeeze-and-excitation networks. In: Proceedings of the IEEE Conference on Computer Vision and Pattern Recognition, pp. 7132–7141 (2018)

7. Hu, J., Chen, Z., Yang, M., Zhang, R., Cui, Y.: A multiscale fusion convolutional neural network for plant leaf recognition. IEEE Sig. Process. Lett. **25**(6), 853–857 (2018)
8. Huang, G., Liu, Z., Van Der Maaten, L., Weinberger, K.Q.: Densely connected convolutional networks. In: Proceedings of the IEEE Conference on Computer Vision and Pattern Recognition, pp. 4700–4708 (2017)
9. Ioffe, S., Szegedy, C.: Batch normalization: accelerating deep network training by reducing internal covariate shift. arXiv preprint arXiv:1502.03167 (2015)
10. Joly, A., et al.: Overview of LifeCLEF 2018: a large-scale evaluation of species identification and recommendation algorithms in the era of AI. In: Bellot, P., et al. (eds.) CLEF 2018. LNCS, vol. 11018, pp. 247–266. Springer, Cham (2018). https:// doi.org/10.1007/978-3-319-98932-7_24
11. Krizhevsky, A., Sutskever, I., Hinton, G.E.: ImageNet classification with deep convolutional neural networks. In: Advances in Neural Information Processing Systems, pp. 1097–1105 (2012)
12. Lee, S.H., Chan, C.S., Mayo, S.J., Remagnino, P.: How deep learning extracts and learns leaf features for plant classification. Pattern Recogn. **71**, 1–13 (2017)
13. Mora, C., Tittensor, D.P., Adl, S., Simpson, A.G., Worm, B.: How many species are there on earth and in the ocean? PLoS Biol. **9**(8), e1001127 (2011)
14. Nair, V., Hinton, G.E.: Rectified linear units improve restricted Boltzmann machines. In: Proceedings of the 27th International Conference on Machine Learning (ICML-2010), pp. 807–814 (2010)
15. Sadeghi, M., Zakerolhosseini, A., Sonboli, A.: Architecture based classification of leaf images (2018)
16. Sun, Y., Liu, Y., Wang, G., Zhang, H.: Deep learning for plant identification in natural environment. Comput. Intell. Neurosci. **2017**, 1–6 (2017)
17. Wäldchen, J., Mäder, P.: Plant species identification using computer vision techniques: a systematic literature review. Arch. Comput. Methods Eng. **25**(2), 507–543 (2018). https://doi.org/10.1007/s11831-016-9206-z
18. Wu, S.G., Bao, F.S., Xu, E.Y., Wang, Y.X., Chang, Y.F., Xiang, Q.L.: A leaf recognition algorithm for plant classification using probabilistic neural network. In: 2007 IEEE International Symposium on Signal Processing and Information Technology, pp. 11–16. IEEE (2007)

Semantic Segmentation for Evaluation of Defects on Smartphone Screens

Huijie Zhu[1,2], Zhuohao Shen[3], Shenggui Yuan[1], Fuliang Chen[1], and Jinhui Li[1(✉)]

[1] Science and Technology on Near-Surface Detection Laboratory,
Wuxi 214035, China
[2] Department of Automation, Shanghai Jiao Tong University,
Shanghai 200240, China
[3] School of Software Engineering, Shanghai Jiao Tong University,
Shanghai 200240, China

Abstract. Smartphone recycling is a heated topic recently because of environmental and economical concerns. However, the limited recognition ability of naked eyes to find defects on phones impedes further growth of the second-hand markets. Related work for this problem focuses on detection and feature extraction, which can be tough because of the thin shapes of the defects and similar characteristics obstructing discrimination between scratches and cracks.

In this paper, we propose an algorithm using semantic segmentation based on HRNet to build an effective model to evaluate defects of screens quickly and precisely. We improve the performance of the model by introducing the Lovász-Softmax loss function and data augmentation. Peripheral methods including subdivision and postprocessing are proposed to reduce misprediction on small scratches and enforce reliability in practice. We compare our model with other networks on mIoU and Kappa scores, concluding on an empirical basis.

Keywords: Semantic segmentation · Convolutional neural network · HRNet · Smartphone

1 Introduction

Recycling of smartphones is becoming a new trend with the enormous growth of the mobile phone market and the saturating capacity of consumer demands [1]. As one of the solutions, second-hand markets of smartphones have seen a rapid expansion in recent years.

However, limited methods of detection on defects of phones, which is a crucial part in evaluating devices, stunt further growth of the market, creating chaos of prices and disorders in transactions. Naked eyes can hardly distinct subtle scratches and cracks on screens from inflections of lights, which slows down the process of evaluation. On the other hand, the absence of widely-recognized objective criteria for appraisal invokes distrust between buyers and sellers.

© Springer Nature Singapore Pte Ltd. 2021
F. Sun et al. (Eds.): ICCSIP 2020, CCIS 1397, pp. 437–448, 2021.
https://doi.org/10.1007/978-981-16-2336-3_41

Therefore, it is necessary to find a highly reliable method to efficiently recognize the defects, displaying them in a human-friendly way. Detection and extractions of defects on a phone screen have been discussed heatedly during recent years [2,3], improvements including detection for floating dirt and adding pre-examinations are proposed to speed up the process [4]. Nevertheless, detection models cannot handle the massive variance of the textures of defects satisfactorily, and the uneven distribution of light has a great impact on the detection of glass substrate without a stable illumination system [5]. It is more natural to use segmentation algorithms and neural networks to seek a solution, but the high resolution of the images demands gigantic video memory and computing resources in regular networks, bringing in huge rises in cost and are not practical. Compressing images will lead to more problems because of the fineness of defects.

HRNet (High-Resolution Network), initially developed for human pose estimation [6], is broadly applied in a wide range of vision tasks. One of the branches focuses on segmentation labeling pixels and regions [7]. It maintains characteristics of high-resolution images by connecting high-to-low resolution convolutions in parallel and multi-scale fusions.

We apply the branch of segmentation for HRNet, gearing it to the best performance in this specific task. With peripheral augmentations, we get a highly efficient model to solve the problem.

In the following sections, we firstly introduce our methods in the order of the process of our algorithm. In Sect. 2.1 we discuss the preprocess of images to reduce computational pressure and improve performance. Section 2.2 discusses the backbone network of our algorithm. Sections 2.3, 2.4 and 2.5 are methods for improving performance when training the model. Section 2.6 discusses the postprocess methods to denoise the final output. Finally, we evaluate our algorithm in Sect. 3.

2   Methods

2.1   Subdivision of Images

To keep all the characteristics of defects, input images are often captured by a line-scan camera to an extreme extent of high resolution. Even if our network can handle all the details with reliable capability, the size of images will still impose large pressure to computing units, slowing down the process of training and evaluating and deteriorating the performance of normalization. In production, huge demand for video memory increases costs which can be a nightmare for phone recyclers.

Subdivision of the images is an ideal way to handle this problem. Suppose scratches and cracks distribute evenly on the screen, then dividing the original images into smaller pieces removes no context of recognition thus do no harm to the training process.

We subdivide all the labeled images (2048 × 1024 pixels) into four pieces each with a resolution of 1024 × 512 (pixels). When training, all four parts are treated as input images. Figure 2 shows the training process. During the evaluation, the program first divides the image to be processed into four pieces, then do segmentation in parallel, which is a reverse process of training.

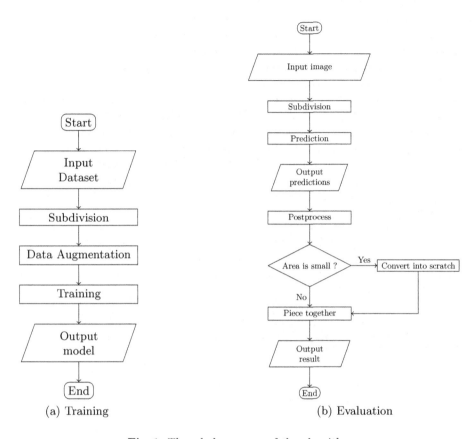

Fig. 1. The whole process of the algorithm

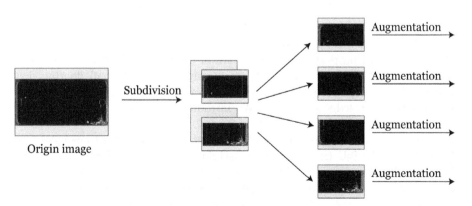

Fig. 2. Subdivision in the training process

The whole process is shown in Fig. 1. When more details are necessary, $\frac{1}{4}$ downsized original images are also inputted as training data.

2.2 HRNet

The key to our problem is that subtle defects are often small on a superficial basis, whose characteristics are often lost in common methods of semantic segmentations. Maintaining details on both large scale stages and low scale stages is vital.

Initially developed from human pose estimation, HRNet adds high-to-low resolution sub-networks each stage, taking a high-resolution sub-network as the first stage, and connects sub-networks with different resolutions in parallel. It keeps the details of origin scales throughout the convolution network. HRNetV2, an extended version of it, exploits other subsets of channels outputted from low-resolution convolutions by rescaling the low-resolution representations through bilinear upsampling to the high resolution and concatenating the subsets of representations [7].

The architecture of HRNetV2 is the same as HRNetV1, composed of four stages, each formed by repeating modularized multi-resolution blocks except the first stage. Each block is a combination of a multi-resolution convolution and a multi-resolution group convolution, which is extended from the group convolution, dividing the input channels into subsets of them and then performing convolution over them separately.

A multi-resolution convolution resembles the multi-branch full-connection manner of the regular convolution, with different resolution levels on input. Thus the connection should handle the variance of resolution by stride convolutions and upsampling.

Modifications of HRNetV2 fully explored the capacity of the multi-resolution convolutions, reducing the loss of other subsets from lower-resolution convolutions.

2.3 Lovász Loss Function

Another problem while training roots in the distribution of target objects. There are fat chances that second-hand phones sold to the recyclers are ill-protected, which leads to disproportionate input data of defects. There are few defects on phone screens while most of whom are merely black and small floating dirt. Moreover, the proportion of scratches and cracks is not even, which leads to poor-learned knowledge on cracks. We introduce a new loss function to solve this problem.

A common way to measure the efficiency of segmentation is to calculate the Jaccard loss, aka IoU (Intersection-over-Union) score. Jaccard loss of class c is calculated by (1)

$$J_c(\boldsymbol{y}^*, \tilde{\boldsymbol{y}}) = \frac{|\{\boldsymbol{y}^* = c\} \cap \{\tilde{\boldsymbol{y}} = c\}|}{|\{\boldsymbol{y}^* = c\} \cup \{\tilde{\boldsymbol{y}} = c\}|}, \tag{1}$$

where $\boldsymbol{y}^*$ is the vector of ground truth labels and $\tilde{\boldsymbol{y}}$ is a vector of predicted labels. It gives a ratio in $[0,1]$ indicating the overlapping efficiency over a union basis, with the convention that $0/0 = 1$. $\varDelta_{J_c}$ is a loss function derived from J_c to be employed in empirical risk minimization defined as

$$\varDelta_{J_c}(\boldsymbol{y}^*, \tilde{\boldsymbol{y}}) = 1 - J_c(\boldsymbol{y}^*). \tag{2}$$

Although $\varDelta_{J_c}$ as a loss function indicates the kernel expectation of segmentation algorithms, it is defined on $\{0,1\}^p$ thus is only assignable to discrete vectors of mispredictions in $\{0,1\}^p$. The general way to continue a set function is to compute its convex closure, which is NP-hard. However, the Jaccard set function has proved submodular and can be continued by Lovász hinge in polynomial time [8].

Definition 1. *The Lovász extension of a set function* $\varDelta$: $\{(0,1)^p\} \to \mathbb{R}$ *such that* $\varDelta(\boldsymbol{0}) = 0$ *is defined by*

$$\bar{\varDelta} : \boldsymbol{m} \in \mathbb{R}^p \mapsto \sum_{i=1}^{p} m_i g_i(\boldsymbol{m}) \tag{3}$$

with $g_i(\boldsymbol{m}) = \varDelta(\{\pi_1, \ldots, \pi_i\}) - \varDelta(\{\pi_1, \ldots, \pi_{i-1}\})$,
$\boldsymbol{\pi}$ *being a permutation ordering the components of* $\boldsymbol{m}$ *in decreasing order.*

When $\varDelta$ is submodular, Lovász extension produces its tight convex closure, and is piecewise linear, interpolating the values of $\varDelta$ in $\mathbb{R}^p \backslash \{0,1\}^p$ [9]. Moreover, $\bar{\varDelta}$ is differentiable, having

$$\frac{\mathrm{d}}{\mathrm{d}\boldsymbol{m}} \bar{\varDelta} = \boldsymbol{g}(\boldsymbol{m}). \tag{4}$$

Synthesizing multiclass cases, using Lovász extension, Lovász-Softmax loss is defined as follows:

$$\mathrm{loss}(\boldsymbol{f}) = \frac{1}{|\mathcal{C}|} \sum_{c \in \mathcal{C}} \overline{\varDelta_{J_c}}(\boldsymbol{m}(c)), \tag{5}$$

where $c \in \mathcal{C}$ and

$$m_i(c) = \begin{cases} 1 - f_i(c), & c = y_i^* \\ f_i(c), & otherwise. \end{cases}$$

2.4   Proportioning Loss Weights

While using Lovász-Softmax in training adjusts the optimization target directly for image-mIoU, it is detrimental to the optimization of dataset-mIoU [10]. The loss considers an ensemble of pixel predictions when computing Lovász extended Jaccard loss, which takes only a small portion of pixel predictions. Thus, optimizing Lovász-Softmax loss cannot directly optimize the dataset-mIoU.

For optimization of the dataset-mIoU, heuristic algorithms and an additional trick to ensure that each lass is visited at least once every $|\mathcal{C}|$ patches. In practice, balancing the two targets by a weighted loss mixed of Lovász-Softmax loss and cross-entropy loss is beneficial.

We test different proportions of the two losses and get roughly optimized weights.

2.5 Data Augmentation

Improving the generalization ability of our models is one of the most difficult challenges, especially in concern of the relatively small size of our dataset. Generalizability is the performance difference of a model between evaluations of training data and alien data. Models with poor generalizability are called overfitting the training data.

One of the measures to improve generalizability is data augmentation. Clipping and translating existing images are the most common ways. In the early phase of the training process, these variations are seen as different types of objects by poor-taught models, which increases the volume of datasets. Moreover, data augmentation adds noises to the model, diluting irrelevant characteristics to avoid overfitting.

In our work, we use clipping, translating, and mirroring methods to augment data.

2.6 Postprocess

The main methods used in our work are mathematical morphology to denoise and connect fragments and Canny edge detector to calculate the area of the object segmented used in substituting smaller cracks with scratches.

In the past few years, mathematical morphology has emerged in the field of shape analysis as a unifying theory. Many key theorems and results in it like generalized dilation and erosion are crucial for upper-class concepts and constructs.

In the context of mathematical morphology, two basic operators are introduced with a kernel-like unit—structuring element.

Definition 2. *Let A be a subset of $\mathbb{Z}^2$, the **translation** of A is defined as*

$$A_x = \{c : c = a + x, a \in A\}. \tag{6}$$

Definition 3. *Let B be a subset of $\mathbb{Z}^2$, the **reflection** of B is defined as*

$$\hat{B} = \{x : x = -b, b \in B\}. \tag{7}$$

Dilation. Dilation produces a thicker version of the original image by extending the edges around each stroke with the same intensity.

Definition 4. *Let A and B be subsets of $\mathbb{Z}^2$, the **dilation** of the object A by structuring element B is given by*

$$A \oplus B = \{x : \hat{B}_x \cap A \neq \varnothing\}. \tag{8}$$

Erosion. A dual operation of the dilation is erosion, which produces a more skinny version of the original image by shrinking the edges around each stroke with the same intensity.

Definition 5. *Let A and B be subsets of $\mathbb{Z}^2$, the **erosion** of the object A by structuring element B is given by*

$$A \ominus B = \{x : B_x \subseteq A\}. \tag{9}$$

In our work, we use operations based on these two basic operations to denoise the output image and connect the gaps and fragments of predicted areas.

3   Results and Discussion

3.1   Apparatus and Materials

Our experiments all execute on the same computer, whose basic hardware information is listed in Table 1.

Table 1. Hardware Information about the Machine Used in Experiment

CPU	Intel® Xeno® Gold 6148
GPU	Nvidia® Tesla V100 32 GB
RAM	32 GB
VRAM	32 GB
Disk	100 GB SSD

We base our experiments on the PaddleSeg framework using PaddlePaddle. Training data are front shot images captured by line scan cameras (Fig. 3). We define two classes of defects to be segmented: scratches and cracks. Cracks are usually long fractures with several branches, while scratches are usually slim and inconspicuous short trails (Fig. 4a). Labeled annotations are converted into pseudocolor images which are more recognizable and straightforward when training and evaluating (Fig. 4b). Note that the scratches are so small that it needs intense magnification for naked eyes to recognize them.

Our dataset contains 212 images, each divided into four pieces. When training, four parts of one image are not relatedly inputted into the network and their losses are also evaluated separately. Thus the actual size of the dataset is equivalent to 848.

Fig. 3. Line scan camera used in the experiment

(a) Origin Image   (b) Labeled Image

Fig. 4. Classes of defects

Table 2. Segmentation results on our dataset

Network		mIoU	Kappa	Average inference time (s)
Name	Backbone			
HRNet-w64	**HRNetV2-W64**	**83.91**	**86.37**	**0.12816**
HRNet-w64 (L80%)	HRNetV2-W64	83.47	85.93	0.12891
HRNet-w48	HRNetV2-W48	82.78	85.26	0.11392
PSPNet	Dilated-ResNet-50	70.31	71.97	0.07738
UNet	ResNet-50	81.44	83.85	0.08655
DeeplabV3+ (ASPP off)	Xception-65	70.56	71.78	0.10249
DeeplabV3+ (ASPP on)	Xception-65	81.61	84.17	0.10140
ICNet (cross-entropy 100%)	ResNet-50	65.31	65.87	0.02003

3.2   Performance Between Networks

The first part of our work is to find the best convolution network as the backbone. Although HRNet maintains the most characteristics from high-resolution, its performance is not certified and the performance can vary when other environmental variables change. Moreover, when it comes to practical applications, efficiency deserves more attention when optimizing accuracy. The data are augmented by step scaling with a minimum factor of 0.8 and a maximum factor of 1.2. Thus the resolution of input images ranges from 819×410 to 1229×614 and it can adapt to different sizes of phone screens. Other augmentations include mirroring and flipping with a ratio of 0.5 with enforced robustness. We use batch normalization with a batch size of 8.

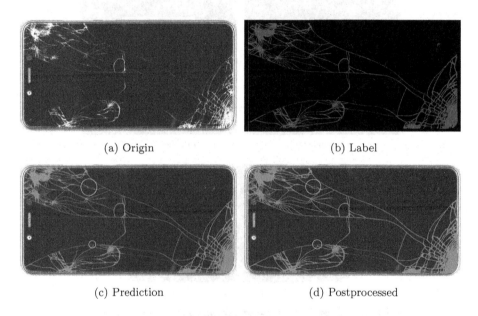

(a) Origin   (b) Label

(c) Prediction   (d) Postprocessed

Fig. 5. Result example 1

All the models of networks used in our experiment are pre-trained with the ImageNet dataset, the loss weights are configured to be 50% Lovász-Softmax loss and 50% cross-entropy if there is no special notation. We set the initial learning rate to 0.01 with the SGD optimizer and use poly dropping. The momentum is 0.9 and the weight decay is 0.005. All the models are trained for 500 epochs.

Table 2 shows the result of all the network compared on mIoU class, Kappa coefficient, and average inference time.

(i) HRNet-w64 trained with 50% Lovász-Softmax loss outperforms other networks. If we do not apply data augmentations, it performs relatively worse in practice. The reason for this abnormality is overfitting when no augmentation method imposed. (ii) HRNet-w48 loses slight performance on the accuracy, but

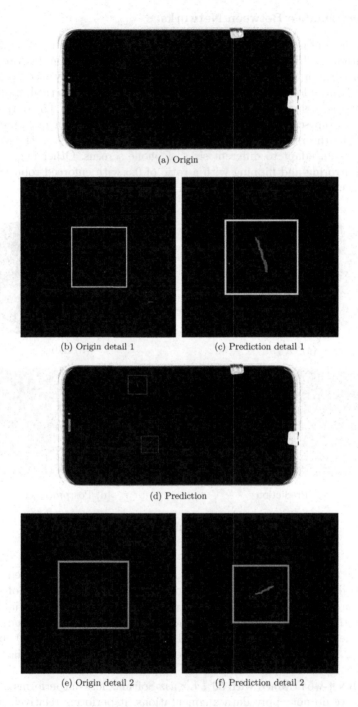

(a) Origin

(b) Origin detail 1   (c) Prediction detail 1

(d) Prediction

(e) Origin detail 2   (f) Prediction detail 2

Fig. 6. Result example 2

it gets faster than w64 for more than 11%. Although the data shown in Table 2 indicates little cost in time per image, when we apply the model into production, higher speed means lower cost on equipment and a larger amount of phones examined.

Comparing between different networks, it is obvious that the more details in high-resolution a network maintains, the better it will perform. UNet's performance is surprisingly outstanding compared to its scale and speed. Skip connection strategy endows it with the ability to maintain some of the characteristics in high-resolution stages. When DeeplabV3+ is trained without ASPP, its performance decreases sharply because of the absence of dilated convolutions from large scales.

The two major objects we want to segment in this problem—scratches and cracks—are both acerose and tapering. Especially considering scratches, which are nearly tracks of pixels on an image, they vanish in the first stage of downsampling mostly. Only when details are kept as much as possible throughout the convolution, can the network learn enough from labeled images.

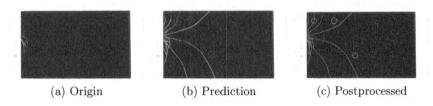

(a) Origin   (b) Prediction   (c) Postprocessed

Fig. 7. Result example 3

3.3   Comprehensive Suggestions

Network. Concerned with choosing the network to train a model for the problem, HRNet owes to be considered because of its performance. However, the number of channels in HRNet depends on practical demands in production. More channels bring higher accuracy while reducing the number of channels brings more speed and loss in precision. Moreover, UNet is an ideal surrogate with a smaller size but a relatively good score on mIoUs.

Postprocess. After our model outputs predictions on the images, there are still nasty problems that improvements of the network can hardly solve. (i)Predictions on a single long crack are often fragments which violate evaluation caused inevitably by subdivisions of the images and thin parts of the cracks lost in downsampling. By extending our prediction area using mathematical morphology, the results are more clear and some breakpoints can be connected. (ii)There are slim chances that a short and small defect on the screen is a crack, but the model often mispredicts in such scenarios. We simply use the Canny edge detector [11] to calculate the area of cracks and substitute all predictions on cracks of area less than 50 pixel^2 with scratch predictions.

Figure 5 and Fig. 6 are examples of our output. Figure 7 is another example for post-process. Note that the scratches are so small that it needs scaling largely to recognize them.

4 Conclusions

In this paper, we empirically study a semantic segmentation based algorithm for evaluation of defects on smartphone screens with introducing HRNet, Lovász-Softmax loss, and postprocessing. Experimental results produce fine details for this problem and feasible suggestions for practical usages. HRNet achieves high performance with the proportionate new loss function compared to other networks. In practice, we post-process the prediction to enforce robustness and clarity, connecting fragments and reducing structural mispredictions, which shows high clarity and is more accurate.

Acknowledgement. This work was supported by the Postdoctoral Science Foundation of China (Grant No. 2019M661510), Science and Technology on Near-Surface Detection Laboratory (Grant No. 6142414180203, 6142414190203), and the Young Scientists Fund of the National Natural Science Foundation of China (Grant No. 41704123).

References

1. Sarath, P., Bonda, S., Mohanty, S., Nayak, S.K.: Mobile phone waste management and recycling: views and trends. Waste Manage. **46**, 536–545 (2015)
2. Jian, C.X., Gao, J., Chen, X.: A review of TFT-LCD panel defect detection methods. In: Advanced Materials Research, vol. 734, pp. 2898–2902. Trans Tech Publications (2013)
3. Lei, J., Gao, X., Feng, Z., Qiu, H., Song, M.: Scale insensitive and focus driven mobile screen defect detection in industry. Neurocomputing **294**, 72–81 (2018)
4. Li, C., Zhang, X., Huang, Y., Tang, C., Fatikow, S.: A novel algorithm for defect extraction and classification of mobile phone screen based on machine vision. Comput. Ind. Eng. **146**, 106530 (2020)
5. Ming, W., et al.: A comprehensive review of defect detection in 3C glass components. Measurement **158**, 107722 (2020)
6. Sun, K., Xiao, B., Liu, D., Wang, J.: Deep high-resolution representation learning for human pose estimation. arXiv:1902.09212 (2019)
7. Sun, K., et al.: High-resolution representations for labeling pixels and regions. arXiv:1904.04514 (2019)
8. Yu, J., Blaschko, M.: The lovász hinge: a novel convex surrogate for submodular losses. arXiv:1512.07797 (2015)
9. Lovász, L.: Submodular Functions and Convexity. Springer, Heidelberg, pp. 235–257 (1983). https://doi.org/10.1007/978-3-642-68874-4_10
10. Berman, M., Triki, A.R., Blaschko, M.B.: The lovász-softmax loss: a tractable surrogate for the optimization of the intersection-over-union measure in neural networks. arXiv:1705.08790 (2017)
11. Canny, J.: A computational approach to edge detection. IEEE Trans. Pattern Anal. Mach. Intell. **PAMI-8**(6), 679–698 (1986)

Image Clipping Strategy of Object Detection for Super Resolution Image in Low Resource Environment

Lei Huang[1,3]([⊠]), Xiaokai Zhang[2,3], Baohua Qiang[1], Jinlong Chen[1], Hongbo Yang[2], and Minghao Yang[3]

[1] Guilin University of Electronic Technology, Guilin 541000, China
[2] Beijing Information Science and Technology University, Beijing 100192, China
[3] Institute of Automation, Chinese Academy of Sciences, Beijing 100190, China

Abstract. Nowadays, deep learning based object detection algorithms have been widely discussed in various application fields. Some super resolution images are not fully supported by the deep learning network structure in low resource hardware devices. An example is the embedded hardware installed on satellite with the super resolution image as input. Traditional methods usually clip the large scale image into small multiple block images, and merge the detect results from clipped images. However, there is still a lack of corresponding strategy to analyze the relationship between detection efficient, including cost time, detection accuracies and the size of block images. To this end, this paper proposes a strategy of image clipping for super resolution images on low resource hardware environment of object detection algorithm. In methodology, we consider the relationship among the number of chip cores, the number of image targets, image input resolution, image block numbers and propose an evaluation method for the optimal efficiency of object detection on low resource hardware. In experiments, the classic Haar detection algorithm runs on TI6678 chips with 8 CPU cores shared with 2.0 G RAM. It shows that the utilization efficiency of object detection algorithm in chip is related to the ratio of segmentation, the number of partitions and the number of CPU cores used. The exploration in this work is also helpful for researchers and developers optimize other algorithms, such as Fast R-CNN, YOLO, on other similar low resource environment in the future.

Keywords: Object detect · Low resources · Embedded hardware

1 Introduction

In recent years, object detection algorithms have been widely discussed in various field, such as security monitoring, gate face recognition, SAR satellite detection and so on. Among which deep learning based object detection algorithms have been widely discussed, among which quit a few methods have been adopt in low resource environment, e.g. traditional face recognition has been transplanted to smart phones and in RISC

L. Huang and X. Zhang—The authors contribute equally to this paper.

© Springer Nature Singapore Pte Ltd. 2021
F. Sun et al. (Eds.): ICCSIP 2020, CCIS 1397, pp. 449–456, 2021.
https://doi.org/10.1007/978-981-16-2336-3_42

Machine (ARM), DSP, ADSP chip and other embedded devices [10], etc.,. In addition, deep architecture based object detection algorithm, such as YOLO V1-V4 object detection algorithms have achieved good detection results [9] on ARM, DSP, field programmable gate array (FPGA). However, since the deep learning network structure requires high power consumption and computing power, some low resource hardware devices do not fully support the deep learning network structure. In addition, some low resource hardware devices could not obtain super resolution images. In this paper, the super-resolution image and "large format" have different meanings. They all refer to the images over 10240×10240 [2]. In such super-resolution images, the target is small and sparse [3]. However, in low resource hardware, computing resources are scarce. It is a challenge to realize the target detection in high-resolution images on low resource hardware devices.

Traditional methods usually clip the large scale image into small multiple block images, and merge the detect results from clipped images [2]. However, there is still a lack of corresponding strategy to analyze the relationship between detection efficient, including cost time, detection accuracies and the size of block images. To this end, this paper proposes a schema to evaluate the correlation between the efficiency on low resource hardware environment of traditional object detection algorithm. We consider the relationship among the number of chip cores, the number of image targets, image input resolution, image block numbers and propose an evaluation method for the optimal efficiency of object detection on low resource hardware.

The remains of the paper are organized as follows: we first introduce the related work in Sect. 2, and we present the workflow in Sect. 3, experiments and discussion are five in Sect. 4, finally, we conclude the paper in Sect. 5.

2   Related Work

2.1   Application Background

The target detection algorithms have widely deployed on various low resource devices. In the second half of 2015, the mobile phone carries the latest face recognition algorithm, which has become the starting point for object detection algorithms to mature and land on low resource devices. Some foreign scholars have studied transplanting machine learning algorithms to low resource hardware and applying them to genome classification [9]. There are also many scholars studying the adaptation of object detection algorithms with low resource devices to complete the "customization" of object detection algorithms for low resource devices, such as the neural processing released by Qualcomm snapdragon in the second half of 2017 Engine (NPE). It supports deep learning and traditional target detection [11].

Whether it is at home and abroad, transplanting the object detection algorithm to low resource chip is the development trend. In the future, more chips will apply these technologies and produce corresponding products to use in various industrial scenarios. Due to the current technical bottleneck, deep learning were not fully supported to DSP chip, especially in some application field, such as object detection in super resolution image, faster detection speed and higher resource utilization rate.

2.2 Low Resource Environment

There are various low resource devices in history, in which some classic object detection algorithms were successfully deployed, such as Texas Instruments (TI) DSP multi-core chip tms320c6678 (c6678), Fast R-CNN, YOLO V2 on Hi3559 chips. In this paper, we choose c6678 [1] as the low resource devices, which does not support deep learning but support the cascade Haar feature extraction algorithm. C6678 is an 8-core DSP processor based on tms320c6678 keystone architecture. The frequency of each core is up to 1.25 GHz, which provides powerful fixed-point core floating-point operation capability. At the same time, the chip integrates multi core navigator, RapidIO and enhanced direct memory with Gigabit Ethernet core Access (EDMA) and other peripherals can be widely used in communication, radar, sonar, fire control, electronic countermeasures and other fields due to its strong chip processing ability, rich peripheral functions, and integration of a large number of hardware accelerators, such as packet accelerator, multicore navigator, etc. From the current situation, due to the above excellent characteristics of c6678, the hardware and software platform based on tms320c6678 will be the mainstream of signal processing platform in the next 5–10 years [1].

The ide of c6678 embedded processor includes debugger, compiler, editor, DSP/BIOS operating system, etc. Studio (CCS) V5 is based on the original eclipse [1]. The c6678 chip development environment is divided into analog chip environment and simulation environment. The former uses CCS software to simulate DSP resource environment on $\times 86$ architecture for virtual debugging, which is similar to the principle of virtual machine; the latter connects DSP chip with CCS development environment through simulator and debugs in real chip environment. In this paper, the latter is used to debug multiple object detection algorithm on real c6678 chip.

3 Method

3.1 Work Flow

The workflow and the evaluation of this paper is given in Fig. 1. We divide the super-resolution image into multiple blocks with equal proportion according to the pyramid overlap rule (the flow chart takes $M \times N$ blocks as an example), and binds the multiple sub images to the specified CPU core on the multi-core CPU bus. Each core uses Haar target detector, and the detected target output result stack is completed after classification. The target is visualized on the original super-resolution image on PC.

Let W, H are the with and high of large image K, and w, h are those of small block images clipped in large scale image, and O_w, O_h are the overlapped width and high among small block images in K. Then we have $m = (H - h)/(h - O_h) + 1$, and $n = (W - w)/(w - O_w) + 1$, and m, n are the number of small image blocks along vertical and horizontal coordinate respectively. Then the relationship between efficiency and block number m, n, single core detection time f_c on the $c^{th}(1 \leq c \leq C)$ core, total parallel detection time T are given as Eq. (1).

$$T = max\left(\forall_{c=1}^{C} f_c\right) \times \frac{(m \times n)}{C} \tag{1}$$

The total time of parallel detection is equal to the maximum value of the product of the cth core time and the optimal coefficient of single kernel.

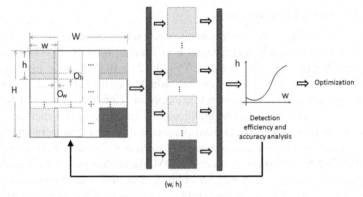

Fig. 1. The proposed objection and efficient analysis evaluation workflow.

3.2 Haar Cascade Target Detection Classifier

Since C6678 does not support deep learning method, we use the Haar cascade target detection classifier, a classic object detection method in efficiency analysis of super resolution image in this work. Haar feature is an image feature extraction algorithm proposed by in 2001 [5]. After several iterations, the algorithm has been well applied to face recognition and object recognition technology [6]. Moreover, several computer vision databases such as opencv have provided training and reasoning tools for the algorithm. Haar feature object detection algorithm has been applied to various detection scenarios, and has been applied in various detection scenarios. Embedded end has good adaptability in low resource environment.

Haar cascade target detection classifier was optimized with AdaBoost [7]. The algorithm adaptively adjusts the error rate of hypothesis according to the result of weak learning. Therefore, AdaBoost does not need any prior knowledge of weak machine performance, and has the same efficiency as boosting algorithm. Each strong classifier is composed of several weak classifiers. The algorithm connects multiple strong classifier together. C6678 chips support opencv and boosting Haar cascade target detection classifier.

4   Experiments

4.1   Super Resolution Images

One of the super resolution image is shown in Fig. 3, which is located in the sea area near Tianjin Port (left). The super resolution images in this work are sampled from Baidu and Google map. A block image of the large scale image is shown as the right image of Fig. 2. We will use Haar cascade target detection classifier to detect ship in parallel on c6678 chips.

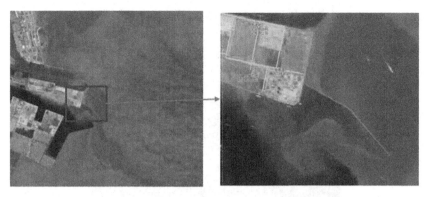

Fig. 2. One of the super resolution image is shown in Fig. 3, which is located in the sea area near Tianjin Port (left) with 16000 × 12000 resolution, and a block image of the large scale image (right) with 3200 × 2800 resolution.

4.2 Multi Core Parallel Detection of Sub Image

The multi DSP parallel computing structure of c6678 is composed of eight DSP chips. It has the characteristics of strong computing power and wide I/O band [8], and high parallel computing performance. Therefore, the algorithm adopts the parallel idea and cuts the super-resolution image into multiple blocks according to the pyramid superposition principle. In order to ensure that the algorithm can be executed independently in multiple cores, the program memory space and sub image storage space need to be planned. In 2G memory space, the allocation scheme is as follows.

Within the available RAM range of DSP, we assign stack space address (using CPU memory), start address in SDRAM and read image address for multi-core program according to the following scheme. The image format is fixed, and the starting address is 0b00x0000, and the image is read from this position. Through the tool, the image data is converted into binary format and loaded into the corresponding memory address of DSP. Each core is assigned the sub image detection task averagely. The sub image has the same header data (width, height and sub image data length), and the second image data is followed by the first image data, so as to complete the splicing of all sub image data.

4.3 Visualization of the Detect Results

There is no operating system and graphical interface on c6678 chip, so the detection results are saved to a fixed memory address, and the multi-core CPU uses the same stack to store the results. On the 8-core chip, only 6 CPU cores are used, and the other two are respectively responsible for preprocessing the input image and collecting the output results. We use a third-party tool to read the memory block of DSP detection results and restore it to the original image to view the detection effect. The visualization result on the image block showed in Fig. 2 on c6678 is given as Fig. 3.

Fig. 3. Visualization of test results of one block on c6678 with 3200 × 2800 resolution, which is coincident with the results detected on PC.

4.4 Optimal Efficiency

We select the image with the ratio of less than 5600 × 4200 as the input image of multi-core parallel detection. We need to determine an optimal ratio to ensure the maximum efficiency of the algorithm. Therefore, we randomly select images with different proportions from 16000 × 12000 super-resolution images and analyze the relationship between image resolution, detection time and detection rate in Table 1. The relationship between them does not grow nonlinearly, so we do many experiments to obtain the optimal sub image ratio. The research methods are as follows:

1) Refine the image scale of 4 × 3 in the range of 400 × 300 ~ 5600 × 4200.
2) Taking 400 × 300 as the unit image, other scale images are represented by integral multiple of the unit.
3) Randomly selected multi-scale images are input to c6678 single core processing.
4) The detection time is divided by the multiple of image blocks, and the result is the normalized detection time.

The smaller the normalized detection time, the higher the chip utilization rate and the better the algorithm efficiency. Therefore, we select the optimal ratio 1440 × 1080 as the sub image ratio of super-resolution image, that is, the optimal coefficient $\varepsilon = 0.340$.

4.5 Discussions

W and H are taken as the super-resolution image size of 16000 × 12000. The Haar algorithm found that the detection time of more than 5600 × 4200 on low resource chip tends to infinity, and the sub image size is analyzed and the optimal image clipping strategy is about 1440 × 1080. The hyperbolic relationship between the number of cuts in the horizontal direction and the length of the overlay buffer is obtained. By analyzing the detection efficiency of multi-scale input image, the detection rate of super-resolution

Table 1. Normalized image scale and algorithm efficiency.

Image block scale	Multiple times of basic block	Detection time one core (in seconds)	Normalized detection time one core
400 × 300	1.00	1.01	1.01
800 × 600	4.00	2.31	0.58
1000 × 750	6.25	3.32	0.53
1200 × 900	9.00	4.16	0.51
1440 × 1080	**12.96**	**5.17**	**0.40**
1600 × 1200	16.00	9.86	0.62
2400 × 1800	36.00	18.10	0.50
3200 × 2400	64.00	30.47	0.48
400 × 3000	100.00	156.00	1.56
4800 × 3600	144.00	279.00	1.93
5600 × 4200	196.00	∞	∞
6800 × 5100	289.00	∞	∞

image reaches 91% and the speed is 30–35 FPS (Frames Per Second), A method that can be used to find the optimal utilization of low resource chips is obtained, The utilization efficiency of object detection algorithm in chip is related to the ratio of segmentation, the number of partitions and the number of CPU cores used. This conclusion is helpful for researchers and developers in this field to set and allocate these dependencies reasonably in the development of low resource chips, so as to optimize the chip utilization.

5 Conclusion

This paper proposes a schema of image clipping for super resolution images on low resource hardware environment of object detection algorithm. In methodology, we consider the relationship among the number of chip cores, the number of image targets, image input resolution, image block numbers and propose an evaluation method for the optimal efficiency of target detection on low resource hardware. In experiments, the classic Haar detection algorithm runs on TI6678 chips with 8 CPU cores shared with 2.0 G RAM. It shows that the utilization efficiency of target detection algorithm in chip is related to the ratio of segmentation, the number of partitions and the number of CPU cores used.

Due to the low power consumption of low resource devices, more and more embedded hardware such as ARM and DSP are used in some specific target detection scenarios. Especially in the context of mobile Internet, the target detection algorithm is becoming more and more accurate. The exploration in this work is also helpful for researchers and developers optimize other algorithms, such as Fast R-CNN, YOLO, on other similar low resource environment for super resolution image in the future.

456   L. Huang et al.

References

1. Tms320 c6678 eight core fixed point and floating point digital signal processor. http://china.findlaw.cn/fagui/p-1/39934.html
2. Chen, G., Ye, F.: Block thinning acceleration algorithm for large image. Comput. Eng. Appl. **37**(023), 101–102 (2001)
3. Wang, T., Sun, H., Sun, J.: Small target detection based on sparse representation. Terahertz J. Sci. Electron. Inf. **17**(5), 794–797 (2019)
4. Jing, R., Tai, X., Cheng, Z., et al.: Optimization method of AdaBoost detection algorithm based on Haar feature (2015)
5. Viola, P.A., Jones, M.J.: Rapid object detection using a boosted cascade of simple features. In: Proceedings of the 2001 IEEE Computer Society Conference on Computer Vision and Pattern Recognition, CVPR 2001. IEEE (2001)
6. Lienhart, R., Kuranov, A., Pisarevsky, V.: Empirical analysis of detection cascades of boosted classifiers for rapid object detection (2003)
7. Xu, W.: Research on target detection system based on AdaBoost algorithm University of Electronic Science and technology
8. Wang, Z., Peng, Y., Wang, X., et al.: A new multi DSP parallel computing architecture and its application. Syst. Eng. Electron. Technol. (03), 20–23 (2001)
9. Randhawa, G.S., Hill, K.A., Kari, L.: ML-DSP: machine learning with digital signal processing for ultrafast, accurate, and scalable genome classification at all taxonomic levels. BMC Genomics **20**(1) (2019)
10. Xie, S.: Design of radar target recognition system based on ADSP-TS101. Xi'an University of Electronic Science and Technology
11. Lu, H.: Research on automatic driving target recognition system. Liaoning University of Engineering and Technology
12. Yu, G., Tan, X., Huo, C.: Design and implementation of ISAR based on tms320 c6678 Special Issue of the 11th National Conference on Signal and Intelligent Information Processing and Application (2017)

Image Quality Assessment with Local Contrast Estimator

Yulian Li, Jun Wang$^{(\boxtimes)}$, and Guoqing Wang$^{(\boxtimes)}$

School of Information Control and Engineering, China University of Mining and Technology,
Xuzhou 221000, China

Abstract. In this paper, a simple, yet effective no-reference image sharpness index for both local and global image sharpness assessment is calculated as the maximized local between-class variation, which is generated by the introduced Fisher discriminant criterion. On the other hand, the idea of dividing the local region into two classes, which we define as content part and background, is adopted to obtain improved Local Binary Pattern (LBP). Based on such LBP and its ability to describe local structure information, a reduced-reference image quality assessment model is realized by combining the shift of LBP histograms and image sharpness index for describing the spatial distribution and structural intensity respectively. Rigorous experiments with three large benchmark databases demonstrate the effectiveness of the two proposed models for both no-reference sharpness and reduced-reference image quality assessment.

Keywords: Image sharpness · Local contrast estimator · Image quality assessment

1 Introduction

With the popularization of multimedia communication, image quality assessment (IQA) is needed as prior knowledge for image restore and image reconstruction because various distortions may be introduced by the acquisition, transmission, and processing of images [1–4]. To our knowledge, a variety of robust and accurate IQA models have been proposed covering full-reference(FR) metrics [5], reduced-reference(RR) metrics [6], and no-reference(NR) metrics [7]. The idea to design an outperformed IQA system is realized by way of mimicking subjective perception of the human visual system (HVS). Regarding all the published IQA systems, FISH [7] is the fastest no-reference IQA model for both local and global sharpness assessment. To propose another fast and effective no-reference IQA system, the local contrast estimator (LCE) based on the idea of HVS is proposed to act as the FISH for IQA, and the idea of LCE is inspired by the fact that the low-level of HVS tends to see things as the background part and the real content, no matter how many things are included in the content, while the degree of contrast between the background and the content could well represent the sharpness of the image. Thus, calculation of maximized between-class variation after clustering image into two parts as background

© Springer Nature Singapore Pte Ltd. 2021
F. Sun et al. (Eds.): ICCSIP 2020, CCIS 1397, pp. 457–463, 2021.
https://doi.org/10.1007/978-981-16-2336-3_43

and content could well represent the contrast information, and the maximization of between-class variation is realized by maximizing the Fisher discriminant score [8].

On the other hand, it is reported that the HVS is highly adapted to capture structural information for better content understanding, and consequently structural degradation model based on LBP is proposed [6] by defining LBP pair shifts between reference and distorted images as spatial distribution degradation. However, the traditional LBP may miss some shifts due to its disadvantage of setting the central pixel as the binarization threshold, followed by resulting in the same codes even distortion occurred as illustrated in Fig. 1(a). Inspired by the method to generate LCE, the procedure, which in terms of classifying images into two parts is realized by finding out the optimal threshold by way of maximizing between-class variance, could be adopted to optimize the LBP coding by selecting a better threshold instead of the central pixel. After obtaining the optimized LBP model, a reduced-reference IQA system is realized by combining the LCE and optimized LBP for both structural intensity and spatial distribution degradation assessment. As for the construction of spatial distribution degradation evaluation model, it is realized by following the whole procedure of [6] except taking the place of traditional LBP with optimized LBP.

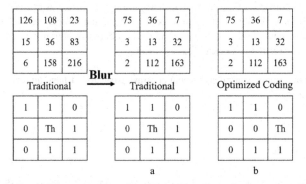

Fig. 1. Comparison of different LBP coding when blur distortion occur, a) Coding result of traditional LBP, b) Coding result of optimized LBP based on LCE theory.

2 Formulation of Local Contrast Estimator

Supposing that local region of input image have been classified into the content and background part with initial threshold, and then the quality of the classification could be measured with the following residual error:

$$\varepsilon(th) = \frac{1}{N}\left\{\sum_{x=1}^{N_b}(I_x - \mu_b)^2 + \sum_{x=1}^{N_c}(I_x - \mu_c)^2\right\} \tag{1}$$

$$\mu_b = \frac{1}{N_b}\sum_{x=1}^{N_b}I_x, \ \mu_c = \frac{1}{N_c}\sum_{x=1}^{N_c}I_x \tag{2}$$

Where N_b is the total number of pixels belonging to background part, while N_c is that of the content part, and N is the total pixels of the local region. By defining μ_b and μ_c to represent the two modes, the constructed residual error could be regarded as the expression of within-class variation $\sigma_w{}^2$ for classes that are partitioned by initial threshold th. The theory that the smaller for the value of residual error, the better effect of the classification, indicates the necessity to minimizing the residual error. According to Fisher discriminant criterion, minimization of residual error is equivalent to maximization of Fisher discriminant score, actually maximization of between-class variance $\sigma_B{}^2$, which are expressed as follows:

$$\sigma_B^2(th) = \frac{N_c}{N}(\mu_c - \mu)^2 + \frac{N_b}{N}(\mu_b - \mu)^2 = \frac{N_c N_b}{N^2}(\mu_c - \mu_b)^2 \qquad (3)$$

Based on the conversion, the sharpness index with LCE for no-reference sharpness assessment could be calculated as the log-energy of the maximized between-class variation:

$$LCE = \log_2 \max{}_{th \in [I_{\min}, I_{\max}]} \sigma_B^2(th) \qquad (4)$$

$I_{\min}$ and $I_{\max}$ represent the minimum and maximum value of the selected local region.

3   Optimized Local Binary Pattern

As the model in [6], the rotation invariant LBP is adopted here for generating optimized local binary pattern, and we name the original LBP and optimized LBP as $LBP_{P,R}^{ri}$ and $OLBP_{P,R}^{ri}$.

It could be inferred from (4) that optimal threshold could be obtained with the maximization of between-class variance. Based on such a threshold calculated as (5), traditional $LBP_{P,R}^{ri}$ with setting threshold as the central pixel could be improved to make up for the disadvantage of Fig. 1(a) to obtain the satisfied result as shown in Fig. 1(b) because the generation of the new threshold is sensitive to local change brought by distortions.

$$th_{optimal} = arg \max{}_{th \in \{I_x\}_{x=1}^N} \sigma_B^2(th) \qquad (5)$$

To further evaluate the superiority of the optimized threshold with $OLBP_{P,R}^{ri}$ against other $LBP_{P,R}^{ri}$ methods, more general coding experiment compared with Fig. 1 is designed as illustrated in Fig. 2 and the different coding results fully show that more stable patterns could be obtained with the optimized threshold generated by maximizing the Fisher discriminant score.

Apart from the advantages of being more discriminative by optimal threshold and weight, and robust to noise, rotation influence, it is also analyzed that the proposed textural descriptor is also affine invariant. Suppose affine change is represented as $ar_i + b$, and it is obvious that different value of coefficient in terms of a and b would generate the same threshold.

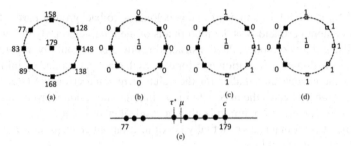

Fig. 2. Example of circle LBP coding with different threshold set, (a) Local 3 * 3 vein patch, (b) $\tau = r(c)$; (c) $\tau = \mu$, (d) $\tau = \tau^*$, (e) threshold distribution

By adopting the local contrast estimator for both contrast evaluation and optimizing formulation of traditional LBP, an improved reduced-reference IQA system could be realized by combining the LCE and optimized LBP for both structural intensity and spatial distribution degradation assessment, and it should be noted that the spatial distribution degradation is realized by following the procedure of [6] and the only modification is to replace the original LBP with the proposed OLBP.

4   No-reference Sharpness Assessment Experiment

The evaluation experiment with LCE for no-reference sharpness assessment is conducted from viewpoint of both global and local evaluation. The LCE with the local region is calculated for local assessment while the average one with the overall image is for global assessment. To comprehensively evaluate the performance of the proposed no-reference sharpness index, six state-of-the-art sharpness estimators including JNBM, CPBD, LPCM, ST, FISH, S_3 together with LCE are tested with the blurred subsets of three benchmark image databases covering LIVE(145 blurred images), TID(96 blurred images), CSIQ(150 blurred images). As for the performance evaluation rules, two classical criterion including Pearson linear correlation (CC) and Spearman rank-order correlation coefficient (SRCC) are adopted for gauging both the prediction consistency and monotonicity.

It can be concluded from Table 1 that the proposed LCE outperforms all the other listed NR sharpness indexes with LIVE and CSIQ databases in terms of CC value contributing to the better performance of average value. As for SRCC, LCE achieves the best performance with both TID and CSIQ databases. Apart from the stressed outperformance value, all the other values, which belong to the two best and highlighted results, are also competitive and fully demonstrate the effectiveness of the proposed no-reference sharpness index. On the other hand, the experiment setup for local sharpness evaluation is completely the same with reference [7], and the specific evaluation result is as illustrated in Table 2, and the competitive results compared with the two state-of-the-art local sharpness evaluation protocols prove the effectiveness of LCE for no-reference local sharpness evaluation task.

Table 1. Performance comparison of various no-reference IQA models with blurred subsets of three benchmark databases. Two best results are highlighted.

	LIVE	TID	CSIQ	Average
	CC			
JNBM	0.816	0.727	0.806	0.786
CPBD	0.895	0.848	0.882	0.875
LPCM	0.917	0.811	0.911	0.892
ST	0.704	0.621	0.690	0.674
FISH	0.904	0.816	**0.923**	0.893
S_3	**0.943**	**0.877**	0.911	**0.914**
Proposed	**0.943**	**0.872**	**0.932**	**0.917**
	SRCC			
JNBM	0.787	0.714	0.762	0.755
CPBD	0.919	**0.854**	0.885	0.884
LPCM	0.928	0.803	0.905	0.886
ST	0.702	0.516	0.705	0.645
FISH	0.881	0.786	0.894	0.866
S_3	**0.944**	0.850	**0.906**	**0.904**
Proposed	**0.935**	**0.863**	**0.912**	**0.903**

5   Reduced-Reference IQA Experiment

In this part, the final IQA score consists of two part including LCE for structural intensity evaluation and distance of optimized LBP histograms between distorted and reference images for spatial distribution degradation evaluation and the calculation of LCE is the same with NR experiment. As for the second score, it is obtained by the way consistent with that of [8], where SVR is adopted to pool the histogram features and return the quality score, and the only changing part is replacing the traditional LBP with the optimized LBP for the more accurate description of the distortion, the weight for LCE and optimized LBP is set as 0.3 and 0.7 empirically. The databases are different from the above one where all the examples but not the blurred subsets are adopted for evaluation. The performance evaluation criterion is the same with the first experiment while the compared methods are replaced by four reduced-reference ones including IGM, ADM, FSIM, and the traditional LBP based metric [6].

Because the SVR model is employed to generate the spatial structural degradation score, a training experiment with 80% random-selected images including both reference images and corresponding distorted images is conducted firstly to obtain the regression model, followed by a testing experiment with the remaining 20% images. To obtain more reliable results, the 80%–20% training-testing experiments are repeated 100 times and then the average values are adopted as the final prediction results as shown in Table 3.

Table 2. Comparison of local sharpness assessment performance

	Proposed	S_3	$FISH_{bb}$
Image	**SRCC**		
Dragon	0.928	**0.931**	0.923
Flower	0.745	0.712	**0.749**
Monkey	0.836	**0.916**	0.897
Orchid	**0.923**	0.920	0.910
Peak	0.910	0.901	**0.912**
Squirrel	0.835	0.794	**0.854**
Average	0.863	0.862	**0.874**
	CC		
Dragon	**0.951**	0.947	0.950
Flower	0.929	**0.936**	0.927
Monkey	0.937	0.944	**0.959**
Orchid	0.924	0.914	**0.929**
Peak	0.927	**0.928**	0.927
Squirrel	**0.958**	0.958	0.954
Average	0.935	0.938	**0.941**

Table 3. Performance comparison with other Reduced-reference IQA

	LIVE	TID	CSIQ	Average
	CC			
IGM	0.958	0.886	0.928	0.914
ADM	0.936	0.869	0.928	0.900
FSIM	0.960	0.874	0.912	0.905
LBP [3]	0.961	0.914	0.960	0.937
Proposed	**0.968**	**0.918**	**0.962**	**0.941**
	SRCC			
IGM	0.958	0.890	0.940	0.919
ADM	0.954	0.862	0.933	0.902
FSIM	0.963	0.881	0.924	0.912
LBP [3]	0.964	0.908	**0.965**	0.936
Proposed	**0.970**	**0.910**	**0.965**	**0.948**

Judging by the results listed in Table 3, it could be concluded that both the values in terms of CC and SRCC obtained by the proposed RR-IQA model are larger than that of the state-of-the-art models, which means the proposed model outperforms the seven famous reduced-reference IQA models, and achieve the best-ever RR-IQA results.

6 Conclusions

In this paper, a novel local contrast estimator instead of the traditional variance is calculated as the local maximized between-class variance, which is generated by adopting the Fisher discriminant criterion. Based on the LCE theory, two image quality assessment systems are realized in terms of no-reference sharpness assessment IQA and reduced-reference image distortion IQA. The log-energy of local between-class variation is calculated as sharpness index for both local and global no-reference sharpness assessment. On the other hand, the threshold corresponding to the one resulting in maximized local between-class variation is adopted to optimize the traditional LBP so as to obtain the optimized LBP which is more sensitive to image distortion, thus a more accurate reduced-reference image distortion IQA system is realized by adopting LCE for structural intensity degradation evaluation and distance of optimized LBP histograms between distorted and reference images for spatial distribution degradation evaluation. Rigorous experimental results have demonstrated that the proposed two IQA systems outperform most state-of-the-art IQA models and are highly consistent with the HVS perception.

References

1. Bong, D., Khoo, B.: An efficient and training-free blind image blur assessment in the spatial domain. IEICE Trans. Inf. Syst. **7**, 1864–1871 (2014)
2. Wang, Y., Ren, S., Dong, F.: A transformation-domain image reconstruction method for open electrical impedance tomography based on conformal mapping. IEEE Sens. J. **19**(5), 1873–1883 (2019)
3. Chow, C.W., Shi, R.J., Liu, Y.C., et al.: Non-flickering 100 m RGB visible light communication transmission based on a CMOS image sensor. Opt. Express **26**(6), 7079 (2018)
4. Xie, H., Lei, H., He, Y., et al.: Deeply supervised full convolution network for HEp-2 specimen image segmentation. Neurocomputing **351**(25), 77–86 (2019)
5. Li, L., Zhou, Y., Wu, J., Qian, J., Chen, B.: Color-enriched gradient similarity for retouched image quality evaluation. IEICE Trans. Inf. Syst. **3**, 773–776 (2016)
6. Wu, J., Lin, W., Shi, G.: Image quality assessment with degradation on spatial structure. IEEE Signal Proc. Lett. **21**(4), 437–440 (2014)
7. Phong, V., Damon, M.C.: A fast wavelet-based algorithm for global and local image sharpness estimation. IEEE Signal Proc Lett. **19**(7), 423–426 (2012)
8. Gao, Q., Wang, Q., Huang, Y., Gao, X., Hong, X., Zhang, H.: Dimensionality reduction by integrating sparse representation and fisher criterion and its application. IEEE Trans. Image Process. **24**(12), 5684–5695 (2015)

Application of Broad Learning System for Image Classification Based on Deep Features

Dan Zhang[1,2], Yi Zuo[1(⊠)], Philip C. L. Chen[1,3,4], Chiye Wang[2(⊠)], and Teishan Li[1,5]

[1] Navigation College, Dalian Maritime University, Dalian 116026, China
zuo@dlmu.edu.cn
[2] Innovation and Entrepreneurship Education College,
Dalian Minzu University, Dalian 116600, China
[3] Computer Science and Engineering College, South China University of Technology,
Guangzhou 510641, China
[4] Department of Computer and Information Science, Faculty of Science and Technology,
University of Macau, Macau 99999, China
[5] School of Automation Engineering, University of Electronic Science and Technology
of China, Chengdu 610054, China

Abstract. Due to large amount of image data, the accuracy and real-time performance of classification are difficult problems in image classification. On the one hand, the broad learning system (BLS) has achieved good results in the timeliness of classification. On the other hand, deep learning feature extraction effect is good, but its structure is complex and the training time is long. Therefore, based on the above advantages of both methods, this paper proposed BLS based on deep features for image classification. Firstly, a feature extractor is constructed based on the ResNet101 to obtain the deep features of the classification image. Then, the feature nodes and enhancement nodes of BLS are constructed based on the deep features. Through the experiment, our method has two performance on benchmark datasets: high classification accuracy, good real-time.

Keywords: Broad learning · Deep features · Image classification

1 Introduction

Image classification is a hotspot and focus in the field of computer vision. It has important applications in intelligent transportation, detection, medical and other fields. Traditional image classification methods are mainly based on the difference of shallow features. It is difficult to extract features manually from massive data, which requires a lot of work and

This work is supported in part by the National Natural Science Foundation of China (under Grant Nos. 51939001, Natural Foundation Guidance Plan Project of Liaoning 61976033, U1813203, 61803064, 61751202); (2019-ZD-0151, 2020-HYLH-26); Science & Technology Innovation Funds of Dalian (under Grant No. 2018J11CY022); The Liaoning Revitalization Talents Program (XLYC1807046, XLYC1908018); Fundamental Research Funds for the Central Universities (under Grant No. 3132019345).

F. Sun et al. (Eds.): ICCSIP 2020, CCIS 1397, pp. 464–471, 2021.
https://doi.org/10.1007/978-981-16-2336-3_44

lacks generalization ability. The classifiers used mainly include support vector machine (SVM) [1], decision tree [2], multiple kernel learning (MKL) [3], and artificial neural network (ANN) [4–7]. The image classification method based on ANN has achieved good results.

With the progress of recent technology, ANN has been greatly developed, and deep learning [8] method has been paid more and more attention. Due to its strong feature extraction ability and semantic expression ability, it solves the problems of high labor cost and high-dimensional data difficulty in image classification feature extraction. According to the learning model, deep learning can be divided into generative model, discriminant model and hybrid model. The generation models include Self Encoder [9], Deep Belief Network (DBN) [10], and Deep Boltzmann Machine (DBM) [11]. The discriminant models include deep feedforward network [12], convolution neural network (CNN) [13–15], etc. The hybrid model consists of a generative model and a discriminant model, as shown in [16]. The main network structures are LeNet-5 [17], AlexNet [18], VGG [19], ResNet [20], GoogLeNet [21], etc. The deepening of CNN structure and network improves the performance of image classification, but the complexity of network structure increases the time cost, and the efficiency of classification becomes the main problem of classification based on deep learning. Therefore, the research of lightweight network model and the construction of network structure has become a new research direction.

BLS was proposed in [22–24]. This network has less layer network structure, which requires less calculation parameters, high efficiency and good image classification effect. Some improvements are made in the later stage [25–28]. The BLS changes the deep network structure, constructs feature nodes and enhances nodes for feature mapping, which has obvious advantages in computing time. Image classification based on deep learning effect is good, due to its strong feature extraction ability. Deep features can extract semantic information better without the influence of image appearance, but the network structure is complex, the amount of calculation is large. Therefore, the classification time is long. We proposed a new method by incorporating the deep features into the feature nodes and enhancement nodes. The automatic feature learning based on overcomes the difficulties of manual feature extraction and long training time, and improves the adaptability of feature extraction for image classification. The combination of deep features and BLS makes full use of the advantages of each system to meet the accuracy and real-time requirements of image classification. Firstly, ResNet101 was used to extract deep features. Then, feature nodes and enhancement nodes were constructed. Finally, all the enhancement nodes and feature nodes are connected to the output layer. Experimental results show that the classification accuracy of our method is high and the real-time performance is good.

The arrangement of the paper is as follows. The preliminaries of the proposed algorithm is introduced in Sect. 2. Our method is introduced in Sect. 3. The experimental results are presented in Sect. 4. The conclusion are given in Sect. 5.

2 Preliminaries

BLS [22–24] is a flat network, which is established feature nodes and enhancement nodes, the original inputs as mapped features. BLS is different from deep network structure, there are fewer layers and fewer parameters to calculate. The pseudo-inverse method is used to solve the parameters, which does not need the calculation of gradient descent and saves time in training.

The input data is X ($X \in \mathbb{R}^{N \times M}$), ϕ_i is the transformation, $Z_i = \phi_i(XW_{ei} + \beta_{ei})$ is the ith mapped feature, $i = 1, \cdots, n$, where W_{ei} is the random weights with the proper dimensions, the vector β_{ei} is the bias. $Z^n \equiv [Z_1, \cdots, Z_n]$, which is the result n groups of feature nodes. For the enhancement nodes, the jth group of the n feature maps together, $H_j = \xi_j(Z^n W_{hj} + \beta_{hj})$, ξ_j is the transformation, the matrix W_{hj} is the parameters, the vector β_{hj} is the bias. So all the result groups of enhancement nodes as $H^m = [H_1, \cdots, H_m]$, $j = 1, \cdots, m$. We suppose that the Y is the output ($Y \in \mathbb{R}^{N \times C}$). Therefore, the final BLS has the following formulation:

$$
\begin{aligned}
Y &= [Z_1, \cdots, Z_i, H_1, \cdots, H_m]W_m \\
&= [Z^n, H^m]W_m
\end{aligned}
\tag{1}
$$

Where W_m are the weights. Pseudo inverse is used to solve the formulation, so $W_m \triangleq [Z^n, H^m]^+ Y$.

The structure of BLS is shown in Fig. 1. From the frame of BLS, we can know that the original inputs is transferred by feature nodes and then input to the system. This indicates that the input data can be previously acquired characteristics, the quality of feature acquisition also affects the subsequent mapping and sparse representation of feature nodes. Therefore, extracting high-quality features will affect the result of image classification. Deep features are less affected by image appearance changes, and will promote the classification effect, the BLS will save the time of training and classification and enhance the real time.

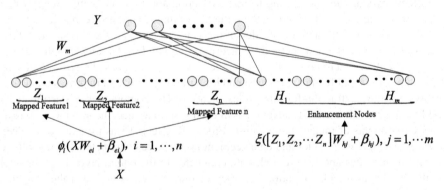

Fig. 1. The structure of BLS

3   BLS Based on Deep Features

The deep features which are used in our paper are derived from ResNet101 network, extract the global_pool layer features. Although ResNet101 network adopts full connection layer for classification, in order to ensure the accuracy and real-time performance of classification, this paper constructs the BLS based on deep features. The system uses the network trained by ImageNet as feature extractor to extract deep features. Then the obtained features is used as the training and input vector for the BLS.

Through the TensorFlow framework, ResNet101 network was trained on the ImageNet data set. As a feature extractor for BLS, the initialization condition of the model remained unchanged. The feature nodes of BLS are obtained through the transformation of random function, and the enhancement nodes are generated by the enhancement of the obtained deep random features. The number of feature nodes was 4,608 and the number of enhancement nodes was 256. They are generated automatically by setting the number of mappings to 18. The specific algorithm flow is shown in Table 1.

Table 1. The specific algorithm flow of our method

Algorithm: broad learning method based on deep features

Input: deep features obtained through ResNet101 network, D; feature maps, n; groups of enhancement nodes, m.

Output: W_m

for $i = 0$, $i \leq n$ do

    Random W_{ei}, β_{ei};

    Calculate $Z_i = \phi_i(DW_{ei} + \beta_{ei})$;

end

$Z^n \equiv [Z_1, \cdots, Z_i]$;

for $j = 1$, $j \leq m$ do

    Random W_{hj}, β_{hj};

    Calculate $H_j = \xi_j(Z^n W_{hj} + \beta_{hj})$;

end

$H^m = [H_1, \cdots, H_m]$;

Calculate $W_m \triangleq [Z^n, H^m]^+ Y$ with ridge regression approximation of the pesudoinverse

---

4 Experimental Analysis

In our paper, the bald and Dogs vs Cats data sets are selected as the experimental datasets. In order to demonstrate the effectiveness of our method, several algorithms are used to compare with our method, including SVM(SKlearn), MKL(MKLpy: a python-based framework for Multiple Kernel Learning), and ResNet101. The above comparing experiments are tested on python 3.7 software platform. The computer equips with 3.5 GHz E5-1620V4. ResNet101 runs on the GPU.

A. Bald Data

Some of the comparative experiments in this section were carried out on the bald classification dataset. There are 160,000 pictures in this datasets, including 3656 positive samples and 156344 negative samples. Image size is 178 × 218. We chose 6,000 for training (3000 positive samples, 3000 negative samples) and 800 for testing. OpenCV resize is used to adjust the size of the image to 224 × 224 and input it into ResNet101 to obtain the deep features. In our comparative experiment, the parameter settings of SVM, MKL refer to the original code version. The classification testing accuracy, training time and testing time of each method as shown in Table 2. The classification accuracy and time were the average of 5 experiments.

Table 2. The performance of each method on bald dataset

Algorithm	Testing accuracy (%)	Training time (s)	Testing time (s)
MKL	85.6%	24.22	0.23
SVM	92.10%	115.18	2.71
ResNet101	92.87%	3108.75	6.26
Ours	91.53%	11.38	0.31

B. Dogs vs Cats Data

Some of the comparative experiments in this section were carried out on the Dog vs Cats dataset. There are 25000 pictures in this datasets, including 12500 positive samples and 12500 negative samples. The picture size is inconsistent. We chose 24160 for training (12080 positive samples, 12080 negative samples) and 840 for testing. OpenCV resize is used to adjust the size of the image to 224 × 224 and input it into ResNet101 to obtain the deep features. The comparison experimental methods on this data set are optimized. During the training process of MKL method, when the training reaches 6000, it is memory overflow, so the training set of this method on the Dogs vs Cats data set is 6000. The classification testing accuracy, training time and testing time of each method as shown in Table 3. These are the average results of 5times.

Table 3. The performance of each method on Dogs vs Cats dataset

Algorithm	Testing accuracy (%)	Training time (s)	Testing time (s)
MKL	99.50%	24.00	0.29
SVM	99.10%	365.07	2.61
ResNet101	97.12%	11626.8	5.48
Ours	99.40%	29.75	0.42

The effectiveness of our method is shown in Table 2 and 3. From those table we could find that our method has the minimum training time and testing time on both datasets except MKL (but there is an out of memory situation in MKL). At the same time, our method also has high classification accuracy. The method in this paper have no other optimization after selecting the number of feature nodes and enhancement nodes. Even so, this method still has a high classification accuracy. Deep features are helpful to obtain more image information and improve the result of classification. The network structure and calculation method of broad learning reduce the time consumption of classification and improve the efficiency of classification.

5   Conclusions

In this paper, a deep features-based BLS is proposed, which combines its own advantages to overcome the time-consuming classification of deep learning and the need for optimization of broad learning data. The classification effect is good on the bald and Dogs vs Cats data sets. In the future, we will further study the adaptive feature extractor to solve the problem of feature optimization, and further optimize the classification algorithm to improve the accuracy of image classification and improve the real-time performance.

References

1. Vapnik, V.: The Nature of Statistical Learning Theory. Springer, New York (1999). https://doi.org/10.1007/978-1-4757-3264-1
2. Beucher, A., Moller, A.B., Greve, M.H.: Artificial neural networks and decision tree classification for predicting soil drainage classes in Denmark. Geoderma **320**, 30–42 (2017)
3. Sonnenburg, S., Ratsch, G., Schafer, C., et al.: Large scale multiple kernel learning. J. Mach. Learn. Res. **7**, 1531–1565 (2006)
4. Wang, Y.F.: Image feature classification based on particle swarm optimization neural network. Metall. Min. Ind. **7**(7), 328–334 (2015)
5. Zheng, Y.G., Wang, P., Ma, J., et al.: Remote sensing image classification based on BP neural network model. Trans. Nonferrous Metals Soc. China **15**(1), 232–235 (2005)
6. Affonso, C., Sassi, R.J., Barreiros, R.M.: Biological image classification using rough-fuzzy artificial neural network. Expert Syst. Appl. **42**(24), 9482–9488 (2015)
7. Tzeng, Y.C., Chen, K.S.: Fuzzy neural network to SAR image classification. IEEE Trans. Geosci. Remote Sens. **36**(1), 301–307 (1998)

8. Hinton, G.E., Salakhutdinov, R.R.: Reducing the dimensionality of data with neural networks. Science **313**(5786), 504 (2006)
9. Rumelhart, D.E., Hinton, G.E., Williams, R.J.: Learning representations by back-propagating errors. Nature **323**(6088), 533–536 (1986)
10. Hinton, G.E., Osindero, S., The, Y.: A fast learning algorithm for deep belief nets. Neural Comput. **18**(7), 1527–1554 (2006)
11. Salakhutdinov, R., Hinton, G.: Deep Boltzmann machines. In: International Conference on Artificial Intelligence and Statistics, Florida, USA, pp. 448–455 (2009)
12. Babri, H.A., Tong, Y.: Deep feedforward networks: application to pattern recognition. In: International Conference on Neural Networks fICNN 1996, pp. 1422–1426. IEEE Press, Washington, USA (1996)
13. Lei, X.Y., Pan, H.G., Huang, X.D.: A dilated CNN model for image classification. IEEE Access **7**, 124087–124095 (2019)
14. Chaib, S., Yao, H.X., Gu, Y.F. et al.: Deep feature extraction and combination for remote sensing image classification based on pre-trained CNN models. In: Proceedings of SPIE - The International Society for Optical Engineering. Ninth International Conference on Digital Image Processing ICDIP 2017, vol. 10420 (2017)
15. Zhang, M.M., Li, W., Du, Q.: Diverse region-based CNN for hyperspectral image classification. IEEE Trans. Image Process. **27**(6), 2623–2634 (2018)
16. Zhong, P., Gong, Z.Q., Schönlieb, C.: A diversified deep belief network for hyperspectral image classification. Int. Arch. Photogram. Remote Sens. Spatial Inform. Sci. **41**, 443–449 (2016). 23rd ISPRS Congress, Commission VII
17. Lecun, G.E., Bottou, L., Bengio, Y., et al.: Gradient-based learning applied to document recognition. Proc. IEEE **86**(11), 2278–2324 (1998)
18. Krizhevsky, A., Sutskever, I., Hinton, E.G.: ImageNet classification with deep convolutional neural networks. In: International Conference on Neural Information Processing Systems, LakeTahoe, Nevada, pp. 1097–1105. Curran Associates Inc, Red Hook (2012)
19. Simonyan, K., Zisserman, A.: Very deep convolutional networks for large-scale image recognition. In: Intenational Conference of Learning Representation, San Diego, CA (2015)
20. He, K.M., Zhang, X.Y., Ren, S.Q. et al.: Deep residual learning for image recognition. In: IEEE Conference on Computer Vision and Pattern Recognition, Las Vegas, Nevada, pp. 770–778. IEEE Computer Society, Los Alamitos (2016)
21. Szegedy, C., Liu, W., Jia, Y.Q., et al.: Going deeper with convolutions. In: IEEE Conference on Computer Vision and Pattern Recognition, Boston, MA, USA, pp. 1–9. IEEE Press, Piscataway (2015)
22. Chen, P.C.L., Liu, Z.L.: Broad learning system: an effective and efficient incremental learning system without the need for deep architecture. IEEE Trans. Neural Netw. Learn. Syst. **29**, 10–24 (2018)
23. Chen, P.C.L., Liu, Z., Feng, S.: Universal approximation capability of broad learning system and its structural variations. IEEE Trans. Neural Netw. Learn. Syst. **30**, 1191–1204 (2018)
24. Chen, P.C.L., Liu, Z.: Broad learning system: a new learning paradigm and system without going deep. In: 2017 32nd Youth Academic Annual Conference of Chinese Association of Automation, YAC 2017, pp. 1271–1276 (2017)
25. Feng, S., Chen, P.C.L.: Fuzzy broad learning system: a novel neuro-fuzzy model for regression and classification. IEEE Trans. Cybern. **50**, 414–424 (2018)
26. Jin, J.W., Chen, P.C.L., Li, Y.T.: Regularized robust broad learning system for uncertain data modeling. Neurocomputing **322**, 58–69 (2018)

27. Jin, J.W., Liu, Z.L., Chen, P.C.L.: Discriminative graph regularized broad learning system for image recognition. Sci. China Inf. Sci. **61**(11), 1–14 (2018)
28. Liu, Z., Chen, P.C.L., Zhang, T., et al.: Multi-kernel broad learning systems based on random features: a novel expansion for nonlinear feature nodes. In: Conference Proceedings - IEEE International Conference on Systems, Man and Cybernetics, IEEE International Conference on Systems, Man and Cybernetics, SMC 2019, pp. 193–197 (2019)

Emotion Recognition Based on Graph Neural Networks

Junjie Zhang, Guangmin Sun$^{(\boxtimes)}$, Kun Zheng, Sarah Mazhar, Xiaohui Fu,
and Dong Yang

Faculty of Information Technology, Beijing University of Technology, Beijing, China
gmsun@bjut.edu.cn

Abstract. Emotion recognition is widely used in many areas, such as medicine
and education. Due to the obvious difference in duration and intensity between
micro and macro expression, the same model cannot be used to classify emotions
precisely. In this paper, an algorithm for emotion recognition based on graph neural network is proposed. The proposed method involves four key steps. Firstly, data
augmentation is used to increase the diversity of original data. Secondly, graph
network is built based on feature points. The feature points Euclidean distance is
calculated as the initial value of the matrix. Thirdly, Laplacian matrix is obtained
according to the matrix. Finally, graph neutral network is utilized to bridge the
relationship between feature vectors and emotions. In addition, a new dataset
named FEC-13 is provided by subdivided traditional six kinds of emotions to thir-
teen categories according to the intensity of emotions. The experimental results
show that a high accuracy is reached with a small amount of training data, especially CASME II dataset, which achieves an accuracy of 95.49%. A cross-database
study indicates that proposed method has high generalization performance and the
accuracy of FEC-13 dataset is 74.99%.

1 Introduction

The change in emotion reflects the fluctuations of state during the learning process [1].
However, it is not easy to quickly discover and capture emotion at the same time during
learning process. With the development of digital technologies, it is possible to record
student behaviors using camera equipment. Analyzing the record video can tackle the
problem mentioned above. Emotions are composed of macro-expressions and micro-
expressions. As compared to macro-expressions, micro-expressions have two characteristics: short duration and small intensity. Analyzing macro and micro expressions
simultaneously can reflect students' true emotions.

Current emotion recognition methods include the traditional method of 'fea-
ture+classifier' and deep learning. Features include Haar, SIFT, LBP and their improvement methods. The extracted features have a high dimension. In particular, existing
studies have shown that traditional features are affected by illumination and posture so
they have poor robustness [2]. Hence, deep learning method is used to emotion recognition [3]. However, this method requires much data to train the model and there are a
few public emotion datasets. Importantly, due to the particularity of micro expressions,

© Springer Nature Singapore Pte Ltd. 2021
F. Sun et al. (Eds.): ICCSIP 2020, CCIS 1397, pp. 472–480, 2021.
https://doi.org/10.1007/978-981-16-2336-3_45

macro expression model cannot be directly applied to micro expression recognition and vice versa. Graph neural networks (GNN) was proposed by Kipf in 2017 [4]. GNN has good reasoning ability, which can process non-European data effectively and get better results with small quantities of training data. Many methods on applying GNN for vision tasks have been developed. Such as temporal action location [5], emotion recognition in conversation [6] et al. The face is a non-European structure and GNN can be used in the field of emotion recognition. Thus, graph neural network based on spectral domain (FDGNN) is proposed.

The major contribution of this paper can be summarized as follows. (1) Features are extracted automatically using FDGNN. This method can classify macro and micro expressions precisely while keeping the model structure unchanged. (2) A high classification accuracy can be reached with low volume data. (3) A high cross-database accuracy and good generalization performance is obtained.

Experiments were carried out on multiple macro and micro expression databases to verify the effectiveness of proposed method and compared with existing algorithms of the past 5 years. The remaining part of this paper is organized as follows. In Sect. 2, FDGNN model for emotion classification is proposed. In Sect. 3, four experiments are conducted to confirm the effective of proposed method based on four macro expression datasets and four micro expression datasets. Finally, the conclusions are drawn in Sect. 4.

2 Materials and Method

2.1 Dataset Analysis

There are eight expression datasets which are used to evaluate proposed algorithm, including four micro-expression datasets CASME II [7], SMIC [8], SAMM [9], SPOS [10] and four macro-expression datasets CK+ [11], JAFFE [12], TFEID [13], RAF [14]. All micro expression datasets are collected in an ideal environment. Images in SMIC and SPOS database have three formats, which are collected by visual, near-infrared and high-speed camera respectively. Macro expression images are rich, including different races, postures, light intensity and image resolution. There are two ways used to obtain macro expression images, one way is through the laboratory environment and the other way is through internet. In reality, emotions are rich and vary in intensity. Current dataset only owns basic expressions. Thus, the raw data is collected from internet and some existing databases and then is subdivided in seven basic emotions except neutral to 13 categories. The emotions are surprise/surprise+ , fear/fear+ , disgust/disgust+ , happiness/happiness+ , sadness/sadness+ , anger/anger+ and neutral, where '+' represents high intensity. Summarize of datasets can be seen in Table 1.

2.2 Graph Neural Network Based on Spectral Domain

In this section, FDGNN is proposed mathematically. The GNN algorithm, which is proposed by Kipf, has been successfully applied in many research areas. GNN has good reasoning ability especially in less public emotion training data. Hence, in this paper, FDGNN is used to classify micro and macro emotions under the same network structure.

Table 1. Summarize of datasets

Type	Database	Samples	Subject	Condition	Elicit	Emotions	Resolution	FPS
Micro-expression	CASMEII	247	26	Lab	S	6	640 × 480	200
	SMIC	164	16	Lab	S	3	640 × 480	100
	SAMM	159	32	Lab	S	7	2040 × 1080	200
	SPOS	231	7	Lab	P&S	6	640 × 480	25
Macro-expression	CK+	593	123	Lab	P&S	6	48 × 48	Image
	JAFFE	213	10	Lab	P	6	256 × 256	Image
	TFEID	7200	40	Lab	P	8	480 × 600	Image
	RAF	29672	–	Web	P&S	6	100 × 100	Image
	FEC-13	9723	–	Web	P	13	100 × 100	Image

The flow chart of proposed algorithm is shown in Fig. 1. Firstly, an undirected weight graph is established, which can be expressed as $G = (V, E)$, where V represents node and E represents edge. The adjacent node of j can be expressed as $N_k = \{i \in V | W_{ij}\rangle k\}$. Where the size of V is m and the size of W is m × m$_o$.

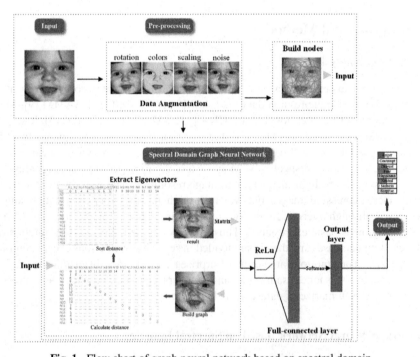

Fig. 1. Flow chart of graph neural network based on spectral domain

Secondly, feature points or image pixels are selected as node V and the distance between each node as edge E, graph can be established according to node and edge. The data dimension will be too high if each node is connected to other nodes. To solve the problem mentioned above, each node is connected to the nearest K nodes and here it is 8. Euclidean distance between the nodes is used as the initial value of the matrix M.

Thirdly, adjacency matrix M and degree matrix D can be calculated after matrix M is obtained. Adjacency matrix and degree matrix can be expressed respectively as:

$$A_{i,j} = \begin{cases} 1 \ if \ i \in N_k[j] \\ 0 \ otherwise \end{cases} \tag{1}$$

and

$$D_{i,i} = \sum_j A_{i,j} \tag{2}$$

Laplacian matrix L can be given by $L = D - A$. Since G is an undirected graph, L is a symmetric matrix. Eigen decomposition of L can be expressed as:

$$L = U \Lambda U^T \tag{3}$$

Where $U = [u_1, u_2, \ldots, u_n]$. Input x_i is converted from spatial domain to spectral domain for graph convolution can be respectively given by:

$$F(x_i) = U^T x_i \tag{4}$$

and

$$(x_i * h)_G = U \begin{pmatrix} \hat{h}(\lambda_1) & & \\ & \ldots & \\ & & \hat{h}(\lambda_n) \end{pmatrix} F(x_i) \tag{5}$$

Finally, the convolution operation on the Kth channel can be expressed as:

$$R_k = h \left(U \sum_{i=1}^{f_{k-1}} \begin{pmatrix} \hat{h}(\lambda_{1,k,i}) & & \\ & \ldots & \\ & & \hat{h}(\lambda_{n,k,i}) \end{pmatrix} F(x_{k,i}) \right) \tag{6}$$

Where the activation function h is Relu. FDGNN can be given by $y = argmax(WR + B)$.

3   Results and Discussion

3.1   Data Augmentation

Data augment can increase the richness of original data. Emotion recognition accuracy will be affected by face posture, face size, brightness and noise. Hence, it is useful to increase accuracy using data augment, which can enrich original data. Data augment imply in this paper include image rotation within the range of $-20°$ to $20°$, image scaling between 0.5 times and 1.5 times, image brightness change and add Gaussian noise with a mean value of 0. Examples of data augment are shown in Fig. 2.

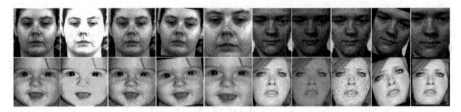

Fig. 2. Example of data augment (images from left to right are original image, brightness change, add noise, rotation and scaling)

3.2 Performance of Different Ratio and Cross-Database Based on Eight Expression Databases

Deep learning requires a lot of data to train the model and there are few expression databases. Thus, it is difficult to train the model fully. GNN has good reasoning ability with a small amount of training data. In order to verify the accuracy of classification in the case of few training data, the ratio of training data to testing data is set to 0.1, 0.2...,1.0 respectively and results can be seen in Table 2. The results show that an accuracy of 89.91% is reached when ratio equals 0.2 based on SPOS NIR dataset and a high accuracy can be reached based on SPOS VIS dataset when ratio equals 0.4. Compared with macro expression dataset, the proposed method has a better effect on micro expression classification. Analysing Table 2, we can find that feature vector may affect classification accuracy. Such as SPOS NIR database, the test accuracy is only 39.79 when the ratio is 1.0. It can be concluded that FDGNN is sensitive to feature vectors.

Next, we list the results of some methods that have been applied for emotion recognition in Table 3. Best results are received with CASME II and SMIC dataset with an accuracy of 95.49% and 82.30% respectively. At the same time, high classification accuracy can be achieved on other databases and the effect of micro expression is better than macro expression.

We then performed a cross-database experiment based on micro expression databases to verify the performance of generalization. 'Cross-database' means the images from one database are used for training and images from the other are used for testing. In order to eliminate the deviation caused by the different resolutions of pictures between different databases, the pictures in all databases are normalized to 400 × 400. GCN based on spectral or spatial domain is efficient for emotion recognition task. Whereas, the former has better generalization in cross-database experiment and the average accuracy can be increased by 2.67%. The results can be seen in Fig. 3. The row represents training dataset and the column represents test dataset. The results show that the model has better generalization performance. The average accuracy and variance of cross-validation model that are calculated, indicates that smic hs model can get best generalization performance and stability with highest average accuracy 53.90% and lowest variance of 7.4305.

Table 2. Expression recognition performance of different training/testing ratios

Dataset	Ratio	0.1	0.2	0.3	0.4	0.5	0.6	0.7	0.8	0.9	1.0
CASME	Spectral	0.5346	0.4618	0.5634	0.5513	0.3969	0.5723	0.5607	0.5661	0.4156	0.5680
CASME CROP	Spectral	0.8733	0.3995	0.9264	0.9810	0.9956	0.9762	0.9784	0.9431	0.9988	0.9983
SMIC DETECT	Spectral	0.6820	0.9325	0.9511	0.8187	0.9892	0.8308	0.9853	0.9915	0.9439	0.9939
SMIC VIS	Spectral	0.4169	0.8040	0.4331	0.4293	0.4135	0.9963	0.4195	0.9781	1.0	0.9765
SMIC NIR	Spectral	0.6602	0.7349	0.5052	0.4341	0.7456	0.7664	0.4341	0.9562	0.4348	0.7862
SMIC HS	Spectral	0.7982	0.8910	0.7922	0.9032	0.9117	0.4012	0.4870	0.9584	0.9060	0.8864
SMIC 2CLASS	Spectral	0.8252	0.7802	0.9526	0.9707	0.5117	0.9146	0.9902	1.0	0.4854	0.9941
SMIC 5CLASS	Spectral	0.7348	0.7474	0.2942	0.9318	0.8909	0.9586	0.9821	0.7421	0.8398	0.8042
SAMM ORI	Spectral	0.7226	0.9830	0.5352	0.5302	0.9160	0.9979	0.6906	0.9979	0.5516	0.9180
SAMM CROP	Spectral	0.9079	0.5432	0.9468	0.9165	0.8746	0.8699	0.8525	0.6134	0.9704	0.9617
SPOS VIS	Spectral	0.8640	0.8584	0.8903	0.9663	0.3641	0.8623	0.8780	0.3826	0.9030	0.9225
SPOS NIR	Spectral	0.7160	0.8991	0.7783	0.4172	0.8259	0.3996	0.8567	0.3938	0.8029	0.3979
JAFFE	Spectral	0.2513	0.3706	0.2886	0.4766	0.4623	0.4588	0.5469	0.3023	0.4545	0.3443
TFEID	Spectral	0.5710	0.4684	0.8432	0.8218	0.8869	0.8815	0.8515	0.8971	0.4706	0.9673
RAF	Spectral	0.4255	0.3906	0.3951	0.4105	0.4947	0.4920	0.4605	0.3862	0.3879	0.5605
CK+	Spectral	0.7203	0.8497	0.8690	0.9083	0.7698	0.9593	0.9729	1.0	0.9899	0.9980

(Note: CROP represent extract face region from original image, the resolution of CASME CROP and SAMM CROP is 250×250 and 400×400 respectively. SMIC DETECT is used to detect whether the emotion is micro or non-micro. VIS, NIR and HS represent visual, near-infrared and high speed respectively. ORI means original)

Table 3. Expression recognition performance with other algorithms

Dataset	Reference	Accuracy	Dataset	Reference	Accuracy	Dataset	Reference	Accuracy
CASMEII	[7]	63.41%	SAMM	[9]	91.52%	JAFFE	[17]	96.20%
	[15]	67.37%		[16]	83.60%		[18]	93.90%
	Proposed	95.49%		Proposed	82.73%		Proposed	53.61%
SMIC	[8]	65.49%	SPOS	[10]	80%	CK+	[19]	94.40%
	[15]	80.00%		[10]	72.00%		[20]	96.70%
	Proposed	82.30%		Proposed	73.56%		Proposed	79.11%
RAF	[21]	67.37%	TFEID	[23]	95.00%	FEC-13	[25]	69.32%
	[22]	84.22%		[24]	91.47%		[26]	70.69%
	Proposed	48.07%		Proposed	78.68%		Proposed	74.99%

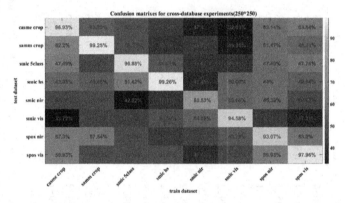

Fig. 3. Confusion matrixes for cross-database experiments based on micro expression

3.3 Performance of Proposed FEC-13 Dataset

Finally, FEC-13 dataset [27] is tested using proposed method and results are shown in Fig. 4. Analysing the diagonals of this matrix, we can see that happiness and neutral are the emotions with the highest recognition rates. But fear+ , disgust+ , sadness+ and anger+ are the emotions with the lowest recognition rates, meanwhile the 13 types of emotions are easily mistakenly divided into happiness, sadness and anger+ .

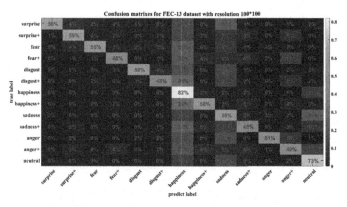

Fig. 4. Confusion matrix for FEC-13 dataset

4 Conclusion

In this paper, FDGNN is proposed for both micro and macro expression classification and we subdivided the seven basic emotions to 13 categories forming a new dataset, named FEC-13. The advantages of the method are summarized as follows. Firstly, macro and micro expressions can be classified using the same network. Secondly, a high classification accuracy can be obtained with a small amount of training data. Thirdly, the performance of generalization is high. Finally, an accuracy of 74.99% is received for FEC-13 dataset.

Acknowledgment. This work was supported in part by the Planning Subject for the 13th Five Year Plan of Beijing Education Sciences (CADA18069).

References

1. Zeng, H., Shu, X., Wang, Y., et al.: EmotionCues: emotion-oriented visual summarization of classroom videos. IEEE Trans. Visual Comput. Graphics. https://doi.org/10.1109/tvcg.2019.2963659

2. Zhao, G., Pietikainen, M.: Dynamic texture recognition using local binary patterns with an application to facial expressions. IEEE Trans. Pattern Anal. Mach. Intell. **29**(6), 915–928 (2007)

3. Song, B., Li, K., Zong, Y., et al.: Recognizing spontaneous micro-expression using a three-stream convolutional neural network. IEEE Access **7**, 184537–184551 (2019)

4. Kipf, T.N., Welling, M.: Semi-supervised classification with graph convolutional networks. In: ICLR 2017 (2017)

5. Zeng, R., Huang, W., Tan, M., et al.: Graph convolutional networks for temporal action localization. In: Proceedings of the IEEE International Conference on Computer Vision, pp. 7094–7103. IEEE (2019)

6. Ghosal, D., Majumder, N., Poria, S., et al.: Dialoguegcn: a graph convolutional neural network for emotion recognition in conversation. arXiv preprint arXiv:1908.11540 (2019)

7. Yan, W.J., Li, X., Wang, S.J., et al.: CASME II: an improved spontaneous micro-expression database and the baseline evaluation. PLoS ONE **9**(1), (2014)

8. Li, X., Pfister, T., Huang, X., et al.: A spontaneous micro-expression database: inducement, collection and baseline. In: 2013 10th IEEE International Conference and Workshops on Automatic Face and Gesture Recognition(fg), pp. 1–6. IEEE (2013)
9. Davison, A.K., Lansley, C., Costen, N., et al.: SAMM: a spontaneous micro-facial movement dataset. IEEE Trans. Affect. Comput. 9(1), 116–129 (2016)
10. Pfister, T., Li, X., Zhao, G., et al.: Differentiating spontaneous from posed facial expressions within a generic facial expression recognition framework. In: 2011 IEEE International Conference on Computer Vision Workshops (ICCV Workshops), pp. 868–875. IEEE (2011)
11. Lucey, P., Cohn, J.F., Kanade, T., et al.: The extended Cohn-Kanade dataset (CK+): a complete dataset for action unit and emotion-specified expression. In 2010 IEEE Computer Society Conference on Computer Vision and Pattern Recognition-Workshops, pp. 94–101. IEEE (2010)
12. Lyons, M., Akamatsu, S., Kamachi, M., et al.: Coding facial expressions with gabor wavelets. In: Proceedings of the Third IEEE International Conference on Automatic Face and Gesture Recognition, pp. 200–205. IEEE (1998)
13. Chen, L.-F., Yen, Y.-S.: Taiwanese facial expression image database. Brain Mapping Laboratory, Institute of Brain Science, National Yang-Ming University, Taipei, Taiwan (2007)
14. Li, S., Deng, W.: Reliable crowdsourcing and deep locality-preserving learning for unconstrained facial expression recognition. IEEE Trans. Image Process. 28(1), 356–370 (2018)
15. Liu, Y.J., Zhang, J.K., Yan, W.J., et al.: A main directional mean optical flow feature for spontaneous micro-expression recognition. IEEE Trans. Affect. Comput. 7(4), 299–310 (2015)
16. Xia, Z., Hong, X., Gao, X., et al.: Spatiotemporal recurrent convolutional networks for recognizing spontaneous micro-expressions. IEEE Trans. Multimedia 22(3), 626–640 (2019)
17. Zavaschi, T.H.H., Britto, A.S., Oliveira, L.E.S., et al.: Fusion of feature sets and classifiers for facial expression recognition. Expert Syst. Appl. 40(2), 646–655 (2013)
18. Wang, X., Jin, C., Liu, W., et al.: Feature fusion of HOG and WLD for facial expression recognition. In: Proceedings of the 2013 IEEE/SICE International Symposium on System Integration, pp. 227–232. IEEE (2013)
19. Ouellet, S.: Real-time emotion recognition for gaming using deep convolutional network features. arXiv preprint arXiv:1408.3750 (2014)
20. Liu, P., Han, S., Meng, Z., et al.: Facial expression recognition via a boosted deep belief network. In: Proceedings of the IEEE Conference on Computer Vision and Pattern Recognition, pp. 1805–1812 (2014)
21. Azadi, S., Feng, J., Jegelka, S., et al.: Auxiliary image regularization for deep CNNs with noisy labels. arXiv preprint arXiv:1511.07069 (2015)
22. Goldberger, J., Ben-Reuven, E.: Training deep neural-networks using a noise adaptation layer. In: International Conference on Learning Representations (2017)
23. Zhang, Z., Fang, C., Ding, X.: Facial expression analysis across databases. In: 2011 International Conference on Multimedia Technology, pp. 317–320. IEEE (2011)
24. Xie, S., Hu, H., Wu, Y.: Deep multi-path convolutional neural network joint with salient region attention for facial expression recognition. Pattern Recogn. 92, 177–191 (2019)
25. Simonyan, K., Zisserman, A.: Very deep convolutional networks for large-scale image recognition. arXiv preprint arXiv:1409.1556 (2014)
26. He, K., Zhang, X., Ren, S., et al.: Deep residual learning for image recognition. In: Proceedings of the IEEE Conference on Computer Vision and Pattern Recognition, pp. 770–778 (2016)
27. Yang, C.Y., Zheng, K., Zhou, J., et al.: Video-based meticulous classification of facial expressions reflecting psychological status in the classroom. Basic Clinical Pharmacol. Toxicol. 125(066), 42–43 (2019)

A Light-Weight Stereo Matching Network with Color Guidance Refinement

Jiali Wang, Zhansheng Duan$^{(\boxtimes)}$, Kuizhi Mei, Hongbin Zhou, and Chenhui Tong

Faculty of Electronic and Information Engineering,
Xi'an Jiaotong University, Xi'an, China
lvb111@stu.xjtu.edu.cn, {zsduan,meikuizhi}@mail.xjtu.edu.cn

Abstract. Deep-learning-based stereo matching methods have achieved significant improvement over traditional methods and obtained great successes in recent years. However, how to trade off accuracy and speed and predict accurate disparity in real time has been a long-standing problem in the stereo matching area. We present an end-to-end light-weight convolutional neural network (CNN) to quickly estimate accurate disparity maps. Our proposed model is based on AnyNet, a real-time network which generates disparity in stages to achieve anytime prediction. Hourglass architecture with dilated convolutional layers is exploited to extract richer features of input stereo images. We also introduce residual connections in 2D CNN and 3D CNN to avoid information loss. Besides, we adopt a color guidance refinement to improve disparity performance. Depthwise separable convolution is used to replace standard convolution in color guidance refinement to sharply decrease the number of parameters and computational complexity. We refer to our proposed model as Light-Weight Stereo Network (LWSN). LWSN is trained and evaluated on three well-known stereo datasets. Experiments indicate that our model is effective and efficient.

Keywords: Stereo matching · Deep learning · Light-weight network

1 Introduction

Stereo matching is one of the most important computer vision technologies and it plays an essential role in a large variety of fields such as 3D reconstruction, object detection and tracking, scene understanding, robotics and autonomous driving. Stereo matching is the process of estimating depth information from a pair of stereo images taken by two cameras at different horizontal positions. In details, stereo images are first rectified, making the matching pixels of two images on the same horizon so that the 2D problem can be cast into a 1D problem and

This work was supported by National Key Research and Development Plan under Grant 2017YFB1301101, and in part by the National Natural Science Foundation of China through grant 61673317, 61673313 and 62076193.

© Springer Nature Singapore Pte Ltd. 2021
F. Sun et al. (Eds.): ICCSIP 2020, CCIS 1397, pp. 481–495, 2021.
https://doi.org/10.1007/978-981-16-2336-3_46

the search space is reduced to a horizontal line. Given a rectified stereo pair of images, the aim of stereo matching is to estimate the disparity for all pixels in the reference image. Disparity refers to the distance on the horizontal line between the corresponding pixels in the binocular images. This means that a pixel at position (x, y) in the left image locates in position $(x - d, y)$ in the right image (see Fig. 1).

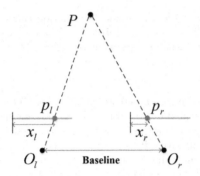

Fig. 1. The stereo matching problem. Corresponding pixels p_l and p_r in the rectified stereo images are on the same horizon. Disparity is $x_l - x_r$.

Recently, deep learning methods have become increasingly popular in lots of computer vision tasks including stereo matching. Convolutional neural networks (CNNs) can be used to predict dense disparity maps in supervised learning, unsupervised learning and semi-supervised learning manners. Earlier methods used CNNs to learn richer feature representations [1]. In these methods, CNNs learn the similarity score on a pair of small image patches for matching cost computation. While others train end-to-end networks to directly compute a disparity map from the input binocular image pair without traditional methods used. CNNs have made significant progress in the stereo matching field in terms of accuracy and efficiency compared to traditional methods.

However, current state-of-the-art disparity computation networks are mostly computationally complex and time-consuming, making it difficult to exploit these approaches in real-time computer vision tasks such as localization, mapping, navigation, obstacle avoidance, and some other robotic applications. To tackle the real-world application problem, there have been successive methods to speed up the process of disparity estimation.

In this paper, we propose a novel light-weight stereo network (LWSN) based on AnyNet [2]. AnyNet is a real-time and stage-wise model which can perform anytime prediction and generate the current best disparity estimate within permitted inference time. In LWSN, hourglass feature extractor is used to generate left and right feature maps at three different resolutions. The feature extractor also contains several dilated convolutional layers with different dilation factors to enlarge the receptive fields and skip connections to aggregate context information. Besides, we add a color guidance refinement step with depthwise separable convolutions to improve the disparity prediction performance. Our main contributions are listed as follows:

(1) We exploit the hourglass architecture with skip connections and dilated convolutions in feature extractor to capture global context information from input stereo images.
(2) We introduce a color guidance refinement step with depthwise convolutions to sharpen predicted disparity without much complexity increase.
(3) LWSN is trained and evaluated on three datasets and experimental results show that our model can achieve state-of-the-art performance but with low inference time.

2 Related Work

2.1 Traditional Methods

According to [3], traditional stereo matching methods generally perform four steps: matching cost computation, cost aggregation, disparity (support) computation and optimization, and disparity refinement. Computation of the matching cost is the process of computing the cost or similarity score at each pixel over the range of all disparity values. Cost aggregation can be done by summing or averaging the matching cost over a local region. The disparity computation and optimization step predicts the initial coarse disparity map. Disparity refinement mainly includes sub-pixel disparity computation, left and right consistency check, occluded areas filling and mismatches correction.

The traditional methods can be further classified into local methods, global methods and semi-global methods. Local methods concentrate on the matching cost computation and cost aggregation steps [4]. The disparity estimation are done on small local box windows under smoothness assumption within the windows. They simply select the disparity value associated with the lowest matching cost at each pixel, which perform a "winner-takes-all" (WTA) solution. The limitation of local methods is that the disparity estimates are usually very noisy. On the contrary, global methods usually skip the cost aggregation step. Instead, they formulate disparity estimation as an energy-minimization problem, the goal of which is to find a disparity which minimizes the energy function containing the data term and smoothness term. Global algorithms mainly include dynamic programming [5], graph cuts [6], belief propagation [7] and so on. Global methods are more accurate than local methods whereas most of them suffer from high computational complexity and time latency. Semi-Global Matching (SGM) proposed in [8] calculates the cost with Mutual Information (MI). It sums matching cost along 1D paths from eight directions towards each pixel via dynamic programming to form the global energy. Semi-global methods are more robust than local methods and less complex than global methods.

2.2 Deep Learning Methods

In recent years, convolutional neural networks (CNNs) have achieved significant successes in the stereo matching field. Early studies applied CNNs to learn image features in the matching cost computing step while traditional methods are still used for cost aggregation, disparity computation and refinement to get the final disparity maps. Zbontar and LeCun [9] proposed two network architectures to generate a similarity measure on small image patches to compute matching cost. The first network is a Siamese network with two shared-weights sub-networks and a score computation layer. The second one, which is more accurate, replaces the last layer with several fully-connected layers. Luo et al. [10] further promoted their work. They formulated the matching cost computation problem as a multi-label classification problem and proposed a faster Siamese network.

Motivated by the significant improvement CNNs had achieved in the stereo matching field, many researchers have developed end-to-end networks to directly predict the entire disparity maps without any additional regularization and post-processing. Typically, end-to-end methods includes several modules as follows: feature extractor, cost volume construction, disparity computation and aggregation, and disparity regression. Mayer et al. [11] proposed DispNet predicting the whole disparity maps with the adoption of the encoder-decoder structure. Kendall et al. [12] presented GC-Net, which consists of a Siamese 2D residual network operating on the input image pair, a cost volume built by the left and right feature maps, a 3D CNN for cost volume regularization, and a disparity regression operation. Chang and Chen [13] proposed PSMNet, consisting of spatial pyramid pooling (SPP) and 3D stacked hourglass architecture. The spatial pyramid pooling module can learn the relationship between an object and its sub-regions to incorporate hierarchical context information by involving different level of features. The 3D hourglass architecture can integrate top-down and bottom-up information by shortcut connections to leverage global context. Yang et al. [14] presented SegStereo model which integrates semantic segmentation and disparity estimation in one framework. Their model exploits the semantic information to rectify and improve the accuracy of disparity computation.

Our work is inspired by and based on AnyNet. AnyNet can trade off accuracy and computation which first outputs a coarse disparity prediction at a lower resolution and successively up-samples the coarse disparity and predicts a residual error at a higher resolution to correct the disparity map of the previous stage. The network adds a Spatial Propagation Network (SPNet) to sharpen the disparity performance. AnyNet is the first model for anytime disparity estimation with competitive accuracy and low computation.

3 Light-Weight Stereo Network with Color Guidance

As illustrated in Fig. 2, the rectified left and right stereo images first pass through two shared-weights pipelines to extract left and right image features. The 2D CNN consists of several dilated convolutional layers and an hourglass architecture which generates feature maps at three different resolutions, i.e. 1/8, 1/4,

1/2 to both capture global and local information. Then, we predict the whole disparity map at the lowest-scale resolution of 1/8 in Stage 1 and compute the residual error maps at the resolutions of 1/4 and 1/2 in Stages 2 and 3 by feeding the stereo feature maps into disparity network. In Stage 4, considering that continuous pixels with similar RGB values are much likely to have similar disparities and reference image is set to the left image, we further refine the Disparity Stage 3 via color guidance of the left image input.

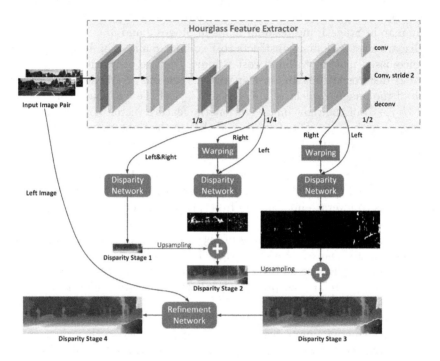

Fig. 2. Overall network architecture of LWSN for disparity prediction.

3.1 Hourglass Feature Extractor

The feature extractor processes left and right input images with the same weights. The hourglass module is a symmetrical structure which is capable of capturing information from all scales of the input image [15]. In particular, feature maps with higher resolutions capture the local information while those of lower resolutions capture the global information. As denonstrated in Fig. 2, the input image is first fed into several dilated convolutions. According to [16], dilated convolutions can obtain exponential expansion of receptive fields without losing resolution or coverage to gather multi-scale context information and dense features. Then, the hourglass module processes the feature maps in a top-down/bottom-up manner to utilize the global context information. Specifically, the feature maps are processed by two convolutional layers of stride 2 from scale

1/2 to 1/4 and from 1/4 to 1/8 and then operated with deconvolutions from scale 1/8 to 1/4 and from 1/4 to 1/2. Shortcut connections are applied in hourglass module to avoid information loss [17]. The feature extractor produces three feature maps of different resolutions (of scale 1/8, 1/4, 1/2).

3.2 Disparity Network and Residual Computation

As shown in Fig. 3, disparity network processes the feature maps of input stereo image pair extracted by the hourglass architecture and generates a whole disparity map in Stage 1 and residual maps in Stages 2 and 3.

Disparity network first constructs cost volume. Same as in AnyNet, we adopt distance-based method to build cost volume, the size of which is $D \times H \times W$, where D denotes the maximum disparity we set and H, W denote height and width of the image, respectively. Let pixel (i, j) of the left image correspond to pixel $(i, j - d)$ of the right image so that the feature vector of pixel (i, j) in the left image can be represented as $\mathbf{p}_{ij}^L$ and that in the right image as $\mathbf{p}_{i(j-d)}^R$. The cost of two pixels in the left and right images can be computed by L_1 distance, i.e. $C_{ijd} = \|\mathbf{p}_{ij}^L - \mathbf{p}_{i(j-d)}^R\|_1$.

And then the cost volume is aggregated and regularized by a 3D residual block. We modified AnyNet's disparity network by adding residual connections in 3D CNNs to leverage information from previous layers.

In Stages 2 and 3, we first up-sample the disparity of the previous stage and use it to warp the right feature maps of higher resolution. The disparity network takes left feature maps and warped right feature maps as input and produces a residual map. Then we add the residual map to the up-sampled disparity in previous stage to refine the previous predicted disparity, which is the output disparity of the current stage.

By computing residuals instead of full disparity maps at higher resolutions, we can limit the maximum disparity to a small number so that the computational complexity of cost volume construction and 3D CNNs can be decreased considerably. For example, let the maximum disparity be 192 pixels in the input images and the size of cost volume be $D \times H \times W$. At the resolution of 1/8 in Stage 1, D will be $192/8 = 24$. If we predict the whole disparities in Stages 2 and 3 the same way as in Stage 1, D will be 48 and 96, respectively. While in LWSN, in Stages 2 and 3, if we restrict the range of residual to $[-3, 3]$, D will just be 7, far too smaller than those in whole disparity computation.

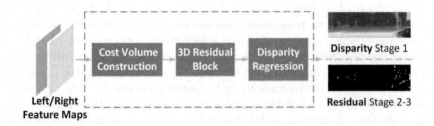

Fig. 3. Disparity network.

For disparity regression, we compute a weighted summation of each d where the weight is the probability computed by the softmax function $\sigma(\cdot)$ operated on cost C_{ijd}. The estimated continuous disparity $\hat{d}_{ij}$ is described as

$$\hat{d}_{ij} = \sum_{d=0}^{D} d \times \sigma(-C_{ijd}) \tag{1}$$

3.3 Color Guidance Refinement

The fourth stage is used to refine our predicted disparity and increase the accuracy of LWSN via color guidance of the left input image. This stage is partially inspired by [18]. As shown in Fig. 4, the left input image and Disparity Stage 3 are fed into two 2D networks and then concatenated for feature fusion. The combined feature maps are further processed by several 2D convolutions to generate the final disparity. Dilated convolutions are applied in refinement to expand the receptive fields so that the network are able to capture more context information and boost the performance. The dilated rates are set to 1, 2, 4, 8, 16, 8, 4, 2 and 1.

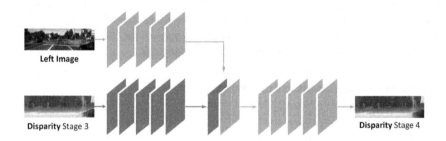

Fig. 4. Color guidance refinement. (Color figure online)

We modified the refinement module in [18] by replacing all the standard convolutions with depthwise separable convolutions. A standard convolution can be decomposed into a depthwise separable convolution and a pointwise 1×1 convolution [19]. The depthwise convolution is a two dimensional convolution operated separately on input channels. Let C_{in} and C_{out} denote the number of input channels and output channels. A standard convolution of 3×3 kernel size has $3 \times 3 \times C_{in} \times C_{out}$ parameters while a depthwise separable convolution layer only has $(3 \times 3 \times C_{in} + C_{in} \times C_{out})$ parameters. Consequently, adopting depthwise separable convolutions rather than standard convolutions can decrease the number of parameters and computational complexity significantly without much accuracy reduction, making our model more efficient but still effective.

3.4   Loss Function

Same as in AnyNet, we adopt the smooth L_1 loss function to train LWSN because it is robust and insensitive to outliers. All output disparities are up-sampled to the original resolution for loss computation. Let N denote the number of valid pixels, d denote the ground truth disparity and $\hat{d}$ denote the estimated disparity. The smooth L_1 loss function can be described as

$$L(d, \hat{d}) = \frac{1}{N} \sum_{i=1}^{N} smooth_{L_1}(d_i - \hat{d}_i) \tag{2}$$

where

$$smooth_{L_1}(x) = \begin{cases} 0.5x^2, & if |x| < 1 \\ |x| - 0.5, & otherwise \end{cases} \tag{3}$$

The network outputs four results so that the loss is computed by summing the four smooth L_1 losses with different weights during training.

4   Experiments

In this section, we evaluate performance of LWSN on three public stereo datasets: Scene Flow [11], KITTI 2015 [20] and KITTI 2012 [21]. We also compare the network with the current state-of-the-art models in terms of accuracy and efficiency. Besides, an ablation study is conducted to evaluate the modules of LWSN with different settings of architectures and parameters.

4.1   Dataset and Evaluation Metrics

We trained and evaluated LWSN on three benchmark datasets, i.e., Scene Flow, KITTI 2015 and KITTI 2012.

Scene Flow. A large scale synthetic dataset which contains $35,454$ training and $4,370$ testing image pairs with $H = 540$ and $W = 960$. This dataset has full, accurate ground truth disparity maps. Pixels with larger disparities than our limits set are excluded in the loss computation. The end-point-error (EPE) is used as the evaluation metric which refers to the average difference of the estimated disparity map and the ground truth disparity map.

KITTI 2015. A real-world dataset with street views captured from a driving car. It contains 200 stereo image pairs for training with sparse ground truth disparity maps obtained by LiDAR and 200 stereo image pairs for testing without ground truth disparity maps given. Each image has a resolution of 1242×375 pixels. In this paper, the training data is divided into training set (160 image pairs) and validation set (40 image pairs). 3-Pixel-Error (3PE) is used as the evaluation metric which computes the percentage of pixels for which the predicted disparity is off the ground truth by more than 3 pixels and more than 5%.

KITTI 2012. A real-world dataset with street views captured from a driving car. It contains 194 stereo image pairs for training with sparse ground truth disparity maps obtained by LiDAR and 195 stereo image pairs for testing without ground truth disparity maps given. Each image has a resolution of 1242 × 375 pixels. In this paper, the training data is divided into training set (160 image pairs) and validation set (34 image pairs). Same as in KITTI 2015, 3-Pixel-Error is used as the evaluation metric.

4.2   Experimental Details

LWSN was implemented in Pytorch framework and was trained end-to-end with Adam ($\beta_1 = 0.9, \beta_2 = 0.999$). We trained our network on patches with the resolution of 512 × 256 pixels randomly cropped from the original images. The maximum disparity D was set to 192 pixels in the original images. All inputs are of original image resolutions and are normalized to be zero-mean with unit variance. On the Scene Flow dataset, we trained LWSN with learning rate of 5×10^{-4} for 10 epochs. The batch size was set to 8 for training and 8 for testing. For KITTI 2015 and KITTI 2012 datasets, we fine-tuned the model pre-trained with the Scene Flow for 300 epochs. The learning rate was set to 5×10^{-4} for the first 200 epochs and 5×10^{-5} for the remaining epochs. The batch size was 6 for training and 8 for testing. The training process took 15.56 h for the Scene Flow dataset and 1.15 h for the KITTI datasets using one GeForce RTX 2080Ti GPU.

4.3   Experimental Results

Table 1 lists the average validation end point error for Scene Flow dataset, 3-pixel error for KITTI 2015 and KITTI 2012 datasets and average inference time for KITTI 2015. Figure 5 shows three testing examples for the KITTI 2015 dataset of disparity maps generated by our model at all four stages associated with 3-pixel errors of the input stereo pairs. LWSN can process images of 1242 × 375 resolutions within 24−52 FPS and generate disparity maps with 3-pixel error within the range [2.68%, 4.75%] on a Geforce RTX 2080Ti GPU. The network generates more accurate disparity as inference time increases. In addition, we also present some examples of predicted disparities of Stage 4 for KITTI 2012 and Scene Flow datasets in Figs. 6 and 7.

We also compare LWSN with some competitive methods and numerical results are shown in Table 2. Besides, in Fig. 8, we visualize some examples of disparity maps for KITTI 2015 predicted by LWSN, AnyNet and PSMNet. Results show that LWSN can achieve the state-of-the-art performance at low inference time.

4.4   Ablation Study

In this section, we conduct an ablation study for KITTI 2015 and Scene Flow datasets to examine the effectiveness of some components of our network,

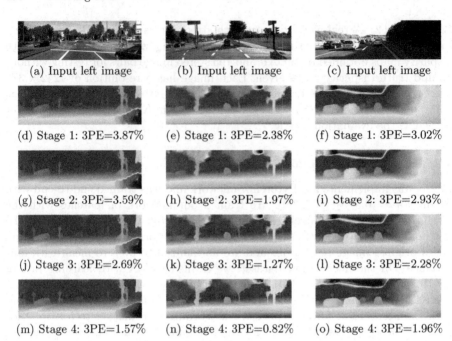

(a) Input left image   (b) Input left image   (c) Input left image

(d) Stage 1: 3PE=3.87%   (e) Stage 1: 3PE=2.38%   (f) Stage 1: 3PE=3.02%

(g) Stage 2: 3PE=3.59%   (h) Stage 2: 3PE=1.97%   (i) Stage 2: 3PE=2.93%

(j) Stage 3: 3PE=2.69%   (k) Stage 3: 3PE=1.27%   (l) Stage 3: 3PE=2.28%

(m) Stage 4: 3PE=1.57%   (n) Stage 4: 3PE=0.82%   (o) Stage 4: 3PE=1.96%

Fig. 5. Input KITTI 2015 left images and associated predicted disparity maps using LWSN in all four stages. Each column shows the left image of input stereo pair and output results. 3 pixel errors are also presented.

Table 1. The average end point error for Scene Flow, 3-pixel error for KITTI 2012 and KITTI 2015 and inference time for KITTI 2015.

Dataset	Stage1	Stage2	Stage3	Stage4
Scene Flow EPE (px)	2.94	2.84	2.62	1.97
KITTI 2012 3PE (%)	6.37	6.25	5.15	3.94
KITTI 2015 3PE (%)	4.75	4.60	3.68	2.68
KITTI 2015 Inference Time (ms)	19.08	21.74	39.74	41.98

including the usage of dilated convolutions in hourglass network, residual blocks in 2D CNN and 3D CNN, color guidance refinement, depthwise separable convolution in refinement.

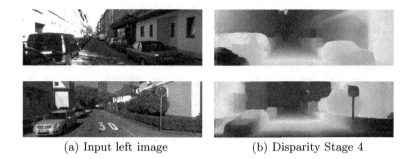

(a) Input left image   (b) Disparity Stage 4

Fig. 6. Visualizations of estimated disparities of LWSN for the KITTI 2012 dataset in Stage 4.

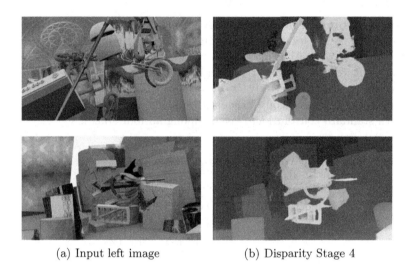

(a) Input left image   (b) Disparity Stage 4

Fig. 7. Visualizations of estimated disparities of LWSN for the Scene Flow dataset in Stage 4.

Table 2. The average 3-pixel error and runtime of different methods for KITTI 2015. Data of other methods are from the KITTI 2015 leaderboard.

Method	3PE (%)	Runtime (s)
Our LWSN	2.68	0.04
AnyNet	6.20	0.02
PSMNet	2.32	0.41
GCNet	2.87	0.90
FBA-AMNet-32	1.84	0.90
CSPN	1.74	1.00
StereoNet	4.83	0.02

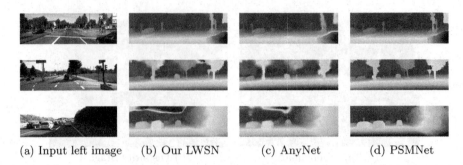

(a) Input left image   (b) Our LWSN   (c) AnyNet   (d) PSMNet

Fig. 8. Testing examples of disparity maps using LWSN, PSMNet and AnyNet for KITTI 2015. For LWSN and AnyNet, we only present results in Stage 4.

Dilated Convolution in Hourglass Network. We compared LWSN with the method where the dilation factors of convolutions were all set to 1 in hourglass feature extractor to test the performance of dilated convolution. In our network, the dilation factors were set to 2, 4, 2 and 2 for the first four convolutional layers of feature extractor, respectively. It can be seen from Table 3 that the hourglass architecture with dilated convolutional layers achieve better performance than that with standard convolutional layers among all four stages.

Table 3. Comparison of LWSN with or without dilated convolutions in 2D CNN. Only results in Stage 4 are listed.

Model	Dataset	
	Scene Flow EPE (px)	KITTI 2015 3PE (%)
LWSN	1.97	2.68
Model without dilated convolutions	2.14	3.98

Residual Blocks. We deleted the shortcut connections in 2D CNN and 3D CNN respectively to evaluate the effects of the residual blocks. We list the Stage 4 results in Table 4. It can be seen that shortcut connections in 2D CNN and 3D CNN can both gather context information and improve estimation accuracy.

Color Guidance Refinement. We evaluated LWSN by comparing it with the model without Stage 4 color guidance refinement. Results in Table 5 show that color guidance refinement plays a significant role in improving accuracy of predicted disparity without much runtime increase.

Table 4. Comparison of LWSN with or without residual connections in 2D CNN and 3D CNN. Only results in Stage 4 are listed.

Residual connections		Scene Flow	KITTI 2015
2D CNN	3D CNN	EPE (px)	3PE (%)
✓	✓	1.97	2.68
✓		2.02	2.72
	✓	2.87	3.07
		2.27	3.24

Table 5. Comparison of LWSN with or without color guidance refinement. Only results in final stage are listed.

Model	Scene Flow	KITTI 2015	
	EPE (px)	3PE (%)	Runtime (ms)
LWSN	1.97	2.68	41.98
Model without Stage 4	2.83	3.51	39.85

Depthwise Separable Convolution. We modified the color guidance refinement in Stage 4 by replacing all the depthwise separable convolutions with the standard convolutions. Table 6 illustrates the number of model parameters, the error rate and inference time of the two models. It can be seen that adopting depthwise separable convolution rather than standard convolution can obtain higher speed without too much accuracy reduction.

Table 6. Comparison of LWSN using depthwise separable or standard convolutions. Only results in Stage 4 are listed.

Model	No. of	KITTI 2015	
	parameters	3PE (%)	Runtime (ms)
Depthwise separable convolution	176, 579	2.68	41.98
Standard convolution	263, 523	2.67	45.95

5   Conclusion

In this paper, we present a novel end-to-end light-weight deep network for the stereo matching problem. We exploit hourglass feature extractor, shortcut connections and dilated convolutions to learn global context information and color guidance refinement is applied to sharpen and boost the disparity performance. Depthwise separable convolution is used in color guidance refinement to reduce the number of parameters and computational complexity. Numerical results demonstrate that LWSN is competitive with the current state-of-the-art methods in terms of both accuracy and speed.

References

1. Janai, J., et al.: Computer vision for autonomous vehicles: problems, datasets and state-of-the-art arXiv:1704.05519 (2017)
2. Wang, Y., et al.: Anytime stereo image depth estimation on mobile devices. In: International Conference on Robotics and Automation (ICRA), pp. 5893–5900 (2019)
3. Scharstein, D., Szeliski, R., Zabih, R.: A taxonomy and evaluation of dense two-frame stereo correspondence algorithms. In: Proceedings IEEE Workshop on Stereo and Multi-Baseline Vision, pp. 131–140 (2001)
4. Heiko, H., Scharstein, D.: Evaluation of cost functions for stereo matching. In: IEEE Conference on Computer Vision and Pattern Recognition, pp. 1–8 (2007)
5. Birchfield, S., Tomasi, C.: Depth discontinuities by pixel-to-pixel stereo. In: Sixth International Conference on Computer Vision, pp. 1073–1080 (1998)
6. Boykov, Y., Veksler, O., Zabih, R.: Fast approximate energy minimization via graph cuts. In: Proceedings of the Seventh IEEE International Conference on Computer Vision, pp. 377–384 (1999)
7. Felzenszwalb, P.F., Huttenlocher, D.R.: Efficient belief propagation for early vision. In: Proceedings of the 2004 IEEE Computer Society Conference on Computer Vision and Pattern Recognition (2004)
8. Hirschmuller, H.: Stereo processing by Semiglobal matching and mutual information. IEEE Trans. Pattern Anal. Mach. Intell. **30**(2), 328–341 (2008)
9. Zbontar, J., LeCun, Y.: Stereo matching by training a convolutional neural network to compare image patches. arXiv:1510.05970 (2016)
10. Luo, W., et al.: Efficient deep learning for stereo matching. In: IEEE Conference on Computer Vision and Pattern Recognition, vol. 2016, pp. 5695–5703 (2016)
11. Mayer, N., et al.: A large dataset to train convolutional networks for disparity, optical flow, and scene flow estimation. In: IEEE Conference on Computer Vision and Pattern Recognition (CVPR), vol. 2016, pp. 4040–4048 (2016)
12. Kendall, A., et al.: End-to-end learning of geometry and context for deep stereo regression. In: IEEE International Conference on Computer Vision (ICCV), vol. 2017, pp. 66–75 (2017)
13. Chang, J., Chen, Y.: Pyramid stereo matching network. In: IEEE/CVF Conference on Computer Vision and Pattern Recognition, vol. 2018, pp. 5410–5418 (2018)
14. Yang, G., Zhao, H., Shi, J., Deng, Z., Jia, J.: SegStereo: exploiting semantic information for disparity estimation. In: Ferrari, V., Hebert, M., Sminchisescu, C., Weiss, Y. (eds.) ECCV 2018. LNCS, vol. 11211, pp. 660–676. Springer, Cham (2018). https://doi.org/10.1007/978-3-030-01234-2_39
15. Newell, A., Yang, K., Deng, J.: Stacked hourglass networks for human pose estimation. In: Leibe, B., Matas, J., Sebe, N., Welling, M. (eds.) ECCV 2016. LNCS, vol. 9912, pp. 483–499. Springer, Cham (2016). https://doi.org/10.1007/978-3-319-46484-8_29
16. Yu, F., Koltun, V.: Multi-scale context aggregation by dilated convolutions. CoRR:1511.07122 (2016)

17. He, K., et al.: Deep residual learning for image recognition. In: IEEE Conference on Computer Vision and Pattern Recognition, vol. 2016, pp. 770–778 (2016)
18. Park, K., Kim, S., Sohn, K.: High-Precision Depth Estimation Using Uncalibrated LiDAR and Stereo Fusion. IEEE Trans. Intell. Transp. Syst. **21**(1), 321–335 (2020)
19. Chollet, F.: Xception: deep learning with depthwise separable convolutions. In: IEEE Conference on Computer Vision and Pattern Recognition, vol. 2017, pp. 1800–1807 (2017)
20. Menze, M., Andreas, G.: Object scene flow for autonomous vehicles. In: IEEE Conference on Computer Vision and Pattern Recognition, vol. 2015, pp. 3061–3070 (2015)
21. Geiger, A., et al.: Are we ready for autonomous driving? The KITTI vision benchmark suite. In: IEEE Conference on Computer Vision and Pattern Recognition, vol. 2012, pp. 3354–3361 (2012)

Vision B

version B

Overview of Monocular Depth Estimation Based on Deep Learning

Quanfu Xu[1,2], Chuanqi Tan[2(✉)], Tao Xue[2], Shuqi Mei[2], and Yan Shan[3]

[1] Aerospace Information Research Institute, Chinese Academy of Sciences,
Beijing 100190, China
xuquanfu18@mails.ucas.ac.cn
[2] Tencent, Beijing, China
{emmaxue,shawnmei}@tencent.com
[3] Beihang University, Beijing 100191, China
shanyan@buaa.edu.cn

Abstract. Monocular depth estimation aims to estimate depth information from a single image. It plays an important role in various applications including SLAM, robotics and autonomous driving and so on. Monocular depth estimation is often described as an ill-posed problem. With the rise of deep neural networks, monocular depth estimation based on deep learning have also developed greatly. In this paper, we review some representative monocular depth estimation methods based on deep learning according to different training manners: supervised, self-supervised and weakly supervised. We then compare these three types of methods and illustrated their application scenarios. Finally, we separately analyze the potential improvements of the three types of methods.

Keywords: Monocular depth estimation · Deep learning · Single image depth estimation

1 Introduction

Depth estimation is one of the important tasks in computer vision, which can be used in robotics [4], SLAM [9] and autonomous driving [13] and so on. Traditional depth estimation has geometry-based methods and sensor-based methods [16]. Geometry-based methods can recover 3D structures from a series of images based on geometric constraints, like structure from motion (SfM) and stereo vision matching. Sensor-based methods use depth sensors, like RGB-D cameras and LIDAR, to get the depth information of the imagey. These methods require many corresponding images for geometric constraints or expensive sensors. In life, we can easily obtain a large number of monocular images, so it is very challenging and meaningful for the computer to estimate the depth from a single image like a human.

Monocular depth estimation is often described as an ill-posed problem. The task can be framed as: given a single RGB image as input, estimate the corresponding depth of each pixel of the image. With the rise of deep learning, monocular depth estimation based on convolutional deep networks has also developed

F. Sun et al. (Eds.): ICCSIP 2020, CCIS 1397, pp. 499–506, 2021.
https://doi.org/10.1007/978-981-16-2336-3_47

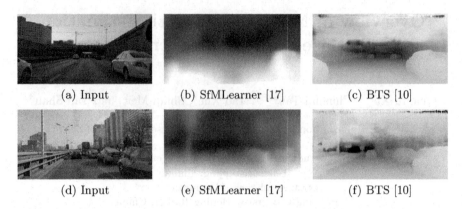

(a) Input   (b) SfMLearner [17]   (c) BTS [10]

(d) Input   (e) SfMLearner [17]   (f) BTS [10]

Fig. 1. Examples of monocular depth estimetion. The models of SfMLearner (self-supervised) and BTS (supervised) are trained by KITTI dataset [7]. In order to validate the effectiveness and robustness of the algorithms, the input images are collected in road scenes rather than KITTI test dataset.

rapidly. As shown in Fig. 1, the results of some monocular depth estimation methods are satisfactory. According to the supervision information, we divide the monocular depth estimation methods based on deep learning into supervised monocular depth estimation, self-supervised monocular depth estimation and weakly supervised monocular depth estimation. Supervised monocular depth estimation methods require depth maps as supervision information. The network structure is generally end-to-end (similar to the semantic segmentation model) and the results of the model are better than other methods. However, the labelled dataset need to be acquired by RGB-D cameras or LIDAR, which is difficult to obtain. In addition, the different application scenarios of the dataset also limit the transfer effect of the model. The self-supervised methods aim to overcome the lack of labelled depth dataset, and estimate the depth map by mining the geometric relationship between video frames. These methods greatly alleviate the short of labelled depth dataset, but they need continuous video frames to train the model and the output depth map of these methods is scale ambiguity. In fact, humans are better at judging relative depth: "Is point A closer than point B?" is often a much easier question for humans [2]. So the methods based on the relative depth between points has been studied by scholars. We classify these methods into weakly supervised monocular depth estimation. As far as we know, we are the first to summarize and discuss such methods which estimate the depth map through relative depth.

This overview is organized in the following way: Sect. 2 introduces some widely used datasets and evaluation indicators in monocular depth estimation. Section 3 reviews reviews the deep learning architectures for monocular depth estimation categorised in supervised, self-supervised and weakly supervised methods. Discussion and potential future research directions are presented in Sect. 4.

2   Datasets and Evaluation Indicators

2.1   Datasets

There are many datasets for monocular depth estimation. As shown in Table 1, KITTI [7] and NYU-v2 [12] are usually used in supervised and self-supervised methods. There are no monocular sequences in Make3D dataset, so Make3D dataset can not be used as training dataset for self-supervised learning, but it can be used to verify the generalization performance of self-supervised models. DIW, ReDWeb and HR-WSI annotated with relative depth information. They are typical datasets for weakly supervised methods.

Table 1. Datasets for monocular depth estimation.

Dataset	Labelled images	Application	Brief description
KITTI [7]	94K	Supervised Self-supervised	RGB and depth from 394 road scenes
NYU-v2 [12]	1449	Supervised Self-supervised	RGB and depth from indoor scenes
Make3D [11]	534	Supervised	RGB and depth from different scenes
DIW [2]	495K	Weakly supervised	Relative depth, an image and a point pair
ReDWeb [14]	3600	Weakly supervised	Dense relative depth
HR-WSI [15]	20378	Weakly supervised	Dense relative depth, more samples and higher resolution

2.2   Evaluation Indicators

The most commonly used evaluation indicators for evaluating the performance of monocular depth estimation methods are Mean Square Error (RMSE), RMSE (log), Absolute Relative Difference (AbsRel), Root and Square Relative Error (SqRel) and Accuracies [5].

In addition, the evaluation indicators of the model based on relative depth information are Weighted Human Disagreement Rate (WHDR) and Ordinal Error [2, 14, 15].

3   Monocular Depth Estimation Based on Deep Learning

3.1   Supervised Monocular Depth Estimation

Supervised monocular depth estimation require labelled depth map as supervisory signal to regress the depth.

Eigen *et al.* [5] composes an end-to-end architecture which is composed of two component stacks (the global coarse-scale network and the local fine-scale network) to predict the depth map. The coarse-scale network is designed to predict the overall depth map structure using a global view of the scene and the local fine-scale network is designed to edit the coarse prediction to align with local details such as object and wall edges. During the training process, they define the scale-invariant mean squared error (in log space) as

$$D(y, y^*) = \frac{1}{n} \sum_{i=1}^{n} (\log y_i - \log y_i^* + \alpha(y, y^*))^2$$

$$\alpha(y, y^*) = \frac{1}{n} \sum_{i=1}^{n} \log y_i^* - \log y_i \tag{1}$$

where y is predicted depth map, y^* is ground truth.

Fu *et al.* [6] composes a supervised method which discretize continuous depth into a number of intervals and cast the depth network learning as an ordinal regression problem to estimate depth maps. The framework consists of a dense feature extractor, multi-scale feature learner, cross channel information learner, a full-image encoder and an ordinal regression optimizer. The ordinal regression optimizer which conbines spacing-increasing discretization(SID) is the main innovation. Assuming that a depth interval $[\alpha, \beta]$ needs to be discretized into K sub-intervals, SID can be formulated as:

$$t_i = e^{\log(\alpha) + \frac{\log(\beta/\alpha) * i}{K}} \tag{2}$$

where $t_i \in \{t_0, t_1, ..., t_K\}$ are discretization thresholds. The SID approach discretizes a given depth interval in log space to down-weight the training losses in regions with large depth values, so that the depth estimation network is capable to more accurately predict relatively small and medium depth and to rationally estimate large depth values.

It can be found from the above introduction that the depth estimation based on CNNs generally compose of two parts: an encoder for dense feature extraction and a decoder for predicting the desired depth. In [10], Lee *et al.* composes a network architecture that utilizes novel local planar guidance layers located at multiple stages in the decoding phase, which can more effectively guide densely encoded features to the desired depth prediction. As far as we known, it is the state-of-the-art method on KITTI dataset according to the published literature.

3.2 Self-supervised Monocular Depth Estimation

The methods of self-supervised monocular depth estimation is generally based on SfMLearner [17] and SfMLearner use view synthesis as supervision. Let $\langle I_1, ..., I_N \rangle$ denotes a training image sequence. The view synthesis objective can be formulated as:

$$L_{vs} = \sum_{s} \sum_{p} |I_t(p) - \hat{I}_s(p)| \tag{3}$$

where I_t is the target view in the sequence and the rest being the source views $I_s(1 \leq s \leq N, s \neq t)$, p indexes over pixel coordinates, and $\hat{I}_s$ is the source view I_s warped to the target coordinate frame based on a depth image-based rendering module. The key component of SfMlearner is a differentiable depth image-based renderer that reconstructs the target view I_t by sampling pixels from a source view I_s based on the predicted depth map $\hat{D}_t$ and the relative pose $T_{t \rightarrow s}$. Let p_t denote the homogeneous coordinates of a pixel in the target view, and K denote the camera intrinsics matrix. The pixel correspondences between p_s and p_t are built up:

$$p_s \sim K\hat{T}_{t \rightarrow s}\hat{D}_t(p_t)K^{-1}p_t \tag{4}$$

Therefore, if we can obtain $\hat{D}_t$ and $\hat{T}_{t \rightarrow s}$, the corresponce between the pixels on different images (I_s and I_t)are established by above projection function. Furthermore, SfMLearner has the explainability mask to reduce the effect of the position of dynamic objects on neighboring frames.

Since then, there are many algorithms based on SfMLearner. Bian et al. [1] focous on scale-consistent of the output of the model. Therefore, they propose a geometry consistency loss and an induced self-discovered mask for scale-consistent predictions and handling moving objects and occlusions, respectively. Godard et al. [8] pay attention to the problem of occlusion and relative motion, and propose Monodepth2. Monodepth2 has three contributions: 1) A novel appearance matching loss to address the problem of occlusion. 2) A novel and simple auto-masking approach to alleviate the effect of no relative camera motion. 3) Multi-scale estimation to reduce depth artifacts.

All of the above self-supervised methods require camera intrinsic parameters as the prerequisite, which limits the application scenario. Chen et al. [3] extend the pose network to estimate the camera intrinsic parameter and achieved satisfactory results. Therefore, they can estimate depth from videos in the wild.

3.3   Weakly Supervised Monocular Depth Estimation

Depth maps need to be acquired by RGB-D cameras or LIDAR in supervised monocular depth estimation, which is difficult to obtain. As for self-supervised methods, they suffer from scale ambiguity, scale inconsistency, occlusions and other problems. Scholars consider how to obtain a compareable result under a lower labeling cost. It is easier for human to estimate relative depth than absolute depth. So estimating the relative depth may be more reasonable than estimating the absolute depth. Furthermore, it is easy to obtain relative depth dataset. As long as the relative depth of all pixels in a image is obtained, we can obtain the final absolute depth maps by monotonic transformations or fine-tuning. We classify this approach as weakly supervised monocular depth estimation.

As far as we know, [18] is the first method to estimate metric depth using only annotations of relative depth, but the result of [18] is not very smooth. Chen et al. [2] improve this method in two aspects: 1) A new dataset called"Depth in the Wild" (DIW) which consists of 495K diverse images with relative depth annotations is open source. 2) They use hourglass network to extract the features, which is an end-to-end design to predict the depth of each pixel. The rest is how to train the network using only ordinal annotations. Consider a training image I and its K queries $R = \{(i_k, j_k, r_k)\}, k = 1, ..., K$, where i_k is the location of the first point in the k-th query, j_k is the location of the second point in the k-th query, $r_k \in \{+1, -1, 0\}$ is the ground-truth depth relation between i_k and j_k: closer $(+1)$, further (-1), and equal (0). Let z be the predicted depth map and z_{ik}, z_{jk} be the depths at point i_k and j_k. The ranking loss function can be formulated as:

$$L(I, R, z) = \sum_{k=1}^{K} \psi_k(I, i_k, j_k, r, z),$$ (5)

where $\psi_k(I, i_k, j_k, r, z)$ is the loss for the k-th query

$$\psi_k(I, i_k, j_k, r, z) = \begin{cases} \log(1 + exp(-z_{ik} + z_{jk})), & r_k = +1 \\ \log(1 + exp(z_{ik} - z_{jk})), & r_k = -1 \\ (z_{ik} - z_{jk})^2, & r_k = 0 \end{cases}$$ (6)

Different from annotating relative depth of two points which use in DIW, Xian et al. [14] introduce a method to automatically generate dense relative depth annotations from web stereo images (ReDWeb). In order to pay more attention on a set of hard pairs, they improve the ranking loss to deal with imbalanced ordinal relations.

Table 2. Evaluation results on KITTI dataset with supervised learning (SL), self-supervised learning (SSL) and weakly supervised learning (WSL). Experimental results of SL and SSL using KITTI's Eigen split. In WSL, DIW, ReDWeb and HR-WSI are used for training in their respective models, KITTI dataset is used to evaluate the robustness of trained models.

Type	Method	Lower is better				Higher is better		
		AbsRel	SqRel	RMSE	RMSE(log)	$thr < 1.25$	$thr < 1.25^2$	$thr < 1.25^3$
SL	Eigen et al. [5]	0.190	1.515	7.156	0.270	0.692	0.899	0.967
	Fu et al. [6]	0.072	0.307	**2.727**	0.120	0.932	0.984	0.994
	Lee et al. [10]	**0.059**	**0.245**	2.756	**0.096**	**0.956**	**0.993**	**0.998**
SSL	Zhou et al. [17]	0.208	1.768	6.865	0.283	0.678	0.885	0.957
	Bian et al. [1]	0.137	1.089	5.439	0.217	0.830	0.942	0.975
	Godard et al. [8]	0.115	0.903	4.863	0.193	**0.877**	**0.959**	0.981
	Chen et al. [3]	**0.100**	**0.811**	**4.806**	**0.189**	0.875	0.958	**0.982**
WSL	Method				Ordinal error			
	Chen et al. [2] (DIW)				29.92			
	Xian et al. [14] (ReDWeb)				16.40			
	Xian et al. [15] (HR-WSI)				**14.01**			

In [15], HR-WSI is open source, it has more training samples (20378 vs. 3600) and higher resolution (833×1251 vs. 408×65) than ReDWeb. To more effectively learn from HR-WSI, they propose a structure-guided ranking loss formulation with two novel sampling strategies (Edge-guided sampling and Instance-guided sampling). Edge-guided sampling focuses on point pairs that are on boundaries and instance-guided sampling is intended for improving depth structural accuracy regarding salient object instances.

Table 2 illustrates evaluation results on KITTI dataset with supervised learning, self-supervised learning and weakly supervised learning.

4 Discussion

4.1 Comparisons of Three Types of Methods

Supervised monocular depth estimation generally has satisfactory results and can obtain absolute depth maps, but it relies heavily on the dataset. Fine tuning or different datasets is needed in different application scenarios.

Self-supervised methods do not require depth maps but require continuous video sequences during training. The results obtained by self-supervised methods are comparable to supervised methods. But they suffer from scale ambiguity, scale inconsistency, occlusions and other problems.

As for weakly supervised monocular depth estimation, they are not rely on depth maps, but they also suffer from scale ambiguity.

In specific application scenarios, we can choose a specific method or combine several methods to achieve good results.

4.2 Analysis of Potential Improvements

Previous supervised methods generally adopt new loss functions or network frameworks (like ordinal regression and local planar guidance layers) to improve the accuracy of depth estimation, which is similar to semantic segmentation. Therefore, we can follow the semantic segmentation methods to improve the supervised depth estimation.

Self-supervised methods mainly suffer from scale ambiguity, scale inconsistency, occlusions and other problems. Finding more geometric constraints between frames may be an important way to deal with these problems.

As for weakly supervised methods, effective supervision information may be an important way to imporve the accurate. In terms of relative depth estimation, sampling strategies, networks and loss functions are three directions to improve the algorithm.

References

1. Bian, J., et al.: Unsupervised scale-consistent depth and ego-motion learning from monocular video. In: Advances in Neural Information Processing Systems, pp. 35–45 (2019)
2. Chen, W., Fu, Z., Yang, D., Deng, J.: Single-image depth perception in the wild. In: Advances in Neural Information Processing Systems, pp. 730–738 (2016)

3. Chen, Y., Schmid, C., Sminchisescu, C.: Self-supervised learning with geometric constraints in monocular video: connecting flow, depth, and camera. In: Proceedings of the IEEE International Conference on Computer Vision, pp. 7063–7072 (2019)

4. Diamantas, S.C., Oikonomidis, A., Crowder, R.M.: Depth estimation for autonomous robot navigation: a comparative approach. In: 2010 IEEE International Conference on Imaging Systems and Techniques, pp. 426–430. IEEE (2010)

5. Eigen, D., Puhrsch, C., Fergus, R.: Depth map prediction from a single image using a multi-scale deep network. In: Advances in Neural Information Processing Systems, pp. 2366–2374 (2014)

6. Fu, H., Gong, M., Wang, C., Batmanghelich, K., Tao, D.: Deep ordinal regression network for monocular depth estimation. In: Proceedings of the IEEE Conference on Computer Vision and Pattern Recognition, pp. 2002–2011 (2018)

7. Geiger, A., Lenz, P., Urtasun, R.: Are we ready for autonomous driving? the kitti vision benchmark suite. In: 2012 IEEE Conference on Computer Vision and Pattern Recognition, pp. 3354–3361. IEEE (2012)

8. Godard, C., Mac Aodha, O., Firman, M., Brostow, G.J.: Digging into self-supervised monocular depth estimation. In: Proceedings of the IEEE International Conference on Computer Vision, pp. 3828–3838 (2019)

9. Hu, G., Huang, S., Zhao, L., Alempijevic, A., Dissanayake, G.: A robust RGB-D slam algorithm. In: 2012 IEEE/RSJ International Conference on Intelligent Robots and Systems, pp. 1714–1719. IEEE (2012)

10. Lee, J.H., Han, M.K., Ko, D.W., Suh, I.H.: From big to small: multi-scale local planar guidance for monocular depth estimation. arXiv preprint arXiv:1907.10326 (2019)

11. Saxena, A., Sun, M., Ng, A.Y.: Make3D: learning 3D scene structure from a single still image. IEEE Trans. Pattern Anal. Mach. Intell. **31**(5), 824–840 (2008)

12. Silberman, N., Hoiem, D., Kohli, P., Fergus, R.: Indoor segmentation and support inference from RGBD images. In: Fitzgibbon, A., Lazebnik, S., Perona, P., Sato, Y., Schmid, C. (eds.) ECCV 2012. LNCS, vol. 7576, pp. 746–760. Springer, Heidelberg (2012). https://doi.org/10.1007/978-3-642-33715-4_54

13. Wang, Y., Chao, W.L., Garg, D., Hariharan, B., Campbell, M., Weinberger, K.Q.: Pseudo-lidar from visual depth estimation: bridging the gap in 3D object detection for autonomous driving. In: Proceedings of the IEEE Conference on Computer Vision and Pattern Recognition, pp. 8445–8453 (2019)

14. Xian, K., et al.: Monocular relative depth perception with web stereo data supervision. In: Proceedings of the IEEE Conference on Computer Vision and Pattern Recognition, pp. 311–320 (2018)

15. Xian, K., Zhang, J., Wang, O., Mai, L., Lin, Z., Cao, Z.: Structure-guided ranking loss for single image depth prediction. In: Proceedings of the IEEE/CVF Conference on Computer Vision and Pattern Recognition, pp. 611–620 (2020)

16. Zhao, C., Sun, Q., Zhang, C., Tang, Y., Qian, F.: Monocular depth estimation based on deep learning: an overview. Sci. China Technol. Sci. 1–16 (2020)

17. Zhou, T., Brown, M., Snavely, N., Lowe, D.G.: Unsupervised learning of depth and ego-motion from video. In: Proceedings of the IEEE Conference on Computer Vision and Pattern Recognition, pp. 1851–1858 (2017)

18. Zoran, D., Isola, P., Krishnan, D., Freeman, W.T.: Learning ordinal relationships for mid-level vision. In: Proceedings of the IEEE International Conference on Computer Vision, pp. 388–396 (2015)

Non-contact Physiological Parameters Detection Based on MTCNN and EVM

Jinfa Zhao[1,2], Wenchang Zhang[3], Rongxuan Chai[1,2], Hang Wu[3(✉)], and Wei Chen[1,2(✉)]

[1] Tianjin Key Laboratory for Advanced Mechatronic System Design and Intelligent Control, School of Mechanical, Tianjin University of Technology, Tianjin 300384, China
[2] National Demonstration Center for Experimental Mechanical and Electrical Engineering Education, Tianjin, China
[3] Institute of Medical Support Technology, Academy of Military Sciences of Chinese PLA, Tianjin, China

Abstract. Non-contact physiological parameters detection has become an important but challenging task. This paper proposes a novel framework for Non-contact physiological parameters detection, which is based on MTCNN (Multi-task convolutional neural network) and EVM (Eulerian Video Magnification). The MTCNN is applied to compensate negative effects of the pseudo motion for improving the efficiency of face detection. The Laplacian pyramid of EVM is added to our framework to perform motion amplification to achieve simultaneous extraction of heart rate and respiration rate, which improves the accuracy of non-contact physiological parameter detection. Then we use FFT to analyze the relevant frequency bands in time domain and calculate the heart rate and breathing rate. In order to improve efficiency, GPU acceleration is implemented under the TensorRT framework. The experimental results based on data sets DUSS (detection under slight shaking) and DUO (detection under occlusion) show the effectiveness of this method. The average error of the heart rate and respiration rate are −0.1 and 0.6, respectively. Our method achieves comparable performance to finger clip oximeter with a good consistency, even in the case of wearing a mask.

Keywords: Multi-task convolutional neural network · Eulerian video magnification · Non-contact detection · Physiological parameters

1 Introduction

With the development of society, the progress of technology and the increasing demand of specific scene detection, the shortcomings and limitations of contact detection have gradually emerged [1].

In 2020, it is extremely dangerous for medical staff to conduct contact physiological testing on COVID-19 patients. At this time, non-contact physiological parameter detection becomes very important.

The ROI area needs to be selected before extracting the physiological signal and most of the areas are human face [2, 3] and wrist radial artery [4, 5]. Face detection is more

© Springer Nature Singapore Pte Ltd. 2021
F. Sun et al. (Eds.): ICCSIP 2020, CCIS 1397, pp. 507–516, 2021.
https://doi.org/10.1007/978-981-16-2336-3_48

convenient compared with detecting the wrist. Up to now, most of the face detection for non-contact physiological parameter detection uses Haar-like feature detection [6–8]. This method was proposed by Paul Viola and Michael Jones in 2001 and implemented based on the AdaBoost algorithm [9]. However, the detection of this method in the case of a person's side face and occlusions may have missed detection and false detection. With the outbreak of COVID-19, testing under masks has become particularly important.

There are three main contributions of our work:

- A new framework constructed MTCNN (Multi-task convolutional neural network) and EVM (Eulerian Video Magnification) was first introduced to achieve simultaneous detection of heart rate and respiration rate.
- The embedded modules were used to facilitate later deployment for increasing practicability. GPU acceleration is achieved under the TensorRT framework, which increases the efficiency of image processing.
- The test results had been analyzed by Bland-Altman consistency analysis, and had a good consistency with traditional contact testing, even in the case of wearing a mask.

2   Related Work

In recent years, non-contact detection which can detect the corresponding physiological parameters without contacting the patient has developed rapidly. It can be divided into the following detection methods based on the measurement principle:

- Laser detection: Doppler Vibrometer LDV is used to measure skin vibration.
- Electromagnetic detection: Use microwave Doppler radar to measure skin vibration.
- Infrared detection: Use infrared sensors to detect human body temperature.
- Visual inspection: Use a camera to collect relevant parts of the human body to detect skin changes.

The advantages and disadvantages of non-contact physiological sign parameter detection are shown in Table 1.

Table 1. Comparison of non-contact physiological sign parameter detection

Detection method	Advantage	Disadvantage
Laser inspection [10, 11]	High accuracy of test results	The equipment is expensive and cannot be tested for a long time
Electromagnetic detection [12, 13]	Testing under non-ideal environment	The equipment is large and the operation steps are complicated
Infrared detection [14, 15]	High efficiency	Single detection parameter
Visual inspection	Low cost, high efficiency, simple operation	Affected by light environment and artificial shaking

Compared with laser and electromagnetic detection, non-contact detection is more convenient to popularize and deploy. Compared with infrared detection, multiple parameters can be detected. As can be seen from Table 1, the advantages of visual non-contact detection are more prominent.

3 MTCNN-EVM Method

3.1 The Overall Process of the Experiment

This paper proposes a novel framework based on MTCNN (Multi-task convolutional neural network) and EVM (Eulerian Video Magnification) to non-contact detect the heart rate and breathing rate. The framework is shown in Fig. 1.

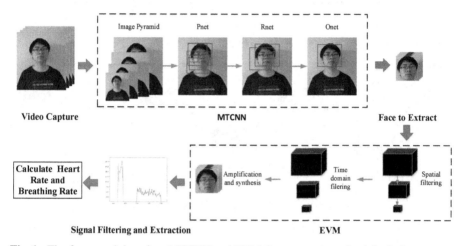

Fig. 1. The framework based on MTCNN and EVM for non-contact physiological parameters detection

3.2 MTCNN Face Detection

Compared with traditional face detection methods, MTCNN has better performance. It can accurately locate faces faster and more accurately.

This method is based on the face detection of deep learning, which can perform face area detection and face key point detection at the same time. It is more robust to light, angle and expression changes in the natural environment, and has a better face detection effect [16].

MTCNN is a multi-task neural network model for face detection tasks proposed by Shenzhen Research Institute of Chinese Academy of Sciences in 2016 [20]. Realize the detection of occluded faces based on the MTCNN algorithm in the railway scene. The model mainly uses three cascaded networks, and adopts the idea of candidate box plus classifier to perform fast and efficient face detection.

As shown in Fig. 2, the algorithm is mainly divided into four parts [17]:

1. Generate image pyramid: detect faces of different sizes.
2. P-Net: Generate face candidate frames. Non-maximum suppression (NMS) is used to remove face images with a high degree of coincidence, and the regression vector is used for correction.
3. R-Net: Judge the face in the face candidate frame and correct the original face candidate frame area.
4. O-Net: The face in the picture is judged again, and the face candidate frame area is corrected.

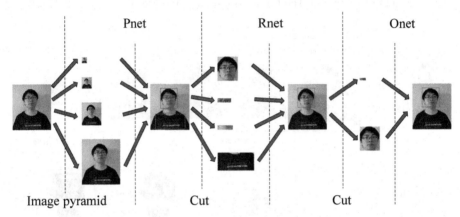

Fig. 2. MTCNN working principle diagram

3.3 EVM

EVM can amplify the changes of color and movement in the video, so that the naked eye can observe small changes that are easily overlooked. Compared with the previous magnification technology based on the Lagrangian perspective, EVM has lower complexity, fewer computing resources, and better magnification effect. Therefore, the Euler image magnification method has been applied to the detection of non-contact physiological parameters [18, 19].

Spatial Filtering

The input video sequence is spatially filtered through image pyramids. Gaussian pyramids or Laplace pyramids can be used as image pyramids. The purpose of spatial filtering is to obtain basebands of different spatial frequencies to reduce the influence of noise. The Laplacian image sequence is used as the motion amplification in the video. The image sequence mainly saves the pixel value change of the boundary part, so it can be used to enhance or extract the pixel value change information related to the displacement movement of the object.

In order to detect the heart rate and respiration rate at the same time, as shown in Fig. 3, the motion magnified Laplace pyramid image sequence are used as information extraction.

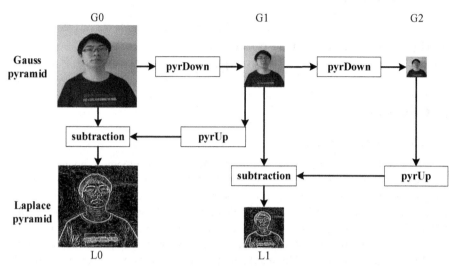

Fig. 3. Extraction of Laplace pyramid

Time Domain Filtering
After the pyramid decomposition, the signal needs to be further filtered in the time domain, that is, in the frequency domain. The signal of interest is retained through filtering, and the signal outside the band pass is eliminated to reduce noise interference.

Amplification and Synthesis
After time domain filtering, the frequency domain signal is subjected to inverse Fourier transform and magnified by α times, and then linearly superimposed with the original video to obtain the magnified and reconstructed video.

3.4 Calculation of Heart Rate and Breathing Rate

After determining the range of detection parameter, the signal in a specific interval is extracted. In this paper, the detection range of adult heart rate and respiratory rate and the corresponding frequency domain range are shown in Table 2.

Table 2. Heart rate and breathing rate selection range

Detection parameters	Detection ranged (bmp)	Frequency domain range (Hz)
Heart rate	60–120	1–2
Respiration rate	12–24	0.2–0.4

According to the frequency domain interval of heart rate and respiratory rate, the frequency corresponding to the maximum peak value is extracted, and the corresponding parameters are calculated based on formulas (1) and (2).

The calculation formula for heart rate is:

$$V_{hr} = 60 \cdot f_{hr} \tag{1}$$

The formula for respiration rate calculation is:

$$V_{rr} = 60 \cdot f_{rr} \tag{2}$$

4   Experiment

4.1   Experimental Setup

As shown in Fig. 4, for hardware, we used Jetson TX2 development board, Logitech C922pro camera and finger clip oximeter. Jetson TX2 is one of the quickest, embedded AI computing devices which is highly power-efficient. This supercomputing module helps in bringing genuine AI processing at the end devices, with a low power consumption of 7.5 W. The Jetson TX2 features a NVIDIA Pascal GPU with 256 CUDA capable cores. The GPU has a compute capability of 6.2. The camera supports up to 1080p resolution and 30 fps video recording. The heart rate test results were based on the finger clip oximeter and respiration rate test results are compared by counting.

Fig. 4. Jetson TX2, C922pro and finger clip oximeter

On the software side, this paper took python as the programming language. The OpenCV and the python correlation library were used for carrying on the image and the signal processing. GPU acceleration of the MTCNN algorithm based on TensorRT reduced the processing time for face recognition. Bland-Altman consistency between the experimental test results and the traditional test results was evaluated to verify the effectiveness of the method.

The camera recording distance was 0.5 m, the resolution was 1920 × 1080, and the frame rate was 30. This paper conducted 3 groups of experiments on 3 adults. The first group was the impact of different time periods in the same video on the results. The recording time was determined to prepare for the next experiments. The second group was the detection of heart rate and breathing rate while wearing a mask. Used the DUSS data set to test in the second group with slight shaking. Used the DUO data set to detect when wearing a mask.

4.2   Face Detection and Time Period Selection

With the outbreak of COVID-19 in 2020, occlusion detection had become particularly important. The traditional Haar face detection algorithm could not detect the occluded face well, so we needed a better face recognition algorithm.

It can be seen from Fig. 5 that MTCNN had good detection results for front face, side face and mask occlusion.

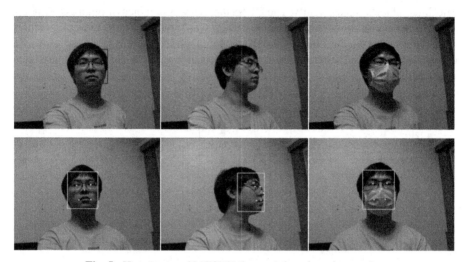

Fig. 5.   Haar (top) and MTCNN (bottom) face detection results.

Too short detection time was an important factor for inaccurate detection results, especially for the detection of respiration rate. Too long detection time would increase the amount of calculation and increase the calculation time. Therefore, it was necessary to find a suitable time period for detection.

As shown in Fig. 6, the heart rate and respiration rate were tested for 3 adults within 1 min. Then the test results at different time periods were compared.

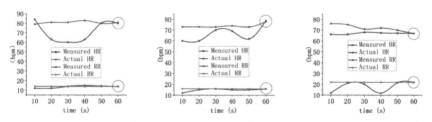

Fig. 6.   3 sets of test results at different time periods

It can be seen from the Fig. 6 that the detection accuracy in a short time was low. This was because the video duration was too short, besides the number of sampling points was small. Due to the non-stationary of the heart rate and respiration rate, accurate results cannot be obtained. When the video duration gradually increased, the number of sampling points increased. Most important of all, the detection result at 60 s had the highest accuracy. Therefore, the next two sets of experiments were recorded with 60-s video as the standard.

4.3 Detection Under Slight Shaking

The three subjects shake slightly. The DUSS data set was obtained through experiments. The corresponding Bland-Altman analysis chart was shown in Fig. 7. Only one point of heart rate was outside the consistency limit. More than 95% of the data were within the consistency limit. The results showed that the detection method had a good consistency with traditional detection.

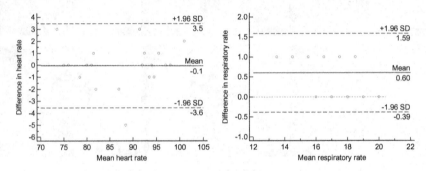

Fig. 7. Consistency analysis of heart rate and respiratory rate test results under slight shaking

Table 3. Comparison of MTCNN and other detection results

Face detection	Average heart rate error	Average respiratory rate error
Haar [3]	0.79	1.85
Haar+Mean-shift [8]	0.18	–
Haar+KLT [21]	0.5	–
MTCNN	−0.1	0.6

Table 3 lists the comparison results of the two algorithms. The results showed that the average error of the heart rate and respiratory rate of the MTCNN algorithm were −0.1 and 0.6, respectively. The detection accuracy had been improved.

The powerful computing ability of GPU had been fully utilized in face image matching and recognition. Under parallel computing, the time for searching and matching the feature data of the face image with the feature template stored in the database would be greatly reduced. As shown in Table 4, for the non-contact physiological parameter extraction of the 10-s video at 1920 × 1080 resolution, the running time of this method was spent sharply less than the Haar method.

Table 4. Comparison of the running time of different detection methods.

Face detection	Time (s)
MTCNN-EVM	40.295722
Haar-EVM	159.135272

4.4 Detection Under Occlusion

There were two difficulties in non-contact detection under occlusion. First, the face area couldnot be accurately recognized. Second, it was impossible to use skin color changes for heart rate extraction. This paper used MTCNN and EVM video motion amplification to overcome the above problems.

Three subjects wore masks. The DUO data set was obtained through experiments. The corresponding Bland-Altman analysis chart is shown in Fig. 8.

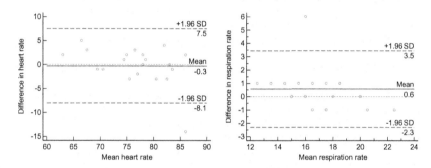

Fig. 8. Consistency analysis of the test results of heart rate and respiration rate wearing a mask

Both heart rate and breathing rate only had one point each outside the limits of consistency. More than 95% of the data were within the consistency limit. The results showed that the non-contact detection with mask wearing had good consistency with the standard testing.

5   Conclusions

Aiming at the difficulty of detecting heart rate and breathing rate under slight shaking and obstruction, this paper proposes a novel framework based on MTCNN and EVM for Non-contact physiological parameters detection. MTCNN is applied to compensate negative effects of the pseudo motion. EVM is added to our framework to improve the accuracy of non-contact physiological parameter detection. In addition, GPU acceleration is implemented under the TensorRT framework to improve efficiency. The experimental results on data sets DUSS and DUO show the effectiveness of this method. Our method achieves comparable performance to finger clip oximeter with good consistency, even in the case of wearing a mask.

Acknowledgments. This work was supported by the Project (19YFZCSF01150) in the Science & Technology Pillar Program of Tianjin, in part by the Tianjin Natural Science Foundation of China under Grant 18JCZDJC40300, in part by Innovation cultivation Foundation 19-163-12-ZT-006-007-06.

References

1. Wang, J., Xue, H., Lu, H., et al.: Non-contact physiological signal detection technology. China Med. Equip. **11**, 5–8 (2013)
2. Liu, Y.: Non-contact heart rate and respiratory rate detection based on FastICA algorithm. Nanchang University, Nanchang (2015)
3. Liu, H., Wang, X., Chen, G.: Non-contact fetal heart rate detection. Comput. Syst. Appl. **28**(8), 204–209 (2019)
4. Su, P., Liang, X., Liang, Y.: Non-contact heart rate measurement method based on Euler image magnification. J. Comput. Appl. **35**(3), 916–922 (2018)
5. Li, J.: Research on pulse wave extraction method based on video amplification. Hefei University of Technology, Hefei (2019)
6. Ma, L.: Research on non-contact physiological parameter detection technology based on ordinary camera. Shandong University, Shandong (2017)
7. Deng, Q.: Research and implementation of heart rate detection based on face video images. Wuhan University of Technology, Wuhan (2017)
8. Hui, P.: Research on non-contact heart rate measurement method based on face image. Southeast University, Nanjing (2017)
9. Viola, P., Jones, M.: Rapid object detection using a boosted cascade of simple features. In: Proceedings of CVPR, vol. 1, pp. 511 (2001)
10. Liu, X., Cui, H., Liu, Z., et al.: Human body sign detection based on Doppler radar sensor. Sens. Microsyst. **2020**(39), 137–139 (2020)
11. Cui, C., Zhao, Q.: Design of vital signs detection system based on micro-Doppler Radar. Control Eng. **26**, 105–107 (2019)
12. Zhou, Y., Pang, L., Zhang, H., et al.: Experimental research on non-contact life detection based on bio-radar technology. Sci. Technol. Vis. 181–182
13. Zhang, Y., Lu, H., Liang, F., et al.: Current status and application prospects of non-contact battlefield injury detection technology. Med. Med. Equip. **40**(07), 99–103 (2019)
14. Cai, S., Men, X., Wang, S., et al.: Research on rapid and accurate measurement of temperature in dense populations during the epidemic of new coronavirus pneumonia. West China Med. **35**, 385–390 (2020)
15. Ge, Z.: Research on medical infrared thermometer and its key technology. Changchun University of Science and Technology, Changchun (2019)
16. Ku, H., Dong, W.: Face recognition based on MTCNN and convolutional neural network. Front. Sig. Process. **4**(1), 37–42 (2020)
17. Wu, J., Chen, S.: An improved MTCNN face detection algorithm. Softw. Guide **18**(12), 78–81 (2019)
18. Cai, K.: Research on non-contact heart rate measurement technology. Nanjing University of Posts and Telecommunications (2019)
19. Liu, Y.: Human heart rate measurement based on facial video. Shanghai Normal University, Shanghai (2018)
20. Yi, S., Zhu, J., Jing, H.: Research on face occlusion recognition based on MTCNN in railway face brushing scene. Comput. Simul. **37**(5), 96–99 (2020)
21. Chen, D.: Research on non-contact heart rate measurement based on video. South China University of Technology, Guangdong (2016)

Texture Classification of a Miniature Whisker Sensor with Varied Contact Pose

Shurui Yan[1,2](✉), Zihou Wei[1,2], Yi Xu[1,2], Guanglu Jia[1,2], Qiang Huang[2,3], Toshio Fukuda[2,3], and Qing Shi[1,2]

[1] School of Mechatronical Engineering, Beijing Institute of Technology, Beijing 100081, China
[2] Beijing Advanced Innovation Center for Intelligent Robots and Systems, Beijing Institute of Technology, Beijing 100081, China
[3] Key Laboratory of Biomimetic Robots and Systems, Beijing Institute of Technology, Ministry of Education, Beijing 100081, China

Abstract. Tactile perception using whisker sensor is widely applied to robots under dark and narrow environments. However, most of the existing whisker sensors are relatively large. Meanwhile, most experiments of texture classification using whisker sensors are carried under relatively constrained conditions. In this paper, we developed an ultra-small whisker sensor consisting of a sensing unit and a nylon whisker (3 cm in length) on a circular PCB with diameter of 1.5 cm. The sensor transforms the deflection of whisker into voltage by Wheatstone bridge. In the experiment, the whisker sensor was controlled to contact the surface of four different materials with varied contact pose (different distances and contact angles). The collected data were classified with SVM corresponding to different contact distances and contact angles. The results show that a larger distance and a smaller angle have impact on the amplitude of whisker vibration, resulting in low accuracy. Furthermore, we proposed a thresholding method to confirm the starting point of contact and extract the steady output signal automatically. Eventually, the classification process can be finished within 1 s after contact and the mean classified accuracy is 88.3% for different contact distances, and 85.2% for different contact angles.

Keywords: Whisker sensor · Texture classification · SVM

1 Introduction

Tactile perception is an important source of information and the whiskers are typical tactile organs. In nature, many mammals have whiskers used for collecting a variety of information. For example, relying on their whiskers, seals can detect water movement to hunt and navigate [1], rats can even discriminate different shapes and textures in the dark [2]. It has been demonstrated that rats' whiskers and the human fingertips are of about the same ability with respect to sensing textures. Therefore, whisker sensors are widely studied and applied to robots [3, 4] for texture and shape recognition [5], navigation [6], and mapping [7]. For example, William et al. applied their whisker sensor on the small aircraft to detect contact and pre-contact forces such that the robot could maneuver

© Springer Nature Singapore Pte Ltd. 2021
F. Sun et al. (Eds.): ICCSIP 2020, CCIS 1397, pp. 517–526, 2021.
https://doi.org/10.1007/978-981-16-2336-3_49

to avoid dangerous interactions [11]. Mohammed et al. mounted their active whisker sensors on a 6-DoF manipulator to building a map of its environment and maintain an accurate estimate of its location [6]. In this paper, we mainly focus on the whisker sensor's ability of texture classification which is also an important component of tactile object recognition [8]. A common working model for the biological whisker system is that as the whisker sweeping the surface, the relative motion between the whisker and the surface generates a vibration along the whisker shaft, which is characteristic of the texture [9]. The internal nerves encode the vibration signal, from which the classification is made. Many effective artificial whisker systems are based on this model [10–13]. However, there are two common problems. The first one is that most of them are large and some whisker sensors use the electric motor as the actuator which is also bulky. For example, the sensor designed by Charles Sullivan et al. has a 5-centimeter-long whisker and a $2 \times 2 \times 2$ cm actuator [14]. These result in a complex system that is difficult to be integrated into small robots. These may also limit the ability of the sensor to explore narrow environments. When an object comes too close, the sensor probably loses the ability of classification because of the too large deformation which will affect the vibration of the whisker.

It has been shown that variable contact parameters make it difficult to classify textures [10]. But few experiments have studied this influence systematically. Charles et al. used a whiskered mobile robot to collect data with different positions and movements of the robot relative to the surface and combined them to classification textures [9]. But they did not present more systematic researches on the relevant factors and the number of control groups is relatively less. Mathew et al. changed the movement speed of the sensor and the angle of the surface with no thought of contact distance [16]. In the unknown static environment, the contact speed is mainly dependent on the speed of the mobile robot which is easy to measure and control. We thus do not consider the various moving speed and keep it constant. By taking the contact distance into account, we can further save the time of repositioning the robot which is mentioned in [15].

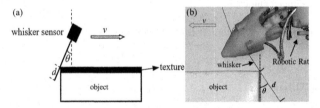

Fig. 1. Whisker pose geometry. a): Whisker contacts the object at an angle θ and a distance d. θ and d affect texture classification. b) Robotic rat's whisker contacts the object with certain contact pose.

To find the influence of variable contact parameters on finishing texture classification with brief contact in limited space, we firstly define the pose by the contact angle and the contact distance with which the whisker contacts a textured surface (Fig. 1). Then we develop an ultra-small whisker sensor and an X-Y-Z positioning platform to generate different datasets with different poses. This system will help us to understand how contact pose affects whisker deflections. We also try to make the classifier keep relatively high accuracy with different contact poses by training. Some common methods to achieve the classification are k-means [17], neural network (NN) [10], template matching [18], and Gaussian mixture model (GMM) [19]. However, these methods have some disadvantages respectively. For example, k-means is sensitive to outliers, NN needs large amounts of training data, and the computational load of template matching and GMM are relatively high. Thus, we chose support vector machine (SVM) based on features which can achieve the task with the small-scale dataset and better robustness.

The remainder of the paper focuses on data collection procedure, feature extraction and results analysis.

2 SVM-Based Texture Classification

2.1 Feature Extraction

Relevant features used in SVM should be specifically selected, which is concerned with generalization performance, computational efficiency and feature interpretability [21]. The paper aims to find the effects of different contact poses on texture classification and try to gain a powerful classification system that keeps relatively high accuracy in different situations. The variation of the pose mainly causes the change of signal amplitude, we thus tried to extract features that are independent of the amplitude for the same class or have a great difference for different classes.

The variance (VAR) of the signal indicates the vertical motion of the whisker, which is larger for uneven textures.

Peak (PEA) is a common feature used for texture classification [22]. But the value of peak varies much with contact pose for the same texture. Considering the cause of the peak is that the whisker gets stuck on the texture and then slips off the stick point, it is reasonable to think the average interval of peaks can reflect the surface texture and is relatively stable. We also set limit to the prominence of a peak (measuring how much the peak stands out due to its intrinsic height and its location relative to other peaks). These temporal features are shown in (1) and (2).

$$VAR = \frac{1}{T} \sum_{t=1}^{T} (x(t) - \mu)^2 \tag{1}$$

$$PEA = \frac{\sum_{i=2}^{N} (P_i - P_{i-1})}{N} \tag{2}$$

where T is the length of the signal, $x(t)$ is signal amplitude at time t, μ is the mean of $x(t)$, P_i is the ith peak and N is the total number of peaks.

Signal energy (ENG) is another popular feature used in texture classification. It has been shown that signal of rough texture tended to have higher energy, which is shown in (3).

$$ENG = \sum_{t=1}^{T} x^2(t) \tag{3}$$

To perform a feature-based classification for texture classification, spectral features are also important. The spectral centroid (SCE) is the center of 'gravity' of the spectrum, which is widely used in speech recognition and EEG-based diagnosis. It also has been shown that the centroid could correspond to the roughness of the textured surface [23].

The spectral entropy (SEN) of a signal is a measure of its spectral power distribution. It treats the signal's normalized power distribution in the frequency domain as a probability distribution and calculates the Shannon entropy of it. All these spectral features are calculated after making hamming window processing of the signal. These two spectral features are shown in (4) and (5).

$$SCE = \frac{\sum_{f=0}^{F} f \cdot s_f}{\sum_{f=0}^{F} s_f} \tag{4}$$

$$SEN = \frac{-\sum_{f=0}^{F} s_f \log(s_f)}{\log(F)} \tag{5}$$

where s_f is the amplitude at frequency f in DFT of the signal and F is the Nyquist frequency, which is the half of the sample rate.

Finally, all the above features compose a feature vector shown in below:

$$x = [VAR, PEA, ENG, SCE, SEN]^T$$

2.2 SVM Classifier

The SVM binary classifier searches for an optimal hyperplane to separate the data into two classes. This optimal hyperplane can be defined as,

$$f(x) = \sum_{i=1}^{m} \alpha_i y_i x_i^T x + b \tag{6}$$

where α is weight vector and b is bias.

As a summary, the whole process of texture classification is shown in Fig. 2. The training data is firstly filtered by a high-pass filter. The Short Time Fourier Transform is then conducted to get the spectrum. Features in different domains are extracted used for SVM training. Before training, data of each feature in the training set were scaled to [0,1] by Eq. (7),

$$\tilde{X}_i = \frac{X_i - \min(X_i)}{\max(X_i) - \min(X_i)} \tag{7}$$

where X_i is the vector of ith feature, consisting of the all training set or test set.

It is obvious that our dataset was linearly inseparable, so we imposed the kernel function and slack variables to finish classification and improve robustness. For the multi-class classification task, we applied OvA (One versus All) strategy to train M classifiers (M is the total number of classes), one for each class. The nth classifier constructs a hyperplane between class m and $M - 1$ other classes. Finally, for a new unknown sound, we can calculate the scores of different textures and then A majority vote is applied. When the scores for all categories are below 0.3, the classifier will output "unknown" which indicates that this sample is not within classification scope.

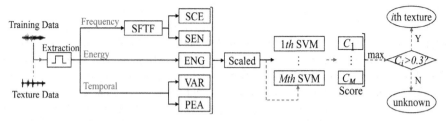

Fig. 2. The flow chart of SVM-based texture classification. The red dash line represents flows when using SVM to identify a new texture data.

3 Experiments

3.1 Experimental Setup

The ultra-small whisker sensor consists of a sensing unit, a nylon whisker (3 cm in length), and a circular PCB with diameter of 1.5 cm, which meets the need of miniaturization. Two crossed two-end fixed beams and two Wheatstone bridges in the sensing unit are used to measure the deflection of the whisker shaft. The circuits generate two voltages, corresponding to the whisker deflection in two directions, x and y. The whisker sensor is shown in Fig. 3(b). The fabrication of the whisker sensor can be seen in our previous work [24]. The platform we used is an XYZ-table (Fig. 3(a)), having a movement range of $32 \times 15 \times 10$ cm. The controller takes instructions from the PC and then drives the motors to complete the specified trajectory. The repeatability of this platform is ± 0.1 mm.

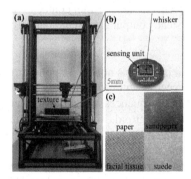

Fig. 3. System setup. a) XYZ-table platform. b) Whisker sensor. c) Four textures selected for texture classification: paper, sandpaper, facial tissue, and suede.

3.2 Data Collection and Preprocessing

The whisker sensor is fixed on the top mobile platform which can sweep the bottom surface with the speed of 2 cm/s. A set of materials were glued on the horizontal fixed bottom platform. Four materials were chosen, which were shown in Fig. 3(c). Contact distance ranged from 1 mm to 5 mm, in increments of 1 mm. Contact angle ranged from 0° to 20° in increments of 5°. An amplifier-filter circuit was designed for signal processing. The output gain is 50.4 and the filter is a low-pass filter with 2 kHz cut-off frequency. Data collection was performed using an Oscilloscope at 1 kHz per channel. Data for each pose were divided into training and test sets randomly.

The original signal shown in Fig. 4 usually contains three segments: contact, stabilization and separation. However, the contact section is affected by speed and the separation section leads to time-delay. Therefore, the suitable section used for classification is the stabilization section.

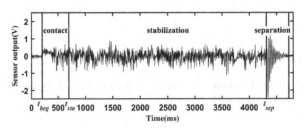

Fig. 4. Typical original signal. t_{beg} indicates the time when the whisker starts to contact the object. t_{sta}, 500 ms after t_{beg}, indicates the time when the output begins to be steady. t_{sep} indicates the time when the whisker leaves the object.

It is also important to extract signal fast enough to meet real-time demand. Generally, the sensor signal is certainly stabilized within 500 ms after contact, as shown is Fig. 4. We intercept 500 millisecond-long signal after t_{sta} for classification, which ensures that it could conduct classification in one second after contact. We improved the thresholding approach [20] to extract the steady output signal automatically. The steps of the approach are as follows:

Step 1. Break the raw signal into 20 ms non-overlapping frames.
Step 2. Extract energy and spectral centroid sequences from the raw signal. Through the statistical analysis of the sample sequences, we carefully selected two thresholds—0.025 for energy and 0.3 for spectral centroid. The "useful region" was present for samples where energy was above its threshold and spectral centroid was below its threshold.
Step 3. Identify the end time t of the first "useful region", which indicates the time when the whisker sensor starts to contact the object. Then we can get the target signal by extracting signal segment between $t + 500$ ms and $t + 1000$ ms.

Typical steady output signals for each texture are shown in Fig. 5.

3.3   The Influence of the Contact Distance

Table 1 shows the confusion matrix for texture classification with different contact distances and fixed contact angle ($\theta = 0°$). The confusion matric columns represent the true classes and the rows represent the predicted classes. This system achieved 95.3% of the classification accuracy on average.

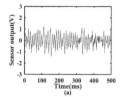 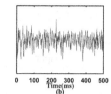 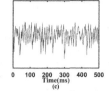 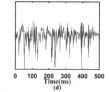

Fig. 5. Typical steady output signals ($d = 3$ mm, $\theta = 0°$) for four textures: a) Paper. b) Sandpaper. c) Facial tissue. d) Suede.

Table 1. Confusion matrix for distance classifier ($\theta = 0°$)

	Paper	Sandpaper	Point paper	Suede
Paper	199	3	0	0
Sandpaper	1	195	0	1
Point paper	0	2	189	20
Suede	0	0	11	179

We also calculate the hit rate of each contact distance, as shown in Table 2. It can be seen that the accuracy firstly decreased, and then increased with the increasing of contact distance. The reason for this is that samples in the middle of the interval are more likely to be disturbed by that from both sides. For example, samples from 3 mm dataset are easily affected by that from 2 mm and 4 mm dataset, which results in decreased accuracy. Though the accuracy does not keep decreasing as the contact distance increases, we can still find that too long contact distance badly affects texture classification. We then tested this system with data collected at random contact distances within 5 cm and the accuracy is 88.3%.

Table 2. Accuracy of different contact distances

Contact distance (mm)	1	2	3	4	5
Accuracy (%)	98.8	94.4	94.4	93.8	95.0

3.4 The Influence of the Contact Angle

Table 3 shows the confusion matrix for texture classification with different contact angles and fixed contact distance ($d = 4$ mm) and the accuracy is 93.08% on average.

Table 3. Confusion matrix for angle classifier

	Paper	Sandpaper	Point paper	Suede
Paper	199	0	0	0
Sandpaper	0	182	14	7
Point paper	0	10	180	10
Suede	0	8	6	183

The hit rate of each contact angles is shown in Table 4. The accuracy changes first decreased and then an upward trend. The accuracy at $0°$ is lower than that at $20°$, which further indicates that large deformation affects the texture classification performance. The accuracy with data collected at random angle within $20°$ is 85.2%.

Table 4. Accuracy of different contact angles ($d = 4$ mm)

Contact distance (°)	0	5	10	15	20
Accuracy (%)	93.7	93.1	87.5	93.6	97.5

4 Conclusion and Future Work

In this paper, we have studied the influence of different contact poses on texture classification. We firstly define contact pose by distance and angle. Then, a preprocessing method and five different features are proposed for the SVM identification. These features are selected in the view of temporal, energy, and spectrum so that they can fully reflect the characters of the target signal. Two classifiers are trained for contact distance and angel separately. The final classification results show that the accuracy of the two classifiers is 88.3% and 85.2% respectively. A larger distance and a smaller angle affect vibration of the whisker, resulting in low accuracy.

The presented work can be extended in several directions. We will introduce more similar or complex textures to expand the scope of the classification. Another interesting direction involves incorporating visual perception to facilitate the texture classification. Finally, we would like to combine the texture information with our previous work on shape information [24] and apply it to our miniature robotic rat WR-5M [25, 26].

Acknowledgments. This work was supported in part by the National Natural Science Foundation of China (NSFC) under grant No. 62022014 and grant No. 61773058.

References

1. Wieskotten, S., Dehnhardt, G., Mauck, B., Miersch, L., Hanke, W.: Hydrodynamic determination of the moving direction of an artificial fin by a harbour seal (Phoca vitulina). J. Exp. Biol. **213**(13), 2194–2200 (2010)
2. Grant, R.A., Mitchinson, B., Fox, C.W., Prescott, T.J.: Active touch sensing in the rat: anticipatory and regulatory control of whisker movements during surface exploration. J. Neurophysiol. **101**(2), 862–874 (2009)
3. Pearson, et al.: Whiskerbot: a robotic active touch system modeled on the rat whisker sensory system. Adapt. Behav. **15**(3), 223–240 (2007)
4. Prescott, T.J., Pearson, M.J., Mitchinson, B., Sullivan, J.C.W., Pipe, A.G.: Whisking with robots. IEEE Robot. Autom. Mag. **16**(3), 42–50 (2009)
5. Jiang, Q., Wei, G., Zhao, C.: Fiber Bragg grating-based biomimetic whisker for shape and texture recognition. J. Instrum. **13**(11), P11013–P11013 (2018)
6. Salman, M., Pearson, M.J.: Advancing whisker-based navigation through the implementation of bio-inspired whisking strategies. In: 2016 IEEE International Conference on Robotics and Biomimetics (ROBIO), Qingdao, pp. 767–773 (2016)
7. Fox, C.W., Evans, M.H., Pearson, M.J., Prescott, T.J.: Towards hierarchical blackboard mapping on a whiskered robot. Robot. Auton. Syst. **60**(11), 1356–1366 (2012)
8. Fox, C., Evans, M., Pearson, M., Prescott, T.: Tactile SLAM with a biomimetic whiskered robot. In: 2012 IEEE International Conference on Robotics and Automation, Saint Paul, MN, pp. 4925–4930 (2012)
9. Arabzadeh, E., Petersen, R.S., Diamond, M.E.: Encoding of whisker vibration by rat barrel cortex neurons: implications for texture discrimination. J. Neurosci. **23**(27), 9146–9154 (2003)
10. Fend, M.: Whisker-based texture discrimination on a mobile robot. In: Advances in Artificial Life, pp. 302–311 (2005)
11. Deer, W., Pounds, P.E.I.: Lightweight whiskers for contact, pre-contact, and fluid velocity sensing. IEEE Robot. Autom. Lett. **4**(2), 1978–1984 (2019)
12. Lepora, N.F., Evans, M., Fox, C.W., Diamond, M.E., Gurney, K., Prescott, T.J.: Naive Bayes texture classification applied to whisker data from a moving robot. In: The 2010 International Joint Conference on Neural Networks (IJCNN), Barcelona, pp. 1–8 (2010)
13. Fries, F., Valdivia, P., Alvarado: Whisker-like sensors with soft resistive follicles. In: 2017 IEEE International Conference on Robotics and Biomimetics (ROBIO), Macau, pp. 2038–2043 (2017)
14. Sullivan, J.C., et al.: Tactile discrimination using active whisker sensors. IEEE Sens. J. **12**(2), 350–362 (2012)
15. Fox, C.W., Mitchinson, B., Pearson, M.J., Pipe, A.G., Prescott, T.J.: Contact type dependency of texture classification in a whiskered mobile robot. Auton. Robots **26**(4), 223–239 (2009)
16. Evans, M.H., Pearson, M.J., Lepora, N.F., Prescott, T.J., Fox, C.W.: Whiskered texture classification with uncertain contact pose geometry. In: 2012 IEEE/RSJ International Conference on Intelligent Robots and Systems, Vilamoura, pp. 7–13 (2012)
17. Ju, F., Ling, S.-F.: Bioinspired active whisker sensor for robotic vibrissal tactile sensing. Smart Mater. Struct. **23**(12), (2014)
18. Evans, M.H., Fox, C.W., Pearson, M.J., Prescott, T.J.: Tactile discrimination using template classifiers: towards a model of feature extraction in mammalian vibrissal systems. In: Doncieux, S., Girard, B., Guillot, A., Hallam, J., Meyer, J.-A., Mouret, J.-B. (eds.) SAB 2010. LNCS (LNAI), vol. 6226, pp. 178–187. Springer, Heidelberg (2010). https://doi.org/10.1007/978-3-642-15193-4_17

19. Dallaire, P., Giguère, P., Émond, D., Chaib-draa, B.: Autonomous tactile perception: a combined improved sensing and Bayesian nonparametric approach. Robot. Auton. Syst. **62**(4), 422–435 (2014)
20. Giannakopoulos, T.: A method for silence removal and segmentation of speech signals, implemented in MATLAB. University of Athens, Athens (2009)
21. Nguyen, M.H., de la Torre, F.: Optimal feature selection for support vector machines. Pattern Recognit. **43**(3), 584–591 (2010)
22. Bernard, M., N'Guyen, S., Pirim, P., Guillot, A., Meyer, J.-A., Gas, B.: A supramodal vibrissa tactile and auditory model for texture recognition. In: Doncieux, S., Girard, B., Guillot, A., Hallam, J., Meyer, J.-A., Mouret, J.-B. (eds.) SAB 2010. LNCS (LNAI), vol. 6226, pp. 188–198. Springer, Heidelberg (2010). https://doi.org/10.1007/978-3-642-15193-4_18
23. Hipp, J., et al.: Texture signals in whisker vibrations. J. Neurophysiol. **95**(3), 1792–1799 (2006)
24. Wei, Z., et al.: Development of a MEMS based biomimetic whisker sensor for tactile sensing. In: 2019 IEEE International Conference on Cyborg and Bionic Systems (CBS), Munich, Germany, pp. 222–227 (2019)
25. Shi, Q., et al.: A modified robotic rat to study rat-like pitch and yaw movements. IEEE/ASME Trans. Mechatron. **23**(5), 2448–2458 (2018)
26. Shi, Q., et al.: Implementing rat-like motion for a small-sized biomimetic robot based on extraction of key movement joints. IEEE Trans. Robot. https://doi.org/10.1109/tro.2020.303 3705

Semantic-Based Road Segmentation
for High-Definition Map Construction

Hanyang Zhuang[1,2], Chunxiang Wang[3,4(✉)], Yuhan Qian[4,5], and Ming Yang[1,3,4]

[1] University of Michigan-Shanghai Jiao Tong University Joint Institute, Shanghai Jiao Tong University, Shanghai 200240, China
[2] Guangxi Key Laboratory of Automobile Components and Vehicle Technology, Guangxi University of Science and Technology, Liuzhou 545006, China
[3] Department of Automation, Shanghai Jiao Tong University, Shanghai 200240, China
wangcx@sjtu.edu.cn
[4] Key Laboratory of System Control and Information Processing, Ministry of Education of China, Shanghai 200240, China
[5] School of Mechanical Engineering, Shanghai Jiao Tong University, Shanghai 200240, China

Abstract. The development of autonomous driving technology proposes higher requirements of the fidelity of the high-definition maps (HD maps). The construction of HD map based on orthophotos generated from panoramic images is the state-of-the-art approach. However, in this process, the dynamic obstacles and shadows on the road captured by the panoramic camera has significant impact on reducing the map quality. Moreover, the GNSS signal may inevitably unavailable or have jitter error, leading to the unsatisfactory of the orthophoto mosaic. Therefore, an approach is proposed to tackle these problems of HD map construction. The semantic segmentation of the panoramic images is firstly implemented to extract the dynamic obstacles such as vehicles and the road segments. Then the shadows on the road segments are removed through GAN networks to generate clean orthophotos. Afterwards, the clean orthophotos are used for feature extraction and image registration based on the road segmentation to provide finer pose estimations. Finally, the GNSS data, odometer data, and estimated poses are combined to optimize the vehicle pose for orthophoto mosaic. The experimental results illustrate that the proposed approach can improve the HD map construction accuracy under the congested environment.

Keywords: High-definition map · Road segmentation · Dynamic obstacle removal · Shadow removal · Image registration

1 Introduction

As the core of autonomous driving system, high-definition map (HD map) provides rich geographic location information. HD map not only plays an important role in the localization, path planning, and motion control [1], but also improves the driving safety of the vehicle in severe weather (such as rainy day and night) [2]. On one hand, "high-definition" refers to the high positioning accuracy of the data contained in the map. On

© Springer Nature Singapore Pte Ltd. 2021
F. Sun et al. (Eds.): ICCSIP 2020, CCIS 1397, pp. 527–537, 2021.
https://doi.org/10.1007/978-981-16-2336-3_50

the other hand, it means that the data contained in the map has fine granularity and rich information types.

HD map is divided into visual map [3] and point cloud map [4, 5]. Compared to point cloud HD map, visual HD map is widely used because of its advantages of fast acquisition speed, obvious semantic information, and less data size. The visual HD map is usually constructed using panoramic camera and high precision GNSS (Global Navigation Satellite System). After the image acquisition, the panoramic images are projected to orthophoto followed by the orthophoto mosaic to get the entire orthophoto map.

In the panoramic image acquisition step, there unavoidably exist some obstacles blocking the image, which leads to the loss of information. The worst but most common case is that the dynamic obstacles (e.g. other vehicles) drive at the same speed as the acquisition platform. This will result in the loss of large-scale ground information for map construction. In addition to the dynamic obstacles, the shadows caused by the dynamic or static obstacles may also lead to the partial blockage on the image.

In the orthophoto mosaic step, the acquired series of orthophoto is stitching together through the acquisition platform poses, which is usually obtained through GNSS. But, the GNSS signal may be blocked or have jitter error that strongly affects the image mosaic process. Therefore, filtered pose estimation by GNSS and image registration is an efficient way to reduce the mosaic error when GNSS signal is degraded. Image registration has good local consistency by registering the features through adjacent images. The features extraction may be biased by the dynamic obstacles and shadows, therefore, the removal of these two types of objects is even more meaningful.

2   Related Works

After analyzing the problems encountered in the HD map construction, the removal of dynamic obstacles and shadows is the first priority. These information are hard to be extracted through conventional computer vision methods such as thresholding [6] or boundary detection [7]. Semantic segmentation has been considered to be the most suitable solution to the find the moving vehicles and pedestrians on the road [8–10]. But the semantic segmentation on panoramic image does not perform well due to the image distortion and structure are different from plane image. It requires specific training on panoramic image dataset.

Shadow is also a kind of semantic information. For the shadow removal task, GAN (Generative Adversarial Network) is one of the most effective way. But most GAN based works only mask out the shadow area without making up the shadowed area [11, 12]. In order to get a smooth and continuous image, the shadow image shall be converted to shadow-free image. Conventional methods to make up shadow area does not adapt to complex environment where has many shadows or shadow boundaries are not clear [13]. ST-CGAN (STacked Conditional GAN) is proposed to remove and make up the shadows through two CGANs which leads to a good performance [14].

To deal with GNSS error, one solution is to use filters such as EKF (Extended Kalman Filter) to predict the pose according to the current state when the GNSS signal is poor [15]. This scheme has a large error when GPS is blocked for a long time. The other solution is to estimate the relative pose of the image according to the registration of feature points [16, 17]. However, the scheme requires a high acquisition environment. If the image is seriously blocked by dynamic obstacles or shadows, the effective feature points will be reduced and the matching accuracy will be reduced.

The above problems existing in the HD map construction limits the map quality. So, this paper proposes a framework to utilize the semantic information to remove the dynamic obstacles and shadows, then optimize the orthophoto mosaic process. Firstly, the framework of DeepLab V3+ [9] is adopted to semantically segment the panoramic image for dynamic obstacles removal which is presented in Sect. 3. The road segmentation result is obtained at the same time using the semantic label. Then in Sect. 4, ST-CGAN [14] is implemented to remove the shadows. The last chain of the framework is in Sect. 5 where orthophoto mosaic through the fusion process of image registration, odometer data, and the GNSS signals are implemented. The framework shall construct the base image for HD map with higher accuracy and without dynamic obstacles and shadow interferences.

3   Dynamic Obstacles Removal and Road Segmentation

The semantic segmentation can achieve pixel level vehicle recognition, and remove dynamic obstacles, mainly the vehicles and pedestrians. Because of the large distortion in panoramic images and lack of panorama training dataset, the semantic segmentation of panorama is challenging. In order to tackle this issue, the semantic segmentation based on DeepLab V3+ is applied to the raw images of the panoramic camera. Then, the semantically segmented images are spliced into the panoramic image with semantic information. The semantic segmentation framework used in this paper is shown in Fig. 1.

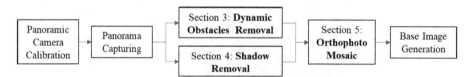

Fig. 1. Framework of the HD map base image generation

DeepLab V3+ is one of the most excellent segmentation networks in Pascal VOC 2012 and Cityscapes. It combines the advantages of pyramid pooling module and encoder-decoder, also, it can segment the target boundary accurately. At the same time, it further explores the xception model by applying the depth separable convolution to the pyramid like cavity pooling and encoder. It is clear to see from Fig. 1 that the semantic segmentation results are quite good for each raw image, and the constructed panorama also has sound quality even though there exists large distortion, unbalanced light, and complex scenes in the raw images.

The semantic segmentation of each individual raw image of the panorama may have errors. But the raw images have significant overlay with each other, therefore, this feature can be utilized to filter the semantic label to reach a better consistency. A weighted average is calculated for the overlaid regions. Since the semantic segmentation has higher confidence in the center of the image while the segmentation result has lower confidence near the edge, the weights of the same point on two different raw images are proportional to the distance from the image centers respectively. Through this filtering, the semantic label is more consistency. Then the pixels of dynamic obstacles are removed based on its label equal to vehicle or pedestrian. The blank area left behind after the removal is theoretically unreachable by single image, but it will be compensated during the orthophoto mosaic process.

4   Shadow Removal on Road Segment

After the removal of dynamic obstacles, the shadows are still left on the road segment. The shadows have strong features that affects the accuracy of image registration. Moreover, the shadows may cause dark zones in the orthophoto to make the lines or lane markings unclear reducing the map model extraction. Therefore, it is essential to remove the shadows to obtain a "clean" orthophoto. The ST-CGAN has been introduced to remove and make up the shadow areas as shown in Fig. 2. It is similar to the semantic segmentation process. The raw images of the panoramic camera are used due to the limitation of lack of training dataset on panorama directly.

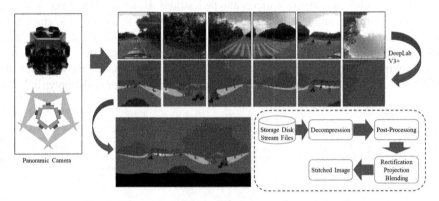

Fig. 2. Flow chart of the panorama semantic segmentation

In the shadow detection framework proposed in this paper there are two CGAN models. The generator G1 and discriminator D1 of the first CGAN are used for shadow region detection. While, the generator G2 and discriminator D2 of the second network are used for shadow removal. The results of G1 come into two usages: to generate the detected shadow region in the image; and to serve as the input of G2 for shadow removed image generation. The D1 is used to discriminate the detected shadow from the ground truth until the discriminator cannot tell the differences. The D2 works in a similar way by discriminating the shadow removed image from ground truth image until it is hard to differentiate real or fake. At last, the raw images after shadow removal are constructed into the panorama for projection.

The orthophoto is made through projection of panorama onto the ground. In this orthophoto, the shadows are removed and the dynamic obstacles are left blank. Also, the parts outside of the road edge is masked out. Gaussian filter and binarization are used to smooth the road edge caused by the projection. The blank areas caused by dynamic occlusion on the road surface can be completed by image superposition of consecutive time steps. For static object occlusion, images taken from different angles can be used to complete the road around the static object. Since now, a "clean" orthophoto is obtained.

5   Orthophoto Mosaic Optimization by Image Registration

The image registration for orthophoto mosaic is utilized to optimize the image stitching to prevent the pose errors from GNSS data. The SIFT(Scale-Invariant Feature Transform) algorithm [17] is used to select the feature points, which has good applicability to rotation and brightness change, and also has a certain degree of stability to the angle of view change and noise. Firstly, feature points are extracted directly from orthophoto. Then the feature points in the overlapped part of adjacent orthophoto are retained while points in the non-overlapped area are discarded. The road segment is extracted from the semantic labels to generate a mask of road-only area. The feature points on the road segment is finally retained and used for registration. The framework is shown in Fig. 3.

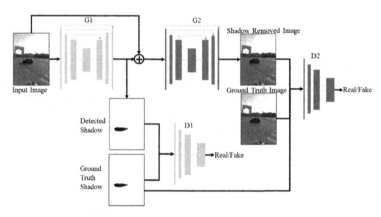

Fig. 3. ST-CGAN shadow detection framework

The extracted feature points are firstly denoised through RANSAC (Random Sample Consensus) [18]. Then the feature points of adjacent orthophotos are matched through ICP (Iterative Closet Point) algorithm [19]. The image registration result is shown in Fig. 4. The estimated transformation including rotation and translation is calculated by ICP and used for image registration.

The image registration result has good local consistency to estimate the relative transformation of poses between adjacent orthophoto. Also, the availability of pose estimation by image registration is ensured since the ICP process has good stability. On the other hand, GNSS has good consistency in global pose determination but may suffer from local signal blockage or error. Therefore, in order to achieve an optimized way to estimate the acquisition platform poses for image stitching, a fusion process to

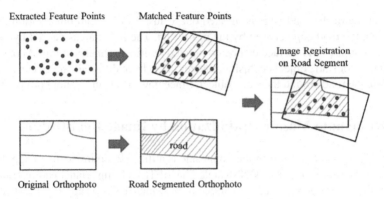

Extracted Feature Points   Matched Feature Points

Image Registration
on Road Segment

Original Orthophoto   Road Segmented Orthophoto

Fig. 4. Image registration framework of road segments

estimate the pose is implemented. The judge of GNSS reliability is simply set as the number of satellites in acquisition. And, the judge of image registration reliability is calculated according to the amount of matched points and the linear correlation between the matched points:

$$
P_i = \begin{cases} P_{GPS,i} & m \geq M \ and \ |\Delta x| < \varepsilon \\ P_{i-1} + \frac{p \cdot s}{L} \cdot \Delta P_{ICP} + \left(1 - \frac{p \cdot s}{L}\right) \cdot \Delta P_{GPS} & m < M \ or \ |\Delta x| \geq \varepsilon \end{cases} \tag{1}
$$

where Pi is the fused pose of the i-th frame image, $P_{GPS,i}$ is the pose obtained from GNSS during data acquisition, ΔP_{ICP} is the pose estimated by ICP, m is the number of satellites connected by GNSS, M is the minimum number of satellites when GNSS is considered to be reliable, s is the amount of matched points of ICP, p is the linear correlation of the matched points of ICP, Δx is the difference between the distance of odometer measurement and linear distance of adjacent GNSS poses, ε and L are the empirical parameter for thresholding.

When the amount of GNSS satellite is larger and the distance measured by GNSS poses is consistent to the odometer, the GNSS pose is directly used. If the amount of GPS satellite is less than the threshold or the distance measured by GNSS poses is inconsistent to the odometer, the pose of the previous frame is added by the weighted local transformations calculated by ICP and GNSS poses at the same time. The weighting function ensures that good ICP results can be used to dominate the pose estimation when GNSS data is poor.

6   Experimental Results

The experiment was carried out in real environment. The panoramic camera used here is Ladybug5 of PointGrey. The panoramic camera was installed on the roof of the acquisition platform. The platform is also equipped with a high precision RTK (Real-Time Kinetic) GNSS and odometry. Panoramic camera and acquisition platform are shown in Fig. 5:

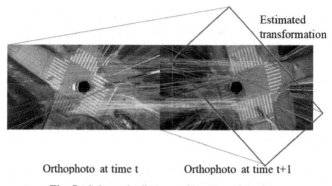

Estimated
transformation

Orthophoto at time t   Orthophoto at time t+1

Fig. 5. Schematic diagram of image registration.

The experimental results contain two aspects: The first is to illustrate the performance of removal mechanism used for panorama and generate "clean" orthophoto; The second is to proof that the orthophoto mosaic optimization process has higher accuracy.

6.1 Dynamic Obstacles and Shadow Removal

The experimental scene is selected on the elevated road. During the acquisition process, many moving vehicles at similar speed surrounded the acquisition platform. Therefore, it is a representative scenario to implement the experiment. The surrounding dynamic obstacles cover significant portion of the ground leading to the lack of ground information. According to the aforementioned method, the semantic segmentation was carried out in each raw image separately before reconstruct to the panorama without dynamic obstacles. Then the panorama was projected on the ground to form the orthophoto, as shown in Fig. 6. The dynamic obstacles are removed from the orthophoto even though the surrounding vehicles are strongly distorted.

Fig. 6. (a) Panoramic camera, (b) Acquisition platform, (c) Part of experiment route

The shadow removal is in a similar form, so the single frame result will not be presented for brevity. As shown in Fig. 6, the blank area left by the removed dynamic obstacles will be completed through orthophoto stitching by a series of images. In the actual experiment, the orthophoto was captured every 6.85 m, and the image has a span of about 30 m in the driving direction of the car, so there are about 77% overlapping areas in two consecutive images, and 54.3% overlapping areas in one frame. The area that is removed can search for the complementary orthophoto in the adjacent 6 frames.

In Fig. 7, the results of the dynamic obstacles and shadow removal compared to the raw orthophoto mosaic on a piece of straight road are presented. It is clear to see that a moving vehicle was taking over the acquisition platform. In Fig. 7(b), the vehicle is removed and the blank area is complemented through mosaic. But there is still some unbalanced area left by the moving vehicle's shadow. In Fig. 7(c), the shadow area is filtered out leading to a light-balanced, clean orthophoto which can be used for further HD map construction.

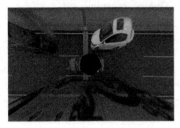 

(a) Raw Orthophoto   (b) Dynamic Obstacle Removal

Fig. 7. Dynamic obstacle removal in single frame orthophoto

6.2 Orthophoto Mosaic Optimization

The core of orthophoto mosaic process is to put the consecutive orthophoto together based on the pose at each orthophoto is captured. Therefore, the critical problem is how to optimize a series of pose so that the orthophoto can be stitched with the smallest error. In current state, GNSS data still has to be used as the ground truth for comparison, so an alternative way is used to simulate GNSS data errors by introducing artificial random noises.

The total length of acquisition path is about 4315 m. According to the data of odometer, data acquisition is carried out every 6.85 m, and a total of 630 panorama and GNSS data are collected. Among all the data, 100 points are randomly selected for adding error. The error is a normal distribution with the maximum distance less than 15 m, and heading angle deviation less than 30°. This "error" GNSS before optimization is evaluated to have the error distribution shown in the left part of Fig. 8. Then the aforementioned orthophoto mosaic optimization method is applied to the "error" GNSS data. The fused poses after optimization comparing to the ground truth can be found in the right part of Fig. 8. The error distribution has been limited in a much lower region after the optimization (Fig. 9).

If we look at some detail data comparison shown in Table 1, it can be seen that the overall error after optimization has been reduced by more than 70%, so as the mean squared error. However, if the GNSS data error exists for a long time, the cumulative error introduced by ICP can be magnified. There is currently no good solution yet to deal with the global consistency of image registration pose estimation. But, the feasibility of the proposed framework has been proved to be able to improve the mosaic accuracy.

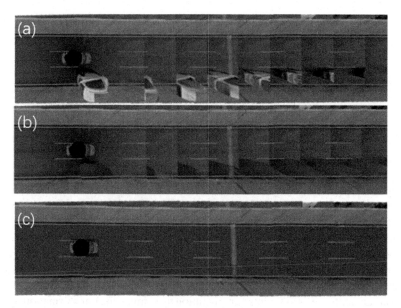

Fig. 8. (a) Raw orthophoto mosaic, (b) Dynamic obstacles removed, (c) Shadows removed

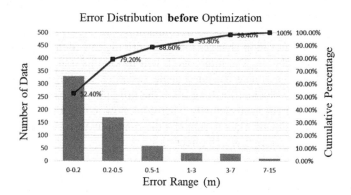

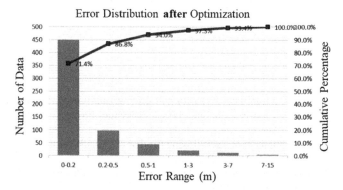

Fig. 9. Error contrast before and after orthophoto mosaic optimization

Table 1. Error data comparison before and after optimization

	Average error/m	Mean squared error/m	Maximum error/m
Before	1.53	3.46	14.81
After	0.42	1.10	8.75

7 Conclusion

Aiming at the problems of dynamic obstacles and shadows as well as the GNSS signal errors for HD map construction, this paper proposes a framework to tackle this issue by semantic-based road segmentation, dynamic obstacles and shadow removal, and image registration. Firstly, the semantic segmentation is used to extract the road segments to remove the blind area and dynamic obstacles. Then the shadows caused by dynamic and static obstacles are removed by ST-CGAN approach. Afterwards, the panorama is projected to orthophoto before overlapping together to complete the road segmentation. The road segments are used for image registration to estimate the transformation of poses. This approach complements the errors caused by GNSS signal blockage or disturbance. The fusion of image registration results, GNSS data, and odometer data can significantly improve the overall accuracy for HD map construction.

This work only focuses on the conditions that the road has no significant elevation. However, if the road elevation changes along the driving direction, the panorama projection is no longer reliable. The future work will tackle this issue by utilizing image registration method to estimate the pitch angle variation. Moreover, in the condition where GNSS signal is blocked for long time, the orthophoto mosaic optimization by image registration degrades substantially. Therefore, how to use some prior knowledge such as road edge or light direction to suppress the cumulative error caused by the image registration is another future research direction.

Acknowledgements. The research work presented in this paper is sponsored by National Natural Science Foundation of China (U1764264/61873165), Shanghai Automotive Industry Science and Technology Development Foundation (1807), and Guangxi key laboratory of Automobile Components and Vehicle Technology Research Project (2020GKLACVTKF02).

References

1. Häne, C., et al.: 3D visual perception for self-driving cars using a multi-camera system: Calibration, mapping, localization, and obstacle detection. Image Vis. Comput. **68**, 14–27 (2017)
2. Lee, U., et al.: Development of a self-driving car that can handle the adverse weather. Int. J. Autom. Technol. **19**(1), 191–197 (2018)
3. He, Y., et al.: Generation of precise lane-level maps based on multi-sensors. J. Chang'an Univ. (Nat. Sci. Edn.) **S1**, 274–278 (2015)

4. Li, L., et al.: An overview on sensor map based localization for automated driving. In: 2017 Joint Urban Remote Sensing Event (JURSE), pp. 1–4 (2017)
5. Lindong, G., et al.: Occupancy grid based urban localization using weighted point cloud. In: 2016 IEEE 19th International Conference on Intelligent Transportation Systems (ITSC), pp. 60–65 (2016)
6. Otsu, N.: A threshold selection method from gray-level histograms. IEEE Trans. Syst. Man Cybern. **9**(1), 62–66 (1979)
7. Lakshmi, S., Sankaranarayanan, D.V.: A study of edge detection techniques for segmentation computing approaches. In: IJCA Special Issue on "Computer Aided Soft Computing Techniques for Imaging and Biomedical Applications", pp. 35–40 (2010)
8. Chen, L., et al.: DeepLab: semantic image segmentation with deep convolutional nets, atrous convolution, and fully connected CRFs. IEEE Trans. Pattern Anal. Mach. Intell. **40**(4), 834–848 (2018)
9. Chen, L.-C., Zhu, Y., Papandreou, G., Schroff, F., Adam, H.: Encoder-decoder with atrous separable convolution for semantic image segmentation. In: Ferrari, V., Hebert, M., Sminchisescu, C., Weiss, Y. (eds.) ECCV 2018. LNCS, vol. 11211, pp. 833–851. Springer, Cham (2018). https://doi.org/10.1007/978-3-030-01234-2_49
10. Shelhamer, E., Long, J., Darrell, T.: Fully convolutional networks for semantic segmentation. IEEE Trans. Pattern Anal. Mach. Intell. **39**(4), 640–651 (2017)
11. Goodfellow, I., et al.: Generative adversarial nets. In: Advances in Neural Information Processing Systems 27 (NIPS 2014), pp. 2672–2680 (2014)
12. Nguyen, V., et al.: Shadow detection with conditional generative adversarial networks. In: Proceedings of the IEEE International Conference on Computer Vision (ICCV), pp. 4510–4518 (2017)
13. Fredembach, C., Finlayson, G.: Simple shadow removal. In: 18th International Conference on Pattern Recognition (ICPR 2006), pp. 832–835 (2006)
14. Wang, J., Li, X., Yang, J.: Stacked conditional generative adversarial networks for jointly learning shadow detection and shadow removal. In: IEEE Conference on Computer Vision and Pattern Recognition (CVPR), pp. 1788–1797 (2018)
15. Shen, K., Guang, X., Li, W.: Application of EKF in integrated navigation system. Trans. Microsyst. Technol. **36**(8), 158–160 (2017)
16. Fan, Y., et al.: Study on a stitching algorithm of the iterative closest point based on dynamic hierarchy. J. Opt. Technol. **82**(1), 28–32 (2015)
17. Lowe, D.G.: Distinctive image features from scale-invariant keypoints. Int. J. Comput. Vis. **60**(2), 91–110 (2004)
18. Fischler, M.A., Bolles, R.C.: Random sample consensus: a paradigm for model fitting with applications to image analysis and automated cartography. Commun. ACM **24**(6), 381–395 (1981)
19. Besl, P.J., McKay, N.D.: A method for registration of 3-D shapes. IEEE Trans. Pattern Anal. Mach. Intell. **14**(2), 239–256 (1992)

Transformer Region Proposal for Object Detection

YiMing Jiang[1], Jinlong Chen[1], Minghao Yang[2(✉)], and Junwei Hu[1]

[1] Guangxi Key Laboratory of Trusted Software, Guilin University of Electronic Technology, Guilin, Guangxi 541004, China
[2] Research Center for Brain-inspired Intelligence (BII), Institute of Automation, Chinese Academy of Sciences (CASIA), Beijing 100190, China

Abstract. We present a method for detecting objects in images using Transformer and Region Proposal. Our method discards the traditional convolution neural network, obtain the positional information and category of the detection object by finding the correspondence between the images through the self-attention mechanism. We extract the region proposal by setting anchors, and combine the positional encoding obtained by the image auto-encoder. Then input the features into the transformer encoder and decoder network to obtain the corresponding information of the target object, and obtain the positional information and category of target object. The experimental results on the public dataset proved, our method's detection speed can reach 26 frames per second, which can meet the needs of real-time detection. In terms of detection accuracy, our method's average precision can reach the 31.4, and under the large object can reach 55.2, which can reach the detection effect of the current mainstream convolutional neural network detection algorithm.

Keywords: Object detection · Region proposal · Transformer · Real-time

1 Introduction

Object detection has always been one of the research hotspots of computer vision and digital image processing, and is widely used in many fields such as intelligent monitoring, driverless and industrial detection. Recent years, Object detection algorithm has made great breakthroughs. The current object detection algorithms can be roughly divided into two categories. One is the R-CNN (Region Convolutional Neural Networks) [1] series algorithm based on region proposal, this algorithm calculate the region proposal, and then evaluate the selective area to get the positional information and category of target object. Another method is one-stage algorithm, such as YOLO (You Only Look Once) [2], SSD (Single Shot MultiBox Detector) [3]. This method directly predicts the object through a convolutional neural network to obtain the category and positional information. The above two types of algorithms have been continuously researched and improved since they were proposed, and the detection results have made great progress compared with the beginning. However, the research situation has gradually slowed down

© Springer Nature Singapore Pte Ltd. 2021
F. Sun et al. (Eds.): ICCSIP 2020, CCIS 1397, pp. 538–547, 2021.
https://doi.org/10.1007/978-981-16-2336-3_51

in recent years, and there is almost no breakthrough progress. This shows the method use convolutional neural networks to extract features and obtain the result through anchor regression and classification has encountered a bottleneck, it is urgent to find a new way to solve such problems.

The Transformer [4] structure has made significant progress in many complex prediction tasks, such as machine translation and speech recognition. Especially in machine translation tasks, the transformer performs better than RNN (Recurrent Neural Network) and CNN (Convolutional Neural Networks) through the combination of encoder-decoder and self-attention mechanisms. In addition, it can be calculated in parallel, which greatly improves the operating efficiency compared to R-CNN which needs cyclic input. However, this structure has not had a lot of attempts in object detection. We believe that its self-attention mechanism and parallel operation method have a certain degree of compatibility with object detection algorithms, and it is a new direction worth exploring.

Our object detection algorithm based on transformer abandoned the traditional operation of convolutional neural network to extract image features, quoted and modified the transformer structure with outstanding performance in the field of NLP (Natural Language Processing), combined it with the anchor, and designed a new object detection algorithm. We extract region proposal by pre-setting anchor boxes for the two input 2d images, pass the obtained regions into transformer network, and add the positional encoding obtained by auto-encoder to provide the positional information of these regions. Through the transformer encoder-decoder process, we realize the end-to-end connection of the anchor in two images, then using match operation to obtain the target object's positional information and category. Unlike most existing algorithms, our algorithm need not any custom layer and can be quickly converted between different frameworks. Through the verification on the public dataset, our method has a good effect on the large object. This algorithm greatly improved the mean average precision of target detection, which was of great significance at the time. However, R-CNN performs a large number of repeated calculations when extracting the proposal, and the detection time is too long to meet the needs of real-time detection.

2 Related Work

In recent years, the object detection algorithm has made a great breakthrough, and it has been studied and improved continuously. Ross Girshick et al. proposed R-CNN [1], using the Selective Search algorithm to get region proposal, inputting the extracted regions into AlexNet to extract features, and then using SVM (Support Vector Machines) for classification. In response to the above problem, Ross Girshick proposed FAST R-CNN [5]. This algorithm improves the input part, input the entire image into the convolutional neural network, and then extracts the feature map to performs classification and regression. Although FAST R-CNN greatly improves the detection speed, it still takes a lot of time to select feature regions. So Shaoqing Ren et al. proposed Faster R-CNN [6]. This algorithm adds the RPN (Region Proposal Network) layer and introduces the RPN layer on the feature map extracted by the convolutional neural network, which improves the detection speed once again.

The R-CNN algorithms mentioned above are all two-stage detection algorithms. These algorithms have a low detection error and a low miss detection, but the speed is slow and cannot meet real-time detection. Therefore, the one-stage algorithm came into being. This type of algorithm does not require the region proposal stage, directly obtains the target object's category and positional information. Only a single detection, the final result can be directly obtained, so it has a faster detection speed. Joseph Redmon proposed the YOLO [2]. The core of this algorithm is to solve the object detection as a regression problem, which greatly improves the detection speed, but its accuracy and recall are relatively low compared to fast R-CNN, and it is less effective in the detection of small objects and overlapping objects. Subsequently, Wei Liu et al. proposed the SSD (Single Shot MultiBox Detector) [3] algorithm, this method uses the anchor ideas in Faster R-CNN, and does feature hierarchical extraction and sequentially calculates box regression and classification to adapt to the training and inference of multiple scale targets task. But the recall of SSD on small objects is still weak, its advantage over Faster R-CNN is not obvious. Joseph Redmon has improved on the original YOLO and proposed the YOLOv2 [7] and YOLOv3 [8]. The YOLOv3 introduces feature pyramids to achieve cross-scale prediction, which improves the detection effect of small targets. For overlapping targets, it uses multi-label analysis. The processing has achieved a balance of speed and precision. Recently, Alexey Bochkovskiy et al. proposed the YOLOv4 [9] model. This model adds a large number of tricks to improve the detection accuracy on the basis of YOLOv3, improves the regularization method of the network, loss function, data enhancement, etc., and mentions a new object detection height.

Although the accuracy and speed of object detection are constantly improving, the pace is getting smaller and smaller. Most of the research continues with the two-stage fast R-CNN series algorithm and the one-stage YOLO series algorithm, and it is hard to obtain a breakthrough. Therefore, a new detection method is urgently needed to solve this problem. Recently, Nicolas Carion et al. proposed the DETR (DEtection TRansformer) [10] method, which obtains image features through convolution, and then directly obtains the category and positional information of the target through the modified transformer structure. The biggest feature of this algorithm is to directly predict through image information. However, this algorithm is first calculated by convolution and then calculated by encoder-decoder, which has the problem of too long training and inference time. Besides, the DETR algorithm still uses CNN to extract features, and the video memory consumption are very large. Therefore, our object detection based on transformer proposed in this paper still has certain advantages.

3   Transformer Region Proposal for Object Detection

3.1   Network Design

Our model sets dual image inputs during the training phase according to the structure of transformer. By inputting processed image feature blocks in the encoder and decoder respectively, the information of the object will be obtained through the correlation between the images. In the inference phase, the input of the decoder part is removed, and the result can be output only by inputting the image in the encoder part (Fig. 1).

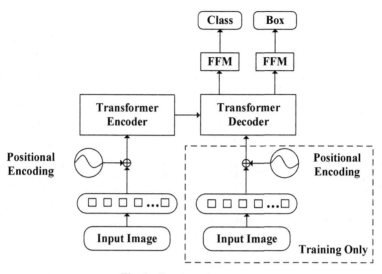

Fig. 1. Our detection system.

The Encoder part is composed of three identical encoder layers, and each layer is composed of two sub-layers, which are multi-head self-attention mechanism and fully connected feed-forward network, each of them has a residual connection and normalization. Among them, the multi-head self-attention mechanism is an important part of the algorithm. The multi-head attention mechanism projects Q, K, and V through h different linear transformations, and finally concatenates the different attention results. The Decoder part is roughly the same as the Encoder part, but there is one more attention layer than the encoder part to calculate the incoming data of the encoder part. The output processed by the decoder passes through an FFM layer to extract the positional information and category. The FFM layer consists of two full connect layers and a MISH activation layer.

$$MultiHead(Q, K, V) = Concat(head_1, head_2, \ldots, head_h)W^O \tag{1}$$

$$head_i = Attention\left(QW_i^Q, KW_i^K, VW_i^V\right) \tag{2}$$

$$Attention(Q, K, V) = softmax\left(\frac{QK^T}{\sqrt{d_k}}\right)V \tag{3}$$

Where: Q, K, V are all vectors of image features, d_k is a scaling factor (Fig. 2).

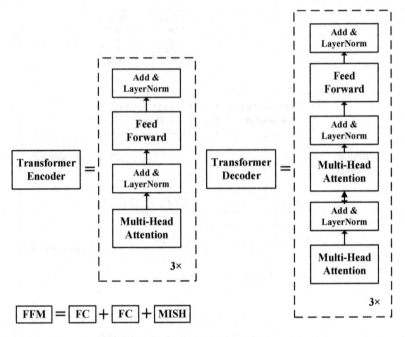

Fig. 2. The concrete structure of the model.

3.2 Feature Extraction

Our method abandons the traditional step of extracting features by convolution neural network. We get the region proposal by setting anchors [11, 12]. Our detection model's input uses image feature pyramids [13], setting three input sizes (320×320, 160×160, 80×80), each size set an anchor at 10 pixels. The size of the anchors is obtained by Kmeans calculation on the ground truth in the training set. The part of the edge anchor beyond the input image is stretched by bilinear interpolation to fill the anchor completely (Fig. 3 and Fig. 4).

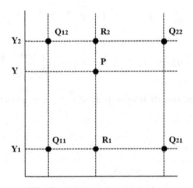

Fig. 3. Bilinear Interpolation

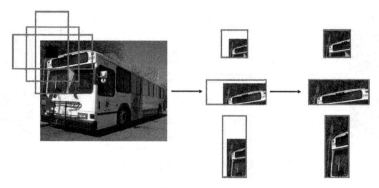

Fig. 4. The Feature extraction process

$$f(R_1) \approx \frac{x_2 - x}{x_2 - x} f(Q_{11}) + \frac{x - x_1}{x_2 - x_1} f(Q_{21}) \ where R_1 = (x, y_1) \tag{4}$$

$$f(R_2) \approx \frac{x_2 - x}{x_2 - x} f(Q_{12}) + \frac{x - x_1}{x_2 - x_1} f(Q_{22}) \ where R_1 = (x, y_1) \tag{5}$$

$$f(P) \approx \frac{y_2 - y}{y_2 - y_1} f(R_1) + \frac{y - y_1}{y_2 - y_1} f(R_2) \tag{6}$$

3.3 Positional Encoding

Our model refers to the original positional encoding structure of the transformer. Aiming at the characteristics of image processing, combined with auto-encoder to design a new positional encoding suitable for image processing. The original positional encoding calculated using the sin cos function cannot fully reflect the positional information on the image, so we input the positional information into the network in the form of images.

This structure generates a corresponding number of positional information images according to the preset amount of anchor frames on the input picture as shown in Figure 6 below. Each image corresponds to an anchor at one position, and the block in the picture is obtained by calculating the current position and the ground truth IOU (Intersection over Union). The larger the IOU, the smaller the gray value. The input image is trained by the auto-encoder network to obtain the positional encoding required in the transformer structure (Fig. 5).

3.4 Loss Function

The loss function used in training stage in our model consists of three parts, which respectively calculate the three losses of target category, confidence and bounding box regression. Among them, the category and confidence are calculated using cross entropy, and the regression box is calculated by CIOU (Complete Intersection over Union) [14].

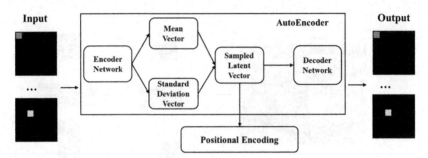

Fig. 5. The structure of auto-encoder

Bounding Box Regression Loss

$$L_{CIoU} = 1 - IoU + \frac{\rho^2(b, b^{gt})}{c^2} + \alpha\upsilon \tag{7}$$

$$\upsilon = \frac{4}{\pi^2}\left(arctan\frac{w^{gt}}{h^{gt}} - arctan\frac{w}{h}\right)^2 \tag{8}$$

Where: α is the weight parameter, υ used to measure the similarity of length-width ratio.

Classification Loss

$$L_{cls} = \lambda_{class}\sum_{i=0}^{S^2}\sum_{j=0}^{B} 1_{i,j}^{obj}\sum_{c\in class} p_i(c)\log(\hat{p}_i(c)) \tag{9}$$

Where: S is the size of the input image, B is the bounding box, $1_{i,j}^{obj}$ means if the box at I, j has a target, its value is 1, otherwise it is 0.

Confidence Loss

$$L_{obj} = \lambda_{nobj}\sum_{i=0}^{S^2}\sum_{j=0}^{B} 1_{i,j}^{nobj}\left(c_i - \hat{c}_i\right)^2 + \lambda_{obj}\sum_{i=0}^{S^2}\sum_{j=0}^{B} 1_{i,j}^{nobj}\left(c_i - \hat{c}_i\right)^2 \tag{10}$$

Where: $1_{i,j}^{nobj}$ means If the box at I, j has no target, its value is 1, otherwise it is 0.

Total Loss

$$Loss = L_{CIoU} + L_{obj} + L_{cls} \tag{11}$$

4   Experiment and Analysis

4.1   Dataset

We use the COCO2017 dataset for experiments [15]. COCO's full name is Common Objects in COntext, a dataset provided by the Microsoft team that can be used for object detection and image recognition. We use the 123K training pictures and 5K test pictures included in the instance section. Each image is marked with bounding boxes. On average, there are 7 instances on each image, and there are up to 63 objects of different sizes on a single image. We randomly divide the training image into a training set and a validation set at a ratio of 7:3, and test our method on the remaining 5K test images. Since the training set and the validation set are randomly divided, the results of each experiment may be different.

4.2   Training

We use the Adam optimizer, set the initial learning rate to $1e-4$, set the decay rates beta1 to 0.9, beta2 to 0.95 and set epsilon to $1e-8$. In order to enhance the detection effect, we carried out image processing to expand the sample, enhanced the sample by randomly shifting, rotating, zooming, and adding Gaussian blur to the input image to adapt to extreme situations. We also use the Mosaic data enhancement method to randomly scale, randomly crop, and randomly arrange four images to be spliced, which greatly enriches the detection data set and improves the robustness of the network.

4.3   Result Analysis

The following Table 1 shows frames per second and average precision including different size of image and IOU thresholds totally seven indicators to evaluate the experimental results. From the experimental results, our method has improved in some indicators, but there are also shortcomings.

Table 1.   Experiment result.

Model	FPS	AP	AP50	AP75	APS	APM	APL
Fast R-CNN	4	30.8	50.4	31.2	11.6	32.4	45.6
Faster R-CNN	16	34.9	54.3	36.5	16.3	37.7	51.2
YOLOv2	20.3	21.2	43.5	18.2	5.6	22.4	34.5
SSD	16.3	31.3	50.7	34.3	10.6	34.7	48.8
DETR	28	35.4	56.4	39.2	17.5	39.8	54.1
Ours	26	31.4	51.4	33.6	13.3	37.6	55.2

By comparing with the two-stage Fast R-CNN and Faster R-CNN, our model has obvious advantages in detection speed, and also has a certain improvement in the accuracy of large targets, but the accuracy of small objects is slightly weaker than Faster

Fig. 6. Detection results

R-CNN. By comparing with the one-stage YOLOv2 and SSD algorithms, it can be seen that our model has some advantages in detection speed, which can meet the needs of real-time detection. It also has some advantages in the accuracy of detection. Since the one-stage detection method simultaneously obtains the target's category and positional information, it is slightly insufficient in accuracy. Compared with the DETR model that also uses the transformer idea, our model has the similar effect, but we have a slight advantage in detection accuracy under large targets.

5 Conclusion

This paper presents an object detection method based on transformer. This method refers to the structure of the transformer, uses anchors and image pyramids to extract region proposal, and performs matching calculations on the extracted regions to get the result. We also present a new method to obtain the positional encoding by autoencoding a special image to enhance the position information of the image, thereby improving the detection effect. In terms of training, we introduce the current Mosaic data enhancement method and the loss function composed of three parts: classification, regression box, and confidence, to enhance the detection effect. Overall, our model introduces a self-attention mechanism to calculate the correlation between preselected regions, so the detection accuracy of large objects has been improved to a certain extent. But for the small objects, only contained in one region proposal which cannot combined with surrounding position information, so the detection accuracy is slightly lower. By comparing with existing detection methods that use convolutional neural networks, our method has a good performance in detection speed and accuracy except for small targets. What's more, our method discards the traditional convolutional neural network, obtains the object positional information and category by calculating the correlation between the images, which is innovative.

Acknowledgements. This work is supported by the National Key Research & Development Program of China (No. 2018AAA0102902), the National Natural Science Foundation of China (NSFC) (No. 61873269), the Beijing Natural Science Foundation (No. L192005), the Guangxi Key Research and Development Program (AB18126053, AB18126063, AD18281002, AD19110001, AB18221011), the Natural Science Foundation of Guangxi of China (2019GXNSFDA185007, 2019GXNSFDA185006), Guangxi Key Laboratory of Intelligent Processing of Computer Images and Graphics (No. GIIP201702), Guangxi Key Laboratory of Trusted Software(No. kx201621, kx201715), and Guangxi Science and Technology Planning Project(No. AD19110137).

References

1. Girshick, R., Donahue, J., Darrell, T., Malik, J.: Rich feature hierarchies for accurate object detection and semantic segmentation. In: CVPR 2014 (2014)
2. Redmon, J., Divvalas, G.R., et al.: You only look once: unified, real-time object detection. In: Proceedings of the IEEE Computer Society Conference on Computer Vision and Pattern Recognition, pp. 779–788. IEEE Computer Society, Washington (2016)
3. Liu, W., et al.: SSD: single shot MultiBox detector. In: Leibe, B., Matas, J., Sebe, N., Welling, M. (eds.) ECCV 2016. LNCS, vol. 9905, pp. 21–37. Springer, Cham (2016). https://doi.org/10.1007/978-3-319-46448-0_2
4. Vaswani, A., Shazeer, N., Parmar, N., et al.: Attention is all you need. arxiv (2017)
5. Girshick, R.: Fast R-CNN. In: ICCV 2015 (2015)
6. Ren, S., He, K., Girshick, R., et al.: Faster R-CNN: towards real-time object detection with region proposal networks. In: PAMI 2015 (2015)
7. Redmon, J., Farhadi, A.: YOLO9000: better, faster, stronger. In 2017 IEEE Conference on Computer Vision and Pattern Recognition (CVPR), pp. 6517–6525. IEEE (2017)
8. Redmon, J., Farhadi, A.: YOLOv3: an incremental improvement. arXiv:1804.02767 (2018)
9. Bochkovskiy, A., Wang, C.-Y., Mark Liao, H.-Y.: YOLOv4: optimal speed and accuracy of object detection. arXiv:2004.10934 (2020)
10. Carion, N., Massa, F., Synnaeve, G., Usunier, N., Kirillov, A., Zagoruyko, S.: End-to-end object detection with transformers. In: Vedaldi, A., Bischof, H., Brox, T., Frahm, J.-M. (eds.) ECCV 2020. LNCS, vol. 12346, pp. 213–229. Springer, Cham (2020). https://doi.org/10.1007/978-3-030-58452-8_13
11. Zhu, C., He, Y., Savvides, M.: Feature selective anchor-free module for single-shot object detection. In: CVPR 2019 (2019)
12. Zhong, Z., Sun, L., Huo, Q.: An anchor-free region proposal network for faster R-CNN based text detection approaches. arXiv preprint arXiv:1804.09003 (2018)
13. Lin, T.-Y., Dollar, P., Girshick, R.B., He, K., Hariharan, B., Belongie, S.J.: Feature pyramid networks for object detection. In: CVPR, p. 3 (2017)
14. Tychsen-Smith, L., Petersson, L.: Improving object localization with fitness NMS and bounded iou loss. In: IEEE Conference on Computer Vision and Pattern Recognition (CVPR), June 2018
15. Lin, T.-Y.: Microsoft COCO: common objects in context. In: Fleet, D., Pajdla, T., Schiele, B., Tuytelaars, T. (eds.) ECCV 2014. LNCS, vol. 8693, pp. 740–755. Springer, Cham (2014). https://doi.org/10.1007/978-3-319-10602-1_48

A Feature Fusion Based Object Tracking Algorithm

Junwei Hu[1], Jinlong Chen[1(✉)], Minghao Yang[2], and Yiming Jiang[1]

[1] Guangxi Key Laboratory of Trusted Software, Guilin University of Electronic Technology, Guilin, Guangxi 541004, China
[2] Research Center for Brain-inspired Intelligence (BII), Institute of Automation, Chinese Academy of Sciences (CASIA), Beijing 100190, China

Abstract. At present, most of the networks used to extract features in tracking algorithms are pre-trained on the ImageNet classification data set, such as VGG-16, AlexNet, etc. Most of the features used are feature maps output by the highest convolutional layer, so as to make full use of the powerful expressive power of convolutional features. But it will bring certain problems. The spatial resolution ability of convolutional neural network is not strong. If the target moves fast, exceeds the sampling area of the picture, or the target is occluded by background objects, the target tracking algorithm will fail. In order to further improve the spatial resolution ability of the convolutional neural network and solve the problem of tracking failure that may be caused by local cutting, a single target tracking algorithm based on feature fusion is proposed here. The feature map of the last layer is up-sampled and merged with the feature map of the previous layer to improve the spatial resolution ability. At the same time, the information of different feature models is used to improve the accuracy of the tracking algorithm. In addition to the local detection model, this article also proposes a classification detection model. When the local detection model cannot perform effective detection, multiple detection models are used instead to detect within the entire image to find the location where the target may appear. If the location where the target appears is found, the local detection model continues to be used at that location.

Keywords: Feature fusion · Object tracking · Local detection model

1 Introduction

In many works, feature fusion of different scales is an important means to improve segmentation performance. The low-level features have a higher resolution and contain more position and detail information, but due to fewer convolutions, they have lower semantics and more noise. High-level features have stronger semantic information, but the resolution is very low, and the perception of details is poor. How to efficiently integrate the two, taking the advantages and discarding the bad ones, is the key to improving the segmentation model.

© Springer Nature Singapore Pte Ltd. 2021
F. Sun et al. (Eds.): ICCSIP 2020, CCIS 1397, pp. 548–557, 2021.
https://doi.org/10.1007/978-981-16-2336-3_52

Many works have improved the performance of detection and segmentation by fusing multiple layers. According to the order of fusion and prediction, they are classified into early fusion and late fusion.

Early fusion: First fusion of multi-layer features, and then train the predictor on the fused features. This type of method is also called skip connection, which uses concat and add operations. Representatives of this idea are Inside-Outside Net (ION) and HyperNet.

Late fusion: Improve detection performance by combining the detection results of different layers. There are two representatives of this type of research thinking:

(1) Features are not fused, and multi-scale features are predicted separately, and then the prediction results are synthesized, such as Single Shot MultiBox Detector (SSD).
(2) Feature performs pyramid fusion and prediction after fusion, such as Feature Pyramid Network (FPN).

2   Related Work

When discussing the defects of Fast RCNN and RPN, Kong [1] et al. pointed out that the deep convolutional layer can find the object of interest with a high recall rate, but the positioning accuracy is very low; while the shallow convolutional layer can be more The low recall rate locates the object of interest, and the network used for detection and localization should use both deep and shallow convolutional layers. Based on the assumption that "useful features should be distributed in each convolutional layer of the convolutional neural network", the author designed a feature called Hyper Feature, which is composed of deep coarse-grained features and shallow fine-grained features. Fusion of features, making the feature more robust.

There are several advantages to using Hyper Feature:

a) Extracting from multiple levels, you can take advantage of the different properties of multiple levels of features;
b) For positioning accuracy will be higher;
c) No additional complexity is introduced in the process of fusing features Calculation has no major impact on the efficiency of the algorithm.

Wang [2] et al. pointed out that when solving the single-target tracking problem, the characteristics of the feature maps output by different convolutional layers are different: deep convolutional layers will extract more abstract features and contain richer semantic information. It has strong ability to distinguish different kinds of objects, and is relatively robust to deformation and occlusion, but it is slightly weaker when distinguishing different objects of the same object; shallow convolutional layer features will provide more specific local features, They are more capable of distinguishing different individuals of similar objects, but they are not robust to sharp appearance changes [15]. Therefore, the author proposes an indicator to automatically select which layer of features to use for tracking.

3 Framework Design

The process of target tracking is divided into two stages.

In the position stage, considering that the tracking target may be blocked by the background or the tracking fails, the positioning is divided into two parts: the first part is the local detection model, which uses only partial pictures for detection, and upsampling increases the picture Size, and use multi-level feature fusion to get the precise target position and size (see Fig. 1. Feature fusion process.); the second part is the global detection model, when the tracking target is lost, the current frame is input into the global detection network to find the possible position of the target, if it can be detected The location where the target appears is then tracked based on this location (see Fig. 2. Tracking framework).

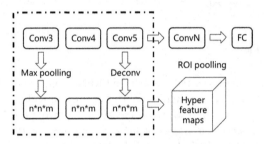

Fig. 1. Feature fusion process.

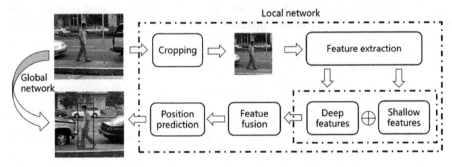

Fig. 2. Tracking framework.

Update. During the tracking process, because the appearance of the object is constantly changing, the model parameters need to be fine-tuned online, and the successful tracking results are expanded to the training set to train the model, so that the model gradually adapts to the gradual change of the appearance of the object.

4 Method and Steps

4.1 Position Stage

Local Detection Model. In the local detection process, first stretch the cropped pictures, adjust the image size to the input size of the VGG network, and input the convolutional neural network to extract different levels of depth features, and then merge the depth features. When fusing the depth features, the feature map output by Conv5 is up-sampled (bilinear interpolation) through a deconvolution layer, and then the up-sampled feature map is cropped through the crop layer to make the up-sampled feature The map size is the same as the feature map size of the Conv4 layer, and then the two feature maps are added to obtain the fusion depth feature. Finally, a convolutional layer is used to convolve on the fused depth features to obtain the output of the local detection model. The algorithm proposed in this paper trains the local detection network by optimizing the following loss function:

$$L_{local} = \left\| \bar{M}_1 - M_1 \right\|_2^2 \tag{1}$$

In this formula, $\bar{M}_1$ is the output of the local detection model, and M_1 is the target heat map, which is a two-dimensional Gaussian distribution centered at the center of the real frame. The parameters use the stochastic gradient descent method in the training process [14].

Global Search Model. In the local detection process, the target may be lost. In this case, this article adjusts the region generation network and training strategy as follows: 1) For single target tracking algorithm, only the foreground and the background need to be distinguished. 0 represents the background and 1 represents the prospect. 2) The purpose of using the region generation network is to generate a series of rectangular boxes with scores. Therefore, only the region generation network can be trained.

The training of the global search model is also completed in the first frame, and the training process is similar to that of RPN. Combining the real frame of the object given in the first frame, and the anchor point of the area generation network design, the area generation network can be trained. When generating the network in the training area, it is necessary to assign a label to each anchor point. A positive sample corresponds to two cases [13]: 1) the IOU ratio of the anchor point and the label frame is the largest, 2) the IOU ratio of the anchor point and the label frame is greater than 0.7; Negative samples are anchor points whose IOU with the label box is less than 0.3, and other anchor points will not be used in the training process.

After allocating the labels of the anchor points, use the stochastic gradient descent method to optimize the following loss function to complete the training of the global search model:

$$L(\{p_i\}, \{t_i\}) = \frac{1}{N_{cls}} \sum_i L_{cls}(p_i, p_i^*) + \lambda \frac{1}{N_{reg}} \sum_i p_i^* L_{reg}(t_i, t_i^*) \tag{2}$$

In formula 2, i is the label of the drawing point, p_i is the probability that the anchor point labeled i contains the target, p_i^* is the pre-assigned label, when the anchor point is a positive sample, p_i^* is 1, and when the anchor point is negative In the sample, p_i is 0, t_i is the offset of the target frame relative to the anchor point predicted by the region generation network, and t_i^* is the offset of the label frame relative to the anchor point.

When the highest value of the feature map output by the local detection model is higher than the given threshold, it can be considered that the local detection model has detected the target, and this position is regarded as the position of the target; otherwise, it is considered that the local detection model cannot detect the object. Global detection model to find the position of the object. Enter the entire image into the global detection network, predict a series of rectangular boxes with scores, and sort the scores to get the rectangular box with the highest score. If the score of the rectangular box is higher than the given threshold, the rectangular box is considered to contain The target to be tracked, and the center of the rectangular box is taken as the position of the target in the current frame, and the local detection network is used to continue tracking the given object with this position as the center.

4.2 Update

In the tracking process, first use the local detection model and the global detection model to determine the position of the object, calculate the coordinates of the target frame in combination with the target frame scale of the previous frame [12]. Then extract feature descriptors according to different scales, use the calculated scale-related filters to find the scale with the largest response value, and then calculate the target frame of the current frame.

In the update process, the target frame predicted by the current frame is first used as the real frame, cropped to obtain the input of the local detection model, and the target Gaussian distribution is constructed, and the local detection model is updated through iteration.

For the update of the scale-dependent filter, follow the incremental update principle of the correlation filter as the Eq. 3.

$$A_t^l = (1 - \eta)A_{t-1} + \eta \bar{G} F_t^l, l = 1, \cdots, d$$

$$B_t = (1 - \eta)B_{t-1} + \eta \sum_{k=1}^{d} \bar{F}_t^k F_t^k \tag{3}$$

In Eq. 3, η represents the learning rate, A_t^l and B_t represents filters. After the update is completed, a new correlation filter is used to calculate the scale of the object in the next frame.

5 Experiment

5.1 Experimental Setup

In order to test the algorithm proposed in this paper, we selected 12 challenging video sequences on the OTB data set for testing, and compared them with the best-known algorithms. Algorithms used for comparison include Struck [4], KCF [9], DSST [10], and RPT [11]. The video sequences used for comparison and related descriptions are shown in the table.

Table 1. Video sequence and related instructions.

Video sequence	Frames	Challenge factor
Car4	659	Lighting change, Scale change
CarDark	393	Messy background, Lighting change
Crossing	120	Scale change, Occlude, Messy background
David	770	Rotate in plane, Occlude, deformation
David3	252	Messy background, Motion blur
Deer	71	Deformation, Rotate in plane
Jogging	307	Motion blur, Messy background, Lighting change
Jump	122	Messy background, Lighting change
Liquor	1741	Rotate in plane, Scale change
Singer1	351	Lighting change, Motion blur
Skaing1	400	Low resolution, Occlude
Walking2	500	Scale change, Occlude

5.2 Evaluation Standard

In this experiment, overlap rate (OR) and center point error (Center Location Error, CLE) are selected as quantitative analysis standards. Among them, the overlap rate is defined as $OR = \frac{B_T \cap B_G}{B_T \cup B_G}$, B_T represents the prediction frame obtained by the algorithm in this paper, and B_G refers to the real frame. The evaluation standard reflects the ratio of the overlap area and the union of the two, and the accuracy of the tracking algorithm to predict the position and scale All have a greater impact on this indicator. The center point error refers to the Euclidean distance between the coordinates of the center points of B_T and B_G. The accuracy of the tracking algorithm's predicted position has a greater impact on this index. The two evaluation indicators are calculated on each frame of the video, and then the average value is calculated as an indicator for evaluating the effect of the algorithm.

6   Experimental Results and Analysis

The results of the analysis are shown in Table 2, Table 3, Fig. 3 and Fig. 4. Our algorithm outperforms the selected comparison algorithm in terms of OR and CLE. It can be seen that by adding feature fusion and global detection models, the algorithm improves performance. The data set selected in the experiment contains multiple and diverse challenge factors, and our algorithm has achieved good results on different sequences. Therefore, it can show that our algorithm is robust.

Some representative frames are selected from the selected test video sequence to compare the tracking results of different algorithms. Our algorithm is more robust in OR and CLE compared with other algorithms (see Fig. 5. Results of different algorithms on video sequences).

Table 2. The average overlap rate of each algorithm (bold indicates the best result, italic indicates the second best result).

	Struck	DSST	RPT	KCF	Ours
Car4	0.75	*0.80*	0.73	**0.83**	0.78
CarDark	**0.87**	0.80	0.82	0.77	*0.85*
Crossing	0.69	0.72	*0.76*	0.74	**0.78**
David	0.65	0.67	0.64	*0.70*	**0.74**
David3	0.70	0.65	**0.78**	0.72	*0.76*
Deer	0.74	*0.80*	0.78	0.71	**0.81**
Jogging-1	*0.69*	0.65	0.67	0.68	**0.79**
Jogging-2	0.64	0.62	0.54	*0.65*	**0.70**
Liquor	0.68	0.75	0.70	*0.78*	**0.84**
Singer1	0.64	**0.78**	0.69	*0.73*	0.72
Skaing1	0.50	0.53	*0.61*	0.56	**0.67**
Walking2	0.59	0.65	**0.78**	0.64	*0.76*
avg	0.68	0.70	0.71	*0.71*	**0.76**

Table 3. The average center location error of each algorithm (bold indicates the best result, italic indicates the second best result).

	Struck	DSST	RPT	KCF	Ours
Car4	9.7	**3.7**	9.1	5.7	*4*
CarDark	**2**	3.7	5.2	5.3	*2.1*
Crossing	3.8	3.8	2.7	6.2	**2.5**
David	13.8	8.9	**6.1**	6.9	*6.2*
David3	17.5	27.5	*5.4*	9.2	**5.1**
Deer	6.3	5.4	5.2	8.7	**4.7**
Jogging-1	8.9	13.7	12	7.2	**5.9**
Jogging-2	17.2	25.6	22	*16.3*	**7**
Liquor	92	54	*12.8*	32.4	**5.4**
Singer1	15.7	**4.5**	11.4	*6.4*	7
Skaing1	83.4	**7.2**	7	15.2	9.2
Walking2	12.3	58.1	18.1	**5.9**	*8.2*
avg	23.5	18	9.8	*10.45*	**5.6**

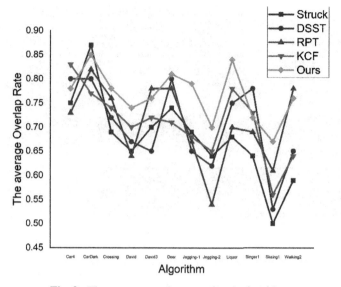

Fig. 3. The average overlap rate of each algorithm.

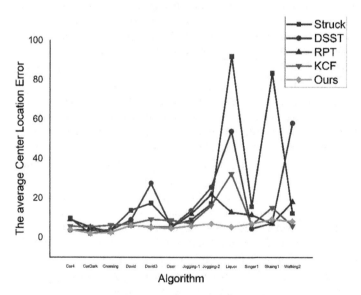

Fig. 4. The average center location error of each algorithm.

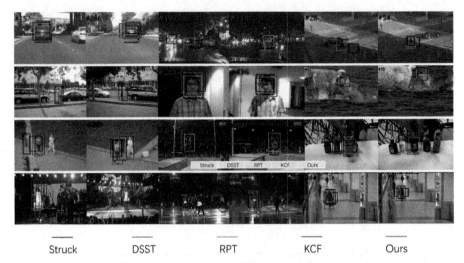

Struck   DSST   RPT   KCF   Ours

Fig. 5. Results of different algorithms on video sequences.

7   Conclusion

Our paper focuses on the first problem of single target tracking under complex background: the interference caused by similar background to target tracking, the existing single target tracking algorithm has poor distinguishing ability, and at the same time, it cannot continue to track effectively after the interference is caused. To solve this problem, our paper proposes a single target tracking algorithm based on feature fusion, which is different from the current single target tracking algorithm based on depth features. The algorithm proposed in this paper fully considers the characteristics of different levels of depth features when using depth features to construct a target model. Using high-level features that have a strong ability to discriminate objects of different types and shallow features that have a strong ability to discriminate between different objects of the same type, the depth features of different levels are merged to enhance the ability to discriminate deep features. In order to prevent the tracking algorithm from losing the target after the object interference, the algorithm proposed in this paper introduces a global detection model to find the possible position of the object through the region generation network, and then continue tracking. The results of comparative experiments on selected video sequences show that thanks to the deep feature fusion algorithm, the single target tracking algorithm proposed in this paper can better distinguish a given target and similar background, obtain better results. For a good scale estimation effect, the algorithm proposed in this paper is improved compared with related comparison algorithms in terms of overlap rate and center point error.

Acknowledgment. This work is supported by the National Key Research & Development Program of China (No. 2018AAA0102902), the National Natural Science Foundation of China (NSFC) (No.61873269), the Beijing Natural Science Foundation (No: L192005), the Guangxi Key Research and Development Program (AB18126053, AB18126063, AD18281002, AD19110001, AB18221011), the Natural Science Foundation of Guangxi of China (2019GXNSFDA185007,

2019GXNSFDA185006), Guangxi Key Laboratory of Intelligent Processing of Computer Images and Graphics (No GIIP201702), and Guangxi Key Laboratory of Trusted Software(NO kx201621, kx201715).

References

1. Kong, T., Yao, A., et al.: HyperNet: towards accurate region proposal generation and joint object detection. In: Proceedings of the IEEE Conference on Computer Vision and Pattern Recognition, pp. 845–853 (2016)
2. Wang, L., Ouyang, W., Wang, X., et al.: Visual tracking with fully convolutional networks. In: Proceedings of the IEEE International Conference on Computer Vision, pp. 3119–3127 (2015)
3. Danelljan, M., Hager, G., Khan, F., et al.: Accurate scale estimation for robust visual tracking. In: British Machine Vision Conference, Nottingham, 1–5 September 2014 (2014)
4. Hare, S., Golodetz, S., Saffari, A., et al.: Struck: structured output tracking with kernels. IEEE Trans. Pattern Anal. Mach. Intell. **38**(10), 2096–2109 (2016)
5. Kalal, Z., Mikolajczyk, K., Matas, J.: Tracking-learning-detection. IEEE Trans. Pattern Anal. Mach. Intell. **34**(7), 1409–1422 (2012)
6. Bao, C., Wu, Y., Ling, H., et al.: Real time robust l1 tracker using accelerated proximal gradient approach. In: 2012 IEEE Conference on Computer Vision and Pattern Recognition (CVPR), pp. 1830–1837. IEEE (2012)
7. Henriques, João F., Caseiro, R., Martins, P., Batista, J.: Exploiting the circulant structure of tracking-by-detection with kernels. In: Fitzgibbon, A., Lazebnik, S., Perona, P., Sato, Y., Schmid, C. (eds.) ECCV 2012. LNCS, vol. 7575, pp. 702–715. Springer, Heidelberg (2012). https://doi.org/10.1007/978-3-642-33765-9_50
8. Adam, A., Rivlin, E., Shimshoni, I.: Robust fragments-based tracking using the integral histogram. In: 2006 IEEE Computer Society Conference on Computer Vision and Pattern Recognition, vol. 1, pp. 798–805. IEEE (2006)
9. Henriques, J.F., Caseiro, R., Martins, P., et al.: High-speed tracking with kernelized correlation filters. IEEE Trans. Pattern Anal. Mach. Intell. **37**(3), 583–596 (2015)
10. Danelljan, M., Hager, G., Khan, F., et al.: Accurate scale estimation for robust visual tracking. In: British Machine Vision Conference, Nottingham, 1–5 September 2014. BMVA Press (2014)
11. Li, Y., Zhu, J., Hoi, S.C.: Reliable patch trackers: robust visual tracking by exploiting reliable patcher. In: 2015 IEEE Conference on Computer Vision and Pattern Recognition (CVPR), pp. 353–361. IEEE (2015)
12. Gongde, G., Nan, L., Lifei, C.: Concept drift detection for data streams based on mixture model. J. Comput. Res. Dev. **51**(4), 731–742 (2014)
13. Klinkenberg, R.: Learning drifting concepts: example selection vs example weighting. Intell. Data Anal. **8**(3), 200–281 (2004)
14. Widmer, G., Kubat, M.: Learning in the presence of concept drift and hidden contexts. Mach. Learn. **23**(1), 69–101 (1996)
15. Sripirakas, S., Russel, P., Albert, B., et al.: Use of ensembles of Fourier spectra in capturing recurrent concepts in data streams. In: International Joint Conference on Neural Networks. Killarney, Ireland, pp. 1–8. IEEE (2015)

Detection and Reconstruction of Transparent Objects with Infrared Projection-Based RGB-D Cameras

Philipp Ruppel[✉], Michael Görner, Norman Hendrich, and Jianwei Zhang

Universität Hamburg, Hamburg, Germany
{ruppel,goerner,hendrich,zhang}@informatik.uni-hamburg.de

Abstract. Robotic manipulation systems frequently utilize RGB-D cameras based on infrared projection to perceive three-dimensional environments. Unfortunately, this technique often fails on transparent objects such as glasses, bottles and plastic containers. We present methods to exploit the perceived infrared camera images to detect and reconstruct volumetric shapes of arbitrary transparent objects. Our reconstruction pipeline first segments transparent surfaces based on pattern scattering and absorption, followed by optimization-based multi-view reconstruction of volumetric object models. Outputs from the segmentation stage can also be utilized for single-view transparent object detection. The presented methods improve on previous work by analyzing infrared camera images directly and by successfully reconstructing cavities in objects such as drinking glasses. A dataset of recorded transparent objects, autonomously gathered by a robotic camera-in-hand setup, is published together with this work.

Keywords: Multi-view 3D reconstruction · Projection-based RGB-D cameras · Transparent object detection · Transparent object reconstruction

1 Introduction

While RGB-D image recognition methods already achieve very good results for detecting opaque objects, detecting transparent objects still remains a challenge. In some cases, transparent objects can be detected using pattern-based depth cameras by looking for holes in the reconstructed depth images. When the projection pattern reaches a transparent surface, some of the light is reflected and some of it is refracted. Thick transparent objects with multiple surface layers and high indices of refraction scatter the projection pattern enough that depth values cannot be reconstructed anymore, and holes appear in the depth image around parts of the transparent object. However, since projection-based depth

This research was funded by the German Research Foundation (DFG) and the National Science Foundation of China in project Crossmodal Learning, TRR-169.

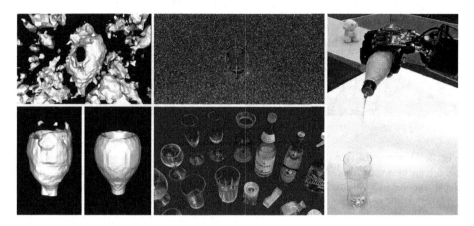

Fig. 1. Our iterative volumetric reconstruction method generates 3D models of transparent objects with cavities (left). We use raw infrared images from pattern-based RGB-D cameras (top) to detect transparent objects (bottom). The technique is used to locate glasses in a robotic bartender scenario (right).

cameras typically combine information from multiple pixels, the locations and extents of the holes in the depth images do not accurately represent the shapes of transparent objects. In addition, many objects (e.g. thin transparent plastic cups) do not cause sufficiently strong scattering to produce holes in the depth image at all, preventing such objects from being detected. To overcome these issues, our method directly works on raw infrared images. Scattering of the projection pattern can be observed over the entire transparent surface, even for thin objects with low indices of refraction. Therefore, localization does not suffer from spatial filtering performed by depth reconstruction algorithms, projector shadows can be distinguished from transparent surfaces, and object detection or reconstruction can use continuous transparency scores instead of having to rely only on binary error masks.

The rest of this paper is structured as follows: First, we give an overview of related work and existing glass detection methods. Next, we describe our method and its different processing steps, from raw infrared images to reconstructed mesh representations. We collected a dataset of IR recordings for various transparent objects with an Orbbec Astra mounted on a UR5 robot (Fig. 1). We validate our reconstruction methods on the dataset.

2   Related Work

Detection and volumetric reconstruction of transparent and specular objects remains a long-standing challenge in computer vision. Approaches include photometrics, analysis of specular flow and distortions, highlight-detection, and custom hardware such as polarized light projectors [5].

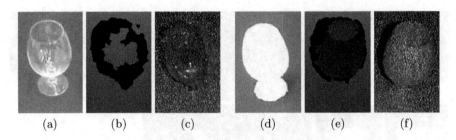

(a)   (b)   (c)   (d)   (e)   (f)

Fig. 2. Transparent (left) and corresponding opaque (right) glass on top of a table, as perceived by an Orbbec Astra camera. (a, d) RGB image, (b, e) the camera's native depth reconstruction, and (c, f) IR channel image showing the projection pattern.

With the widespread availability of cheap projection-based RGB-D sensors, such as the Microsoft Kinect, Asus Xtion and Orbbec Astra, many robotic setups adopted this technique for its ease of use and the overall high quality depth perception. However, for transparent objects, such as glasses, the sensors can produce different artifacts: the projection passes through the glass, resulting in depth measurements of an opaque surface behind; the projection is refracted by the glass, usually resulting in underestimated distances to the surface behind; or the projection is dispersed/absorbed, such that no depth estimate is possible and characteristic holes occur in the depth reconstruction (Fig. 2).

Lysenkov et al. [9] were among the first to exploit these artifacts for model-based pose estimation through template matching. Klank et al. [7] utilized the property of glass to absorb infrared light [3] and analysed the intensity images of an infrared time-of-flight camera. To quickly generate models from only two views of a glass, they deliberately oversimplify their models and reconstruct a two-dimensional representation of the glass only. Evaluating their detection algorithm in a robotic grasping setup, they demonstrated a success rate of 41% for grasping. Sajjan et al. [12] use color information to fill in missing or potentially incorrect depth values in RGB-D images. Saygili et al. [13] presented a hybridization of Kinect-based reconstruction and stereo matching with smoothness-based CRF refinement to fill in gaps in the depth image.

Ham et al. [4] noted that occlusion boundaries, unlike texture, are view-dependent and could be exploited for object reconstruction. Milan et al. presented various insights and tricks for semantic object segmentation in their computer vision pipeline winning the Amazon Robotics Challenge 2017 [10]. Combining a light field camera with structure from motion was proposed in [14]. An optimization-based approach for 3D reconstruction of transparent objects was described in [15]. However, since the method relies on placing an LCD screen behind the transparent object to display known scanning patterns and due to high runtime (5–6 h for full object reconstruction), it is not suitable for most robotics applications.

In the context of data-driven object detection, transparent objects are usually treated the same as opaque objects. For example, YOLO9000 [11] contains

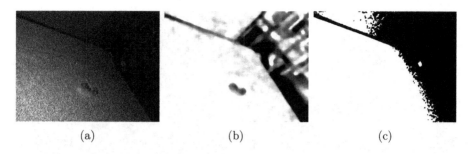

(a)   (b)   (c)

Fig. 3. Infrared image from depth camera (a), high-pass and median filter (b), median filter and threshold (c).

multiple class labels for transparent object classes, including "bottle", "glass", etc., and the system succeeds in predicting approximate bounding boxes for these classes. Chen et al. [2] train deep neural networks on synthetic data to detect transparent surfaces in RGB images. The mentioned approaches operate on single RGB images and generate bounding boxes in image space. Thus, they are not applicable for manipulation tasks in unknown environments where 3D object positions are required. Other projects tried to detect artifacts and perform reconstruction based on silhouette [1, 6, 16].

In contrast to all works known to the authors, the presented paper is the first to reconstruct volumetric object shapes with cavities through optimization on multiple object views with adequate performance for online robot applications.

3   Methods

3.1   Transparency Segmentation

We first want to detect image areas that may correspond to transparent surfaces. Each image is first preprocessed by applying dilation and median blur filters and then dividing the value of each image pixel by the value of the corresponding dilated and blurred image. The projection pattern can typically be observed clearly across the entire scene, with the exception of projector shadows, very dark or distant surfaces, and transparent objects. While projector shadows and very dark surfaces do not show the projection pattern, their overall brightness is also relatively low. In contrast to this, on transparent surfaces, the projection pattern is scattered while the overall brightness remains relatively high. To detect the presence or absence of the projection pattern, we first apply a Difference-of-Gaussians high-pass filter with a standard deviation of 1 pixel. Applying the filter repeatedly leads to better separation between the projection pattern and surface textures. Too many iterations, however, wash out object contours and increase image noise. For the experiments shown in this paper, we use three iterations. After high-pass filtering, we apply a local median filter with a circular kernel both to the original image and to the filtered image. Transparent surfaces now appear relatively dark in the transparency candidate map that was previously high-pass

Fig. 4. Glass detection (right) during our bartender demo (left) at the IROS 2018 Mobile Manipulation Hackathon. The detected glass is marked with a green circle. The small red circle represents the point on the base of the glass that is closest to the camera. The large red circle represents an object candidate which has been rejected during transparency validation. (Color figure online)

filtered (Fig. 3b), but still relatively bright in the transparency validation map that was not previously high-pass filtered (Fig. 3c). Very dark surfaces, as well as projector shadows, appear dark in both images. A simple "glass score" could now be computed for each pixel as a weighted difference between both images. However, we found that even better results can be achieved if the next processing steps use both filtered images separately.

3.2   Transparent Object Detection

To detect transparent objects, we first generate object candidates by applying a standard blob detection algorithm to the previously high-pass and median-filtered transparency candidate map. Different binarizations with different thresholds are created and contiguous dark areas are selected as hypotheses. Object candidates are then filtered. Candidates are rejected if they are either too large or too small, or if their shape does not match additional constraints on circularity, convexity, and inertia. If candidates overlap, the smaller overlapping ones are removed. To validate if an object consists of a transparent material, we sample image pixels inside and around each object candidate and compare their averages. First, two circular masks are constructed from the object candidate centers, their areas, and two scaling factors. One smaller mask lies inside the object for sampling the object surface and one larger mask encompasses the object with a sufficient margin to sample the objects surroundings. An object candidate is now classified as consisting of a transparent material if the brightness difference between the inner circle and the outer circle is sufficiently large for the transparency candidate map and if the difference is sufficiently small for the transparency validation map. Figure 4 illustrates the detection and a rejected candidate on a realistic picture taken during a robotic bartender demonstration.

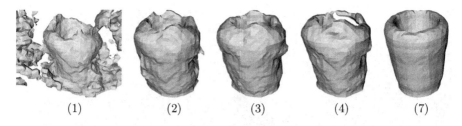

$$(1) \qquad (2) \qquad (3) \qquad (4) \qquad (7)$$

Fig. 5. Iterative reconstruction of a drinking glass (iteration 1, 2, 3, 4, 7).

3.3   Volumetric Reconstruction

In this section, we present an optimization-based reconstruction method for unknown transparent objects. Each infrared camera image that will be used for object reconstruction is preprocessed as described above. To reconstruct the shape of an unknown transparent object, we optimize a density distribution across a 3D voxel grid to match the previously computed 2D transparency maps and to minimize a set of regularizers. One free variable $v_{x,y,z}$ is created for every grid cell. The value of each variable represents an estimate for the amount of transparent material that is located within the corresponding voxel. We assume that this amount cannot be negative and add a soft non-negativity constraint with a quadratic penalty function $g_{x,y,z}$.

$$g_{x,y,z} = \max(0, {v_{x,y,z}}^2) \tag{1}$$

The transparency maps, which are computed from the infrared camera images, are incorporated into the optimization by casting rays through the voxel grid and minimizing errors $e_{u,v}$ between ray integrals $I_{u,v}$ and transparency map pixels $p_{u,v}$ for randomly selected pixel indices u, v. Pixels for which the corresponding values in the transparency validation map are below a threshold are ignored. To increase resistance against image or transparency detection errors, we use a robust Huber loss h with parameter δ.

$$e_{u,v} = h(p_{u,v} - I_{u,v}) \tag{2}$$

$$h(x) = \begin{cases} \dfrac{1}{2}x^2 & \text{if } x < \delta \\ \delta(\|x\| - \dfrac{1}{2}\delta) & \text{otherwise} \end{cases} \tag{3}$$

Most of the scanned volume will typically be empty. We therefore add a sparse regularization term $r_{x,y,z}$.

$$r_{x,y,z} = h(v_{x,y,z}) \tag{4}$$

We further assume that the amount of transparent material within adjacent voxels is likely to be similar. However, at the same time, we still want to allow for hard object boundaries. We therefore add an additional outlier resistant loss

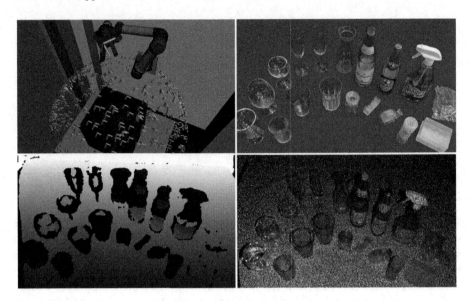

Fig. 6. Observation poses for an in-hand camera attached to the gripper of a UR5 arm (top-left). RGB (top-right), depth (bottom-left) and IR (bottom-right) images of objects from our dataset.

function $l_{x,y,z}$ between the variable corresponding to each voxel and the median value of the variables corresponding to the voxels within a local neighborhood.

$$l_{x,y,z} = h\big(v_{x,y,z} - \text{median}(v_{x-1,y-1,z-1}, v_{x,y-1,z-1}, ..., v_{x+1,y+1,z+1})\big) \quad (5)$$

Many transparent objects (glasses, etc.) are rotationally symmetric and we can exploit this symmetry to further improve the reconstruction. This additional cost function $s_{x,y,z}$ reduces the difference between the value $v(x,y,z)$ assigned to a voxel and the average value of other voxels sampled on a circle around a center point c.

$$s_{x,y,z} = h\left(v_{x,y,z} - \int_0^{2\pi} v\Big(\sin(a)\|x - c_x\| + c_x, \cos(a)\|y - c_y\| + c_y, z\Big) da\right) \quad (6)$$

We combine the previously described cost terms into a single loss function by summation over the voxels and image pixels.

$$\min_v \sum_{u,v \in \mathbb{N}} e_{u,v} + \sum_{x,y,z \in \mathbb{N}} \Big(g_{x,y,z} + l_{x,y,z} + r_{x,y,z} + s_{x,y,z}\Big) \quad (7)$$

Before starting the optimization process, all variables are zero-initialized. The combined non-linear optimization problem is solved through iteratively reweighted least squares. The solution to each quadratic approximation is found using sparse conjugate gradient descent. Each iteration considers a randomly selected subset of rays and the number of conjugate gradient descent steps per quadratic approximation is limited to reduce runtime. The resulting density distribution can be used to generate surface models, for example using the marching cubes method. Figure 5 illustrates reconstruction results at multiple iteration steps and demonstrates convergence to the final object shape.

3.4   Dataset

To extend the amount of real-world data available for qualitative comparison, we collected a dataset composed of 18 everyday objects, depicted in Fig. 6. The set includes standard versions of many types of drinking glasses, as well as several objects with attached labels and composite objects which are only partially transparent. For evaluation purposes, we additionally wrapped six of the glasses in thin opaque tape (compare Fig. 2) and recorded the native depth-reconstruction generated by the camera.

3.5   Data Acquisition

To record images of these objects from many perspectives, we mounted an Orbbec Astra camera in the gripper of a UR5-based robotic setup. This obviously restricts possible camera poses by the kinematic structure of the robot arm. To generate an approximately even distribution of 100 camera poses within the reachable workspace of the setup, we perform rejection-based hypercube sampling of poses pointing to the center of the workspace from a distance of 0.65 m. Additionally, we reject samples which cannot be reached with the end-effector by inverse kinematics. We calibrate intrinsic and extrinsic camera parameters through bundle adjustment. An illustration of the resulting solution space is given in Fig. 6.

4   Baseline Reconstruction Method

As a baseline reconstruction method, we also implemented a technique similar to [1]. Since we are using raw infrared images, we use our pre-processing method described above and subsequent thresholding to obtain binary masks. We then classify a voxel as being part of a transparent object if it lies within the convex hull of the binary transparency mask for 90% of the images. While this method is able to determine the position of a transparent object, and for simple objects a rough approximation of the objects shape, it fails to correctly reconstruct cavities within concave objects such as drinking glasses, which are reconstructed correctly by our proposed reconstruction method (see Fig. 8).

Table 1. Average MSE and RMSE distances between transparent reconstructions and opaque reconstructions for the geometric baseline method and our optimization-based approach.

	MSE [m^2]		RMSE [mm]	
	Baseline	Ours	Baseline	Ours
Small IKEA glass	4.83×10^{-5}	2.09×10^{-5}	6.953	4.569
Big IKEA glass	8.53×10^{-5}	2.31×10^{-5}	9.240	4.808
Red wine glass	9.02×10^{-5}	2.05×10^{-5}	9.499	4.523
White wine glass	6.29×10^{-5}	0.69×10^{-5}	7.931	2.628
Sparkling wine glass	3.25×10^{-5}	1.40×10^{-5}	5.699	3.743
Average	6.38×10^{-5}	1.71×10^{-5}	7.864	4,054

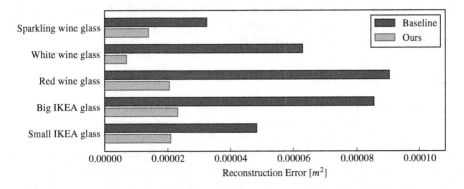

Fig. 7. Average reconstruction errors for the geometric baseline method and our optimization-based approach (lower is better).

5   Evaluation

Figure 8 shows photos and 3D reconstructions of different transparent household objects. The 3D reconstructions are rendered as binarized voxel grids and as smooth marching cubes surface models. Our reconstruction method was able to capture the general appearance of each object and the models seem to be accurate enough for robotic manipulation. For most objects we tested, the baseline method misses key features which are successfully reconstructed by our method. Unlike previous approaches, our method is able to reconstruct cavities within glasses. While the baseline method reconstructs the sparkling wine glass as a cone, our method correctly reproduces a round bowl on a thin stem. Small inaccuracies can be seen in the reconstructions from our method for the bottle and at the feet of the wine glasses. The feet of the wine glasses are too thin and too close to the table to cause sufficient scattering of the projection pattern. Inaccuracies during bottle reconstruction are caused by the opaque labels since the reconstruction method only considers transparent materials (Fig. 7).

Photo	Baseline	Our method	Photo	Baseline	Our method

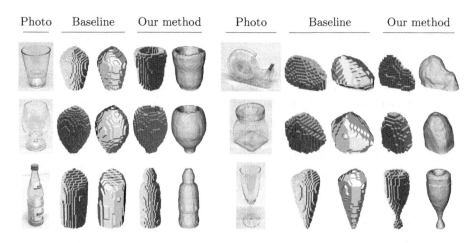

Fig. 8. Photos and 3D reconstructions of different transparent household objects. Reconstructions are visualized as binarized voxel grids and as marching cubes surface reconstructions.

For quantitative evaluation, we generate 3D reconstructions of transparent objects using our optimization-based approach and using the geometric baseline method, then cover the objects in thin opaque tape, scan the objects again using the native reconstruction procedures of the depth camera, and compute MSE and RMSE distances between each transparent object reconstruction and the opaque reconstruction. See Table 1 and Fig. 4 for results. The transparent object reconstructions are generated with a voxel size of 5 mm. Our method consistently outperforms the baseline method and achieves average reconstruction errors close to and below the grid resolution. As our current implementation has not yet been optimized for parallel execution, we only report initial performance results. On a standard desktop computer (Intel Core-i5 8500, 3 GHz), one iteration of the reconstruction algorithm takes about 11 s (5 s for solving the equation, about 6 s to generate rays and build the gradient matrix), and one full object reconstruction takes about one minute.

6   Conclusion and Future Work

We presented an approach for reconstructing transparent objects from multiview observations using a typical low-cost projection-based RGB-D camera. In contrast to previous projects with similar ideas, our approach does not rely on pure silhouette reconstruction but describes an optimization problem based on non-binary maps of the perceived IR images. The resulting system successfully reconstructs the shape of transparent objects, including cavities which could not be reconstructed from silhouettes. If available, additional prior knowledge, such as symmetry assumptions, can be readily included to refine object models.

Future directions for this research include the integration of *Next Best View* mechanisms, such as [8], where adapted definitions of information gain would need to account for the transparency of perceived surfaces. While this research makes the simplifying assumption that filtered transparency values from the IR image behave additively when passing through multiple transparent voxels, it remains an open question how this behavior can be modeled in the presence of different transparent materials. Reconstruction of objects with transparent as well as opaque parts could be improved by combining our transparent object reconstruction method with existing depth reconstruction methods for opaque objects. The source code and the collected dataset are available at https:// github.com/TAMS-Group/tams_glass_reconstruction.

References

1. Albrecht, S.: Transparent object reconstruction and registration confidence measures for 3D point clouds based on data inconsistency and viewpoint analysis. Ph.D. thesis, Osnabrück University (2018)
2. Chen, G., Han, K., Wong, K.Y.K.: TOM-Net: learning transparent object matting from a single image. In: The IEEE Conference on Computer Vision and Pattern Recognition (CVPR), pp. 9233–9241, June 2018
3. Eren, G., et al.: Scanning from heating: 3D shape estimation of transparent objects from local surface heating. Opt. Express **17**, 11457–11468 (2009). https://doi.org/10.1364/OE.17.011457
4. Ham, C., Singh, S., Lucey, S.: Occlusions are fleeting – texture is forever: moving past brightness constancy. In: 2017 IEEE Winter Conference on Applications of Computer Vision (WACV), pp. 273–281 (2017). https://doi.org/10.1109/WACV.2017.37
5. Ihrke, I., Kutulakos, K., Lensch, H., Magnor, M., Heidrich, W.: Transparent and specular object reconstruction. Comput. Graph. Forum **29**, 2400–2426 (2010). https://doi.org/10.1111/j.1467-8659.2010.01753.x
6. Ji, Y., Xia, Q., Zhang, Z.: Fusing depth and silhouette for scanning transparent object with RGB-D sensor. Int. J. Opt. **2017**, 9796127 (2017). https://doi.org/10.1155/2017/9796127
7. Klank, U., Carton, D., Beetz, M.: Transparent object detection and reconstruction on a mobile platform. In: Proceedings of the IEEE International Conference on Robotics and Automation (ICRA), pp. 5971–5978 (2011). https://doi.org/10.1109/ICRA.2011.5979793
8. Kriegel, S., Rink, C., Bodenmüller, T., Suppa, M.: Efficient next-best-scan planning for autonomous 3D surface reconstruction of unknown objects. J. Real-Time Image Proc. **10**(4), 611–631 (2013). https://doi.org/10.1007/s11554-013-0386-6
9. Lysenkov, I., Eruhimov, V., Bradski, G.: Recognition and pose estimation of rigid transparent objects with a Kinect sensor. In: Proceedings of Robotics: Science and Systems, Sydney, Australia, July 2012. https://doi.org/10.15607/RSS.2012.VIII.035
10. Milan, A., et al.: Semantic segmentation from limited training data. In: 2018 IEEE International Conference on Robotics and Automation (ICRA), pp. 1908–1915 (2018). https://doi.org/10.1109/ICRA.2018.8461082
11. Redmon, J., Farhadi, A.: YOLO9000: better, faster, stronger. In: The IEEE Conference on Computer Vision and Pattern Recognition (CVPR), pp. 7263–7271, July 2017

12. Sajjan, S.S., et al.: ClearGrasp: 3D shape estimation of transparent objects for manipulation (2019)
13. Saygili, G., van der Maaten, L., Hendriks, E.: Hybrid Kinect depth map refinement for transparent objects. In: Proceedings of the International Conference on Pattern Recognition, pp. 2751–2756 (2014). https://doi.org/10.1109/ICPR.2014.474
14. Tsai, D., Dansereau, D.G., Peynot, T., Corke, P.: Distinguishing refracted features using light field cameras with application to structure from motion. IEEE Robot. Autom. Lett. **4**(2), 177–184 (2019). https://doi.org/10.1109/LRA.2018.2884765
15. Wu, B., Zhou, Y., Qian, Y., Cong, M., Huang, H.: Full 3D reconstruction of transparent objects. ACM Trans. Graph. **37**(4), 103:1–103:11 (2018). https://doi.org/10.1145/3197517.3201286
16. Yun, Y., Seo, D., Kim, D.: Recognition of transparent objects using 3D depth camera. In: 2017 14th International Conference on Ubiquitous Robots and Ambient Intelligence (URAI), pp. 882–883, June 2017. https://doi.org/10.1109/URAI.2017.7992854

Autonomous Vehicles

A Simulation-to-Real Autonomous Driving System Based on End-to-End Learning

Yifan Zhang, Bo Wang, Jian Li, and Yang Yu$^{(\boxtimes)}$

College of Intelligence Science and Technology, National University of Defense Technology, Changsha, China

Abstract. In this study, an automatic driving system based on end-to-end learning from simulation to reality was proposed, which integrates simulation platform, network model and on-road test platform. The purpose is to verify that the trained model can be directly deployed on the real vehicle using the dataset that is completely collected in the simulation platform. The simulation platform is implemented by calibrating the camera and environment and modeling the vehicle according to its motion characteristics. It is used to collect data and test the trained model preliminarily, where the benchmark is the deviation between the virtual vehicle location and the tracking path. The network model uses a lightweight convolution neural network with image data as input and steering prediction as output. The performance of the network model is also tested in the on-road test platform, and the criteria is the proportion of the vehicle's autonomous driving time during the whole driving. The results show that the path deviation of simulation test is less than 10 pixels, corresponding to about 5 cm on the real road. And the proportion of automatic driving time is more than 98% in the on-road test. The evaluation results can meet the automatic driving requirements. Collecting large amount of synthesized image and calculating the theoretical steering in the simulation platform can improve the certainty and accuracy of model output, and reduce the labor cost. In addition, the end-to-end lightweight network model reduces the demand for computing resources and sensor hardware. On the indoor or park scenes with structured roads as the main elements, this automatic driving system can promote the large-scale use of logistics vehicles or transport vehicles.

Keywords: Simulation · Reality · End-to-end · Autonomous

1 Introduction

At present, the structure of automatic driving system can mainly be divided into two types: hierarchical and end-to-end. The hierarchical system structure usually consists of three sub-modules: perception, decision and control [1], and the end-to-end system structure directly constructs the mapping relationship from sensor input to control command [2]. The hierarchical system structure has clear module division, clear task division and strong interpretability. However, due to the differences in the implementation of each module, it needs to be equipped with a variety of sensors and high-performance computing resources. But the end-to-end system directly obtains the control signal from

© Springer Nature Singapore Pte Ltd. 2021
F. Sun et al. (Eds.): ICCSIP 2020, CCIS 1397, pp. 573–583, 2021.
https://doi.org/10.1007/978-981-16-2336-3_54

the perceived information, thus reducing the hardware cost and simplifying the complex processing steps among the modules in the traditional hierarchical framework and shortening the development cycle. In this paper, we focus on an auto driving system based on the end-to-end learning.

In recent years, researchers have done a lot of work on end-to-end automatic driving systems. Some known solutions in [3, 6, 7] for autonomous driving system based on end-to-end learning work well in real vehicles by imitating the recorded behavior of human drivers in large image datasets. These end-to-end network models are able to learn the entire task of lane and road following without manual decomposition into road or lane marking detection, semantic abstraction, path planning, and control.

Even though the efforts mentioned above have made significant progress, current works of end-to-end automatic driving systems pay little attention to the collection and labeling of data. They usually collect the images captured by camera and record the corresponding steering as label in real time, but do not take into account that different drivers may make different decisions for the same scene, even if the same driver passes through the same scene again. In this way, the network model essentially learns the average control signal of drivers, so it is difficult to give a definite and accurate output for a road scene.

We propose an automatic driving system based on end-to-end learning from simulation to reality. Different from the above methods, the system builds a simulation platform by calibrating camera, environment and modeling vehicle to match the real world to collect data in all kinds of scenes. At the same time, when collecting the image in simulation environment, the theoretical accurate steering calculated according to the vehicle characteristics and reference path is used as a label instead of recording the control behavior of human drivers, which can reduce the ambiguity of the model output on the intersection and other scenes. After simulation test and on-road test, we prove that the system which collects data in simulation environment and trains the weights of network model using the dataset can be directly transplanted to the embedded platform to complete the real-world driving task.

2   Related Work

End-to-End Automatic Driving System. At present, researchers have realized the end-to-end automatic driving controller using convolutional neural network. Pomerleau D A et al. from Carnegie Mellon University first proposed a three-layer back propagation full-link network, which maps camera and radar data to vehicle steering control signal [3]. Todd M. Jochen et al. then improved this method by introducing virtual cameras to detect more road features [4]. Lecun Y et al. used convolution neural network to build an end-to-end convolution neural network model with the images collected by binocular cameras as input and the front wheel angle as output, and completed the low-speed driving of vehicles in the field environment [5]. An end-to-end network model called PilotNet [6] is proposed by NVIDIA, which takes images collected by three cameras as input and steering wheel angle as output. It is tested in both simulation and on-road environment. After the PilotNet was proposed, researchers at Google Research Institute, NVIDIA and New York University visualized the characteristics learned by model to explain the factors that affect decision-making [7]. Since then, end-to-end network models have become richer. The FCN-LSTM network [8] proposed by Berkeley, California, uses a memory network that combines current and previous features and outputs control signals. The Multi-modal multi-task network [9] proposed by the University of Rochester, based on the previous work, not only outputs the steering signal, but also gives the speed, which fully constitutes the basic signal required for vehicle control. Jelena et al. proposed a lighter end-to-end shallow network that is better suited for embedded platforms [10]. Current methods of automatic driving based on end-to-end network model mostly use images collected by monocular camera as input, and gradually add data information from other sensors, such as stereo vision camera [5], radar [11], lidar [12] etc.

Simulation in Automatic Driving System. It is difficult to cover all conditions by manual data collection, which affects the improvement of end-to-end controller performance and leads to poor generalization ability of trained model. Therefore, the simulation environment is used to collect data and test the trained model preliminarily. A method based on reinforcement learning [13] was used to learn and test with the open racing car simulator (TORCS). A conditional learning method [14] using CARLA open-source simulator [15] for data collection was proposed. In addition, A combination of rules and end-to-end approach [16] maps the image to the affordance indicators instead of the control signal, which completes the data collection in TORCS according to the defined indicators.

3   Method

3.1   The Overview of Automatic Driving System

The automatic driving system framework is presented in Fig. 1. The system is mainly divided into three modules: simulation platform, convolutional neural network model for end-to-end training and on-road test platform.

The simulation platform is constructed by calibrating the camera, environment and modeling vehicle. In the simulation environment, the reference path is marked and the virtual vehicle is disturbed by the position and attitude along the reference path to get the image under this perspective. Combined with the vehicle position and kinematic characteristics, the theoretical steering corresponding to this image can be calculated. Taking the image and the corresponding steering as a pair of samples, a large number of samples are collected in this simulation environment. After the completion of the samples collection, the dataset is obtained by the processing methods such as scale division and data augmentation, and the end-to-end lightweight convolution neural network model is trained by the dataset. The trained network model is tested in the simulation platform to simulate automatic driving task. After verification, it is deployed to the real vehicle for on-road test.

3.2   The Simulation Platform

The simulation platform is the most important module in the automatic driving system. Its function is to collect data and carry out simulation test. Its main characteristic is that a synthetic dataset from the simulation environment can replace real scene.

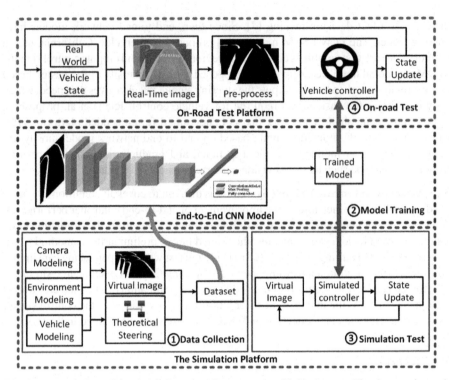

Fig. 1. An **overview** of the simulation-to-real autonomous driving system. The three main modules are: the simulation platform including data collection and simulation test, the end-to-end convolutional neural network model and on-road test platform. We use the labels to indicate the execution order of the system, that is, first to collect data in the simulation platform, then to use the dataset for supervised learning of the model, third to validate the trained model in the simulation platform, and finally to transplant to a real vehicle for on-road test.

Image Synthesizing. In order to simulate the process of image captured by camera, it is necessary to calibrate the camera and the environment. After getting the simulated image, the steering label can be calculated according to the vehicle motion model, instead of fuzzy driver decision.

Environment Modeling. The modeling of the environment mainly includes the following steps: first, take a top view of the environment as a map, then extract the main factors that affect steering (we only retain the binary lane), finally mark the middle line of lane on both sides as the reference path for driving, as shown in Fig. 2. In our work, the real scene is arranged as a 6 m × 8 m site, including lane and several other road elements. The aerial view of the real scene is taken, and a 1200px × 1800px image is obtained, which is used as a map image in the simulation environment. We can get a pixel in the simulation environment that represents 5 mm of the real world. The world coordinate system and the map coordinate system differ only in the location of the origin. Mask the map according to the lane color and only lane lines are retained. For other complex structured road scenes, other lane detection related algorithms can be used to obtain the map containing only lane elements. The top view can be used here because the lane lines are in the same plane, and it includes all the road information, so that the lane lines in the real world can be mapped to the top view, otherwise it is necessary to establish a 3D map model of the environment. The mapping of a point in the real world (x_w, y_w, z_w) to the simulation map (x_s, y_s, z_s) has the following relationship.

$$\begin{bmatrix} x_s \\ y_s \\ z_s \\ 1 \end{bmatrix} = T_{ws} \begin{bmatrix} x_w \\ y_w \\ z_w \\ 1 \end{bmatrix} = \begin{bmatrix} R_{ws} & T_{ws} \\ 0 & 1 \end{bmatrix} \begin{bmatrix} x_w \\ y_w \\ z_w \\ 1 \end{bmatrix}, R_{ws} = \mathbf{0}, z_s = 0 \qquad (1)$$

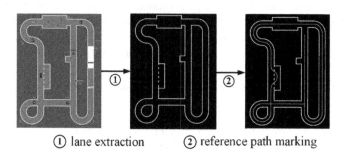

① lane extraction   ② reference path marking

Fig. 2. The process of modeling the environment

Camera Calibration. The relationship between the camera coordinate and the world coordinate can be obtained through the camera external parameter matrix T_{cw}, the relationship between the camera coordinate and the pixel coordinate in image can be obtained through the camera internal parameter matrix K, and the relationship between the distorted image and the undistorted image can be obtained through the distortion coefficient k_1, k_2. Figure 3 shows the change process of a red marked point from the world coordinates (x_w, y_w, z_w) to camera coordinates (x_c, y_c, z_c), and then through the image coordinates (x_i, y_i) to pixel coordinates (u, v), the process is as formula(2), where s is the scale factor, f is the effective focal length, d_x and d_y is the physical size of two axes directions in the image coordinate system, (u_0, v_0), are the coordinates of the origin of the image coordinate system in the pixel coordinate system [17].

$$s \begin{bmatrix} u \\ v \\ 1 \end{bmatrix} = \begin{bmatrix} \frac{1}{dx} & 0 & u_0 \\ 0 & \frac{1}{dy} & v_0 \\ 0 & 0 & 1 \end{bmatrix} \begin{bmatrix} x_i \\ y_i \\ 1 \end{bmatrix} = \begin{bmatrix} \frac{1}{dx} & 0 & u_0 \\ 0 & \frac{1}{dy} & v_0 \\ 0 & 0 & 1 \end{bmatrix} \begin{bmatrix} f & 0 & 0 & 0 \\ 0 & f & 0 & 0 \\ 0 & 0 & f & 0 \end{bmatrix} \begin{bmatrix} x_c \\ y_c \\ z_c \\ 1 \end{bmatrix}$$

$$= \begin{bmatrix} f_x & 0 & u_0 & 0 \\ 0 & f_y & v_0 & 0 \\ 0 & 0 & 1 & 0 \end{bmatrix} \begin{bmatrix} R & T \\ 0 & 1 \end{bmatrix} \begin{bmatrix} x_w \\ y_w \\ z_w \\ 1 \end{bmatrix} = K T_{cw} \begin{bmatrix} x_w \\ y_w \\ z_w \\ 1 \end{bmatrix} \qquad (2)$$

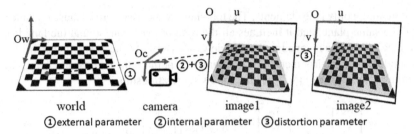

world   camera   image1   image2
①external parameter   ②internal parameter   ③distortion parameter

Fig. 3. The process of mapping a point from the world to an image

In the ideal case, the coordinates of the point (x_i, y_i) in the undistorted image (image 2 in Fig. 3) are obtained, but the real pixel coordinates are $(\overline{x}_i, \overline{y}_i)$ in the distorted image (image 1 in Fig. 3). This is due to the optical distortion caused by the essential character-istics of lens. In this work, only the radial distortion is considered, and the coefficients are K1 and K2, then the following relationship is obtained.

$$\overline{x}_i = x_i + \left[k_1\left(x_i^2 + y_i^2\right)\right] + k_2\left(x_i^2 + y_i^2\right)^2] \tag{3}$$

$$\overline{y}_i = y_i + \left[k_1\left(x_i^2 + y_i^2\right)\right] + k_2\left(x_i^2 + y_i^2\right)^2] \tag{4}$$

When synthesizing an image in a simulation environment, simulate the characteristics of the camera to get a distorted image, the reverse process mentioned above. A blank image is generated firstly, then the corresponding point on the simulated map can be filled in each pixel point on the blank image. That is, make points $(\overline{x}_i, \overline{y}_i)$ in our synthesized image mapping to undistorted points (x_i, y_i) according to formulas (3) and (4), and then deduce the corresponding points in the simulation environment according to the formulas (1) and (2), and fill the pixel values on the synthesized image.

Steering Calculation. After the modeling of the camera and environment, the virtual camera can be placed at any position in the virtual environment to capture the image. According to the deviation between the current position and the target point on the reference path, the steering corresponding to the current image can be calculated as a label. In this paper, a simple pure tracking algorithm is used to calculate the steering. The relationship between the deviation and the steering is obtained by kinematic model of the vehicle. The kinematic model of the vehicle is abstracted into a simplified Ackermann steering structure. From Fig. 4, the position of the target point is found according to the forward-looking distance. According to the geometric relationship, the relationship between the radius corresponding to the path arc R and the forward-looking distance l and lateral deviation d is as follows:

$$\frac{1/2}{R} = \frac{d}{l} \tag{5}$$

The relationship between the front wheel angle θ and the arc radius R is:

$$tan\theta = \frac{L}{R} \tag{6}$$

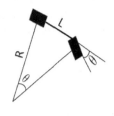

(a)The tracking trajectory. (b)Vehicle kinematics model.

Fig. 4. The calculation of theoretical steering. The yellow position icon represents the position of the center of the vehicle's rear wheel axle. The yellow arrow represents the vehicle heading.

So the steering corresponding to the current image is calculated as:

$$\theta = arctan\frac{2Ld}{l^2} \tag{7}$$

After calibrating the camera, environment and modeling vehicle respectively, the simulation platform is basically completed. At this time, the virtual camera can be placed in a specific position of the virtual environment in a certain posture to capture the image, and the corresponding steering signal can be obtained as a label through simple calculation. Suppose that the vehicle starts from the start position of the reference path, drives along the reference path in the center of the lane, and gives the vehicle position and heading deviation according to certain conditions to collect the images. When the vehicle reaches the destination, a large number of samples collected form the dataset for end-to-end learning.

3.3 The End-to-End Model

The dataset collected by the simulation platform is used to train weights of the end-to-end network model to minimize the mean square error between the output from the model and the label obtained by theoretical calculation. The task of supervised learning can be described as formula (8), where o_i represents the observed image at time i, and a_i represents the steering decision.

$$\text{minimize}_\theta \sum_i \ell(F(o_i; \theta), a_i) \tag{8}$$

The network model consists of 15 layers, including 5 blocks. The first 4 blocks are composed of a convolutional layer, a batch normalization layer and a pooling layer. The last block processes the output. The input of the network model is a one-channel picture composed of three 161×97 grayscale images. The convolution layer in the first block is composed of 32 convolution cores of 5×5, in which strip is 2 and padding is 1. In the second and third block, the convolution layer is composed of 64 convolution kernels with the size of 3×3, the stride of 1 and padding of 1. In the fourth and fifth block, the convolution layer is composed of 128 convolution kernels with the size of 3×3, the stride of 1 and padding of 1. During training, the loss function is the mean square error function, the optimization method is Adam optimizer [18], and the learning rate is set to 0.001.

3.4 On-road Test Platform

We use an Ackermann steering vehicle as the basic hardware to build an on-road test platform. The kinematic model of the vehicle is described in Sect. 3.2. The main computing resources on the vehicle adopts the EdgeBoard embedded development board provided by Baidu, which can directly transplant the network model trained for real-time reasoning. We use an Ardiuno microcomputer as the central control system to output steering for vehicle control.

4 Experiments

At a certain point on the reference path, its vertical section intersecting with the left and right lane are evenly divided 31 location points. Each location point is set with 31 camera orientations 0 to $\pm 15°$ in step of $1°$. Therefore, when the vehicle passes a certain point along the reference path, a simulation image captured. By disturbing the position and heading, a total of 961 (31×31) images can be obtained. For each image obtained, the corresponding steering is calculated by the method in Sect. 3.2, and the image and corresponding steering control signal constitute a pair of samples. The reference path consists of 1800 points from the start to the end. If two points are stepped each time, a total of 864,900 (900×961) samples can be collected. The total time required for data generation is about 74 min.

4.1 Simulation Test

In the simulation platform, the virtual camera collects the image in real time, and the image is reasoned by trained model to get the steering control signal. Under the effect of control period, speed and steering, the position of the vehicle next moment in the simulation environment is calculated. From the start position to the end position of the simulation environment, the comparison between the vehicle path in the simulation test and the reference path is obtained, as shown in Fig. 5.

4.2 On-road Test

Different from the simulation platform, the embedded EdgeBoard is used to reason of network model in the real vehicle. Although the development cost is reduced, the calculation accuracy and speed are also damaged. At the same time, the test in the real world will be affected by many external factors, such as the mechanical structure of the vehicle, the friction of the ground and so on. The sensor equipment used in the real vehicle platform is only a monocular camera, without positioning equipment, so it is impossible to record the accurate driving position of the vehicle in real time. Also

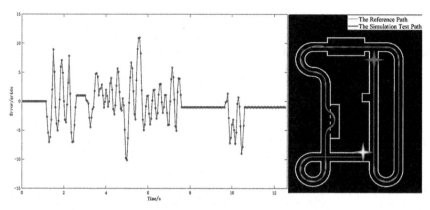

Fig. 5. The deviation and visualization results between simulation test route and reference path. The yellow star represents start and the blue star represents end.

considering that the vehicle is not required to always perform in the middle of the lane in the actual scene, the test criteria is the proportion of autonomous driving time (that is, total time excluding manual intervention time) during the whole driving time. In our on-road test, the manual intervention conditions used are the wheels pressing on the lane or driving out of the lane. In order to improve the generalization ability of the model to transplant to the real vehicle, we use the data augmentation in the training, and compare the effect of the model trained by the original data. A total of 10 tests were carried out, and the proportions of autonomous driving time were statistically analyzed, as shown in Table 1.

Table 1. The result of on-road test. The Interventions index represents the number of human interventions, and Time represents time in seconds from start to end, and Automatic proportion (%) represents the proportion of automatic driving time in the whole driving.

Method	No.	Interventions	Time	Automatic proportion
No augmentation	1	6	40	70.0
	2	5	39	74.36
	3	6	40	70.0
	4	6	40	70.0
	5	4	39	79.49
With augmentation	1	1	35	94.29
	2	1	36	94.4
	3	2	36	88.9
	4	0	33	100
	5	1	35	94.29

It can be seen that in the real environment, the captured images will be affected by noise and illumination and so on, while the simulation environment is the most ideal. Therefore, considering the data enhancement processing before training, the trained model will perform better in the real world.

5 Conclusion

In this paper, an automatic driving system based on end-to-end learning from simulation to reality is proposed. The system is mainly composed of simulation platform, network model training and on-road test platform. The simulation platform completes the data collection by calibrating the camera, environment and modeling vehicle, and can test the performance of model in the simulation environment; the end-to-end network model means that the steering can be directly inferred from the image collected by the monocular camera; the on-road test platform carries the trained model to make the vehicle run in the real environment, which shows the availability of the trained model with the dataset completely collected in the simulation platform, so as to verify the portability from simulation to reality. In conclusion, the automatic driving system has the following advantages:

- The images are collected in the simulation platform to ensure the completeness in different positions and orientations, without using real vehicle equipment and driver operation, which is convenient and efficient.
- In the simulation platform, the accurate steering control signal can be calculated in real time according to the vehicle kinematics model, so as to avoid the fuzzy operation of the driver or remote operator during the real vehicle labels collection.
- The end-to-end model is used to obtain the steering control signal directly from the RGB image captured by the camera, which simplifies the intermediate module of automatic driving, thus greatly reducing the hardware cost.
- The availability of porting to embedded computing unit is verified by using lightweight network model.

In the future work, embedded computing equipment and simple monocular camera can be configured on the logistics vehicle or transport vehicle, and the lightweight end-to-end network model can be carried out. The automatic driving system based on end-to-end learning from simulation to reality can reduce the manpower and development cost, which is of great significance for practical industrial application.

References

1. Scott, P., Hans, A., Xinxin, D., et al.: Perception, planning, control, and coordination for autonomous vehicles. Machines 5(1), 6 (2017)
2. Lei, T., Liu, M.: Deep-learning in mobile robotics - from perception to control systems: a survey on why and why not. J. Latex Class Files 14(8) (2016)
3. Pomerleau, D.A.: Alvinn: an autonomous land vehicle in a neural network. In: Advances in Neural Information Processing Systems 1, pp. 305–313, Colorado, USA (1988)

4. Jochem, T., Pomerleau, D.: Vision-based neural network road and intersection detection and traversal. In: IEEE Conference on Intelligent Robots and Systems (1995)
5. Lecun, Y., Muller, U., Ben, J., et al.: Off-road obstacle avoidance through end-to-end learning. In: International Conference on Neural Information Processing Systems, vol. 1, pp. 305–313 (2005)
6. Bojarski, M., Del Testa, D., Dworakowski, D., et al.: End to end learning for self-driving cars. Preprint at https://arxiv.org/abs/1604.07316 (2016)
7. Bojarski, M., Yeres, P., Choromanska, A., et al.: Explaining how a deep neural network trained with end-to-end learning steers a car. arXiv:1704.07911 (2017)
8. Xu, H., Gao, Y., Yu, F., Darrell, T.: End-to-end learning of driving models from large-scale video datasets. In: Proceedings of IEEE Conference on Computer Vision and Pattern Recognition (2017)
9. Yang, Z., Zhang, Y., Yu, J., et al.: End-to-end multi-modal multi-task vehicle control for self-driving cars with visual perceptions (2018)
10. Kocic, J., Jovicic, N., Drndarevic, V.: An end-to-end deep neural network for autonomous driving designed for embedded automotive platforms. Sensors (2019). https://doi.org/10.3390/s19092064
11. Pfeiffer, M., Schaeuble, M., Nieto, J., et al.: From perception to decision: a data-driven approach to end-to-end motion planning for autonomous ground robots. In: IEEE International Conference on Robotics and Automation (2017)
12. Patel, N., Choromanska, A., Krishnamurthy, P., et al.: Sensor modality fusion with CNNs for UGV autonomous driving in indoor environments. In: IEEE/RSJ International Conference on Intelligent Robots and Systems (2017)
13. Sallab, A., Abdou, M., Perot, E., et al.: Deep reinforcement learning framework for autonomous driving. Electron. Imaging 19, 70–76 (2017)
14. Codevilla, F., Müller, M., López, A., et al.: End-to-end driving via conditional imitation learning, pp. 1–9 (2018)
15. Dosovitskiy, A., Ros, G., Codevilla, F., et al.: CARLA: an open urban driving simulator. In: Conference on Robot Learning (CoRL), Mountain View, California, pp. 1–16 (2017)
16. Chen, C., Seff, A., Kornhauser, A., et al.: DeepDriving: learning affordance for direct perception in autonomous driving. In: International Conference on Computer Vision (ICCV) (2015)
17. Zhang, Z.: A flexible new technique for camera calibration. IEEE Trans. Pattern Anal. Mach. Intell. 22(11), 1330–1334 (2000)
18. Kingma, D., Ba, J.: Adam: a method for stochastic optimization. arXiv preprint arXiv:1412.6980 (2014)

Underwater SLAM Based on Forward-Looking Sonar

Chensheng Cheng, Can Wang, Dianyu Yang, Weidong Liu,
and Feihu Zhang$^{(\boxtimes)}$

Northwestern Polytechnical University, Xi'an, China
wangcan2017@mail.nwpu.edu.cn, {liuwd,feihu.zhang}@nwpu.edu.cn

Abstract. This paper presents a Simultaneous Localization And Mapping (SLAM) algorithm in the underwater environment. In this paper, forward-looking sonar is used to extract environmental features to establish a 2D grid map. The SLAM algorithm estimates the AUV's (Autonomous Underwater Vehicle) pose by fusing multi-sensor data, including IMU data and the DVL data. To verify the algorithm, we simulated the experimental environment using the UUV-Simulator software. The results show that the algorithm can effectively suppress divergence and accurately locate the AUV.

Keywords: Forward-looking sonar · SLAM · Grid map · UUV-Simulator

1 Introduction

AUV plays an essential role in the underwater environment. The most important thing is that it can automate complex tasks independently without any control. To achieve the autonomy issue, the first thing to solve is its navigation capability. For accurate navigation, accurate positioning and map information is needed. Therefore, the simultaneous positioning and map construction of AUV capabilities are particularly important. However, the underwater environment has more complexity and unpredictability than the terrestrial environment. Some general-purpose sensors, such as GPS positioning modules, vision sensors, and lidar, often cannot achieve satisfactory results underwater. Therefore, it is incredibly essential to use sonar to effectively extract underwater features in unknown underwater environments.

So far, there are many kinds of researches on underwater SLAM using sonar, and they have been successfully applied to the field of AUV [1–4]. David Rabis et al. described a system for underwater navigation with AUVs in partially structured environments, such as dams, ports, or marine platforms and test the SLAM algorithm with the Ictineu AUV equipping with an MSIS [3,5]. Angelos Mallios et al. proposed a pose-based algorithm to solve the full SLAM problem for an AUV, navigating in an unknown and possibly unstructured environment [6]. Konstantinos Siantidis described a SLAM system suitable for an AUV equipped

© Springer Nature Singapore Pte Ltd. 2021
F. Sun et al. (Eds.): ICCSIP 2020, CCIS 1397, pp. 584–593, 2021.
https://doi.org/10.1007/978-981-16-2336-3_55

with a dead reckoning system and a side-scan sonar (SSS). The system was developed to compensate for position drifts of an AUV navigation system during a mission [7]. Qiang Zhang et al. presented a SLAM algorithm towards a structured underwater environment using Mechanical Scanning Imaging Sonar (MSIS). An adaptive Hough transform integrating with the method of Random Sampling Consensus (RANSAC) is used to extract the line feature of sonar scanning data and build the geometric feature map in this paper [8]. Sharmin Rahman et al. used a combination of sonar and visual sensors to complete underwater reconstruction, and experiments on underwater wrecks, underwater caves, and buses submerged in water prove their effectiveness method [9].

These articles have given the results of using sonar for localization, but could not establish two-dimensional grid maps that can be used for path planning. This paper establishes an two-dimensional grid map and analyzes the positioning accuracy, proving that it can well correct the deviation originated from the odometer.

Section 2 introduces the algorithm used in this article. Section 3 describes the construction of the experimental environment. The experimental results are shown in Sect. 4. Section 5 presents the conclusions.

2 SLAM Algorithm Based on Particle Filter

The SLAM algorithm we used in this paper is based on the RBPF particle filter, that is, the positioning and mapping processes are separated, the positioning is performed before the mapping. The SLAM algorithm then made two significant improvements to the RBPF algorithm: improved proposal distribution and adaptive resampling [10].

The key idea of the RBPF particle filter for SLAM is to estimate the joint posterior $p(x_{1:t}, m|z_{1:t}, u_{1:t-1})$ and AUV trajectory $x_{1:t} = x_1, ..., x_t$ on the map m. Observation $z_{1:t} = z_1, ..., z_t$ and odometer measurement $u_{1:t-1} = u_1, ..., u_{t-1}$ are known data obtained from the measurement. The RBPF particle filter for SLAM can be broken down into the following representations:

$$p(x_{1:t}, m|z_{1:t}, u_{1:t-1}) = p(m|x_{1:t}, z_{1:t}) \cdot p(x_{1:t}|z_{1:t}, u_{1:t-1}) \qquad (1)$$

This decomposition allows us to estimate only the AUV's trajectory and then calculate the map based on the given trajectory. Since the map depends heavily on the AUV's pose estimation, this method can provide efficient calculations. This technique is commonly referred to as Rao-Blackwellization.

In general, Eq. (1) can use the "known pose mapping" to analytically calculate the map posterior probability $p(m|x_{1:t}, z_{1:t})$, and $x_{1:t}$ and $z_{1:t}$ are known so that this equation can be calculated efficiently.

To estimate the posterior $p(x_{1:t}|z_{1:t}, u_{1:t-1})$ on the potential trajectory, a particle filter can be applied. Each particle represents the potential trajectory of the AUV. These maps are also built from observations and the corresponding particles' trajectories, so each map is associated with each sample.

Sample-based Importance Resampling (SIR) filters are one of the most common particle filtering algorithms. RaoBlackwellized SIR filters are used for incremental mapping to process sensor observations and odometer readings, if available. It updates the sample set representing map posteriors and AUV trajectories. This process can be summarized in the following four steps:

- Sampling: The next generation particle $\left\{x_t^{(i)}\right\}$ is obtained from $\left\{x_{t-1}^{(i)}\right\}$ by sampling from the proposed distribution π. Usually, a probabilistic odometer motion model is used as the proposed distribution.
- Importance weighting: each particle is assigned a separate importance weighting based on the importance sampling principle $w_t^{(i)}$.

$$w_t^{(i)} = \frac{p(x_{1:t}^{(i)}, m|z_{1:t}, u_{1:t-1})}{\pi(x_{1:t}^{(i)}, m|z_{1:t}, u_{1:t-1})} \tag{2}$$

The weights explain that the proposed distribution π is usually not equal to the subsequent target distribution.
- Resampling: The particles are replaced in proportion to their importance weight when drawing. This step is necessary because only a limited number of particles are used to approximate the continuous distribution. Resampling allows us to apply particle filters when the target distribution is different from the proposed distribution. After resampling, all particles have the same weight.
- Map estimation: For each particle, the corresponding map estimation $p(m^{(i)}|x_{1:t}^{(i)}, z_{1:t})$ is calculated based on the sample's trajectory $x_{1:t}^{(i)}$ and observation history $z_{1:t}$.

As the length of the trajectory increases over time and the implementation of this architecture requires the trajectory's weight to be evaluated from zero when there are new observations, this process will significantly reduce algorithm efficiency. According to the research of Doucet et al., We can obtain the recursive formula by limiting proposal π, and then calculate the importance of weight.

$$\pi(x_{1:t}|z_{1:t}, u_{1:t-1}) = \pi(x_t|x_{1:t-1}, z_{1:t}, u_{1:t-1}) \\ \cdot \pi(x_{1:t-1}|z_{1:t-1}, u_{1:t-2}) \tag{3}$$

Based on the Eq. (2) and (3), the weight calculation formula is as follows:

$$w_t^{(i)} = \frac{p(x_{1:t}^{(i)}, m|z_{1:t}, u_{1:t-1})}{\pi(x_{1:t}^{(i)}, m|z_{1:t}, u_{1:t-1})} \tag{4}$$

$$= \frac{\eta p(z_t|x_{1:t}^{(i)}, z_{1:t-1})p(x_t^{(i)}|x_{t-1}^{(i)}, u_{t-1})}{\pi(x_t^{(i)}|x_{1:t-1}^{(i)}, z_{1:t}, u_{1:t-1})} \cdot \\ \underbrace{\frac{p(x_{1:t-1}^{(i)}|z_{1:t-1}, u_{1:t-2})}{\pi(x_{1:t-1}^{(i)}|z_{1:t-1}, u_{1:t-2})}}_{w_{t-1}^{(i)}} \tag{5}$$

$$\propto \frac{p(z_t|m_{t-1}^{(i)}, x_t^{(i)})p(x_t^{(i)}|x_{t-1}^{(i)}, u_{t-1})}{\pi(x_t|x_{1:t-1}^{(i)}, z_{1:t}, u_{1:t-1})} \cdot w_{t-1}^{(i)} \qquad (6)$$

Here, $\eta = 1/p(z_t|z_{1:t-1}, u_{1:t-1})$ is the normalization factor produced by Bayes' rule where all particles are equal.

Existing particle filtering applications mostly rely on the recursive structure of the Eq. (6). Although the general algorithm specifies a framework that can be used to learn maps, it is still open to how to calculate the proposed distribution and when to perform the resampling step.

3   The Construction of the Experimental Environment

The UUV-Simulator model library was originally developed for the EU ECSEL project 662107SWARMs. After the end of the project, the model library was converted to open source for the majority of UUV enthusiasts to use for secondary programming. Users can pull the model library on https://github.com/uuvsimulator. The model library is only applicable to the Linux development environment. The models of UUV-Simulator are built on the Gazebo platform of the ROS system, including UUV entity models, underwater environment models, UUV sensor models, et al.

3.1   Underwater Environment

UUV-Simulator provides a variety of underwater environments for developers to use, including ideal underwater flat environment, underwater sandy environment, lake environment (as shown in Fig. 1 and Fig. 2). We can also build mazes, mountains, and other underwater environments by itself. Under the environment, it can simulate the field lake environment for experiments.

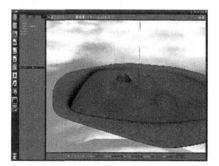

Fig. 1. Underwater sand environment   **Fig. 2.** Lake environment

3.2   Sonar Model

UUV-Simulator provides many optional sensor plug-ins for the Rexrov2 model. For underwater obstacle avoidance tasks, the most critical sensor is the sonar. We use the Rexrov2 model equipped with analog sonar to perceive environmental information and perform SLAM experiments.

The model simulation sonar is modified based on the ROS lidar plug-in. In this article, it is set to single-line scanning. When the obstacle information in the Z-axis direction needs to be scanned, it can be set to multi-line scanning. In the simulation test, Rexrov2 is equipped with a simulation sonar on the front, which can feedback the distance and angle information of surrounding obstacles in time.

3.3   Underwater Vehicle Model

UUV-Simulator contains a series of different types of UUV solid models. In the experiments, we used the Rexrov2 model, which is a full-propeller-driven UUV, and it is equipped with four cameras, four lights, and a wide range of sensors, including sonar, doppler, altimeter, etc. The real model is 2.5 m in length, 1.5 m in width, 1.6 m in height, and 1850 kg in weight.

The difference between ROV and AUV is that ROV needs to provide power source and control commands through cables, so there is no need to consider too much about the experimental carrier's shape. In this paper, Rexrov2 is used as the experimental simulation model, as shown in Fig. 3. The reason is that compared with the cylindrical shape of the traditional AUV, its four-degree-of-freedom motion stability is higher, the possibility of rolling and pitching is low, the ability to resist interference from ocean currents is strong, and it is easy to control in the simulation environment to achieve better SLAM effect.

4   SLAM Simulation Experiment

Based on the above experiment, we continue to carry out the simulation experiment of autonomous underwater vehicle SLAM. In order to better verify the performance of SLAM in complex environments, a 50×50 m underwater maze was built in the underwater environment, and some features were placed on the walls to verify the effect of SLAM.

First, use Blender to build a topographic map, as shown in Fig. 4. Then export the established environment graph model, and use the launch file to load it into the Gazebo, and at the same time import the underwater ROV model. The water layer environment has been established in UUV-Simulator, and the force of water flow has also been added. The final underwater environment in the Gazebo is shown in Fig. 5.

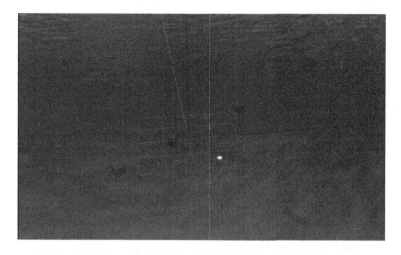

Fig. 3. ROV model in simulation environment.

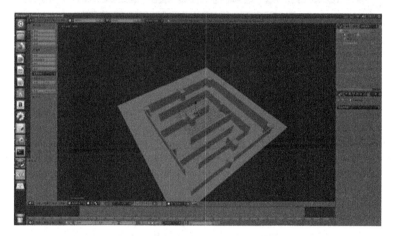

Fig. 4. Environmental model of underwater topographic Map.

The darker layer in the picture is the water layer. Set the ROV to be 2m underwater for depth movement. In the picture, Revrov2 will be operated to scan the entire environment, and a grid map that can be used for path planning will be obtained finally. In the experiment, the scanning angle of the sonar is set from −45° to 45°.

Now that the simulation environment has all the conditions for SLAM. First, we launch SLAM algorithm to start to build a map. The mapping effect of the initial position is shown in Fig. 6. In the algorithm, the mapping range is set to 10 m. The grid map will be filled when the distance between the Rexrov2 and the obstacle is less than or equal to 10 m to determine whether this area is feasible. When the distance exceeds 10 m, the area between Rexrov2 and the obstacle is considered undetected.

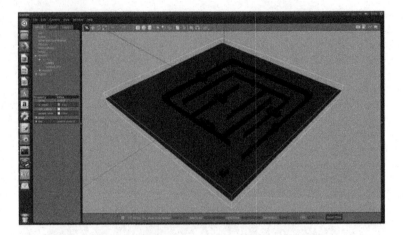

Fig. 5. Final experimental environment and ROV model.

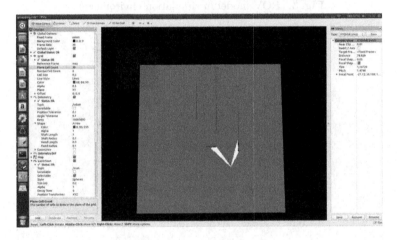

Fig. 6. Map of initial location.

After the ROV scans the entire scene, a complete grid map that can be used for path planning can be established. The effect is shown in Fig. 7.

Figure 7 is a map created after Rexrov2 scanned the environment once. The blue line in the figure represents the odometer's trajectory. The black part represents the obstacle-free and non-driving area, the white part represents the barrier-free driving area, and the gray part represents the undetected area. Based on this information, AUV can make path planning to avoid obstacles and reach the designated position. It can be seen that there are some undetected areas on the path of the Rexrov2. The simulated sonar did not scan some places too close to itself, and it is also affected by the map update frequency, resulting in these undetected areas. Control the Rexrov2 to scan the map for the second time, and we will find that all these undetected areas have become navigable areas.

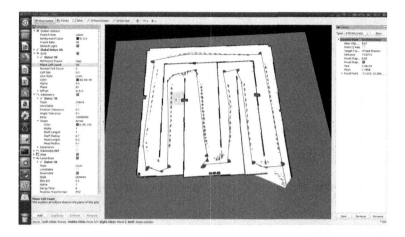

Fig. 7. Two-dimensional grid map of scanning environment once.

The effect is shown in Fig. 8. The comparison between the ROV position calculated by the SLAM algorithm and the real position is shown in Fig. 9 and Fig. 10. The error between the two is tiny, which proves the accuracy of our method.

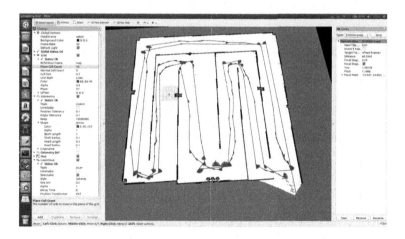

Fig. 8. Two-dimensional grid map of scanning environment twice.

The above experimental results show that under high sensor accuracy and stable data, multiple repeated data collection of the environment will better mapping effects.

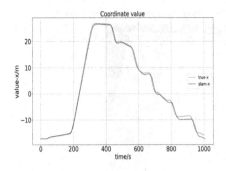
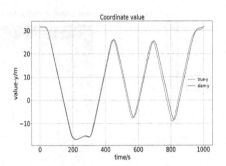

Fig. 9. Coordinate curve of x   **Fig. 10.** Coordinate curve of y

5   Conclusions

This paper proposes an underwater SLAM algorithm based on forward-looking sonar. Simultaneously, we build an ROV model and simulation environment based on the ROS operating system and UUV-Simulator underwater simulation platform. Then, we completed the underwater SLAM experimental verification, detailed analysis of the experimental results, verified the feasibility of the particle filter-based SLAM algorithm in the underwater environment, and provided theoretical support for future actual underwater SLAM experiments.

Acknowledgment. This work was supported by the National Natural Science Foundation of China (NSFC) under Grants 61703335.

References

1. Burguera, A., Cid, Y., Oliver, G.: Underwater SLAM with robocentric trajectory using a mechanically scanned imaging sonar. In: 2011 IEEE/RSJ International Conference on Intelligent Robots and Systems vol. 10, no. 1, pp. 3577–3582 (2011)
2. Burguera, A., González, Y., Oliver, G.: A probabilistic framework for sonar scan matching localization. Adv. Robot. **22**(11), 19 (2008)
3. Ribas, D., Ridao, P.: Underwater SLAM in man-made structured environments. J. Field Robot. **25**(11–12), 898–921 (2010)
4. Wu, M., Yao, J.: Adaptive UKF-SLAM based on magnetic gradient inversion method for underwater navigation. In: Liu, H., Kubota, N., Zhu, X., Dillmann, R., Zhou, D. (eds.) ICIRA 2015. LNCS (LNAI), vol. 9245, pp. 237–247. Springer, Cham (2015). https://doi.org/10.1007/978-3-319-22876-1_21
5. Ribas, D., Ridao, P., Neira, J.: Underwater SLAM for Structured Environments Using an Imaging Sonar. Springer, Heidelberg (2010). https://doi.org/10.1007/978-3-642-14040-2
6. Mallios, A., Ridao, P., Ribas, D., et al.: Probabilistic sonar scan matching SLAM for underwater environment. In: OCEANS 2010 IEEE - Sydney. IEEE (2010)
7. Siantidis, K.: Side scan sonar based onboard SLAM system for autonomous underwater vehicles. In: IEEE/OES Autonomous Underwater Vehicles, pp. 195–200 (2016)

8. Zhang, Q., Niu, B., Zhang, W., Li, Y.: Feature-based UKF-SLAM using imaging sonar in underwater structured environment. In: 2018 IEEE 8th International Conference on Underwater System Technology: Theory and Applications (USYS), Wuhan, China, pp. 1–5 (2018)
9. Rahman, S., Li, A.Q., Rekleitis, I.: Sonar visual inertial SLAM of underwater structures. In: 2018 IEEE International Conference on Robotics and Automation (ICRA), Brisbane, QLD, pp. 5190–5196 (2018)
10. Grisetti, G., Stachniss, C., Burgard, W.: Improved techniques for grid mapping with Rao-Blackwellized particle filters. IEEE Trans. Robot. **23**(1), 34–46 (2007)
11. Dellaert, F., Fox, D., Burgard, W., et al.: Monte Carlo localization for mobile robots. In: Proceedings of the 1999 IEEE International Conference on Robotics and Automation. IEEE (1999)
12. Montemarlo, M.: FastSLAM : a factored solution to the simultaneous localization and mapping problem. In: Proceedings of the AAAI National Conference on Artificial Intelligence, Edmonton, Canada, 2002. American Association for Artificial Intelligence (2002)
13. Kuang, C., Chen, W., Jie, G.U., et al.: FastSLAM 2.0: an improved particle filtering algorithm for simultaneous localization and mapping that provably converges. In: Proceedings of the International Conference on Artificial Intelligence, vol. 133, no. 1, pp. 1151–1156 (2003)
14. Liu, J.S.: Metropolized independent sampling with comparisons to rejection sampling and importance sampling. Stat. Comput. **6**(2), 113–119 (1996)
15. Doucet, A., de Freitas, N., Gordan, N. (eds.): Sequential Monte-Carlo Methods in Practice. Springer, New York (2001). https://doi.org/10.1007/978-1-4757-3437-9

Robust Visual Odometry Using Semantic Information in Complex Dynamic Scenes

Hao Wang[1,2], Le Wang[1,2], and Baofu Fang[1,2(✉)]

[1] Key Laboratory of Knowledge Engineering with Big Data, Ministry of Education,
Hefei University of Technology, Hefei 230009, Anhui, China
fangbf@hfut.edu.cn
[2] Department of Computer Science and Technology,
Hefei University of Technology, Hefei 230009, Anhui, China

Abstract. Traditional vision-based simultaneous localization and mapping (SLAM) technology cannot obtain the semantic information of the surrounding environment, which will cause the robot to fail to complete intelligent grasping, human-computer interaction, and other advanced decision tasks. There are many challenges to solve this problem, such as obtaining less semantic information of the environment with low precision and being unable to deal with dynamic objects in a real environment quickly and effectively. In this paper, a robust visual odometry using semantic information in complex dynamic scenes was designed. Specifically, we present a refined instance segmentation method based on the contextual information of the frame to improve the accuracy of segmentation. On this basis, a feature detection and elimination algorithm for dynamic objects based on instance-level semantic information is proposed to improve the localization accuracy of camera pose. We extensively evaluate our system on the public TUM data set and compare it with ORB-SLAM2 and other methods. Experiments show that our methods greatly improve the localization accuracy of the camera pose and the robustness of the system, which verifies that our system is effective in complex dynamic scenes.

Keywords: Visual odometry · Simultaneous localization and mapping · Dynamic scene · Semantic information

1 Introduction

The SLAM was first proposed in the field of robotics, mainly used to solve the problem of the localization and mapping of robot in unknown environments [1]. According to different types of sensors, SLAM can be divided into two methods: laser-based and visual-based. With the continuous reduction of cameras cost, visual SLAM (vSLAM) has become a current research hotspot [2]. The vSLAM framework generally consists of five parts: reading sensor data, visual odometry (VO), optimization, loop closing, and mapping.

Klein et al. [3] present the PTAM in 2007. This system established parallel threads for tracking and mapping, and introduced back-end nonlinear optimization method, which

© Springer Nature Singapore Pte Ltd. 2021
F. Sun et al. (Eds.): ICCSIP 2020, CCIS 1397, pp. 594–601, 2021.
https://doi.org/10.1007/978-981-16-2336-3_56

was of great significance. Based on PTAM, Artal et al. [4, 5] proposed ORB-SLAM and ORB-SLAM2 in 2015 and 2017. In the front-end and back-end of the system, ORB feature points [6] were used for matching, which had achieved good results in processing speed and map accuracy. However, these methods either cannot obtain the semantic information in the environment, or assume that the scene is static [7, 8]. This will not only reduce the accuracy of the pose estimation but also cannot provide the basis for the robot to perform advanced tasks. Recently, researchers have proposed to combine deep learning technology to detect dynamic objects. Yu et al. [9] combined results of SegNet and the optical flow to eliminate dynamic objects. Xiao et al. [10] proposed an SSD object detector to detect dynamic objects at semantic level. These detection methods have low accuracy and poor time performance.

In this paper, we propose a robust visual odometry using semantic information in complex dynamic scenes. The main contributions of our work are summarized as follows:

- A robust visual odometry using semantic information was proposed, which can work well in highly complex dynamic environments.
- A refined instance segmentation method based on the contextual information of frame was introduced to improve the accuracy of segmentation.
- A feature detection and elimination algorithm for dynamic objects based on instance-level semantic information was designed to improve the localization accuracy of camera pose. This will enhance the robustness of the system.

The rest chapters are as follows. Section 2 describes the details of our works. Section 3 designs extensive experiments. We conclude the paper in Sect. 4.

2   Our Works

Our work is built on ORB-SLAM2. Based on the original thread, we modified the tracking thread and added an instance segmentation thread. In the thread of instance segmentation, the images of two adjacent frames collected by the camera have a great similarity. Therefore, the segmentation results of the previous frame can be used to refine the results of the current frame, and then the accuracy of overall segmentation can be improved. The refined segmentation results can not only reduce the interference of features extracted from dynamic objects, but also can be used to build instance-level semantic maps. Figure 1 shows the data flow between threads.

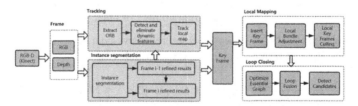

Fig. 1. Data flow of work between threads.

2.1 A Refined Instance Segmentation Method

Aiming to obtain the instance-level semantic information of objects, so we use the Mask R-CNN [11] network in the instance segmentation thread. Figure 2 shows the RGB images and the segmentation results of the Mask R-CNN network for two adjacent frames. (a) And (b) represent the original RGB image of the frame K-1 and K respectively, and (c) and (d) represent the segmentation results corresponding to the RGB images. As can be seen from (d) that the keyboard, mouse, book, and chair are missed in the frame K.

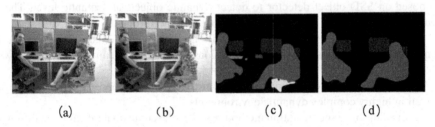

(a)   (b)   (c)   (d)

Fig. 2. RGB images and Mask R-CNN network segmentation results of two adjacent frames.

In view of the above problems, we propose a refined instance segmentation method based on the contextual information of frame. The refined instance segmentation results can be used to eliminate the features extracted from dynamic objects in the tracking thread to improve the localization accuracy of camera pose. In this paper, F is the frame, F^K is the RGB image of the K-th frame, and the $\mathbb{O}^K_{object}$ set denotes the instance segmentation result of the frame and the $\mathbb{B}^K_{j,bounding\_box}$ set denotes the corresponding object candidate bounding box. We can calculate the Euclidean distance D_{ij} between the centroid of the bounding box of object j in the frame F^{K-1} and the centroid of the bounding box of object i in the frame F^K. Then we use formula (1) to evaluate the contextual relevance of the two objects in the adjacent frames by calculating the IoU of the area of the $B^{K-1}_{j,bounding\_box}$ of object j in the frame F^{K-1} and the area of the $B^K_{i,bounding\_box}$ in the frame F^K. Where $A^K_{j,bounding\_box}$ represents the area of the bounding box $B^K_{j,bounding\_box}$.

$$IoU_{ij} = \frac{A^{K-1}_{j,bounding\_box} \cap A^K_{i,bounding\_box}}{A^{K-1}_{j,bounding\_box} \cup A^K_{i,bounding\_box}}, \left(0 \leq i \leq N^K, 0 \leq j \leq N^{K-1}\right) \quad (1)$$

In the above formula, N^K represent the total number of objects segmented in frame F^K. If the D_{ij} is less than $\frac{b^K_{i,w}+b^{K-1}_{i,w}}{2}$ then the comprehensive contextual relevance R_{ij} of the two objects in adjacent frames is calculated by formula (2).

$$R_{ij} = \varepsilon_{ij} * (\alpha * \frac{2D_{ij}}{b^K_{i,w} + b^{K-1}_{j,w}} + \beta * IoU_{ij}), \ (0 \leq i \leq N^K, \ 0 \leq j \leq N^{K-1}) \quad (2)$$

Where α and β are the corresponding weights; ε_{ij} is used to determine whether two objects in adjacent frames are of the same category. If it is the same, ε_{ij} is taken as 1, otherwise it is taken as 0. When R_{ij} is greater than the threshold θ_1, the two objects are regarded as the same object in the adjacent frame. Otherwise, when all objects in $\mathbb{O}_{object}^{K}$ are traversed and no object corresponding to the object $\mathbb{O}_{j,object}^{K-1}$ in $\mathbb{O}_{object}^{K-1}$ is found, the object $\mathbb{O}_{j,object}^{K-1}$ is added to the $\mathbb{O}_{object}^{K}$.

2.2 A Feature Detection and Elimination Algorithm for Dynamic Objects

Dynamic objects will cause the large error between the estimated camera motion. Therefore, before feature matching, we should eliminate the features extracted from dynamic objects to improve the accuracy of VO as much as possible.

To solve this problem, we propose a feature detection and elimination algorithm for dynamic objects based on instance-level semantic information. According to the prior knowledge, we divide 80 object classes that can be recognized by the Mask R-CNN network into three categories. The first is the set of active moving objects (such as people), which has a high possibility of movement. The second is the set of highly passive moving objects (such as books), whose movement possibility is determined by the active moving objects. The third is the set of low passives moving objects (such as sofas, dining tables), which has a low probability of movement.

In Fig. 3(a), if there is no active moving object in the segmentation results, all features extracted are considered static. In Fig. 3(b), if the bounding box of the people does not intersect with the bounding box of a non-active moving object, only the features extracted from the people are regarded as dynamic. In Fig. 3(c), if the result $R_{ij\_inter\_ratio}^{K}$ calculated by formula (3) between the active moving object $O_{i,object}^{K}$ and the non-active moving object $O_{j,object}^{K}(j \neq i)$ is greater than the threshold θ_2, the average pixel depth difference $D_{ij\_ave\_depth}^{K}$ of the two objects in the Depth image is calculated. If $\left| D_{ij\_ave\_depth}^{K} \right|$ is less than the threshold θ_3, and the result $D_{j,dynamic\_object}^{K}$ calculated by formula (4) is greater than the threshold θ_4, then the features extracted in the non-active moving object are also considered dynamic. In the formula (4), the $P_{i,object}^{K}$ is the motion probability score function for each object.

$$R_{ij\_inter\_ratio}^{K} = \frac{A_{i,bounding\_box}^{K} \cap A_{j,bounding\_box}^{K}}{A_{j,bounding\_box}^{K}}, \left(0 \leq i,j \leq N^K \text{ and } i \neq j \right) \quad (3)$$

$$D_{j,dynamic\_object}^{K} = P_{j,object}^{K} \left(R_{ij\_inter\_ratio}^{K} + \left| D_{ij\_ave\_depth}^{K} \right| \right), \left(0 \leq i,j \leq N^K \text{ and } i \neq j \right) \quad (4)$$

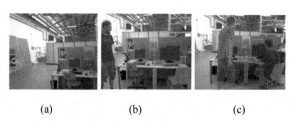

(a)   (b)   (c)

Fig. 3. Examples of judging dynamic and static features.

3   Experiments and Results

The TUM RGB-D data set [12] is the sequence images of 39 different indoor scenes collected by Microsoft Kinect sensors. It contains static, dynamic, and dynamic-static combined scenes sequences. The metrics of the data set mainly includes two types: The Relative Pose Error (RPE) and the Absolute Trajectory Error (ATE). In the TUM RGB-D data set, the dynamic scenes mainly include two series of "walking" and "sitting". The algorithm proposed in this paper is tested on an AMD 2990wx processor, 32 GB RAM, and GeForce RTX 2080Ti GPU.

3.1   The Results of the Refined Instance Segmentation

Figure 4 shows the experimental results of the method on some frames in the sequence "fr3_sitting_static". The sub-figures from top row to bottom row are the original RGB images, the initial segmentation of Mask R-CNN, and the refined segmentation of Mask R-CNN respectively. As we can see, our method improves the accuracy of segmentation to a certain extent. For example, in frame 7, we refined the missing keyboard (dark yellow) and chairs (bright yellow) of Mask R-CNN.

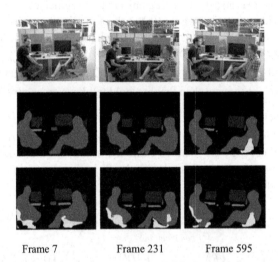

Frame 7   Frame 231   Frame 595

Fig. 4. Experimental results of some frames in the "fr3_sitting_static" sequence.

3.2   Evaluation Results of VO in Dynamic Scenes

From the results in Table 1, our system greatly reduces the translation and rotation drift of the VO of ORB-SLAM2 in a dynamic environment. Among them, the reduction results are most obvious in the highly complex dynamic environment "walking". According to the experimental results, two conclusions can be drawn: one is that ORB-SLAM2 is suitable for static and low dynamic environments, and its robustness is poor in highly complex dynamic environments; the other is that the algorithm proposed in this paper is effective in dynamic environment, which can detect and eliminate the features in dynamic objects, and solve the problem of poor accuracy of VO of ORB-SLAM2 in dynamic scenes.

Table 1. Comparisons of translation drift of ORB-SLAM2 and ours (RPE, unit m/s).

Sequences	ORB-SLAM2		Ours		Improvements	
	RMSE	S.D.	RMSE	S.D.	RMSE	S.D.
fr3_walking_static	0.2015	0.1823	**0.0099**	**0.0050**	**95.09%**	**97.26%**
fr3_walking_half	0.3418	0.2712	**0.0272**	**0.0133**	**92.04%**	**95.10%**
fr3_sitting_static	0.0091	0.0043	**0.0074**	**0.0035**	**18.68%**	**18.60%**
fr3_sitting_half	0.0315	0.0232	**0.0189**	**0.0089**	**40.00%**	**61.64%**

Table 2 shows the comparison results between ours and other systems in dynamic scenes. Yu et al. [9] designed an algorithm using a combination of optical flow method and SegNet network. Sun et al. [13] proposed a dynamic region judgment algorithm based on the difference of images. Li et al. [14] introduced an algorithm to reduce the impact of dynamic objects by weighting the edge points of key frames. From Table 2, it can be seen that our algorithm is mostly better than other algorithms in different dynamic environment scenes.

Table 2. Comparisons of RMSE of RPE between ours and other algorithms.

Sequences	Translation drift in m/s				Rotation drift in °/s			
	Yu [9]	Sun [13]	Li [14]	Ours	Yu [9]	Sun [13]	Li [14]	Ours
fr3_walking_static	0.0102	0.0842	0.0327	**0.0099**	0.2690	2.0487	0.8085	**0.2601**
fr3_walking_half	0.0297	0.1672	0.0527	**0.0272**	0.8142	5.0108	2.4048	**0.7658**
fr3_sitting_static	0.0078	–	0.0231	**0.0074**	0.2735	–	0.7228	**0.2718**
fr3_sitting_half	–	0.0458	0.0389	**0.0189**	–	2.3748	1.8836	**0.6398**

3.3 Overall Performance Evaluation of System

From Table 3, we can see that our system has improved a lot of performance compared with ORB-SLAM2 in dynamic scenes. Figures 5 and 6 show the results of comparisons between the estimated and real values of the trajectory. From the results, it can be seen our system can track the camera's trajectory well than ORB-SLAM2. The experimental data in Table 4 shows the analysis and comparison of ate between our system and other SLAM systems in dynamic environment, from which we can see that the system proposed in this paper has better performance than other systems.

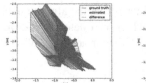 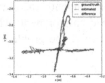

Fig. 5. Estimated trajectories on fr3_walking_xyz: ORB-SLAM2 (left) and ours (right).

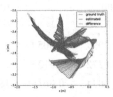 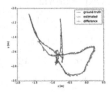

Fig. 6. Estimated trajectories on fr3_walking_halfsphere: ORB-SLAM2 (left) and ours (right).

Table 3. Comparisons of ATE of ORB-SLAM2 and ours (ATE, unit m/s).

Sequences	ORB-SLAM2		Ours		Improvements	
	RMSE	S.D.	RMSE	S.D.	RMSE	S.D.
fr3_walking_static	0.3575	0.1490	**0.0078**	**0.0034**	**97.82%**	**97.72%**
fr3_walking_half	0.5186	0.2424	**0.0277**	**0.0141**	**94.66%**	**94.18%**
fr3_sitting_static	0.0082	0.0039	**0.0062**	**0.0030**	**24.39%**	**23.08%**
fr3_sitting_half	0.0452	0.0180	**0.0159**	**0.0074**	**64.82%**	**58.89%**

Table 4. Comparisons of RMSE of ATE between ours and other systems (unit m).

Sequences	Yu [9]	Sun [13]	Li [14]	Ours
fr3_walking_static	0.0081	0.0656	0.0261	**0.0079**
fr3_walking_half	0.0303	0.1252	0.0489	**0.0277**
fr3_sitting_static	0.0065	–	–	**0.0062**
fr3_sitting_half	–	0.0470	0.0432	**0.0159**

4   Conclusion

In this article, a robust visual odometry using semantic information in complex dynamic scenes is proposed. Aiming at the problem that the accuracy of segmentation is not high, a refined instance segmentation method is presented. In view of the poor localization accuracy of camera pose in dynamic scenes, a feature detection and elimination algorithm for dynamic objects is proposed, which greatly improves the localization accuracy of camera pose. We have carried out many experimental evaluations, and most of results indicate that our system outperforms ORB-SLAM2 and other systems. In the future, we will design a complete semantic SLAM system, including building instance level semantic map without dynamic objects.

Acknowledgments. The author(s) disclosed receipt of the following financial this article: This work was supported by National Natural Science Foundation of China (No.61872327), Fundamental Research Funds for Central Universities (No. ACAIM190102), Natural Science Foundation of Anhui Province (No. 1708085MF146), the Project of Collaborative Innovation in Anhui Colleges and Universities (Grant No.GXXT-2019-003), the Open Fund of Key Laboratory of Flight Techniques and Flight Safety, (Grant No.2018KF06), Scientific Research Project of Civil Aviation Flight University of China (Grant No.J2020-125) and Open Fund of Key Laboratory of Flight Techniques and Flight Safety, CAAC (Grant No. FZ2020KF02).

References

1. Garcia-Fidalgo, E., Ortiz, A.: Vision-based topological mapping and localization methods: a survey. Robot. Auton. Syst. **64**, 1–20 (2014)
2. Fuentes-Pacheco, J., Ascencio, J., Rendon-Mancha, J.: Visual simultaneous localization and mapping: a survey. Artif. Intell. Rev. **43**, 55–81 (2015)
3. Klein, G., Murray, D.: Parallel tracking and mapping for small AR workspaces. In: ISMAR, IEEE, pp. 225–234, January, 2007
4. Mur-Artal, R., Tardos, J.: Orb-slam2: an open-source slam system for monocular, stereo and RGB-D cameras. IEEE Trans. Robot. **33**, 1255–1262, October, 2016
5. Mur-Artal, R., Montiel, J., Tardos, J.: ORB-SLAM: a versatile and accurate monocular slam system. IEEE Trans. Robot. **31**, 1147–1163, October, 2015
6. Rublee, E., Rabaud, V., Konolige, K., et al.: ORB: an efficient alternative to SIFT or SURF. In: International Conference on Computer Vision, IEEE (2012)
7. Cadena, C., Carlone, L., et al.: Simultaneous localization and mapping: present, future, and the robust-perception age. IEEE Trans. Robot. **32**(6), 1309–1332 (2016)
8. Younes, G., Asmar, D., Shammas, E.: A survey on non-filter-based monocular visual slam systems. Robot. Auton. Syst. **98**, 67–88 (2016)
9. Yu, C., et al.: DS-SLAM: a semantic visual slam towards dynamic environments, pp. 1168–1174, October, 2018
10. Xiao, L., Wang, J., Qiu, X., Rong, Z., Zou, X.: Dynamic-SLAM: semantic monocular visual localization and mapping based on deep learning in dynamic environment. Robot. Auton. Syst. **117**, 1–16 (2019)
11. He, K., Gkioxari, G., Dollar, P., Girshick, R.: Mask R-CNN. IEEE Trans. Pattern Anal. Mach. Intell. **42**, 386–397, June, 2018
12. Sturm, J., Engelhard, N., et al.: A benchmark for the evaluation of RGB-D SLAM systems. In: 2012 IEEE/RSJ International Conference on Intelligent Robots and Systems, IEEE (2012)
13. Sun, Y., Liu, M., Meng, M.: Improving RGB-D slam in dynamic environments: a motion removal approach. Robot. Auton. Syst. **89**, 110–122 (2016)
14. Li, S., Lee, D.: RGB-D SLAM in dynamic environments using static point weighting. IEEE Robot. Autom. Lett. **2**, 2263–2270, July, 2017

A Multi-sensor Data Fusion Method Based on Improved XGBoost Model for AGV Localization

Honglei Che[1], Gang Wang[2(✉)], and Congling Shi[1]

[1] Beijing Key Laboratory of Metro Fire and Passenger Transportation Safety, China Academy of Safety Science and Technology, Beijing 100012, China
[2] School of Automation, Beijing University of Posts and Telecommunications, Beijing 100876, China

Abstract. High-precision positioning technology is one of the key technologies for automated guided vehicle (AGV). This paper presents a positioning system based on multi-sensor data fusion using improved XGBoost model. Specially, the quartile based amplitude change limited sliding filtering algorithm is designed to preprocess the data collected by each time-varying sensor. The processed sensor data is facilitated for XGBoost model training. The loss function and the evaluation function are tailored for XGBoost in order to make the model applicable to the positioning system. The simulation results show our algorithm can achieve the average positioning accuracy of 4.8 mm for a 5-fold cross-validation and also achieve 5.2 mm positioning accuracy on the independent testing set. To further verify the positioning accuracy of the proposed model, comparison results are conducted with the conventional Kalman method and XGBoost model without the filtering.

Keywords: Multi-sensor data fusion · AGV positioning · XGBoost model

1 Introduction

With advantages such as mobility, flexibility, efficiency and so on, the automatic guided vehicles (AGV) are playing a more and more important role in modern manufactory system [1]. The use of AGV is the one of the most preferred means to reduce the operation costs by helping the factories to automate a manufacturing facility or warehouse [2]. The common challenges related with AGV applications are positioning, path planning, obstacle avoidance and trajectory tracking, while positioning is the foundation of other problems [3].

The commonly used positioning methods in AGV were camera-based visual navigation system [4], encoder-based positioning system, laser navigation system [5] and positioning system based on gyroscope attitude calculation [6]. Although these methods can each obtain AGV coordinates, the positioning accuracy is not high due to their respective defects. Therefore, multi-sensor data fusion technology [7] came into being.

© Springer Nature Singapore Pte Ltd. 2021
F. Sun et al. (Eds.): ICCSIP 2020, CCIS 1397, pp. 602–610, 2021.
https://doi.org/10.1007/978-981-16-2336-3_57

The most important evaluation indicator is the accuracy and speed of the fusion system. The results are shown to be more accurate than any single sensor positioning system. Furthermore, it has a better precision than the multi-sensor data fusion positioning system based on Kalman filter, which proves the feasibility and effectiveness of the proposed algorithm.

The remainder of this paper is organized as follows. In Sect. 2, the theoretical basis and system description of this paper are proposed. The simulation experiment is shown in Sect. 2.5 to verify the effect of the improved method proposed in this paper on the accuracy of the positioning model and the performance comparisons with unfiltered system and the Kalman filter system by experiment are proved in Sect. 3. Finally, the conclusions are drawn in Sect. 4.

2 Background of AGV Positioning System

Positioning system based on multi-sensor data fusion using improved XGBoost model is studied in this section. First, the system framework of this research is presented. The next is the introduction of a preprocessing method for raw positioning data before the model training. Then, briefly introduce the XGBoost model. In the last part, we propose the loss function and evaluation function of the XGBoost model for positioning system training.

2.1 System Framework

The framework of our AGV positioning system is illustrated in Fig. 1. Two critical steps are data preprocessing and model building. In our system, we let the AGV move along the set path, use several sensors to locate separately, and preprocess the positioning data. Generate data sets in combination with real coordinates. After that, our system uses 5-fold cross-validation method to divide the data into training sets and verification sets. These two sets are used to train XGBoost model repeatly. In addition, we also improved the loss function and evaluation function of the XGBoost model before training. With supervised learning, parameters of the model can be adjusted to the best state. The fused position coordinates of the new track then can be output in real time.

2.2 Data Preprocessing with Quartile Based Amplitude Change Limited Sliding Filtering Algorithm

Before the data fusion, for the position coordinates calculated by the single sensor through the respective methods, the filtering process needs to be performed first. The purpose of filtering is to deal with some abnormal data caused by the instability of the sensor itself or measurement noise. After pre-processing, the training effect of the XGBoost model can be better, and the position coordinates obtained by the fusion are more accurate. This system proposes a quartile based amplitude change limited sliding filtering algorithm (QCLS algorithm) for the above problems. The specific steps are as follows:

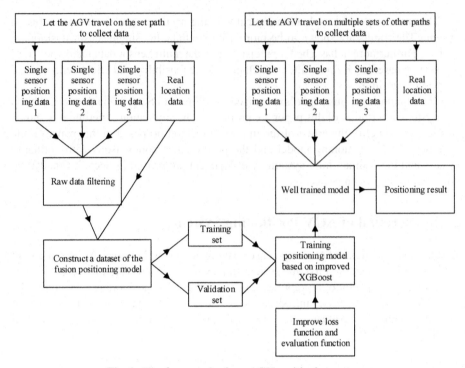

Fig. 1. The framework of our AGV positioning system

(1) $S = \{x_1, x_2, \cdots, x_n\}$ is a continuous sample taken from the original data set. Set the number of truncated samples $N = 20$, and reorder each element of the sample set in ascending sequence from small to large:

$$x_{(1)} < x_{(2)} < \ldots < x_{(20)} \tag{1}$$

(2) Calculate the quartile value of the current sample. The first quartile (Q1) is equal to the 25% of the numbers in the sample from small to large. The second quartile (Q2) is equal to the 50% of the numbers in the sample from small to large. The third quartile (Q3) is equal to the 75% of the numbers in the sample from small to large. When $N = 20$,

$$Q_1 = \frac{x_5 + x_6}{2} \tag{2}$$

$$Q_3 = \frac{x_{15} + x_{16}}{2} \tag{3}$$

(3) Calculate the interquartile range (IQR) of the sample:

$$IQR = Q_3 - Q_1 \tag{4}$$

(4) At the next moment, x_{n+1} is the newly obtained sample, and the difference between it and the observation of the sample at the previous moment is calculated. When the

difference is less than IQR, it is judged as a normal sample. Otherwise it is judged as an abnormal value, and the cull is replaced by the previous time sample x_n. As shown in Eq. (5)

$$x_{n+1} = \begin{cases} x_{n+1}, x_{n+1} - x_n < IQR \\ x_n, x_{n+1} - x_n > IQR \end{cases} \tag{5}$$

(4) Next, update the sample sequence S.

2.3   Training with the XGBoost Model

XGBoost method is a kind of gradient tree boosting method, the full name is XGBoost, which was proposed by T. Chen et $al.$ [23, 24]. The main idea of this gradient tree boosting method is that the results of the algorithm are given by the sum of many tree learners.

For a training data set with n samples, the prediction is given by a function of the sum of several learner:

$$\hat{\mathbf{y}}\mathbf{i} = \sum_{k=1}^{K} fk(\mathbf{xi}), fk \in F \tag{6}$$

where Xi represents the i-th sample in the training set, f_k is a function in function space F, each of which corresponds to a structure parameter s and leaf weights w, and F is a function space containing all regression trees. K is the number of trees used to regress the data set. The purpose of the algorithm is to minimize the loss function. The objective function contains the loss function and the regularization term.

$$Obj = \sum_{i=1}^{n} l(\mathbf{yi}, \hat{\mathbf{y}}\mathbf{i}) + \sum_{k=1}^{K} \Omega(fk), fk \in F \tag{7}$$

with

$$\Omega(fk) = \gamma T + \lambda \|w\|^2 \tag{8}$$

where $l(y_i, \hat{y}_i)$ represents the loss function between the real coordinates of data and the predicted coordinates. The latter function $\Omega(fk)$ is the penalise term. T is the number of leaves in the tree. γ, λ are two parameters to control the complexity of the tree. We adopt an addition strategy, which is to fix the already learned tree, keep the original model unchanged, and add a new tree to the model at a time. Generally assumed model to predict initialization $\hat{y}_i^{(0)} = 0$, each time adding a new function (tree), the t-th iteration round prediction model output value $\hat{y}_i^{(t)}$

$$\hat{\mathbf{y}}\mathbf{i}^{(t)} = \sum_{k=1}^{t} fk(xi) = \hat{\mathbf{y}}\mathbf{i}^{(t-1)} + ft(\mathbf{xi}) \tag{9}$$

where $\hat{y}_i^{(t)}$ represents the model prediction for the t-th round, $\hat{y}_i^{(t-1)}$ denotes the model prediction for the previous $t-1$ round, and $f_t(x_i)$ denotes the addition of a new function. In the experiment, generally by the Eq. (10)

$$\hat{\mathbf{y}}^{(t)} = \hat{\mathbf{y}}^{(t-1)} + \varepsilon f_t(\mathbf{x_i}) \tag{10}$$

where ε is the step size, which means that we won't be fully optimized in each step to reserve opportunities for future rounds, helping to prevent overfitting. The model prediction Eq. (9) is substituted into the objective Eq. (7), we obtain

$$Obj^{(t)} = \sum_{i=1}^{n} l\left(y_i, \hat{y_i}^{(t-1)} + f_t(\mathbf{x_i})\right) + \Omega(f_t) + C \tag{11}$$

According to Taylor's second-order exhibition, Simplify the loss function in the objective function and redefine the objective function:

$$Obj^{(t)} \approx \sum_{i=1}^{n} \left[l\left(y_i, \hat{y_i}^{(t-1)}\right) + g_i f_t(\mathbf{x_i}) + \frac{1}{2} h_i f_t^2(\mathbf{x_i}) \right] + \Omega(f_t) + C \tag{12}$$

where $g_i = \partial_{\hat{y}^{(t-1)}} l(y_i, \hat{y}^{(t-1)})$, $h_i = \partial_{\hat{y}^{(t-1)}}^2 l(y_i, \hat{y}^{(t-1)})$, C is a constant. After removing the constant term, the final objective function depends only on the first-order derivative g_i and second-order derivative h_i of each sample point on the error function.

Thus, the tree can be calculated by minimizing Eq. (12). More details of the algorithm can be found. Through several rounds of iterative training, the final learned XGBoost model can be regarded as a piecewise integrated model based on the linear tree model, which can well fuse the position coordinates according to the input set of single sensor positioning data.

2.4   The Tailored Loss Function and Evaluation Function

(1) Loss function

The loss function is a tool that can well reflect the gap between the model results and the actual data. In order to enhance the robustness of the model to smaller outliers, we constructively use Log-Cosh as the loss function. The Log-Cosh loss function is a smoother loss function than $L2$, which uses the hyperbolic cosine to calculate the prediction error, as follows:

$$l(\mathbf{xi}, \hat{\mathbf{xi}}) = \sum_{i=1}^{n} \log(cosh(\mathbf{xi} - \hat{\mathbf{xi}})) \tag{13}$$

where

$$cosh(\mathbf{xi} - \hat{\mathbf{xi}}) = \frac{e^{(\mathbf{xi} - \hat{\mathbf{xi}})} + e^{(\hat{\mathbf{xi}} - \mathbf{xi})}}{2} \tag{14}$$

In order to optimize the model structure, the g_i and h_i of the improved objective function are respectively obtained:

$$g_i = \frac{e^{(\hat{x}_i - x_i)} - e^{(x_i - \hat{x}_i)}}{2\ln 10 * (e^{(x_i - \hat{x}_i)} + e^{(\hat{x}_i - x_i)})} \tag{15}$$

$$h_i = \frac{2}{\ln 10 * (e^{(x_i - \hat{x}_i)} + e^{(\hat{x}_i - x_i)})^2} \tag{16}$$

(2) Evaluation function

Different from the one-dimensional data often used in the field of data analysis, the positioning data of the AGV system we want to merge is a set of 2D data, in the form of:

$$\mathbf{y_i} = (\mathbf{x_{i1}}, \mathbf{x_{i2}}) \tag{17}$$

where x_{i1}, x_{i2} represent the x-axis and y-axis position of the position in the world coordinate system.

So we have improved the evaluation function of the positioning model. The euclidean metric between the predicted coordinates and the real coordinates is used as the evaluation function, as follows:

$$E(\mathbf{y_i}, \mathbf{\hat{y}_i}) = \sqrt{(\hat{x}_{i1} - x_{i1})^2 + (\hat{x}_{i2} - x_{i2})^2} \tag{18}$$

2.5   Comparative Methods

In order to verify the data preprocessing and improve the role of the XGBoost model objective function and evaluation function, we carried out simulation experiments and compared verification. Collecting a total of more than 3000 sets of data of the AGV moving on the trajectory as a data set, we randomly select 80% of the samples in the data set as the training set and 20% as the test set according to the stratified sampling method. And make sure that the data distribution of the positioning data in the training set and the test set is roughly the same. Based on this division, we performed a set of experiments using the data filtering method mentioned in Sect. 2.2 and the traditional median filtering and without preprocessing.

Figure 2 shows the experimental results of different experimental data preprocessing methods used in this experiment. It can be seen from the figure that the positioning model based on the quadrant-based limit-width sliding filter algorithm which is more sensitive to abnormal data obtains the best performance in the test set.

Finally, we evaluated the results of the improved XGBoost model of the objective function, as shown in Fig. 3. The positioning accuracy of the XGBoost model using log-cosh as the objective function is improved compared with the original XGBoost model. The average error is reduced by 1 mm and the maximum error is reduced by 37 mm. Simulation experiments show that the improved model has achieved better results and can reduce the positioning error.

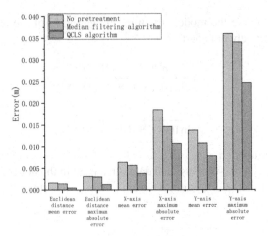

Fig. 2. Comparative Experiment result

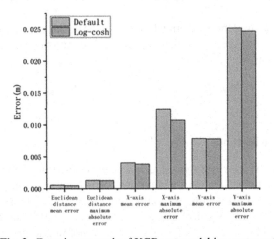

Fig. 3. Experiment result of XGBoost model improvement

3   Experimental Work

3.1   Experimental Program

Figure 4 presents the experiment platform for evaluating the feasibility and practicality of the proposed positioning approach. The dimension of the AGV is 70 cm × 70 cm × 40 cm, equipped with high-precision encoders, gyroscope sensors, and laser radar for positioning. Furthermore, we use the StarGazer as a calibration tool to get the real coordinates of the AGV in real time. Experimental field size is 600 cm × 200 cm. Under this condition, we let AGV travel along any path different from the original set path, and collect position coordinate data in real time for experiment.

Before the experiment started, we set the system sampling frequency to be fixed at 500 Hz. To start the experiment, we let AGVtravel along any path different from

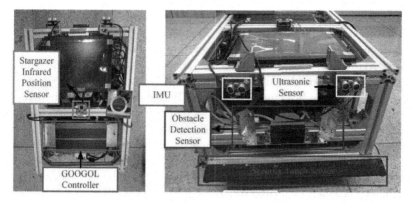

Fig. 4. AGV model

the simulation experiment path, and collect position coordinate data every 2 ms. The data to be collected includes the real position coordinates, the single sensor positioning system coordinates, the fusion position coordinates of the model, and the Kalman fusion system coordinates. Simultaneously record the time spent calculating each coordinate. Also record the time spent calculating each coordinate. The experimental results will be introduced in the next section.

3.2 Experimental Results

In this section, we evaluated the positioning accuracy of several different positioning models for AGV running on any path. Figure 5 and Fig. 6 show the positioning results of the positioning system proposed in this paper, the positioning results of the positioning system using the classic Kalman fusion, and the positioning results of the single sensor positioning system. Furthermore, the accuracy of each model is the best of several experiments with different parameters.

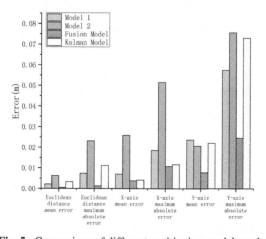

Fig. 5. Comparison of different positioning model results

4 Conclusion

The paper presents a positioning system based on multi-sensor data fusion using the improved XGBoost model. To facilitate the improved XGBoost model training, the quartile based amplitude change limited sliding filtering algorithm is designed to pre-process the sensor data from multiple sensors. The processed form of the sensor data is used for XGBoost model training. The loss function and the evaluation function are tailored for XGBoost in order to make the model applicable to the positioning system. The simulation results show our model can achieve the average positioning accuracy of 4.8 mm for a 5-fold cross-validation and also achieve 5.2 mm positioning accuracy on the independent testing set. Besides, experiments show the new model gets a better positioning accuracy compared with the single sensor positioning system and some conventional methods such as Kalman filter.

References

1. Tong, F., Tso, S.K., Xu, T.Z.: A high precision ultrasonic docking system used for automatic guided vehicle. Sens. Actuators, A **118**(2), 183–189 (2005)
2. Ng, P.P., Yucel, G., Duffy, V.G.: Modelling the effect of AGV operating conditions on operator perception of acceptability and hazard. Int. J. Comput. Integr. Manuf. **22**(12), 1154–1162 (2009)
3. Pratama, P.S., Nguyen, T.H., Kim, H.K., Kim, D.H., Kim, S.B.: Positioning and obstacle avoidance of automatic guided vehicle in partially known environment. Int. J. Control Autom. Syst. **14**(6), 1572–1581 (2016)
4. Doan, P.T., Nguyen, T.T., Dinh, V.T., Kim, H.K., Kim, S.B.: Path tracking control of automatic guided vehicle using camera sensor. In Proceedings of the 1st International Symposium on Automotive and Convergence Engineering, pp. 20–26 (2011)
5. Pratama, P.S., Luan, B.T., Tran, T.P., Kim, H.K., Kim, S.B.: Trajectory tracking algorithm for automatic guided vehicle based on adaptive backstepping control method. In: Zelinka, I., Duy, V.H., Cha, J. (eds.) AETA 2013: Recent Advances in Electrical Engineering and Related Sciences. LNEE, vol. 282, pp. 535–544. Springer, Heidelberg (2014). https://doi.org/10.1007/978-3-642-41968-3_53
6. Shi, E., Wang, Z., Huang, X., Huang, Y.: Study on AGV posture estimating based on distributed Kalman fusion for multi-sensor. In: IEEE International Conference on Robotics and Biomimetics (ROBIO), pp. 1219–1223 (2009)
7. Zhao, X., Luo, Q., Han, B.: Survey on robot multi-sensor information fusion technology. In: 2008 7th World Congress on Intelligent Control and Automation, pp. 5019–5023 (2008)

Multi UAV Target Tracking Based on the Vision and Communication Information

Chang Liu[1], Dongsheng Wang[1], Yong Tang[2], and Bin Xu[1(✉)]

[1] School of Automation, Northwestern Polytechnical University, Xi'an 710072, China
liuchang111@nwpu.edu.cn
[2] Chengdu Aircraft Design and Research Institute of AVIC, Chengdu 610065, China

Abstract. This paper investigates the multi Unmanned Aerial Vehicle (UAV) target tracking mission based on the vision and communication information. Firstly, the multiple UAV platform is established to achieve the target tracking mission. Furthermore, utilizing deep learning algorithm, target detection is accomplished based on UAV vision. Thirdly, each UAV could communicate with others to share target information and track it by maintaining the certain distance. Finally, the effectiveness of multi UAV target tracking system is verified on the actual test.

Keywords: Multi UAV · Target tracking · Target localization

1 Introduction

With the development of electronic information technology, a large number of advanced control algorithms could be implemented by digital controllers, which has promoted the research and development of control algorithms for lightweight UAV. At present, the control technology of drones is becoming more and more mature, and multi-rotor have begun to emerge in all areas of people's lives. The UAV were used in the military field at first, engaged in reconnaissance, strike, search and other tasks, then gradually developed into the civilian field. For example, power line and bridge inspection [1,2], visual navigation [3], etc. In addition to these applications, multiple drones coordinated tracking is also a hot research area in the UAV vision field.

In the industrial application field of drones, many tasks depend on object detection and tracking. In order to realize the real-time track, the combination of background subtraction detection and directional gradient histogram can achieve the required accuracy and meet real-time requirements [4]. Building on the pictorial structures framework [5,6], an object detection system is proposed which based on mixtures of multiscale deformable part models, the system is able to achieve state-of-the-art results in object detection challenges [7].

Obtaining the position of target in the real world is the basis for tracking, and the distance between UAV and target is a significant parameter to estimate the position. Many related technologies have been employed [8,9]. In [10], The target location is estimated by the combination of a monocular camera and sonar, and

© Springer Nature Singapore Pte Ltd. 2021
F. Sun et al. (Eds.): ICCSIP 2020, CCIS 1397, pp. 611–620, 2021.
https://doi.org/10.1007/978-981-16-2336-3_58

an attempt is made to reduce the influence of the proportional non-linear factor of the camera. In order to improve the location accuracy, Lidar is installed to provide more accurate relative vehicle height [11]. In [18], stereo camera is used to estimate the human posture and control a hexacopter.

To achieve continuous tracking of the target, many studies have made good progress. In [12], the Cam Shift algorithm is proposed on the basis of Mean Shift. The algorithm uses the position of the target in the current frame as the starting position to search in the next frame. In order to solve the problem of long-term object tracking, the Tracking-Learning-Detection (TLD) algorithm was proposed to combine the tracking, detection and learning process, which has attracted wide attention from scholars [13].

Because of the movement of drone and target, a single drone may lose target even though the gimbal camera could adjust its attitude angle to point to the target [14]. There are many reasons for this problem [15], such as occlusion of the target, excessive relative movement between target and UAV, and the change of the target's imaging angle which causes the visual algorithm to fail [16]. One of the solutions is to use multiple UAV clusters to coordinate the tracking of the target [17]. This paper use the multi-UAV to carry out coordinated targets tracking.

This study establishes a target tracking-oriented UAV platform and a corresponding multi-UAV coordinated tracking method was proposed. The main contributions are as follows:

1) Based on deep neural networks and face recognition, target localization is achieved;
2) Target position is obtained through the monocular camera localization algorithm, and the Zigbee communication module is used to encode and decode target information to achieve communication between drones;
3) Target tracking is achieved by the coordinated of multi UAV.

This paper is organized as follows: In Sect. 2, the workflow and the configuration of the UAV system are introduced. Object detection and localization given in Sect. 3. In Sect. 4, the implementation details of the communication and target following are shown. The experiment of implemented algorithms is presented and analyzed in Sect. 5. The conclusion is drawn in Sect. 6.

2   System Configuration

The target tracking system consist of detection, localization, cooperation and tracking. The system workflow of multi UAV target tracking is presented in Fig. 1. The input of system are target face image and camera streaming. The target detection section could find every person in the image and find target by the face recognition. The Kernelized Correlation Filters (KCF) tracker would track target in the image coordination and output is bounding box. The target position could be obtained by the distance estimating system based on the Principle of Camera Imaging. At the same time, target position would be send to other UAV by the Zigbee module. Finally the feedback control was used to track the target.

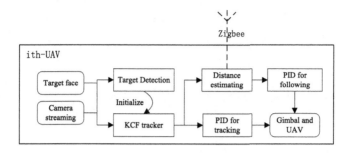

Fig. 1. Target tracking workflow.

The hardware configuration of the single UAV consists a quad-rotor platform, a gimbal with camera which could change the angle of camera, an intelligent processor and Zigbee communication module. The main processor of tracking system is NVIDIA TX2, which is lightweight, power-efficient and easy to deploy AI computer for UAV platform. Since the TX2 should process the video streaming and make decision on time, some simple control task would be assigned to a STM32 microcontroller. At the same time, TX2 could control the microcontroller by the pre-defined protocol. The gimbal could be controlled by the TX2 through STM32, which is used to change the angle of camera. Zigbee module is used to communicate with other UAV to share the target information. The hardware configuration is presented in Fig. 2.

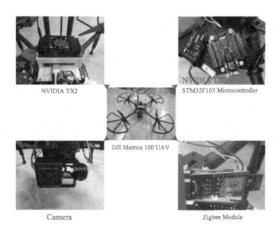

Fig. 2. Hardware configuration.

3   Detection and Localization

Based on the vision information, the target person could be identified by the Deep Learning algorithm. Furthermore, the target location in the image could be used to compute the target location in real world based on the Principle of Camera Imaging.

3.1   Detection

The input of detection subsystem are target face image and a sequence of images sampled from video. And the output of this subsystem is the target's location and size in the image.

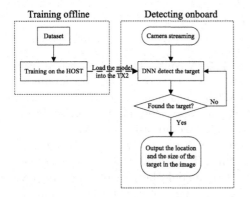

Fig. 3. Target detect workflow.   **Fig. 4.** Face recognition diagram.

Pedestrian Detect Based on Deep Learning. This paper use the DetectNet to detect person on the TX2, which is recommended by the TX2 official forum. This network could be trained on the personal computer and deployed on TX2 efficiently. The cost time of model training process could be reduce by the pre-defined network. After the training, the network parameters could load in the TX2 and could be complied by the TensorRT engine. The workflow of target detection is presented in Fig. 3. The output of DetectNet is the target location in the image coordinate, names bounding box, which contains following elements.

1) F_x: x-coordinate;
2) F_y: y-coordinate;
3) F_w width of the bounding box;
4) F_h height of the bounding box.

Face Recognition. This paper use the **face_recognition** python package to recognize faces, which is a powerful, simple and easy-to-use face recognition open source project. The workflow of face recognition is presented in Fig. 4.

3.2   Target Localization Based on Principle of Camera Imaging

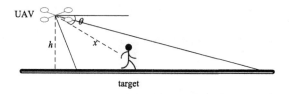

Fig. 5. Target localization.

To obtain the localization after find target, the distance between UAV and target should be estimated. This paper estimate the distance by the Principle of Camera Imaging, which is presented in Fig. 5.

The target distance x could be calculated by the following equation:

$$x = \frac{h_i}{\sin \theta} \tag{1}$$

where h represents the i-th UAV altitude above ground and θ is the Angle between target line and the horizontal plane. The angel θ could be obtained by the location of target in the image coordinate system. The Fig. 6 shows the target position on the image coordinate with a red point. The camera angel is 2λ and the target location is (a, b) in the image. Then the angle θ could be calculated by the following equation:

$$x = \frac{2\lambda b}{height} \tag{2}$$

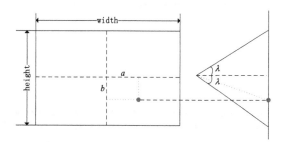

Fig. 6. Camera imaging.

4   Communication and Tracking

After the detection and localization, the target position relative to UAV has obtained. At the same time, UAV should send the target global position to the others. Each UAV could know the relative position with target by this way. Every UAV could tarck target at different height and angle to obtain different information.

4.1   Information Exchange Based on Zigbee

Since position of target should send to other UAV, the relative position would transform to global position such as longitude and latitude. The transform equation is showed as following:

$$lo = UAV_{lo} + \frac{d\sin\alpha}{111\cos UAV_{la}} \qquad (3)$$

$$la = UAV_{la} + \frac{d\cos\alpha}{111} \qquad (4)$$

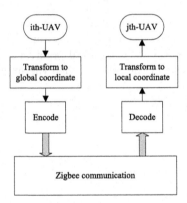

Fig. 7. Communication flow.

where the lo, la, UAV_{lo} and UAV_{lo} are the target longitude and latitude, UAV longitude and latitude respectively. α is the course of UAV. Futhermore, the target global location lo and la should be encoded to character type array since the Zigbee module could send the character type data to other Zigbee nodes. And the receiver node should decode the character array to longitude and latitude. The workflow of communication is represented in the Fig. 7. After knowing the latitude and longitude of target and UAV, the relative position and azimuth angle can be obtained by the following formula:

$$cosC = cos(90 - lo)cos(90 - UAV_{lo}) + sin(90 - lo)sin(90 - UAV_{lo})cos\gamma \qquad (5)$$

$$C_d = \pi C/180, d = RC_d \tag{6}$$

$$\alpha = arctan\frac{(lo - UAV_{lo})cosla}{la - UAV_{la}} \tag{7}$$

where γ is the degree of the difference between lo and UAV_{lo}.

4.2   Target Tracking Based on Feedback Control

Before the target tracking in real world by the mutil UAV, the KCF tracker is used to track target location in image coordinate. Each UAV should maintain the certain distance and height to the target pedestrian.

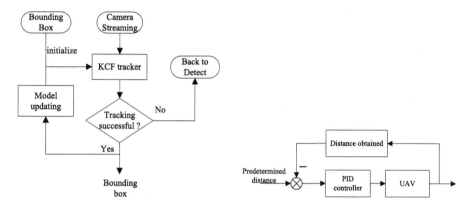

Fig. 8. KCF tracking algorithm.   **Fig. 9.** Target following control.

KCF Tracking in Image. KCF tracker is used to track the target in each frame of camera streaming because the DetectNet could not find target in each frame. Once the target is locked by the KCF tracker, the target location in the frame would be predicted with the less computational burden.

The KCF is a target tracking algorithm, which could distinguish the target and surrounding. The input of KCF is the bounding box which contains target. This bounding box could initialize the tracker, which could find the target location on the next frame. If the tracker loss target in the next frame, the detection section would be used to find target again. If the tracker find target in the next frame, the target location would be used to tracking the target in real world.

The KCF tracking flow is presented in Fig. 8.

Target Tracking. When the target relative position is obtained, the UAV could keep a certain distance to track the target.

The predetermined distance of ith-UAV is d_i and the current distance is d, the error of target following is represented as follow.

$$e_i = d - d_i \tag{8}$$

The PID controller is used to track the target by maintaining the certain distance:

$$u(k) = K_p e(k) + K_i \sum_{i=0}^{k} e(i) + K_d [e(k) - e(k-1)] \tag{9}$$

where $u(k)$ is the output of system at time k, K_p, K_i and K_d represent the PID parameters of distance maintaining system, $e(k)$ is the error which means the difference to determined distance at time k. The PID control algorithm is presented in Fig. 9.

5   Experiment

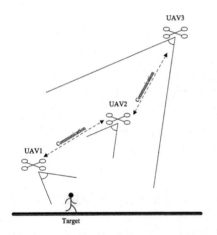

Fig. 10. Test scenario.

Fig. 11. Test scenario.

At the test step, target pedestrian face is load in the tracking system before the experiment. The initial parameters of system are given in Table 1. The DetectNet and Face_recognition is used in target detect. KCF tracker is subsequent step, finally each UAV would track the target pedestrian, these algorithm were test on the three UAV target tracking experiment. The test scheme is showed in Fig. 10 and Fig. 11.

In the test, UAV_1 finds the target person firstly, then UAV_2 and UAV_3 obtain target position by the Zigbee communication. UAV_1 and UAV_2 maintain certain to track target person, UAV_3 fly around target at a certain radius, which is showed in Fig. 12. The trajectory of UAV_3 is a circle.

Table 1. Initial parameters.

Parameters	Value	Parameters	Value	Parameters	Value
K_p	0.03	d_1	4 m	h_1	3 m
K_i	0.004	d_2	8 m	h_2	5 m
K_d	0.03	d_3	10 m	h_3	8 m

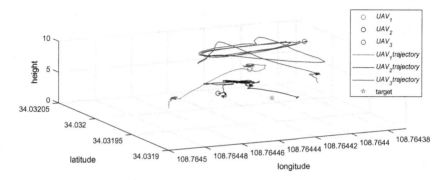

Fig. 12. Tracking trajectory.

6   Conclusion

This paper presented the multi UAV target detect and track based on the vision information and communication. The multi UAV tracking platform is established and realize the target detect and tracking by several useful algorithm. The DetectNet could detect the pedestrian efficient and the face recognition could find the target pedestrian. Furthermore, KCF tracker demonstrates a good performance in real time test. Finally, according the Zigbee communication, each could tracking the target by maintaining a certain distance once one UAV find target.

The limitation of these algorithms in the application of multi UAV target tracking is that the detect algorithm could not find target when it is partially occluded and the network training is time-consuming. Meanwhile, the target localization algorithm would fail to work when the KCF tracker obtain a inaccurate bounding box.

References

1. Li, Z., Liu, Y., Walker, R., et al.: Towards automatic power line detection for a UAV surveillance system using pulse coupled neural filter and an improved Hough transform. Mach. Vis. Appl. **21**(5), 677–686 (2010)
2. Metni, N., Hamel, T.: A UAV for bridge inspection: visual servoing control law with orientation limits. Autom. Constr. **17**(1), 3–10 (2007)

3. Krajník, T., Nitsche, M., Pedre, S., et al.: A simple visual navigation system for an UAV. In: International Multi-Conference on Systems, Signals & Devices, pp. 1–6. IEEE (2012)
4. Zhang, S., Wang, X.: Human detection and object tracking based on Histograms of Oriented Gradients. In: 2013 Ninth International Conference on Natural Computation (ICNC) (2013)
5. Felzenszwalb, P.F., Huttenlocher, D.P.: Pictorial structures for object recognition. Int. J. Comput. Vision **61**(1), 55–79 (2005)
6. Fischler, M.A., Elschlager, R.A.: The representation and matching of pictorial structures. IEEE Trans. Comput. **100**(1), 67–92 (1973)
7. Felzenszwalb, P.F., Girshick, R.B., McAllester, D., et al.: Object detection with discriminatively trained part-based models. IEEE Trans. Pattern Anal. Mach. Intell. **32**(9), 1627–1645 (2009)
8. Xie, G., Li, X., Peng, X., et al.: Estimating the probability density function of remaining useful life for wiener degradation process with uncertain parameters. Int. J. Control Autom. Syst. **17**(11), 2734–2745 (2019)
9. Xie, G., Sun, L., Wen, T., et al.: Adaptive transition probability matrix-based parallel IMM algorithm. IEEE Trans. Syst. Man Cybern. Syst. **51**(3), 2980–2989 (2019)
10. Gavish, M., Weiss, A.J.: Performance analysis of bearing-only target location algorithms. IEEE Trans. Aerosp. Electron. Syst. **28**(3), 817–828 (1992)
11. Liu, C., Song, Y., Guo, Y., et al.: Vision information and laser module based UAV target tracking. In: IECON 2019–45th Annual Conference of the IEEE Industrial Electronics Society. IEEE, vol. 1, pp. 186–191 (2019)
12. Bradski, G.R.: Computer vision face tracking for use in a perceptual user interface (1998)
13. Kalal, Z., Mikolajczyk, K., Matas, J.: Tracking-learning-detection. IEEE Trans. Pattern Anal. Mach. Intell. **34**(7), 1409–1422 (2011)
14. Huang, S., Hong, J.: Moving object tracking system based on camshift and Kalman filter. In: 2011 International Conference on Consumer Electronics, Communications and Networks (CECNet), pp. 1423–1426. IEEE (2011)
15. Wei, D.: Multi-target visual positioning technology of four-wing UAV based on VI-SLAM. Comput. Measur. Control. **27**(11), 224–227 (2019)
16. Guerra, E., Munguía, R., Grau, A.: UAV visual and laser sensors fusion for detection and positioning in industrial applications. Sensors **18**(7), 2071 (2018)
17. Dong, X., Yu, B., Shi, Z., et al.: Time-varying formation control for unmanned aerial vehicles: theories and applications. IEEE Trans. Control Syst. Technol. **23**(1), 340–348 (2014)
18. Jiao, R., Wang, Z., Chu, R., et al.: An intuitional end-to-end human-UAV interaction system for field exploration. Front. Neurorobotics **13**, 117 (2019)

An Accurate Positioning Method for Robotic Manipulation Based on Vision and Tactile Sensors

Dan Zhao[(✉)] and Fuchun Sun

Department of Computer Science and Technology, Beijing National Research Center for Information Science and Technology, Tsinghua University, Beijing 100083, China
fcsun@mail.tsinghua.edu.cn

Abstract. To improve the positioning accuracy of the robotic system, a novel positioning method based on vision and tactile sensors is proposed for robotic manipulation which consists of two stages: the vision-based positioning stage and the tactile-based positioning stage. The tactile sensor used in the paper and the proposed methodology are introduced in detail. Furthermore, experiments have been performed in the real platform to verify the effectiveness of the proposed method. The results show that the positioning accuracy has been largely improved with the proposed method.

Keywords: Robotic manipulation · Computer vision · Tactile sensor · Object positioning

1 Introduction

Great progress has been made after robots were introduced into the manufacturing industry which are widely used to improve working conditions, efficiency and quality. Traditional robotic systems are usually preprogrammed to move and operate in structured environment [1]. Nowadays, modern production requires more complex processes and manipulations in open environment which make great challenge for traditional robot systems, and this has led to increased interest in intelligent robotic systems in various fields [2, 3].

The performance of robotic system depends on its ability to accurately position the end-effector respect to the required object dimension, which is called the positioning accuracy. It is greatly constrained by the errors either built into the robot itself or occurring in the manipulation process such as geometric and force-induced errors [4]. In the positioning process of a robotic manipulation, it is the fundamental task to determine the position and orientation relationship between the robot's end and the target object to be operated.

There are many researchers contributed to solve this problem. From the published literatures, the main ideas can be divided into two categories. One is trying to improve the positioning accuracy of the robot itself to accurately describe the position and orientation

© Springer Nature Singapore Pte Ltd. 2021
F. Sun et al. (Eds.): ICCSIP 2020, CCIS 1397, pp. 621–631, 2021.
https://doi.org/10.1007/978-981-16-2336-3_59

of the robot's end respect to its base which can be calculated by kinematics [5–7]. The other one is trying to directly describe the relative position and orientation between the robot's end and the target object which are usually measured by camera or other sensors [8, 9].

In a robotic manipulation system, the desired position and orientation of the robot's end-effector should be equal to the real position and orientation of the target object in ideal condition. However, due to the inaccuracy of robot, measurement, and other disturbance in the environment, the relative position and orientation errors between the robot's end-effector and target object will be generated and may cause serious quality and safety problems in real application. Therefore, it is the primary problem for a robotic system to effectively improve its positioning accuracy in precise manipulation application especially in assembly manufacturing fields.

2 Related Works

To improve the positioning accuracy of robotic systems, many attempts have been made over past few decades. Some researchers have improved design methodologies and advanced materials technology to achieve high accuracy of robots. However, the effectiveness is limited and cost will be considerably large. Besides, it is much easier to measure or monitor the amount of inaccuracy and compensate it through the changes of the commanded positions of different joints which is especially applicable to robots.

Vision-Based Method. Researchers have developed some measurement methods for robotic systems to determine the position and orientation of target object in three-dimensional space. In this aspect, vision-based positioning technique has been greatly developed in recent years which include camera calibration, digital image processing, feature extraction, visual measurement, and control algorithms, etc. adopted widely for object recognition, positioning and tracking. Liu et al. published a series of papers to research on the pose measurement and visual servoing methods for positioning in aircraft digital assembly [10, 11]. Zhu et al. analyzed the measurement error to improve the accuracy of 2D vision system for robotic drilling [12]. Du et al. published a review for vision-based robotic grasp detection from object localization, object pose estimation to grasp estimation [13]. Besides, there are many other researchers studied on the vision-based methods and applied them in robotic manipulation.

Tactile-Based Method. In recent years, there are many research based on sensors and tactile sensors are important among them. Liu et al. proposed several kernel sparse coding methods to address the tactile data representation and classification problem in object recognition using tactile measurements of the BarrettHand [14]. Hogan et al. develops closed-loop tactile controllers for dexterous robotic manipulation with a dual-palm robotic system [15]. Dong et al. studied the tactile-based insertion for dense box-packing with two GelSlim fingers in which the error direction and magnitude of the grasped object were estimated based on the neural networks [16]. The methods have been verified by the robotic manipulation experiments, however, the focused dimension of the error space is small which only consider translation errors in axis x and rotation errors in yaw θ. A more advanced method for robotic precise positioning and manipulation would consider all translation and rotation errors of the target object, which increases not only the dimension of the error space but also the action space for error compensation. In this paper, we proposed an accurate positioning method based on vision and tactile sensors for robotic manipulation, which contains the vision-based positioning stage and touch-based positioning stage. The proposed methodology will be introduced in the next part.

3 The Proposed Methodology

As the eyes and skins of a robot, vision and tactile sensors play important roles for robotic systems, especially in precise manipulation fields. In this paper, a precise positioning method with vision and tactile sensor is proposed for dexterous and accurate manipulation applications. The proposed method consists of two stages, vision-based positioning stage and tactile positioning stage, which will be introduced in detail in this part.

3.1 Vision-Based Positioning Stage

In this stage, the robotic manipulation system will capture the images of the manipulation platform, detect the target object in the scene and calculate the position and orientation of the object using the vision-based method.

Firstly, before data capture process, the camera calibrations are needed to determine the internal and external parameters which represent the relationships between the camera and the robot system. Nowadays, there have been many published methods to solve this problem [17, 18]. Then, the three dimensional coordinates of arbitrary point in the scene can be obtained in the camera coordinate system.

In data capture process, the RGB and depth images of scene will be obtained with the vision-based measurement. Then, a background subtraction method are used in the paper for the target object detection. The equation will be described as follow

$$S(k) = |N(k) - B(k)| \tag{1}$$

$$G(k) = \begin{cases} 1, S(k) \geq \delta \\ 0, S(k) < \delta \end{cases} \tag{2}$$

where $B(k)$ is the depth value at point k in background image, $N(k)$ is the depth value at point k in current image, $S(k)$ is the difference of depth value at point k between current and background images, and δ is the threshold. When $S(k) \geq \delta$ and $G(k) = 1$, it means that the point k is the one on the target object. When $S(k) < \delta$ and $G(k) = 0$, it means that the point k is on the background.

The center point on the top surface of the target object is set as O_1 (x_1, y_1, z_1), and its position in camera coordinate system can be determined by the outlines of the target object on the captured images. The orientation of the target object is regarded as the unit normal vector $R_1(\alpha_1, \beta_1, \gamma_1)$ of the top surface which can be calculated as:

$$
\begin{cases}
\alpha = arctan(\Delta U(k)/D \sin \rho) \\
\beta = arctan(\Delta U(k)/D \cos \rho) \\
\gamma = \rho \\
\alpha_1 = \alpha/\sqrt{\alpha^2 + \beta^2 + \gamma^2} \\
\beta_1 = \beta/\sqrt{\alpha^2 + \beta^2 + \gamma^2} \\
\gamma_1 = \gamma/\sqrt{\alpha^2 + \beta^2 + \gamma^2}
\end{cases}
\tag{3}
$$

where $\Delta U(k)$ is the largest difference of depth value between the points or on the top surface of the target object, D is the straight line through the points with the largest difference of depth value, and ρ is the angle between the line D and the x axis of the camera coordinate system. The brief schematic diagram is shown in Fig. 1. Therefore, the position and orientation of the target object can be represented as $T_1 = (x_1, y_1, z_1, \alpha_1, \beta_1, \gamma_1)$ which is also the desired position and orientation of the robot system in manipulation.

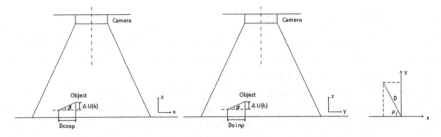

Fig. 1. The brief schematic diagram of vision-based positioning stage.

Considering the safety distance between the robot and the target object, the robot should firstly arrive at a position and orientation $T_2 = (x_2, y_2, z_2, \alpha_2, \beta_2, \gamma_2)$ which is near the desired pose T_1 and then approach the target object at a safe speed to perform the manipulations. The position and orientation T_2 can be calculated as:

$$
T_2 = T_1 + \Delta d =
\begin{cases}
x_2 = x_1 + \Delta d \alpha_1 \\
y_2 = y_1 + \Delta d \beta_1 \\
z_2 = z_1 + \Delta d \gamma_1 \\
\alpha_2 = \alpha_1 \\
\beta_2 = \beta_1 \\
\gamma_2 = \gamma_1
\end{cases}
\tag{4}
$$

where Δd is the safety distance between the robot and the target object which is usually set by experience as 10–15 mm. The position and orientation T_2 can be transformed into the robotic coordinate system, and used to control the robot to move to the desired pose. Therefore, the vision-based positioning stage has been done.

3.2 Tactile-Based Positioning Stage

It is known that the accuracy of depth measurement with camera is limited which depends on the measurement distance between the camera and target object [19]. Besides, the errors introduced in the camera calibration process will also lead to the deviations of the visual measurement results. Therefore, due to the inaccuracy of the vision-based positioning method, a precise positioning method based on tactile sensor is proposed in this section to improve the positioning accuracy of the target object for the robotic manipulation.

Tactile Sensor. To realize the tactile perception of the robot, a vision-based tactile sensor was developed in our research team. The structure of tactile sensor and the principle of its tactile perception will be introduced in this section. As shown in Fig. 2, the tactile sensor is mainly composed of support component, a camera, light sources, acrylic board, an elastomer and surface attachment.

When the tactile sensor contact with the object, the deformations of its elastomer and surface attachment will be generated due to their softness which can reflect the outline and geometric features of the object's contact surface. Then, with the light provided by the internal LEDs in the sensor, the micro camera can capture the images of these deformations. Besides, the object surface properties like the temperature and texture of the object can also be measured with the appropriate materials of the sensor's surface attachment. In this paper, we aim to improve the positioning accuracy of the desired object in robotic manipulation, and will not focus its temperature and texture of the surface.

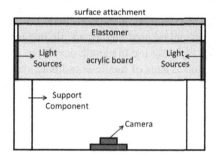

Fig. 2. The structure of the tactile sensor.

Positioning Method. After the vision-based positioning stage, the end of the robot has been arrived at the position and orientation T_2, which considers the safety distance Δd between the robot and the target object in application. In this stage, the deviations of relative position and orientation between the target object and robot end will be obtained.

At the beginning of this stage, the orientation of tactile sensor is the same as that of robot end which is named as $R_2 = (\alpha_2, \beta_2, \gamma_2)$. Then, the robot end with the tactile sensor moves along the axis of last joint, keeping the tactile sensor at the same orientation when moving, until the tactile sensor touch the target object. When the force at the robot end reaches a certain threshold, the displacement of movement is recorded as d, and the deviation along the Z-axis in tactile coordinate system between the target object and robot end can be obtained as $\Delta z = (d - \Delta d)$ in which Δd is the safety distance.

The surface of tactile sensor will be deformed due to the contact with target object, and the tactile images of these deformations will be captured by the inner camera. In captured tactile image, the image center is represented as the point P whose position in tactile coordinate system is (x_p, y_p), and the center of contact surface of target object is represented as the point C whose position in the tactile coordinate system is (x_c, y_c). According to the displacement between the points P and C, the deviations along X- and Y-axis in tactile coordinate system between the target object and robot end can be calculated as $(\Delta x, \Delta y) = (x_c - x_p, y_c - y_p)$. Therefore, the relative position deviations between target object and robot end can be obtained as $\Delta_{pos} = (\Delta x, \Delta y, \Delta z)$.

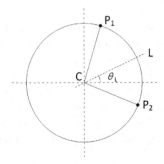

Fig. 3. The brief schematic diagram of angle deviations calculation.

Furthermore, the relative orientation deviations between target object and robot end in tactile coordinate system can be predicted by tactile image and described as $\Delta_{ori} = (\Delta \alpha, \Delta \beta, \Delta \gamma)$ where $\Delta \alpha, \Delta \beta, \Delta \gamma$ are the angle deviations between target object and robot end around X-, Y- and Z-axes of tactile coordinate system. The angle deviation between X-axes of tactile and object coordinate systems can be defined as $\Delta \gamma$. The points with maximum and minimum deformation on the surface of tactile sensor is P_1 and P_2, and the center of surface is C. The angle between CP_1 and CP_2 is θ whose angular bisector is L. The angle between L and X-axis of tactile coordinate system is θ_L. The brief schematic diagram is shown in Fig. 3. Therefore, the angle deviations between tactile sensor and target object can be calculated as:

$$\theta_{xy} = f(\Delta B) \tag{5}$$

$$\Delta \alpha = \theta_{xy} \cos \theta_L \tag{6}$$

$$\Delta \beta = \theta_{xy} \sin \theta_L \tag{7}$$

where ΔB is the maximum displacement deviation on the surface of tactile sensor which usually reflects as the brightness deviation at different points in tactile image, θ_{xy} is the angle deviation in XOY plane of tactile coordinate system, and $f(\Delta)$ represents the relationship between brightness deviation and angle deviation which can be modeled as an end-to-end model by deep learning method. In this paper, we use a convolutional neural networks model to establish this mapping relationship which is suitable for the tactile image processing.

Therefore, the relative position and orientation deviations between target object and robot end in tactile coordinate system is obtained as:

$$\Delta T = \left(\Delta_{pos}, \Delta_{ori}\right) = (\Delta x, \Delta y, \Delta z, \Delta \alpha, \Delta \beta, \Delta \gamma) \tag{8}$$

4 Experiments and Results

To verify the effectiveness of the proposed method, experiments have been performed in the paper and the experimental platform is shown in Fig. 4. In this experimental platform, it mainly consists of a Kinect DK camera, a UR5 robot, a tactile sensor connected with the robot's end, several target objects and a control computer.

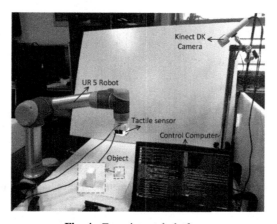

Fig. 4. Experimental platform.

Firstly, the camera calibration has been performed. Referring to literatures [17, 18], we selected several points in the workspace of the UR5 robot and the vision range of the Kinect DK camera. Then, the relative position and orientation relationship between camera and robot can be obtained as following:

$$R = \begin{bmatrix} -0.0401 & 0.8671 & -0.4966 \\ 0.9992 & 0.0372 & -0.0157 \\ 0.0049 & -0.4968 & -0.8678 \end{bmatrix} \tag{9}$$

$$T = \begin{bmatrix} 0.7869 & 0.0063 & 0.7816 \end{bmatrix} \tag{10}$$

After the camera calibration, the points in camera coordinate system can be described in robot coordinate system through matrix transformation. With measurement of camera and the proposed algorithm in Part 3.1, the position and orientation of target object can be obtained to determine the desired pose of robot. Then, the robot move to the object with a safe distance and the vision-based positioning stage is completed. With the measurement of tactile sensor and proposed method in Part 3.2, the relative position and orientation between target object and robot end will be obtained and the tactile-based positioning stage is completed.

The experimental results are shown in the following figures and tables. Figures 5 and 6 show the position and orientation error prediction with the proposed method. From the Fig. 5, we can see that the predicted values in blue line are similar as the true values in red line. The predicted error of position shown in green line is almost within 1 mm which show the effectiveness of the proposed method. From the Fig. 6, we can see that the predicted values in orange line are similar as the true values in light blue line. The predicted error of orientation shown in purple line is almost within 1° which show the effectiveness of the proposed method. The predicted error represents the deviation between the predicted and true value which can be calculated as:

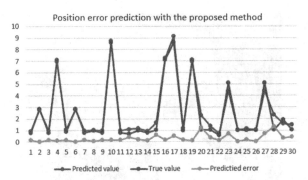

Fig. 5. Position error prediction with the proposed method. The ordinate unit is millimeter. (Color figure online)

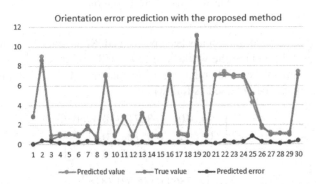

Fig. 6. Orientation error prediction with the proposed method. The ordinate unit is degree. (Color figure online)

$$E = \left| E_{pred} - E_{true} \right| \tag{11}$$

From the Table 1, we can see the experimental results that the average values of the prediction error for position and orientation are 0.3044 mm and 0.2186° respectively, which improved 87.73% and 93.42% compared with the initial error. To further analyze the experimental results, we calculate the error distribution for the position and orientation prediction with the proposed method which are shown in Figs. 7 and 8.

Table 1. The position and orientation error prediction results.

Mean value	Predicted	True	Error	Improved
Position (mm)	2.6482	2.4813	0.3044	87.73%
Orientation (°)	3.3813	3.3253	0.2186	93.42%

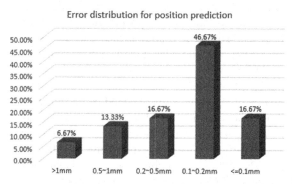

Fig. 7. The error distribution for position prediction.

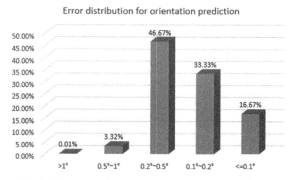

Fig. 8. The error distribution for orientation prediction.

In Table 2, we further conclude the results and we can see that more than 90% of the prediction errors for position and orientation are less than 1 mm or 1° which are enough to meet the accuracy requirements for manipulation applications. Therefore, these experimental results have verified the effectiveness of the proposed method successfully.

Table 2. The error distribution for position and orientation prediction.

Error (mm/°)	≤ 1	≤ 0.5	≤ 0.2	≤ 0.1
Position	93.33%	80.00%	63.33%	16.67%
Orientation	99.99%	96.67%	50.00%	16.67%

5   Conclusion

In the robotic manipulation, it is important to accurately determine the position and orientation of target object. To improve the positioning accuracy of robotic system, an accurate positioning method based on vision and tactile sensors is proposed in this paper. Firstly, the research background and related works are introduced. Then, the proposed methodology is introduced which consists of two stages: the vision-based positioning stage and the tactile-based positioning stage. In the vision-based positioning stage, the position and orientation of target object is obtained using camera and the robot moves near the target object considering the safety distance. In the tactile-based precise positioning stage, the designed tactile sensor is introduced and used to improve the positioning accuracy. To validate the proposed method, experiments have been performed in the real platform. The results show that the positioning accuracy is largely improved and more than 90% of the prediction errors for position and orientation are less than 1 mm or 1° which are enough to meet the accuracy requirements for manipulation applications.

Acknowledgement. This research was sponsored by the Major Project of the New Generation of Artificial Intelligence (No. 2018AAA0102900) and the China Postdoctoral Science Foundation Grant (No. 2019TQ0170).

References

1. Gan, Y., Dai, X.: Base frame calibration for coordinated industrial robots. Robot. Auton. Syst. **59**(7), 563–570 (2011)
2. Argall, B., Chernova, S., Veloso, M., Browning, B.: A survey of robot learning from demonstration. Robot. Auton. Syst. **57**(5), 469–483 (2009)
3. Lars, K., Nick, H., Tom, D., Marc, H., Tomas, K.: Artificial intelligence for long-term robot autonomy: a survey. IEEE Robot. Autom. Lett. **3**, 4023–4030 (2018)
4. Zhao, D., Bi, Y., Ke, Y.: An efficient error compensation method for coordinated CNC five-axis machine tools. Int. J. Mach. Tools Manuf. **123**, 105–115 (2017)
5. Li, R., Qu, X.: Study on calibration uncertainty of industrial robot kinematic parameters. Yi Qi Yi Biao Xue Bao/Chin. J. Sci. Instrum. **35**(10), 2192–2199 (2014)

6. Zhao, D., Bi, Y., Ke, Y.: Kinematic modeling and base frame calibration of a dual-machine-based drilling and riveting system for aircraft panel assembly. Int. J. Adv. Manuf. Technol. **94**(5–8), 1873–1884 (2018)
7. Oh, S., Orin, D., Bach, M.: An inverse kinematic solution for kinematically redundant robot manipulators. J. Robot. Syst. **1**(3), 235–249 (2010)
8. Chen, W., Jiang, M., Wang, H., Liu, Y.: Visual servoing of robots with uncalibrated robot and camera parameters. Mechatron. Sci. Intell. Mach. **22**(6), 661–668 (2012)
9. Nubiola, A., Bonev, I.: Absolute calibration of an ABB IRB 1600 robot using a laser tracker. Robot. Comput. Integr. Manuf. **29**(1), 236–245 (2013)
10. Liu, H., Zhu, W., Ke, Y.: Pose alignment of aircraft structures with distance sensors and CCD cameras. Robot. Comput. Integr. Manuf. **48**, 30–38 (2017)
11. Liu, H., Zhu, W., Dong, H., Ke, Y.: An adaptive ball-head positioning visual servoing method for aircraft digital assembly. Assembly Autom. **39**(2), 287–296 (2019)
12. Zhu, W., Mei, B., Yan, G., Ke, Y.: Measurement error analysis and accuracy enhancement of 2D vision system for robotic drilling. Robot. Comput. Integr. Manuf. **30**(2), 160–171 (2014)
13. Du, G., Wang, K., Lian, S., Zhao, K.: Vision-based robotic grasping from object localization, object pose estimation to grasp estimation for parallel grippers: a review. Artif. Intell. Rev. **54**, 1677–1734 (2021)
14. Liu, H., Guo, D., Sun, F.: Object recognition using tactile measurements: kernel sparse coding methods. IEEE Trans. Instrum. Meas. **65**(3), 656–665 (2016)
15. Hogan, F., Ballester, J., Dong, S., Rodriguez, A.: Tactile dexterity: manipulation primitives with tactile feedback. In: 2020 IEEE International Conference on Robotics and Automation, pp. 1–7. IEEE, Paris, France (2020)
16. Dong, S., Rodriguez, A.: Tactile-based insertion for dense box-packing. In: 2019 IEEE/RSJ International Conference on Intelligent Robots and Systems, pp. 1–8. IEEE, Macau, China (2020)
17. Wang, Y., Li, Y., Zheng, J.: Camera calibration technique based on OpenCV. In: The 3rd International Conference on Information Sciences and Interaction Sciences, pp. 1–4. IEEE, Chengdu, China (2010)
18. Zhang, Z.: Flexible camera calibration by viewing a plane from unknown orientations. In: Proceedings of the Seventh IEEE International Conference on Computer Vision, pp. 1–8. IEEE, Kerkyra, Greece (1999)
19. Poggi, M., Aleotti, F., Tosi, F., Mattoccia, S.: On the uncertainty of self-supervised monocular depth estimation. In: 2020 IEEE Conference on Computer Vision and Pattern Recognition, pp. 1–26. IEEE, China (2020)

Author Index

Printed in the United States
by Baker & Taylor Publisher Services